"On the broad shoulders of William Perkins, epoch-making pioneer, stood the entire school of seventeenth-century Puritan pastors and divines, yet the Puritan reprint industry has steadily bypassed him. Now, however, he begins to reappear, admirably edited, and at last this yawning gap is being filled. Profound thanks to the publisher and heartfelt praise to God have become due."
—J. I. Packer, Board of Governors' Professor of Theology,
Regent College, Vancouver, British Columbia

"Without a doubt, the Puritans were theological titans. The Puritan theological tradition did not emerge out of a vacuum. It was shaped by leaders and theologians who set the trajectory of the movement and shaped its commitments. William Perkins was one of those men. Perkins's contribution to Puritan theology is inestimable, and this new reprint of his collected works is a much-awaited addition to all who are still shaped and influenced by the Puritans and their commitment to the centrality of the grace of God found only in Jesus Christ. Even now, every true gospel minister stands in debt to Perkins, and in his shadow."
—R. Albert Mohler Jr., president, The Southern
Baptist Theological Seminary

"The list of those influenced by the ministry of William Perkins reads like a veritable Who's Who of the Puritan Brotherhood and far beyond. This reprinting of his works, so long unobtainable except by a few, is therefore a publishing event of the first magnitude."
—Sinclair B. Ferguson, professor of systematic theology,
Redeemer Theological Seminary, Dallas

"The father of Elizabethan Puritanism, Perkins presided over a dynasty of faith. The scope of his work is wide, yet on every topic he treats one discovers erudition and deep reflection. He was the first in an amazing line of ministers at Cambridge University's main church. A pastor to pastors, he wrote a bestseller on counseling, was a formative figure in the development of Reformed orthodoxy, and a judicious reformer within the Church of England. I am delighted to see Perkins's works made available again for a wide audience."
—Michael Horton, J. Gresham Machen Professor of Theology
and Apologetics, Westminster Seminary California

"William Perkins was a most remarkable Christian. In his relatively short life he was a great preacher, pastor, and theologian. His prolific writings were foundational to the whole English Puritan enterprise and a profound influence beyond his own time and borders. His works have become rare, and their republication must be a source of real joy and blessing to all serious Christians. Perkins is the first Puritan we should read."

—W. Robert Godfrey, president, Westminster Seminary California

"This is a welcome collection of the gospel-saturated writings of William Perkins. A faithful pastor, Puritan leader, prolific author, and lecturer, Perkins defended the doctrines of the Protestant Reformation throughout his life. Giving particular emphasis to *solus Christus* and *sola Scriptura*, these Reformed doctrines drove him as a pastor to preach the unsearchable riches of God's truth with confidence and assurance. Sadly, Perkins is unknown to the modern Christian. However, throughout the centuries, the writings, meditations, and treatises of this Puritan luminary have influenced Christians around the world. It is my hope that many will be introduced and reintroduced to the writings of this Reformed stalwart. May his zeal for gospel advance awaken a new generation of biblical preachers and teachers to herald the glory of our sovereign God in this present day."

—Steven J. Lawson, president, OnePassion Ministries, and professor of preaching at The Master's Seminary

"Relatively few in the church's history have left a written legacy of enduring value beyond their own time. Perkins is surely among that select group. Reformation Heritage Books is to be commended for its commitment to making his *Works* available in this projected series, beginning with this volume."

—Richard B. Gaffin Jr., professor of biblical and systematic theology emeritus, Westminster Theological Seminary

"Christians have heard about William Perkins, especially that he was an extraordinary preacher whose sermons made a deep impression on Cambridge and that they were still impacting the town in the decades that followed Perkins's death at a mere forty-four years of age in 1602. He was at the heart of the revival of truth and holy living that made the Reformation a glorious work of God. He was the outstanding Puritan theologian of his time, but most of us have not had the opportunity to study his works because of their rarity. After more than three hundred years, this ignorance is going to be ended with the remarkable appearance during the next decade of the complete works of this man of God. We are looking forward to their appearance very much. There will be sufficient gaps between their publication to ensure a sincere attempt at imbibing the truths of each volume, and then we face the challenge of translating Perkins's teaching into flesh-and-blood living."

—Geoff Thomas, pastor, Alfred Place Baptist Church, Aberystwyth, Wales

The Works of
WILLIAM PERKINS

The Works of
WILLIAM PERKINS

—=··=—

VOLUME 5

Exposition of the Symbol or Creed of the Apostles
Exposition of the Lord's Prayer
Foundation of Christian Religion Gathered into Six Principles

EDITED BY RYAN HURD

General editors:
Joel R. Beeke and Derek W. H. Thomas

REFORMATION HERITAGE BOOKS
Grand Rapids, Michigan

The Works of William Perkins, Volume 5
© 2017 by Reformation Heritage Books

Reformation Heritage Books
2965 Leonard St. NE
Grand Rapids, MI 49525
616-977-0889 / Fax 616-285-3246
orders@heritagebooks.org
www.heritagebooks.org

Printed in the United States of America
17 18 19 20 21 22/10 9 8 7 6 5 4 3 2 1

ISBN 978-1-60178-568-8 (vol. 5)
ISBN 978-1-60178-569-5 (vol. 5) epub

Library of Congress Cataloging-in-Publication Data

Perkins, William, 1558-1602.
 [Works]
 The works of William Perkins / edited by J. Stephen Yuille ; general editors: Joel R. Beeke and Derek W. H. Thomas.
  pages cm
 Includes bibliographical references and index.
 ISBN 978-1-60178-360-8 (v. 1 : alk. paper) 1. Puritans. 2. Theology—Early works to 1800. I. Yuille, J. Stephen, 1968- editor. II. Beeke, Joel R., 1952- editor. III. Thomas, Derek, 1953- editor. IV. Title.
 BX9315.P47 2014
 230—dc23
                        2014037122

For additional Reformed literature, request a free book list from Reformation Heritage Books at the above regular or e-mail address.

Contents

General Preface

William Perkins (1558–1602), often called "the father of Puritanism," was a master preacher and teacher of Reformed, experiential theology. He left an indelible mark upon the English Puritan movement, and his writings were translated into Dutch, German, French, Hungarian, and other European languages. Today he is best known for his writings on predestination, but he also wrote prolifically on many doctrinal and practical subjects, including extended expositions of Scripture. The 1631 edition of his English *Works* filled over two thousand large pages of small print in three folio volumes.

It is puzzling why his full *Works* have not been in print since the early seventeenth century, especially given the flood of Puritan works reprinted in the mid-nineteenth and late twentieth centuries. Ian Breward did much to promote the study of Perkins, but Breward's now rare, single-volume compilation of the *Work of William Perkins* (1970) could only present samplings of Perkins's writings. We are extremely pleased that this lacuna is being filled, as it has been a dream of many years to see the writings of this Reformed theologian made accessible again to the public, including laymen, pastors, and scholars.

Reformation Heritage Books is publishing Perkins's *Works* in a newly typeset format with spelling and capitalization conformed to modern American standards. The old forms ("thou dost") are changed to the modern equivalent ("you do"), except in Scripture quotations and references to deity. Punctuation has also been modernized. However, the original words are left intact, not changed into modern synonyms, and the original word order retained even when it differs from modern syntax. Pronouns are capitalized when referring to God. Some archaic terms and obscure references are explained in the editor's footnotes.

As was common in his day, Perkins did not use quotation marks to distinguish a direct quotation from an indirect quotation, summary, or paraphrase, but simply put all citations in italics (as he also did with proper names). We have removed such italics and followed the general principle of placing citations in quotation marks even if they may not be direct and exact quotations. Perkins generally quoted the Geneva Bible, but rather than conforming his quotations to any particular translation of Scripture, we have left them in his words. Scripture references in the margins are brought into the text and enclosed in square brackets. Parenthetical Scripture references in general are abbreviated and punctuated according to the modern custom (as in Rom. 8:1), sometimes corrected, and sometimes moved to the end of the clause instead of its beginning. Other notes from the margins are placed in footnotes and labeled, "In the margin." Where multiple sets of parentheses were nested within each other, the inward parentheses have been changed to square brackets. Otherwise, square brackets indicate words added by the editor. An introduction to each volume by its editor orients the reader to its contents.

The projected *Works of William Perkins* will include ten volumes, including four volumes of biblical exposition, three volumes of doctrinal and polemical treatises, and three volumes of ethical and practical writings. A breakdown of each volume's contents may be found inside the cover of this book.

If it be asked what the center of Perkins's theology was, then we hesitate to answer, for students of historical theology know that this is a perilous question to ask regarding any person. However, we may do well to end this preface by repeating what Perkins said at the conclusion of his influential manual on preaching, "The sum of the sum: preach one Christ by Christ to the praise of Christ."

—Joel R. Beeke and Derek W. H. Thomas

Preface to Volume 5 of
William Perkins's *Works*

———— ⇒•◦•⇐ ————

As is indicated by the title frequently given him, "father of Puritanism," William Perkins (1558–1602) exercised intense influence on the rise of the Post-Reformation Puritan movement in England, an influence some have considered superlative, at least during the Elizabethan period.[1] The later Gisbertus Voetius (1589–1676), in his own right a significant figurehead in the Continental further reform across the sea, placed Perkins on par with such theologians as Beza, Vermigli, Daneau, Ames, Ursinus, Zanchius, and Rivet.[2]

As an important progenitor in the English Puritan movement, Perkins, we might say, wore several different hats, one of which was that of an apologist or defender of the faith "once delivered to the saints." The works included in this volume, the fifth of a projected ten, are examples of such contribution: an *Exposition of the Apostles' Creed*; an *Exposition of the Lord's Prayer*; and the catechism *Foundation of Christian Religion*. In this short introduction I want to give a sketch of each, with priority on Perkins's more substantial work on the Creed.

Exposition of the Apostles' Creed

The 1595 *Exposition of the Symbole or Creed of the Apostles* is the latest and largest of the three works included in this volume.[3] Arguably the closest Perkins ever came to writing a systematics proper—at least according to modern sensibilities—Perkins summarizes basic Christian teachings following the redemptive-historical order of the Apostles' Creed. Perkins's own succinct summary of this work would be stated later in his *Cloud of Faithful Witnesses*,

---

1. Raymond A. Blacketer, "William Perkins (1558–1602)," in *The Pietist Theologians: An Introduction to the Theology of the Seventeenth and Eighteenth Centuries* (Oxford: Blackwell, 2005), 41.

2. Gisbert Voetius, *Disputationes*, in *Reformed Dogmatics*, ed. John W. Beardslee (Oxford: OUP, 1965), 289–90.

3. William Perkins, *An Exposition of the Symbole or Creed of the Apostles, According to the Tenour of the Scriptures and the Consent of Orthodoxe Fathers of the Church* (Cambridge: John Legatt, Printer to the University of Cambridge, 1595).

where he points out that the *Exposition of the Creed* presents the whole "doctrine of faith," while his exposition of Hebrews 11 in the *Cloud* is its "practice."[4]
This pigeon-holing is not unhelpful, as it is clear that doctrine is a point of
critical concern for Perkins in this present work. This is further evident in that
he argues that of the "two heads," that is, faith and love, of Paul's exhortation
(2 Tim. 1:13), only that of faith is presented in the Creed. However, and rather
predictably, Perkins also treats the Creed as serving an important practical
function, as we will see below.

The text as a document that received Perkins's particular attention, that
of the Apostles' Creed, is complex and difficult to trace as to its own origin,
though its theology is clear as faithful to the earliest of the church's teaching.[5]
Though the first fully developed version of the Creed appeared in the eighth
century in Saint Priminius's *De Singulis Libris Canonicis Scarapsus*,[6] its Latin
formulation, used yet today, has been taken from the writings of Melchior Hit-
torp in 1568.[7] This text was viewed as authoritative in the Western church
in the late Medieval period and would have been adopted by the Reformers,
including Perkins.[8]

As a tool for the church, the Creed was in its earliest codifications deployed
in baptismal preparation for new converts, who, upon being queried, would
respond with the positive *credo*. The use of the Creed quickly extended beyond
preparation for baptism into a more broadly catechetical function, and this
England enjoyed long prior to the Reformation and beyond Perkins's own day.
Its presence was felt especially from the 1215 Fourth Lateran Council onward,
with the 1271 Council of Lambeth providing a further impetus for its presence and use in the English church. The latter council, in outlining its *De
Informatione Simplicitum*, contains the well-known *ignorantia sacerdotum*,
the council's ninth canon. Therein, the council required that every priest provide a quarterly exposition of the Articles of Faith (in which the Creed would
be included), and that in the vernacular (though precisely *what* vernacular

---

4. William Perkins, *A Cloud of Faithful Witnesses* (1607; London: John Legatt, 1618), 1.

5. For a helpful summary of the history of the Creed, see Jaroslav Pelikan, *Credo: Historical
and Theological Guide to Creeds and Confessions of Faith in the Christian Tradition* (New Haven:
Yale University Press, 2003); Ferdinand Kattenbusch, *Das apostolische Symbol; seine Entstehung,
sein Geschichtlicher Sinn, seine ursprüngliche Stellung im Kultus und in der Theologie der Kirche;
ein Beitrag zur Symbolik und Dogmengeschichte* (Leipzig: J. C. Hinrichs, 1894–1900); and John
Norman Davidson Kelly, *Early Christian Creeds* (London: Longmans, 1950).

6. Kelly, *Early Christian Creeds*, 398–99.

7. Kelly, *Early Christian Creeds*, 369.

8. For a helpful survey of the use of Apostles' Creed in the period, see Joseph de Ghellinck,
Patristique et Moyen-Age (Paris: Descle de Brower, 1949–1961), 1:18–28.

is difficult to determine).[9] From these two councils, the groundwork was laid for English catechesis through the end of the Medievals, of which the Reformation would have been heir, and was built up especially through the efforts of the Franciscan, Dominican, and Augustinian canons of the Roman Catholic church.[10]

Perkins, also, deploys the Creed in a catechetical way and presents it early in his exposition as the way one may know to whom he belongs and from what he is distinguished, like a soldier who wears a "badge" that proclaims his allegiance. The doctrinal allegiance of the Christian is to Christ and the foundation of the apostles, the "truth faith" expressed in abbreviated form in the aptly named Apostles' Creed. As Perkins writes, the Christian must "hold, believe, and maintain, and preach the true faith, that is, the ancient doctrine of salvation by Christ, taught and published by the prophets and apostles, as the book of the articles of faith agreed upon in open Parliament do fully show"—the "book of the articles of faith" being a reference to the 1571 Thirty-Nine Articles of the Church of England.

Perkins's exposition of the Creed begins with him handling an objection, one that is not unheard of in our own day of the creedal antipathy extant in broad evangelicalism:[11] whether it is proper to "treat of the doctrine of faith without a text," or, to phrase it in common parlance, what value is there in handling a creed over the positive theology of the Word of God? Perkins's response is simple and clear: the use of the Apostles' Creed as a way of systematically expositing Christian teaching was the practice of the early church, and therefore is lawful—an answer that purportedly targets a (misguided) biblicism. Perkins will later note that this was also the practice of "teachers both in the New and Old Testament" as well, thus there is scriptural basis for his present work.

Having dealt with the objection and established that the minister "has his liberty to follow or not...a certain text of Scripture," and, after recognizing that the Creed itself commences with a statement of belief in God, Perkins starts with, first, *belief,* that is the "nature, properties, and kinds of faith," and then proceeds to *God.*

It is important to note that the Creed summarizes the flow of redemptive history, and thus Perkins's exposition is historically rooted and oriented. This

---

9. See *Councils and Synods, with other Documents Relating to the English Church, II: Ad 1205-1313,* eds. F. M. Powicke and C. R. Cheney (Oxford: Clarendon Press, 1964), 2:900.

10. See Andrew B. Reeves, "Teaching the Creed and Articles of Faith in England: Lateran IV to *Ignorantia Sacerdotum,*" PhD diss., University of Toronto, 2009.

11. See for a useful introductory critique, Carl R. Trueman, *The Creedal Imperative* (Wheaton, Ill.: Crossway, 2012).

is particularly crucial in that some have pitted Perkins's work here against, e.g., his *Golden Chaine*, that follows a different ordering of topics.[12] It is clear there are differences at least to the degree that, for instance, the *Golden Chaine* treatment of the covenant follows Christology, while in the *Exposition* it precedes it. However, this is not an example of two competing systems of theology, but differences in the *ordo docendi*, and thus differences that are not substantial. Perkins's departure from what may be a more creed-based ordering (as, e.g., the *Golden Chaine*) is due to his commitment to how the Creed itself progresses (recall the work is an *exposition*). As Richard Muller has noted, Perkins here "move[s] from the statement of principia, through creation, fall, and redemption, to the last things with an emphasis on the covenant as the historical or economic form of the divine work of salvation."[13] Thus, the *Golden Chaine* follows Pauline soteriology while the *Exposition*, following the Creed, the history of redemption. Hence the "peculiar" (from one perspective) ordering of, e.g., discussing faith at the beginning before his doctrine of God. The Creed itself reveals "peculiarities," introducing, say, eschatology at the end of the Christology section ("to judge the quick and the dead") and then returning again to it in the Creed's closing.

But the question of faith, introduced at the start, is Perkins's nod to the issue of the *duplex cognitio Dei*.[14] While it is not here necessary to trace out Perkins's definition(s) of faith in all their nuances, it is at least important to note that the phrase *credo in Deum*,[15] a la the Creed, indicates not simply the belief that a God (or even this God) exists, so much as it indicates a trust in Him. Or at least it should; that is to say, the Creed intends you to confess by affirming *credo*. Perkins capitalizes on this issue of faith and, after outlining the "three sorts of common [non-saving] faith," defines the "faith of the elect" thus: "a supernatural gift of God in the mind, apprehending the saving promise with all the promises that depend on it," and further, faith's "place and seat" is located in the mind, not will.

After defining and distributing faith, Perkins turns to *an sit Deus*, which he passes over with an affirmation but no explanation, proofs or otherwise. Then, *quid sit Deus*, and notes properly that we cannot define God, but "by His

---

12. On the other hand, some have argued that the *Golden Chaine* is a "truncated version" of Perkins's work on the Creed. David M. Barbee, "A Reformed Catholike: William Perkins' Use of the Church Fathers," PhD diss., University of Pennsylvania, 2013, 137.

13. Richard A. Muller, *Post-Reformation Reformed Dogmatics* (Grand Rapids: Baker Academic, 2006), 1:447.

14. See Richard A. Muller, "'*Duplex Cognitio Dei*' in the Theology of Early Reformed Orthodoxy," *Sixteenth Century Journal* 10 (1979): 51–62.

15. At times the Latin phrase was used to distinguish to what type of faith one referred, e.g., a distinction between *credere deum*, *credere deo*, and *credere in Deum*.

effects and properties" we may describe Him, that is He is an "essence spiritual, simple, infinite, most holy." Finally, *quantus sit*, to which he naturally answers in the singular.

The remainder of the *Exposition* proceeds in similar fashion. A couple of things to note. Union with Christ, some have pointed out, plays an important role in the *Exposition*,[16] a union by which a person derives "virtue" that "warms our benumbed hearts dead in sin and revives us to newness of life," like the sunlight of spring brings to life the worms and flies that lie dead through the winter months. Expectedly, Perkins also handles the descent clause; and, after presenting four views—a literal local descent; a synonym for "buried"; a metaphor for suffering; a way of speaking of His continuance under death's curse—Perkins allows for either of the two last as possible interpretations, with his personal preference being for the final option.[17] And the *Exposition of the Apostles' Creed* also provides a healthy development of Perkins's pneumatology, one of the most extensive in his works.

But as we noted earlier, the Creed does not only serve a doctrinal function. For Perkins, it is also to be used practically. From the start, introducing the first article on God, Perkins noted his method or "order" of handling each article of the Creed: first its meaning, then the duties, and last the consolations. And he follows this throughout. But he also closes the entire work with a lengthy paragraph outlining how the Creed is a "storehouse of remedies against all troubles and temptations whatsoever"—of which he gives ten examples: e.g., the Creed supplies help for those who grieve the "loss of earthly riches," who should thus consider that God is the Creator who guides and preserves; those who receive "outward disgrace and contempt," they should recall Christ crucified; those who have lost friends may find help in the communion of saints; those who face bodily captivity, let them recall that serving Christ is "perfect liberty," and so on.

Exposition of the Lord's Prayer
Moving to the second work included in this volume, Perkins's *Exposition of the Lords Prayer in the Way of Catechising, Serving for Ignorant People* was published in 1592,[18] and again the emphasis of catechesis is clearly notable in

---

16. See John Fesko, *Beyond Calvin: Union with Christ and Justification in Early Modern Reformed Theology (1517–1700)* (Gottingen: Vanderhoeck & Ruprecht, 2012), 254–68. See also Fesko's summary article, "William Perkins on Union with Christ and Justification," *MidAmerica Journal of Theology* 21 (2010): 21–34.

17. See Dewey Wallace, "Puritan and Anglican: The Interpretation of Christ's Descent into Hell in Elizabethan Theology," *Archiv für Reformationgeschichte* 69 (1978): 248–87.

18. William Perkins, *An Exposition of the Lords Prayer in the Way of Catechising, Serving for Ignorant People* (London: Robert Bourne and John Porter, 1592).

xvi   Preface to Volume 5 of William Perkins's *Works*

the title. In point of fact the combination of the Creed with the Lord's Prayer as dual catechetical tools was something that was done far earlier than Perkins, e.g., the Carolingian period saw numerous councils and synods which presented both the Creed and the Lord's Prayer as the foundational knowledge for all believers.[19] Even today, Thomas Cranmer's injunction to the parents of the child to be baptized still is read in many churches whose historical roots lay in the Church of England: namely, that they be taught the Apostles' Creed and the Lord's Prayer.

Before expositing that prayer, Perkins identifies another reason for publishing the work, as he explains in the prefatory pages. He protests a "book of late published in London" that claimed his name for authorship, which he claims commits the double sin of (1) being printed without his knowledge or consent and (2) being faulty. After pointing out some of these faults, more or less significant, he concludes clearly that the present volume serves as his "redress."

The exposition itself is a fairly extensive examination of each word/phrase of the Lord's Prayer, as well as the "manifold uses" for each—the writing of which is many times longer than that of the text's meaning. And after the prayer itself, there is an extensive and summary "use of the Lord's Prayer," as well as the "circumstances," or, ways in which one prays.

To this section is also appended a collection of prayers (with short expositions) from the Bible and a short, poetic song "gathered out of the Psalms, containing the sobs and sighs of all repentant sinners."

Foundation of Christian Religion

The last of the works included here is Perkins's 1590 *Foundation of Christian Religion Gathered into Six Principles*,[20] drafted in a catechetical form, to which copious biblical references and quotations are supplied.

As we have noted of the other works as well, Perkins's intent here is for instruction in knowledge and application, with an eye to the audience of "all ignorant people that desire to be instructed," to instruct them out of their "great ignorance." It appears that Perkins intended the *Foundation* to be something of a foundation for understanding the basics of theology, especially in its application, which he notes is the "very point in which you fail." He expressly states that the work's goal is that the "Ten Commandments, the Creed, the Lord's Prayer, and the institution of the two sacraments" will be "more easily"

---

19. Susan Keefe, *Water and the Word: Baptism and the Education of Clergy in the Carolingian Empire* (Notre Dame: University of Notre Dame, 2002).

20. William Perkins, *The Foundation of Christian Religion, Gathered into Six Principles: and It Is to Be Learned of Ignorant People, that They May Be Fit to Heare Sermons with Profit, and to Receive the Lords Supper with Comfort* (London: John Porter, 1590).

understood—but includes in this understanding not just "true knowledge" but both "unfeigned faith" and "sound repentance." His list of thirty-two "common"—and regrettably, erroneous—"opinions" held by the people he wishes to instruct support this idea, and confront the errors of Roman Catholicism, what we would call today "easy believism," issues of assurance, and various other problems—running the gamut from "drinking and bezelling in the alehouse or tavern" to the issue of magic and witchcraft to wrong views on what preachers are and what they do.

The catechism that follows was to be first memorized, and then studied in its exposition that followed every point. The initial, what we might term "shorter" catechism is quite lucid, and has six sections that proceed from knowledge of God, to man, Christ, salvation, obtaining/growing in faith, and the final state of humanity. The answers are short and abbreviated—e.g., "what do you believe concerning God?": "There is one God, Creator and Governor of all things, distinguished into the Father, the Son, and the Holy Ghost." Each phrase is supported by a proof text or texts.

The exposition of the six principles has the feeling of a larger catechism, and follows a question format as well: "What is God? God is a spirit, or a spiritual substance, most wise, most holy, eternal, infinite." By far the longest section is the fourth principle, covering soteriology, handling the meaning of the Ten Commandments under repentance, as well as the nature and definition of faith.

Conclusion

All projects owe both their genesis and conclusion, as also the steps between the two termini, to many in different ways. Of special note are the thanks due to the RHB crew, in particular Linda and Gary den Hollander, the tireless typesetting team; Ann Dykema, Stephen Mouring, and Linda Rudolph, who labored in typing up the script in the first place; and also to Joel Beeke and Derek Thomas, the general editors of the series, for permission to work on this volume and patience in its completion. May many through this work be helped to come further "to the knowledge of the truth" (1 Tim. 2:1), and that according to godliness (Titus 1:1).

—Ryan M. Hurd

AN EXPOSITION OF THE SYMBOL, OR CREED OF THE APOSTLES

According to the tenor of the Scripture, and the consent of Orthodox Fathers of the Church

Reviewed and corrected by WILLIAM PERKINS

Aug. lib. Quæst. in Matthew 11
They are good catholics, which are of good faith and good life.

LONDON
Printed by JOHN LEGATT

1635

To the Right Honorable, Edward Lord Russell, Earl of Bedford,
grace, and peace, etc.

Right Honorable, excellent is the saying of Paul to Titus: "To the pure all things are pure but to the impure and unbelieving is nothing pure, but even their minds and consciences are defiled" [Titus 1:15]. In which words he determines three questions. The first, whether things ordained and made by God, may become unclean or no? His answer is, that they may, and his meaning must be conceived with a distinction. *By nature* things ordained of God are not unclean, for Moses in Genesis says, that God saw all things which He had made, and they were very good; yet they may become unclean either by law, or *by the fault of men. By law*, as when God forbids us the things which in themselves are good: without whole commandment, they are as pure things not forbidden. Thus, for the time of the Old Testament, God forbade the Jews the use of certain creatures; not because they were indeed worse than the rest, but because it was His pleasure upon special cause to restrain them, that He might put a difference between His own people, and the rest of the world: that He might exercise their obedience, and advertise them of the inward impurity of mind. Now this *legal impurity* was abolished at the ascension of Christ. *By the fault of men* things are unclean when they are abused, and not applied to the ends for which they were ordained. The second question is, to whom things ordained of God are pure? He answers, *to the pure*: that is, to them whose persons stand justified and sanctified before God in Christ in whom they believe, who also do use God's blessings in a holy manner to His glory and the good of men. [Acts 15:10; 1 Tim. 4:3]. The third question is, who they are to whom all things are unclean? His answer is, *to the unclean*, by whom he understands all such: (1) Whose persons displease God, because they do not indeed believe in Christ. (2) Who use not the gifts of God in holy manner, sanctifying them by the word and prayer. (3) Who abuse them to bad ends, as to riot, pride, and oppression of men, etc. Now that to such, the use of all the creatures of God is unclean, it is manifest, because all their actions are sins, in that they are not done of faith; and a man's person must first please God in Christ, before his action or work done can please Him. Again, they use the blessings and creatures of God with evil conscience, because so long as they are forth of Christ, they are but usurpers thereof before God. For in the fall of the first Adam, we lost the title and interest to all good things; and though God permit the use of many of them to wicked men, yet is not the former title recovered but in Christ the second Adam, in whom we are advanced to a better state than we had by creation.

Hence it follows necessarily, that (to omit all other things) nobility, though it be a blessing and ordinance of God in itself, is but an unclean thing, if the enjoyers thereof be not truly engrafted into Christ, and made bone of His bone, and flesh of His flesh. The blood unstained before men is stained blood before God by the fall of Adam, if it be not restored by the blood of Christ, the Lamb of God. And hence it follows again, that nobility must not dwell solitary, but combine herself in perpetual fellowship with hearty love and sincere obedience of pure and sound religion: without which all pleasant pastimes, all sumptuousness of building, all bravery in apparel, all glistering gold, all delicate fare, all delightful music, all reverence done with cap and knee, all earthly pleasures and delights that heart can wish, are but as a vanishing shadow, or like the mirth, that begins with laughing, and ends with woe. A happy thing were it, if this consideration might take place in the hearts of all noble men: it would make them honor God, that they might be honored of God with everlasting honor, and it would make them kiss the Son lest He be angry, and they perish in the way [1 Sam. 2:22, 26; Ps. 2:12].

I speak not this as though I doubted of your lordship's care in this very point, but my only meaning is, to put you in mind, that as you have begun to cleave unto Christ with full purpose of heart, so you would continue to do it still, and do it more; and withal to manifest the same unto the whole world, by honoring Christ with your own honor, and by resembling Him especially in one thing, in that as He grew in stature and years, He also grew in grace and favor with God and men [Prov. 3:9–10; Luke 2:15]. And for this very cause (without any further consideration of earthly respects) I further present unto you an exposition of another part of the catechism, namely, the Symbol or Creed of the Apostles: which is indeed the very pith and substance of Christian religion, taught by the apostles, embraced by the ancient fathers, sealed by the blood of martyrs, used by Theodosius the Emperor[1] as a means to end the controversies of his time, and hereupon hath been called the *rule of faith*,[2] the *key of faith*.[3] And furthermore, I hope that your lordship will accept the same in good part, the rather because you vouchsafed when you were in Cambridge, to be an hearer thereof when it was taught and delivered. Thus craving pardon for my boldness, I take my leave, commending your lordship and yours to the protection of the Almighty. Anno Apr 2, 1595.

Your Lordship to command,
William Perkins

---

1. Socrat. hist. Eccl. 1.5 cap. 10.
2. Aug. de temp. serm. 119.
3. Ambros. Serm. 38.

An Exposition of the Creed

"I believe in God," etc.

No man justly can be offended at this, that I begin to treat of the doctrine of faith without a text, though some be of mind that in catechizing the minister is to proceed as in the ordinary course of preaching only by handling a set portion of Scripture, and therefore that the handling of the Creed, being no Scripture, is not convenient. Indeed, I grant that other course to be commendable. Yet I doubt not but in catechizing the minister has his liberty to follow or not to follow a certain text of Scripture, as we do in the usual course of preaching. My reason is taken from the practice of the primitive church, whose catechism (as the author of the epistle to the Hebrews shows) was contained in six principles or grounds of religion, which were not taken out of any set text in the Old Testament but rather was a form of teaching gathered out of the most clear places thereof. Hence I reason thus: that which in this point was the use and manner of the primitive church is lawful to be used of us now. But in the primitive church it was the manner to catechize without handling any set text of Scripture. And therefore the ministers of the gospel at this time may with like liberty do the same, so be it they do confirm the doctrine which they teach with places of Scripture afterward.

Now to come to the Creed, let us begin with the name or title thereof. That which in English we call the Apostles' Creed in other tongues is called "symbolum"—that is, a "shot" or a "badge." It is called a shot, because as in a feast or banquet every man pays his part, which being all gathered, the whole (which is called the shot) amounts. And so out of the several writings of the apostles arises this creed or brief confession of faith. It is a badge, because as a soldier in the field by his badge and livery is known of what band he is and to what captain he does belong, even so by this belief a Christian man may be distinguished and known from all Jews, Turks, atheists, and all false professors. And for this cause it is called a badge.

Again, it is called the Creed of the Apostles not because they were the penners of it, conferring to it besides the matter the very style and frame of words[1] as we have them now set down. *Reason 1.* There are in this Creed

---

1. Russin. in expos. Smyb & Hieron. ad Pam.

certain words and phrases which are not to be found in the writings of the apostles—namely, these: "he descended into hell"; the "catholic church." The latter whereof no doubt first began to be in use when after the apostles' days the church was dispersed into all quarters of the earth.[2] *[Reason] 2.* If both matter and words had been from the apostles, why is not the Creed canonical Scripture, as well as any other writings? *[Reason] 3.* The apostles had a summary collection of the points of Christian religion which they taught and also delivered to others to teach by, consisting of two heads, faith and love, as may appear by Paul's exhortation to Timothy, wishing him "to keep the pattern of wholesome words, which he had heard of him, in faith and love, which is in Christ Jesus" [2 Tim. 1:13]. Now the Creed consists not of two heads but of one—namely, of faith only, and not of love also. Wherefore, I rather think that it is called the Apostles' Creed because it does summarily contain the chief and principal points of religion, handled and propounded in the doctrine of the apostles, and because the points of the Creed are conformable and agreeable to their doctrine and writings.

And thus much of the title. Now let us hear what the Creed is. It is a sum of things to be believed concerning God and concerning the church, gathered forth of the Scriptures. For the opening of this description, first, I say it is a sum of things to be believed or an abridgement. It has been the practice of teachers both in the New and Old Testament to abridge and contract summarily the religion of their time. This the prophets used. For when they had made their sermons to the people, they did abridge them and penned them briefly, setting them in some open places, that all the people might read the same. So the Lord bade Habakkuk to write the vision which he saw and to make it plain upon tables, "that he may run that reads it" [Hab. 2:2].[3] And in the New Testament the apostles did abridge those doctrines which otherwise they did handle at large, as may appear in the place of Timothy aforenamed [2 Tim. 1:13]. Now the reason why both in the Old and New Testament the doctrine of religion was abridged is that the understanding of the simple as also their memories might be hereby helped, and they better enabled to judge of the truth and to discern the same from falsehood. And for this end the Apostles' Creed, being a summary collection of things to be believed, was gathered briefly out of the Word of God for helping of the memory and understanding of men.[4] I add that this Creed is concerning God and the church, for in these two points consists the whole sum thereof. Lastly, I say that it is gathered forth of the Scripture to make

2. Pacianus epist. 1. ad Symp.
3. Originally, "Hab. 3:2."
4. Aug. serm. 119. de temp. cassian l.6. de in car. dom.

a difference between it and other writings and to show the authority of it, which I will further declare on this manner.

There be two kinds of writings in which the doctrine of the church is handled, and they are either divine or ecclesiastical. Divine are the books of the Old and New Testament, penned either by prophets or apostles. And these are not only the pure word of God but also the scripture of God, because not only the matter of them but the whole disposition thereof with the style and the phrase was set down by the immediate inspiration of the Holy Ghost. And the authority of these books is divine—that is, absolute and sovereign—and they are of sufficient credit in and by themselves, needing not the testimony of any creature, not subject to the censure either of men or angels, binding the consciences of all men at all times, and being the only foundation of our faith and the rule and canon of all truth.

Ecclesiastical writings are all other ordinary writings of the church consenting with [the] Scriptures. These may be called the word or truth of God, so far forth as their matter or substance is consenting with the written Word of God; but they cannot be called the scripture of God, because the style and phrase of them was set down according to the pleasure of man, and therefore they are in such sort the word of God, as that also they are the word of men. And their authority in defining of truth and falsehood in matters of religion is not sovereign but subordinate to the former, and it does not stand in the authority and pleasure of men and counsels but in the consent which they have with the Scriptures.

Ecclesiastical writings are either general, particular, or proper. General are the creeds and confessions of the church, dispersed over the whole world; and among the rest [is] the Creed of the Apostles, made either by the apostles themselves or by their hearers and disciples, apostolical men, delivered to the church and conveyed from hand to hand to our times. Particular writings are the confessions of particular churches. Proper writings are the books and confessions of private men. Now between these we must make difference. For the general Creed of the Apostles (other universal creeds in this case not excepted), though it be of less authority than Scripture, yet has it more authority than the particular and private writings of churches and men. For it has been received and approved by universal consent of the catholic church in all ages, and so were never these. In it the meaning and doctrine cannot be changed by the authority of the whole catholic church. And if either the order of the doctrine or the words whereby it is expressed should upon some occasion be changed, a particular church of any country cannot do it without catholic consent of the whole church. Yet particular writings and confessions made by some special churches may be altered in the words and in the points of doctrine by the same churches without offence to the catholic church. Lastly, it is received as a rule of faith among all churches to try doctrines and interpretations of Scriptures by, not because it is a rule of itself—for that the Scripture is alone—but because it borrows its[5] authority from Scripture with which it agrees. And this honor no other writings of men can have.

Here some may demand [what is] the number of creeds. *Answer.* I say but one creed, as there is but one faith. And if it be alleged that we have many creeds, as besides this of the apostles, the Nicene Creed and Athanasius Creed, etc., I answer, the several creeds and confessions of churches contain not several faiths and religions but one and the same. And this, called the Apostles' Creed, is most ancient and principal. All the rest are no new creeds in substance, but in some points penned more largely for the exposition of it, that men might better avoid the heresies of their times.

Further, it may be demanded, in what form this Creed was penned? *Answer.* In the form of an answer to a question. The reason is this. In the primitive church, when any man was turned from gentilism[6] to the faith of Christ and was to be baptized, this question was asked him: what do you believe?[7] Then, he answered according to the form of the Creed, "I believe in God," etc. And this manner of questioning was used even from the time of [the] apostles. When the eunuch was converted by Philip, he said, "What doth let me to be baptized?" Philip said, "If thou dost believe with all thine heart, thou mayest" [Acts 8:37]. Then he answered, "I believe that Jesus Christ is the Son of God." By this it appears that although all men for the most part among us can say this Creed, yet not one of a thousand can tell the ancient and first use of it; for commonly at this day of the simpler sort it is said for a prayer, being indeed no prayer. And when it is used so, men make it no better than a charm.

Faith Described Generally[8]

Before we come to handle the particular points of the Creed, it is very requisite that we should make an entrance thereto by describing the nature, properties, and kinds of faith, the confession and ground whereof is set forth in the Creed. Faith therefore is a gift of God, whereby we give assent or credence to God's word. For there is a necessary relation between faith and God's word. The common property of faith is noted by the author to the Hebrews, when he says, "Faith is the ground of things hoped for: and the demonstration of things that are not seen" [Heb. 11:1]. For all this may be understood not only of justifying

---

5. Originally, "his."
6. *Gentilism*: paganism.
7. Cyrill catec. 1. Mystag. Tert. de resurrect. Origen. hom. 5. in Num.
8. This heading appears in the margin.

faith but also of temporary faith and the faith of miracles. Where faith is said to be a ground, the meaning is that though there are many things promised by God which men do not presently enjoy but only hope for, because as yet they are not, yet faith does after a sort give subsisting or being unto them. Secondly, it is an evidence or demonstration, etc.—that is, by believing a man does make a thing as it were visible, being otherwise invisible and absent.

Faith is of two sorts: either common faith or the faith of the elect—as Paul says he is an apostle according "to the faith of God's elect" [Titus 1:1], which is also called "faith without hypocrisy" [1 Tim. 1:5]. The common faith is that which both the elect and reprobate have, and it is threefold. The first is historical faith, which is when a man does believe the outward letter and history of the Word. It has two parts—knowledge of God's Word and assent unto the same knowledge. And it is to be found in the devil and his angels. So St. James says, "The devils believe, and tremble" [James 2:19]. Some will say, what a faith have they? *Answer.* Such as whereby they understand both the law and the gospel. Besides, they give assent to it to be true, and they do more yet in that they tremble and fear. And many a man has not so much. For among us, there is many a one which has no knowledge of God at all, more than he has learned by the common talk of the world—as, namely, that there is a God, and that He is merciful, etc. And yet this man will say that he believes with all his heart. But without knowledge it cannot be that any should truly believe, and therefore he deceives himself. *Question.* But whence have the devils historical faith? Were they illuminated by the light of the Spirit? *Answer.* No, but when the gospel was preached, they did acknowledge it and believed it to be true, and that by the virtue of the relics of God's image, which remained in them since their fall. And therefore this their faith does not arise from any special illumination by His Spirit, but they attain to it even by the very light of nature, which was left in them from the beginning.

The second kind of faith is temporary faith, so called because it lasts but for a time and season and commonly not to the end of a man's life. This kind of faith is noted unto us in the parable of the seed that fell in the stony ground. And there be two differences or kinds of this faith. The first kind of temporary faith has in it three degrees. The first is to know the Word of God and particularly the gospel. The second, to give an assent unto it. The third, to profess it, but to go no further. And all this may be done without any love to the Word. This faith has one degree more than historical faith. Examples of it we have in Simon Magus (Acts 8:13), who is said to believe because he held the doctrine of the apostle to be true and withal professed the same. And [it is] in the devils also, who in some sort confessed that Christ was the Son of the Most Highest and yet looked for no salvation by Him (Mark 5:7; Acts 19:15). And this is the common faith that abounds in this land. Men say they believe as the prince believes; and if religion change, they will change. For by reason of the authority of princes' laws, they are made to learn some little knowledge of the Word. They believe it to be good, and they profess it. And thus for the space of thirty or forty years men hear the word preached and receive the sacraments, being for all this as void of grace as ever they were at the first day. And the reason is because they do barely profess it without either liking or love of the same.

The second kind of temporary faith has in it five degrees.[9] For by it, first, a man knows the Word. Secondly, he assents unto it. Thirdly, he professes it. Fourthly, he rejoices inwardly in it. Fifthly, he brings forth some kind of fruit. And yet for all this [he] has no more in him but a faith that will fail in the end, because he wants the effectual application of the promise of the gospel and is without all manner of sound conversation. This faith is like corn on the housetop, which grows for awhile, but when heat of summer comes it withers. And this is also set forth unto us in the parable of the seed, which fell in stony ground, which is hasty in springing up; but because of the stones, which will not suffer it to take deep root, it withers. And this is a very common faith in the church of God, by which many rejoice in the preaching of the word and for a time bring forth some fruits accordingly with show of great forwardness, yet afterward shake off religion and all [Luke 8:13]. But (some will say) how can this be a temporary faith, seeing it has such fruits? *Answer.* Such a kind of faith is temporary because it is grounded on temporary causes, which are three. (1) A desire to get knowledge of some strange points of religion. For many a man does labor for the five former degrees of temporary faith only because he desires to get more knowledge in Scripture than other men have. [2] The second cause is a desire of praise among men, which is of that force that it will make a man put on a show of all the graces which God bestows upon His own children, though otherwise he want them, and to go very far in religion, which appears thus. Some there are which seem very bitterly to weep for the sins of other men and yet have neither sorrow nor touch of conscience for their own, and the cause hereof is nothing else but pride. For he that sheds tears for another man's sins should much more weep for his own, if he had grace. Again, a man for his own sins will pray very slackly and dully when he prays privately, and yet when he is in the company of others he prays very fervently and earnestly. From whence is this difference? Surely, often it springs from the pride of heart and from a desire of praise among men. [3] The third cause of temporary faith is profit, commodity, the getting of wealth and riches, which are common occasions to move to choose or refuse religion, as the time serves. But such a

---

9. This paragraph break was not in the original.

kind of believers embrace not the gospel because it is the gospel—that is, the glad tidings of salvation—but because it brings wealth, peace, and liberty with it. And these are the three causes of temporary faith.

The third kind of faith is the faith of miracles, when a man, grounding himself on some special promise or revelation from God, does believe that some strange and extraordinary thing which he has desired or foretold shall come to pass by the work of God. This must be distinguished from historical and temporary faith. For Simon Magus, having both these kinds of faith, wanted this faith of miracles and therefore would have bought the same of the apostles for money [Acts 8:19]. Yet we must know that this faith of miracles may be in hypocrites, as it was in Judas, and at the last judgment it shall be found to have been in the wicked and reprobate, which shall say to Christ, "Lord, in Thy name we have prophesied and cast out devils and done many great miracles" [Matt. 7:22; 1 Cor. 13:2].

And thus much for the three sorts of common faith. Now we come to true faith, which is called the faith of the elect. It is thus defined: faith is a supernatural gift of God in the mind, apprehending the saving promise with all the promises that depend on it. First, I say it is a gift of God (Phil. 1:29) to confute the blind opinion of our people that think that the faith whereby they are to be saved is bred and born with them. I add that this is a gift supernatural, not only because it is above the corrupt nature in which we are born, but also because it is above that pure nature in which our first parents were created; for in the state of innocency they wanted this faith, neither had they then any need of faith in the Son of God as He is Messiah. But this faith is a new grace of God added to regeneration after the fall and first prescribed and taught in the covenant of grace. And by this one thing faith differs from the rest of the gifts of God, as the fear of God, the love of God, the love of our brethren, etc. For these were in man's nature before the fall; and after it, when it pleases God to call us, they are but renewed. But justifying faith admits no renewing. For the first engrafting of it into the heart is in the conversion of a sinner after his fall.

The place and seat of faith (as I think) is the mind of man, not the will; for it stands in a kind of particular knowledge or persuasion, and there is no persuasion but in the mind. Paul says indeed that we believe with the heart (Rom. 10:9). But by the heart he understands the soul, without limitation to any part. Some do place faith partly in the mind and partly in the will, because it has two parts: knowledge and affiance. But it seems not greatly to stand with reason that one particular and single grace should be seated in divers parts or faculties of the soul.

The form of faith is to apprehend the promise. "That we might receive the promise of the Spirit through faith" (Gal. 3:14) and "to receive Christ"

(John 1:12) and "to believe" are put one for another. And to believe is to eat and drink the body and blood of Christ. To apprehend properly is an action of the hand of man, which lays hold of a thing and pulls [it] to himself; and by resemblance it agrees to faith, which is the hand of the soul, receiving and applying the saving promise.

The apprehension of faith is not performed by any affection of the will, but by a certain and particular persuasion whereby a man is resolved that the promise of salvation belongs unto him, which persuasion is wrought in the mind by the Holy Ghost (1 Cor. 2:12). And by this the promise which is general is applied particularly to one subject.

By this one action saving faith differs from all other kinds of faith. From historical, for it wants all apprehension and stands only in a general assent. From temporary faith, which though it make a man to profess the gospel and to rejoice in the same, yet does it not thoroughly apply Christ with His benefits. For it never brings with it any thorough touch of conscience or lively sense of God's grace in the heart. And the same may be said of the rest.

The principal and main object of this faith is the saving promise: "God so loved the world, that he gave his only begotten Son, that whosoever believes in him, should not perish, but have everlasting life" [John 3:16]. But some will say, Christ is commonly said to be the object of faith. *Answer.* In effect it is all one to say "the saving promise" and "Christ promised," who is the substance of the covenant. Christ then, as He is set forth unto us in the word and sacraments, is the object of faith. And here certain questions offer themselves to be scanned.

The first, what is that particular thing which faith apprehends? *Answer.* Faith apprehends the whole Christ, God and man. For His Godhead without His manhood and His manhood without His Godhead does not reconcile us to God. Yet this which I say must be conceived with some distinction according to the difference of His two natures. His Godhead is apprehended not in respect of His efficacy or nature, but in respect of His efficacy manifested in the manhood, whereby the obedience thereof is made meritorious before God. As for His manhood, it is apprehended both in respect of the substance or thing itself and also in respect of the efficacy and benefits thereof.

The second, in what order faith apprehends Christ? *Answer.* First of all, it apprehends the very body and blood of Christ. And then in the second place the virtue and benefits of His body and blood, as a man that would feel in his body the virtue of meat and drink must first of all receive the substance thereof.

To go forward, besides this main promise, which concerns righteousness and life everlasting in Christ, there be other particular promises touching strength in temptations, comfort in afflictions, and such like, which depend on the former. And they also are the object of justifying faith; and with the very same faith we believe them, wherewith we believe our salvation. Thus, Abraham by the same faith wherewith he was justified believed that he should have a son in his old age (Rom. 4:9, 22). And Noah by that faith whereby he was made heir of righteousness believed that he and his family should be preserved in the flood—this conclusion being always laid down, that to whom God gives Christ, to them also He gives all things needful for this life or the life to come in and by Christ. And hereupon it comes to pass that in our prayers, besides the desire of things promised, we must bring faith, whereby we must be certainly persuaded that God will grant us such things as He has promised. And this faith is not a new kind or distinct faith from justifying faith. Thus, we see plainly what saving faith is.

Whereas some are of opinion that faith is an affiance or confidence, that seems to be otherwise; for it is a fruit of faith. And indeed no man can put any confidence in God, till he be first of all persuaded of God's mercy in Christ toward him [Eph. 3:12].

Some again are of mind that love is the very nature and form of faith, but it is otherwise. For as confidence in God, so also love is an effect which proceeds from faith. "The end of the law is love from a pure heart, and good conscience, and faith unfeigned" (1 Tim. 1:5). And in nature they differ greatly. Christ is the fountain of the water of life. Faith in the heart is as the pipes and leads that receive in and hold the water. And love in some part is as the cock[10] of the conduit, that lets out the water to every comer. The property of the hand is to hold, and of itself it cannot cut. Yet by a knife or other instrument put into the hand it cuts. The hand of the soul is faith, and its[11] property is to apprehend Christ with all His benefits and by itself can do nothing else. Yet join love unto it, and by love it will be effectual in all good duties [Gal. 5:6].

Now to proceed further, first, we are to consider how faith is wrought; secondly, what be the differences of it. For the first, faith is wrought in and by the outward ministry of the gospel, accompanied by the inward operation of the Spirit, and that not suddenly but by certain steps and degrees—as nature frames the body of the infant in the mother's womb (1) by making the brain and heart; (2) by making veins, sinews, arteries, bones; (3) by adding flesh to them all. And the whole operation of the Spirit stands in two principal actions: first, the enlightening of the mind; the second, the moving of the will. For the first, the Holy Ghost enlightens men's minds with a further knowledge of the law than nature can afford and thereby makes them to see the sins of their hearts and lives with the ugliness thereof and withal to tremble at the curse of

---

10. *Cock*: ?.
11. Originally, "his."

the law. Afterward, the same Spirit opens the eye to understand and consider seriously of righteousness and life eternal promised in Christ. This done, then comes the second work of the Holy Ghost, which is the inflaming of the will, that a man, having considered his fearful estate by reason of sin and the benefit of Christ's death, might hunger after Christ and have desire not so much to have the punishments of sin taken away as God's displeasure and also might enjoy the benefits of Christ. And when He has stirred up a man to desire reconciliation with God in Christ, then withal He gives him grace to pray not only for life eternal but especially for the free remission and pardon of all his sins. And then the Lord's promise is, "Knock and it shall be opened, seek and ye shall find" [Matt. 7:7]. After which He further sends His Spirit into the same heart that desires reconciliation with God and remission of sins in Christ and does seal up the same in the heart by a lively and plentiful assurance thereof.

The differences and degrees of faith are two: (1) a weak faith; (2) a strong faith. Concerning the first, this weak faith shows itself by this grace of God—namely, an unfeigned desire not only of salvation (for that the wicked and graceless man may have), but of reconciliation with God in Christ. This is a sure sign of faith in every touched and humbled heart, and it is peculiar to the elect. And they which have this have in them also the ground and substance of true saving faith, which afterward in time will grow up to great strength. *Reason 1.* Promise of life everlasting is made to the desire of reconciliation. "Lord, thou hast heard the desire of the poor" (Ps. 10:17). "My soul desires after thee, as the thirsty land" (143:6).[12] "He will fulfill the desire of them that fear him" (145:19). "Blessed are they that hunger and thirst after righteousness, for they shall be satisfied" (Matt. 5:6). "I will give unto him which is athirst, of the well of the water of life freely" (Rev. 21:6). *[Reason] 2.* The hungering desire after grace is a sanctified affection. Where one affection is sanctified, all are sanctified. Where all are sanctified, the whole man is sanctified. And he that is sanctified is justified and believes. *[Reason] 3.* God accepts the will and desire to repent and believe for repenting and believing indeed. Wherefore, this desire of reconciliation (if it be soundly wrought in the heart) is in acceptation with God as true faith indeed. But carnal men will say, "If faith, yea, true faith show itself by a desire of reconciliation with God in Christ for all our sins, then we are well enough, though we live in our sins; for we have very good desires." I answer that there be many sundry, fleeting motions and desires to do good things, which grow to no issue or head but in time vanish as they come. Now such passions have no soundness in them and must be distinguished from the desire of reconciliation with God that comes from a bruised heart and brings

---

12. Originally, "Ps. 14:36."

always with it reformation of life. Therefore, such, whosoever they are, that live after the course of this world and think notwithstanding that they have desires that are good deceive themselves.

Now faith is said to be weak when a man either fails in the knowledge of the gospel or else, having knowledge, is weak in grace to apply unto himself the sweet promises thereof. As, for example, we know that the apostles had all true saving faith (except Judas), and when our Savior Christ asked them whom they thought He was, Peter in the person of the rest answered for them all and said, "Thou art Christ, the Son of the living God" [Matt. 16:16]; for which our Savior commended him and in him them all, saying, "Thou art Peter, and upon this rock"—that is, upon Christ, which Peter confessed in the name of them all— "will I build my church" [v. 18; 8:26]. And yet about that time we shall find in the Gospel that they are called men of "little faith" [16:8]. Now they failed in knowledge of the death of Christ and of His passion and resurrection and were carried away with a vain hope of an earthly kingdom. And therefore when our Savior showed them of His going down to Jerusalem and of His sufferings there, Peter a little after his notable confession began to rebuke Christ and said, "Master, have pity on thyself, this shall not be unto thee" [16:22].[13] And until He had appeared unto them after His death, they did not distinctly believe His resurrection.

Again, weak faith, though it be joined with knowledge, yet it may fail in the applying or in the apprehension and appropriating of Christ's benefits to a man's own self. This is to be seen in ordinary experience. For many a man there is of humble and contrite heart that serves God in spirit and truth, yet is not able to say without great doubtings and waverings, "I know and am fully assured that my sins are pardoned." Now shall we say that all such are without faith? God forbid. Nay, we may resolve ourselves that the true child of God may have a hungering desire in his heart after reconciliation with God in Christ for all his sins, with care to keep a good conscience, and yet be weak sometimes in the apprehension of God's mercy and the assurance of the remission of his own sins.

But if faith fail either in the true knowledge or in the apprehension of God's mercies, how can a man be saved by it? *Answer.* We must know that this weak faith will as truly apprehend God's merciful promises for the pardon of sin as strong faith, though not so soundly—even as a man with a palsy hand can stretch it out as well to receive a gift at the hand of a king as he that is more sound, though it be not so firmly and steadfastly. And Christ says that He will not break the bruised reed nor quench the smoking flax.

---

13. Originally, "Matt. 16:21."

The Church of Rome bears men in hand that they are good Catholics if they believe as the Church believes, though in the mean season[14] they cannot tell what the Church believes. And some Papists commend this faith by the example of an old, devout father, who, being tempted of the devil and asked how he believed, answered that he believed as the Church believed. Being again asked how the Church believed, he answered, "As I believe," whereupon the devil (as they say) was fain[15] to depart. Well, this fond and ridiculous kind of faith we renounce as being a means to muzzle men in blindness, superstition, and perpetual ignorance. Yet withal we do not deny but there is an implicit or infolded faith, which is when a man as yet having but some little portion of knowledge in the doctrine of the gospel does truly perform obedience according to the measure thereof and withal has care to get more knowledge and shows good affection to all good means whereby it may be increased. In this respect, a certain ruler who by a miracle wrought upon his child was moved to acknowledge Christ for the Messiah and further to submit himself to His doctrine is commended for a believer, and so are in like case the Samaritans [John 4:33, 42].

And thus much of weak faith, which must be understood to be in a man not all the days of his life, but while he is a young babe in Christ. For as it is in the state of the body—first we are babes and grow to greater strength as we grow in years—so it is with a Christian man. First, he is a babe in Christ, having weak faith, but after grows from grace to grace till he come to have a strong faith, an example whereof we have in Abraham, who was strong and perfect both in knowledge and apprehension. This strong faith is when a man is endued with the knowledge of the gospel and grace to apprehend and apply the righteousness of Christ unto himself for the remission of his own sins, so as he can say distinctly of himself and truly that he is fully resolved in his own conscience that he is reconciled unto God in Christ for all his sins and accepted in Him to life everlasting. This degree of faith is proper to him that begins to be a tall man and of ripe years in Christ. And it comes not at the first calling of a man unto grace. And if any shall think that he can have it at the first, he deceives himself; for as it is in nature—first we are babes, and then as we increase in years, so we grow in strength—so it is in the life of a Christian. First, ordinarily, he has a weak faith and after grows from grace to grace, till he come to stronger faith and at the last he be able to say he is fully assured in his heart and conscience of the pardon of his sins and of reconciliation to God in Christ. And this assurance arises from many experiences of God's favor and love in the course of his life by manifold preservations and other blessings, which, being

14. *Mean season*: meantime.
15. *Fain*: to desire or will.

deeply and duly considered, bring a man to be fully persuaded that God is his God, and God the Father his Father, and Jesus Christ his Redeemer, and the Holy Ghost his Sanctifier.

Now howsoever this faith be strong, yet is it always imperfect, as also our knowledge is, and shall so long as we live in this world be mingled with contrary unbelief and sundry doubtings more or less. A great part of men among us, blinded with gross ignorance, say they have faith and yet indeed have not. For ask them what faith they have, they will answer they believe that God is their Father, and the Son their Redeemer, etc. Ask them how long they have had this faith; they will answer, ever since they could remember. Ask them whether they ever doubt of God's favor; they will say they would not once doubt for all the world. But the case of these men is to be pitied; for howsoever they may persuade themselves, yet true it is that they have no sound faith at all, for even strong faith is assaulted with temptations and doubtings. And God will not have men perfect in this life, that they may always go out of themselves and depend wholly on the merit of Christ.

And thus much of these two degrees of faith. Now, in whomsoever it is, whether it be a weak faith or a strong, it brings forth some fruit, as a tree does in the time of summer. And a special fruit of faith is the confession of faith, "I believe in God," etc. So Paul says, "With the heart a man believeth unto righteousness, and with the mouth man confesseth to salvation" [Rom. 10:10]. Confession of faith is when a man in speech and outward profession does make manifest his faith for these two causes: (1) that with his mouth outwardly he may glorify God and do Him service both in body and soul; (2) that by the confession of his faith he may sever himself from all false Christians, from atheists, hypocrites, and all false seducers whatsoever. And as this is the duty of a Christian man to make profession of his faith, so here in this Creed of the Apostles we have the right order and form of making confession set down, as we shall see in handling[16] the parts thereof.

The Creed therefore sets down two things concerning faith—namely, the action of faith and its[17] object, which also are the parts of the Creed: the action, in these words, "I believe"; the object, in all the words following, "in God the Father Almighty, Maker," etc. And first let us begin with the action.

"I believe in God." We are taught to say, "I believe," not, "We believe," for two causes: first, because (as we touched before) in the primitive church this Creed was made to be an answer to a demand or question, which was demanded of every particular man that was baptized; for they asked him thus,

---

16. Originally, "handing."
17. Originally, "his."

"What do you believe?" Then he answered, "I believe in God the Father," etc. And thus did everyone of years make profession of his faith, and it is likely that Peter alluded hereunto, saying, "The stipulation or answer of a good conscience makes request to God" [1 Peter 3:21]. The second cause is, howsoever we are to pray one for another by saying, "Our Father," etc., yet when we come to years, we must have a particular faith of our own. No man can be saved by another man's faith, but by his own, as it is said, "The just shall live by his faith" [Hab. 2:4]. But some will say, this is not true, because children must be saved by their parents' faith. The answer is this: the faith of the parent does bring the child to have a title or interest to the covenant of grace and to all the benefits of Christ; yet does it not apply the benefits of Christ's death, His obedience, His merits, and righteousness unto the infant, for this the believer does only unto himself and to no other. Again, some may say, if children do not apprehend Christ's benefits by their parents' faith, how then is Christ's righteousness made theirs, and they saved? *Answer.* By the inward working of the Holy Ghost, who is the principal applier of all graces, whereas faith is but the instrument. As for the places of Scripture that mention justification and salvation by faith, they are to be restrained to men of years. Whereas infants, dying in their infancy and therefore wanting actual faith, which none can have without actual knowledge of God's will and Word, are no doubt saved by some other special working of God's Holy Spirit not known to us.

Furthermore, to believe signifies two things: to conceive or understand anything and withal to give assent unto it to be true. And therefore in this place "to believe" signifies to know and acknowledge that all the points of religion which follow are the truth of God. Here therefore we must remember that this clause, "I believe," placed in the beginning of the Creed, must be particularly applied to all and every article following. For so the case stands, that if faith fail in one main point, it fails a man in all. And therefore faith is said to be wholly copulative.[18] It is not sufficient to hold one article, but he that will hold any of them for his good must hold them all; and he which holds them all in show of words, if he overturn but one of them indeed, he overturns them all.

Again, to believe is one thing, and to believe in this or that is another thing; and it contains in it three points or actions of a believer: (1) to know a thing; (2) to acknowledge the same; (3) to put trust and confidence in it. And in this order must these three actions of faith be applied to every article following which concerns any of the persons in [the] Trinity. And this must be marked as a matter of a special moment.[19] For always by adding them to the words fol-

---

18. Fides est tota copulativa.
19. *Moment*: importance.

lowing we do apply the article unto ourselves in a very comfortable manner: "As I believe in the Father and do believe that He is my Father, and therefore I put my whole trust in Him"—and so of the rest.

The Object of Faith

Now we come to the object of general faith, which is either God or the church, in handling of both which I will observe this order: (1) I will speak of the meaning of every article; (2) of the duties which we ought to learn thereby; (3) and, lastly, of the consolations which may be gathered thence. Concerning God, three things are to be considered. And, first, by reason of manifold doubtings that rise in our minds, it may be demanded, whether there be a God? Many reasons might be used to resolve those that have scruple of conscience. Otherwise we are bound to believe that there is a God without all doubting. As for the atheists which confidently avouch there is no God, by God's law they ought to die the death. Nay, the earth is too good for such to dwell on. Malefactors, as thieves and rebels, for their offences have their reward of death; but the offence of those which deny that there is a God is greater and therefore deserves a most cruel death.

The second point follows—namely, what God is? *Answer.* Moses, desiring to see God's face, was not permitted but to see His hinder parts [Ex. 33:20, 23]. And therefore no man can be able to describe God by His nature, but by His effects and properties, on this or such like manner: God is an essence spiritual, simple, infinite, most holy. I say first of all that God is an essence to show that He is a thing absolutely subsisting in Himself and by Himself, not receiving His being from any other. And herein He differs from all creatures whatsoever, which have subsisting and being from Him alone. Again, I say He is an essence spiritual because He is not any kind of body. Neither has He the parts of the bodies of men or other creatures, but is in nature a spirit invisible, not subject to any man's senses. I add also that He is a simple essence because His nature admits no manner of composition of matter or form of parts. The creatures are compounded of divers parts and of variety of natures, but there is no such thing in God. For whatsoever thing He is, He is the same by one and the same singular and indivisible essence. Furthermore, He is infinite, and that divers ways: infinite in time, without any beginning and without end; infinite in place, because He is everywhere and excluded nowhere, within all places and forth of all places. Lastly, He is most holy—that is, of infinite wisdom, mercy, love, goodness, etc. And He alone is rightly termed "most holy" because holiness is of the very nature of God Himself, whereas among the most excellent creatures it is otherwise. For the creature itself is one thing, and the holiness of the creature another thing. Thus, we see what God is; and to this effect God describes

Himself to be "Jehovah Elohim" [3:6, 14],[20] and Paul describes Him to be a king "everlasting, immortal, invisible, and only wise, to whom is due all honor and glory for ever" [1 Tim. 1:17].

The third point is touching the number of gods—namely, whether there be more gods than one or no. *Answer.* There is not, neither can there be any more gods than one. Which point the Creed avouches in saying, "I believe in God," not, "in gods"; and yet more plainly the Nicene Creed and the Creed of Athanasius, both of them explaining the words of the Apostles' Creed in this manner, "I believe in one God." Howsoever some in former times have erroneously held that two gods were the beginning of all things—one of good things, the other of evil things. Others, that there was one God in the Old Testament, another in the New. Others again—namely, the Valentinians—that there were thirty couples of gods. And the heathen people (as Augustine reports) worshipped thirty thousand gods. Yet we that are members of God's church must hold and believe one God alone, and no more. "Understand this day and consider in thine heart, that Jehovah, he is God in heaven above, and upon the earth beneath: there is none other" (Deut. 4:39). "One God, one faith, one baptism" (Eph. 4:6). If it be alleged that the Scripture mentions many gods because magistrates are called gods [Ps. 82:6], Moses is called Aaron's god [Ex. 4:16], the devil and all idols are called gods [2 Cor. 4:4], [then] the answer is this: they are not properly or by nature gods, for in that respect there is only one God. But they are so termed in other respects. Magistrates are gods because they are vicegerents placed in the room of the true God to govern their subjects. Moses is Aaron's god because he was in the room of God to reveal His will to Aaron. The devil is a god because the hearts of the wicked world give the honor unto him which is peculiar to the ever-living God. Idols are called gods because they are such in men's conceits and opinions, who esteem of them as gods. Therefore, Paul says an idol is nothing in the world [1 Cor. 8:4]—that is, nothing in nature subsisting, or nothing in respect of the divinity ascribed to it.

To proceed forward, to believe in this one God is in effect thus much: (1) to know and acknowledge Him as He has revealed Himself in His Word; (2) to believe Him to be my God; (3) from mine heart to put all mine affiance in Him. To this purpose Christ says, "This is eternal life, to know thee the only God, and whom thou hast sent, Jesus Christ" [John 17:3]. Now the knowledge here meant is not a bare or general knowledge, for that the devils have, but a more special knowledge whereby I know God not only to be God but also to be my God and thereupon do put my confidence in Him.

20. Originally, "Ex. 36:14."

And thus much of the meaning of the first words, "I believe in God," etc. Now follow the duties which may be gathered hence. First of all, if we are bound to believe in God, then we are also bound to take notice of our natural unbelief, whereby we distrust God, to check ourselves for it and to strive against it. Thus dealt the father of the child that had a dumb spirit. "Lord," says he, "I believe. Lord, help mine unbelief" [Mark 9:24]. And David, "Why art thou cast down my soul? and why art thou so disquieted within me? wait on God" [Ps. 42:11].[21] And that which our Savior Christ said once to Peter, men should daily speak to themselves: "O thou of little faith! why hast thou doubted?" [Matt. 14:31]. But some may say, wherein stands our unbelief? *Answer.* It stands in two things: (1) in distrusting the goodness of God—that is, in giving too little or no affiance to Him or in putting affiance in the creature. For the first, few men will abide to be told of their distrust in God, but indeed it is a common and rife corruption. And though they soothe themselves never so, yet their usual dealings proclaim their unbelief. Go through all places; it shall be found that scarce one of a thousand in his dealings makes conscience of a lie. A great part of men get their wealth by fraud and oppression and all kinds of unjust and unmerciful dealings. What is the cause that they can do so? Alas, alas, if there be any faith, it is pinned up in some by-corner of the heart, and unbelief bears sway as the lord of the house. Again, if a man had as much wealth as the world comes to, he could find in his heart to wish for another. And if he had two worlds, he would be casting for the third, if it might be compassed. The reason hereof is because men have not learned to make God their portion and to stay their affections on Him—which if they could do, a mean[22] portion in temporal blessings would be enough. Indeed, these and such like persons will in no wise yield that they do distrust the Lord, unless at some time they be touched in conscience with a sense and feeling of their sins and be thoroughly humbled for the same. But the truth is that distrust of God's goodness is a general and a mother sin, the ground of all other sins, and the very first and principal sin in Adam's fall. [2] And for the second part of unbelief, which is an affiance in the creatures, read the whole Book of God, and we shall find it a common and usual sin in all sorts of men—some putting their trust in riches, some in strength, some in pleasures, some placing their felicity in one sin, some in another. When King Asa was sick, he put his whole trust in the physicians and not in the Lord [2 Chron. 16:12]. And in our days the common practice is when crosses and calamities fall, then there is trotting out to that wise man, to this cunning woman, to this sorcerer, to that wizard—that is, from God to the devil. And their counsel is received and practiced without making any

---

21. Originally, "Ps. 24:11."
22. *Mean*: small.

bones [about it]. And this shows the bitter root of unbelief and confidence in vain creatures, let men smooth it over with goodly terms as long as they will. In a word, there is no man in the world, be he called or not called, if he look narrowly unto himself, but he shall find his heart filled almost with manifold doubtings and distrustings, whereby he shall feel himself even carried away from believing in God. Therefore, the duty of every man is, that will truly say that he believes in God, to labor to see his own unbelief and the fruits thereof in his life. And for such as say they have no unbelief nor feel none, more pitiful is their case, for so much greater is their unbelief.

Secondly, considering that we profess ourselves to believe in God, we must every one of us learn to know God. As Paul says, "How can they believe in him whom they have not heard? and how can they hear without a preacher?" [Rom. 10:14], therefore none can believe in God, but he must first of all hear and be taught by the ministry of the word to know God aright. Let this be remembered of young and old. It is not the pattering over the Belief[23] for a prayer that will make a man a good believer, but God must be known of us and acknowledged as He has revealed Himself, partly in His Word and partly in His creatures. Blind ignorance and the right use of the Apostles' Creed will never stand together. Therefore, it stands men in hand to labor and take pains to get knowledge in religion, that, knowing God aright, they may come steadfastly to believe in Him and truly make confession of their faith.

Thirdly, because we believe in God, therefore another duty is to deny ourselves utterly and become nothing in ourselves. Our Savior Christ requires of us to become as little children, if we would believe. The beggar depends not upon the relief of others, till he find nothing at home. And till our hearts be purged of self-love and pride, we cannot depend upon the favor and goodness of God. Therefore, he that would trust in God must first of all be abased and confounded in himself and in regard of himself be out of all hope of attaining to the least spark of the grace of God.

Fourthly, in that we believe in God and therefore put our whole trust and assurance in Him, we are taught that every man must commit his body, his soul, goods, life, yea, all that he has into the hands of God and to His custody. So Paul says, "I am not ashamed of my sufferings, for I know whom I have believed, and am persuaded, that he is able to keep that which I have committed unto him against that day" [2 Tim. 1:12]. A worthy saying, for what is the thing which Paul committed unto the Lord? It was his own soul and the eternal salvation thereof. But what moves him to trust God? Surely, his persuasion whereby he knew that God would keep it. And Peter says, "Let them that suffer

---

23. Editor's note: the Apostles' Creed.

according to the will of God commit their souls to him in well doing, as unto a faithful creator" [1 Peter 4:19]. Look as one friend lays down a thing to be kept of another, so must a man give that he has to the custody of God. Few or none can practice this; and therefore when any evil befalls them either in body or in goods or any other way whatsoever, then they presently show themselves rather beasts than men in impatience. For in prosperity they had no care to put their trust in God; and therefore in adversity, when crosses come, they are void of comfort. But when a man has grace to believe and trust in God, he commits all into God's hands; and though all the world should perish, yet he would not be dismayed. And undoubtedly, if a man will be thankful for the preservation of his goods or of his life, he must show the same by committing all he has into God's hands and suffer himself to be ruled by Him.

Now follows the consolations and comforts which God's church and children reap hereby. He that believes in God and takes God for his God may assure himself of salvation and of a happy deliverance in all dangers and necessities. When God threatened a plague upon Israel for their idolatry, good King Josiah humbled himself before the Lord his God; and he was safe all his days [2 Chron. 34:27]. And so King Hezekiah, when Sennacherib, the king of Assyria, offered to invade Judah, trusted likewise in the Lord and prayed unto Him and was delivered [c. 32].[24] Whereby we see if a man puts his whole trust in God, he shall have security and quietness, as Jehoshaphat said to the men of Judah [20:20]. And our Savior Christ, when He was upon the cross and felt the whole burden of the terrible wrath of God upon Him, cried, "My God, my God, why hast thou forsaken me?" [Mark 15:34]. And it appears in the epistle to the Hebrews that Christ "was heard in that he feared" [Heb. 5:7], whereby we are given to understand that they shall never be utterly forsaken that take God for their God. And King David, having experience of this, uses most excellent speeches for this end, to show that the ground of his comfort was that God was his God [Psalm 22].[25] And it is said that Daniel had no manner of hurt in the lions' den because he trusted in the Lord his God [Dan. 6:23].[26] And contrariwise, such as distrust God are subject to all miseries and judgments. The Israelites in the wilderness "believed not God, and trusted not in his help. Therefore, fire was kindled in Jacob, and wrath came upon Israel" [Ps. 78:21–22].

"God, the Father, Almighty." Some have thought that these words are to be coupled to the former without distinction, as if the title of God had been proper to the first person, the Father, and not common to the rest; and thus have some

---

24. Originally, "2 Chron. 3:2."
25. Originally, "Ps. 21:10."
26. Originally, "Dan. 6:2–3."

heretics thought. But indeed there must a pause or distinction be made, that the name or title of God may be set in the forefront as common to all the three persons following. For that is the very intent of the order of this Creed, to teach us to believe in one God, who is distinct in three subsistences or persons, called the Father, the Son, and the Holy Ghost. And here offers itself to be considered even one of the greatest mysteries of our religion—namely, that God is the Father, the Son, and the Holy Ghost; and again, that the Father, the Son, and the Holy Ghost are one and the same God. Some at the first may possibly say that this cannot stand, because it is against all reason that one should be three, or three one. The answer is that indeed, if one and the same respect be kept, it is not possible; but in diverse considerations and respects it may. And thus the Father, the Son, and the Holy Ghost are three—namely, in person. And again, they three are one not in person, but in nature. By "nature" is meant a thing subsisting by itself that is common to many, as the substance of man, consisting of body and soul, common to all men, which we call the "humanity" of a man, is the nature of man. By "person" is meant a thing or essence subsisting by itself not common to many but incommunicable—as among men, these particulars, Peter, John, Paul, are called persons. And so in the mystery of the Trinity the divine nature is the Godhead itself, simply and absolutely considered; and a person is that which subsists in that Godhead, as the Father, the Son, and the Holy Ghost. Or again, a person is one and the same Godhead not absolutely considered but in relation and as it were restrained by personal or characteristical properties—as the Godhead or God begetting is the Father; God, again considered not simply, but so far forth as He is begotten, is the Son; and God proceeding of the Father and the Son, the Holy Ghost. And if any man would conceive in mind rightly the divine nature, he must conceive God or the Godhead absolutely. If any of the persons, then he must conceive the same Godhead relatively with personal proprieties. Thus, the Godhead considered with the property of fatherhood or begetting is the Father; and conceiving the same Godhead with the property of generation we conceive the Son; and the Godhead with the property of proceeding we conceive the Holy Ghost. Neither must it seem strange to any that we use the names of "nature" and "person" to set forth this mystery by; for they have been taken up by common consent in the primitive church, and that upon weighty consideration, to manifest the truth and to stop the mouths of heretics. And they are not so used against the proper sense of the Scriptures; nay, they are therein contained [Gal. 4:8; Heb. 1:3]. Thus, we see how it comes to pass that the three things signified by these names, Father, Son, and Holy Ghost, are each of them one and the same God. And this mystery may well be conceived by a comparison borrowed from light. The light of the sun, the light of the moon, and the light of the air for nature and substance are one and the same light; and yet they are three distinct lights—the light of the sun being of itself and from none, the light of the moon from the sun, and the light of the air from them both. So the divine nature is one, and the persons are three, subsisting after a diverse manner in one and the same nature.

And for the further clearing of this point, we must yet further mark and remember two things—namely, the union and the distinction of the persons. The union is whereby three persons are not one simply but one in nature—that is, coessential or consubstantial, having all one Godhead. For the Father is God, the Son is God, and the Holy Ghost is God. Now there are not three distinct Gods, but one God, because there is one God and no more in nature, considering that the thing which is infinite is but one and is not subject to multiplication. And the Father is this one God, as also the Son and the Holy Ghost. And as these three persons are one in nature, so whatsoever agrees to God simply considered agrees to them all three. They are all coequal and coeternal; all most wise, just, merciful, omnipotent by one and the same wisdom, justice, mercy, power. And because they have all one Godhead, therefore they are not only one with another but also each in [the] other—the Father in the Son, and the Son in the Father, and the Holy Ghost in them both. And we must not imagine that these three are one God, as though the Father had one part of the Godhead, the Son another part, and the Holy Ghost a third. For that is most false, because the infinite and the most simple Godhead is not subject to composition or division; but every person is whole God, subsisting not in a part but in the whole Godhead. And the whole entire Godhead is communicated from the Father to the Son, and from both Father and Son to the Holy Ghost. But some may yet say that this doctrine seems to be impossible, because three creatures, as, for example, Peter, Paul, [and] Timothy, be three persons and so remaining cannot have one and the same nature—that is, the same body and the same soul. *Answer.* Three or more men may have the same nature in kind,[27] but the truth is they cannot possibly have a nature which shall be one and the same in number[28] in them all three. For a man is a substance created and finite, and the bodies of men are quantities and therefore divisible and separable one from another. Hereupon it comes that the persons of men are not only distinguished by property, but also divided and sundered one from another. And though Peter, Paul, and Timothy have all one common and universal form, yet they three are not one man, but three men. Now it is otherwise with the divine nature or Godhead, which is uncreated and infinite and therefore admits

---

27. Specie.
28. Numero.

neither composition nor division but a distinction without any separation, so as the three persons subsisting in it shall not be three Gods but one and the same God.

Yet further, some will object that it is truly said of the Father that He is God; but the same Godhead is not in the Son nor in the Holy Ghost, for the Son and the Holy Ghost have their beginning from the Father. *Answer.* The Son and the Holy Ghost have not a beginning of their nature or of their Godhead from the Father, but of their person only. The person of the Son is from the Father, and the person of the Holy Ghost is both from the Father and from the Son. But the Godhead of all three persons is uncreate[d] and unbegotten and proceeding from none. Yet some may say both the Son and the Holy Ghost have received from the Father all their attributes, as wisdom, knowledge, power, etc. Now he that receives anything from another is in that respect inferior to him that gives it, and therefore the Son and the Holy Ghost are not God as He is. *Answer.* We must know that that which the Son receives of the Father, He receives it by nature and not by grace; and He receives not a part but all that the Father has, saving the personal property. And the Holy Ghost receives from the Father and the Son by nature and not by grace. And therefore, though both the Son and the Holy Ghost receive from the Father, yet they are not inferior to Him but equal with Him. And thus much is both necessary and profitable to be learned of the union between the three persons in [the] Trinity, whereby they being three have all one and the same Godhead.

The second point to be considered is that though these three have but one Godhead and all make but one God, yet they are distinguished one from another—for the Father is the Father and not the Son or the Holy Ghost; the Son is the Son and not the Father nor the Holy Ghost; and the Holy Ghost is the Holy Ghost, not the Father nor the Son. This distinction of the persons is notably set forth unto us in the baptism of our Savior Christ, where it is said that "when Jesus was baptized, he came out of the water" [Matt. 3:16–17]—there is the second person. And the Holy Ghost descended upon Him in the form of a dove—there is the third person. And the Father, the first person, pronounced from heaven that He was His only beloved Son in whom He was well pleased. And we must not conceive this distinction in such manner as though these three, Father, Son, and Holy Ghost, were three names of one God, for the three persons do not in name or word but really in truth distinctly subsist in the same divine nature. Neither must we imagine that the three persons are three forms or differences of one God, as some heretics have dreamed, who taught that the Father alone is God and that He is called a father in one respect, the Son in another, and the Holy Ghost in a third. For this were nothing else but to make the personal properties to be nothing but imaginary accidents, which indeed, or at the least in man's conceit, might come and go and be either in the persons or forth of them. For the personal relations, though in mind[29] they may be distinguished from the divine essence, yet indeed[30] they are one with it. But some will say, if they make this distinction, there is rather a quaternity than a Trinity; for the Godhead is one, the Father another, the Son a third, and the Holy Ghost a fourth. Thus, some heretics have objected against the distinction of the Trinity, but it is untrue which they say. For the Godhead must not be severed from the Father nor from the Son nor from the Holy Ghost; for as the Father is God or the whole Godhead, so also is the Son and the Holy Ghost. And the Godhead likewise is in every one of these three persons; and every one of them subsisting in the Godhead, the same must be conceived to be in them all and not as a fourth thing out of them. And therefore we must still maintain that these three persons are distinguished and not divided, as three men are divided in being and substance; for this division cannot be in them, because all three have one divine nature and one Godhead. This is the mystery of all mysteries to be received of us all—namely, the Trinity of the persons in the unity of the Godhead. This form of doctrine must be retained and held for these causes: (1) because by it we are able to distinguish this true God from all false gods and idols; (2) because among all other points of religion this is one of the chiefest, being the very foundation thereof. For it is not sufficient for us to know God as we can conceive of Him in our own imagination, but we must know Him as He has revealed Himself in His Word. And it is not sufficient to salvation to believe in God confusedly, but we must believe in one God distinct in three persons, the Father, the Son, and the Holy Ghost. Yea, and more than this, we must hold and believe that God the Father is our Father, the Son our Redeemer, the Holy Ghost our Sanctifier and Comforter. Well then, if we must in this manner believe in God, then we must also know Him; for we can have no faith in the thing which is utterly unknown. Wherefore, if we would believe in the Father, Son, or Holy Ghost, we must know them in part. "This is life eternal, to know thee the only God, and whom thou hast sent, Jesus Christ" [John 17:3]. "The world cannot receive the spirit of truth, because it hath neither seen him, nor known him" [14:17]. "Whosoever denieth the Son, hath not the Father" [1 John 2:23]. Thirdly, this doctrine directs us in worshipping God aright; for unity in Trinity and Trinity in unity is to be worshipped. One God must be worshipped in the Father, in the Son, and in the Holy Ghost. And if we worship God the Father without the Son and the Holy Ghost, or if we worship the Son without the Father and the Holy Ghost, and the Holy Ghost without the Father and the

---

29. τῷ λογῳ.
30. τῷ ειναι.

Son, we worship nothing but an idol. Again, if we worship the three persons not as one God but as three Gods, then likewise we make three idols.

Note further that of all the three persons, the first person of the Father is set in the first place and described to us by three things: (1) by His title, that He is a father; (2) by His attribute, that He is almighty; (3) by His effect, that He is maker of heaven and earth. Of these in order, as they lay in the Creed. And first of the title, "Father." It may seem that He has some prerogative over the Son and the Holy Ghost, because He is set before them; but we must know that He is set before them neither in regard of time nor of dignity, for therein all three are equal, but in regard of order only. The Father is the first, the Son the second, and the Holy Ghost the third, as may appear by this similitude. If three emperors equal in dignity should meet all in one place, being equal also in power and majesty, if all three should sit down, though one be no better than another, yet one of them must needs sit down in the first and another in the second place, and then the third. But yet we cannot say that he which sat down first is the chiefest. And so it is in the Trinity; though none be greater or above another, yet the Father is in the first place, not because He is before the Son or the Holy Ghost in dignity and honor, but because He is the fountain of the deity, the Son being from Him and the Holy Ghost from them both.

The Meaning of Father

Now let us come to the title of the first person.[31] The name "Father" in Scripture is ascribed either to God taken indefinitely, and so by consequent to all the three persons in [the] Trinity, or particularly to the first person alone. For the first, God is a father properly and principally, according to the saying of Christ: "Call no man father upon earth, for there is but one, your Father which is in heaven" [Matt. 23:9]—that is, principally, whereas earthly parents, whom we are commanded to worship and honor, are but certain images or resemblances of our heavenly Father, having this blessing that they are fathers from Him. And hereupon this title agrees to men not simply but so far forth as God honors them with fatherhood in calling them to be fathers, whereas God Himself receives this honor from none. God is termed a father in respect both of nature and grace. He is a father in regard of nature, because He created and governs all things. In this regard, He is called the "Father of spirits" [Heb. 12:9], and "Adam" [Luke 3:38] is called "the son of God." He is a father in respect of grace because we are regenerate by Him, accepted to be His sons by adoption through the merits of Christ. And in this respect the second person as well as the first is called a father [Isa. 9:6] and said to have an offspring [53:10] or seed

---

31. The meaning.

and children [8:18]. But when the name of Father is given to the first person, it is done upon a special consideration, because He is a father by nature to the second person, begetting Him of His own substance before all worlds. By this it appears that out of the title of the first person we may fetch a description thereof on this manner. The Father is the first person in [the] Trinity, begetting the Son. Now to beget is the personal property whereby He is distinguished from the other two. If it be said that creatures do beget and that therefore to beget is not proper to the Father, the answer is that in this point there are many differences between God the Father and all creatures. First, the Father begets the Son before all eternity. And therefore God the Father begetting and the Son begotten are equal in time, whereas in earthly generation the father is before the son in time. Secondly, God the Father begets His Son by communicating to Him His whole essence or Godhead, which cannot be in earthly parents, unless they should be abolished and come to nothing. Whereas nevertheless, God the Father, giving His whole nature to His Son, retains the same still, because it is infinite. Thirdly, the Father begets the Son in Himself and not forth of Himself; but in earthly generation the father begetting is forth of the child, and the child forth of the father. And that must not trouble us which heretics allege against this doctrine—namely, that if the Father, who is of one nature with the Son, did beget the Son, then He did beget Himself. For the Godhead of the Father does not beget either the Godhead or the person of the Son. The person of the Father begets the person of the Son, both which in one Godhead are really distinct.

Thus we see what the Father is. Now to believe in the Father is to be persuaded that the first person in [the] Trinity is the Father of Christ and in Him my Father particularly, and that for this cause I intend and desire forever to put my trust in Him [Jer. 24:7;[32] Matt. 6:4].

Duty 1.[33] The duties which we may learn hence are manifold. And here we have occasion offered first of all to consider who is our father by nature. "I shall say to corruption," says Job, "thou art my father: and to the worm, thou art my mother" [Job 17:14]. Seeing God vouchsafes this great prerogative to them that love Him, that He will be their Father, therefore Job in consideration hereof would have every man to have recourse to his own natural condition to see who is his father by nature. Job says corruption is his father; but if we mark well the condition of our nature, we shall further see every man to be the child of wrath, and that Satan is his father. For so long as a man walks in his sins (which every man does by nature), so long does he show himself to be the lively child of the devil. And thus Christ reasons against the scribes and Pharisees: "Ye are of your

---

32. Originally, "Jer. 24:9."
33. This was originally in the margin, as are the following five duties.

father the devil, and the lusts of your father, ye will do" [John 8:44]. And true it is that no child is so like his father that begot him, as every man by nature is like the devil. And the whole tenor and course of his natural life without grace is a lively resemblance of the disposition of Satan.

[Duty] 2. Secondly, everyone that believes God to be a father and in Christ his Father must as a good child be obedient to his Father's will. So Solomon says, "A wise son makes a glad father" [Prov. 10:1]. How? By doing his will. And therefore when one told our Savior Christ that His mother and brethren stood without, desiring to speak with Him, He said, "Whosoever shall do my Father's will which is in heaven, the same is my brother, my sister, and mother" [Matt. 12:50], wherein we may note that he that will have God the Father to be his Father and Christ Jesus his brother must do the will of God the Father. And hence God says, "If I be a master, where is my fear? If I be a father, where is my honor?" [Mal. 1:6]. Where is plainly taught this second duty, that if God be our Father, then as good children we must show obedience unto Him. But if we disobey Him, then we must know that that former saying of Christ will be verified upon us, that because men do the lusts of the devil, therefore they are the children of the devil. But lest this fearful sentence be verified of us, it is the duty of every man that makes this confession that he believes God to be his Father, first, to labor to know God's will and, secondly, to perform continual obedience unto the same, like unto a good child that would fain please his father and therefore is always ready to do the best he can. And without doubt, that man which unfeignedly takes God for his Father is then most grieved when as by any sin he displeases Him, and no other cross or calamity is so grievous unto him. The greatest grief that the prodigal son upon his repentance had was that he had offended his father by sinning against heaven and against him. The same also must be our grief. And all our care must be set on this, to consider how we may be obedient children to this our loving Father.

[Duty] 3. Thirdly, that man that believes God to be his Father must imitate and follow Him, for it is the will of God that His children should be like unto Himself. Now we follow God specially in two things. (1) In doing good to them that persecute us. So says our Savior Christ: "Pray for them that hurt you, that you may be the children of your Father which is in heaven: for he maketh the sun to rise on the evil and on the good, and sendeth rain on the just and unjust" [Matt. 5:45]. (2) Our heavenly Father is merciful, for He is the Father of the fatherless. And therefore he that will be a son of this Father must be merciful to his poor brethren, as Job says of himself: "I was eyes to the blind, and I was feet unto the lame, I was a father to the poor" [Job 29:15–16]

[Duty] 4. Fourthly, seeing we believe God to be our Father, we are hereby taught to use moderate care for the things of this life; for if a man know himself to be the child of God, then he also knows that God will provide for him, as we know in a family the father provides for all. Now God is a father, and His church is this family. Therefore, if you will be a member of God's church and a child of God, you must cast your care on God and follow the counsel of Christ: "Be not too careful for your life, what ye shall eat, or what ye shall drink" [Matt. 6:25]. And mark His reason drawn from the point which we have in hand: "The fowls of the heaven," says He, "they neither sow, nor reap, nor carry into barns: and yet your heavenly Father feedeth them: are ye not much better than they?" [v. 26]. But alas, the practice of the world is contrary, for men have no care for the knowledge of God's Word nor the means of their salvation. All their minds are set on the things of this life, when as Christ says, "First seek the kingdom of heaven, and the righteousness thereof, and all these things shall be ministered unto you" [v. 33]. If we should see a young man provide for himself, and no man else for him, we should presently say [that] surely his father is dead. Even so, when a man's care is set wholly both day and night for the things of this life, it argues that God has either cast him off, or else that he takes Him for no Father of his.

[Duty] 5. Fifthly, if God be our Father, then we must learn to bear any cross patiently that He shall lay upon us, either in body or in mind, and always look for deliverance from Him; for whom the Lord loves, them He chastises. And "if ye endure chastising," says the apostle, "God offereth himself unto you as unto children" [Heb. 12:7], which may appear more plainly by this comparison: if two children should fight, and a man coming by should part them and after beat the one and let the other go free, [then] every man that sees this will say that that child which he beats is his own son. Even so, when God chastises us, He shows Himself unto us a father, if we submit ourselves. "Now if our earthly fathers corrected us, and we gave them reverence, taking it patiently, should we not much rather be in subjection to the Father of spirits, that we may live?" [v. 9]. Therefore, the conclusion is this: if we displease God, be you sure, He will correct us. And when His hand is upon us, we must not murmur against Him but bear it with a mild spirit. And furthermore, when we are under the cross, we must always look for deliverance from this Father only. If a son when he is beaten should fly to his father's enemies for help and counsel, it would argue that he were but a graceless child. Sundry and divers calamities and crosses befall men in this life which they cannot brook. And therefore it is a common practice of many among us in these days, when God's hand is upon them, to go for help to the devil. They seek for counsel at witches and wise men (as I have said); but let them look unto it, for that is the right way to double their misery and to show themselves lewd children.

[*Duty*] 6. Lastly, if we confess and believe God to be the Father of Christ and in Him our Father also, then in regard of our conversation we must not frame ourselves like unto the world; but the course of our lives must be in righteousness and true holiness. Paul exhorts the Corinthians to separate themselves from idolaters [2 Cor. 6:17], alleging the place out of the Old Testament where the Lord bids the Israelites "to come out from idolaters, and to touch no unclean thing" [Isa. 52:11]. And the reason follows out of Jeremiah, that if they do so, "then God will be their Father, and they shall be his children, even his sons and daughters" [Jer. 31:1], which reason Paul urges in the next chapter to this effect: considering we have these promises, that therefore we should cleanse ourselves from all filthiness of the flesh and spirit and grow up unto holiness in the fear of the Lord [2 Cor. 7:1]. Where if we mark the place diligently, we shall find this lesson: that every man who takes God for his Father must not only in this sin of idolatry but in all other sins separate himself, that men by his godly life may know whose child he is. But some will say this exhortation is needless among us, for we have no cause to separate ourselves from others, because all among us are Christians—all believe in God and are baptized and hope to be saved by Christ. *Answer.* In outward profession, I confess we carry the show of Christians; but in deed and truth, by our lives and conversations, very many among us deny Christ. For in every place the common practice is to spend the time in drunkenness and surfeiting, in chambering and wantonness. Yea, great is the company of those that make a trade of it. Take this lewd conversation from many men, and take away their lives. And on the Lord's Day it may be seen both publicly and privately, in houses and in the open streets. There is such revel, as though there were no God to serve. In the six days of the week, many men walk very painfully in their calling, but when the Lord's Day comes, then every man takes license to do what he will. And because of the prince's laws, men will come formally to the church for fashion's sake; but in the meantime how many do nothing else but scorn, mock, and deride, and as much as in them lies disgrace both the word and the ministers thereof, so that the common saying is this: "Oh, he is a precise fellow; he goes to hear sermons; he is too holy for our company." But it stands men in hand to take out a better lesson, which is, if we will have God to be our Father, we must show ourselves to be the children of God by repentance and newness of life. He cannot be but a graceless child that will lead a rebellious life flat against his Father's mind. Let us then so behave ourselves that we may honor our Father which is in heaven and not dishonor Him in our lives and callings. Rather, let us separate ourselves from the filthiness of the flesh, loathing those things which our Father loathes and flying from those things which our Father abhors.

And thus much for the duties.[34] Now follow the consolations which arise from this point. But first we are to know that there are three sorts of men in the world. The first are such as will neither hear nor obey the word of God. The second sort are those which hear the word preached unto them, but they will not obey. Both these sorts of men are not to look for any comfort hence. Now there is a third sort of men, which as they hear God's word, so they make conscience of obeying the same in their lives and callings. And these are they in whom the consolations that arise out of this place do rightly belong and must be applied.

[Consolation] 1.[35] First, therefore, seeing God the Father of Christ and in Him the Father of all that obey and do His will is our Father, here note the dignity and prerogative of all true believers; for they are sons and daughters of God, as says St. John, "So many as received him, to them he gave a prerogative to be the sons of God: even to them that believe in his name" [John 1:12]. This privilege will appear the greater if we consider our first estate; for as Abraham says, "We are but dust and ashes" [Gen. 18:27], and in regard of the depravation of our natures we are the children of the devil. Therefore, of such rebels to be made the sons of God—it is a wonderful privilege and prerogative, and no dignity like unto it. And to enlarge it further, he that is the son of God is the brother of Christ and fellow heir with Him, and so heir apparent to the kingdom of heaven and in this respect is not inferior to the very angels. This must be laid up carefully in the hearts of God's people to confirm them in their conversation among the company of ungodly men in this world.

[Consolation] 2. Secondly, if a man do endeavor himself to walk according to God's Word, then the Lord of His mercy will bear with his wants; for as a father spares his own son, so will God spare them that fear Him [Ps. 103:13; Mal. 3:17].[36] Now a father commands his child to write or to apply his book; though all things herein be not done according to his mind, yet if he find a readiness with a good endeavor, he is content and falls to praise his child's writing or learning. So God gives His commandments; and though His servants fail in obedience, yet if the Lord see their hearty endeavor and their unfeigned willingness to obey His will, though with sundry wants, He has made this promise and will perform it, that as a father spares his son, so will He spare them. If a child be sick, will the father cast him off? Nay. If through the grievousness of his sickness he cannot take the meat that is given him, or if he take it and for faintness pick it up again, will the father of the child thrust him out of doors? No, but he will rather pity him. And so, when a man does endeavor himself through the whole course of his life to keep God's commandments, God will

---

34. Consolations.

35. This was originally in the margin, as the following four conclusions.

36. Originally, "Mal. 3:27."

not cast him away, though through weakness he fail in sundry things and displease God. This prerogative can none have, but he that is the child of God. As for others, when they sin, they do nothing else but draw down God's judgments upon them for their deeper condemnation.

[Consolation] 3. Thirdly, hence we learn that the child of God cannot wholly fall away from God's favor. I do not say that he cannot fall at all, for he may fall away in part; but he cannot wholly. Indeed, so oft as he sins, he deprives himself wholly of God's favor as much as in him lies. Yet God for His part still keeps the mind and purpose of a father. David loved his son Absalom wonderfully; but Absalom, like a wicked son, played a lewd prank and would have thrust his father out of his kingdom. And David, although he was sore offended with Absalom and showed tokens of his wrath, yet in heart he loved him and never purposed to cast him off. Hereupon, when he went against him, he commanded the captains to "entreat the young man Absalom gently for his sake" [2 Sam. 18:5]. And when he was hanged by the hair of the head in pursuing of his father, then David wept and cried, "O my son Absalom, my son Absalom, would God I had died for thee, Absalom my son" [v. 33]. And so it is with God, our heavenly Father. When His children sin against Him and thereby lose His love and favor and fall from grace, He forsakes them—but how far? Surely, He shows signs of anger for their wickedness, and yet indeed His love remains toward them still; and this is a true conclusion. The grace of God in the adoption of the elect is unchangeable, and he that is the child of God can never fall away wholly or finally. On the contrary, that is a bad and comfortless opinion of the Church of Rome, which holds that a man may be justified before God and yet afterward by a mortal sin finally fall from grace and be condemned.[37]

[Consolation] 4. Fourthly, the child of God that takes God the Father for his Father may freely come into the presence of God and have liberty to pray unto Him. We know it is a great privilege to come into the chamber of presence before an earthly prince, and few can always have this prerogative, though they be great men. Yet the king's own son may have free entrance and speak freely unto the king himself, because he is his son. Now the children of God have more prerogative than this, for they may come into the presence not of an earthly king, but of Almighty God, the King of kings. And as they are the sons of God in Christ, so in Him they may freely speak unto God, their Father, by prayer. And this overthrows the doctrine of such as be of the Church of Rome, which teach and hold that a man must come to speak to God by prayer through the intercession of saints; for, say they, the presence of God is so glorious that

---

37. Torren. confess. August.

we may not be so bold as of ourselves to speak unto Him, but must needs have the intercession of others.

[Consolation] 5. Lastly, God will provide for all His church and children all things needful both for their bodies and souls. So our Savior Christ bids His disciples take no thought what they should eat or what they should drink or wherewith they should be clothed, adding this reason: "for your heavenly Father knoweth all your wants" [Matt. 6:32]. And if we take thought, it must be moderate and not distrustful. It is a part of the father's duty to provide for his family and children, and not the children for the father. Now shall an earthly father have this care for his children, and shall not our heavenly Father much more provide for those that fear and love Him? Nay, mark further, in God's church there be many hypocrites, which receive infinite benefits from God by reason of His elect children with whom they live. And we shall see this to be true, that the wicked man has ever fared better for the godly man's cause. Sodom and Gomorrah received many benefits by reason of righteous Lot. And when the Lord was purposed to destroy Sodom, He was feign to pull Lot forth of the city; for the text says the Angel of the Lord "could not do anything, till he was come out of it" [Gen. 19:22]. So also in Paul's dangerous voyage toward Rome all the men in it fared better for Paul's company; for the Lord told Paul by an angel that there should be no loss of any man's life, for the Lord had given to him all that sailed with him [Acts 27:24]. And undoubtedly, if it were not for some few that fear God, He would pour down His vengeance upon many nations and kingdoms, [as] there is such excess of wickedness in all sorts. Again, if the Lord does thus carefully provide for His children all kinds of benefits, what a wonderful wickedness is this for men to get their living by ungodly means, as usury, carding, dicing, and such like exercises? If a man were persuaded that God were his Father and would provide sufficiently both for his body and soul, so that using lawful means he should ever have enough, out of all doubt he would never after the fashion of the world use unlawful and profane means to get a living. But this proves that howsoever many men say God is their Father, yet indeed they deny Him.

The Father's Omnipotence
And thus much of this title "Father," the first thing whereby the first person is described. Now follows the second point—namely, His attribute of omnipotence, in the word "almighty." And whereas the Father is said to be almighty, it is not so to be understood as though the Son were not almighty, or the Holy Ghost not almighty; for every property or attribute (save the personal properties) is common to all the three persons. For as God the Father does impart His

Godhead unto the Son and to the Holy Ghost, so does He communicate the properties of the Godhead to them also.

God is omnipotent two ways: (1) because He is able to do whatsoever He will; (2) because He is able to do more than He will do. For the first, that God is able to do whatsoever He will, David says, "Our God is in heaven, and he doth whatsoever he will" [Ps. 115:3]. For there is nothing that can hinder God, but as He wills, so everything is done. Secondly, that God can do more than He wills to be done, it is plain where John [the] Baptist says, "God is able of these stones to raise up children unto Abraham" [Matt. 3:9]; for though God can do thus much, yet He will not do it. So likewise when Christ was betrayed, the Father could have given Him more than twelve legions of angels to have delivered Him out of their hands; but yet He would not [26:53]. And the like may be said of many other things. The Father is and was able to have created another world, yea, a thousand worlds; but He would not, nor will not. And likewise Christ, being upon the cross, was able at their bidding to have come down and saved Himself from death; but He would not. And therefore this is true: the Lord can do anything that He wills to be done actually, yea, and more than He will. But some will say God cannot do some things which man can do, as God "cannot lie" [Titus 1:2] nor "deny himself" [2 Tim. 2:13]. And therefore He is not omnipotent. *Answer.* Although some have thought that God could do even these things, and He did them not because He would not, yet we must know and believe that God can neither lie nor deny Himself. Indeed, man can do both; but these and many other such things, if God could do them, He could not be God. God indeed can do all things which show forth His glory and majesty. But such things as are against His nature He cannot do, as, for example, God cannot sin and therefore cannot lie. And because He cannot do these things, for this very cause He is omnipotent; for these and such like are works of impotency, which, if God could do, He should even by His own word be judged impotent. Secondly, He cannot do that which implies contradiction, as when a thing is, to make it at the same time to be and not to be—as when the sun does shine, to make it at the same instant to shine and not to shine. And therefore false is the doctrine of that Church [of Rome] which in their transubstantiation make the body of Christ (whose essential property is to be only in one place at once) to be circumscribed and not to be circumscribed, to be in one place and not to be in one place.

And thus much for the meaning. Now follow the duties whereunto we are moved by this doctrine of God's omnipotency.

First, whereas God the Father is said to be almighty, we are taught true humiliation. "Humble yourselves under the mighty hand of God," says Peter [1 Peter 5:6], where he gives an exhortation to humility and alleges the cause:

because God is almighty. To make this more plain, every one of us was born in sin, and by nature we are most wretched in ourselves. Now what a one is God? Surely, He is able to do whatsoever He will, yea, and more than He will, and is able to destroy such as rebel against Him every moment. Therefore, our duty is to cast down ourselves for our sins in His presence. This true humiliation was that which our Savior Christ would have brought the young man in the gospel unto, when He bade him go sell all that he had and give to the poor. Therefore, whosoever you are, take heed you must. For if you run on in your wickedness and still rebel against God, it is a thousand to one at length He will destroy you. For He is an almighty God and able to do whatsoever He will. His hand is mighty. It boots not a man to strive with Him, for He was never yet overmastered, and for this cause we must needs cast down ourselves under His hands. It is a "fearful thing," says the Holy Ghost, "to fall into the hands of the living God" [Heb. 10:31]. Therefore, if we would escape His heavy and terrible displeasure, the best way for us is to abase ourselves and be ashamed to follow our sins. Christ bids us not to fear him that is able to kill the body and can go no further. But we must fear Him "that is able to cast both body and soul into hellfire" [Matt. 10:28]. [An] example of this we have in David, who, when he was persecuted by his own son Absalom, he said unto the Lord, "If he thus say, I have no delight in thee, behold here I am, let him do to me as seemeth good in his eyes" [2 Sam. 15:26]. But some will say, "I will live a little longer in my sins, in lying, pride, Sabbath breaking, in swearing, dicing, gaming, and wantonness; for God is merciful, and in my old age I will repent." *Answer.* Well, soothe not yourself; but mark, usually when God holds back His hand for a season, He does as it were fetch a more mighty blow for the greater confusion of a rebellious sinner. Therefore, humble, submit, and cast down yourself before God and do not strive against Him. His hand is mighty and will overthrow you. Though you have all learning, wisdom, might, riches, etc., yet (as Christ said to the young man) one thing is wanting, that you should be humbled. And until you be humbled, nothing is to be looked for but God's judgments for sin.

Secondly, seeing God is almighty, we must tremble and fear at all His judgments. We must stand in awe, quake, and quiver at them, as the poor child does when he sees his father come with the rod. Example of this we have often in God's Word, as when the sons of Aaron offered strange fire before the Lord, He sent fire from heaven and burned them up. And though Aaron was very sorry for his sons, yet when Moses told him that the Lord would be "glorified in all that came near him," then the text says, "Aaron held his peace" [Lev. 10:3]. So also we read that the apostles reproved Peter for preaching unto the Gentiles; but when Peter had expounded the things in order which he had seen, then "they held their peace and glorified God" [Acts 11:18]. As also David says, "I held my tongue, O Lord; because thou didst it" [Ps. 39:9]. Isaiah says, "In hope and silence is true fortitude" [Isa. 30:15]. If a man be in trouble, he must hope for deliverance and be quiet and patient at God's judgments. But the practice of the world is flat contrary; for men are so far from trembling at them that they use to pray to God that plagues, curses, and vengeance may light upon them and upon their servants and children. Now the Lord, being a mighty God, often does answerably bring His judgments upon them. Again, many, carried away with impatience, wish themselves hanged or drowned, which evils they think shall never befall them. Yet at the length God does in His justice bring such punishments upon them according as they wished. And (which is more) in all ages there have been some which have scorned and mocked at God's judgments. Hereof we had not far hence a most fearful example. One being with his companion in a house drinking on the Lord's Day, when he was ready to depart thence, there was great lightning and thunder. Whereupon his fellow requested him to stay, but the man, mocking and jesting at the thunder and lightning, said (as report was) it was "nothing but a knave cooper knocking on his tubs."[38] Come what would, he would go, and so went on his journey. But before he came half a mile from the house, the same hand of the Lord, which before he had mocked, in a crack of thunder struck him about the girdle-stead, that he fell down stark dead. Which example is worthy of our remembrance to put us in mind of God's heavy wrath against those which scorn His judgments; for our duty is to tremble and fear, and it were greatly to be wished that we could with open eye behold the terribleness and fearfulness of God's judgments. It would make a man to quake and to leave off sin. If a man pass by some high and dangerous place in the night when he cannot see, he is not afraid. But if you bring him back again in the day and let him see what a steep and dangerous way he came, he will not be persuaded to pass the same way again for anything. So is it in sinning. For men, living in ignorance and blindness, practice any wickedness and do not care for God's judgments; but when God of His goodness brings them back and opens their eyes to see the downfall to the pit of hell and the judgments of God due to their sins, then (they say) they will never sin as they have done, but become new men and walk in the way to eternal life.

Thirdly, we are taught by the apostle Paul that if we be to do any duty to our brethren, as to relieve them, we must do it with cheerfulness; for he labors to persuade the Corinthians to cheerful liberality, and the reason of his persuasion is because God is able to make "all grace to abound toward them" [2 Cor. 9:7–8]. Where also this duty is taught us, that seeing God is omnipotent and

---

38. Anno 1592 in Cambridgeshire.

therefore able to make us abound, therefore we must give cheerfully to our poor brethren which want.

Fourthly, whereas there are many in every place which have lived long in their sins, even from their cradle—some in wantonness, some in drunkenness, some in swearing, some in idleness, and such like—out of this place to all such there is a good lesson, namely, that every one of them do now become new men and repent of all their sins for all their life past. For mark what Paul says of the Jews, which are cut off from Christ through unbelief and have continued in hardness of heart and desperate malice against Him almost sixteen hundred years. "If," says he, "they abide not still in unbelief, they may be grafted in their olive again." And his reason is this: "because God is able to graft them in again" [Rom. 11:23]. Even so, though we have lived many years in sin (and sure it is a dangerous and fearful case for a man to live twenty, thirty, or forty years under the power of the devil), yet we must know that if we will now live a new life, forsake all our sins, and turn to God, we may be received to grace and be made a branch of the true olive, though we have borne the fruits of the wild olive all our life long. But some will object that they have no hope of God's favor, because they have been so grievous sinners and continued in them so long. *Answer.* But know it, whosoever you are, God is able to graft you in. And if you repent, He will receive you to His love and favor. This must be observed of all, but especially of such as are old in years and remain ignorant without knowledge. They must turn to the Lord by repentance. Otherwise, if they continue still profane and impenitent, they must know this, that their damnation comes posthaste to meet them, and they to it.

And thus much for the duties. Now follow the consolations which God's church reap from this, that God the Father is omnipotent. First, the wonderful power of God serves to strengthen us in prayer unto God; for he that will pray truly must only pray for those things for which he has warrant in God's Word. All our prayers must be made in faith; and for a man to pray in faith, it is hard. Therefore, a special means to strengthen us herein is the mighty power of God. This was the ground and stay of the leper whom our Savior Christ cleansed: "Lord," says he, "if thou wilt, thou canst make me clean" [Matt. 8:2]. And in the Lord's Prayer, when our Savior Christ has taught us to make six petitions, in the end He gives us a reason or motive to induce us to stand upon and to wait for the benefits before craved, in these words: "Thine is the kingdom. Thine is the power," etc.

Secondly, hence we learn this comfort, that all the gates of hell shall never be able to prevail against the least member of Christ. I do not say they shall never be able to assault or tempt them, for that may be. But they shall never overcome them. How (will some say) may we be resolved of this? I answer, by reason of faith; for if a Christian man do believe that God the Father and Christ, His Son, is almighty, no enemy shall ever be able to prevail against him. So St. John reasons, "Little children, ye are of God, and have overcome them"—that is, all false teachers—"because greater is he that is in you [Christ Jesus by His Holy Spirit, who is God and therefore almighty] than he that is in the world," that is, the spirit of Satan [1 John 4:4]. Therefore, you need not to fear. So David compares himself to a silly sheep and says, "Though I should walk through the valley of the shadow of death"—that is, as it were in the mouth of the lion—"yet I would fear none evil." Why so? Because the Lord is with him. "Thy rod," says he, "and thy staff comfort me" [Ps. 23:4].

Thus much for the benefits. Now whereas it is said the first person is a father and also almighty, join these two together, and hence will arise singular benefits and instructions. First, whereas we are taught to confess that the first person is a father almighty, we and every man must learn to have experience in himself of the mighty power of this almighty Father. Why, will some say, that is nothing; for the devil and all the damned souls feel the power of the Almighty. True indeed they feel the power of God—namely, as He is an almighty judge condemning them. But they feel not the power of an almighty father. This is the point whereof we must endeavor to have experience in ourselves. Paul prays that the God of our Lord Jesus Christ, the Father of glory, would give unto the Ephesians "the spirit of wisdom, to see what is the exceeding greatness of his power in them which believe, according to the working of his mighty power, which he wrought in Christ" [Eph. 1:19]. Which place must be considered, for here the apostle would have us have such a special manifestation of God's power in ourselves, like to that which He did once show forth in Christ. But how did Christ see and find the power of God as He was man? *Answer.* Divers ways. (1) On the cross, He died the first death, which is the separation of body and soul; and He suffered the sorrows of the second death. For in His soul He bare the whole wrath of God and all the pangs of hell and after was buried and laid in the grave, where death triumphed over Him for the space of three days. Now in this extremity God did show His power in that He raised Christ from death to life. And look as His power was manifested in Christ, the head, so must it be manifested in all His members; for every man has his grave, which is natural sin and corruption, which we draw from our first parents. And look as a man lies dead in the grave and can move neither hand nor foot, so every man by nature lies dead in sin. Now as God did show His power in raising Christ from death, so everyone must labor to have this knowledge and experience in himself of the mighty power of God in raising him from the grave of sin to newness of life. For thus Paul makes a special request, that he might know Christ and "the virtue of his resurrection" [Phil. 3:10]—that is, that he might feel in himself that power whereby Christ was raised from death to life, to raise him also from the bondage of his sins to a new life more and more. Furthermore, when Christ was upon the cross, and all the gates of hell were open against Him, then did He vanquish Satan. He bruised the serpent's head. And, as Paul says, He "spoiled principalities and powers, and made a show of them openly, and hath triumphed over them on the cross" (Col. 2:15). He overcame the devil and all his angels by the power of His almighty Father and by His own power as He is God. And even so must Christian men labor to find the same power in themselves of this almighty Father by which Christ did triumph over Satan, that by it they may tread him under their feet, which men can never do by any power in themselves. Again, Christ prays that that cup might pass from Him; and yet He says, "Not my will, but thy will be fulfilled" (Luke 22:42). For it was necessary that Christ should suffer. And this request was heard, not because He was freed from death, but because God, His Father almighty, gave Him power and strength in His manhood to bear the brunt of His indignation. Now look as this power was effectual in Christ Jesus, the head, to make Him able and sufficient to bear the pangs of hell, so the same power of God is in some measure effectual in all the members of Christ, to make them both patient and of sufficient strength to bear any affliction, as St. Paul says, "Being strengthened with all might through his glorious power, unto all patience, and longsuffering, with joyfulness" (Col. 1:11). And this is a notable point which everyone ought to learn, that whereas they confess God to be their almighty Father, they should here withal labor to feel and have experience in themselves that He is almighty in the beginning and continuing of grace unto them and in giving them power and patience to suffer afflictions. Further, Christ Jesus, when the work of our redemption was accomplished, was lifted up into heaven and "set at the right hand of God in heavenly places far above all principalities and powers," etc. [Eph. 1:20–21], even by the power of His Father. Well, as this power was made manifest in the Head, so must it be in the members thereof. Every child of God shall hereafter see and feel in himself the same power to translate him from this vale of misery in this life to the kingdom of heaven. Wherefore, to conclude, we have great cause to be thankful and to praise God for this privilege, that He shows His power in His children in regenerating them, in making them die unto sin and to stand against the gates of hell and to suffer afflictions patiently, as also that He translates them from death to life. And everyone should show his thankfulness in laboring to have experience of this power in himself, as Paul exhorts us in his epistles to the Colossians and Ephesians. Yea, read all his epistles, and we shall find he mentions no point so often as this—namely, the mighty power of God, manifested first in Christ and secondly in His members. And he accounts "all things loss that he might know Christ, and the virtue of his resurrection" [Phil. 3:10]. This point is the rather to be marked because this power in the matter of grace is not to be seen with [the] eye; and few there be in respect that have felt the virtue thereof in themselves, for the devil does mightily show his contrary power in the greatest part of the world in carrying them to sin and wickedness.

Secondly, hence we learn that which Paul teaches—namely, to know that all things work together for the best unto them that love God [Rom. 8:28]. God is almighty and therefore able to do whatsoever He will. He is also a father and therefore is willing to do that which is for our good. But some will say, "We are subject to many crosses, yea, to sin. What? Can our sins turn to our good?" *Answer*. If God Almighty be your Father, He will turn your afflictions, yea, your sins, which by nature are evil, beyond all expectation unto your salvation. And thus much God will do to all such as be obedient unto Him, yet no man must hereupon presume to sin.

Thirdly, whereas we believe that God is a mighty father, it serves to confirm God's children in the promises of mercy revealed in His Word. The chiefest whereof is that if men will turn from their sins and believe in Christ, they shall not perish but have life everlasting. I know some men will make it an easy thing to believe, especially those which never knew what faith meant. But such persons need no means of confirmation of faith. Therefore, let all those which have tasted of the hardness of attaining unto it learn how to establish their wavering hearts in the promise of God by the consideration of these two points: God is a father, and therefore He is willing; He is almighty, and therefore He is able to perform His promise. He that will be resolved of God's promises must have both those settled in his heart and build on them as on two foundations.

The Father as Creator
It follows, "Creator of heaven and earth." We have spoken of the title of the first person and of His attributes. Now we come to speak of His effect—namely, the creation. But before we come to it, we are to answer a certain objection which may be made. At the first, it may seem strange to some that the work of creation is ascribed to the first person in [the] Trinity, the Father, whereas in the Scripture it is common to them all three equally. And first, that the Father is Creator, it was never doubted; as for the second person, the Son, that He is Creator, it is evident: "All things are made by it"—that is, by the Son, who is the substantial Word of the Father—"and without it was made nothing that was made" [John 1:3]. And again it is said that God "by his Son made the world" [Heb. 1:2]. As for the Holy Ghost, the work of creation is also ascribed unto Him. And therefore Moses says, "The spirit moved upon the waters" [Gen. 1:2]; and Job says, "His spirit has garnished the heavens" [Job 26:13]. How then is this

peculiar to the Father, being common to all the three persons in [the] Trinity? I answer, the actions of God are twofold: either inward or outward. The inward actions are those which one person does exercise toward another, as the Father does beget the Son; and this is an inward action peculiar to the Father. And all inward actions are proper to the persons from whom they are. So the Son does receive the Godhead by communication from the Father, and the Holy Ghost from them both. And these are inward actions peculiar to these persons. So likewise, for the Father to send His Son, it is an inward action proper to the Father and cannot be communicated to the Holy Ghost; and the Son to be sent by the Father only is a thing proper to the Son and not common to the Father or to the Holy Ghost. Now outward actions are the actions of the persons in the Trinity to the creatures, as the work of creation, the work of preservation, and of redemption. These and all such actions are common to all the three persons: the Father creates, the Son creates, and the Holy Ghost creates. And so we may say of the works of government and of redemption and of all outward actions of the persons to the creatures. But some again may say, how then can the work of creation, being an outward action of God to the creature, be peculiar to the first person, the Father? I answer, the work of creation is not so proper to the first person as that it cannot also be common to the rest; for all the three persons jointly created all things of nothing. Only they are distinguished in the manner of creating. For the Father is the cause that begins the work; the Son puts it in execution; the Holy Ghost is the finisher of it.[39] And again, the Father creates by the Son [Rom. 11:36; Col. 1:16] and by the Holy Ghost. The Son creates by the Holy Ghost and from the Father. The Holy Ghost creates not by the Father nor by the Son, but from the Father and the Son. And this is the reason why the work of creation is ascribed here unto the Father, because He alone creates after a peculiar manner—namely, by the Son and by the Holy Ghost. But the Son and the Holy Ghost create not by the Father, but from Him.

Thus, having answered the objection, we come to speak of the creation itself. In handling whereof, we must withal treat of the counsel of God, as being the cause thereof, and of the government of the creatures, as being a work of God whereby He continues the creation. And the order which I will observe is first to speak of the counsel of God and secondly of the execution of His counsel, which has two special branches: the first, the creation; the second, the preservation or government of things created.

The counsel of God is His eternal and unchangeable decree whereby He has ordained all things either past, present, or to come for His own glory. First, I call it a decree because God has in it set down with Himself as appointed

---

39. Basil. de spirit. sanct. cap. 16.

sovereign Lord what shall be [and] what shall not be. I add further that all things whatsoever come under the compass of this decree, as Paul says, "He worketh all things according to the counsel of his will" [Eph. 1:11]. And our Savior Christ says that a sparrow cannot fall on the ground without the heavenly Father [Matt. 10:29]. Yea, further, He tells His disciples that the very hairs of their heads are numbered [v. 30], meaning that they are known and set down in the counsel of God. And considering that God is King over heaven and earth, and that most wise, yea, wisdom itself, and most mighty, yea, might and power itself—it must needs be that He has determined how all things shall come to pass in His kingdom, with all their circumstances, time, place, causes, etc., in such [a] particular manner that the very least thing that may be is not left unappointed and undisposed.

The counsel of God has two properties: eternity and unchangeableness. It is eternal, because it was set down by God from everlasting before all times, as Paul says: God has chosen the Ephesians to "salvation before all worlds" [Eph. 1:4]. And he says of himself that he was called according to "the purpose of God, which was before all worlds" [2 Tim. 1:9]. Again, the same counsel once set down is unchangeable. God says, "I am Jehovah, I change not" [Mal. 3:6]. "With God," says St. James, "there is no variableness, nor shadow of change" [James 1:17]. Now such as God is, such is His decree or counsel. And being unchangeable, His counsels also are unchangeable.

God's counsel has two parts: His foreknowledge and His will or pleasure—His foreknowledge, whereby He did foresee all things which were to come; His will, whereby in general manner He wills and ordains whatsoever is to come to pass. And therefore such things as God altogether nills[40] cannot come to pass. Now these two parts of the counsel of God must be joined together and not severed. Will without knowledge is impotent, and foreknowledge without will is idle. And therefore such as hold that God does barely foresee sundry things to come, no manner of way either willing or decreeing the issue and event of them, do bring in little better than atheism. For if we say that anything comes to pass either against God's will, or God not knowing of it or not regarding it, we shall make Him either impotent or careless and raze the very foundation of God's providence.

And this decree of God must be conceived of us as the most general cause of all things subsisting, being first in order, having all other causes under it, and most principal, overruling all, overruled by none.

Thus, we see what is to be held touching God's counsel. Now for the better clearing of the truth, three objections of some difficulty are to be answered.

---

40. *Nills*: to not will.

First, may some man say, if God decree and ordain all things whatsoever, then He decrees and ordains sin. But God decrees not sin inasmuch as it is against His will, and therefore He decrees not all things. *Answer.* We use not to say that God does simply will or decree sin, but only in part, adding withal these caveats: (1) that God wills and decrees sin not properly as it is sin, but as it has in it sundry regards and respects of goodness, so far forth as it is a punishment or chastisement or trial or action or has an existence in nature.[41] (2) God can so use evil instruments that the work done by them, being a sin, shall nevertheless in Him be a good work, because He knows how to use evil instruments well. If it be further alleged that God wills no wickedness (Ps. 5:5), we must know that God's will is twofold: general and special. General, whereby God wills and decrees that a thing shall be; and by this kind of will He may be said to will sin, and that without sin. For though He decree it thus, yet does He not instill wickedness into the heart of any sinner, and His decree is only for a most excellent end. For in regard of God, which decrees it, it is good that there should be evil.[42] To this purpose Augustine says excellently, "By an unspeakable manner it comes to pass that that which is against God's will is not without His will."[43] Now the special will of God is that whereby He wills anything in such manner that He approves it and delights in it. And thus indeed we cannot say without blasphemy that God wills sin. Thus, then we see in what manner and how far forth God may be said to decree sin—that is, to will and appoint the permission of it.

Again, it may be objected thus: If all things be determined by the unchangeable decree of God, then all things come to pass by an unchangeable necessity. And men in their actions have no free will at all nor liberty in doing anything. *Answer.* This must be learned as a certain rule, that the necessary decree of God does not abolish the nature of the second causes and impose necessity upon the will of man, but only order and incline it without any constraint, to one part. As, for example, when a people is gathered together to hear God's word, there is none of them but they know that they come thither by God's providence (and in that respect necessarily); yet before they come they had all freedom and liberty in themselves to come or not to come. And God's eternal counsel did not hinder the liberty of our wills in coming or not coming nor take away the same, but only incline and turn them to the choice of one part. Another example hereof we may have in our Savior Christ, whose state and condition

---

41. Quatenus habet rationem entis, non quatenus habet rationem defectus. [It is insofar as it possesses the concept of being, not insofar as it possesses the concept of a defect.]

42. Bonum est ut sit malum. [It is good that evil may exist.] *Aug.* Enchir. ad Laur. 101.

43. Voluntate permissiva vult, approbativa non vult. [By His permissive will He wills, but He does not will by His approving will.]

of body if we regard, He might have lived longer. Yet by the eternal counsel of God He must die at that place, at that time, at that hour where and when He died. Whereby we may see that God's counsel does not hinder the will of man, but only order and dispose it. Which answer being well marked, we shall see these two will stand together: the necessary and unchangeable counsel of God and the free will of man. And again, that the same action may be both necessary and contingent: necessary, in regard of the highest cause, the counsel of God; not necessary but contingent, in respect of the second causes, as among the rest, the will of man.

Thirdly, some will yet object against this doctrine that if all things come to pass according to God's unchangeable decree, then what needs the using of any means? What needs the preaching of the word? And receiving of the sacraments? What needs any laws, princes, magistrates, or government? What needs walking in men's ordinary callings? All is to no end; for let men play or work, sleep or wake—let them do what they will; all is one. For God's eternal counsel must needs come to pass. Therefore, it may seem in vain for men to busy themselves about such things. *Answer.* But we must know that as God has appointed all things to come to pass in His eternal and unchangeable counsel, so in the same decree He has together set down the means and ways whereby He will have the same things brought to pass; for these two must never be severed: the thing to be done and the means whereby it is done. We may read in the Acts in Paul's dangerous voyage toward Rome [Acts 27:24–25] an angel of the Lord told Paul that God had given him all that sailed with him in the ship. Now the soldiers and mariners, hearing this, might reason thus with themselves: "Seeing God has decreed to save us all, we may do what we will. There is no danger, for we shall all come to land alive." But mark what Paul says, "Except these abide in the ship, ye cannot be safe" [v. 31],[44] where we see that as it was the eternal counsel of God to save Paul and all that were with him, so He decreed to save all by this particular means of their abode in the ship. King Hezekiah was restored to his health and received from God a promise that he should have fifteen years added to his days, and the promise was confirmed by a sign. Now what does he? Cast off all means? No, but as he was prescribed, so he applies a bunch of dry figs to his sore and uses still his ordinary diet [2 Kings 20:6–7]. Therefore, it is gross ignorance and madness in men to reason so against God's decree: "God in His unchangeable counsel has decreed and set down all things how they shall be. Therefore, I will use no means but live as I list." Nay, rather we must say the contrary: "Because God has decreed this thing or that to be done, therefore I will use the means which God has appointed to bring the same to pass."

---

44. Originally, "v. 32."

Now follows the creation, which is nothing else but a work of the blessed Trinity, forming and framing His creatures which were not before, and that of nothing. The points to be known concerning the creation are many. The first is the thing by which God did begin and finish the creation. And we must understand that at the first God made all things without any instrument or means, and not as men do, which bring to pass their business by servants and helps, but only by His word and commandment—as the psalmist says, "He commanded, and all things were made" [Ps. 148:5]. In the beginning, God said, "Let there be light" [Gen. 1:3], and there was light. And by the same means was the creation of every creature following. The very power of the word and commandment of God was such as by it that thing was made and had a being which before was not. It may be demanded what word this was by which God is said to make all things. *Answer.* The word of God in Scripture is taken three ways: for the substantial Word, for the founding or written word, for the operative or powerful word. The substantial Word is the second person, begotten of the substance of the Father. Now howsoever it be true that God the Father did create all things by His Word—that is, by His Son, yet does it not seem to be true that by these words, "God said, 'Let there be this or that,'" that the Son is meant. For that word which God gave out in the creation was in time, whereas the Son is the Word of the Father before all times. And again, it is a word common to the three persons equally, whereas the Son is the Word of the Father only. Furthermore, it is not like that it was any founding word, standing of letters and syllables and uttered to the creatures after the usual manner of men that was the cause of them. It remains therefore that all things were made by the operative word, which is nothing but the pleasure, will, and appointment of God [Heb. 1:3] and is more powerful to bring a thing to pass than all the means in the world beside. For God's willing of anything is His effecting and doing of it. And this is proved by David when he says, "He spake the word, and they were made: he commanded, and they were created" [Ps. 33:6, 9]. Hence we must take out a special lesson needful to be learned of every man. Look what power God used and showed in making the creatures when they were not; the same power He does, can, and will show forth in recreating and redeeming sinful men by the precious blood of Christ. By His word He created man's heart when it was not. And He can and will as easily create in us all new hearts [51:10], specially when we use the good means appointed for that end. As when Christ said to dead Lazarus, "Lazarus, come forth" [John 11:43],[45] he arose and came forth of his grave, though bound hand and foot, so when the Lord speaks to our dead heart by His word and Spirit, we shall rise forth of the graves of our

---

45. Originally, "John 11:44."

sins and corruptions. In the creation of the great world, God said, "Let there be light," and presently darkness gave place. And the same He can do to the little world—that is, to man. We are by nature darkness, and let God but speak to our blind understandings, our ignorance shall depart, and we shall be enlightened with the knowledge of the true God and of His will, as Paul says, "God that commanded the light to shine out of darkness is he which hath shined in our hearts, to give the light of the knowledge of the glory of God in the face of Jesus Christ" [2 Cor. 4:6].

Secondly, God made all creatures, without motion, labor, or defatigation; for His very bidding of the work to be done was the doing of it. And this thing no creature can do, but God only, though unto Adam labor was without pain before the fall.

Thirdly, the matter and the first beginning of all creatures was nothing— that is, all things were made, when as there was nothing whereof they might be made, as Paul says, "God calleth those things which be not, as though they were" [Rom. 4:17]. And indeed in the first creation all things must be made either of the essence of God or of nothing. But a creature cannot be made of the essence of God, for it has no parts; it is not divisible. And therefore God made all things that were made out[side] of Himself or His own essence. The conclusion then is that the framing of the creatures in the beginning was not of any matter, but of nothing, because before the creation, out[side] of God there was nothing. This must teach us to humble ourselves. Many there be that stand upon their ancestors, but let them here look whence they came first—namely, as Abraham says of himself, "of dust and ashes." And what was this dust and ashes made of? Surely, of nothing; wherefore, every man's first beginning is of nothing. Well then, such men as are carried away with their pedigree and descent, if they look well unto it, they shall find small cause to boast or brag. And this consideration of our first beginning must move us to true humiliation in ourselves.

Fourthly, God in framing His creatures in the beginning made them good, yea, very good. Now the goodness of the creature is nothing else but the perfect estate of the creature, whereby it was conformable to the will and mind of the Creator, allowing and approving of it, when He had made it. For a creature is not first good and then approved of God; but because it is approved of God, therefore it is good. But wherein, will some say, stands this goodness of the creature? I answer, in three things. (1) In the comeliness, beauty, and glory of every work in his kind both in form and constitution of the matter. (2) In the excellency of the virtue which God has given to it, for as He has appointed every creature for some especial end, so He has fitted and furnished it with sufficient power and virtue for the accomplishing of the same end. (3) In the exceeding benefit and profitableness that came by them to man. But since the fall of man, this goodness of the creature is partly corrupted and partly diminished. Therefore, when we see any want, defect, or deformity in any of them, we must have recourse back again to the apostasy of our first parents and remember our fall in them and say with a sorrowful heart [that] this comes to pass by reason of man's most wretched sin, which has defiled heaven and earth and drawn a curse not only upon himself but upon the rest of the creatures for his sake, whereby their goodness is much defaced.

Fifthly, the end of creation is the glory of God, as Solomon says, "God made all things for his own sake, yea even the wicked for the day of evil" [Prov. 16:4]. And God propounds this principal end to Himself, not as though He wanted glory and would purchase it unto Himself by the creation—for He is most glorious in Himself, and His honor and praise, being infinite, can neither be increased nor decreased—but rather that He might communicate and make manifest His glory to His creatures and give them occasion to magnify the same. For the reasonable creatures of God, beholding His glory in the creation, are moved to testify and declare the same among men.

The sixth shall be touching the time of the beginning of the world, which is between five thousand and six thousand years ago. For Moses has set down exactly the computation of time from the making of the world to his own days, and the prophets after him have with diligence set down the continuance of the same to the very birth of Christ. But for the exact account of years chronologists are not all of one mind. Some say there be 3929 [years] from the creation to Christ's birth, as Beroaldus. Some, 3952, as Jerome and Bede. Some, 3960, as Luther and John Lucidus. Some, 3963, as Melanchthon in his chronicle and Fanctius. Some, 3970, as Bullinger and Tremelius. Some, toward 4000, as Buntingus. Now from the birth of Christ to this day are 1592 years, and adding these together, the whole time amounts. And God would have the very time of the beginning of the world to be revealed, first, that it might be known to the church when the covenant of grace was first given by God to man and when it was afterward renewed and how Christ came in the fullness of time (Gal. 4:4). Secondly, that we might know that the world was not made for the eternal and ever-living God, but for man. Thirdly, that we might learn not to set our hearts on the world and on the things therein, which have beginning and end, but seek for things eternal in heaven. And before the time which I have named began, there was nothing besides God. The world itself and all things else were uncreated. Some men used to object and say, "What did God all that while before the world was? How did He employ Himself? What, was He idle?" *Answer.* The Jews to this bad question make as bad an answer. For they say He was continually occupied in making many little worlds, which He continually destroyed as He made them, because none pleased Him till He made this.

But we must rather say that some things are revealed which God did then, as that He decreed what should come to pass when the world was, and that then the blessed persons in [the] Trinity did take eternal delight each in [the] other [Prov. 8:30]. If any man will needs know more, let them hear what Moses says, "Secret things belong to the Lord our God; but things revealed, to us and our children forever" [Deut. 29:29]. And let them mark what one, eluding the question, answered[46]—namely, that God was making hellfire to burn all such curious persons as will needs know more of God than He has revealed to them; for where God has not a mouth to speak, there we must not have an ear to hear. Therefore, our duty is to let such curious questions pass.

Seventhly, some may ask in what space of time did God make the world? I answer, God could have made the world and all things in it in a moment; but He began and finished the whole work in six distinct days. In the first day, He made the matter of all things and the light [Genesis 1]. In the second, the heavens; in the third day, He brought the sea into its[47] compass and made the dry land appear and caused it to bring forth herbs, plants, and trees. In the fourth day, He made the sun, the moon, and the stars in heaven. In the fifth day, He made the fishes of the sea, the fowls of the heaven, and every creeping thing. In the sixth day, He made the beasts of the field and all cattle; and in the end of the sixth day He made man. Thus, in six distinct spaces of time the Lord did make all things, and that especially for three causes. (1) To teach men that they ought to have a distinct and serious consideration of every creature; for if God had made the world in a moment, some might have said this work is so mystical, that no man can speak of it. But for the preventing of this cavil, it was His pleasure to make the world and all things therein in six days. And the seventh day, He commanded it to be sanctified by men, that they might distinctly and seriously meditate upon every day's work of the creation. (2) God made the world and everything therein in six distinct days to teach us what wonderful power and liberty He had over all His creatures; for He made the light when there was neither sun nor moon nor stars to show that in giving light to the world He is not bound to the sun, to any creature, or to any means, for the light was made the first day, but the sun, the moon, and the stars were not created before the fourth day. Again, trees and plants were created the third day; but yet the sun, moon, and the stars and rain, which nourish and make herbs, trees, and plants to grow, were not created till after the third day, which shows plainly that God can make trees, plants, and herbs to grow without the means of rain and without the virtue and operation of the sun, the moon, and the stars. (3)

---

46. August. l. 1. confess. 2. 12.
47. Originally, "his."

He made the world in six distinct days and framed all things in this order to teach us His wonderful providence over all His creatures, for before man was created He provided for him a dwelling place and all things necessary for his perpetual preservation and perfect happiness and felicity. So also He created beasts and cattle, but not before He had made herbs, plants, and grass and all means whereby they are preserved. And if God had this care over man when as yet he was not, much more will God have care over him now when he is and has a being in nature.

And thus much concerning the points of doctrine touching the creation. The duties follow. *Duty 1.*[48] And, first, by the work of creation we may discern the true Jehovah from all false gods and idols in the world. This Isaiah makes plain, bringing in the Lord, reasoning thus: "I am God, and there is none other God besides me." How is that proved? Thus: "I form the light, and create darkness, I make peace, and create evil: I the Lord do all these things" [Isa. 45:6–7]. If a man ask you how you know the true God from all false gods, you must answer, by the work of creation; for He alone is the maker of heaven and earth and all things in them. This property cannot agree to any creature, to any man, saint, or angel—nay, not to all men and all angels. They cannot give being to a creature which before was nothing.

[*Duty*] 2. Secondly, whereas God the Father is Creator of all things and has given unto man reason, understanding, and ability more than to other creatures, we are taught to consider and meditate of the work of God's creation. This the wise man teaches us, saying, "Consider the work of God" [Eccl. 7:13]. And indeed it is a special duty of every man which professes himself to be a member of God's church, as he acknowledges God to be the Creator, so to look upon His workmanship and view and consider all creatures. A skillful workman can have no greater disgrace than when he has done some famous thing to have his friend pass by his work and not so much as look upon it. If it be demanded, for what end we must look upon the work of God's creation, I answer, that in it we may see and discern God's power, wisdom, love, mercy, and providence and all His attributes and in all things His glory. This is a most necessary duty to be learned of every man. We think nothing too much or too good to bestow on vain shows and plays, idle sports and pastimes, which are the vanities of men; and we do most willingly behold them, in the mean season utterly neglecting and contemning the glorious work of God's creation. Well, the Lord has appointed His Sabbath to be sanctified not only by the public ministry of the word and by private prayer, but also by an especial consideration

---

48. This was originally in the margin, as were the following four duties (the fifth is added by the editor).

and meditation of God's creatures. And therefore the duty of every man is this: distinctly and seriously to view and consider the creatures of God and thereby take occasion to glorify His name by ascribing unto Him the wisdom, glory, power, and omnipotency that is due unto Him and appears in the same.

[Duty] 3. Thirdly, we must give God glory in all His creatures, because He is the Creator of them all. So in the Revelation the four and twenty elders fall down before Him and say, "Thou art worthy, O Lord, to receive glory and honor, and power"—giving this reason: "for thou hast created all things, and for thy will's sake they are and have been created" [Rev. 4:11]. Read the Psalms 147 and 148, both which tend to this effect, that God must be praised because He is the Creator of all things, to whom all glory is due. We know that when men behold any curious work of a cunning and skillful craftsman, straightway they will leave the work and inquire after him that made it, that they may praise his skill. The same is our duty in this case. When we come abroad and behold everywhere in all the creatures the admirable and unspeakable wisdom, goodness, and power of God, then we must make haste from the creature and go forward to the Creator to praise and glorify Him. And herein must we show ourselves to differ from brute beasts, in that by the use and view of God's creatures we do return due glory, praise, and honor unto the Creator.

[Duty] 4. Our fourth duty is set down by the prophet Amos, who, moving the people to meet God by repentance, adds a reason taken from the creation: "He that formeth the mountains and createth the winds, which declareth unto man what is his thought, which maketh the morning darkness, etc. The Lord God of hosts is his name" [Amos 4:13]. The meaning of the prophet is this: God is a terrible judge, and we are as traitors and rebels against Him. Therefore, the best way that we can take is this: He is coming to judgment; let us therefore meet Him, fall down before Him, and humble ourselves under His mighty hand. And the Holy Ghost by the prophet would move the people to meet God by serious repentance, by a reason framed thus: if God, who is their Judge, be able to create the winds and to form the mountains and to make the morning darkness, then He is also able to make an eternal judgment for their confusion. And therefore all such as be impenitent sinners, let them prepare themselves to turn unto Him. And surely, if men had grace to lay this to their hearts, they would not live so long in their sins without repentance as they do. Nay, rather they would prepare themselves to meet Him in the way before He come to judgment, because He is a creator and therefore able to bring infinite punishments upon them at His pleasure and to bring them to nothing, as He made them of nothing. And let them know it, whosoever they be that go forward in their sins, that God, the Creator, whensoever He will can open hell to devour them, and that He can show Himself as mighty in His judgments to man's destruction as He was mighty in the beginning in giving us being when we were nothing. Wherefore, notable is the practice of David, who inures himself to the fear of God by the consideration of his creation, saying, "I am fearfully, and wonderfully made," etc. [Ps. 139:14].

[*Duty 5.*] Lastly, those that have been impenitent sinners through all their life past must not only learn to repent for their sins but also endeavor to perform obedience unto God's word. God is a creator, and the thing created should in all respects be conformable to His will; for David says, "Thine hands have fashioned me, and framed me; give me understanding therefore that I may learn thy commandments" [119:73].[49] And good reason, for there is no man of any trade but he would fain have all that he makes and devises to be used, but yet so as the use thereof must be conformable to the will of the maker. For this cause Moses, that faithful servant of God, says that the people of Israel dealt wrongfully with the Lord. Why? "For he hath created them, and proportioned them: he is their father and he bought them: yet they have dishonored him by corrupting themselves toward him by their vice" [Deut. 32:5–6].

All creatures in heaven and earth do the will of the Creator, except man and the devil and his angels; for the sun, the moon, and the stars, they keep that course which God has appointed them. But man, though he be bound to do the will of God because God is his Creator, yet he rebels against Him. The potter, if in tempering his clay he cannot make and frame it according to his mind, at length he will dash it in pieces. So God, He creates man, not that he should do his own will, but God's will. And therefore the Lord in His wrath will confound him eternally, whosoever he be that follows the lusts of his own wicked heart and will not be brought to be conformable to God's will but goes on in his rebellion without stay. For this cause it stands every man in hand to yield himself pliable to God's will and to endeavor to obey it by keeping a good conscience before God and all men and by walking faithfully in his calling, lest the end be confusion. If a man have a trade, and other men come into his shop and use such tools and instruments as be there to wrong ends, he will in no wise brook it, but take the abuse in great displeasure. Now the world is as it were an opened shop, which God has set forth unto His glory and majesty and the creatures of all kinds to be instruments appointed for excellent uses, and specially man for the accomplishment of His will. And therefore, when he rebels against the will of God and by sin puts the creatures to wrong ends, he cannot but most grievously offend God.

---

49. Originally, "Ps. 119:37."

And thus much of the duties. Now in the third place follow the consolations unto God's church and people. *Consolation 1.*[50] First, as St. Peter says, "God is a creator, yea a faithful creator" [1 Peter 4:19]. The properties of a faithful creator are two. (1) He will preserve his creature. No man is so tender over any work as he that made it, for he cannot abide to see it any way abused. God therefore, being a faithful creator, tenderly loves all His creatures. So Job reasons with God that He will not cast him off, "because he is the work of his hands" [Job 10:3]. (2) God will bear with His creature to see whether it will be brought to any good end and use, before He will destroy it. And to use the former comparison, the potter will turn and work the clay every way to make a vessel unto his mind. But if it frame no way, then will he cast it away and dash it against the wall. And so God, who created man, still preserves him and uses all means to make him conformable to His will, before He cast him off. The Lord did long strive with men in the old world to turn them from their wickedness; but when nothing would serve them, it is said, "It repented the Lord that he had made man on the earth" [Gen. 6:6]. And in like manner, if we, which are the creatures of God, shall rebel against this our Creator, it may be He will bear with us for a time. But if we continue therein and do not turn to Him by repentance, He will bring upon us a final destruction both in body and soul. Yet I say, before He do this, His manner is to try all means to preserve us and turn us unto Him. And afterward, if nothing will serve, then will He show forth His power in men's confusion. And therefore it stands us in hand to look unto it betime.

[Consolation 2.] Secondly, look what power the Lord did manifest in the creation of all things, the same power He both can and will make manifest in the redemption of mankind. In the beginning, God made all things by His word; and so likewise He is able still to make by the power of His word of a wicked man that is dead in sin a true and lively member of Christ, which the prophet Isaiah signifies when he says, "The Lord that created the heavens, and spread them abroad, he that stretcheth forth the earth, and the bounds thereof, etc. I the Lord have called thee in righteousness" [Isa. 45:12–13]. This must not encourage evil men in their wickedness, but it serves to comfort the people of God, considering that the same God which once created them is also as able to save them and will show Himself as mighty in their redemption as He was in their creation of nothing.

And thus much of the creation in general. Now it follows that we come to the handling of the parts thereof. For it is not said barely that God is a creator, but particularly that He is a creator "of heaven and earth," of both which we will speak in order, and, first, of the creation of heaven.

---

50. Originally in the margin.

Heaven in God's Word signifies all that is above the earth, for the air wherein we breathe is called heaven. And according to this acceptation of the word, there are three heavens, as Paul says he was taken up "into the third heaven" [2 Cor. 12:2]. The first of these heavens is that space which is from the earth upward unto the firmament, where the stars are. Thus, the birds, which fly in the air between the earth and the stars, are called "the fowls of heaven." And when God sent the flood to drown the old world, Moses says, "The windows of heaven were opened" [Gen. 7:11], meaning that God poured down rain from the clouds abundantly for the making of a flood to drown the world. The second heaven is that which contains the sun, the moon, and the stars. So Moses says that God in the beginning created the sun, the moon, and the stars and placed them in the "firmament of heaven" [1:14]. Besides these two heavens, there is a third, which is invisible; and yet it is the work of God's hands. And it is that glorious place where Christ even in His manhood sits at the right hand of the Father and whither the souls of the faithful departed are carried and placed, and in which at the end of the world shall all the elect both in body and soul have perfect joy and bliss in the glorious sight and presence of God forever. But for the better conceiving the truth, we are to scan and consider diligently three questions. First, whether this third heaven be a creature, for many have thought it was never created but was eternal with God Himself. But it is a gross error contrary to God's Word. For the Scripture says, "Abraham looked for a city"— meaning the heavenly Jerusalem, this third heaven—"having a foundation whose builder and maker is God" [Heb. 11:10]. Further, if it be eternal, it must either be a creator or a creature. But it is no creator, for then it should be God. And therefore it must needs be a creature. But some will say, the Lord is eternal, and this third heaven has always been the place of the Lord's abode, and therefore it is also eternal. *Answer.* True it is indeed that God does show His glory and majesty in the third heaven, but yet that cannot possibly contain His Godhead, as Solomon says: "Behold the heavens, and the heaven of heavens are not able to contain thee" [1 Kings 8:27]. Wherefore, though God does manifest His eternal glory in this third heaven, yet does it not follow that therefore this place should be eternal; for He needs no habitation to dwell in. He is everywhere, filling all things with His presence, excluded from no place. The second question is, where this third heaven is? *Answer.* There are some Protestants [who] say, it is everywhere; and they hold this opinion to maintain the real presence of the Lord's body in or about the sacrament. But if it were everywhere, then hell should be in heaven, which no man will say. But heaven indeed is above these visible heavens which we see with our eyes. So the apostle says, "Christ ascended on high far above all heavens," etc. [Eph. 4:10].[51] And again, it is said of Stephen that, being full of the Holy Ghost, he "looked up steadfastly into the heavens, and saw them open, and the Son of Man standing at the right hand of God" [Acts 7:55–56]. Thirdly, it may be demanded why God created this third heaven? *Answer.* God made it for this cause, that there might be a certain place wherein He might make manifest His glory and majesty to His elect angels and men, for the which cause it was created a thousandfold more glorious than the two former heavens are and in this respect is called "paradise" [Luke 23:43] by reason of the joy and pleasure arising from God's glorious presence. And our Savior Christ calls it the "house of God his Father" [John 14:2] because into it must be gathered all God's children. It is called the "kingdom of heaven" because God is the King thereof and rules there in perfect glory. True it is, God has His kingdom here on earth; but He rules not so fully and gloriously here as He shall in heaven, for this is the kingdom of grace, but that is the kingdom of His glory, where He so reigns that He will be all in all, first in Christ and then in the elect, both angels and men.

Now follow the duties whereunto we are moved principally in consideration of the making of the third heaven. *Duty [1].*[52] First, if God created it especially for the manifestation of His glory unto men, that at the end of the world, by the fruition of God's most glorious presence, there they might have perfect joy and felicity, [then] we have occasion here to consider the wonderful madness and forgetfulness that reigns everywhere among men which only have regard to the estate of this life and cast all their care on this world and never so much as once dream of the joyful and blessed estate which is prepared for God's children in the highest heaven. If a man having two houses, one but a homely cottage and the other a princely palace, should leave the better and take all the care and pains for the dressing up of the first, would not every man say he were a madman? Yes, undoubtedly. And yet this is the spiritual madness that takes place everywhere among men; for God has prepared for us two houses—one is this, our body, which we bear about us, which is a house of clay, as Job says, "We dwell in houses of clay whose foundation is dust, which shall be destroyed before the moth" [Job 4:19],[53] and as Peter says, "a tabernacle or tent" [2 Peter 1:13],[54] which we must shortly take down and wherein we abide but as "pilgrims and strangers" [1 Peter 2:11]. Again, the same God of His wonderful goodness has provided for us a second house in the third heaven, wherein we must not abide for a time and so depart but forevermore

---

51. Originally, "Eph. 4:18."
52. Originally in the margin.
53. Originally, "Job 4:29."
54. Originally, "2 Peter 1:14."

enjoy the blessed felicity of His glorious presence. For all this, mark a spiritual frenzy possessing the minds of men; for they employ all their care and industry for the maintaining of this house of clay, whose foundation is but dust, but for the blessed estate of the second house, which is prepared for them in the kingdom of heaven, they have little regard or care. They will both run and ride from place to place day and night, both by sea and land—but for what? Is it for the preparing of a mansion place in the heavenly Jerusalem? Nothing less, for they will scarce go out of the door to use any means whereby they may come unto it, but all their study is to patch up the ruins and breaches of their earthly cabin. Now, let all men judge in their own consciences whether, as I have said, this be not more than senseless madness. Again, the body is but a tabernacle wherein we must rest as it were for a night, as a stranger does in an inn, and so away. But the second house is eternal in the heavens, an everlasting seat of all felicity and happiness. And therefore our duty is above all things to seek the kingdom of God and His righteousness, as Christ Himself bids us [Matt. 6:33]. And if the Lord have there prepared such a place for us, then we must in this world use all good means whereby we may be made worthy the fruition of it and also fit and ready at the day of death to enter into it, which at the day of judgment we shall fully possess both in soul and body and there reign eternally in all happiness with God Almighty, our Creator, the Father, the Son, and the Holy Ghost. But some may say, how shall a man so prepare himself, that he may be fit for that place? *Answer.* This the Holy Ghost teaches us; for, speaking of this heavenly Jerusalem, He says, "There shall enter into it none unclean thing, neither whatsoever works abomination or lies" [Rev. 21:27]. This means then to make ourselves fit is to seek to be reconciled to God in Christ for our sins past and withal to endeavor to have an assurance of the free remission and pardon of them all in the blood of Christ. And as touching that part of life which is to come, we must remember what St. John says, "Everyone that hath this hope purifieth himself" [1 John 3:3], meaning that he which has hope to reign with Christ in heaven uses the means whereby he may purify and keep himself from sin—as also he says after, that "he which is born of God keepeth himself, and the wicked one toucheth him not" [5:18], signifying that all such persons as are truly justified and sanctified carry such a narrow and strait watch over the whole course of their lives and conversations that the devil can never give them deadly wounds and wholly overcome them. Now the man that is resolved in his conscience of the pardon of his sin for the time past and has a steadfast purpose in his heart to keep himself upright and continually to walk in righteousness and true holiness all the days of his life—this man, I say, is prepared and made fit to enter into the heavenly Jerusalem. Come death when it will, he is ready. And howsoever he must not look for heaven here upon earth, yet he is as it were in the suburbs of this heavenly city. And at the end of this life, the King thereof, the Lord Jesus, will open the gates and receive him into His kingdom, for he is already entered into the kingdom of grace. To conclude this point, let every man in the fear of God be moved hereby to set his heart to prepare himself, that when God shall call him hence, he may be fit to enter into that glory.

[Duty 2.] Secondly, seeing God has prepared the third heaven for us, it teaches every man in this world to be content with the estate wherein God has placed him, whether it be high or low, rich or poor. Why so? Because here he is but a pilgrim and lives in a cottage of clay and in a tent wherein he must abide but a while, as a pilgrim does, oftentimes carrying his house about with him. And we shall in better sort accept the afflictions which God sends us in this life if we remember that there is prepared for us a place of joy which must be our resting place and perfect felicity forevermore. This was the practice of the children of God, especially of Abraham; for when the Lord called him out of his own country, he obeyed and "by faith abode in the promised land, as in a strange country, as one that dwelt in tents with Isaac and Jacob heirs with him in the same promise." And the reason follows: "for he looked for a city having a foundation, whose builder and maker is God" [Heb. 11:9–10]. They believed that these things which the Lord promised were shadows of better things and hereon stayed themselves, being well content with that estate whereto God had called them. So Paul was contented to bear the afflictions which God had laid upon him, and his reason was because, says he, "we look not on things which are seen, but on things which are not seen: for the things which are seen are temporal, but the things which are not seen are eternal" [2 Cor. 4:18]. And in the next chapter, "We know," says he, "that if our earthly house of this tabernacle be destroyed, we have a dwelling given us of God, that is, an house not made with hands, but eternal in the heavens" [vv. 1–2]. And for this cause his desire was rather to remove out of this body and to be with the Lord.

And thus much concerning heaven. Now follows the second part of God's creation in these words:

"And earth." Earth signifies the huge mass or body, standing[55] of sea and land, on which we live, and all things that be in or upon the earth whatsoever—as Paul says, "For by him were created all things that are in heaven or in earth," etc. [Col. 1:16]. In other creeds which were made since this of the apostles, being expositions of that, there is added, "maker of all things visible and invisible." Here we have occasion to speak of all creatures, but that were infinite. Therefore, I will make choice of these two: good angels and men.

---

55. *Standing*: consisting.

(1) That angels had a beginning it is no question; for Paul says that by God all things were created in heaven and earth, things visible and invisible, whether thrones, principalities, or powers [1:16]. And in respect of the creation, angels are called the "sons of God" [Job 38:7]. But the time and day of their creation cannot be set down further than this, that they were created in the compass of the six days. For Moses says, "Thus"—namely, in the compass of the first six days—"the heavens and the earth were fashioned, and all of the host of them" [Gen. 2:1], that is, all variety of creatures in heaven and earth, serving for the beauty and glory thereof, whereof no doubt the angels are the principal.

(2) Touching the nature of angels, some have thought that they are nothing but qualities and motions in the minds of men, as the Sadducees and the Libertines of this time. But the truth is that they are spirits—that is, spiritual and invisible substances created by God and really subsisting. For the Scripture ascribes unto them such kinds of actions which cannot be performed by the creatures, save only such as be substances, as to stand before the throne of God, to behold the face of the Father, to carry men's souls to heaven. Yet we must not imagine that they are bodily substances, consisting of flesh and bone. And though they took upon them visible shapes and forms and did eat and drink in company of men and thereupon are called "men" in Scripture [Luke 24:4], yet they did this by divine dispensation for a time, that they might the better perform the actions and businesses among men to which they were by God appointed. And the bodies of men which they assumed were no parts of their natures united to them, as our bodies are to us; but rather they were as garments are to us, which they might put off and on at their pleasure. If any shall ask, whence they had these bodies, the answer is that either they were created of nothing by the power of God or framed of some other matter subsisting before. If again it be asked, what became of these bodies when they laid them down, because they used them but for a time, the answer may be that if they were made of nothing, they were again resolved into nothing; if made of other creatures, that then they were resolved into the same bodies of which they were first made, though indeed we can define nothing certainly in this point.

(3) Angels are reasonable creatures of excellent knowledge and understanding, far surpassing all men save Christ. Their knowledge is threefold: natural, revealed, experimental. Natural, which they received from God in the creation. Revealed, which God makes manifest to them in process of time, whereas before they knew it not. Thus, God revealed to Gabriel the mystery of the seventy weeks (Daniel 8–9). And in the [Book of the] Apocalypse many things are revealed to the angels that they might reveal them to us. Experimental knowledge is that which they get by observing the dealing of God in the whole world, but especially in the church. And thus Paul says that "to principalities

and powers in heavenly places is known the manifold wisdom of God by the church" [Eph. 3:10].

(4) And as the knowledge, so also the power of the good angels is exceeding great [Ps. 103:20]. They are able to do more than all men can. Therefore, Paul calls them "mighty angels" (2 Thess. 1:7). Yea, their power is far superior to the power of the wicked angels, who since the fall are under them and cannot prevail against them.[56]

(5) The place of the abode of angels is the highest heaven, unless they be sent thence by the Lord to do something appointed by Him. This our Savior Christ teaches when He says that "the angels of little ones do always behold the face of their Father in heaven" [Matt. 18:10]. And the wicked angels before their fall were placed in heaven, because they were cast thence.

(6) That there be certain distinctions and diversities of angels, it is very likely, because they are called thrones and principalities and powers, cherubim and seraphim. But what be the distinct degrees and orders of angels and whether they are to be distinguished by their natures, gifts, or offices, no man by Scripture can determine.

(7) The ministry of angels to which the Lord has set them apart is threefold, and it respects either God Himself or His church or His enemies. The ministry which they perform to God is first of all to adore, praise, and glorify Him continually. Thus, the cherubim in Isaiah's vision cry one to another, "Holy, holy, holy is the Lord God of hosts: the world is full of his glory" [Isa. 6:3]. And when they were to publish the birth of the Messiah, they begin on this manner, "Glory to God in the highest heavens, peace on earth" [Luke 2:14]. And John in his vision heard the angels about the throne, crying with a loud voice, "Worthy is the Lamb, etc., to receive power, riches, and strength, wisdom, and honor, and glory, and praise" [Rev. 5:11–12]. And indeed the highest end of the ministry of angels is the manifestation of the glory of God. The second is to stand in God's presence, evermore ready to do His commandments, as David says, "Praise the Lord, ye his angels that excel in strength, that do his commandments in obeying the voice of his word" [Ps. 103:20].[57] And here is a good lesson for us. We pray daily that we may do the will of God, as the angels in heaven do it. Let us therefore be followers of the holy angels in praising God and doing His commandments as they do.

The ministry of angels concerning the church stands in this, that they are ministering spirits for the good of them which shall be the heirs of salvation [Heb. 1:14]. This good is threefold: in this life, in the end of this life, and in

---

56. Aug. de Trin. lib. 3. cap. 3.
57. Originally, "Ps. 103:26."

the last judgment. Again, the good which they procure to the people of God in this life is either in respect of body or soul. In respect of the body, in that they do most carefully perform all manner of duties which do necessarily tend to preserve the temporal life of God's children, even from the beginning of their days to the end. David said that "they pitch their tents about him that fears the Lord" [Ps. 34:7]. When Hagar was cast forth of Abraham's family and wandered in the wilderness, an angel comes unto her and gives her counsel to return to her mistress and humble herself [Gen. 16:7]. When Elijah fled from Jezebel, he was both comforted, directed, and fed by an angel [1 Kings 19:5, 7]. And an angel bids the same Elijah be of good courage and without fear to go to King Ahaziah and reprove him [2 Kings 1:3]. Angels bring Lot and his family out of Sodom and Gomorrah before they burn the cities with fire and brimstone [Gen. 19:15–17]. When Jacob feared his brother Esau, he saw angels coming unto him; and he plainly acknowledges that they were sent to be his protectors and his guides in his journey [32:1–2]. Abraham, being persuaded of the assistance of God's angels in all his ways, said to his servant [that] the Lord God of heaven, "who took me from my father's house," etc. "will send his angel before thee" [24:7]. The wise men that came to see Christ are admonished by angels to return another way, and Joseph by the direction of an angel fled into Egypt that he might preserve Christ from the hands of the cruel tyrant [Matt. 2:12–13]. The tents of the Israelites were guarded by angels [Ex. 14:19;[58] 23:20]. The three children are delivered from the fiery furnace, and Daniel out of the lions' den by angels [Dan. 3:27; 6:22]. When Christ was in heaviness, they ministered unto Him and comforted Him [Matt. 4:11]; and they brought Peter out of prison and set him at liberty [Acts 12:7].

Again, the angels procure good unto the souls of the godly, in that they are maintainers and furtherers of the true worship of God and of all good means whereby we attain to salvation. The law was delivered in Mount Sinai by angels [Acts 7:38], and a great part of the Revelation of John. They expound to Daniel the seventy weeks [Dan. 9:24].[59] They instruct the apostles touching the return of Christ to the last judgment [Acts 1:11]. An angel forbids John to worship him, but worship God the Creator of heaven and earth [Rev. 21:10]. They fetch the apostles out of prison and bid them teach in the temple [Acts 5:20]. An angel brings Philip to the eunuch, that he may expound the Scriptures to him [8:26]. Lastly, they reveal the mysteries and the will of God, as to Abraham, that he should not kill his son Isaac [Gen. 22:12]; to Mary and Elizabeth, the nativity of John [the] Baptist and of Christ, our Savior [Luke 1:13, 28, 35]. And

---

58. Originally, "Ex. 14:16."
59. Originally, "Dan. 9:22."

all this they do according unto the will of God (Gal 1:8). Besides all this, angels rejoice at the conversion of sinners by the ministry of the gospel. And for the church's sake, they protect not only particular men, but even whole nations and kingdoms [Luke 15:7, 10].

The ministry of angels in the end of this life is to carry the souls of the godly into Abraham's bosom, as they did the soul of Lazarus [16:22]; and in the day of judgment to gather all the elect that they may come before Christ and enter into eternal fruition of glory both in body and soul [Matt. 25:32].

The third and last part of the ministry of angels concerns God's enemies, and it is to execute judgments on all wicked persons and impenitent sinners. Thus, all the firstborn of Egypt are slain by an angel [Ex. 12:23, 29]. When Joshua was about to sack Jericho, an angel appeared unto him as a captain with a drawn sword to fight for Israel [Josh. 5:13]. When the host of Sennacherib came against Israel, the angel of the Lord in one night slew a hundred eighty and five thousand [2 Kings 19:35]. Because Herod gave not glory unto God, the angel of the Lord smote him, so as he was eaten up of worms and died [Acts 12:23].

And thus we see what points we are to mark touching the good angels. Now follows the use which we are to make in regard of their creation. *Duty 1*.[60] First, whereas they are God's ministers to inflict punishments upon the wicked, here is a special point to be learned of us: that every man in the fear of God take heed how he lives and continues in his sins, for the case is dangerous, considering that God has armies of angels, which stand ready everywhere to execute God's heavy judgments upon them that live thus. When the people of Israel had sinned against the Lord, Moses says they were naked [Ex. 32:25]—that is, open to all the judgments of God, even destitute of the guard of His good angels. Wretched Balaam, that wizard, went to Balak to curse the children of Israel. And as he went it is said the angel of the Lord stood in his way with a drawn sword; and if the ass had been no wiser than his master, the angel had slain him [Num. 22:31].[61] Whereby it appears that when we rush on into the practice of any sin, we do as much as in us lies to cause God to send down His judgments upon us for our sins, and that by the ministry of His angels.

[Duty] 2. Secondly, we are taught another lesson by Christ Himself. "See," says He, "that you despise not one of these little ones." Now mark His reason: "for I say unto you, that in heaven their angels do always behold the face of my father" [Matt. 18:10]. By "little ones" He means young infants which are within the covenant, or others which are like to young infants in simplicity and innocency of life and humility. And Christ will not have them to be despised, a duty

---

60. This was in the margin, as were the following three duties.
61. Originally, "Num. 22:31."

very needful to be stood upon in these times. For nowadays, if a man carry but a show of humility, of good conscience, and of the fear of God, he is accounted but a silly fellow. He is hated, mocked, and despised on every hand. But this should not be so. For him whom God honors with the protection of His good angels, why should any mortal man despise? And it stands mockers and scorners in hand to take heed whom they mock. For though men for their parts put up many abuses and injuries, yet their angels may take just revenge by smiting them with plagues and punishments for their offences.

[*Duty 3*]. Thirdly, seeing angels are about us and serve for the good of men, we must do whatsoever we do in [a] reverent and seemly manner, as Paul gives counsel to the Philippians. "Brethren," says he, "whatsoever things are true, whatsoever things are honest, just, pure, and pertain to love, of good report: if there be any virtue, if there be any praise, think on these things" [Phil. 4:8]. Many men do all their affairs orderly for avoiding shame, but we must do the same upon a further ground—namely, because God's holy angels wait on us. And considering that men have care to behave themselves well when they are before men, what a shame is it for a man to behave himself unseemly either in open or in secret, he then being before the glorious angels! Paul says that "the woman ought to have power on her head, because of the angels" [1 Cor. 11:10]—that is, not only the ministers of the church, but God's heavenly angels, which daily wait upon His children and guard them in all their ways.

[*Duty 4*]. Fourthly, this must teach us modesty and humility, for the angels of God are very notable and excellent creatures, and therefore they are called in the Psalms "elohim," "gods." Yet how excellent soever they be, they abase themselves to become guardians and keepers unto sinful men. Now if the angels do so abase themselves, then much more ought every man to abase and humble himself in modesty and humility before God. And whatsoever our calling is, we must not be puffed up but be content. This is a necessary duty for all, but especially for those which are in the schools of the prophets. Whatsoever their gifts or birth be, they must not think themselves too good for the calling of the ministry. And if God have called us thereunto, we must be content to become servants unto all in the matter of salvation, though the men whom we teach be never so base or simple; for no man does so far excel the basest person in the world as the glorious angels of God do exceed the most excellent man that is. Therefore, seeing they vouchsafe to become servants unto us, we must not think ourselves too good to serve our poor brethren.

And thus much of the duties. Now follow the consolations that arise from this, that God has given His glorious angels to serve for the protection and safeguard of His church and people. If men's spiritual eyes were opened, they should see the devil and his angels and all the wicked of this world to fight against them. And if there were no means of comfort in this case, then our estate were most miserable. But mark, as God's servant has all these wicked ones to be his enemies, so he has garrisons of angels that pitch their tents about him and defend him from them all. So David says, "He shall give thy angels charge over thee, and they shall keep thee in all his ways, that thou dash not thy foot against a stone" [Ps. 91:11], where the angels of God are compared to nurses, which carry little children in their arms, feed them, and are always ready at hand to save them from falls and many other dangers. When the king of Syria sent his horses and chariots to take Elisha, the Lord's prophet, because he revealed his counsel to the king of Israel, his servant saw them round about Dothan where he was; and he cried, "Alas, master what shall we do?" Then Elisha answered, "Fear not, for they that be with us, are more than they that be with them." And he besought the Lord to open his servant's eyes, and he looked, and behold, the mountains were full of horses and chariots of fire round about Elisha [2 Kings 6:17]. So likewise not many years ago our land was preserved from the invasion of the Spaniard, whose huge navy lay upon our seacoasts. But how were we delivered from them? Surely, by no strength nor power nor cunning of man; but it was the Lord, no doubt, by His angels that did keep our coasts and did scatter our enemies and drown them.[62] Let enemies rage, and let them do that they will. If a man keep himself in the ways which God prescribes, he has God's angels to guide and preserve him, which thing must move men to love and embrace the true religion and to conform themselves in all good conscience to the rule of God's Word. For when a man does not so, all the angels of God are his enemies and at all times ready to execute God's vengeance upon him. But when men carry themselves as dutiful children to God, they have this prerogative, that God's holy angels do watch about them and defend them day and night from the power of their enemies, even in common calamities and miseries. Before God sends His judgments on Jerusalem, an angel is sent to mark them in the foreheads that mourn for the abominations of the people [Ezekiel 9]. And this privilege none can have, but he whose heart is sprinkled with the blood of Christ, and that man shall have it unto the end [Ex. 12:23 with 1 Cor. 5:7].

And thus much of the creation of angels. Now it follows to speak of the creation of man, wherein we must consider two things: (1) the points of doctrine; (2) the uses. For the points of doctrine, first, man was created and framed by the hand of God and made after the image of God. For Moses brings in the Lord speaking thus, "Let us make man in our image, etc., in the image of God created he them" [Gen. 1:26], which also must be understood of angels. The image

---

62. Editor's note: referring to the destruction of the Spanish Armada in 1588.

of God is nothing else but a conformity of man unto God, whereby man is holy as God is holy; for Paul says, "Put on the new man, which after God"—that is, in God's image—"is created in righteousness and holiness" [Eph. 4:24]. Now I reason thus: wherein the renewing of the image of God in man does stand, therein was it at the first. But the renewing of God's image in man does stand in righteousness and holiness. Therefore, God's image wherein man was created at the beginning was a conformity to God in righteousness and holiness. Now whether God's image does further consist in the substance of man's body and soul or in the faculties of both, the Scripture speaks not. This image of God has two principal parts: (1) wisdom; (2) holiness. Concerning wisdom, Paul says, "Put ye on the new man which is created in knowledge after the image of him which created him" [Col. 3:10]. This wisdom consists in three points. (1) In that he knew God, his Creator, perfectly; for Adam in his innocency knew God so far forth as it was convenient for a creature to know his Creator. (2) He knew God's will so far forth as it was convenient for him to show his obedience thereunto. (3) He knew the wisdom and will of his Creator touching the particular creatures; for after Adam was created, the Lord brought every creature unto him, presenting them unto him as being lord and king over them, that he might give names unto them. Whereby it appears that Adam in his innocency did know the nature of all creatures and the wisdom of God in creating them, else he could not have given them fit names. And when God brought Eve unto Adam, he knew her at the first and said, "This is now bone of my bone and flesh of my flesh, she shall be called woman," etc. [Gen. 2:23].[63] The second part of God's image in man is holiness and righteousness, which is nothing else but a conformity of the will and affections and of the whole disposition of man both in body and soul to the will of God, his Creator. Yet we must remember that Adam in his innocency had a changeable will so as he could either will good or evil. He was created with such liberty of will as that he could indifferently will either. And we must not think that the will of the creature was made unchangeably good, for that is peculiar to the will of God, and hereby is the Creator distinguished from the creature.

And here two things offer themselves to be considered. The first, why the man is called "the image of God," and not the woman. *Answer.* He is so called not because holiness and righteousness is peculiar to him, which is common to both, but because God has placed more outward excellency and dignity in the person of a man than of a woman [1 Cor. 11:7]. The second, how Christ should be called the image of God. *Answer.* He is so called for two special causes. First, because He is of the same substance with the Father and therefore is His most

---

63. Originally, "Gen. 1:23."

absolute image [Col. 1:15] and, as the author of the Hebrews says, "the brightness of his glory, and the engraven form of his person" [Heb. 1:3]. Secondly, because God, being invisible, does manifest Himself in Christ, in whom as in a glass we may behold the wisdom, goodness, justice, and mercy of God.

The second point to be considered in the creation of man is the dignity of his person, for David says, "Thou hast made him little inferior to the angels, and crowned him with glory, and worship" [Ps. 8:5]. This dignity stands in four points. (1) A blessed communion with the true God; for Paul, speaking of the Gentiles which were not called, says they were "strangers from the life of God" [Eph. 4:18]. Where by the contrary we may gather that our first parents in their innocency lived the life of God, which is nothing else but to lead a life here on earth as that the creature shall have a blessed and immediate fellowship with God, which stands in this: that before the fall of man, God revealed Himself in a special manner unto him, so as his very body and soul was a temple and dwelling place of the Creator. This fellowship between God and man in his innocency was made manifest in the familiar conference which God vouchsafed to man; but since the fall, this communion is lost, for man cannot abide the presence of God. And therefore when Peter had fished all night and caught nothing, our Savior bade him cast down his net to make a draught, who did so. But when he saw the great multitude of fishes that were taken, at this sight beholding but as it were some sparks of the glorious majesty of God in Christ, he fell down at His feet, saying, "Lord, depart from me, for I am a sinner" [Luke 5:8]. [2] The second point wherein man's dignity consists is that man was made lord and king over all creatures, as David says, "Thou hast made him to have dominion in the works of thy hands" [Ps. 8:6]. And therefore God, having created him in His image, bids him "rule over the fishes of the sea, over the fowls of the heaven, and over every beast that moves upon the earth" [Gen. 1:28]. And afterward He brought them all to him, as to a sovereign lord and king to be named by him; and answerably every creature in its[64] kind gave reverence and subjection unto man before his fall, as to their lord and king. Where by the way we must remember that when we see any creature that is hurtful and noisome unto man and would rather devour than obey him, it must put us in mind of our sin; for by creation we were made lords and kings over all creatures, and they durst not but reverence and obey us. But the rebellion of man unto God is the cause of the rebellion of the creatures unto us. [3] The third part of man's dignity by creation is that before his fall he had a wonderful beauty and majesty above all creatures in his body, whereupon David says the Lord has crowned him with "glory and worship" [Ps. 8:5]. And in the renewing of the

---

64. Originally, "his."

covenant with Noah, God says that "the dread and fear of man shall be upon all creatures" [Gen. 9:2], which now though it be but small, yet does it plainly show what was the glory and majesty of man's person at the first. [4] The fourth dignity of man's estate in innocency is that his labor was without pain or weariness. If he had never fallen, he should have labored in the garden, but so as he should never have been wearied therewith. For when Adam was fallen, God said, "In the sweat of thy face shalt thou eat thy bread" [3:19].[65] Now if the pain in labor come after as a curse upon man for his transgression, then before his fall man felt no pain in his affairs. And in these four things consists man's dignity which he had in the creation.

Now in the third follows man's calling before his fall, which is twofold: (1) particular; (2) general. Man's particular calling was to come into the garden of Eden, to keep it, and to dress the trees and fruits thereof. This shows unto us a good lesson, that every man must have a particular calling wherein he ought to walk. And therefore such as spend their time idly in gaming and vain delights have much to answer to God at the day of judgment. This will not excuse a man to say then that he had land and living to maintain himself and therefore was to live as he list; for even Adam in his innocency had all things at his will and wanted nothing, yet even then God employed him in a calling. Therefore, none must be exempted, but every man both high and low must walk in his proper calling. Adam's general calling was to worship his Creator, to which he was bound by the right of creation, considering the moral law was written in his heart by nature. Which is signified in the Decalogue, where the Lord requires worship and obedience of His people, because He is Jehovah [Ex. 20:2]—that is, one which has being in Himself and gives being to all men by creation. For the better understanding of this point, we are to consider three things: (1) the place where Adam did worship; (2) the time; (3) the sacraments. For the first, God ever since the beginning had a place where He would be worshipped, and it is called "God's house," which then was the garden of Eden [Gen. 28:17]. For it was unto Adam a place appointed by God for His worship, as church assemblies are unto us, where also the Lord at some time did in a special manner show Himself unto His creature. Touching the time of God's worship, it was the seventh day from the beginning of the creation, the Sabbath Day. And here we must note that the keeping of the Sabbath is moral. Some indeed do plead that it is but a ceremony, yet falsely; for it was ordained before the fall of man, at which time ceremonies signifying sanctification had no place. Nay, mark further: Adam in his innocency was not clogged with sin as we are; yet then he had a set Sabbath to worship God, his Creator. And therefore much more need

---

65. Originally, "Gen. 3:29."

has every one of us of a Sabbath Day, wherein we may sever ourselves from the works of our callings and the works of sin to the worship of God in the exercise of religion and godly meditation of our creation. This point must be learned of us, for when no occasion is offered of business, then men will formally seem to keep the Sabbath. But if there come occasion of breaking the Sabbath, as traffic, gaming, and vain shows, then Sabbath farewell. Men will have their pleasures, let them worship God that will. But let us remember in the fear of God that whosoever continue in the breach of this law, being moral, God will no less pour forth His punishments upon them, than for the breach of any other commandment—the consideration whereof must move every man to a reverent sanctifying of the Lord's Day.

Now for Adam's sacraments, they were two: the tree of life and the tree of knowledge of good and evil. These did serve to exercise Adam in obedience unto God. The tree of life was to signify assurance of life forever, if he did keep God's commandments. The tree of knowledge of good and evil was a sacrament to show unto him that if he did transgress God's commandments, he should die [Gen. 2:17].[66] And it was so called because it did signify that if he transgressed this law, he should have experience both of good and evil in himself.

Now in the fourth place follows the end of the creation of man, which is twofold. First, that there might be a creature to whom God might make manifest Himself, who in a special manner should set forth and acknowledge His wisdom, goodness, mercy in the creation of heaven and earth and of things that are in them, as also His providence in governing the same. Secondly, God, having decreed to glorify His name in showing His mercy and justice upon His creature, hereupon in time creates men to show His mercy in the salvation of some and to show His justice in the just and deserved damnation of other some. And therefore He has appointed the creation specially of man to be a means of manifestation and beginning of the execution of His eternal counsel.

Thus much concerning man's creation in general. The special parts of man are two: body and soul. And the reason why the Lord would have him stand on these two parts is this: some creatures made before him were only bodily, as beasts, fishes, fowls; some spiritual, as angels. Now man is both—spiritual in regard of his soul; corporal and sensible in regard of his body—that nothing might be wanting to the perfection of nature. If it be alleged that man consists of three parts, body, soul, and spirit, because Paul prays that the Thessalonians "may be sanctified, in body, soul, and spirit" (1 Thess. 5:23), the answer is that "the spirit" signifies the mind, whereby men conceive and understand such things as may be understood, and "the soul" is there taken for the will and

---

66. Originally, "Gen. 2:7."

affections. And therefore these twain are not two parts but only two distinct faculties of one and the same soul.

The body of man at the first was formed by God of clay, or of the dust of the earth, not to be the grave of the soul, as Plato said, but to be an excellent and most fit instrument to put in execution the powers and faculties of the soul. And howsoever in itself considered it is mortal, because it is compounded of contrary natures called elements, yet by the appointment and blessing of God in the creation it became immortal till the fall of man.

As for the soul, it is no accidentary quality but a spiritual and invisible essence or nature, subsisting by itself. Which plainly appears in that the souls of men have being and continuance as well forth of the bodies of men as in the same [Zech. 12:1] and are as well subject to torments as the body is. And whereas we can and do put in practice sundry actions of life, sense, motion, understanding, we do it only by the power and virtue of the soul.

Hence arises the difference between the souls of men and beasts. The souls of men are substances; but the souls of other creatures seem not to be substances because they have no being out of the bodies in which they are, but rather they are certain peculiar qualities arising of the matter of the body and vanishing with it. And it may be for this cause that "the soul of the beast is said to be in the blood" [Gen. 9:4], whereas the like is not said of the soul of man.

And though men's souls be spirits as angels are, yet a difference must be made. For angels cannot be united with bodies, so as both shall make one whole and entire person, whereas men's souls may. Yea, the soul coupled with the body is not only the mover of the body but the principal cause that makes man to be a man.

The beginning of the soul is not of the essence of God, unless we will make every man's soul to be God. Neither does it spring of the soul of the parents, for the soul can no more beget a soul than an angel can beget an angel. And Adam is called a living soul and not a quickening soul [1 Cor. 15:45]. And earthly fathers are called the fathers of our bodies and not of our souls [Heb. 12:9]. It remains therefore as being most agreeable to the Scriptures that the souls of men are then created by God of nothing when they are infused into the body.

And though the souls of men have a beginning, yet they have no end but are eternal. And when they are said to die, it is not because they cease at any time to subsist or have being in nature, but because they cease to be righteous or to have fellowship with God.

Whereas our bodies are God's workmanship, we must glorify Him in our bodies. And all the actions of body and soul, our eating and drinking, our living and dying, must be referred to His glory [1 Cor. 10:31]. Yea, we must not hurt or abuse our bodies but present them as holy and living sacrifices unto God

[6:20]. And whereas God made us of the dust of the earth, we are not to glory and boast ourselves,[67] but rather to take occasion to praise the great goodness of God that has vouchsafed to honor us, being but dust and ashes. And after that man is created, what is his life? Alas, it is nothing but a little breath. Stop his mouth and his nostrils, and he is but a dead man. By this we are put in mind to consider of our frail and uncertain estate and to lay aside all confidence in ourselves, and for this cause the prophet Isaiah teaches us to have no confidence in man, because his breath is in his nostrils [Isa. 2:22]. Again, let us mark the frame and shape of man's body. All other creatures go with their bodies and eyes to the ground-ward, but man was made to go upright. And whereas all other creatures have but four muscles to turn their eyes round about, man has a fifth to pull his eyes up to heavenward.[68] Now what does this teach us? Surely, that howsoever we seek for other things, yet first of all and above all we should seek for the kingdom of heaven and the righteousness thereof, and that our whole desire should be set to enjoy the blessed estate of God's children in heaven. Secondly, it teaches us in receiving God's creatures to return thankfulness unto God by lifting up the heart to heaven for the same. These are very needful and profitable lessons in these days; for most men indeed go upright, but look into their lives, and they might as well go on all four[s]. For in their conversation they set their whole hearts upon the earth, as the beast does, and their eyes upon the things of this world. Hereby they do abase themselves and deface their bodies and, being men, make themselves as beasts. We shall see great numbers of men that run and ride from place to place to provide for the body. But to seek the kingdom of heaven, where their souls should dwell after this life in joy forever, they will not stir one foot.

Thirdly, man's body by creation was made a temple framed by God's own hands for Himself to dwell in. Therefore, our duty is to keep our bodies pure and clean and not to suffer them to be instruments whereby to practice the sin of the heart [1 Cor. 6:19].[69] If a man had a fair house wherein he must entertain a prince and should make thereof a swine sty or a stable, would not all men say that he did greatly abuse both the house and the prince? Even so, man's body being at the first made a palace for the ever-living God, if a man shall abuse it by drunkenness, swearing, lying, fornication, or any uncleanness, he does make it instead of a temple for the Holy Ghost to be a sty or stable for the devil. For the more filthy a man's body is, the more fit it is to be a dwelling place for sin and Satan.

---

67. There is a marginal note to Romans 22:1 here, which is incorrect.
68. Columb. l. 5. cap. 9.
69. Originally, "1 Cor. 16:19."

Fourthly, man by creation was made a goodly creature in the blessed image of God, but by Adam's fall men lost the same and are now become the deformed children of wrath. Our duty therefore is to labor to get again our first image and endeavor ourselves to become new creatures. If a nobleman should stain his blood by treason, after his death the posterity will never be at rest till they have got away the spot. Man by Adam's fall is become a limb of the devil, a rebel and traitor against God's majesty. And this is the state of every one of us. By nature we are at enmity with God, and therefore we ought to labor above all things in the world to be restored in Christ to our first estate and perfection, that so we may become bone of His bone, flesh of His flesh, being justified and sanctified by His obedience, death, and passion.

Fifthly, man was created that there might be a way prepared whereby God might show His grace and mercy in the salvation of some and His justice in the deserved damnation of others for their sins. And in the creation of man God's eternal counsel begins to come into execution. Hereupon it stands us in hand to make conscience of every evil way, being repentant for all our sins past and having a constant purpose never to sin more as we have done, that by our good conversation here in this life we may have assurance that we be eternally chosen to salvation by the Lord Himself.

Lastly, whereas we have learned that the soul of man is immortal, we are hereby taught to take more care for the soul than for the body, for it cannot be extinguished. When it is condemned, even then it is always in dying and can never die. But alas, in this point the case is flat contrary in the world; for men labor all their lives long to get for the body, but for the soul they care little or nothing at all. Whether it sink or swim, go to heaven or hell, they respect not. This does appear to be true by the practice and behavior of men on the Lord's Day; for if the number of those which come to hear God's word were compared with those which run about their worldly wealth and pleasure, I fear me the better sort would be found to be but a little handful to a huge heap or as a drop to the ocean sea in respect of the other. But will you go a hundred miles for the increase of your wealth and delight of your body? Then think it not much to go ten thousand miles (if need were) to take any pains for the good of your soul and to get food for the same, it being everlasting.

And thus much for the duties. Now follow the consolations. Although by reason of the fall of man we can have but little comfort now, yet the creation does confirm the unspeakable providence of God over His creatures, but especially over man, in that the Lord created him the sixth day and so before he was made prepared him a paradise for his dwelling place and all creatures for his use and comfort. And if He were thus careful for us when we were not, then no doubt He will be much more careful for us at this present in which we live and have being. Nay, mark further: since the fall, man cares and drinks in quantity a great deal which in common reason should rather kill him than turn to the strength and nourishment of his body. Yet herein does the wonderful power of the Creator most notably appear, who has made man's stomach as a limbeck or style to digest all meats that are wholesome for his nourishment and preservation.

God's Providence Proved[70]

And thus much for the creation. Now in these words "maker of heaven and earth," [there] is more to be understood than the work of creation—namely, God's providence in governing all things created, as He appoints in His eternal decree. And therefore St. Peter says, "God is a faithful Creator" [1 Peter 4:19]—that is, God did not only make heaven and earth and so leave them, as masons and carpenters leave houses when they are built; but by His providence He does most wisely govern the same. Now therefore let us come to speak of God's providence. And first of all the question offers itself to be considered, whether there be any providence or no? For the minds of men are troubled with many doubtings hereof. And to make the question out of all doubt, I will use four arguments to confirm the providence of God.

[Argument] 1.[71] The first is the testimony of the Scripture, which ascribes the event of all particular actions, even such as are in themselves casual, as the "casting of lots" [Prov. 16:33] and such like, to the disposition of God—which very thing also teaches that even men themselves, indued with reason and understanding, have need to be guided in all things [20:24] and governed by God [Jer. 10:23], and it serves to confute those that deny God's providence. "Why sayest thou, O Jacob, and speakest, O Israel, my way is hid from the Lord, and my judgment is passed over by my God?" [Isa. 40:27].

[Argument] 2.[72] The second argument may be taken from the order which appears in the whole course of nature. First, to begin with families, there is to be seen an eutaxy[73] or seemly order in which some rule and some obey; and the like is to be found in towns, cities, countries, and kingdoms—yea, even in the whole world, in which all things are so disposed that one serves for the good of another. Trees and herbs and grass of the field serve for beasts and cattle; beasts and cattle serve for men; the heavens above serve for them which are beneath; and all the creatures which are above and beneath serve for God.

---

70. Originally in the margin.
71. Originally in the margin, as the additional three arguments following. This paragraph break is not in the original.
72. This paragraph break is not in the original.
73. *Eutaxy*: arrangement or order.

This argues that God is most wise and provident in ordering and disposing all things whatsoever.

[*Argument*] 3.[74] The third argument is taken from the conscience specially of malefactors. Suppose a man that commits a murder so closely[75] that no man knows thereof, and that the party himself is free from all the danger of the law. Yet shall he have his own conscience to accuse, upbraid, and condemn him, yea, even to fright him out of his wits and to give him no more rest than he can find upon the rack or gibbet. Now this accusation and terror of conscience is nothing else but the forerunner of another most terrible judgment of God, who is Lord of all creatures and Judge of all men. And this also proves the providence of God. For if the conscience can find a man out and lay his faults to his charge, how much more shall God Himself, the Creator of the conscience, see and consider all his doings?

[*Argument*] 4.[76] The fourth and last argument is this: the prophecies of things to come should be uncertain or false, if God governed not the world. But now considering things many years ago foretold come to pass in the same manner as they were foretold by the prophets and apostles, hereby we must certainly conclude that there is a providence of God, whereby all and everything is governed.

Against the providence of God sundry things be alleged. [*Objection*] 1.[77] The first and special is that providence and disorder, confusion and order cannot stand together. Now in the world there is nothing but disorder and confusion in seditions, treasons, conspiracies, and subversions of kingdoms, where also sin and wickedness prevails. *Answer*. It is true indeed there has been confusion in the world ever since the fall of man and angels; and it arises not from God, but from them alone, who as they did at the first transgress the will of God, so they do what they can to turn all upside down. Now then, confusion and disorder is only in respect of the devil and his instruments. But in regard of God in the very midst of all confusion there is order to be found, because He can and does dispose it to the glory of His own name and to the good and salvation of His chosen, as also to the confusion of His enemies.

[*Objection*] 2. Again, it may be objected that with ungodly and wicked men all things go well, and contrariwise with the godly all things go hardly—for through the world none are more molested and more under outward misery than they. But if there were any providence in God, then it should be otherwise.

---

74. This paragraph break is not in the original.
75. *Closely*: secretly.
76. This paragraph break is not in the original.
77. "Objections answered 1" originally in margin, as also the additional two objections following.

The godly should flourish, and the wicked perish. *Answer.* The consideration of the outward estate of men in the world was to David an occasion of a sore temptation. For when he saw the wicked to prosper always, and their riches to increase, he brake forth and said, "Certainly I have cleansed my heart in vain, and washed my hands in innocency" [Ps. 73:13]. Now if we would repel this temptation, as David afterward did, then we must go into the Lord's sanctuary [v. 17] with him and learn to be resolved in these points. (1) Though the godly be laden with miseries, yet even that by the especial providence of God turns to their great good. For every man since the fall of Adam is stained with the loathsome contagion of sin. Now the child of God, that is truly regenerate and must be fellow heir with Christ after this life in the kingdom of glory, must in this life be cast into the Lord's furnace, that in the fire of affliction he may more and more be scoured and purified from the corruption of his nature and be estranged from the wickedness of the world. (2) The prosperous success of the wicked, their spoils, their revenues, and all their honor turns to their greater woe in the end—as does appear in Job's history and in the examples of the Chaldeans, of David's enemies, and of Dives and Lazarus.

[Objection] 3. Thirdly, it may be objected that many things come to pass by chance and therefore not by God's providence, because chance and providence cannot stand together. *Answer.* We must distinguish between chance and mere chance. Chance is when anything comes to pass, the cause thereof being unknown not simply, but in respect of man. And therefore in regard of men, which know not the reason of things, we may say there is chance. And so the Spirit of God speaks, "Time and chance come to them all" [Eccl. 9:11], and again, "By chance there came down a priest the same way" [Luke 10:31]. Now this kind of chance is not against the providence of God, but is ordered by it. For things which in regard of men are casual are certainly known and determined by God. Mere chance is when things are said or thought to come to pass without any cause at all. But that must be abhorred of us as an overturning the providence of God.

Providence Described[78]

Thus, seeing it is plain that there is a providence, let us in the next place see what it is. Providence is a most free and powerful action of God whereby He has care over all things that are.

---

78. Originally in the margin.

The Parts of It[79]

Providence has two parts: knowledge and government. God's knowledge is whereby all things from the greatest to the least are manifest before Him at all times. As David says, "His eyes will consider, his eyelids will try the children of men" [Ps. 11:4]. And again, "He abaseth himself to behold the things that are in the heaven and the earth" [113:6]. And the prophet Hanani said to Asa, "The eyes of the Lord behold all the earth" [2 Chron. 16:9]. And St. James says, "From the beginning of the world God knoweth all his works" [Acts 15:18]. This point has a double use, as St. Peter says: it must move us "to eschew evil and do good." Why? "Because," says he, "the eyes of the Lord are upon the just, and his countenance against evildoers" [1 Peter 3:11–12]. Secondly, it must comfort all those that labor to keep a good conscience. For the eyes of God behold all the earth "to shew himself strong with them that are of perfect heart toward him" [2 Chron. 16:9].

Government is the second part of God's providence, whereby He orders all things and directs them to good ends. And it must be extended to the very least thing that is in heaven or earth, as to the sparrows [Matt. 6:26] and to oxen [Deut. 25:4] and the hairs of our heads [Matt. 10:30]. And here we must consider two things: the manner of government and the means.

The manner of government is diverse, according as things are good or evil. A good thing is that which is approved of God, as first of all the substances of all creatures, even of the devils themselves, in whom whatsoever is remaining since their creation is in itself good. Secondly, the quantities, qualities, motions, actions, and inclinations of the creatures in themselves considered with all their events are good. Again, good is either natural or moral—natural, which is created by God for the lawful use of man; moral, which is agreeable to the eternal and unchangeable wisdom of God, revealed in the moral law.

Now God governs all good things two ways: first, by sustaining and preserving them that they decay not; secondly, by moving them that they may attain to the particular ends for which they were severally ordained. For the quality and virtues which were placed in the sun, moon, stars, trees, plants, seeds, etc., would lie dead in them and be unprofitable, unless they were not only preserved but also stirred up and quickened by the power of God so oft as He employs them to any use.

Evil is the destruction of nature, and it is taken for sin or for the punishment of sin. Now sin is governed of God by two actions. The first is an operative permission. I so call it, because God partly permits sin and partly works in it. For sin as it is commonly taken has two parts: the subject or matter and the

---

79. Originally in the margin.

form of sin. The subject of sin is a certain quality or action; the form is the anomy[80] or transgression of God's law. The first is good in itself; and every quality or action, so far forth as it is a quality or action, is existing in nature and has God to be the author of it. Therefore, sin, though it be sufficiently evil to eternal damnation, yet can it not be said to be absolutely evil as God is absolutely good, because the subject of it is good, and therefore it has in it respects and regards of goodness. In respect of the second—that is, the breach of the law itself—God neither wills nor appoints nor commands nor causes nor helps sin, but forbids, condemns, and punishes it, yet so as withal He willingly permits it to be done by others, as men and wicked angels, they being the sole authors and causes of it. And this permission by God is upon a good end, because thereby He manifests His justice and mercy. Thus, it appears that in original sin the natural inclination of the mind, will, and affections in itself considered is from God, but the ataxy[81] or corruption of the inclination is in no wise from Him, but only permitted. Again, that in actual sin the motion of the body or mind is from God, but the evilness and disorder of the motion is not from Him, but freely permitted to be done by others. As, for example, in the act of murder, the action of moving the whole body, of stirring the several joints, and the fetching of the blow whereby the man is slain is from God; for "in him we live, move, and have our being" [Acts 17:28]. But the disposing and applying of all these actions to this end—that our neighbor's life may be taken away, and we thereby take revenge upon him—is not from God, but from the wicked will of man and the devil.

God's second action in the government of sin is after the just permission of it partly to restrain it more or less according to His good will and pleasure and partly to dispose and turn it against the nature thereof to the glory of His own name, to the punishment of His enemies, and to the correcting and chastisement of His elect.

As for the second kind of evil, called the punishment of sin, it is the execution of justice and has God to be the author of it. And in this respect Isaiah says that "God createth evil" [Isa. 45:7], and Amos, that "there is no evil in the city which God hath not done" [Amos 3:6]. And God as a most just judge may punish sin by sin, Himself in the mean season free from all sin. And thus the places must be understood in which it is said that God gives kings in His wrath, hardens the heart, blinds the eyes, mingles the spirit of errors, gives up men to a reprobate sense, sends strong illusions to believe lies, sends evil spirits giving

80. *Anomy*: sin (literally, against the law, *nomos*).
81. *Ataxy*: the opposite of eutaxy.

them commandment to hurt, and leave to deceive, etc. [Hos. 13:11; Neh. 9:37; Exodus 4; 7; Isa. 19:14; Rom. 1:28; 2 Thess. 2:11; 1 Kings 22:22].

Thus, having seen in what manner God governs all things, let us now come to the means of government. Sometimes God works without means. Thus, He created all things in the beginning, and He made trees and plants to grow and flourish without the heat of the sun or rain. Sometimes He governs according to the usual course and order of nature, as when He preserves our lives by meat and drink, yet so as He can and does most freely order all things by means either above nature or against nature, as it shall seem good unto Him—as when He caused the sun to stand in the firmament [Josh. 10:12] and to "go back in Ahaz's dial" [Isa. 38:8]; when He caused the fire not to burn the three children [Dan. 3:27]; when He kept back dew and rain three years in Israel [1 Kings 18:45]; when He made waters to flow out of the rock [Ex. 17:6]; when He caused Elijah's cloak to divide the waters of Jordan [2 Kings 2:8]; when He caused iron to swim [6:6]; when He preserved Jonah alive three days and three nights in the whale's belly [Jonah 1:17]; when He cured diseases by the strength of nature incurable [Matt. 9:12], as the leprosy of Naaman [2 Kings 5:14], the issue of blood, and blindness, etc. [John 9:6–7].

Among all the means which God uses, the special are the reasonable creatures, which are no passive instruments, as the tool in the hand of the workman, but active, because as they are moved by God, so again being indued with will and reason, they move themselves. And such instruments are either good or evil. Evil, as wicked men and angels. And these He uses to do His good will and pleasure, even then when they do least of all obey Him. And considering that the sinning instrument which is moved by God does also move itself freely without any constraint on God's part, God Himself is free from all blame, when the instrument is blameworthy. In directing the instrument, God sins not. The action indeed is of Him, but the defect of the action from the instrument, which, being corrupt, can itself do nothing but that is corrupt. God in the mean season by it brings that to pass which is very good. The whole cause of sin is in Satan and in us. As for God, He puts no wickedness into us; but the evil which He finds in us He moves—that is, orders and governs—and bends it by His infinite wisdom, when and in what manner it pleases Him, to the glory of His name, the evil instrument not knowing so much, nay, intending a far other end. As in the mill, the horse blindfolded goes forward and perceives nothing but that he is in the ordinary way, whereas the miller himself whips him and stirs him forward for another end—namely, for the grinding of corn. And this is that which we must hold touching God's providence over wicked men and angels, and it stands with the tenor of the whole Bible. Joseph's brethren sold him to Egypt very wickedly, even in the testimony of their own consciences. Yet

Joseph, having respect to the counsel and work of God which He performed by his brethren, says that the Lord sent him thither [Gen. 45:7–8]. And the church of Jerusalem says that Herod and Pontius Pilate did nothing in the death of Christ, but that which "the hand and the counsel of God had determined to be done" [Acts 4:28], because though they wickedly intended nothing but to show their malice and hatred in the death of Christ, yet God, propounding a further matter by them than ever they dreamed of, showed forth His endless mercy to man in the work of redemption. On this manner must all the places of Scripture be understood, in which it is said that God gave the wives of David to Absalom [2 Sam. 12:11]; that God moved David to number the people [24:1]; that He commanded Shimei to rail on David [16:11]; that the Medes and Persians are His sanctified ones [Isa. 13:3];[82] that the revolt of the ten tribes was done by God [2 Chron. 11:4], etc. By all these examples it appears that we must not sever God's permission from His will or decree, and that we must put difference between the evil work of man and the good work of God which He does by man. And the whole matter may yet be more clearly perceived by this comparison: a thief at the day of assize is condemned, and the magistrate appoints him to be executed. The hangman, owing a grudge to the malefactor, uses him hardly and prolongs his punishment longer than he should. Now the magistrate and the hangman do both one and the same work—yet the hangman for his part is a murderer, [and] the magistrate in the mean season no murderer but a just judge putting justice in execution by the hangman. So God, though He use evil instruments, yet is He free from the evil of the instruments.

And further we must here mark the difference which must be made in God's using of all kinds of instruments. When He uses good creatures, as angels, He works His will not only by them, but also in them, because He inspires them and guides them by His Spirit, so as they shall will and do that which He wills and intends. As for evil instruments, He works by them only and not in them, because He holds back His grace from them and leaves them to themselves, to put in practice the corruption of their own hearts.

The Kinds of God's Providence[83]

Thus much of the parts of God's providence. Now follow the kinds thereof. God's providence is either general or special. General is that which extends itself to the whole world and all things indifferently, even to the devils themselves [Job 37–38; Acts 17:28; Heb. 1:3]. By this providence God continues and maintains the order which He set in nature in the creation; and He preserves

---

82. Originally, "Isa. 10:5; 23:6."
83. Originally in the margin.

the life, substance, and the being of all and every creature in its[84] kind [Psalm 104].

The special providence is that which God shows and exercises toward His church and chosen people in gathering and guiding them and in preserving them by His mighty power against the gates of hell [Zech. 2:8; Isa. 43:1–2]. And therefore God's church here upon earth is called the kingdom of grace, in which He shows not only a general power over His creatures, but withal the special operation of His Spirit in bowing and bending the hearts of men to His will.

Duties from God's Providence[85]

Thus much concerning the doctrine of God's providence. Now follows the duties. *[Duty] 1.*[86] First, seeing there is a providence of God over everything that is, we are hereby taught to take good heed of the transgression of the least of God's commandments. If men were persuaded that the prince had an eye everywhere, doubtless many subjects in England would walk more obediently to the laws of the land than they do and durst in no wise work such villanies as are daily practiced. Well, howsoever it is with earthly princes, yet this all-seeing presence is least wanting in God. He has an eye everywhere. Wheresoever you are, there God beholds you, as David says, "God looked down from heaven upon the children of men, to see if there were any that would understand and seek God" [Ps. 53:2]. Therefore, except you be brutish and past shame, take heed of sin. If men had but a spark of grace, the consideration of this would make them loath the practice of any evil work. Elijah says to Ahab, "As the Lord God of Israel liveth before whom I stand, there shall be neither dew nor rain these three years." Where the prophet confirms his speech with an oath, saying, "As the Lord of hosts liveth it shall be so" [1 Kings 17:1]. And lest Ahab should think he made no conscience what he said, he adds this clause, that he stood in the presence of God. As if he should say, "Howsoever you think of me, yet as it stands me in hand, so do I make conscience of my word; for I stand in the presence of God. And therefore know it, as the Lord lives there shall be no rain nor dew these three years." So Cornelius, having an eye to God's providence, does move himself and all his household to a solemn hearing of the word of God delivered by the mouth of Peter, saying that "they were all present before God, to hear all things commanded of him" [Acts 10:33]. As these men had regard to God's providence, so we likewise must behave ourselves reverently, making conscience of our behavior both in words and works, because wheresoever we be, we are in the presence of God.

---

84. Originally, "his."
85. Originally in the margin.
86. Originally in the margin, as the next duty following.

[Duty] 2. Secondly, if there be a providence of God over everything, then we must learn contentation of mind in every estate. Yea, in adversity under the cross when all goes against us we must be content, because God's providence has so appointed. So David in the greatest of his griefs was dumb and spoke nothing. His reason was because "thou Lord didst it" [Ps. 39:9]. And when Shimei cursed David, Abishai would have had the king to have given him leave to have slain him; but David would not suffer it, but said, "He curseth even because the Lord hath bidden him curse David: who dare then say, wherefore hast thou done so?" [2 Sam. 16:10]—in whose example we may see a pattern of quietness of mind. When a cross comes, it is a hard thing to be patient; but we must draw ourselves thereunto by consideration of God's especial providence.

[Duty 3]. Thirdly, when outward means of preservation in this life do abound, as health, honor, riches, peace, and pleasure, then we must remember to be thankful, because these things always come by the providence of God. Thus, Job was thankful both in prosperity and adversity. "The Lord," says he, "gave, and the Lord taketh away. Blessed be the name of the Lord" [Job 1:21].[87] Indeed, to be patient in every estate and thankful to God is a very hard matter, yet will it be more easy if we learn in all things that befall us in this life never to sever the consideration of the things that come to pass from God's providence. For as the body and soul of man (though we see only the body) are always together as long as a man lives, so is God's providence joined with the thing done. Wherefore, as we look on the thing done, so we must also in it labor to see and acknowledge the good pleasure and appointment of God. As, for example, a man's house is set on fire, and all his goods consumed. This very sight would make him at his wits' end. But now as he beholds this event with one eye, so with the other eye he must at that very instant look upon God's blessed providence. When a man beholds and feels the loss of his friends, he cannot but grieve thereat, unless he be more senseless than stock or stone. Yet that he may not be overwhelmed with grief, he must ever with one eye look at the pleasure of God herein. This will be an especial means to slay the rage of any headstrong affection in all our afflictions. In the world the manner of men is, if health, wealth, and ease abound, to think all is well. But if crosses come, as loss of friends and loss of goods, then men cry out as being straught[88] of their wits. The reason is because they look only at the outward means and tie God's providence to them, not being able to see any goodness or providence of God out of ordinary means. Again, when a man is stored with riches, honor, wealth, and prosperity, he must not barely look on them but behold withal God's goodness and blessing

---

87. Originally, "Job 1:22."
88. *Straught*: distraught.

in them; for if that be wanting, all the riches in the world are nothing. Likewise, in receiving your meat and drink, you must look further into the blessing of God upon it, which if it be away, your meat and your drink can no more nourish you than the stone in the wall. And the same must we do in every business of our callings, which if men could learn to practice, they would not so much trust to the means, as honor, wealth, favor, etc., but rather to God Himself. The Lord by the prophet Habakkuk reproves the Chaldeans for offering "sacrifice unto their nets" [Hab. 1:16], which sin they committed because they looked only upon outward things and like moles had no power to see further into them and to behold the work of God in all their proceedings. And this is the very cause why we are unthankful for God's benefits; for though we behold the bare creatures, yet are we so pure blind that we cannot discern any blessing and providence of God in them. Therefore, let us learn to look upon both jointly together, and so shall we be thankful unto God in prosperity and patient in adversity with Job and David. This lesson Paul learned. "I can be abased," says he, "and I can abound; everywhere in all things I am instructed, both to be full and to be hungry: and to abound, and to be in want" [Phil. 4:12–13].

[Duty] 4.[89] Fourthly, seeing God's providence disposes all things, we are taught to gather observations of the same in things both past and present, that we may learn thereby to be armed against the time to come. Thus, David, when he was to encounter with Goliath, gathered hope and confidence to himself for the time to come by the observation of God's providence in the time past; for, says he, "When I kept my father's sheep, I slew a lion and a bear that devoured the flock: now the Lord that delivered me out of the paw of the lion, and out of the paw of the bear, he will deliver me out of the hand of this Philistine" [1 Sam. 17:37].

[Duty] 5. Fifthly, because God's providence disposes all things, when we make lawful promises to do anything, we must put in or at the least conceive this condition: "if the Lord will." For St. James says that we ought to say, "If the Lord will, and if we live, we will do this or that" [James 4:15]. This also was David's practice, for to all the congregation of Israel he said, "If it seem good to you, and if it proceed from the Lord our God, we will send to and fro," etc. [1 Chron. 13:2].

[Duty] 6. Sixthly, seeing God's providence is manifest in ordinary means, it behooves every man in his calling to use them carefully. And when ordinary means be at hand, we must not look for any help without them, though the Lord be able to do what He will without means. Joab, when many Ammonites came against him, he heartened his soldiers, though they were but few in number,

---

89. Originally in the margin, as the additional two duties following.

bidding them "be strong and valiant for the people, and for the cities of their God, and then let the Lord do that which is good in his eyes" [2 Sam. 10:12]. And our Savior Christ avouches it to be flat tempting of God for Him to leap down from the pinnacle of the temple to the ground [Matt. 4:6], whereas there was an ordinary way at hand to descend by stairs. Hence it appears that such persons as will use no means whereby they may come to repent and believe do indeed no more repent and believe than they can be able to live which neither eat nor drink.

Consolations[90]

And thus much of the duties. Now follow the consolations. First, this very point of God's special providence is a great comfort to God's church; for the Lord moderates the rage of the devil and wicked men, that they shall not hurt the people of God. David says, "The Lord is at my right hand, therefore I shall not slide" [Ps. 16:8]. And when Joseph's brethren were afraid because they had sold him into Egypt, he comforts them, saying that "it was God that sent him before them for their preservation" [Gen. 45:7]. So King David, when his soldiers were purposed to stone him to death, he was in great sorrow. But it is said, "He comforted himself in the Lord his God" [1 Sam. 30:6],[91] where we may see that a man which has grace to believe in God and rely on His providence in all his afflictions and extremities shall have wonderful peace and consolation.

Before we can proceed to the articles which follow, it is requisite that we should intreat of one of the greatest works of God's providence that can be, because the opening of it gives light to all that ensues. And this work is a preparation of such means whereby God will manifest His justice and mercy. It has two parts: the just permission of the fall of man and the giving of the covenant of grace. For so Paul teaches when he says that "God shut up all under unbelief, that he might have mercy upon all" [Rom. 11:32]. And again, "The Scripture hath concluded all under sin, that the promise by the faith of Christ Jesus should be given to them that believe" [Gal. 3:22].

Sin[92]

Touching the first, that we may rightly conceive of man's fall, we are to search out the nature and parts of sin. Sin is anything whatsoever is against the will and word of God. As St. John says, sin is "the transgression of the law" [1 John 3:4]. And this definition Paul confirms when he says that "by the law comes the

---

90. Originally in the margin.
91. Originally, "1 Sam. 3:86."
92. Originally in the margin.

knowledge of sin" [Rom. 3:20],[93] and, "where no law is, there is no transgression" [4:15], and, "sin is not imputed, where there is no law" [5:13].

In sin, we must consider three things: the fault, the guilt, the punishment. The fault is the anomy or the disobedience itself; and it comprehends not only huge and notorious offences, idolatry, blasphemy, theft, treason, adultery, and all other crimes that the world cries shame on, but every disordered thought, affection, inclination, yea, every defect of that which the law requires.

The guilt of sin is whereby a man is guilty before God—that is, bound and made subject to punishment. And here, two questions must be scanned: where man is bound, and by what. For the first, man is bound in conscience. And hereupon the conscience of every sinner fits within his heart as a little judge to tell him that he is bound before God to punishment. For the second, it is the order of divine justice set down by God which binds the conscience of the sinner before God; for He is Creator and Lord, and man is a creature and therefore must either obey His will and commandment or suffer punishment. Now then, by virtue of God's law, conscience binds over the creature to bear a punishment for his offence done against God. Yea, it tells him that he is in danger to be judged and condemned for it. And therefore the conscience is as it were the Lord's sergeant to inform the sinner of the bond and obligation whereby he always stands bound before God.

The third thing which follows sin is punishment, and that is death. So Paul says, "The stipend of sin is death" [Rom. 6:23], where by "death" we must understand a double death, both of body and soul. The death of the body is a separation of the body from the soul. The second death is a separation of the whole man but especially of the soul from the glorious presence of God. I say not simply from the presence of God, for God is everywhere, but only from the joyful presence of God's glory. Now these two deaths are the stipend or allowance of sin, and the least sin which a man commits does deserve these two punishments. For in every sin the infinite justice of God is violated, for which cause there must needs be inflicted an infinite punishment, that there may be a proportion between the punishment and the offence. And therefore that distinction of sin which Papists make—namely, that some are in themselves venial, and some mortal—is false and hereby confuted. Otherwise, in respect of the diverse estate and condition of men, sins are either venial or mortal. Venial they are to the elect, whose sins are pardonable in Christ; but to the reprobate all sins are mortal.

Nevertheless, we hold not all sins equal, but that they are greater or less according to the diversity of objects and other circumstances.

---

93. Originally, "Rom. 3:10."

Thus much of sin in general. Now we come to the parts of it. The first sin of all that ever was in man is the sin of Adam, which was his disobedience in eating the forbidden fruit [Rom. 5:15][94]—in handling whereof sundry points are to be opened, but let us begin with the causes thereof.

The outward efficient cause was the devil. And though he be not named by Moses in the history of the fall, yet that is not to trouble us; for we must not conceive otherwise of the serpent than of the instrument and mouth of the devil. For it is not likely that it, being a brute creature, should be able to reason and determine of good and evil, of truth and falsehood. Now in the temptation the devil shows his malice and his fraud. His malice, in that whereas he cannot overturn God Himself, yet he labors to disturb the order which He has set down in the creation and especially the image of God in the most excellent creatures on earth, that they may be in the same miserable condition with himself. His fraud, first, in that he begins his temptation with the woman, being the weaker person, and not with the man, which course he still continues, as may appear by this: that more women are entangled with witchcraft and sorcery than men [Ex. 22:18].[95] Secondly, he shows his fraud in that he proceeds very slyly and entangles Eve by certain steps and degrees. For, first, by moving a question he draws her to listen unto him and to reason with him of God's commandment. Secondly, he brings her to look upon the tree and wishly to view the beauty of the fruit. Thirdly, he makes her to doubt of the absolute truth of God's word and promise and to believe his contrary lies. Fourthly, having blinded her mind with his false persuasion, she desires and lusts after the forbidden fruit and thereupon takes it, eats it, and gives it to her husband.

The inward cause was the will of our first parents, even in the testimony of their own consciences, as Solomon says, "This have I found, that God made man righteous, but they have found many inventions" [Eccl. 7:29].[96] But it may be objected that if Adam were created good, he could not be the cause of his own fall, because a good tree cannot bring forth evil fruit. *Answer.* Freedom of his will is fourfold. (1) Freedom to evil alone. This is only in wicked men and angels and is indeed a bondage. [2] The second is freedom to good alone, and that is in God and the good angels by God's grace. [3] The third is freedom to good in part, joined with some want of liberty by reason of sin; and this is in the regenerate in this life. [4] The fourth is freedom either to good or evil indifferently. And this was in Adam before his fall, who, though he had no inclination to sin but only to that which was acceptable to God, yet was he not bound by any necessity but had his liberty freely to choose or refuse either good or evil.

---

94. Originally, "Rom. 5:5."
95. A witch named in the feminine gender Mechashepha.
96. Originally, "Eccl. 7:31."

And this is evident by the very tenor of God's commandment, in which He forbids Adam to eat the forbidden fruit, and thereby showing that he, being created righteous and not prone to sin, had power to keep or not to keep the commandment, though since the fall both he and we after him cannot but sin. Wherefore, Adam, being allured by Satan, of his own free accord changed himself and fell from God. Now then, as the good tree, changed from good to evil, brings forth evil fruit, so Adam, by his own inward and free motion changing from good to evil, brings forth evil.

As for God, He is not to be reputed as an author or cause [in] any way of this sin; for He created Adam and Eve righteous, endued them with righteous wills, and He told them what He would exact at their hand and what they could perform. Yea, He added threatenings, that with the fear of danger He might terrify them from sin. Some may say, whereas God foresaw that Adam would abuse the liberty of his will, why would He not prevent it? *Answer.* There is a double grace: the one to be able to will and do that which is good; the other to be able to persevere in willing and doing the same.[97] Now God gave the first to Adam, and not the second. And He is not to be blamed of us, though He confirmed him not with new grace, for He is debtor to no man to give him so much as the least grace, whereas He had already given a plentiful measure thereof to him. And God did hold back to confer any further grace upon just cause. (1) It was His pleasure that this fact should be an occasion or way to exercise His mercy in the saving of the elect and His justice in the deserved condemnation of impenitent sinners. And unless Adam had fallen for himself and others, there should have been found no misery in men on whom God might take pity in His Son, nor wickedness which He might condemn—and therefore neither manifestation of justice nor mercy. (2) It was the will of God in part to forsake Adam to make manifest the weakness that is in the most excellent creature without the special and continual assistance of God. (3) There is a double liberty of will. One is to will good or evil; this belongs to the creature in this world, and therefore Adam received it. The other is to will good alone. This he wanted, because it is reserved to the life to come. And though we knew no cause of this dealing of God, yet is it one step to the fear of God for us to hold that good and righteous which He appoints or wills, and not to square the works and judgments of God by our crooked reason. And yet to come to reason itself, who can here complain of God? Can the devil? But God did not cause him to tempt or deceive our first parents. Can Adam and Eve? But they fell freely without any motion or instigation from God, and their own conscience accused them for it. Can the posterity of Adam? But the elect receive more in Christ than they

97. Dedit Adamo posse perseverare si: vellet, non & posse & velle.

lost in Adam; and the reprobate, overwhelmed with the burden of their own sins and thereupon receiving nothing but due and deserved damnation, cannot find fault. But some may further reply and say, he that foresees an evil and does not prevent it is a cause of it. But God did foresee the fall of man and did not prevent it. *Answer.* The rule is generally true in man that the foreseer of an evil not preventing it is in some sort a doer of it, for it is the sentence of the law of God, to which man is bound from the first creation. But God is above all His laws and not bound to them. He is an absolute lord and lawgiver, and therefore His actions are not within the compass of moral laws as men's are. Whereupon it follows that though He did foresee man's defection, yet is He free from all blame in not preventing it. For with Him there be good causes of permitting evil.

How God Willed Adam's Fall[98]

And though God be no cause of man's fall, yet must we not imagine that it came to pass by chance or fortune, whereas the least things that are come to pass with God's providence. Neither was it by any bare permission without His decree and will, for that is to make an idle providence. Neither did it happen against the will of God, He utterly nilling it; for then it could not have been, unless we deny God to be omnipotent. It remains therefore that this fall did so proceed of the voluntary motion of Adam[99] as that God did in part ordain and will the permitting of it, not as it was a sin against His commandment, but as it was further in the counsel of God a way to execute His justice and mercy. Against this which I say, diverse things are objected.

Objection 1.[100] First, that if Adam did that which God in any respect willed, then he did not sin at all.[101] *Answer.* He that wills and does that which God wills, for all that sins, unless he will it in the same manner which God [did], and for the same end. Now in the permitting of this fact, God intended the manifesting of His glory; but our first parents, intending no such thing, fought not only to be like but also to be equal with God.

[Objection] 2. Secondly, it is alleged that Adam could not but fall necessarily if God decreed it. *Answer.* Adam's fall, that came not to pass without God's decree and therefore in that respect was necessary, was nevertheless in respect of Adam's free will contingent and not necessary—God's decree not taking away the freedom of will, but only ordering it.

---

98. Originally in the margin.
99. Aug. Ench. ad Laur. chapter 99.
100. "Objection 1" originally in the margin, as the additional two objections following.
101. This paragraph break, as the additional two following, is not in the original.

[*Objection*] 3. Lastly, it is alleged that God's will is the cause of Adam's will, and Adam's will the cause of his fall, and that therefore God's will shall be the cause of the fall. *Answer.* It must needs be granted that God's will is a moving cause of the wills of evil men, yet mark how: not as they are evil wills simply, but as they are wills. And therefore when God inclines the evil will of His creature to His good purpose, He is nothing at all entangled with the defect or evil of his will.

Time of Adam's Fall[102]

Touching the time of the fall, the received opinion in former ages has been that our first parents fell the same day in which they were created, and therefore Augustine writes that they stood but six hours. And though we cannot determine of the certain time, yet in all likelihood it was very short. For Moses presently after that he had set down the creation of man without the interposition of anything else comes immediately to the fall. And considering the nature of the devil is without ceasing to show his malice, no doubt he took the first occasion that possibly might be had to bring man to the same damnation with himself. And our Savior Christ says that the devil was a manslayer from the beginning [John 8:44]—namely, from the beginning not of the creation of the world or of time, but of man. And Eve says, "We shall eat of the fruit of the trees of the garden" [Gen. 3:2]—it may be insinuating that as yet she had not eaten when the devil tempted her.

Particular Sins in Adam's Fall[103]

Touching the greatness of man's fall, some have made a small matter of it because it was the eating of an apple or some such fruit. But we must not measure the greatness or smallness of a sin by the object or matter whereabout it is occupied, but by the commandment of God and by the disobedience or offence of His infinite majesty. And that this fact of Adam and Eve was no small fault but a notorious crime and apostasy in which they withdrew themselves from under the power of God, nay, reject and deny Him, will evidently appear if we take a view of all the particular sins that be contained in it. (1)[104] The first is unbelief, in that they doubted and distrusted of the truth of God's word which He spoke to them. (2) The second is contempt of God, in that they believed the lies of the devil rather than Him. For when God says, "In the day that ye shall eat thereof, ye shall die the death," it is as nothing with Eve; but when

---

102. Originally in the margin.
103. Originally in the margin.
104. Originally in the margin, as the additional seven sins following.

the devil comes and says, "Ye shall not die at all" [3:4], that she takes hold on. (3) The third is pride and ambition; for they did eat the forbidden fruit that they might be "as gods" [v. 5]—namely, as the Father, the Son, the Holy Ghost. (4) The fourth is unthankfulness. God had made them excellent creatures in His own image. That is nothing with them to be like unto Him, unless they may be equal with Him. (5) The fifth is curiosity, whereby they affected greater wisdom than God had given them in creation and a greater measure of knowledge than God has revealed to them. (6) The sixth is reproachful blasphemy, in that they subscribe to the saying of the devil in which he charged God with lying and envy. (7) The seventh is murder, for by this means they bereave themselves and their posterity of the fellowship and graces of God's Spirit and bring upon their own heads the eternal wrath of God. (8) The eighth is discontentation, in that they fought for a higher condition than that was in which God had placed them. In a word, in this one single fact is comprised the breach of the whole law of God. And we should often think upon this, that we may learn to wonder at the just judgments of God in punishing this fall and His unspeakable goodness in receiving men to mercy after the same.

And here we must not omit to remember the largeness of Adam's fall. Sins are either personal or general: personal are such as are peculiar to one or some few persons and make them alone guilty; general, that be common to all men—and such is Adam's fall. It is a sin not only of the person of one man but of the whole nature of man. And Adam must be considered not as a private man, but as a root or head bearing in it all mankind, or as a public person, representing all his posterity. And therefore when he sinned, all his posterity sinned with him, as in a parliament whatsoever is done by the burgess of the shire is done by every person in the shire. As Paul says, "By one man sin entered into the world, and so death went over all forasmuch as all have sinned" [Rom. 5:12]. And here lies the difference between Adam's fall and the sins of men, as Cain's murder, which makes not the posterity of Cain guilty, because he was never appointed by God to be the root of his posterity, as Adam was. And therefore his sin is personal, whereas Adam's is not. Yet this which I say must not be understood of all the sins of Adam, but only of the first.

Original Sin[105]

From the fall of Adam springs original sin, so commonly called not only as a fruit thereof but also as a just punishment of it. And after the foresaid fall, it is in Adam and his posterity as the mother and root of all other sin—yet with this

---

105. Originally in the margin.

distinction: that actual sin was first in Adam, and then came original; but in us, first is original sin, and then after follows actual.

Original sin is termed diversely in Scriptures, as the flesh;[106] the old man, because it is in us before grace; concupiscence [Rom. 7:13]; sin that is ready to compass us about; the sinning sin. And it is termed "original," because it has been in man's nature ever since the fall, and because it is in every man at the very instant of his conception and birth, as David plainly says, "Behold, I was born in iniquity, and in sin hath my mother conceived me" [Ps. 51:5], not meaning properly his parents' sin (for he was born in lawful marriage), but his own hereditary sin, whereof he was guilty in his mother's womb.

But let us a little search the nature of it. Considering it has place in man, it must be either the substance of body or soul, or the faculties of the substance, or the corruption of the faculties. Now it cannot be the substance of man corrupted, for then our Savior Christ in taking our nature upon Him should also take upon Him our sins and by that means should as well have need of a redeemer as other men. And again, the souls of men should not be immortal. Neither is it any one of all the faculties of men. For every one of them—as, namely, the understanding, will, affections, and all other powers of body or soul—were in man from the first creation, whereas sin was not before the fall. Wherefore, it remains that original sin is nothing else but a disorder or evil disposition in all the faculties and inclinations of man, whereby they are all carried inordinately against the law of God.

Propagation of Original Sin[107]

The subject or place of this sin is not any part of man, but the whole body and soul. For first of all, the natural appetite to meat and drink and the power of nourishing is greatly corrupted, as appears by diseases, aches, surfeits, but specially by the abuse of meat and drink. Secondly, the outward senses are as corrupt; and that made David to pray that God "would turn his eyes from beholding of vanity" [119:37], and St. John to say, "Whatsoever is in the world, is the lust of the flesh, the lust of the eye, and the pride of life" [1 John 2:16]. Thirdly, touching the understanding, the Spirit of God says that the "frame of the heart of man is only evil continually" [Gen. 6:5; 8:21], so as we are "not able of ourselves to think a good thought" [2 Cor. 3:5]. And therefore withal, the will of man and his affections are answerably corrupt. And hereupon the doctrine of Christ is that we must renounce our own wills. Lastly, all men's strength to good things is nothing out of Christ. The propagation of this sin is the

---

106. There is a marginal note to Heb. 12:1.
107. Originally in the margin.

deriving of it from Adam to all his posterity, whereby it runs as a leprosy over all mankind. But in what manner this propagation is made, it is hard to define. The common opinion of divines is that it may be done two ways. The first is this: God when He created Adam in the beginning set down this appointment and order touching the estate of man, that whatsoever Adam received of God, he should receive it not only for himself but for his posterity, and whatsoever grace of God he lost, he should lose not only to himself but to all his posterity. And hereupon Adam when he sinned, he deprived first of all himself and then secondly all his posterity of the image of God, because all mankind was in his loins when he sinned. Now then upon the former appointment, when the souls of men are created and placed in the body, God forsakes them, not in respect of the substance of the soul or the faculties, but only in respect of His own image, whereof the souls are deprived, after which follows the defect or want of righteousness, which is original sin. And God in depriving man of that which Adam lost is not therefore to be thought to be the author or maintainer of sin, but a judge. For this deprivation of the image of God, so far forth as it is inflicted by Him upon mankind, it must be conceived as a deserved punishment for the sin of Adam and all men in him [Rom. 5:12], which punishment they pulled upon themselves. The second way is that the corruption of nature is derived from the parents in generation by the body; for as a sweet oil poured into a fusty[108] loses its[109] pureness and is infected by the vessel, so the soul created good and put into the corrupt body receives contagion thence. And this conjunction of the pure soul with the corrupt body is not against the goodness of God, because it is a just punishment of the sin of all men in Adam. It may be this which has been said will not satisfy the minds of all; yet if any will be curious to search further into this point, let them know that there is another matter which more concerns them to look unto. When a man's house is on fire, there is no time then to inquire how and which way and whence the fire came; but our duty is with all speed and expedition to use all good means to stay it. And so, considering that our whole natures are really infected and poisoned with the loathsome contagion of original sin, which is a weight sufficient to press down the soul to the gulf of hell, it stands us in hand a thousandfold more to use the means whereby it may be taken away than to dispute how it came.

Some may allege against the propagation of sin that holy parents beget holy children, which are void of original sin, because it stands not with reason that parents should convey that to their children which they themselves want— namely, the guilt and the punishment and the fault of sin in part. *Answer.*

---

108. *Fusty*: a cask.
109. Originally, "his."

(1) Men are not in this life perfectly holy. For sanctification is but in part, and therefore they cannot possibly beget children pure from all sin. [2] Secondly, parents beget children as they are men and not as they are holy men. And by generation they derive unto their children nature with the corruption thereof, and not grace, which is above nature. Take any corn, yea, the finest wheat that ever was. Winnow it as clean as [it] possibly may be. Afterward, sow it, weed it also when it is sown, reap it in due time, and carry it to the barn. When it is threshed, you shall find as much chaff in it as ever was before—and why? Because God has set this order in the creation, that it shall spring and grow, so oft as it is sowed, with the stalk, ear, blade, and all. So likewise, though the parents be never so holy, the children as they come of them are conceived and born wholly corrupt, because God took this order in the creation, that whatsoever evil Adam procured, he should bring it not only on himself but upon all his posterity, by virtue of which decree the propagation of sin is continued without any interruption, though parents themselves be born anew by the Spirit of God.

Greatness of Original Sin[110]

And here we must not omit to speak of the quantity or greatness of original sin, for the opening whereof we must consider three points. (1)[111] The first, that original sin is not diverse but one and the same in kind in every man, as the general and common nature of man is one and the same in all men. (2) The second, that this sin is not in some men more, in some men less, but in every man equally, as all men do equally from Adam participate [in] the nature of man and are equally the children of wrath. Some, it may be, will say that this cannot be true, because some men are of better natures than others are: some of disposition cruel and severe; some again gentle and mild; some very licentious and disordered; some very civil. *Answer.* The differences that be in men wanting the fear of God arise not of this, that they have more or less original corruption, but of the restraint and limitation of man's corruption. For in some God bridles sin more than in others, and in them is found civility, and again in some less, and in such the rebellion of nature breaks forth unto all misdemeanor. And indeed, if God should not keep the untoward disposition of men within compass, otherwhiles more, otherwhiles less, as shall seem good unto His majesty, [then] impiety, cruelty, injustice, and all manner of sins would break out into such a measure that there should be no quiet living for men in the world and no place for God's church. And thus it is manifest that although all men be not equal in the practice of wickedness, yet that is no hindrance but they may be

---

110. Originally in the margin.
111. Originally in the margin, as the additional two points following.

equal in the corruption of nature itself. (3) The third point is that original sin is so huge and large every way, that it may truly be termed the root or seed not of some few sins but of all sins whatsoever, even of the very sin against the Holy Ghost. We must not imagine it to be an inclination or proneness to one or two faults, but a proneness to all and every sin that is practiced in the world, and that in all persons young and old, high and low, male and female. It is a most horrible villainy for a man to kill his father or mother or his child, yet some there be that do so. At the hearing whereof we used to wonder and to testify our dislike by saying that the doers thereof were wicked and devilish persons, and it is truly said. Nevertheless, we must understand that although we abstain from such heinous practices, yet the very root of such sins—that is, a disposition unto them—is found in us also. Julian the Apostate, both living and dying, blasphemed Christ. Herod and Pontius Pilate and the wicked Jews crucified Him, and Judas betrayed Him. Men used to say that if Christ were now alive, they would not do so for all the world. But let us better consider of the matter. The same natural corruption of heart that was in them is also in us, we being the children of Adam as well as they. And by force of this corruption, if Christ were now living on earth, you would if like occasion were offered either do as Judas did in betraying Him; or as Pilate did, deliver Him to be crucified; or as the soldiers, thrust Him through with their spears; or as Julian, pierce Him with all manner of blasphemies, if God withhold His graces from you and leave you to yourself. In a word, let men conceive in mind the most notorious trespass that can be, though they do it not nor intend to do it and never do it, yet the matter, beginning, and seed thereof is in themselves. This made Jeremiah say, "The heart of man is deceitful and wicked above all things, who can know it?" [Jer. 17:9]. It is like a huge sea, the banks whereof cannot be seen, nor the bottom searched. In common experience, we see it come to pass that men [are] Protestants today, tomorrow Papists; of Christians, heretics; now friends, but presently after foes; this day honest and civil men, the next day cruel murderers. Now what is the cause of this difference? Surely, the hidden corruption of the heart that will thrust a man forward to any sin when occasion is offered. This point must be remembered and often thought on.

Actual Sin[112]

From original sin springs actual, which is nothing else but the fruit of the corrupt heart either in thought, word, or deed.

---

112. Originally in the margin.

Use of Man's Fall[113]

Thus much touching man's fall into sin by God's just permission. Now follows the good use which we must make thereof.

[Use] 1.[114] First, by this we learn to acknowledge and bewail our own frailty.[115] For Adam in his innocency, being created perfectly righteous, when he was once tempted by the devil fell away from God. What shall we do then in like case which are by nature sold under sin and in ourselves a thousand times weaker than Adam was? Many men there be that mingle themselves with all companies. Tell them of the danger thereof, [and] they will presently reply that they have such a strong faith that no bad company can hurt them. But alas, [they are] silly people. Satan bewitches them and makes them to believe falsehood to be truth. They know not their miserable estate. "If Adam," says Bernard, "had a downfall in paradise, what shall we do that are cast forth to the dunghill?" Let us therefore often come to a serious consideration of our own weakness and follow withal the practice of David, who, being privy to himself touching his own corruption, prays to God in this manner, "Knit my heart to thee, O Lord, that I may fear thy name" [Ps. 86:11].

[Use] 2. Secondly, we learn hereby absolutely to submit ourselves to the authority of God and simply to resolve ourselves that whatsoever He commands is right and just, though the reason of it be not known to us. For Eve condescended to listen to the speech of the serpent, and without any calling she reasoned with it of a most weighty matter, and that in the absence of Adam, her head and husband—namely, of the truth and glory of God. And hereby [she] was brought to doubt of God's word and so overturned.

[Use] 3. Thirdly, if all men by Adam's fall be shut up under damnation, there is no cause why any of us should stand upon his birth, riches, wisdom, learning, or any other such gifts of God. There is nothing in us that is more able to cover our vileness and nakedness than fig tree leaves were able to cover the offence of Adam from God's eyes. We are under the wrath of God by nature and cannot attain to everlasting life of ourselves. Wherefore, it does stand every one of us in hand to abase ourselves under the mighty hand of God, in that we are become by our sins the very basest of all the creatures upon earth; yea, utterly to despair in respect of ourselves and with bleeding hearts to bewail our own case. There is no danger in this. It is the very way to grace. None can be a lively member of Christ till his conscience condemn him and make him quite out of heart in respect of himself. And the want of this is the cause why so few

---

113. Originally in the margin.
114. Originally in the margin, as the additional two uses following.
115. This paragraph break is not in the original, as the additional three following.

perceive any sweetness or comfort in the gospel, and why it is so little loved and embraced nowadays.

[Use 4.] Lastly, if all mankind be shut up under unbelief, the duty of every man is to labor in using all good means whereby he may be delivered from this bondage and to pray to God with David, "Create in me a clean heart, O God, and renew a right spirit within me" [51:10], and cry out with Paul, "O wretched man that I am, who shall deliver me from this body of death?" [Rom. 7:24]. And we must never be at rest till we have some assurance in conscience that in Christ we have freedom from this bondage and can with the Colossians give thanks that we are delivered from the power of darkness and translated into the kingdom of Christ [Col. 1:13]. This should be the affection of every man, because the spiritual thraldom under sin is of all miseries most loathsome and burdensome. And in this respect the day of death should be unto us most welcome, because it does unloose us from this miserable estate in which we do almost nothing but displease God. For this is the greatest grief that can be to such as are indeed the children of God: by their sins to offend their merciful Father. As for those which feel not the weight of their natural guiltiness and corruption but lie slumbering in the security of their own hearts, they are therefore the more miserable in that, being plunged in the gulf of all misery, yet they feel no misery.

Covenant of Grace[116]

Thus much of the permission of the fall of man. Now we come to the covenant of grace, which is nothing else but a compact made between God and man touching reconciliation and life everlasting by Christ. This covenant was first of all revealed and delivered to our first parents in the garden of Eden immediately after their fall by God Himself, in these words, "The seed of the woman shall bruise the serpent's head" [Gen. 3:15].[117] And afterward it was continued and renewed with a part of Adam's posterity, as with Abraham, Isaac, Jacob, David, etc.; but it was most fully revealed and accomplished at the coming of Christ.

Parties Covenanting[118]

In the covenant, I will consider two things: the parties reconciled, between whom the covenant is made, and the foundation thereof. The parties are God and man. God is the principal, and He promises righteousness and life eternal in Christ. Man again binds himself by God's grace to believe and to rest

---

116. Originally in the margin.
117. Originally, "Gen. 3:25."
118. Originally in the margin.

upon the promise. Here, it may be demanded why man is more in the covenant than angels. *Answer*. The will of God in this point is not revealed, unless it be because angels fell of themselves not moved by any other, but man did fall by them. Again, it may be asked whether all mankind were ever in the covenant or no? *Answer*. We cannot say that all and every man has been and now is in the covenant, but only that little part of mankind which in all ages has been the church of God and has by faith embraced the covenant, as Paul plainly avouches. "The scripture," says he, "hath concluded all under sin: that the promise of the faith of Jesus Christ should be given"—not unto all men—"but to them that believe" [Gal. 3:22]. "Without faith no man can please God" [Heb. 11:6]. And therefore God makes no covenant of reconciliation without faith. Again, since the beginning of the world, there has been always a distinction between man and man. This appears in the very tenor of the words of the covenant made with our first parents, where God says He will put difference "between the seed of the woman and the seed of the serpent" [Gen. 3:15], meaning by the seed of the woman, Christ with all the elect whom the Father has given unto Him, who shall bruise the serpent's head and "tread Satan under their feet" (Rom. 16:20). And by the seed of the serpent, He means wicked men that live and die in their sins. St. John says, "He that committeth sin is of the devil" (1 John 3:8). And according to this distinction in times following was Abel received into the covenant and Cain rejected. Some were the sons of God in the days of Noah; some, the sons of men [Gen. 6:2]. In Abraham's family, Ishmael is cast out, and the covenant established in Isaac [17:21]. Jacob is loved; Esau is hated [Rom. 9:13]. And this distinction in the families of Abraham, Isaac, and Jacob, Paul approves when he makes some to be the children of the flesh and some other the children of the promise (v. 8); and again, the Jews, a people of God in the covenant; the Gentiles, no people. For Paul makes it a privilege of the Jews to have the "adoption, and covenant, and the service of God, and the promises" belonging unto them [vv. 3–4], whereas he says of the Ephesians that they were "aliens from the commonwealth of Israel" and were "strangers from the covenants of promise, and had no hope, and were without Christ, and without God in the world" (Eph. 2:12).[119] And the same may be said of the whole body of the Gentiles, excepting here and there a man who was converted and became a proselyte. And this is manifest in that they wanted the word and the sacraments and teachers. And this saying of the prophet Hosea, "I will call them my people, which were not my people: and her beloved, which was not beloved," is alleged by Paul to prove the calling of the Gentiles [Rom. 9:25]. *Objection 1*. Some do allege to the contrary, that when the covenant was

---

119. Originally, "Eph. 1:12."

made with our first parents, it was also in them made with all mankind, not one man excepted; and that the distinction and difference between man and man arises of their unbelief and contempt of the covenant afterward. *Answer.* Indeed, in the estate of innocency, Adam by creation received grace for himself and his posterity; and in his fall he transgressed not only for himself, but for all his posterity. But in receiving the covenant of grace it cannot be proved that he received it for himself and for all mankind. Nay, the distinction between the seed of the woman and the seed of the serpent, mentioned in the very first giving of the covenant, shows the contrary; for if after the fall all and every part of mankind were received into the covenant, then all men without restraint should be the seed of the woman, bruising the serpent's head, and the serpent should have no seed at all. And again, all men cannot be charged with unbelief and contempt in respect of the evangelical covenant, but only such persons as have known it, or at the least heard of it. And therefore sundry heads of the nations may be charged with unbelief, as Cain, Ham, Japheth, Ammon, Moab, Ishmael, Esau, [and] Midian; for they, being near to the fathers, heard the promises concerning Christ, offered sacrifices, and observed external rites of the church, but afterward fell away from the sincere worship of the true God to idolatry and all manner of wickedness and became enemies of God and His people. But we plainly deny that there was or could be the like unbelief and contempt of God's grace in their posterity which for the most part never so much as heard of any covenant, their ancestors endeavoring always to bury and extinguish the memory of that which they hated. *Objection 2.* It is objected again that the covenant was made with Abraham and with all mankind after him, because, says the Lord, "thou hast obeyed my voice, in thy seed shall all the nations of the earth be blessed" (Gen. 22:18). *Answer.* Paul gives a double answer: first, that the place must be understood of many nations; secondly, that it must be understood not of all nations in all ages but of all nations of the last age of the world. For says he, "The Scripture foreseeing that God would justify the Gentiles through faith, preached before the gospel unto Abraham, saying, in thee shall all the nations be blessed" (Gal. 3:8). Well, to conclude this point, in the making of the covenant there must be a mutual consent of the parties on both sides; and besides the promise on God's part, there must be also a restipulation on man's part. Otherwise, the covenant is not made. Now then, it must needs follow that all unbelievers, contemning grace offered in Christ, are out of the covenant, as also such as never heard of it; for where there is no knowledge, there is no consent; and before the coming of Christ the greatest part of the world never knew the Messiah nor heard of the covenant, as Paul says to the learned Athenians, "The time of this ignorance God regarded not, but now he admonisheth all men everywhere to repent" (Acts 17:30).

The Foundation of the Covenant[120]

The foundation and groundwork of the covenant is Christ Jesus, the Mediator, in whom all the promises of God are yea and amen. And therefore He is called the "angel of the covenant" [Mal. 3:1] and the "covenant of the people" [Isa. 49:8][121] to be made with all nations in the last age. Now then, that we may proceed at large to open the substance of the covenant, we are in the next place to come to that part of the Creed, which concerns the second person in [the] Trinity set down in these words: "and Jesus Christ, his only Son," etc., from which words to the very end of the Creed such points only are laid down as do notably unfold the benefits and the matter of the covenant. Now the second person is described to us by three things: first, His titles; secondly, His incarnation; thirdly, His twofold estate. His titles are in number four: (1) Jesus; (2) Christ; (3) His only Son; (4) our Lord. His incarnation and His twofold estate are set down afterward.

To come to His titles, the first is Jesus, to which if we add the clause, "I believe," on this manner, "I believe in Jesus," etc., the article which we now have in hand will appear to be most excellent, because it has most notable promises annexed to it. When Peter confessed Christ to be the Son of the living God, He answered, "Upon this rock will I build my church, and the gates of hell shall not prevail against it" [Matt. 16:18]. And again, "He that confesseth that Christ is the Son of God, God dwelleth in him, and he in God" [1 John 4:15]. And again, "To him give all the prophets witness, that through his name all that believe in him shall receive remission of sins" [Acts 10:43]. Paul says, "Believe in the Lord Jesus, and thou shalt be saved, and all thy household" [Acts 16:31]. Thus then, the confession in which we acknowledge that we believe in Jesus Christ has a promise of fellowship with God and of life everlasting. But it may be objected that every spirit (as St. John says) which confesses that "Jesus Christ is come in the flesh, is of God" [1 John 4:2]. Now the devil and all his angels and unbelievers do thus much. Therefore, why may not they also have the benefit of this confession? *Answer.* By "spirit" in that place is neither meant angels nor men nor any creature, but the doctrine which teaches that Jesus Christ is come in the flesh. And it is of God because it is holy and divine and has God to be the author of it. As for the devil and his angels, they can indeed confess that Christ, the Son of God, was made man, and a wicked man may teach the same. But unto the confession whereunto is annexed a promise of eternal life is required true faith, whereby we do not only know and acknowledge this or that to be true in Christ, but also rest upon Him—which neither Satan nor wicked men

---

120. Originally in the margin.
121. Originally, "Isa. 19:8."

can do. And therefore by this confession the church of God is distinguished from all other companies of men in the world which believe not, as paynims,[122] heretics, atheists, Turks, Jews, and all other infidels.

This name "Jesus" was given to the Son of God by the Father and brought from heaven by an angel unto Joseph and Mary. And on the day when He was to be circumcised as the manner was, this name was given unto Him by His parents, as they were commanded from the Lord by the angel Gabriel. And therefore the name was not given by chance or by the alone will of the parents, but by the most wise appointment of God Himself.

The name in Hebrew is "Jehoscua," and it is changed by the Grecians into "Jesus," which signifies a savior [Matt. 1:21;[123] Luke 1:31]. And it may be called the proper name of Christ, signifying His office and both His natures, because He is both a perfect and absolute savior, as also the alone Savior of man, because the work of salvation is wholly and only wrought by Him, and no part thereof is reserved to any creature in heaven or in earth. As Peter says, "For among men there is no other name given under heaven whereby we may be saved but by the name of Jesus" (Acts 4:12). And the author to the Hebrews says that He is "able perfectly to save them that come unto God by him seeing he ever liveth to make intercession for them" (Heb. 7:25). If any shall object that the promises of salvation are made to them which keep the commandments, the answer is that the law of God does exact most absolute and perfect obedience, which can be found in no man but in Christ, who never sinned. And therefore it is not given unto us now that we might by ourselves fulfill it and work out our own salvation, but that, being condemned by it, we might wholly depend on Christ for eternal life. If any further allege that such as walk according to the commandments of God, though their obedience be imperfect, yet they have the promises of this life and of the life to come [1 Tim. 4:8], the answer is that they have so indeed, yet not for their works but according to their works, which are the fruits of their faith, whereby they are joined to Christ, for whose merits only they stand righteous and are acceptable before God. And whereas it is said by Peter that "baptism saveth us" [1 Peter 3:21],[124] his meaning is not to signify that there is any virtue in the water to wash away our sins and to sanctify us, but that it serves visibly to represent and confirm unto us the inward washing of our souls by the blood of Christ. It may further be said that others have been saviors beside Christ, as Joshua, the son of Nun, who for that cause is called by the same name with Christ. *Answer.* Joshua after the death of Moses was appointed by God to be a guide to the children of Israel, which might defend them from their enemies

---

122. *Paynims*: non-Christians, often Muslims.
123. Originally, "Matt. 1:22."
124. Originally, "1 Peter 3:1."

and bring them to the land of Canaan [Acts 7:45]. But this deliverance was only temporal, and that only of one people [Heb. 4:8]. Now the Son of God is called Jesus, not because He delivers the people of the Jews only, or because He saves the bodies of men only, but because He saves both body and soul not only of the Jews but also of the Gentiles from hell, death, and damnation. And whereas prophets and ministers of the word are called saviors [Obad. 1:21; 1 Tim. 4:16], it is because they are the instruments of God to publish the doctrine of salvation, which is powerful, in men's hearts—not by any virtue of theirs, but only by the operation of the Spirit of Christ. Lastly, it may be objected that the Father and the Holy Ghost are Saviors, and therefore not only the Son. *Answer.* True it is, that in the work of salvation all the three persons must be joined together and in no wise to be severed: the Father saves; the Son saves; the Holy Ghost saves. Yet must we distinguish them in the manner of saving: the Father saves by the Son; the Son saves by paying the ransom and price of our salvation; the Holy Ghost saves by a particular applying of the ransom unto men. Now therefore, whereas the Son pays the price of our redemption and not the Father or the Holy Ghost, therefore in this special respect He is called in Scriptures and entitled by the name of Jesus, and none but He.

By this which has been said the Papists are faulty two ways. First, that they give too much to the name of Jesus; for they write in plain terms that "the bare name itself being used hath great power, and doth drive away devils, though the parties that use it be void of good affection,"[125] whereas indeed it has no more virtue than other titles of God or Christ. Secondly, they are faulty that they give too little to the thing signified. For Christ must either be our alone and whole Savior, or no Savior. Now they make Him but half a savior, and they join others with Him as partners in the work of salvation when they teach that with Christ's merits must be joined our works of grace in the matter of justification, and with Christ's satisfaction for the wrath of God our satisfaction for the temporal punishment; and when they add to Christ's intercession the intercession and patronage of saints, especially of the Virgin Mary, whom they call "the queen of heaven," "the mother of mercy," withal requesting her that "by the authority of a mother, she would command her Son."[126] If this doctrine of theirs may stand, Christ cannot be the only Savior of mankind; but every man in part shall be Jesus to himself.

But let us go on yet further to search the special reason of the name, which is notably set down by the angel. "Thou shalt," says he, "call his name Jesus, for he shall save his people from their sins" [Matt. 1:21]. In which words we

125. Thyrrh. de demon. thes. 567, 569.
126. Officium B. Mariæ reforman. Pio 5. Pont. f.

may consider three points: (1) whom the Son of God shall save; (2) by what; (3) from what. For the first, He shall save His people—that is, the elect of the Jews and Gentiles. And therefore He is called the Savior of His body [Eph. 5:23]. We must not here imagine that Christ is a savior of all and every man; for if that were true, then Christ should make satisfaction to God's justice for all and every man's sins. And God's justice being fully satisfied, He could not in justice condemn any man. Nay, all men should be blessed, because satisfaction for sin and the pardon of sin depend one upon another inseparably. Again, if Christ be an effectual savior of all and every particular man, why is any man condemned? It will be said, because they will not believe. Belike then man's will must overrule God's will, whereas the common rule of divines is that the first cause orders the second.[127]

The means of salvation by Christ are two: His merit and His efficacy. His merit, in that by His obedience to the law and by His passion, He made a satisfaction for our sins, freed us from death, and reconciled us unto God. Some may object that the obedience and passion of Christ, being long ago ended, cannot be able to save us now, because that which He did sixteen hundred years ago may seem to be vanished and come to nothing at this day. *Answer.* If Christ's obedience be considered as an action, and His passion as a bare suffering, they are both ended long ago. Yet the value and price of them before God is everlasting, as in Adam's fall the action of eating the forbidden fruit is ended, but the guilt of his transgression goes all over mankind and continues still even to this hour and shall do so to the end of the world, in those which shall be born hereafter. The efficacy of Christ is in that He gives His Spirit to mortify the corruption of our natures, that we may die unto sin and live unto righteousness and have true comfort in terrors of conscience and in the pangs of death.

The evils from which we are saved are our own sins, in that Christ frees us from the guilt and the punishment and fault of them all, when we believe.

Thus much for the meaning of this title "Jesus." Now follow the uses which arise of it. First of all, whereas we are taught to make confession that the Son of God is Jesus—that is, a savior—hence, it must needs follow that we are lost in ourselves. And indeed before we can truly acknowledge that Christ is our Savior, this confession must needs go before, that we are in truth and therewithal do feel ourselves to be miserable sinners under the wrath of God, utterly lost in regard of ourselves; for "Christ came to save that which was lost" (Matt. 18:11). And when He talked with the woman of Canaan, He checked her and said He was not sent but "to the lost sheep of the house of Israel" (15:24). Christ Jesus came to pour oil into our wounds. Christ came to set them at liberty which are

---

127. Actus primæ causæ ordinatactum secundæ causæ.

in prison and to place them in freedom that are in bondage. Now a man cannot pour oil into a wound before there be a wound or before it be opened, [and] we feel the smart of it. And how can we be set at liberty by Christ, except we feel ourselves to be in bondage, under hell, death, and damnation? When the disciples of Christ were upon the sea in a great tempest, they cried, "Master, save us, we perish" [8:25]. So no man can heartily say, "I believe Jesus Christ to be my Savior," before he feel that in himself he is utterly lost and castaway, without His help. But after that we perceive ourselves to be in danger and to be overwhelmed in the sea of the wrath of God, then we cry out with the disciples, "Lord Jesus, save us. We perish." Many Protestants in these days hold Christ to be their Savior, but it is only formally from the teeth outward and no further; for they were never touched with the sense of their spiritual misery, that they might say with Daniel, "Shame and confusion belongeth unto us" [Dan. 9:7], and with the publican, "I am a sinner, Lord, be merciful to me" [Luke 18:13]. And therefore the conclusion is this, that if we will have Christ to be our Savior, we must first believe that in ourselves we are utterly lost. And so must that place be understood where Christ says He is not sent but to the lost sheep of the house of Israel [Matt. 15:24]—that is, to those which in their own sense and feeling are lost in themselves.

Secondly, if Christ be a savior, then we must acknowledge Him to be so. But how shall we do this? I answer, thus: a man is taken to be a skillful physician by this, that many patients come unto him and seek for help at his hands. And so should it be with Christ. But alas, the case is otherwise. Every man can talk of Christ, but few acknowledge Him to be a savior by seeking to Him for their salvation, because they judge themselves righteous and feel not themselves to stand in need of the help of Christ. Nay, which is more, if a man be known that can cure strange diseases, men will seek to him by sea and land and sell both goods and lands to get help at his hands. Even so, if men were persuaded that Christ were a perfect savior, and that they were sick and utterly unable to be saved without Him, they would never rest nor be quiet but seek unto Him for His help and cry with David, "O Lord, say unto my soul, that thou art my salvation" (Ps. 35:3). The woman that was diseased with an issue of blood came behind our Savior Christ, and when she had but touched Him, she was healed [Matt. 9:20]. In the same manner, if we shall seek to come to Christ and do but touch His precious body and blood by the hand of faith, the issue and the bleeding wounds of our souls shall be dried up. When a man that had been sick eight and thirty years was come to the pool of Bethsaida, he was fain to lie there uncured, because when the angel troubled the water, evermore some stepped before him [John 5:7]. But if we will seek to Christ for the salvation of our souls, no man shall prevent us or step before us. And if we find ourselves to be so laden with the burden of our sins that we cannot draw near unto Him, let us then do as the palsy man did. He got four men to carry him on their shoulders to the place where Christ was. And when they could not by reason of the press of the people enter into the house, they opened the roof and let him down in his bed by cords to Christ that he might be healed [Mark 2:4]. And so let us use the help of such as be godly, that by their instructions and consolations they may as it were put their shoulders and by their prayers, as with cords, bring us to Christ that we may receive eternal salvation, being otherwise dead in sin and subject to damnation.

Lastly, whereas Joseph and Mary gave this name not at their own pleasure but at the appointment of God Himself, this ministers a good instruction to all parents touching the naming of their children when they are baptized, that they are with care and deliberation to give convenient names unto them, which may put them in mind of duties either to God or men. This is worthy our observation, for many care not how they name their children. Yea, it is at this day and ever has been that some give such names to them as that at the very rehearsing thereof laughter ensues. But this ought not to be so; for the name is given unto children at the time of their baptism in the presence of God, of His church, and angels, even then when they are to be entered into the church of God, and that in the name of the Father, the Son, and the Holy Ghost. Therefore, though we do not place religion in titles or names, yet nevertheless a wise and godly choice in this matter is to be had, that the names imposed may be in stead of instructions and admonitions to the parties named. And for this cause in the Old Testament names are given by the prophetical instinct or according to the event of things which came to pass about the time of the birth of children; or they were borrowed from the holy ancestors, to put the posterity in mind to follow their steps [Luke 1:59]. And thus much of the duties. Now follow the consolations that God's church and people reap from this, that the Son of God is our Savior. When as all mankind was included under sin and condemnation, then the Lord had mercy upon us and gave unto man the covenant of grace, in which He promised that His own Son should be our Redeemer. This is a great and unspeakable comfort, as may appear in that the angels so greatly rejoiced herein when Christ was born. "Behold," say they, "I bring you tidings of great joy that shall be to all people"—that is, "that unto you is born in the city of David, a Savior, which is Christ the Lord" (2:10–11). Now if they rejoice thus exceedingly at Christ's birth, who was not their Savior, because they stood not in need to be redeemed, then much more ought the church of God to rejoice herein, whom it does principally concern. And no marvel, for if we had wanted this blessed Savior, it had been better to have been a brute beast or any other creature than a man; for the death of a beast is the end of his woe, but the death of a man without a savior is the beginning of endless misery. Satan and his angels are fallen and have no savior. But when man was fallen, God of His mercy dealt not so with him, but gave His own Son to restore him to a better estate, whereas He might as justly have damned all men for the fall of our first parents, as He did the wicked angels for theirs, for God is not bound to any creature. Behold then a matter of unspeakable joy. Let us therefore receive and embrace Christ, our Savior, fly to Him for the pardon of all our sins, and praise His name therefore.

Now we come to the second title of the Son of God, whereby He is termed "Christ," which title is as it were the surname of the second person, as some do think. Yet according to the opinion of some others, it is no name at all but only a mere appellation, as when in the like case a particular man is called a duke or a king. It is all one with "messiah" in Hebrew wherewith the Redeemer was named in the Old Testament, and both signify "anointed."

Among the Jews before the coming of Christ, three estates or orders of men were anointed with oil. First of all, kings, as Saul, David, and the rest of the kings of Judah. Secondly, the priests that served in the tabernacle and temple before the Lord, when they were ordained and as it were installed into the priesthood, were anointed with oil, as, first of all, Aaron and his sons, but afterward the high priests alone. Thirdly, prophets were thus anointed, as Elisha.[128]

Now this legal anointing was a type and figure of the anointing of Christ, which was not with bodily oil but by the Spirit; and it was more excellent than all other anointings were. For David says He was anointed with the oil of gladness above all His fellows [Ps. 45:7], signifying that neither king, priest, nor prophet was ever anointed in the same manner as He was.

Christ's anointing is according to both His natures; for in what nature He is a mediator, in the same He is anointed. But according to both His natures jointly He is a mediator. The Godhead is no mediator without the manhood, nor the manhood without the Godhead. And therefore His anointing extends itself both to His Godhead and to His manhood.

Christ's anointing has two parts, both of them figured by the anointing of the Jews. The first is His consecration whereby He was set apart to do the office of a mediator between God and man, and therefore to be a king, a priest, a prophet: a king, to gather and withal to govern His church and people; a priest, to make satisfaction and intercession for the sins of the elect; a prophet, to reveal and teach His people the will of God, His Father. And though it be true that Christ is set apart to the work of mediation, as He is a mediator or as He is man, yet as He is God He does design and set Himself apart to the same

---

128. Tertul. contra Praxeam. Dan. 9:25

work. For to design the mediator is a common action of the three persons, the Father, the Son, and the Holy Ghost. And yet considering the Father is first in order and therefore has the beginning of the action, for this cause He is said especially to design, as when St. John says, "Him hath God the Father sealed" [John 6:27].[129]

The second part of Christ's anointing is the pouring out of the fullness of the Spirit of grace into the manhood of Christ, and it was particularly figured by the holy oil [Isa. 61:1]. For first, that oil had no man but God alone to be the author of it. So the most excellent and unspeakable graces of the manhood of Christ have their beginning from the Godhead of Christ. Again, though the same oil was most precious, yet was it compounded of earthly substances, as myrrh, calamus, and cassia, and such like [Ex. 30:23–24], to signify that the spiritual oil of grace, whereof the manhood of Christ was as it were a vessel or storehouse, did not consist of the essential properties of the Godhead, as Eutychus and his followers in these days imagine, but in certain created gifts and qualities placed in His human nature. Otherwise, we should not have any participation of them. Thirdly, the sweet savor of the holy oil figured that the riches of all graces with the effect thereof in the obedience of Christ does take away the noisome scent of our loathsome sins from the nostrils of God and withal does make our persons and all our actions acceptable to Him as a sweet perfume, as Paul says we are unto God "the sweet savor of Christ," etc. [2 Cor. 2:16]. And Christ's death is for this cause termed a sacrifice of a sweet smelling savor.

And we must further understand that these gifts of Christ's manhood are not conferred in small scantling or measure; for John says God gives Him the Spirit "not by measure" [John 3:34], because the graces which are in Christ are far more both in number and degree than all men or angels have or shall have, though the good angels and the saints of God in heaven are very excellent creatures stored with manifold graces and gifts of God. For this cause Christ is called the head of man [1 Cor. 11:4], because He is every way the most principal and glorious man that ever was. Yet for all this are not the gifts of Christ's manhood infinite any way, because it is a creature and finite in nature and therefore not capable of that which is infinite.

By Christ's anointing the people of God reap great benefit and comfort, because they are to be partakers thereof. For this cause the oil wherewith He was anointed is called the oil of gladness [Ps. 45:7], because the sweet savor of it gladdens the hearts of all His members and brings the peace of God which passes all understanding. The holy oil poured upon Aaron's head came down to his beard and to the very skirts of his garments [133:2]; and it signified that the

---

129. Originally, "John 6:17."

spiritual oil of grace was first of all poured upon our Head, Christ Jesus, and from thence consequently derived to all His members, that by this means He might be not only anointed Himself, but also our anointer.

Now the benefits which we receive by His anointing are two. The first is that all the elect when they are called to the profession of the gospel of Christ are in and by Him set apart and made spiritual kings, priests, and prophets, as St. John says, "He hath made us kings and priests unto his Father" [Rev. 1:6]. And St. Peter out of Joel: "I will pour," says the Lord, "my spirit upon all flesh, and your sons and daughters shall prophesy" [Acts 2:17].

The second benefit is that all the faithful receive the same oil—that is, the same Spirit of God—in some little and convenient measure which He received above measure, as St. John says, "The anointing which ye received of him dwells in you, and teaches you all things" [1 John 2:27], where by "anointing" is meant "the Holy Ghost." And hence it is that men are called Christians of the name of Christ—that is, anointed with the same oil wherewith Christ was anointed [Ps. 105:15]. And the holy oil might not be given to a stranger to signify that to have the Spirit of Christ and to be guided by it is peculiar to them that are Christ's [Ex. 30:33]. Now then, let us all lay these things to our hearts and extol the unspeakable goodness of God that has advanced us to the dignity of kings, priests, prophets before Him and has given His Spirit unto us to enable us to be so indeed.

Now follow the duties which are to be learned hence. And, first, whereas all Christians receive anointing from the Holy One, Christ Jesus, to become prophets in a sort, we must do our endeavors that the word of God may dwell plentifully in us [Dan. 9:24; 1 John 2:20]. And for that cause we must search the Scriptures, even as hunters seek for the game and as men seek gold in the very mines of the earth. There is nothing more unbeseeming a man than gross ignorance a Christian. Therefore, the author of the epistle to the Hebrews reproves them, that whereas for the time they ought to have been teachers, they had need again to be taught the first principles of the Word of God [Heb. 5:12].

Again, that portion of knowledge which we have received of God is further to be applied to the benefit and good of others. That is the most precious balm that on our parts should never be wanting to the heads of men [Ps. 141:5]. And here every man that is set over others must remember within the compass of his calling and charge to instruct those that be under him, so far forth as possibly he can. Governors of families must teach their children and servants and their whole household the doctrine of true religion, that they may know the true God and walk in all His ways in doing righteousness and judgment. If householders would make conscience of this their duty and in some sort and measure prepare their families against they come to the public congregation, the ministers of the gospel with greater comfort and far more ease should perform their duty and see far more fruit of their ministry than now they do. But whereas they neglect their duty, falsely persuading themselves that it does not belong to them at all to instruct others, it is the cause of ignorance both in towns and families, in masters themselves, in servants and children, and all. Lastly, by this we are admonished to take all occasions that possibly can be offered mutually to edify each other in knowledge, saying among ourselves (as it was foretold of these times), "Come let us go up to the mountain of the Lord, to the house of the God of Jacob, and he will teach us his ways, and we will walk in his paths" [Isa. 2:3]. And withal we should confirm each other, as Christ says to Peter, "When thou art converted, confirm thy brethren" [Luke 22:32], and be ready at all times to render an account of our faith and religion even before our enemies, when we are justly called so to do.

Spiritual Sacrifices[130]

Secondly, because we are set apart in Christ to become spiritual priests unto God, we must therefore offer spiritual sacrifices acceptable unto Him; and they be in number seven. (1)[131] The first is an affiance whereby we rest upon God, as David says, "Offer the sacrifice of righteousness and trust in the Lord" [Ps. 4:5]. (2) The second is wholly to subject ourselves to the ministry of the gospel, that we may be changed and converted by it, as Paul says that he "ministereth the gospel to the Gentiles, that the offering up of them might be acceptable, being sanctified by the Holy Ghost" [Rom. 15:16]. (3) The third is all manner of prayers and supplications made unto God. "Let my prayer," says David, "be directed in thy sight, as incense, etc., the lifting up of my hands as in evening sacrifice" [Ps. 141:2]. (4) The fourth is praising and thanksgiving unto God. "Let us by him offer the sacrifice of praise always to God, that is, the fruit of the lips which confess his name" (Heb. 13:15). And in the Revelation the "golden vials full of odors" [Rev. 5:8][132] are the prayers of the saints. (5) The fifth is the relief of our poor brethren according to our ability, as Paul says, "I was even filled, after that I had received of Epaphroditus that which came from you, an odor that smelleth sweet, a sacrifice pleasant and acceptable to God" [Phil. 4:18].[133] (6) The sixth is the denial of ourselves with a contrite and broken heart [Ps. 51:17]. (7) The seventh is to resign ourselves, bodies and souls wholly to the service of God. "Set yourselves," says Paul, "to God, as they that are alive from the dead: and your members as weapons of righteousness unto God" [Rom.

---

130. Originally in the margin.
131. Originally in the margin, as the additional six spiritual sacrifices following.
132. Originally, "Rev. 5:7."
133. Originally, "Phil. 4:28."

6:13]—in which words he alludes to the manner of the Old Testament. When a man offered any sacrifice for himself, he brought the beast into the temple or tabernacle and set it before the altar in token that he did resign it unto God. And so we for our parts must not give our bodies and souls to become the instruments of sin and Satan; but we must have them always in readiness, freely presenting them unto God, that He may have the whole disposition of them according to His good pleasure, to the honor and glory of His name. Again, in the whole burnt offering all was consumed and turned to smoke, no man having benefit of it, to signify that we must give ourselves not in part but wholly to the service of God, even to death, if need be. If this be so, miserable is the practice of such that give up their bodies and souls to live in licentious wantonness, in the pleasures of their beastly sins, in idleness. For they offer themselves a sacrifice not to God, but to the devil.

Thirdly, considering we are anointed to be spiritual kings even in this life, we must walk worthy [of] so great a calling. That this may be so, first of all, such as are governors set over others must rule not according to their wills and pleasures, but in the Lord, withal doing homage to their Head and King, Christ Jesus Himself. Secondly, we must every one of us rule and bear sway even as kings over our own thoughts, wills, affections, over-mastering them as much as we possibly can by God's Word and Spirit, withal maintaining and proclaiming continual war against our corrupt natures, the devil, and the world. And truly he which can bear rule over his own heart is a right king indeed; and, having received some measure of grace to reign over himself in this life, he shall reign forever with Christ in the life to come. As for such as are carried away with the swing of their corruptions, having blindness and ignorance to reign in their minds, rebellion in their wills and affection, looseness in their whole lives, they may carry the outward form and show of Christians as long as they will, but indeed they are no spiritual kings, but very bondmen. The strong man, Satan, keeps as yet the hold of their hearts and as lord and king holds up his scepter there. Lastly, seeing Christ is anointed with most precious balm that ever was, and that for our sakes, He must be sweet and savory unto us, and all other things must be as unsavory dross and dung in regard of Him. We must in this case endeavor to say as the spouse of Christ does, "Because of the savor of thy good ointments, thy name is an ointment poured out: therefore the virgins love thee" [Song 1:3].[134] O that we could "savor in the fear of God" [Isa. 11:3] that we might feel "how all his garments smell of myrrh, aloes, and cassia, coming forth of the ivory palaces unto us" [Ps. 45:8].[135]

---

134. Originally, "Song 1:2."
135. Originally, "Ps. 46:8."

And because the holy ointment of Christ is poured forth upon all His members to make them savory and sweet in the presence of God, let us make conscience of all manner of sin, lest by the poison and stink thereof we infect not only ourselves but all the creatures of God which we use, yea, heaven and earth itself. It stands not with equity, that after we have been embalmed and sweetened by the precious merits of Christ, we should make ourselves two-footed swine to return to the mire of our old sins.

The coupling and combining of these two former titles together contains the principal question of the whole Bible, which is whether Jesus, the son of Mary, be Christ or no—as St. John says, "These things are written that ye might believe, that Jesus is the Christ the Son of God, and that in believing ye might have life everlasting" [John 20:31]. This conclusion was denied by the Jews, but avouched and confirmed both by Christ and by His apostles [Acts 18:5]; and their principal argument was framed thus. He which has the true notes of Christ is the Messiah or Christ indeed. But Jesus, the son of Mary, has the true notes of Christ. Therefore, Jesus is Christ. The proposition is opened at large in the prophesies of the Old Testament. The assumption is confirmed in the writings of the New Testament. And the principal reasons of the confirmation are touched in the articles which concern the second person. The conclusion follows, and it is set down, as I have said, in the knitting together of the titles "Jesus" and "Christ."

Thus much of the second title. Now follows the third: His "only Son"—that is, the only Son of the first person, the Father. In this title, we must consider two things: the first, that He is the Son of God; the second, that He is the only Son of God. Touching the first, Christ is called the Son of God because He was begotten of the Father. Now for the opening of this eternal generation, we must consider three points: the thing begotten, the manner of begetting, and the time. For the thing itself, it is Christ, who must be considered two ways: as He is a son, and as He is God.[136] As He is a son, He is not of Himself, but the Son of the Father, begotten of Him. Nevertheless, as He is God, He is of Himself: neither begotten or proceeding. For the essence or Godhead of the Father is of itself without all beginning; but the Godhead of the Son is one and the same with the Godhead of the Father, because by what Godhead the Father is God, by the same and no other the Son is God. Therefore, the Son, as He is God, He is God of Himself without beginning even as the Father. Whereupon it follows that the Son is begotten of the Father as He is a son, but not as He is God.

The manner of this generation is this: the Son is begotten of the substance of the Father not by any flux, as when water is derived from the head of the

---

136. Non αυτουσιος, ταμεν αυτοθεος.

spring to the channel; nor by decision, as when a thing is cut in pieces; nor by propagation, as when a graft is transplanted into a new stock; but by an unspeakable communication of the whole essence or Godhead from the Father to the Son, in receiving whereof the Son does no more diminish the majesty or Godhead of the Father than the light of one candle does the light of the other from which it is taken. Whereupon the Council of Nicaea has said well that "the Son is of the Father as light of light, not proceeding but begotten."

The time of this generation has neither beginning, middle, or end. And therefore it is eternal before all worlds, and it is a thing to be wondered at, that the Father begetting and the Son begotten are coeternal and therefore equal in time. Wisdom in the Proverbs (which with one consent of all divines is said to be Christ) affirms that she was before the world was created—that is, from eternity—for before the world was made there was nothing but eternity [Prov. 8:24]. But it may be alleged to the contrary that the saying of the Father, "This day have I begotten thee" [Ps. 2:7], is expounded by Paul of the time of Christ's resurrection [Acts 13:30, 33]. *Answer.* We must distinguish between generation itself and the manifestation of it; and of the second must the place be understood, which was indeed accomplished at the time of Christ's resurrection in which He was mightily declared to be the Son of God [Rom. 1:4]. And though this be so, yet the generation itself may be eternal. If any man allege further that the person which begets must needs go before the person begotten, the answer is that there is a double priority: one of order; the other of time. Now in the generation of creatures there is priority both of order and time; but in the generation of the second person in [the] Trinity there is priority of order alone—the Father being first, the Son second, without priority of time, because they both in that respect are equal. And neither is before or after [the] other, because the being or subsisting of the persons is not measured by time.

Hence it follows necessarily that Jesus Christ is true God, and the whole tenor of the Scriptures confirm it sufficiently. (1) He is made equal to God the Father, "who being in the form of God, thought it not robbery to be equal with God" [Phil. 2:6]. Again, "All things that the father hath are mine" [John 16:15]. The children of Israel are said to have tempted Jehovah [Num. 14:26–27]. And Paul says that He whom they tempted was Christ [1 Cor. 10:9]. Jehovah founded the earth, and the same is said of Christ [Ps. 102:25 with John 1:3]. (2) Christ, the Son of God, is by name called God. "Jesus Christ is very God and life eternal" [1 John 5:20]. (3) The properties of the Godhead are ascribed unto Him. He is eternal because He was then when there was no creature. "In the beginning was the Word" [John 1:1], and, "Before Abraham was, I am" [8:58]. He is omnipresent. "Where two or three are gathered together in my name, there am I in the midst amongst them" [Matt. 18:20, 26]. Lastly, He is omnipotent.

"Whatsoever things the Father doth, the same doth the Son also" [John 5:17].[137] (4) The works of creation and preservation are as well ascribed to the Son as the Father. By Him the Father made the world, and He bears up all things by His mighty power. And miracles, which are works either above or against the order of nature, peculiar to God, were done by Christ. (5) Divine worship is given to Him; for He is adored, invocated, and believed in, as God the Father. To Him is given a "name at which every knee doth bow, of things in heaven, and things in earth, and things under the earth."

As for the reasons which be alleged to the contrary, they are of no moment. *Objection 1.* The Word of God cannot be God. The Son is the Word of the Father. Therefore, He is not God. *Answer.* The "word" is taken two ways. First, for a founding word, standing of letters and syllables uttered either by God or by the creatures. Now on this manner Christ is not the word of God. Secondly, there is a substantial word, which is of the substance of Him whose word it is. And thus Christ is the Word of God the Father. And He is so termed (1) in respect of the Father; for as reason and speech have their beginning from the mind, without any passion in the mind, so has He beginning from the Father. And as the speech is in the mind, and the mind in the speech, so the Father is in the Son, and the Son in the Father. (2) In respect of all creatures. The Father does all things by the Son [Phil. 2:10], by whose powerful word the world was made, is now preserved, and will be abolished [John 1:1; Heb. 1:3; 2 Cor. 13:3; John 17]. (3) In respect of the church. For the Father by Him speaks unto us both in the outward ministry of the word and by the inward operation of the Spirit; and again, we by Him speak to the Father.

Objection 2. It may be objected thus: God has no beginning from any other. Christ has beginning from the Father. Therefore, He is not God. *Answer.* Christ must be considered both in regard of His Godhead and in regard of His person. In regard of His Godhead, He came not of any but is of Himself, as well as the Father is. Yet in regard of His person, He is from the Father, who is a beginning to the rest of the persons both in respect of order (for the Scripture says not the Holy Ghost, the Son, the Father, but the Father, the Son, the Holy Ghost [Matt 28:19]),[138] as also in respect of the communication of the Godhead. And where it is said that God is of Himself, if the name of God be taken for the Godhead itself absolutely considered, it is true. But if it be taken for any particular person in the Godhead, it is false.

Objection 3. None is greater than God.[139] But the Father is greater than Christ, for so He says, "The Father is greater than I" [John 14:28]. *Answer.*

---

137. Originally, "Joel 5:17."
138. Principium ordinis & originis. [He is the principium of order and origin.]
139. This paragraph break is not in the original, as the additional four following.

Christ there speaks of Himself as He was a man abased in the form of a servant, in which respect He is less than the Father, who was never incarnate and abased in our nature. And though Christ in respect of His nature assumed be inferior to the Father, yet does it not hinder but that He may be equal to Him as He is the second person in [the] Trinity, or as He is God by one and the same Godhead with the Father.

Objection 4. He that is made of God, this or that, is not God.[140] But Christ is made of God, as Paul says, "Christ is made unto us wisdom, righteousness," etc. [1 Cor. 1:30]. *Answer.* Christ is said to be made not because there was any beginning of His Godhead or any change or alteration in His person, but because in the eternal counsel of the Father He was set apart before all times to execute the office of a mediator and was withal in time called and as it were consecrated and ordained thereunto in His baptism. He is made therefore in respect of His office but not in respect of His person or nature.

Objection 5. God has no head. Christ has a head, as Paul says, "God is Christ's head" [11:3]. *Answer.* God—that is, the Father—is head of Christ, not as He is God simply, but as He is God incarnate or made manifest in the flesh and in respect of the office to which He willingly abased Himself.

Objection 6. He which gives up his kingdom is not God. Christ gives up His kingdom. "Then," says Paul, "shall be the end, when he hath delivered up his kingdom to God, even the Father" [15:24]. *Answer.* Christ is King two ways: as He is God; as He is Mediator. As He is God, He reigns eternally with the Father and the Holy Ghost. But as He is Mediator in the end of the world when all the company of the elect are gathered, His kingdom shall cease, not simply, but in respect of the outward manner of administration; for the execution of civil and ecclesiastical functions shall cease. And whereas in the same place it is said that Christ shall be subject unto God eternally after the end [v. 28], it must be understood partly in regard of the assumed manhood, partly in respect of His mystical body, the church, most nearly joined unto Him in heaven.

Objection 7. The firstborn of every creature and of many brethren is a creature and not God. But Christ is the firstborn of every creature and of many brethren [Rom. 8:29; Col. 1:15]. *Answer.* He is called the firstborn by resemblance or allusion to the firstborn in the Old Testament; for as they were principal heirs, having double portions allowed them [Gen. 49:3; Deut. 21:16], and the chief or governors of the family, so Christ is made heir of the world and the Head of God's family, which is His church, elected and adopted in Him. And again, He is called the firstborn of every creature because He was begotten

---

140. This paragraph break is not in the original.

of the substance of His Father before any creature was made. And therefore it is not here said that He was first created, but first begotten.

By the reasons which have been alleged, as also by the sufficiency of the contrary arguments, it is more than manifest against all heretics that Christ is very God. Yet to stop the mouths of all atheists and to satisfy all wavering and doubting minds, I will add one reason further. The Gospel of St. John was chiefly penned for this end, to prove the deity of Christ. And among other arguments alleged this is one, that Christ gave a resolute and a constant testimony of Himself that He was the Son of God and very God. Now, if any man shall say that sundry persons since the beginning of the world have taken upon them, and that falsely, to be gods, I answer that never any creature took this title and honor upon him to be called God, but the fearful judgments of God were upon him for it. In the estate of man's innocency, the devil told our first parents that by eating the fruit of the tree of knowledge of good and evil they should be as gods, knowing good and evil. Now, they believed him and affected divine honor—but what came of it? Surely Adam with all his posterity is shut up for this very cause under eternal damnation. Herod likewise, arrayed in royal apparel and sitting on the judgment seat, made an oration to the men of Tyre and Sidon, who gave a shout, saying, "The voice of God, and not of man" [Acts 12:22–23]. Now because he took the glory of God to himself and did not return it to Him to whom it was due, immediately the angel of the Lord smote him. And so, if Christ had been but a mere man and not very God as He avouched, undoubtedly the hand of God would have been upon Him likewise for His confusion. But when He suffered for us and bare the punishment due for our sins, He most triumphed. And the judgments of God were upon Herod, Pontius Pilate, Caiaphas, and upon all those that were enemies to Him and to His church afterward, and that partly in life, partly in death. Wherefore, considering God cannot abide that His glory should be given to any creature and seeing for that cause He takes revenge on all those that exalt themselves to be gods, it remains that the testimony which Christ gave of Himself that He was God is infallibly true and without all question to be believed of us. And to conclude, I would have all the devils in hell with the cursed orders of Lucians, Porphyrians, and atheists whatsoever to answer this one point: how it could come to pass that Christ by publishing the doctrine of the gospel, that is as contrary to man's reason, will, and affection as water to fire, should win almost the whole world to become His disciples and to give their lives for Him, unless He were God indeed, as He professed Himself to be?

There be sundry special reasons wherefore it was necessary that Christ should be God. (1) There is none which can be a savior of body and soul but God. "I, even I, am the Lord, and besides me there is no Savior" [Isa. 43:11].

And, "I am the Lord thy God from the land of Egypt, and thou shalt know no God but me: for there is no Savior beside me" [Hos. 13:4]. (2) There must be a proportion between the sin of man and the punishment of sin. Now the sin of man in respect of the offence of the majesty of God is infinite, in that He is infinitely displeased with man for the breach of His law. Therefore, the punishment of sin must be infinite. And hence it follows that He which suffers the punishment, being man, must withal be God, that the manhood by the power of the Godhead may be supported, that in suffering it may vanquish death and make a sufficient satisfaction. (3) He that must be a savior must be able first to deliver men from the bondage of their spiritual enemies—namely, sin and Satan; secondly, to restore the image of God, lost by the fall of Adam, and to confer righteousness and life everlasting; thirdly, to defend them from hell, death, damnation, the flesh, the devil, the world; fourthly, to give them full redemption from all their miseries both in body and soul and to place them in eternal happiness—all which none can do, but He which is very God. (4) It was the pleasure of God to show His incomprehensible goodness in this, that His grace should not only be equal to our sin, but also by many degrees go beyond it. And therefore the first Adam being but a mere man, the second Adam must be both God and man, that as the second was more excellent than the first, so our comfort might be greater in our redemption by the second than our misery and discomfort was by the fall of the first.

Hitherto we have showed that Christ is the Son of God. Now let us come to the second point—namely, that He is the only Son of God. And He is so termed because He is the Son of the Father in a special manner, so as no one can be the Son of God as He is. Angels indeed are termed the sons of God [Job 1:6], but that is only in respect of their creation. And all that believe in Christ are sons of God by adoption, being received into the family of God, which is His church, by the merit of Christ, whereas by nature they were the children of wrath. Christ also as He is man (I say not His manhood, which is a nature and no person) is the Son of God by the grace of personal union and not by nature or adoption. Lastly, Christ as He is the second person in [the] Trinity, the eternal Word of the Father coeternal and consubstantial with Him, is also the Son of God. But how? Neither by creation nor adoption nor by the virtue of personal union, but by nature, as He was begotten of the very substance of the Father before all worlds. And therefore He is called the proper and only begotten Son of God [John 1:14; Rom. 8:32]. It may be objected on this manner: if the Father beget the Son, He does it either willingly or against His will. If willingly, then the Son is begotten by the free will of the Father and no Son by nature. *Answer.* The Father did communicate to the Son His whole Godhead willingly without constraint, yet not by His will. And therefore He is the Son of the Father by nature, not by will. It may be further said that if Christ be the Son of God by nature, as He is the essential Word of the Father, and by personal union as He is man, then He is not one but two sons. *Answer.* As He is but one person, so is He but one son, yet not in one but in two respects. Two respects make not two things, whereas one and the same thing not altered but still remaining one may admit sundry respects.

Thus much of the meaning of the third title. Now follow the comforts which may be gathered hence. Whereas Christ Jesus is the Son of God, it serves as a means to make miserable and wretched sinners, that are by nature the children of wrath and damnation, to be the sons of God by adoption, as St. John testifies [John 1:12]. Now what a benefit this is to be the child of God, no tongue can express. Christ says, "Blessed are the peacemakers" [Matt. 5:9][141]—but why are they blessed? "For," says He, "they shall be called the sons of God." Whereby He testifies that the right of adoption is a most excellent privilege, and not without cause. For he which is the child of God is spiritually allied to Christ and to all the saints and servants of God, both in heaven and earth, having his own Redeemer for his elder brother and all His members as his brethren and sisters. Yea, if we be God's adopted children, we are also heirs, even heirs of God and heirs annexed with Christ [Rom. 8:17]. Well, how great soever this prerogative is, yet few there be that rightly weigh it and consider of it. Children of noblemen and princes' heirs are had in account and reputation of all men. They are the very speech and wonder of the world. But it is a matter of no account to be the son of God and fellow heir with Christ. The dearest servants of God have been esteemed but as the off-scouring of the world. And no marvel, for they which are after the flesh savor the things of the flesh. Few men have their understandings enlightened to discern of such spiritual things as these are, and therefore they are little or nothing regarded. A blind man, never seeing the sun, is not brought to wonder at it. And earthly minded men, neither seeing nor feeling what an excellent thing it is to be the child of God, cannot be brought to seek after it. But let all such as fear God enter into a serious consideration of the unspeakable goodness of God, comforting themselves in this, that God the Father has vouchsafed by His own Son to make them of the vassals of Satan to be His own dear children.

Now follow the duties, which are two. First, we believe that Jesus Christ, who was to be the Savior of mankind, must needs be God. What is the reason hereof? Surely because no creature, no, not all the creatures in heaven and earth were able to save one man, so vile, wretched, and miserable is our estate by Adam's fall. And therefore the Son of God Himself pitied our estate and, being

141. Originally, "Matt. 5:7."

King of heaven and earth, was fain to come from heaven and lay down His crown and become a servant and, taking upon Him our nature, was also fain to take upon Him our case and condition and suffer death for our sins, which otherwise every one of us should have suffered both in body and soul, world without end. To make this more plain, let us suppose someone that has committed an offence against a prince, and the trespass to be so grievous that no man can appease the king's wrath, save only the king's only son. And which is more, the king's son himself cannot release him, unless he suffer the punishment for him in his own person which is due unto the malefactor. Now what is to be thought of this man's estate? Surely, all men will say that he is in a most miserable taking, and that his trespass is notorious. And so it is with every one of us by nature, whatsoever we are. No man could save our souls, no, not all the angels of heaven, unless the King of heaven and earth, the only Son of God, had come down from heaven and suffered for us, bearing our punishment. Now the consideration of this must humble us and make us to cast down ourselves under the hand of God for our sins and pray continually that the Lord would send some Moses or other which might smite the rocks of our hearts, that some tears of sorrow and repentance might gush out for this our woeful misery.

Secondly, whereas God the Father of Christ gave His only Son to be our Savior, as we must be thankful to God for all things, so especially for this great and unspeakable benefit. Common blessings of God, as meat, drink, health, wealth, and liberty, must at all times move us to be thankful; but this, that Christ Jesus, the only Son of God, redeemed us, being utterly lost—this, I say, must be the main point of our thankfulness. But alas, men's hearts are so frozen in the dregs of their sins that this duty comes little in practice nowadays. When our Savior Christ cleansed ten lepers, there was but one of them that returned to give Him thanks. And this is as true in the leprosy of the soul, for though salvation by Christ be offered unto us daily by God's ministers, yet not one of ten, nay, scarce one of a thousand gives praise and thanks to God for it, because men take no delight in things which concern the kingdom of heaven. They think not that they have need of salvation, neither do they feel any want of a savior. But we for our parts must learn to say with David, "What shall I render unto the Lord for all his benefits?" [Ps. 116:12]. Yea, we are to practice that which Solomon says, "My son, give me thy heart" [Prov. 23:26]; for we should give unto God both body and soul in token of our thankfulness for this wonderful blessing that He has given His only Son to be our Savior. And we are to hold this for truth, that they which are not thankful for it, let them say what they will, they have no soundness of grace or power of religion at the heart.

And thus much of the third title. The fourth and last title is in these words, "our Lord." Christ Jesus, the only Son of God, is our Lord three ways. First, by creation, in that He made us of nothing when we were not. Secondly, He is our Lord in the right of redemption. In former times the custom has been, when one is taken prisoner in the field, he that pays his ransom shall become always after his lord. So Christ, when we were bondslaves under hell, death, and condemnation, paid the ransom of our redemption and freed us from the bondage of sin and Satan; and therefore in that respect He is our Lord. Thirdly, He is the Head of the church (as the husband is the wife's head) to rule and govern the same by His word and Spirit. And therefore in that respect also Christ is our Lord.

And thus much for the meaning. Now follow the duties. And, first of all, if Christ be our sovereign Lord, we must perform absolute obedience unto Him—that is, whatsoever He commands us, that must we do. And I say, absolute obedience, because magistrates, masters, rulers, and fathers may command and must be obeyed, yet not simply, but so far forth as that which they command does agree with the word and commandment of God. But Christ's will and word is righteousness itself, and therefore it is a rule and direction of all our actions whatsoever; and for this cause He must be absolutely obeyed. Thus, He requires the obedience of the moral law. But why? Because He is "the Lord our God" [Ex. 20:2]. And in Malachi He says, "If I be your Lord, where is my fear?" [Mal. 1:6]. And again, we must resign both body and soul, heart, mind, will, affections, and the course of our whole lives to be ruled by the will of Christ. He is Lord not only of the body but of the spirit and soul of man. He must therefore have homage of both. As we adore Him by the knee of the body, so must the thoughts and the affections of our hearts have their knees also to worship Him and to show their subjection to His commandments. As for such as do hold Him for their Lord in word but in the mean season will not endeavor to show their loyalty in all manner of obedience, they are indeed no better than stark rebels.

Secondly, when by the hand of Christ strange judgments shall come to pass, as it is usual in all places continually, we must stay ourselves without murmuring or finding fault, because He is an absolute lord over all His creatures.[142] All things are in His hands, and He may do with His own whatsoever He will. And therefore we must rather fear and tremble whensoever we see or hear of them. So David says, "I was dumb and opened not my mouth, because thou didst it" [Ps. 39:9]. And again, "My flesh trembles for fear of thee, and I am afraid of thy judgments" [119:120].

Thirdly, before we use any of God's creatures or ordinances, we must sanctify them by the direction of His Word and by prayer. The reason is this: because

---

142. This paragraph break is not in the original, as the additional two following.

He is Lord over all, and therefore from His Word we must fetch direction to teach us, whether we may use them or not, and when and how they are to be used. And, secondly, we must pray to Him that He would give us liberty and grace to use them aright in a holy manner. Also we are so to use the creatures and ordinances of God as being always ready to give an account of our doings at the day of judgment; for we use that which is the Lord's, not our own. We are but stewards over them, and we must come to a reckoning for the stewardship. Have you learning? Then employ it to the glory of God and the good of the church. Boast not of it as though it were your own. Have you any other gift or blessing of God, be it wisdom, strength, riches, honor, favor, or whatsoever? Then look you use it so as you may be always ready to make a good account thereof unto Christ.

Lastly, everyone must in such manner lead his life in this world that at the day of death he may with cheerfulness surrender and give up his soul into the hands of his Lord and say with Stephen, "Lord Jesus, receive my soul" [Acts 7:59].[143] For consider this with yourself, that your soul is none of your own, but His who has bought it with a price. And therefore you must so order and keep it as that you may in good manner restore it into the hands of God at the end of your life. If a man should borrow a thing of his neighbor and afterward hurt it and make a spoil of it, he would be ashamed to bring it again to the owner in that manner. And if he do, the owner himself will not receive it. Ungodly men in this life do so stain their souls with sin that they can never be able willingly to give them up into the hands of God at the day of death. And if they would, yet God accepts them not but casts them quite away. We must therefore labor so to live in the world that with a joyful heart at the day of death we may commend our souls into the hands of our Lord Christ Jesus, who gave them unto us. This is a hard thing to be done; and he that will do it truly must first be assured of the pardon of his own sins, which a man can never have without true and unfeigned faith and repentance. Wherefore, while we have time, let us purge and cleanse our souls and bodies, that they may come home again to God in good plight. And here all governors must be put in mind that they have a higher lord, that they may not oppress or deal hardly with their inferiors. This is Paul's reason: "Ye masters," says he, "do the same things unto your servants, putting away threatening: and know that even your master is also in heaven, neither is there respect of persons with him" (Eph. 6:9). Inferiors again must remember to submit themselves to the authority of their governors, especially of magistrates. For they are set over us by our sovereign Lord and King, Christ Jesus—as Paul says, "Let every soul be subject to the higher powers: for there

---

143. Originally, "Acts 7:56."

is no power but of God, and the powers that be, are ordained of God" (Rom. 13:1). And again, "Servants be obedient to your masters according to the flesh, with fear and trembling, in singleness of your hearts, as unto Christ" (Eph. 6:5).

The comfort which God's church may reap hence is very great; for if Christ be the Lord of lords, and our Lord especially whom He has created and redeemed, we need not to fear what the devil or wicked men can do unto us. If Christ be on our side, who can be against us? We need not fear them that can destroy the body and do no more, but we must cast our fear on Him that is Lord of body and soul and can cast both to hell (Matt. 10:28).

Thus much of the fourth title. Now follows Christ's incarnation, in these words, "conceived by the Holy Ghost, born of the virgin Mary." And they contain in them one of the most principal points of the doctrine of godliness, as Paul says, "Without controversy great is the mystery of godliness, which is, God is made manifest in the flesh, justified in the Spirit," etc. (1 Tim. 3:16). And that we may proceed in order in handling them, I will first speak of the incarnation generally and then after come to the parts thereof. In general, we are to propound three questions, the answering whereof will be very needful to the better understanding of the doctrine following.

The first question is, who was incarnate or made man? *Answer.* The second person in [the] Trinity, the Son of God alone, as it is set down in this first article according to the Scripture. St. John says, "The Word was made flesh" (John 1:14). And the angel says, "The holy One which shall be born of thee, shall be called the Son of the Most High" (Luke 1:35). And Paul says that Christ Jesus our Lord was "made of the seed of Abraham according to the flesh" (Rom. 1:3). And there be sundry reasons why the second person should rather be incarnate than any other. (1) By whom the Father created all things, and man especially, by Him man, being fallen, is to be redeemed and, as I may say, recreated. Now man was at the first created of the Father by the Son, and therefore [ought] to be redeemed by Him. (2) It was most convenient that He who is the essential image of the Father should take man's nature that He might restore the image of God, lost and defaced in man. But the second person is the essential image of the Father, and therefore He alone must take man's nature [Col. 1:15; Heb. 1:3]. (3) It was requisite that that person which was by nature the Son of God should be made the son of men, that we which are the sons of man, yea, the sons of wrath, should again by grace be made the sons of God. Now the second person alone is the Son of God by nature, not the Father nor the Holy Ghost.

As for the Father, He could not be incarnate. For to take flesh is to be sent of another, but the Father cannot be sent of any person, because He is from none. Again, if the Father were incarnate, He should be Father to Him which is by nature God and the son of a creature—namely, the Virgin Mary—which things cannot well stand.

And the Holy Ghost could not be incarnate, for then there should be more sons than one in the Trinity—namely, the second person, the Son of the Father, and the third person, the Holy Ghost, the son of the Virgin Mary.

It may be objected to the contrary on this manner: the whole divine essence is incarnate. Every person in [the] Trinity is the whole divine essence. Therefore, every person is incarnate. *Answer.* The whole Godhead indeed is incarnate, yet not as it is absolutely considered, but so far forth as it is restrained and limited to the person of the Son. And to speak properly, the Godhead itself is not incarnate, but the very person of the Son, subsisting in the Godhead. And though all the persons be one and the same essence, yet do they really differ each from [the] other in regard of the peculiar manner of subsisting. And therefore man's nature may be assumed of the second person and be not assumed either of the Father or of the Holy Ghost, as in the like case, the soul of man is wholly in the head and wholly in the feet, yea, wholly in every part, and yet the soul cannot be said to use reason in the feet or in any other part, but only in the head.

Again, it may be alleged that the incarnation, being an outward action of God to the creature, is not proper to the Son. For the rule is that all outward actions of God are common to all the persons in [the] Trinity equally. *Answer.* The incarnation stands of two actions. The first is the framing and creating of that manhood which was to be assumed by the Son or Word of the Father, and this action is common to all the three persons equally. The second is the limiting or the receiving of it into the unity of any person, and in respect of this action the work of incarnation is peculiar to the Son.[144] To this purpose Augustine speaks: "That creature," says he, "which the Virgin conceived and brought forth, though it appertain to the person of the Son alone, yet was it made by the whole Trinity"[145]—as when three men weave one and the same garment, and the second only wears it.

The second question is, what manner of man the Son of God was made? *Answer.* He was made a proper or particular man and a perfect or a very man. I say that He was a particular man to show that He took not unto Him the general form or idea of man's nature, conceived only in [the] mind, nor the common nature of man as it is existing in every man, but the whole nature of man—that is, both a body and a reasonable soul, existing in one particular subject.[146] I say further that He was and is a true and perfect man, being in

---

144. Inchoative communis, terminative non: sic scholastici. (Common inchoatively, but not terminatively—thus say the scholastics.)

145. August. in Ench. ad Lau. c. 38.

146. In uno individuo.

everything that concerns man's nature like to Adam, Abraham, David, and all other men, saving only in sin. For, first of all, He had the substance of a true body and of a reasonable soul. Secondly, the properties of body and soul— in the body, length, breadth, thickness, circumscription, etc.; in the soul, the faculties of understanding, both simple and compound, will and affections, as love, hatred, desire, joy, fear, etc., the powers also of hearing, feeling, seeing, smelling, tasting, moving, growing, eating, digesting, sleeping, etc. Thirdly, He took unto Him the infirmities of man's nature, which are certain natural effects or passions of body or mind, as to be hungry, thirsty, weary, sad and sorrowful, ignorant of some things,[147] angry, to increase in stature and wisdom and knowledge, etc. Yet this which I say must be understood with two caveats. The first is that infirmities be either certain unblamable passions, or else such defects as are sins in themselves. Now Christ takes the first only and not the second. Secondly, infirmities be either general or personal. General, which appertain to the whole nature of man and are to be found in every man that comes of Adam, as to be born unlearned and subject to natural affections, as sorrow, anger, etc. Personal are such as appertain to some particular men and not to all and arise of some private causes and particular judgments of God, as to be born a fool, to be sick of an ague, consumption, dropsy, pleurisy, and such like diseases. Now, the first sort be in Christ and not the second; for as He took not the person of any man but only man's nature, so was it sufficient for Him to take unto Him the infirmities of man's nature, though He took not the private infirmities of any man's person. And the reason why Christ would put on not only the substance and faculties of a true man but also his infirmities was that He might show Himself to be very man indeed, [and] also that He might suffer for us both in body and soul, and that He might give us an example of patience in bearing all manner of evil for God's glory and the good of our neighbor.

Now, the things which may be alleged to the contrary for the infringing of the truth of Christ's manhood are of no moment. As, first, because Christ appeared in the form of a man in the Old Testament, being no man. Therefore, He did so at His coming in the New Testament. But the reason is not [a]like. For Christ in the Old Testament (Gen. 18:9, 13), as the Angel of His Father in some special affairs, took unto Him the body of a man for some space of time. But He did not receive it into the unity of His person but laid it down when the business which He enterprised with men was ended. Now in the fullness of time He came from heaven as the Angel of the Covenant, and for that cause He was to unite into His own person the nature of man, which thing was never

147. Ignorantia mere privationis non prave dispositionis. (An ignorance merely of privation, not improperly of disposition.)

done before. And when as Paul says that Christ "came in the similitude of sinful flesh" (Rom. 8:3), his meaning is not to signify that He was a man only in resemblance and show, but to testify that, being a true man which was indeed void of sin, He was content to abase Himself to that condition in which He became like to a miserable sinner in bearing the punishment for our sin. For Paul does not say that He took upon Him the similitude of flesh simply as it is flesh, but of the flesh of sin, or sinful.

The third question is, why the Son of God must become man? *Answer.* There be sundry reasons of this point, and the most principal are these. (1)[148] First of all, it is a thing that greatly stands with the justice of God, that in that nature in which God was offended, in the same should a satisfaction be made to God for sin. Now sin was committed in man's nature. Adam sinned first, and in him all his posterity. Therefore, it was necessary that in man's nature there should be a satisfaction made to God's justice, and for this cause the Son of God must needs abase Himself and become man for our sakes.

(2) Secondly, by the right of creation, every man is bound in conscience to fulfill even the very rigor and extremity of the moral law.[149] But considering man is now fallen from his first estate and condition, therefore, it was requisite that the Son of God should become man, that in man's nature He might fulfill all righteousness, which the law does exact at our hands.

(3) Thirdly, He that is our Redeemer must die for our sins, for there is no remission of sins without shedding of blood. But Christ as He is God cannot die, for no passion can befall the Godhead. Therefore, it was needful that He should become man, that in man's nature He might die and fully satisfy God's justice for man's offence.

(4) Lastly, He that must make reconciliation between God and man must be such a one as may make request or speak both to God and man. For a mediator is as it were a middle person, making intercession between two other persons—the one offended; the other offending. Therefore, it is necessary that Christ should not only be God to speak unto the Father for us and to present our prayers unto Him, but also man, that God might speak to us, and we to God by Christ. For howsoever before the fall, man could speak to God even face to face; yet since the fall, such fear possesses man's corrupt nature that he cannot bide the presence of God but flies from it.

Now whereas I say that it was necessary that the Son of God for the causes before alleged must become man, the necessity must be understood in respect of God's will and not in respect of His absolute power. For if it had so pleased

---

148. Originally in the margin, as the additional three reasons following.
149. This paragraph break is not in the original, as the additional two following.

God, He was able to have laid down another kind of way of man's redemption than by the incarnation of the Son of God. And He appointed no other way because He would not.[150]

Thus much of the incarnation in general. Now follow the duties which arise of it. *Duty 1.*[151] And, first, we are taught hereby to come to Christ by faith and with all our hearts to cleave unto Him. Great is the deadness and sluggishness of man's nature, for scarce one of a thousand care for Him or seek to Him for righteousness and life everlasting. But we should excite ourselves every way to draw near to Him as much as possible we may; for when He was incarnate, He came near unto us by taking our nature upon Him, that we again, whatsoever we are, might come near unto Him by taking unto us His divine nature. Again, when Christ was incarnate, He was made bone of our bone and flesh of our flesh; and therefore proportionally we must labor to become bone of His bone and flesh of His flesh, which we shall be when we are mystically united unto Him by faith and born anew by His Spirit. Moreover, Christ by His incarnation came down from heaven to us, that we, being partakers of His grace, might ascend up to heaven by Him. And thus we see how the meditation of Christ's incarnation should be a spur to prick us forward still more and more to come to Christ.

[*Duty 2.*] Secondly, Christ's incarnation must be a pattern unto us of a most wonderful and strange humility. For as Paul says, "Being in the form of God, and thinking it no robbery to be equal with God, he made himself of no reputation: and took on him the form of a servant: and humbled himself, and became obedient to death, even to the death of the cross" (Phil. 2:6–7). Yea, so far forth He abased Himself that as David says He "was a worm and no man" [Ps. 22:6]. And this teaches us to lay aside all self-love and pride of heart and to practice the duties of humility, as the apostle exhorts the Philippians in the same place. And that shall we do, when we begin to cast off that high opinion which every man by nature conceives of himself and become vile and base in our own eyes. Secure and drowsy Protestants think themselves blessed and say in their hearts as the angel of the church of Laodicea said, "I am rich and increased with goods, and have need of nothing" [Rev. 3:17], whereas indeed they are most miserable and wretched and poor and naked and blind. And the same fond opinion possesses the minds of our ignorant people, who chant it in the very same tune, saying that God loves them and that they love God with all their hearts and their neighbors as themselves; that they have perfect faith in Christ and ever had, not once so much as doubting of their salvation; that all is well with them; and that they are past all danger whatsoever in the matter of

---

150. Aug. de Agone Christi.
151. Originally in the margin.

their salvation and therefore need not take so much care for it. Thus, you may see how men are commonly carried away with vain and fond conceits of their own excellency. And truly, so long as this over-weaning of our own righteousness reigns in our hearts, let preachers speak and say what they will, we can never become followers of Christ in the practice of humility. Some will say, peradventure, that they never had any such opinion of their own righteousness. But I answer again that there was never yet any man descended of Adam save Christ, but he had this proud fantasy ruling and reigning in him till such time as God gave grace to change and alter his heart. And this inward pride, the less we discern it, the more it is; and the more we discern it, the less it is. Therefore, though as yet you see it not in yourself, yet labor both to see and to feel it and to strive against it, casting down yourself for your own misery after Christ's own example, who, being God, abased Himself to the condition of a miserable man. For you shall never be filled with the good things of God, till you be emptied of self-love and self-liking. For this cause let us purge and empty ourselves of all conceit of our own righteousness, that God may fill our hearts with His grace.

Furthermore, the incarnation of Christ is the ground and foundation of all our comfort, as the names of Christ, serving to express the same, do testify. Jacob in his last testament says that "the scepter shall not depart from Judah, till Shiloh"—that is, Messiah—"come" [Gen. 49:10]. Now, the name "Shiloh" signifies the tunicle or skin that laps the infant in the mother's womb, called by the physicians the secundine; and by a kind of figure it is put for the Son of God in the womb of the Virgin, made man.[152] And Job to comfort himself in his affliction says, "I know that my redeemer liveth" [Job 19:25]. Now the word which he uses to signify his Redeemer by is very emphatical, for it signifies a kinsman near allied onto him of his own flesh that will restore him to life. And the Lord by the prophet Isaiah calls Christ "Immanuel" [Isa. 7:14], that is, "God with us," which name imports very much—namely, that whereas by nature we have lost our fellowship with God, because our sins are a wall of partition [59:2], severing us from Him, yet nevertheless the same is restored to all that believe by the Mediator, Christ Jesus [Col. 1:22],[153] because His divine nature is coupled to man's nature, and so the Word is made flesh. And this strait conjunction of two natures into one person joins God to men and men to God. Yea, by Christ we are brought to God and have free access unto Him, and again in Him we apprehend God and are made one with Him.

And further, whereas Christ besides our nature took our infirmities also, it is a wonderful comfort to God's church; for it shows that He is not only a savior

---

152. P. Gallat. de occultis cath. veritat. 5. c. 4. Goel.
153. Originally, "Col. 1.2.11."

but also a very compassionate and pitiful savior. As the Holy Ghost says, "In all things it became Christ to be like onto his brethren, that he might be merciful and a faithful high priest in things concerning God" [Heb. 2:17]. Let a man be sick of a grievous disease, and let a friend come that has been troubled with the very same disease, he will presently show more compassion than twenty others. And so Christ, having felt in His own soul and body the anguish and the manifold perplexities that we feel in our temptations and afflictions, has His bowels as it were yearning toward us, evermore being pressed and ready to relieve us in all our miseries. In the days of His flesh, He wept over Jerusalem when He saw it afar off, because she continued in her old sins and did not know the time of her visitation. And no doubt, though now He be exalted in glory in heaven, yet His compassion to His poor members upon earth is no whit diminished.

Now we come to speak of the incarnation more particularly, and the Creed yet further expresses it by two parts. The first is the conception of Christ in these words, "conceived by the Holy Ghost." The second is His birth, in the words following, "born of the virgin Mary."

The conception of Christ is set down with His efficient cause, the Holy Ghost, as the angel said to Joseph, "Fear not to take Mary for thy wife, for that which is conceived in her, is of the Holy Ghost" [Matt. 1:20]. Here it may be demanded why the conception of Christ should be ascribed to the Holy Ghost alone, which is common to all the persons in [the] Trinity, as all other such actions are? *Answer.* (1)[154] It is not done to exclude the Father or the Son Himself from this work; but to signify that it comes of the free gift and grace of God (which commonly is termed by the Holy Ghost) that the manhood of Christ being but a creature should be advanced to this dignity, that it should become a part of the Son of God.[155] (2) And again, the Holy Ghost is the author of His conception in a special manner, for the Father and the Son did cause it by the Holy Ghost from them both immediately.

In the conception of Christ, we must observe and consider three things: the framing of the manhood, the sanctifying of it, and the personal union of the manhood with the Godhead. And howsoever I distinguish these three for order's sake, yet must we know and remember that they are all wrought at one and the same instant of time. For when the Holy Ghost frames and sanctifies the manhood in the womb of the Virgin, at the very same moment it is received into the unity of the second person.

In the framing of Christ's manhood, two things must be considered: the matter and the manner. The matter of His body was the very flesh and blood

---

154. Originally in the margin, as the "2" below.
155. *August. ench.* c. 37. 39.

of the Virgin Mary, otherwise He could not have been the son of David, of Abraham, and Adam according to the flesh. As for His soul, it was not derived from the soul of the Virgin Mary as a part thereof, but it was made as the souls of all other men be—that is, of nothing by the very power of God—and placed in the body, both of them from the first moment of their being having their subsistence[156] in the person of the Son. And here we must take heed of two opinions. The first is of the Anabaptists, which hold that the flesh of Christ came down from heaven and passed through the Virgin Mary as through a pipe without taking any substance from her. The places which they allege for the purpose are manifestly abused. For whereas Christ says of Himself that He "descended from heaven" (John 3:13), His speech must be understood in respect of His Godhead, which may be said in some sort to descend, in that it was made manifest in the manhood here upon earth. And whereas Paul calls Him "heavenly, and the Lord from heaven" [1 Cor. 15:47–48], it is not in respect of the substance of His body but in respect of His glorious qualities which He received after His resurrection. The other opinion is of the Papists, that hold the bread in the Sacrament to be turned substantially into the body of Christ, which thing, if it be true, then the body of Christ is made of bread kneaded and tempered by the hand of the baker and not of the substance of the Virgin Mary.

As for the manner of the making and framing of the human nature of Christ, it was miraculous, not by generation according to the ordinary course of nature, but by an extraordinary operation of the Holy Ghost above nature. And for this cause it is not within the compass of man's reason either to conceive or to express the manner and order of this conception. The angel ascribes two actions to the Holy Ghost in this great work: the one to "come upon the virgin Mary"; the other to "overshadow her" [Luke 1:35]. By the first is signified the extraordinary work of the Holy Ghost in fashioning the human nature of Christ, for so much the phrase elsewhere imports [Judg. 14:6]. The second signifies that the Holy Ghost did as it were cast a cloud over her [Luke 24:4; Acts 1:8], to teach us that we should not search overmuch into the mystery of the incarnation.

It may be objected against this which has been said that if Christ be in this manner conceived by the Holy Ghost, then the Holy Ghost shall be Father to Christ, and Christ, His Son. *Answer.* The reason is not good; for he that is a father is not a bare efficient cause, but one which in the effecting of anything confers the matter unto it from himself, whereof it shall be made. Now the Holy Ghost did not minister any matter unto Christ from His own substance, but did only as it were take the mass and lump of man's nature from the body of the

---

156. Originally, "substance."

Virgin Mary and without ordinary generation made it the body of Christ, as Basil says, "Christ was conceived not of the substance, but of the power, not by any generation, but by the appointment and benediction of the Holy Ghost."[157]

The second point in the conception is the sanctifying of that mass or lump which was to be the manhood of Christ. And that was done upon special cause, first, that it might be joined to the person of the Son, which could not have been, if it had been defiled with sin. Secondly, Christ was a savior as He is both God and man. Now then, being man, if He had been sinful Himself, He could not have saved others but should have stood in need of a savior Himself.

This sanctification has two parts. The first is the stay and stoppage of the propagation of original sin and of the guilt of Adam's sin, which was on this manner: God in the beginning set down this order touching man, that what evil or defect soever he brought upon himself, he should derive the same to every one of his posterity begotten of him. And hereupon when any father begets his child, he is in the room of Adam and conveys unto it besides the nature of man the very guilt and corruption of nature. Now for the preventing of this evil in Christ, God in great wisdom appointed that He should be conceived by the Holy Ghost without any manner of generation by man. And by this means He takes substance from the Virgin without the guilt and corruption of the substance. But it may further be objected thus: all that be in Adam have sinned in him. But Christ was in Adam as He is man. Therefore, He sinned in him. *Answer.* The proposition is false, unless it be expounded on this manner: all that were in Adam have sinned in him, so be it they come of him by generation. Paul says not out of one man but "by one man sin entered into the world" [Rom. 5:12], to show that man propagates his corruption to no more than he begets. Again, Christ is in Adam not simply as other men are, but in some part—namely, in respect of substance which He took from him and not in respect of the propagation of the substance by ordinary generation. Other men are both from Adam and by Adam. But Christ is from him alone and not by him as a begetter or procreant cause. The second part of sanctification is the infusion of all pureness and holiness into the manhood of Christ, so far forth as was meet for the nature of a redeemer.

The duties to be learned hence are these: first, whereas Christ was sanctified in the womb of the Virgin Mary, we likewise must labor to be sanctified in ourselves, following the commandment of God, "Be ye holy as I am holy" (1 Peter 1:16). St. John says that "he which hath hope to be" with Christ in glory in heaven "purifieth himself even as he is pure" [1 John 3:3], no doubt setting before himself the example of Christ as a pattern to follow in all his ways. And

---

157. *Sermon. de S. nativit.*

because our hearts are as it were seas of corruptions, we must daily cleanse ourselves of them by little and little, following the practice of the poor beggar that is always piecing and mending and day by day pulls away some rags and puts better cloth in the room. And if we shall continually endeavor ourselves to cast off the remnants of corruption that hang so fast on and make a supply thereof by some new portions of God's heavenly grace, we shall be vessels of honor sanctified and meet for the Lord and prepared unto every good work. Christ could not have been a fit savior for us, unless He had first of all been sanctified. Neither can we be fit members unto Him, unless we be purged of our sins and in some measure truly sanctified.

The comfort which God's people may reap of the sanctification of Christ's manhood is great. For why was He sanctified? Surely, if we mark it well, we shall find it was for the good and benefit of His elect. For Adam and Christ be two roots, as has been shown. Adam by creation first received God's image and after lost the same for himself and his posterity. Now Christ to remove the sin of man is made the second Adam and the root and very head of all the elect. His manhood was filled with holiness above measure, that from thence as from a storehouse it might be derived to all His members. And therefore by His most holy conception, our sinful birth and conception is sanctified, and His holiness serves as a cover to hide our manifold corruptions from the eyes of God. Yea, it serves as a buckler to thwart the temptations of the devil; for when he shall say to our hearts on this manner, "No unclean thing can enter into the kingdom of heaven. But you by reason of the remnants of original sin are unclean. Therefore, you cannot enter into the kingdom of heaven," [then] we return our answer, saying that Christ's righteousness is our righteousness, serving to make us stand without blame or spot before God. And as Jacob put on Esau's garments that he might get his father's blessing, so if by faith we do put on the white garment of righteousness of our elder brother, Christ Jesus, and present ourselves in it unto our heavenly Father, we shall obtain His blessing, which is eternal happiness.

Now remains the third and last part of the conception, which [concerns] the union of the Godhead and the manhood, concerning which many points are particularly to be handled. The first is, what kind of union this is? *Answer.* In the Trinity there be two sorts of unions: union in nature and union in person. Union in nature is when two or more things are joined and united into one nature, as the Father, the Son, the Holy Ghost, being and remaining three distinct persons, are one and the same in nature or Godhead. Union in person is when two things are in that manner united, that they make but one person or substance—as a body created by God and a reasonable soul joined both together make one particular man, as Peter, Paul, John etc. And this second is the union whereof we entreat in this place, by which the second person in [the] Trinity, the Son of God, did unite unto Himself the human nature—that is, the body and soul of man—so as the Godhead of the Son and the manhood, concurring together, made but one person.

The second point is, in what thing this union does consist? *Answer.* It consists in this, that the second person, the Son of God, does assume unto it a manhood in such order, that it, being void of all personal being in itself, does wholly and only subsist in the same person. As the plant called mistle or mistletoe,[158] having no root of its[159] own, both grows and lives in the stock or body of the oak or some other tree, so the human nature, having no proper subsistence, is as it were engrafted into the person of the Son and is wholly supported and sustained by it so as it should not be at all, if it were not sustained in that manner. And for the better understanding of this point we must consider that there be four degrees of the presence of God in His creatures. The first is His general presence, and it may be called the presence of His providence, whereby He preserves the substances of all creatures and gives unto them to live, move, and have being [Acts 17:28]. And this extends itself to all creatures good and bad. The second degree is the presence of grace, whereby He does not only preserve the substances of all His creatures but also gives grace unto it. And this agrees to the church and people of God upon earth. The third degree is the presence of glory, peculiar to the saints and angels in heaven. And this stands in three things; for God not only preserves their substances and gives them plenty of His grace, but also admits them into His glorious presence so as they may behold His majesty face to face. The fourth and last is that whereby the Godhead of the Son is present and dwells with and in the manhood, giving unto it in some part His own subsistence. Whereby it comes to pass that this manhood assumed is proper to the Son and cannot be the manhood of the Father or of the Holy Ghost or of any creature whatsoever. And this is a thing so admirable and so unspeakable that among all the works of God there cannot be found another example hereof in all the world.

Hence it follows necessarily that the manhood of Christ, consisting of body and reasonable soul, is a nature only and not a person, because it does not subsist alone as other men, Peter, Paul, John do, but wholly depends on the person of the Word, into the unity whereof it is received.

The third point is in what order the divine and human nature of Christ are united together. *Answer.* The common consent of divines is that, albeit all the parts of the manhood and the Godhead of Christ be united at one instant, yet

---

158. Viscus Matthiol.
159. Originally, "his."

in respect of order He unites unto Himself first and immediately the soul and by the soul the body.[160] And it seems unmeet that God, being a most simple essence, should immediately be joined to a compound body. And therefore it may well be said that He is united unto it by the more simple part of man, which is the soul. Again, the manhood of Christ is first and immediately joined to the person of the Son Himself and by the person to the Godhead of the Son.

The fourth point is whether there remain any difference or diversity of the two natures after that the union is made. *Answer.* The two natures concurring make not the person of the Son to be compounded properly, but only by analogy; for as body and soul make one man, so God and man make one Christ. Neither are they turned one into another, the Godhead into the manhood or the manhood into the Godhead, as water was turned into wine at Cana in Galilee. Neither are they confused and mingled together as meats in the stomach. But they now are and so remain without composition, conversion, or confusion really distinct, and that in three respects. First, in regard of essence. For the Godhead of Christ is the Godhead and cannot be the manhood. And again, the manhood of Christ is the manhood and not the Godhead. Secondly, they are distinguished in properties. The Godhead is most wise, just, merciful, omnipotent, yea, wisdom, justice, mercy, and power itself. And so is not the manhood, neither can it be. Again, Christ as He is God has His will eternal and uncreated, which is all one with the will of the Father and the Holy Ghost. And as He is man He has another will created in time and placed in His reasonable soul, and this Christ signifies when He says, "Not my will, but thy will be done" [Luke 22:42]. Thirdly, they are distinct in their actions or operations, which though they go together inseparably in the work of redemption, yet they must in no wise be confounded but distinguished as the natures themselves are. Christ says of Himself, "I have power to lay down my life, and I have power to take it up again" [John 10:18], and hereby He shows the distinctions of operation in His two natures. For to lay down His life is an action of the manhood, because the Godhead cannot die. And to take it up again is the work of the Godhead alone, which reunites the soul to the body after death.

The fifth and last point is, what arises of this union? *Answer.* By reason of this hypostatical union, though the Godhead receive nothing from the manhood, yet the manhood itself, which is assumed, is thereby perfected and enriched with unspeakable dignity. For first of all, it is exalted above all creatures whatsoever, even angels themselves, in that it has subsistence in the second person in [the] Trinity. Secondly, together with the Godhead of the Son it is adored and worshipped with divine honor, as in like case the honor done

---

160. Damas. l. 3. cap 6. Cypr. in Symbol.

to the king himself redounds to the crown on his head. Thirdly, by reason of this union, the Godhead of Christ works all things in the matter of our redemption in and by the manhood. And hereupon the flesh of Christ, though it profit nothing of itself, yet by the virtue which it receives from that person to which it is joined it is quickening flesh and the bread of life [6:35]. Again, from this union of two natures into one person arises a kind of speech or phrase peculiar to the Scripture called the communication of properties, when the property of one nature is attributed to the whole person or to the other nature—as when Paul says that "God shed his blood" [Acts 20:28], that the "Lord of glory was crucified" [1 Cor. 2:8]. And when Christ says that He, talking with Nicodemus, "was then in heaven" [John 3:13].

The use of the personal union is threefold. *Use 1.*[161] First, it serves to show the heinousness of our sins and the greatness of our misery. For it had not been possible to make a satisfaction to God's justice in man's nature for the least offence, unless the same nature had first of all been nearly joined to the Godhead of the Son, that thereby it might be so far forth supported and sustained that it might overcome the wrath of God. *[Use] 2.* Secondly, it sets forth unto us the endless love of God to man. For whereas by reason of Adam's fall we were become the vilest of all creatures, except the devil and his angels, by this mystical conjunction our nature is exalted to such an estate and condition as is far above all creatures, even the angels themselves. *[Use] 3.* Thirdly, it is as it were the key of all our comfort; for all sound comfort stands in happiness; all happiness is in fellowship with God; all fellowship with God is by Christ, who for this cause, being very God, became very man, that He might reconcile man to God and God to man.

Thus much of the conception of Christ. Now follows His birth, whereby in the ordinary time of travail according to the course of nature He was brought forth into the world by the Virgin Mary [Luke 2:6]. And it was the will of God that Christ should not only be conceived but also born, and that after the manner of men, that He might be known to be very man indeed. In the birth, we may consider four things: the time, the place, the manner, the manifestation of it.

The time was in the "last days" [Isa. 2:2], toward the end of the seventy weeks of Daniel [Dan. 9:24], which are to be accounted from the end of the captivity of Babylon and make in all four hundred ninety years, or, more plainly, three thousand nine hundred years and more from the beginning of the world, and as Paul says, "in the fullness of time" [Gal. 4:4]. And the evangelists have noted of purpose the time to have been when Augustus Caesar taxed the Jews and all nations under his dominion [Luke 2:1], to signify that Christ was born

---

161. Originally in the margin, as the additional two uses following.

at the very time foretold by Jacob, when the crown and scepter was taken from Judah, and withal to show that His kingdom was not of this world. And it was the good pleasure of God that Christ should not be born either later or sooner, but so many ages from the beginning of the world. And this consideration of the very time itself serves greatly for the confirmation of our faith. For thus may we reason with ourselves: if God, who in the beginning made a promise to our first parents concerning the seed of the woman, deferred it almost four thousand years and yet at length accomplished the same to the very full, then no doubt God, having promised the resurrection of the dead and life everlasting, will in His good time bring them to pass, though as yet we see them not. And thus by the accomplishment of all things past should we confirm our hopes concerning things to come.

The place was not at Jerusalem nor Nazareth nor any other city, but only a village of Judah called Bethlehem, that the prophecy of Micah might be fulfilled, "Thou Bethlehem Ephrata art little to be among the thousands of Judah, yet out of thee shall he come forth unto me, that shall be ruler in Israel" [Mic. 5:2]. And here we may observe a memorable example of God's providence, which overrules the proceedings of cruel tyrants to the accomplishing of His own will, they themselves for their parts intending nothing less. Augustus, not so much as dreaming of the birth of the Messiah, gave commandment that every man should go to his own city to be taxed. And hereupon Joseph and Mary take their journey from Nazareth to Bethlehem, which journey God Himself appointed and disposed to this end, that the Messiah might be born in the place which He preordained and foretold by His prophets.

The manner of Christ's birth was very base and poor, for the place where He was born was a stable, and the cradle where He lay was a cratch. And He willingly took upon Him this poverty for sundry causes. (1) That the Scripture might be fulfilled, which says that He should be the "shame and contempt of the people" [Ps. 22:6], and that He shall grow up "as a root out of a dry ground, and have neither form nor beauty" [Isa. 53:2]. (2) That He might afterward from this base condition be exalted even in His manhood to that rich and glorious estate in which He should manifest Himself to be Lord of heaven and earth. (3) He was born in exceeding poverty, that He might shame the wise men of this world, who exceedingly esteem of their riches, power, and glory, persuading themselves that without such means nothing can be done. And yet for all this they cannot so much as reconcile one man to God by all their might and wealth, whereas Christ Himself has done the same both in poverty and weakness and can enlarge and preserve His kingdom without earthly helps. When He hung upon the cross, the soldiers stripped Him of His garments, and, being naked, He brought that to pass which all the monarchs of the earth in all their royalties could never have performed. And whether Christ lie in the manger between the ox and the ass or in the palace of the king, it matters not in regard of our salvation. (4) He came in this manner, that there might be a difference between His first coming in the flesh and His last coming to judgment. In the first, He came only for this end, not to make any outward alterations in the world, but to change the conscience and to put in execution the work of our spiritual redemption. And therefore He has reserved the overturning of all earthly estates, with the manifestation of His own glory to the latter. (5) Lastly, He was born in a poor estate, that He might procure true riches for us in heaven and withal sanctify unto us our poverty upon earth. As Paul says, "Ye know the grace of our Lord Jesus Christ, that he being rich, for your sakes became poor, that ye through his poverty might be made rich" [2 Cor. 8:9]. He was content to lie in the manger, that we might rest in heaven.

This serves to teach us to be content to bear any mean condition that the Lord shall send upon us; for this is the very estate of the Son of God Himself. And if for our cause He did not refuse the basest condition that ever was, why should we murmur at the same? For what are the best of us but miserable sinners and therefore utterly unworthy either to go or lie upon the bare earth? And though we fare and lie better than our Lord Himself, yet such is our daintiness [that] we are not pleased therewith—whereas He for His part disdained not the manger of the ox. And if the Lord of heaven and earth, coming into the world, find so little entertainment or favor, we for our parts, being His members, should willingly prepare ourselves to take as hard measure at the hands of men.

The last point is the manifestation of Christ's birth, that it may be known to the world. Where consider two circumstances: the first, to whom? Namely, to poor shepherds, tending their flocks by night [Luke 2:8–9], and not to great or mighty men, lovers of this world, not to the priests at Jerusalem, contemners of God's grace—and that for two causes: one, because the shepherds were the fittest persons to publish the same at Bethlehem; the other, it was God's pleasure to manifest that in the birth of Christ which Paul says, "Not many wise men after the flesh, not many mighty, not many noble are called: but God hath chosen the foolish things of the world to confound the wise" [1 Cor. 1:27]. The second is, by whom? By the angels of the Lord, appearing in great glory unto the shepherds. For the priests of Jerusalem and the rulers of the synagogues to whom this office did belong held their peace, being blinded in their manifold errors and wicked ways.

The duties to be learned from the birth of Christ are these. First, we are admonished hereby to magnify and praise the name of God, saying with Mary, "My soul doth magnify the Lord, and my spirit rejoiceth in God my Savior" [Luke 1:46–47]; and with Zacharias, "Blessed be the Lord God of Israel, for he hath visited and redeemed his people" [v. 68]; and with the angels of heaven, "Glory to God in the highest heavens" [2:14].[162] For in this birth is made manifest the wisdom, the truth, the justice, mercy, and goodness of God toward us, more than ever it was before. Yea, as Christ, God and man, is more excellent than the first Adam, created according to God's own image; and as the spiritual life is better than the natural life; and as the eternal and most holy marriage of Christ, the husband, and His spouse, the church, arising as it were out of the blood that trickled out of His side, is more wonderful than the creation of Eve of the rib of Adam; lastly, as it is a far greater matter by death to overcome death and to turn it unto eternal life than to command that to exist and be, which was not before—so is the work of redemption, begun in the birth of Christ, more unspeakable and admirable than the first creation of man. Hereupon not six cherubim, as in the vision of Isaiah, not twenty-four elders, as in the Apocalypse, but a great multitude of angels like armies were heard to praise God at the birth of Christ. And no doubt the like sight was not seen since the beginning of the world. And the angels by their example put us in mind to consider aright of this benefit and to praise God for it. But alas, this practice is very rare in this fruitless and barren age of the world, where sin and iniquity abounds, as may be seen by experience; for by an old custom we retain still in the church the feast of the nativity of Christ, so commonly called, which nevertheless is not spent in praising the name of God, who has sent His Son from His own bosom to be our Redeemer; but contrariwise in rifling, dicing, carding, masking, mumming, and in all licentious liberty for the most part, as though it were some heathen feast of Ceres or Bacchus.

Secondly, Christ was conceived and born in bodily manner, that there might be a spiritual conception and birth of Him in our hearts, as Paul says, "My little children, of whom I travail till Christ be formed in you" [Gal. 4:19]—and that is, when we are made new creatures by Christ and perform obedience to our Creator. When the people said to Christ that His mother and His brethren sought Him, He answered, "He that doth the will of God, is my brother, my sister, and mother" [Mark 3:35]. Therefore, let us go with the shepherds to Bethlehem, and finding our blessed Savior swaddled and lying in the cratch, let us bring Him thence and make our own hearts to be His cradle, that we may be able to say that we live not, but Christ lives in us. And let us present unto Him ourselves, our bodies and souls, as the best gold, myrrh, and frankincense that may be. And thus conceiving Him by faith, He remaining without change, we shall be changed into Him and made bone of His bone and flesh of His flesh. The world, I know, never so much as dreams of this kind of conception and

---

162. Originally, "Luke 1:14."

birth; for as David says, "Men travail with wickedness, conceive mischief, and bring forth a lie" [Ps. 7:14].[163] And St. James says, "Men are drawn away by their own concupiscence, which when it hath conceived, bringeth forth sin" [James 1:14–15]. And these are the ugly and monstrous births of these days. But let us, I pray you, contrariwise wail and mourn for the barrenness of our hearts, that do so little conceive the grace of Christ in heart and bring it forth in action. The mother of Christ undoubtedly was a blessed woman; but if she had not as well conceived Christ in her heart as she did in her womb, she had not been saved. And no more can we, unless we do the same.

The birth of Christ to them that have touched hearts is the comfort of comforts and the sweetest balm of confection that ever was. "Behold," say the angels to the shepherds, "we bring tidings of great joy that shall be to all people" [Luke 2:10]—but wherein stands the joy? They add further, "Unto you this day is born in the city of David a Savior, which is Christ the Lord" [v. 11]. And no marvel, for in that birth is manifested the good will of God to man. And by it we have peace, first, with God; secondly, with ourselves in conscience; thirdly, with the good angels of God; fourthly, with our enemies; lastly, with all the creatures. For this cause the angels sang, "Peace on earth, good will toward men" [v. 14].

In the last place, the Creed notes unto us the parent or mother of Christ, "the virgin Mary." And here at the very first it may be demanded how He could have either father or mother, because He was figured by Melchizedek, who had neither father nor mother [Heb. 7:3]. *Answer.* Melchizedek is said to be without father and mother not because he had none at all, for according to the ancient and received opinion it is very likely that he was Shem, the son of Noah,[164] but because where he is mentioned under this name of Melchizedek in Genesis 14 there is no mention made of father or mother. And so Christ in some sort is without father or mother. As He is man, He has no father; as He is God, He has no mother. And whereas Christ is called the son of Joseph [Matt. 1:16;[165] Luke 4:22; John 1:45; 6:42], it was not because He was begotten of him, but because Joseph was His reputed father, or, which is more, because he was a legal father—namely, according to the Jews, in that (as sundry divines think) He was the next of his kin and therefore to succeed him as his lawful heir.

Mary became the mother of Christ by a kind of calling thereto, which was by an extraordinary message of an angel concerning the conception and birth of Christ in and by her, to which calling and message she condescended, saying, "Behold, the handmaid of the Lord, be it unto me according to thy word" [Luke 1:38]. And hereupon she conceived by the Holy Ghost. This being so, it is more

---

163. Originally, "Ps. 7:12."
164. Hier. ep. ad Euagr.
165. Originally, "Matt. 13:15."

than senseless folly to turn the salutation of the angel, "Hail freely beloved," etc., into a prayer. For it is as much as if we should still call her to become a mother of a christ. And she must be held to be the mother of whole Christ, God and man; and therefore the ancient church has called her "the mother of God," yet not "the mother of the Godhead."

Furthermore, the mother of Christ is described by her quality, a virgin, and by her name, Mary. She was a virgin, first, that Christ might be conceived without sin and be a perfect savior; secondly, that the saying of the prophet Isaiah might be fulfilled, "Behold, a virgin shall conceive and bear a son" [Isa. 7:14], according as it was foretold by God in the first giving of the promise. The "seed of the woman" [Gen. 3:15], not the seed of the man, shall bruise the serpent's head. Now, the Jews to elude the most pregnant testimony of the prophet say that [the Hebrew] "alma" signifies not a virgin but a young woman which has known a man. But this is indeed a forgery. For Isaiah there speaks of an extraordinary work of God above nature, whereas for a woman having known man to conceive is no wonder. And the word "alma" through the whole Bible is taken for a virgin, as by a particular search will appear [Gen. 24:16; Ex. 2:5].

As Mary conceived a virgin, so it may be well thought that she continued a virgin to the end, though we make it no article of our faith. When Christ was upon the cross, He commended His mother to the custody of John [John 19:27], which probably argues that she had no child to whose care and keeping she might be commended. And though Christ be called her firstborn, yet does it not follow that she had any children after Him; for as that is called last after which there is none, so that is called the first before which there were none. And as for Joseph, when he was espoused to Mary, he was a man of eighty years old.[166]

And here we have an occasion to praise the wisdom of God in the forming of man. The first man, Adam, was born of no man but immediately created of God. The second—that is, Eve—is formed not of a woman, but of a man alone. The third and all after [are] begotten both of woman and man. The fourth, that is Christ, God and man, [is] not of no man as Adam, not of no woman as Eve, nor of man and woman as we, but after a new manner—of a woman without a man He is conceived and born.

And hereupon our duty is not to despise but highly to reverence the Virgin Mary as being the mother of the Son of God [Luke 1:48], a prophetess upon earth, a saint in heaven. And we do willingly condescend to give her honor three ways: first, by thanksgiving to God for her; secondly, by a reverent estimation of her; thirdly, by imitation of her excellent virtues. Yet far be it from us to adore her with divine honor, by prayer to call upon her, as though she knew

166. Epiph. l. 2. to. I.

our hearts and heard our requests, and to place her in heaven as a queen above the Son of God.

The name of the mother of Christ is added to show that He came of the lineage of David, and that therefore He was the true Messiah before spoken of. It may be objected that both Matthew and Luke set down the genealogy of Joseph, of whom Christ was not. *Answer*. Matthew sets down indeed in Christ's genealogy the natural descent of Joseph, the husband of Mary, having Jacob for his natural father. But Luke, taking another course, propounds the natural descent of Mary, the mother of Christ. And when he says that Joseph was the son of Eli, he means of a legal son. For sons- and daughters-in-law are called sons and daughters to their fathers- and mothers-in-law, Mary herself and not Joseph being the natural daughter of Eli.[167] And whereas Luke does plainly say that Mary was the daughter of Eli, but puts Joseph the son-in-law in her room, the reason hereof may be because it was the manner of the Jews to account and continue their genealogies in the male and not in the female sex, the man being the head of the family and not the woman. And though Ruth and Rahab and other women be mentioned by Matthew, yet that is only by the way; for they make no degrees herein. Again, it may be further demanded how Christ could come of David by Solomon, as Matthew says, and by Nathan, as Luke says, they twain being two distinct sons of David. *Answer*. By virtue of the law whereby the brother was bound to raise up seed to his brother there was a double descent in use among the Jews—the one was natural; the other, legal. Natural, when one man descended of another by generation, as the child from the natural father. Legal, when a man not begotten of another yet did succeed him in his inheritance [Deut. 25:5–6]. And thus Salathiel is the natural son of Neri and the legal son of Jechonias. Now, St. Luke sets down a natural descent of Christ from David by Nathan; and St. Matthew the other descent, which is legal, by Solomon [Matt. 1:12; Luke 3:27], whom Christ succeeded in the right of the kingdom, being born the king of the Jews, none that could possibly be named having more right to it than He.

By this descent of Christ, we have occasion to consider that Christ was even in His birth the most excellent and noble man that ever was, descending of the eternal Father as He is the Son of God and as He is man descending of the patriarchs and of the renowned kings of Judah. And this His nobility He conveys in part to His members, in that He makes them the sons of God, a royal priesthood, and a peculiar people to Himself, enriching them also with the revenues of the whole world and with title and right to the kingdom of glory in heaven as their inheritance.

---

167. Aphrie. apud Euseb. Damas. lib. 4. c. 15.

And withal Christ being the lively pattern of true nobility, by His example men of blood are taught not to stand so much on their pedigree and their ancestors, as though nobility stood in this, that man descends of man, but to labor withal that they may be the sons and daughters of God by regeneration in Christ. This indeed is the ornament of the blood, the best part in the nobleman's [e]scutcheon, and the finest flower in his garland. And though a man be never so noble or great in estate, yet if he be not a repentant sinner, he is base and vile, and his nobility stinks in the nostrils of God. Christ in His genealogy does not so much as vouchsafe to name those His ancestors that ruled wickedly; and hereupon St. Matthew omits three kings of Judah, Ahaziah, Joash, and Amaziah, whereas nevertheless heinous offenders that repented are mentioned, as Ruth and Tamar and Bathsheba.

Thus much of the incarnation of Christ. Now follows the third and last point which is to be considered in the description of Christ—namely, the estate of Christ after His birth, which is twofold: the estate of humiliation and the estate of exaltation.

The estate of humiliation is the condition of Christ the Mediator in which He abased Himself even to the death of the cross, that by that means He might perform the office of a priest in making satisfaction to the justice of His Father.

This estate agrees to the whole person of Christ according to both natures. For first of all His manhood was abased and humbled, in that it was made subject to the infirmities of man's nature, as also to the miseries and punishments which were due unto man for sin. Secondly, His Godhead was abased, not as is considered in itself, for so it admits no alteration or change, but in respect of the flesh or manhood assumed, under the which, as under a veil, the Godhead lay hid from the first moment of the incarnation to the time of His resurrection, without any great manifestation of His power and majesty therein.

The order of these two estates must be marked. The first is the estate of humiliation, and then in the second place follows the estate of exaltation—as Christ says of Himself, "O fools, and slow of heart to believe, etc., ought not Christ to have suffered these things, and to enter into his glory?" [Luke 24:26]. And here we for our parts must learn a lesson. The same which was true in Christ, the Head, must be verified in all His members. They must all have their twofold estate—first, in this life the estate of humiliation; secondly, after this life the estate of glory. And as Christ first entered into the estate of His humiliation and then into glory, so it is with His members. First, they must be abased in this life and, secondly, exalted in the world to come. He that will reign with Christ and be exalted must first suffer with Him and be humbled. He that will wear the crown of glory must wear first a crown of thorns. They that will have all tears wiped from their eyes must here first in this life shed them. And the children of God before they can sing the song of Moses and of the servants of God and of the Lamb must first swim through the sea of burning glass [Rev. 15:2–3], whereby is signified that those which after this life would sing songs of praises to Christ must in this life be cast into a sea of misery. And if this be true, then we may here learn that it is a wretched case for a man in this life to have perpetual ease, rest, and quietness both in body and soul, goods, and good name. For we see by Christ's example that through adversity we must come to happiness, and if a man would have rest and peace in the life to come, then in this life he must look for trouble, persecution, and sorrow. Indeed, in the judgment of the world they are blessed that always live at rest, but before God they are most miserable and (as oxen which are made fat in the best pasture) ready for the slaughterhouse every day. Secondly, here is an excellent consolation for those which profess the gospel of Christ. In the time of trouble and persecution, they must rejoice, because the state of humiliation in this life is a sign that they are in the plain and right way to salvation and glory. A man is to take his journey into a far country; and, inquiring for the way, it is told him that there are many plain ways, but the strait and right way is by woods and hills and mountains and great dangers. Now, when he is traveling and comes into those places, he gathers certainly that he is in the right way. So the child of God, that is going to the kingdom of heaven, though there be many ways to walk in, yet he knows that there is but one right way, which is very strait and narrow, full of trouble, sorrow, and persecution, full of all manner of crosses and afflictions. And when in this life he is persecuted and afflicted for good causes, whether in body or in mind, if he be content to bear his cross, it argues plainly that he is in the right way to salvation; for "through many afflictions we must enter into the kingdom of heaven" [Acts 14:22].[168]

The humiliation of Christ is first of all set down in the Creed generally and, secondly, by its parts or degrees. Generally, in these words: "suffered under Pontius Pilate." Where we must consider two things: the passion itself and under whom it was. For the first, that we may the better conceive the passion in its own nature, seven special points must be opened.

(1) The cause efficient.[169] The principal cause of the passion as it is the price of our redemption was the decree and providence of God, as Peter says expressly that Christ was delivered by the determinate counsel and foreknowledge of God [2:23]. The impulsive cause that moved God to work our salvation by this means was nothing in man (for all mankind was shut up under unbelief and therefore unable to procure the least favor at God's hands), but the will and

168. Originally, "Acts 4:12."
169. This paragraph break is not in the original, as the additional six following.

good pleasure of God within Himself. The instruments which the Lord used in this business were the wicked Jews and Gentiles and the devil himself, by whom He brought to pass the most admirable work of redemption, even then when they according to their kind did nothing else but practice wickedness and malice against Christ.

(2) The matter of the passion is the whole malediction or curse of the law, containing in it all manner of adversities and miseries both of body and mind. All which may be reduced to three heads: the temptations of Christ; His ignominies and slanders; His manifold sorrows and griefs, especially those which stand in the apprehension of the unsupportable wrath of God.

(3) The form of the passion is that excellent and meritorious satisfaction which in suffering Christ made unto His Father for man's sin. We do not rightly consider of the passion if we conceive it to be a bare and naked suffering of punishment, but withal we must conceive it as a propitiation or a means satisfactory to God's justice. The passion considered as a passion ministers no comfort. But all our joy and rejoicing stands in this, that by faith we apprehend it as it is a satisfaction or a means of reconciliation for our offences. In this very point stands the dignity of the passion, whereby it differs from all other sufferings of men whatsoever. Therefore, most damnable and wicked is the opinion of the Papists, who besides the alone passion of Christ maintain works of satisfaction partly of their own and partly of the saints departed, which they add to the passion as an appendance thereof.

(4) The end of the passion is that God might bring to pass a work in which He might more fully manifest His justice and mercy than He did in the creation, and that is the reconciliation between God and man. And here remember with the passion to join the active obedience of Christ in fulfilling the law; for Christ in suffering obeyed, and in obeying suffered. And they must be jointly conceived together for this cause. In reconciliation with God, two things are required: the removing of sin in regard of the guilt, of the fault, and the punishment; and the conferring or giving of righteousness. Now the passion of Christ considered apart from His legal obedience only takes away the guilt and punishment, frees man from death, and makes Him of a sinner to be no sinner.[170] And that he may be fully reconciled to God and accepted as righteous to life everlasting, the legal obedience of Christ must also be imputed. And therefore in the Scriptures, where all our redemption is ascribed to the death and passion of Christ, this very obedience which stands in the perfect love of God and man must be included and not excluded.

---

170. 1. Non peccator. 2. Justus.

(5) The time of the passion was from the very birth of Christ to His resurrection, yet so as the beginning only of His sufferings were in the course of His life, and the accomplishment thereof to the very full, upon the cross.

(6) The person that suffered was the Son of God Himself, concerning whom in this case two questions must be resolved. The first, how can it stand with God's justice to lay punishment upon the most righteous man that ever was, and that for grievous sinners, considering that tyrants themselves will not do so? *Answer.* In the passion, Christ must not be considered as a private person—for then it could not stand with equity that He should be plagued and punished for our offences—but as one in the eternal counsel of God set apart to be a public surety or pledge for us [Heb. 7:22] to suffer and perform those things which we in our own persons should have suffered and performed. For this cause God the Father is said to give His Son unto us, and the Son again to give His life for His friends (John 3:16; 15:13). The second question is, how by the short and temporary death of the Son of God any man can possibly be freed from eternal death and damnation which is due unto Him for the least sin? *Answer.* When we say that the Son of God suffered, it must be understood with distinction of the natures of Christ, not in respect of the Godhead but in respect of the assumed manhood. Yet nevertheless the passion is to be ascribed to the whole person of Christ, God and man. And from the dignity of the person which suffered arises the dignity and excellency of the passion, whereby it is made in value and price to countervail everlasting damnation. For when as the Son of God suffered the curse for a short time, it is more than if all men and angels had suffered the same forever.

(7) The difference of the passion of Christ and the sufferings of martyrs, and that stands in two things. First, Christ's passion was a cursed punishment; the sufferings of the martyrs are no curses but either chastisements or trials. Secondly, the passion of Christ is meritorious for us even before God, because He became our Mediator and Surety in the covenant of grace. But the sufferings of martyrs are not of value to merit for us at God's hand, because in suffering they were but private men, and therefore they nothing appertain to us. By this it appears that the treasury of the Church of Rome, which is as it were a common chest containing the overplus of the merits of saints, mingled with the merits of Christ, kept and disposed by the pope himself, is nothing else but a senseless dotage of man's brain. And whereas they say that Christ by His death did merit that saints might merit both for themselves and others, it is as much as if they should say the Son of God became Jesus to make everyone Jesus. And it is a manifest untruth which they say. For the very manhood of Christ, considered apart from the Godhead, cannot merit properly, considering whatsoever it is, has, or does, it is, has, and does the same wholly and only by grace.

Whereas therefore Christ merits for us, it is by reason He is both God and man in one person. For this cause it is not possible that one mere man should merit for another.

The use of the passion follows. It is the manner of friars and Jesuits in the Church of Rome[171] to use the consideration of the passion of Christ as a means to stir up compassion in themselves partly toward Christ, who suffered grievous torments, and partly toward the Virgin Mary, who for the torments of her dear Son was exceedingly troubled, and withal to kindle in their hearts an indignation toward the Jews that put Christ to death. But indeed this kind of use is mere human and may in like manner be made by reading of any human history. But the proper and special use of the passion indeed is this: first of all, we must set it before our eyes as a looking glass in which we may clearly behold the horribleness of our sins, that could not be pardoned without the passion of the Son of God, and the unspeakable love of Christ, that died for us and therefore loved His own enemies more than His own life, and, lastly, our endless peace with God and happiness. In that, considering the person of our Redeemer, who suffered the pangs of hell, we may after a sort find our paradise even in the midst of hell.

Secondly, the meditation of Christ's passion serves as a most worthy means to begin and to confirm grace, specially when it is mingled with faith, and that two ways. For, first, it serves to breed in our hearts a godly sorrow for our sins past when we do seriously with ourselves consider that our own sins were the cause of all the pains and sorrows and calamities which He suffered in life and death. When any man had sinned under the law, he brought unto the temple or tabernacle some kind of beast for an offering according as he was prescribed, laying his hand upon the head of it and afterward slaying it before the Lord (Lev 4:4, 29). Now by the ceremony of laying on the hand, he testified that he for his part had deserved death, and not the beast; and that it, being slain and sacrificed, was a sign unto him of the sacrifice of Christ offered upon the cross for his sins. And hereby we are taught that so oft as we remember the passion of Christ we should lay our hands as it were upon our own heads, utterly accusing and condemning ourselves, evermore keeping this in our hearts, that Christ suffered not for Himself but for our offences, which were the proper cause of all His woe and misery. And as Christ's passion was grievous and bitter unto Him, so should our sins likewise be grievous and bitter unto us. Let us always remember this, otherwise we shall never reap any sound benefit by the passion of Christ.

Again, the passion of Christ is a notable means to stir up in our hearts a purpose and a care to reform ourselves and live in holiness and newness of life,

---

171. Lud. gran.

on this manner. "Has the Son of God so mercifully dealt with me as to suffer the curse of the whole law for my manifold iniquities and to deliver me from just and deserved damnation? Yea, no doubt, He has; I am resolved of it. If I should go on in mine old course, I should be the most ungrateful of all creatures to this my loving Savior. I will therefore by His grace return and reform my life." And in this very point of reformation, the passion of Christ is set before us as a most lively pattern and example to follow. "For as much," says St. Peter, "as Christ hath suffered for us in the flesh, arm yourselves likewise with the same mind, which is, that he which hath suffered in the flesh, hath ceased from sin" (1 Peter 4:1). Where he teaches that there must be in us a spiritual passion answerable to the passion of Christ. For as His enemies did laden Him with miseries even to the death of the cross, so should we laden our own flesh—that is, the corruption of our natures—with all such means as may subdue and weaken, crucify and kill it. To the doing of this, three things especially are required.

First, we must consider that the corruption of our rebellious natures is like the great and mighty Goliath, and the grace of God, which we receive, like young and little David.[172] And therefore, if we desire that grace should prevail against corruption, we must disarm the strong man and strip him of all his weapons, which is done by giving all the members of our bodies to be instruments of the service of God in righteousness and holiness.

Secondly, we must endeavor to keep in the corruption of nature, as it were choking and smothering it in the heart, that by it neither the world nor the devil prevail against us. And this must be done by having a narrow regard unto all the powers and faculties of body and soul, setting a watch before our eyes, ears, lips, and all other parts of the body [Job 31:1; Ps. 119:37] that are in any action the instruments of the soul, and, above all, as Solomon says, "By counterguarding the heart with all diligence" [Prov. 4:23]. By the outward senses of the body as through open windows the devil creeps into the heart, and therefore our duty is to stop all such ways of entrance.

Thirdly, when original corruption begins to rebel either in the mind, will, or any of the affections, then must we draw out the sword of the Spirit, which is the Word of God, and encounter with that hideous giant, laying load upon him by the judgments and threatenings of the law and as it were "beating him down with clubs," as Paul speaks [1 Cor. 9:27].[173] And if it fall out that concupiscence begin to conceive and bring forth any sin, we must bruise it in the head and dash it against the ground as a bird in the shell, lest it grow up to our utter confusion. These are the duties which we should learn by the passion of Christ.

---

172. This paragraph break is not in the original, as the additional two paragraphs following.
173. Originally, "1 Cor. 4:27." ὑπωπιάζω.

But lamentable are our days, in which all for the most part goes contrary; for commonly men are so far from killing and subduing the rebellion of the natural concupiscence that all their study and care is how they may feed and cherish it and make it stronger than the mighty Goliath. But let us for our parts be conformable to Christ in His passion, suffering in our flesh as He suffered in body and soul for us. And let us daily more and more by the hand of faith apprehend and apply to our hearts and consciences the passion of Christ, that it may as a fretting corrosive eat out the poison of our sinful natures and consume it.

Now follows the second point concerning the passion of Christ, which is under whom He suffered—namely, "under Pontius Pilate." And Christ may be said to suffer under him in two respects. First, because he was then the president of Jewry [Luke 3:1]. For a little before the birth of Christ, the kingdom of the Jews was taken away by the Roman emperor and reduced into a province, and Pontius Pilate was placed over the Jews not as king but as the Roman emperor's deputy. And this circumstance is noted in the history of the Gospel and here specified in the Creed to show that the Messiah was exhibited in the time foretold by the prophets. Jacob foretold that Shiloh must be born after the scepter is removed from Judah [Gen. 49:10]. Isaiah says that the family of Jesse shall be worn as it were to the root before Christ as a branch shall spring out of it [Isa. 11:1]. Again, Christ suffered under Pontius Pilate as he was a judge, whereby we are given to understand of a wonder—namely, that Christ, the Son of God, King of heaven and earth, was arraigned at the bar of an earthly judge and there condemned. For thus much the words in meaning import, that Pontius Pilate sat as a judge upon Christ to examine Him, to arraign Him, and give sentence against Him. Wherefore, before we come to speak of the degrees of the passion of Christ, we must needs entreat of His arraignment upon earth. In handling whereof we must generally consider these points. First, that when He was arraigned before Pilate, He was not as a private man but as a pledge and surety that stood in the place and stead of us miserable sinners [Heb. 7:22]. As the prophet Isaiah says, "He bare our iniquities, and carried our sorrows" [Isa. 53:4]; and withal in Him was mankind arraigned before God. Secondly, this arraignment was made not privately in a corner but openly in the public court, and that in a great feast of the Jews, as it were in the hearing of the whole world. Thirdly, though Pilate in citing, examining, and condemning Christ intended not to work any part of man's redemption, yet was this wholly set down in the counsel and good pleasure of God in whose room Pilate sat and whose judgment he exercised [2 Chron. 19:6].

The general use of Christ's arraignment is twofold. First, it is a terror to all impenitent sinners; for there is no freedom or protection from the judgment of God, but by the arraignment of Christ. And therefore such as in this life receive not Him by faith must at the end of this world be brought out to the most terrible bar of the last judgment, there to be arraigned before the King of heaven and earth. And mark the equity hereof. Christ Himself could not have been our Savior and Redeemer, unless He had been brought out to the bar of an earthly judge and arraigned as a guilty malefactor. And there is no man upon earth that lives and dies out of Christ but he must, whether he will or no, hold up his hand at the bar of the great Judge of all mankind, where he shall see hell underneath him, burning red hot and opening itself wide to swallow him up; and on the right hand of God standing all the prophets, apostles, and saints of God, giving judgment against him; on the left hand, the devil and all his angels accusing him; and within him a guilty conscience, condemning him. And thus one day shall the arraignment of those persons be that with full purpose of heart cleave not to Christ. And yet, alas, huge and infinite is the number of those which make more account of transitory and earthly matters, even of their pigs with the Gadarenes, than of Him and His benefits; and such persons should rather be pitied than despised of us all, considering their estate is such that every day they are going as traitors pinioned to their own judgment, that they may go thence to eternal execution.

Secondly, Christ's arraignment is a comfort to the godly. For He was arraigned before Pilate, that all such as truly believe in Him might not be arraigned before God at the day of the last judgment. He was accused before an earthly judge, that they might be cleared and excused before the heavenly Judge. Lastly, He was here condemned on earth, that we might receive the sentence of absolution and be eternally saved in heaven.

The arraignment of Christ has three parts: His apprehension, His accusation, His condemnation. In the apprehension, we must consider two things: the dealing of Christ and the dealing of Judas and the Jews. The dealing and proceeding of Christ was this: when He saw that the time of His apprehension and death was near, He solemnly prepared Himself thereto. And His example must teach every one of us, who know not the shortness of our days, every hour to prepare ourselves against the day of death, that then we may be found ready of the Lord. What? Shall the Son of God Himself make preparation to His own death, and shall not we most miserable sinners do the same, who stand in need of a thousand preparations more than He? Wherefore, let us continually think with ourselves that every present day is the last day of our life, that so we may address ourselves to death against the next day.

The first thing which Christ does in this preparation is to make choice of the place in which He was to be apprehended, as will appear by conferring the evangelists together. St. Matthew says He went to the place called Gethsemane (Matt. 26:36). St. Luke says He went to the Mount of Olives as He "was accustomed" (Luke 22:39). And that we might not imagine that Christ did this that He might escape and hide Himself from the Jews, St. John says that "Judas which betrayed him knew the place, because oftentimes he resorted thither with his disciples" [John 18:2], whereas if He had feared apprehension, He would have rather gone aside to some other secret and unwonted place. This then is the first point to be considered, that Christ, knowing the time of His own death to be at hand, does willingly of His own accord resort to such a place in which His enemies in all likelihood might easily find Him and have fit opportunity to attack Him. For if He should have still remained in Jerusalem, the scribes and Pharisees durst not have enterprised His apprehension because of the people, whom they feared. But out of the city in the garden all occasion of fear is cut off. By this it is manifest that Christ yielded Himself to death willingly and not of constraint; and unless His sufferings had been voluntary on His part, they could never have been a satisfaction to God's justice for our sins. Here a question offers itself to be considered, whether a man may lawfully fly in danger and persecution, seeing Christ Himself does not? *Answer.* When good means of flying and just occasion is offered, it is lawful to fly. When the Jews sought to kill Paul at Damascus, the disciples took him by night and put him through the wall and let him down in a basket to escape their hands [Acts 9:25]. When Moses was called by God to deliver the Israelites after he had slain the Egyptian, and the fact was known, and Pharaoh sought to kill him for it, he fled to the land of Midian [Ex. 2:15]. And our Savior Christ sundry times when He was to be stoned and other ways hurt by the Jews withdrew Himself from among them [John 8:59; 10:31, 39; 11:54]. It is lawful then to fly in persecution, these caveats observed. (1) If a man find not himself sufficiently strengthened to bear the cross. (2) His departure must be agreeable to the general calling of a Christian, serving to the glory of God and the good of his brethren and the hurt of none. (3) There must be freedom at the least for a time from the bond of a man's particular calling. If he be a magistrate, he must be freed from ruling; if a minister, from preaching and teaching—otherwise he may not fly. And in this respect Christ, who withdrew Himself at other times, would not fly at this time, because the hour of His suffering was come wherein He intended most willingly to submit Himself to the good pleasure and will of His Father [18:4].

The second part of the preparation is the prayer which Christ made unto His Father in the garden. And herein His example does teach us earnestly to pray unto God against the danger of imminent death and the temptations which are to come. And if Christ, who was without sin and had the Spirit above measure, had need to pray, then much more have we need to be watchful in all kinds of prayers who are laden with the burden of sin and compassed about with manifold impediments and dangerous enemies.

In this prayer, sundry points worthy our marking are to be considered. The first, who prayed? *Answer.* Christ, the Son of God. But still we must remember the distinction of natures and of their operations in one and the same Christ. He prays not in His Godhead, but according to His manhood. The second is for whom He prays. *Answer.* Some have thought that this and all other His prayers were made for His mystical body the church. But the truth is, He now prays for Himself, yet not as He was God, for the Godhead feels no want, but as He was a man abased in the form of a servant—and that for two causes. First, in that He was a man, He was a creature and in that respect was to perform homage to God the Creator. Secondly, as He was man, He put on the infirmities of our nature and thereupon prayed that He might have strength and power in His manhood to support Him in bearing the whole brunt of the passion to come.

The third point is to whom He prayed. *Answer.* To the Father. Neither must this trouble us, as though Christ in praying to the Father should pray to Himself, because He is one and the same God with Him. For though in essence they admit no distinction, yet in person or in the proper manner of subsisting they do.[174] The Father is one person; the Son, another. Therefore, as the Father saying from heaven, "This is my well beloved Son," spoke not to Himself but to the Son, so again the Son, when He prays, He prays not to Himself but to the Father.

The fourth point [is] what was the particular cause of His prayer. *Answer.* His agony, in which His soul was heavy unto death, not because He feared bodily death, but because the malediction of the law, even the very heat of the fury and indignation of God was poured forth upon Him, wherewith He was affected and troubled, as if He had been defiled with the sins of the whole world. And this appears, first, by the words whereby the evangelists express the agony of Christ, which signify exceeding great sorrow and grief [Matt. 26:37]. Secondly, His doleful complaint to His disciples in the garden: "My soul is heavy unto the death" [v. 38]. Thirdly, by His fervent prayer thrice repeated, full of doleful passions. Fourthly, by the coming of an angel to comfort Him. Fifthly, by His bloody sweat, the like whereof was never heard. And herein lies the difference between Christ's agony and the death of martyrs: He put on the guilt of all our sins; they in death are freed from the same. He was left to Himself void of comfort; they in the midst of their afflictions feel the unspeakable comfort of the Holy Ghost. And therefore we need not marvel why Christ should pray against death, which nevertheless His members have received and borne most joyfully. Again, this most bitter agony of Christ is the ground of all our rejoicing and the cause why Paul bids all the faithful in the person of the

---

174. In personis non est aliud & aliud, est tamen alius & alius. (In the persons there is not one thing and another thing. Nevertheless, there is one and another.)

Philippians to rejoice always in the Lord and again to rejoice. And here we are further taught that when we are plunged into a sea of most grievous afflictions and overwhelmed with the gulfs of most dreadful temptations—even then, then I say, we should not be discouraged but lift up our hearts by fervent prayer to God. Thus did Christ when in the garden He was about to drink the cup of the wrath of God and to suck up the very dregs of it. And David says that "out of the deeps" [Ps. 130:1]. He called on the name of the Lord and was heard.

The fifth point, what is the matter and form of this prayer? *Answer*. Christ prays to be delivered from the death and passion which was to come, saying on this manner, "Father, let this cup pass from me"—yet with two clauses added thereto: "if it be possible" and "not my will, but thy will be done" [Mark 14:35–36]. But it may be demanded how it could be that Christ, knowing that it was His Father's will and counsel that He should suffer death for man and also coming into the world for that end, should make such a request to His Father without sin. *Answer*. The request proceeds only of a weakness or infirmity in Christ's manhood without sin, which appears thus: we must still consider that when He made His prayer to His Father, the whole wrath of God and the very dolors and pangs of hell seized upon Him, whereby the senses and powers of His mind were astonished and wholly bent to relieve nature in His agony. For as when the heart is smitten with grief, all the blood in the body flows thither to comfort it, so when Christ was in this astonishment, the understanding and memory and all the parts of His human nature (as it were for a time suspending their own proper actions) concurred to sustain and support the spirit and life of Christ, as much as possibly might be. Now Christ, being in the midst of this perplexed estate, prays on this manner, "Father, if it be possible, let this cup pass." And these words proceed not from any sin or disobedience to His Father's will [John 12:27], but only from a mere perturbation of mind, caused only by an outward means—namely, the apprehension of God's anger, which neither blinded His understanding nor took away His memory, so as He forgot His Father's will, but only stopped and stayed the act of reasoning and remembering for a little time. Even as in the most perfect clock that is, the motion may be stayed by the air or by man's hand or by some outward cause without any defect or breach made in any part of it. It may be objected that Christ's will is flat contrary to the will of His Father. *Answer*. Christ's will as He is man and the will of His Father in this agony were not contrary but only diverse, and that without any contradiction or contrariety. Now a man may will a diverse thing from that which God wills, and that without sin. Paul desired to preach the word of God in Asia and Bithynia, but he was hindered by the Spirit [Acts 16:6–7]. For all this, there is no contrariety between Paul and the Spirit of God, but in show of discord great consent. For that which Paul wills well, the Spirit of God wills not by a better will, though the reason hereof be secret, and the reason of Paul's will manifest. Again, the minister, in charity reputing the whole congregation to be elect, in holy manner seeks and wills the salvation of everyone, which nevertheless the Lord in His eternal counsel wills not. Now between both these wills there may be and is a difference without contrariety. For one good thing as it is good may differ from another, but it cannot be contrary unto it. It may further be alleged that in this prayer there seems to be a combat and fight in the mind, will, and affections of Christ, and therefore sin. *Answer.* There be three kinds of combats: the one between reason and appetite, and this fight is always sinful and was not in Christ. The second is between the flesh and the Spirit, and this may be in God's child, who is but in part regenerate. But it did not befall Christ, who was perfectly holy. The third is the combat of diverse desires, upon sundry respects drawing a man to and fro. This may be in man's nature without fault, and was in Christ in whom the desire of doing His Father's will, striving and struggling with another desire whereby nature seeks to preserve itself, caused Him to pray in this manner.

The sixth point is in what manner Christ prayed. *Answer.* He prayed to His Father partly kneeling, partly lying on His face, and that with strong cries and tears, sweating water and blood; and all this He did for our sins. Here then behold the agony of Christ as a clear crystal in which we may fully see the exceeding greatness of our sins, as also the hardness of our hearts. We go vaunting with our heads to heaven as though it were nothing to sin against God, whereas the horror of the wrath of God for our rebellions brought down even the Son of God Himself and laid Him groveling upon the earth. And we cannot so much almost as shed one tear for our iniquities, whereas He sweats blood for us. Oh, let us therefore learn to abase ourselves and to carry about us contrite and bleeding hearts and be confounded in ourselves for our sins past.

The last point is the event of the prayer, which is to be heard, as the author to the Hebrews says, "Christ Jesus in the days of his flesh, did offer up unto his Father prayers and supplications, with strong crying and tears, unto him, that was able to save him: and was also heard in that thing which he feared" (Heb. 5:7). But some will say, how was Christ heard, seeing He suffered death and bare the pangs of hell and the full wrath of God? If He had been heard, He should have been delivered from all this. *Answer.* We must know that God hears our prayers two ways: (1) when He directly grants our requests; (2) when, knowing what is good for us, He gives not us our requests directly, but a thing answerable thereunto. And thus was Christ heard; for He was not delivered from suffering, but yet He had strength and power given Him whereby His manhood was made able to bear the brunt of God's wrath. And in the same manner God hears the prayers of His servants upon earth. Paul prayed to be delivered from the angel of Satan that buffeted him; but the Lord answered that it should not so be, because His grace whereby he was enabled to resist his temptation was sufficient. And Paul, finding the fruit of his prayers on this manner, protests hereupon that he will rejoice in his infirmities [2 Cor. 12:9]. Others pray for temporal blessings, as health, life, liberty, etc., which notwithstanding God holds back and gives instead thereof spiritual graces, patience, faith, contentation of mind. Augustine says God hears not our prayers always according to our wills and desires, but according as the things asked shall be for our salvation.[175] He is like the physician, who goes on to lance the wound and hears not the patient though he cry never so, till the cure be ended.

Now follows the second thing to be considered in Christ's apprehension— namely, the dealing of the Jews. Wherein we must consider four things: (1) how they consult together concerning Christ's apprehension; (2) how they came to the place and met Him; (3) how they laid hands on Him; (4) how they bound Him and took Him away. For the first, before they enterprised this matter, they did wisely and warily lay their heads together to consult of the time and place and also of the manner of apprehending Him. So St. Matthew says, "There assembled together the chief priests and the scribes, and the elders of the people into the hall of the chief priest called Caiaphas: and consulted how they might take Jesus by subtlety" (Matt. 26:3–5). Whence we learn two good instructions. First, the Jews, having a quarrel against Christ, could never be at rest till they had His blood; and therefore they consult how they might take Him. But God did so order the matter and dispose of their purposes and consultations that even thereby He did confound them and their whole nation. For by reason of this heinous sin against Christ came the just wrath of God upon them, and so remains unto this day. Whereby we see that the Lord will overthrow such in their own wisdom that will be wise without the direction of God's Word and against Christ. And thus it was with Ahithophel, who for wisdom was as the oracle of God; yet because he rebelled against the Lord's anointed, God confounded him in his own wisdom. For when his counsel which he gave against David was not followed, he thought himself despised, as the text says, "and saddled his ass, and rose and went home into his city, and put his household in order, and hanged himself" (2 Sam. 17:23). And in this action he showed himself [no] more senseless than a brute beast. And in our days the leaguers that have bound themselves by oath to root out the church of God by His most wonderful providence turn their swords against themselves and destroy each other. Therefore, if we would be wise, we must learn to be wise in Christ; for else our

---

175. Audit ad salutem, non audit ad voluntatem. (He listens unto our salvation, and not unto our will.)

counsel will be our own confusion. Secondly, hence we learn that if any shall live in stubbornness and rebellion against Christ, the Lord will so carry and order those men or that people that in the end they shall be the very causes of their own perdition. This we see most plainly in the example of these Jews; for they evermore envied Christ, and now they go on to take counsel against Him. But God so disposed thereof that even by this means they brought destruction upon themselves and their country. This must teach you to take heed how you live in your sins; for if you do so, the Lord has many ways to work your confusion—as your conscience to condemn you; your friends to forsake you; the devil and his angels to torment and molest you; and His creatures to annoy you. Yea, the Lord can leave all these and make your own self to be the direct means of working your own confusion both in body and soul eternally, and that even then when you are most wary and wise in your own behalf. And this is the reward of all those that walk on in their evil ways without any true conversion.

Having consulted, in the next place they come to the garden where Christ was to be apprehended. And here we are to consider who they were that came—namely, the scribes and Pharisees, the high priests and their servants, a band of soldiers, and the servants of Pontius Pilate and the elders of the Jews [Matt. 26:47; Luke 22:47; John 18:3], all which came with one consent to the place where Christ was, that they might attack Him. Where we learn a good lesson, that all sorts of wicked men, disagreeing among themselves, can agree against Christ. The scribes and Pharisees were two contrary sects and at discord one with another in matters of religion. And Judas was one of Christ's disciples. The elders differed from them all. The soldiers were Gentiles. All these were at variance among themselves and could not one brook another. So also we read that Herod and Pontius Pilate were not friends; but at the same time when Christ was apprehended, Pilate sent Him to Herod, and they were made friends [Luke 23:12]. Now as these wicked men did conspire against Christ, so do the wicked ones of this world in all countries and kingdoms band themselves against the church of Christ at this day. And howsoever such be at discord among themselves, yet they do all join hand in hand to persecute Christ in His members. And the reason is plain: because Christ and His religion is as flat opposite to the corrupt disposition of all men as light is to darkness.

Again, whereas we see so many sorts of men so amiably consenting to take Christ, we may note how all men naturally do hate and abhor Him and His religion. And look as then it was with Christ, so has it been with all His members and will be to the end of the world. They are accounted as the off-scouring of the world, men not worthy to live on the face of the earth—as Christ told His disciples, saying, "Ye shall be hated of all nations for my name's sake" [Matt. 24:9].

Let us also mark how all these came furnished to apprehend Christ. The text says, "They came with clubs and staves as unto a thief" [Luke 22:52].[176] All the whole nation of the Jews knew right well that Christ was no man of violence, but meek and lowly; and yet they came armed to apprehend Him, as though He had been some mighty potentate that would not have been apprehended but have resisted them. Where we see the property of an evil conscience, which is to fear where there is no cause at all. This causes some to be afraid of their own shadows; and if they see but a worm peep out of the ground, they are at their wits' end. And, as Solomon says, "The wicked flee when none pursueth them" (Prov. 28:1).

After that they are now come to Christ, we are to consider two things in their meetings: (1) Christ's communication with them; (2) the treason of Judas. Concerning their conference, it is said, "Jesus knowing all things that should come unto him, went forth, and said unto them, whom seek ye? They answered him, Jesus of Nazareth: Jesus answered, I am he" [John 18:4–6]. Now so soon as He had said, "I am he," the stoutest of them fell to the ground, as being astonished at the majesty of His word. Where note that the word of God is a word of power. The same power was in His word when He raised up Lazarus; for when he had lain in the grave and had entered into some degrees of corruption, He did no more but said, "Lazarus come forth" [11:43]. And hence we may also mark what a wonderful might and power is in the word preached; for it is the very word of Christ and therefore, being preached by His ministers lawfully called by Him thereunto, has the same power and force in it which Christ Himself showed when He spoke on earth. It is "the savor of life unto life" to save those that hear it, or "the savor of death unto death" [2 Cor. 2:16]. It is like to a vapor or perfume in the air, which in some men's nostrils is savory and pleasant and does revive them, and others again it strikes dead. And therefore everyone that either now or heretofore has heard this word preached shall find it to be unto them either a word of power to save their souls or through their corruption the ministry of death and condemnation. Again, if a word spoken by Christ, being in a base or low estate, be able to overthrow His enemies, then at the last day, when He shall come in glory and power and majesty to judge both the quick and the dead, what power shall His words have, "Go you cursed of my Father into everlasting fire, which was prepared for the devil and his angels" [Matt. 25:41]? The consideration of this, that the word of Christ shall even be as powerful at that day, must be a motive to every one of us to cause us to come unto Him and while we have time in these days of grace and mercy to seek to be

---

176. Originally, "Luke 21:52."

reconciled unto Him for all our sins, lest at the day we hear that dreadful voice of Christ, sounding against us, "Go ye cursed into everlasting fire," etc.

And thus much for the communication. Now follows Judas's treason, wherein we are to observe these things: (1) the qualities and conditions of the man that did the treason. He was by calling a disciple chosen to be an apostle, which is the chiefest in ecclesiastical callings. And among the disciples he was in some account, because he was as it were a steward in Christ's family and bare the bag. But yet he was a traitor and did more against Christ than all the Jews did. For he brought them to the place where they might apprehend Him and, when they were come, did point Him out unto them and delivered Him into their hands. Nay, he gave them a sign and token, saying, "Whom I kiss, he it is: take him and lead him away warily" [Mark 14:44]. Here we see the cause why Christ called Judas a devil, for He said, "Have I not chosen you twelve, and one of you is a devil?" [John 6:70].[177] He became to be a devil and a traitor by nourishing a wicked and covetous heart. And here we are taught that the ministers of the word, if they make no conscience of sin, by the just judgment of God do prove devils incarnate. This example of Judas does manifest the same; and the reason is plain, for the more knowledge a man has, the more wicked he is, if he want grace. They are like in this case unto a man that has meat and drink enough, but no stomach to digest meat, whereby the more he eats, the more it turns to his hurt. This I speak not to deface the callings of ministers, but that those which preach God's word should not do it with impenitent hearts, living in their own sins. For it is a fearful thing for a man to speak unto the people of the pardon of their sins and yet himself not to apprehend the same by faith [Jer. 15:19]. A lump of wax, if you keep it from heat or from the fire, it keeps its[178] own form still; but if it be held to the fire, it melts and runs abroad. So ministers, who by reason of their callings come near God, if they be lumps of iniquity and live in their sins, they shall find that the corruptions of their hearts will melt abroad as wax at the fire. And therefore everyone that is designed to this calling must first purge himself of his own sin, or else God's judgments shall fall upon him, as they did on Judas that betrayed Christ [Isa. 6:5; Acts 20:28].

Secondly, let us consider what moved Judas to betray his Master—namely, the desire of wealth and gain. And this covetousness, which is an insatiable desire of money, is the root of all sin [1 Tim. 6:10]—not that all sins came of it, but because where it is, there all other sins are preserved and do get strength. The desire of thirty pieces of silver caused Judas to make an agreement with the Jews to betray his Master. Some man will haply say that this practice of Judas

---

177. Originally, "John 6:80."
178. Originally, "his."

was very strange and that no man now living would do the like for any money. *Answer.* Judas is dead indeed, but his practice is yet alive; for in the high and weighty calling of the ministry he that has charge of souls and either cannot teach and feed his flock or else will not, though he betray not Christ in his own person, yet he betrays the members of Christ unto the devil. If a nurse should take a man's child to bring up and yet seldom or never give it milk, insomuch that the child pines away for very hunger, is not she the very cause of the death of it? Yes, verily. And so it is with him that takes upon him the charge of God's people and never feeds them with the milk of God's Word or else so seldom that their souls do famish. He is the murderer of them and has betrayed them into the hands of their enemies and shall be condemned for them as a traitor unto God unless he repent. Besides those that live by traffic in buying and selling, make gain by lying, swearing, and breaking the Lord's Sabbath—even they also are very Judases; for they chop away their souls with the devil for a little gain. And more lamentable is their case because it is hard to find one of a hundred in the world that makes conscience of a lie or of any bad dealing, if any gain at all may come thereby. Men use to cry out on Judas for betraying Christ, and they do well; yet they themselves for a little worldly pelf betray their own souls. If such would not be counted Judases, they must leave off sin and keep a good conscience in God's worship and the works of their callings.

Thirdly, let us consider what course Judas took in betraying Christ. He was very submissive, saying, "Hail, Master, and kissed him" [Luke 22:47]. Why did he so? Herein he played the most palpable hypocrite; for, having gotten a piece of money, he thought that neither Christ nor any of his fellow disciples should have known of it (though Christ knew it well enough). And therefore he comes in this manner to Him, thinking that Christ would have conveyed Himself from among them at the very pinch as He had done sometimes before. And this practice also of Judas is common in the world. Judas, an enemy, unto Christ speaks Him fair and salutes Him; and so do most of our secure and drowsy Protestants in England. They salute Christ both by hearing His word and receiving His sacraments, and as the prophet says, "They honor God with their lips, but their hearts are far from him" [Isa. 29:13]. We may see daily experience of this. Every man will say, "Lord, Lord"; but in their lives and conversations few there be that deny Him not, both in their duties which they owe unto God, as also in their duties toward their brethren. Many come to hear God's word because they are compelled by the magistrate's laws. But when they are come, they worship not God in their hearts, which is plainly seen by the breach of God's holy Sabbath in every place, and that they make more account of a mess of pottage with Esau than of their birthright, and of thirty pieces of silver than of Christ Himself.

The third point to be handled in Christ's apprehension is that they lay hold on Him, wherein we must consider two things: (1) the resistance made by Christ's disciples; (2) their flight. For the first, Christ's disciples resisted, and specially Peter, drawing his sword, stroke one of the high priest's servants and cut off his ear [Matt. 26:51]. This fact our Savior Christ reproves, and that for these causes. First, because His disciples were private men, and they that came to apprehend Him were magistrates. Secondly, He was to work the work of man's redemption. Now Peter by this fact did what he could to hinder Him. And from this practice of Peter we may learn that nothing in the world is so hard to a man as to take up his cross and follow Christ. One would think it should be a hard matter for him to encounter with his enemies, especially they being stronger than he; but Peter stoutly resisting makes nothing of it—whereas a little before when Christ told him and the rest concerning His passion, they were so heavy with grief that they could not hold up their heads, so hard a thing it is to bear the cross. And for this very cause afterward when Christ reproved him for striking, both he and all the rest of the disciples fled away. Secondly, Peter in all man's reason was to be commended because he struck in the defense of his Master, but Christ reproves him for it. Whence we learn that if a man be zealous for Christ, he must be zealous within the compass of his calling and not be zealous first and then look for a calling, but first look for a calling and then be zealous. Which thing if Peter had marked, he had not dealt so rashly; for being without the compass of his calling he could not but do amiss. Here it may be demanded whether Christ and His religion may not be maintained by the sword. I answer that the magistrate, which is the vicegerent of the Lord, is the keeper of both tables and therefore is to maintain religion with the sword and so may put to death atheists, which hold there is no God, of which sort there are many in these days, and heretics, which maliciously maintain and hold anything that overthrows the foundation of religion in the churches whereof they are members. But some object that in the parable of the field the servants are commanded not to pluck up the tares from the wheat but to suffer both to grow till harvest [13:30], and that therefore there must be no separation of heretics and true Christians before the last day of judgment. *Answer.* The scope of that place is not to forbid the execution of heretics, but it speaks only of the final separation which must be in the end of the world. For there the master of the family does signify God Himself; and the field, the church militant spread over the face of the whole earth. And by tares is meant not only heretics but also those that are forth of the church. The servants are God's holy angels, and the harvest is the last judgment. Here further it may be demanded, who may use the sword? *Answer.* All men may use the sword to strike and to kill into whose hands God puts the sword. Now God puts it into the hand first and principally of the public magistrate, who, when just occasion serves, may draw it out. And again, it is put into a private man's hand sometimes. A private man, when he is assailed of his enemy, may take the sword in way of his own defense and may kill his enemy therewith (if there be no other help), not doing it upon malice, but because he can no otherwise escape and save his own life. And so for want of a magistrate, he is a magistrate unto himself.

In the flight of the disciples, we may consider two things: the time and the quality of the persons. The time was at the apprehension of our Lord and Savior. And this came to pass not without the special providence of God, that it might be known that Christ had no helper or fellow in the accomplishment of the work of our redemption, and that, whereas we for our sins deserved to be forsaken of all creatures, He, being our pledge and surety, might be forsaken for us. As for the quality of the persons that fly, they were the chosen disciples of Christ, such as had believed in Him, confessed Him, and preached in His name. And this serves to teach us that God will otherwhiles forsake His own children and servants and leave them to themselves in some part, that they may feel their wants and miseries and their weakness in themselves and by that means be humbled thoroughly and be touched with a hungering desire after Christ. As a mother sets down her child and hides herself, suffering it to cry, fall, and break the face, not because she hates it but that she may teach it to depend upon her and love her—so God gives grace to His children, and yet again sometimes He does in part withdraw it from them, and then they fail in their duties sundry ways. And this He does to make them ashamed of themselves and to cause them to put all their confidence out of themselves in the merits of Christ.

The fourth thing to be considered in Christ's apprehension is their binding of Him. In which action of theirs we are to observe first of all the circumstance of time when this binding was. When our Savior Christ had said unto them, "I am he," they, being astonished, fell to the ground. And withal, when Peter had smitten off Malchus's ear with the sword, Christ healed the same miraculously. Yet for all this, though they had seen His wonderful power both in word and deed, they proceed in malice against Him and lay hands on Him and bind Him as a malefactor [John 18:12]. In this we note what a fearful sin hardness of heart is, the danger whereof appears in this: that if a man be overtaken with it, there is nothing that can stay or daunt him in his wicked proceedings, no, not the powerful words and deeds of Christ Himself. And indeed among God's judgments there is none more fearful than this, and yet (how fearful soever it be) it is a rife sin among us in these our days. For it is very evident by common experience that the more men are taught the doctrine of the law and of the gospel, the more hard and senseless are their hearts—like unto the stithy, which the more it is beaten upon with the iron hammer, the harder it is. And again, it is hard to find men that sorrow for their sins and feel the want of Christ, which argues the exceeding deadness of spirit. And let us be resolved that it is a most terrible judgment of God, the rather to be feared, because it is like a pleasant sleep into which, when a man is fallen, he feels neither pain nor grief. And therefore we for our parts must look unto it with fear and trembling, lest it take such hold of us that we be past all hope of recovery.

Furthermore, this binding of Christ was prefigured unto us in the sacrifices of the Old Testament. For the beast that was to be sacrificed was tied with cords and bound and so brought to the altar. And whereas Christ was bound, we must not consider Him in His own person, but as He, standing in our room and stead, bears the person of all sinners. And therefore, whereas He is thus taken captive by His enemies to be brought before a mortal judge, there to be arraigned for us, hence we learn two good instructions. First, here is a comfort to all the people of God. Christ was bound by His enemies, that they might be unloosed from the bondage of Satan, sin, and their own corruptions (under which they lie bound by nature) and might have free liberty in and by Him. Secondly, all impenitent sinners are taught hereby to reform and amend their hearts and lives. For what exceeding madness is this, that they, by Christ's bonds being set at liberty, will yet live and die in their sins and take pleasure to lie bound hand and foot under the power of sin and Satan. And indeed this shows unto us the fearful and dangerous estate of all those that go on still in their sins. For what can they say for themselves at the day of judgment, when as now they have freedom offered and will not accept of it?

Thus much of Christ's apprehension. Now follows the indictment. For they proceed against Him judicially, after the custom of the Jews. Christ's indictment was twofold: one before Caiaphas, the high priest in the great council at Jerusalem; the second before the civil judge Pontius Pilate, as is plainly set forth by all the evangelists [Matt. 26:57; Mark 14:53; Luke 22:66; John 18:19]. And Christ's arraignment before Caiaphas was a preparation to the second before Pontius Pilate, that the Jews might thoroughly proceed against Him. In the first, we are to consider these points: (1) the time in which Christ was indicted; (2) the end of His indictment; (3) the whole tenor and proceeding thereof. For the first, Christ was indicted early in the morning at the break of the day; for He was apprehended in the night and withal was brought into Caiaphas's hall, where they kept Him all night. And at the break of the day Caiaphas, the high priest, and the elders with the scribes and Pharisees held a solemn council against Him. And there they received accusations and condemned Him before morning, at which time they sent Him to the common hall, as St. Matthew says, "When the morning was come, all the chief priests, and elders of the people took counsel against Jesus to put him to death," and led Him away bound and delivered Him to Pontius Pilate [Matt. 27:1–2]. In which action of theirs we are to mark two points. First, the diligence of ungodly men and the quickness of their nature to practice sin and wickedness—as it was said of the old Jews: their feet run to evil, and they make haste to shed blood [Isa. 59:7]. When the Israelites would sacrifice to the golden calf which they had made, it is said "they rose up early in the morning" [Ex. 32:6]. Hence it appears that, if God leave us to ourselves, we are as ready to practice any mischief as the fire is to burn without delay, and that with much violence. Now the consideration of this must move every one of us to take heed of all occasions and provocations to sin, whatsoever they be, that the corruption of our nature break not forth any way. Secondly, in the circumstance of the time of this council, we may mark the rashness of this solemn assembly in judicial proceedings, whereas they examine Him both of His doctrine and also of His disciples, omitting such circumstances as should have been used, as the serious examining of witnesses and the weighing of His contrary answers; for He is taken and brought before the judge and condemned on the sudden. Now as this was the practice of the council, so on the contrary the common complaint of these times is of the slow dispatch of matters in law and of the long delay, insomuch that some be almost undone before their suits be ended, whereas judicial proceedings were ordained by God not for men's undoing but for the maintaining of the common peace and liberty and wealth. And therefore justice ought to be dispatched with such speed as men thereby might be furthered and not hindered.

The end of Christ's indictment was directly to kill Him and to put Him to death. Here is no indifferent proceeding to be looked for, but plotting on every hand for the very blood of Christ [Matt. 26:59; Mark 14:55].[179] Where note that in the hearts of all wicked men there is an engrafted hatred of Christ and as it were bred in the bone, and the same affection the world carries to the members of Christ. This hatred is manifest in the first giving [of] the promise, "I will put enmity between thee and the woman, between thy seed and her seed" [Gen. 3:15]. It appears in the hatred that Cain bare to his brother Abel; Ishmael toward Isaac; Esau toward Jacob; and the Gentiles that were without the covenant toward the church of God at all times. And to come near to ourselves, this engrafted hatred that is in the heart of the wicked against Christ and His members is as plentiful and as evident as ever it was, even in these our days. For among all men none are more maligned and hated than those that profess Christ—and for none other cause but because they profess Christ.

---

179. Originally, "Matt. 14:55."

And hereupon the very profession of religion is laden with nicknames and reproachful terms by all sorts of men.

And thus much of the end and intent of their council. The proceeding in judgment stands in these points: (1) they examine Christ; (2) they bring witnesses against Him; (3) they adjure Him to tell them who He is. Of these in order. First, they examine our Savior Christ of His doctrine, suspecting Him to be a false prophet. Secondarily, of His disciples, as suspecting Him seditiously to raise up a new sect unto Himself to make a faction among the Jews. Now to this examination let us mark Christ's answer, in which He says nothing at all concerning His disciples [John 18:19]; whereas notwithstanding He might have said that one of them betrayed Him, another denied Him, and the rest fled away. Whereby we note that it is not our duty at all times and in all places to speak of the faults and wants that we know by others. Secondly, the answer which He makes is only concerning His doctrine, whereby the ministers of God and all men else are taught that, being called before their enemies to give a reason of their doctrine, they are (as St. Peter says) "to be always ready to give an account of the hope that is in them" [1 Peter 3:15]. And further we are to consider the wisdom that Christ uses in answering; for He says nothing of His doctrine in particular, but said, "I spake openly in the world, I ever taught in the synagogue, and in the temple whither the Jews resorted: in secret have I taught nothing: ask them therefore what I said which heard me: behold they can tell you what I said" [John 18:19–20]. Now the reason why He answered thus sparingly in general terms is because their examination served only to entangle Him and out of His words to gather matter of accusation. After whose example we may learn that, being called to make answer of our faith and doctrine before our enemies, we are to do it so as thereby we do not entangle ourselves nor give any advantage unto our enemies. And hereof we have a notable example in the apostle Paul (Acts 23:6). Again, in the words of Christ's answer, we must observe two things. First, that the place where Christ taught was public. Now hence it may be demanded whether ministers may handle the Word of God privately or no? *Answer.* The state of God's church is twofold: peaceable or troublesome. In the time of peace, ministers must preach the word publicly. But in time of persecution for the safety and preservation of the church of God they may with good warrant preach privately. And indeed at such times the assemblies of the church make private places public [12:12].[180] And hence we learn that in time of peace all those that are called to the office of the ministry must (if it be possible) spend their labors publicly, so as they may do most good. Secondly, whereas Christ says He preached in their synagogues

---

180. Originally, "Acts 12:18."

and temple, which at that time were places full of disorder, insomuch as He called the temple a "den of thieves" [Matt. 21:13], and the scribes and Pharisees had corrupted the doctrine of the law, "transgressing the commandments of God by their own traditions" [15:3], and they taught justification by the works of the law, as Paul says, "They being ignorant of the righteousness of God, and going about to establish their own righteousness, which is by works, had not submitted themselves to the righteousness of God" [Rom. 10:3]. Besides all this, they were loose and wicked men in their lives and conversations. And therefore Christ commanded the people that they should observe and do whatsoever the scribes and Pharisees bid them, sitting in Moses's chair [Matt. 23:2–3]; but after their works they must not do, because they say and do not. Now although these corruptions and deformities were in the Jewish church, yet our Savior Christ made no separation from it but came and preached both in their temple and synagogues, where these seducers and false teachers were. And hence we gather that the practice of all those men in our church which separate themselves from all assemblies for the wants thereof, holding that our church is no church, that the grace which is wrought by the preaching of the word among us is nothing else but a satanic illusion; that sacraments are no sacraments—I say that their practice is condemned by our Savior Christ's conversing among the Jews. For if Christ should have followed their opinion, He ought to have fled from among the Jews and not so much as once to have come into the temple or taught in their synagogues. But contrariwise He joined Himself with them, and therefore we cannot in good conscience disjoin ourselves from the Church of England. The second thing to be observed in Christ's answer is that He refers Caiaphas to the judgment of His hearers, being resolved of the truth of His own doctrine, though sundry of them were His utter enemies. Behold then a good example for all the ministers of God's word to follow, teaching them to deliver God's word so purely and sincerely that if they be called into question about the same, they may be bold to appeal to the consciences of their hearers, although they be wicked men.

Now after this answer one of the servants of Caiaphas smites Christ with a rod [John 18:22], in whom the saying is verified, "Like master, like servant"— that is, if the masters be wicked, servants commonly will be wicked also. If the master be an enemy to Christ, his servant will be Christ's enemy also. And this is the cause why there are so many lewd apprentices and servants, because there are so many lewd masters. Many masters complain of servants nowadays; but there is more cause why they should complain of themselves, for usually servants will not become obedient to their masters, till their masters first become obedient unto Christ. Therefore, let masters learn to obey God, and then their servants will obey them also.

Further, Christ, being smitten, makes this answer, "If I have evil spoken, bear witness of the evil: but if I have well spoken, why smitest thou me?" [John 18:23], making complaint of an injury done unto Him. Now hereupon scoffing Julian the Apostate says Christ keeps not His own laws, but goes against His own precept, when as He said, "If one strike thee on the one cheek, turn to him the other also" [Matt. 5:39]. But we must know that in these words Christ's meaning is that a man must rather suffer a double wrong than seek a private revenge. And therefore Christ spoke in His own defense, which a man may lawfully do and not seek any revenge; for it is one thing to defend his own cause, and another to seek revenge.

Now follows the second point in their proceeding, which is the producing of false witnesses against Him, as St. Matthew says, "The whole council sought false witness against him, and though many came, yet found they none" [26:60]; for they could not agree together, because they alleged false things against Him, which they could not prove. And thus the members of Christ have often such enemies as make no bones shamefully to avouch that against them which they cannot be able to justify. The ten persecutions which were in the first three hundred years after Christ[181] arose oftentimes of shameless reports that men gave out, which said that (1) Christians lived on man's flesh, and therefore slew their own children; (2) that they lived on raw flesh; (3) that they committed incest one with another in their assemblies; (4) that they worshipped the head of an ass; (5) that they worshipped the sun and moon; (6) that they were traitors and sought to undermine the Roman empire—and [7], lastly, wheresoever was thunder or earthquakes, seditions or tumults, or any disquietness or trouble, Christians were accused as the authors thereof. Such enemies have they had in all ages, and in these our days the same is practiced and will be to the world's end. Now when the first witnesses could not agree among themselves, then two other false witnesses came forth, which avouched that Christ said, "I will destroy this temple made with hands, and within three days will build another made without hands" [Mark 14:58]. Indeed, Christ said some such words; for says He, "Destroy this temple, and within three days I will build it up again" [John 2:19, 21]. But He spoke this of the temple of His body, whereas they maliciously did interpret Him to have spoken of the temple in Jerusalem. And again, they change the words; for Christ said, "Destroy this temple," etc. But these witnesses affirm He said, "I will destroy this temple made with hands," etc. And thus they change both words and meaning, and therefore the Holy Ghost called them false witnesses. By this we must be advertised to take heed how we report men's words; for if we change the meaning, though in

---

181. Tertul. upon contra gent.

part we retain the words, we may soon become slanderers and false witnesses. And as this duty must be performed toward all men, so especially toward the ministers of the gospel, and the neglect of this duty procures many slanders to them in this our church, whereof indeed the reporters are the cause and not the ministers themselves.

Now at this false accusation Christ was silent, so as Caiaphas asked Him "why he answered nothing" [Mark 14:60–61]. Herein we are to consider many things. (1) Why Christ was silent. The causes be two. First, He was to show Himself a pattern of true humility and patience. Therefore, even then would He be silent, when He was most falsely accused of His adversaries. Secondly, He is silent that, standing before the judge to be condemned, the sentence might proceed against Him, and He might suffer the death appointed which was due unto us and so become our Redeemer. And in Christ's example we must note that it is a special duty to know when to speak and when to be silent. The ordering of the tongue is a rare gift, and few attain unto it. Some will peradventure ask what rule we have to direct us herein. *Answer.* The general rule for the ordering of the tongue is the law of God. We are commanded to seek the glory of God in the first table and in the second the good of our neighbor. When your speech therefore will serve either for God's glory or the good of your neighbor, then you must speak. If it serve for neither, then be silent. Again, if your silence be either for God's glory or the good of your neighbor, then be silent; if it will not, then speak. And because it is hard for a man to know when his speech or silence will serve for these two ends, therefore we must pray unto God that He will teach and direct us herein, as David does, "Set a watch," says he, "O Lord, before my mouth, and keep the door of my lips" [Ps. 141:3]; and again, "Open thou my lips, O Lord and my mouth shall show forth thy praise" [51:15].

Thus much for the false witnesses produced. Now follows the third point, which is the adjuring of Christ [Matt. 26:63]; for Caiaphas, the high priest, charged Him to tell him whether He were the Christ, the Son of God, or no. To adjure a man is to charge and command him in the name of God to declare a truth, not only because God is witness thereof but also because He is a judge to revenge, if he speak not the truth. Thus, Paul adjures the Thessalonians, charging them in the Lord, that his epistle should be read unto all the brethren, the saints [1 Thess. 5:27]. And the like does Caiaphas to Christ. And here is a thing to be wondered at. Caiaphas, the high priest, adjures Him in the name of God, who is very God, even the Son of God. And this shows what a small account he made of the name of God; for he did it only to get advantage on Christ's words. And so do many nowadays, who for a little profit or gain make a matter of nothing to abuse the name of God a thousand ways.

Christ, being thus adjured, though silent before, yet now in reverence to God's majesty answered and said, first, "Thou hast said it" [Matt. 26:64], and in St. Mark, "I am he" [Mark 14:62]. In this answer appears the wonderful providence of God. For though Caiaphas take hence the occasion of condemning Christ, yet he has withal drawn from Him a most excellent confession that He is the Son of God and our alone Savior [John 19:7]. And by this means he proceeds to shut heaven against himself and to open the same for us.

Thus, we have ended the first indictment of Christ before Caiaphas. Now follows the second, which was before Pontius Pilate, in the common hall at Jerusalem. The history of it is set down at large in all the evangelists [Matt. 27:2; Mark 15:1; Luke 23:2; John 18:19]. In the second indictment of Christ (that we may refer every matter to its[182] place) we are to observe four things: (1) the accusation of Christ before Pilate; (2) His examination; (3) Pilate's policy to save Christ; (4) Pilate's absolving of Him, and then the condemnation of Christ in both courts, ecclesiastical and civil. Of these in order. In Christ's accusation, we must consider many points. The first is who were His accusers—namely, the high priests, the scribes, and Pharisees and elders of the people and the common people. All these conspired together to accuse Him. The cause that moved the Pharisees and elders of the people hereunto is noted by St. Matthew, who says, "Of envy they delivered him" [Matt. 27:18]. Envy is nothing but a sadness in a man's heart at the prosperity of his better. And it reigned in the scribes and Pharisees, and the occasion was this: Christ had taught most heavenly doctrine and confirmed the same by most wonderful miracles and did greatly exceed them all and was in more account among the people, and for this cause the scribes and Pharisees and high priests repined and grudged at Him. Now their example serves to admonish us to take heed of this sin as being the mother of many mischiefs. And we must rather follow the example of Moses, who when Joshua desired him to forbid Eldad and Medad to prophesy answered, "Enviest thou for my sake? yea I would to God all the Lord's people were prophets" [Num. 11:26–28]. And we must be of the same mind with John [the] Baptist, who, hearing by His disciples that the people left him and followed Christ, said his joy was fulfilled, for Christ must increase, and he must decrease [John 3:29]. And so we must be glad and content when we see the prosperity of our neighbors any way. Now the cause why the common people join with them was because the chief priests and the scribes and elders had persuaded them to a bad conceit of Christ. Hence it appears that it is most requisite for any people, be they never so good, to have good magistrates and godly rulers to govern them by wise and godly counsel. The necessity hereof was well known to Jethro,

---

182. Originally, "his."

Moses's father-in-law, though he were a heathen man. For he bids "Moses to provide among all the people men of courage, fearing God, men dealing truly, hating covetousness, and appoint them to be rulers over the people" [Ex. 18:21], teaching us that if covetous, malicious, and ungodly men, not fearing God, go before the people, they also shall in all likelihood be carried into the like sins by their example.

The next point concerns the place where they accuse Him, which was at the "door of the common hall" [John 18:28]; for, having brought Him before the council at Jerusalem and there condemned Him of blasphemy, afterward they bring Him into the common hall where Pilate sat judge. Yet did they not enter in but stayed without at the door, lest they should be defiled and be made unfit to eat the Passover. In which practice of theirs we are to mark an example of both most notable superstition and most gross hypocrisy. For they make no bones to accuse and arraign a man most just and innocent and yet are very strict and curious in an outward ceremony. And in like manner they make no conscience to give thirty pieces of silver to betray Christ; but to cast the same into the treasury, they make it a great and heinous offence. And for this cause Christ pronounces a "woe unto the scribes and Pharisees, calling them hypocrites: for," says he, "you tithe mint, anise, and cumin, and leave the weighty matters of the law, as judgment, and mercy" [Matt. 23:23; Mark 7:6]. And the very same thing we see practiced of the Church of Rome at this day and of sundry Papists that live among us. They will not eat flesh in Lent or upon any of the pope's fasting days for anything, and yet the same men make no conscience of seeking the blood of the Lord's anointed and their dread sovereign. And in this we see the most palpable and most gross hypocrisy of those that be of that church. But shall we think that our own church is free from such men? No, assuredly; for take a view of the profession that is used among the people of England, and it will appear that they place their whole religion for the most part in the observation of certain ceremonies. The manner of the most men is to come to the place of assemblies, where God is worshipped, and there mumble up the Lord's Prayer, the [Ten] Commandments, and the [Apostles'] Belief instead of prayers, which being done, God is well served think they; whereas in the mean season they neglect to learn and practice such things as are taught them for their salvation by the ministers of God's word. At the feast of Easter, every man will be full of devotion and charity and come to receive the Lord's Supper, as though he were the holiest man in the world; but when the time is past, all generally turn to their old bias again and all the year after live as they list, making no conscience of lying, slandering, fraud, and deceit in their affairs among men. But we must know that there is no soundness of religion but gross hypocrisy in all such men. They worship God with their lips, but there is no power of godliness in their hearts.

The third point is concerning the party to whom they make this accusation against Christ—namely, not to a Jew, but to a Gentile. For, having condemned them in their ecclesiastical court before Caiaphas, the high priest, they bring him to Pontius Pilate, the deputy of Tiberius Caesar in Judea [15:1]. Where we must observe the wonderful providence of God, in that not only the Jews but the Gentiles also had a stroke in the arraignment of Christ, that that might be true which the apostle says, "God shut up all under sin, that he might have mercy upon all" (Rom. 11:32).

The fourth point is the matter of their accusation. They accuse our Savior Christ of three things: (1) that He seduced the people; (2) that He forbad to pay tribute to Caesar [Luke 23:2]; (3) that He said He was a king. Let us well consider these accusations, especially the two last, because they are flat contrary both to Christ's preaching and to His practice. For when the people would have made Him a king, after He had wrought the miracle of the five loaves and two fishes, the text says, "He departed from among them" [John 6:15] unto a mountain Himself alone. Secondly, when tribute was demanded of Him for Caesar, though He were the King's Son and therefore was freed, yet says He to Peter, "Lest we should offend them, go to the sea, and cast in an angle, and take the first fish that cometh up, and when thou hast opened his mouth, thou shalt find a piece of twenty pence, that take, and give unto them for thee and me" (Matt. 17:27). And when He was called to be a judge to divide the inheritance between two brethren, He refused to do it, saying, "Who made me a judge between you?" (Luke 12:14). Therefore, in these two things they did most falsely accuse Him. Whereby we learn that nothing is so false and untrue, but the slanderer dare lay it to the charge of the innocent. The tongues of the slanderers are "sharp swords" and "venomous arrows" [Ps. 120:4] to wound their enemies. Their "throats" are "open sepulchres, the poison of asps is under their lips" [5:9]. If a man speak gracious words, his tongue is touched with the fire of God's Spirit; but, as St. James says, the tongue of the wicked is "fire," yea, "a world of wickedness, and it is set on fire with the fire of hell" (James 3:6). Therefore, let this example be a caveat to us all to teach us to take heed of slandering, for the devil then speaks by us and kindles our tongues with the fire of hell.

The fifth point is the manner of their accusation, which is diligently to be marked; for they do not only charge Him with a manifest untruth, but they beseech Pilate to put Him to death, crying, "Crucify him, crucify him" [Matt. 27:22–23],[183] insomuch that Pontius Pilate was afraid of them. Where we see

---

183. Injustice. For a blasphemer by their law should be stoned, and not crucified.

how these shameless Jews go beyond their compass and the bounds of all accusers, whose duty is to testify only what they know. Now in the matter of this their accusation appears their wonderful inconstancy. For a little before when Christ came to Jerusalem, riding upon an ass, showing some signs of His kingly authority, they cut down branches from the trees and strewed them in the ways, crying, "Hosanna. Blessed is He that comes in the name of the Lord." But now they sing another song, and instead of "hosanna," they cry, "Crucify Him, crucify Him." And the like inconstancy is to be found in the people of these our times. They use to receive any religion that is offered unto them. For in the days of King Edward VI, the people of England received the gospel of Christ; but shortly after, in Queen Mary's time, the same people received the wretched and abominable doctrine of the Church of Rome. And not many years after, when it pleased God to bring again the light of His glorious gospel by our gracious prince, the same people turned from popery and embraced the true religion again. And thus with the Jews, one while they cry, "Hosanna," to Christ and receive His gospel, and shortly after they cry, "Crucify Him, crucify Him," by embracing idolatrous popery. Let us therefore learn in the fear of God by the fickleness of the Jews, that sing two contrary songs in so short a space, to acknowledge our inconstancy and weakness in the matter of religion, whereby if God leave us but a little to ourselves, we shall straightway forsake Christ, His gospel, and all.

Thus much of the accusation. Now follows Christ's examination before Pontius Pilate; for when the Jews had thus falsely accused Him, then Pontius Pilate took Him and brought Him into the common hall and asked Him this question: "Art thou the king of the Jews?" (Luke 23:3). Now Christ, being thus examined, made as Paul also testifies "a good confession" [1 Tim. 6:13]. The sum thereof stands in four heads.

The first is that He confesses Himself to be a king—not such a one as they accused Him to be, yet a true king [John 18:36–37].[184] Whence we may learn divers instructions. First, that every Christian man in the midst of his misery and affliction has one that is most sufficient every way to defend him against all his enemies, the world, the flesh, and the devil. For this King can do whatsoever He will; and therefore when the legion of devils would enter into a herd of swine, they could not without His leave [Matt. 8:31].[185] And when the centurion's daughter was dead, He but spoke the word, and she arose [Mark 5:41–42]. And when Lazarus was dead and had lain in the grave four days, He but said, "Lazarus, come forth," and he came forth bound hand and foot [John 11:43–44]. Yea,

---

184. This paragraph break is not in the original, as the additional one following.
185. Originally, "Mark 8:31."

even hell and death give place to His word, and nothing can resist His power. And therefore he that is a true member of Christ needs not to fear any enemies, be they never so great and many. And again, as Christ is able, so is He ready and willing to save and defend all that believe in Him. For He it is that gave His life for His subjects, which no king would do, and shed His blood for their redemption, which He would never have done if He had not desired their salvation.

Secondly, whereas Christ is a mighty king, which can do whatsoever He will, let all such among us that have hitherto lived in ignorance and by reason of ignorance live in their sins at length begin to come unto Him and do Him homage and with penitent hearts fall down before Him. Otherwise, if they continue in their old rebellions, let them know whatsoever they be, high or low, that He has a rod of iron [Ps. 2:9; 110:2] in His hand to bruise them in pieces. Their souls shall smart for it, as both Pilate, Caiaphas, and the rest of the Jews were with a full cup rewarded for crucifying the Lord of life. And if Christ cannot draw you in this life from your crooked ways, be sure at the hour of death He will break you in pieces like a potter's vessel. This must we learn in regard of the first point, that He said plainly He was a king.

Now follows the second part of His confession—namely, that "his kingdom was not of this world" [John 18:36], where He sets down what kind of king He is. He is no earthly king; His kingdom stands not in the power of men nor in earthly and outward government. But His kingdom is spiritual, and His government is in the very hearts and consciences of men. His kingdom is not outward to be seen of men, but inward in the heart and soul. And therefore it is only begun in this life and is continued and accomplished in the world to come in the kingdom of glory, where Christ shall be all in all in the hearts and consciences of all the elect. Now then, if this be so, howsoever Satan have heretofore reigned in us and made our hearts as it were his palaces, yet now let us prepare a room for Christ that He may come and dwell in us. Let Him rule our hearts, wills, and affections, that they may become conformable to His will. Let us resign ourselves wholly to be ruled by Him, that His spiritual kingdom may be in us. This kingdom in the heart and conscience is the pearl and hid treasure which when a man finds he sells all he has and buys it [Matt. 13:46]. Let us therefore in the fear of God esteem it as the most precious thing that may be and so live in this world, as that Christ may rule inwardly in us by His word and Spirit. And again, seeing this regimen of Christ is heavenly and the full manifestation of it is reserved till the life to come, we must therefore use this world and all things in it, as honor, wealth, ease, and liberty, as though we used them not [1 Cor. 7:31]. As a traveler uses his staff in his journey, as long as it does further him, so long he will carry it with him, but when it hinders him, then he casts it away—so must we use the things of this life, namely, as long as they are helps to further and make us fit for the kingdom of heaven. But if they be any hindrance to this spiritual regimen of Christ, we must renounce them and cast them away, be they never so precious to us.

The third part of Christ's confession is concerning the means whereby He governs His kingdom. "I came," says He, "into this world to bear witness of the truth" (John 18:37)—that is, to preach the gospel and doctrine of salvation. And hereby He teaches that the outward administration of His kingdom stands specially in the preaching of the word, which is a principal ordinance of His, serving to gather His church from the beginning of the world to the end thereof. And for this cause He has in all ages set apart chosen ministers for the publishing of the doctrine of the gospel. And hence it is manifest that the gift of prophecy is the greatest gift that God bestows on His church for the building thereof. And therefore it ought to be most highly esteemed as a most precious jewel. And for this cause also the schools of learning are to be reverenced and maintained and all other means used for the furthering of them, because they are under God the fountains and wellsprings of this gift of prophecy.

The last point is concerning the subjects of Christ's kingdom, expressed in these words, "They which are of the truth hear my voice," in which He sets down the true mark of His servants and subjects, that they are hearers of that heavenly and saving word which He revealed from the bosom of His Father. It may be alleged [that] the most wicked men upon earth, yea, the devils themselves may be hearers of the truth of Christ. *Answer.* There be two kinds of hearers: one which hears only the outward sound of the word with his bodily ears, and he, having ears to hear, does not hear [Matt. 13:9]. The second is he that does not only receive the doctrine that is taught with his ears but also has his heart opened to feel the power of it and to obey the same in the course of his life. This distinction is notably set forth by David, saying, "Sacrifice and burnt offering thou wouldst not have: but my ears hast thou pierced" [Ps. 40:6], whereby he insinuates as it were two kinds of ears: one that is deaf and cannot hear, and thus are the ears of all men by nature in hearing the doctrine of salvation; the other is a new ear pierced and bored by the hand of God, which causes a man's heart to hear the sound and operation of the word and the life to express the truth of it. Now the subjects of Christ's kingdom are such as with the outward hearing of the word have an inward hearing of the soul and grace also to obey. And therefore all those that make no conscience of obedience to the word of God preached unto them are no less than rebels to Christ. We may persuade ourselves that we are good subjects, because we hear the word and receive the sacraments; but if our lives abound with sin, and if our hearts be not pierced through by the sword of God's Spirit, whether we be high or low, rich or poor, let us be what we will be, we are no right subjects indeed but rebels and traitors unto the everlasting God. It may be hereafter God will give further grace; but as yet all impenitent persons, though living in the midst of God's church, are no obedient and faithful subjects. And therefore, while we have time, let us labor to perform in deed what we do in word profess.

Thus much of the examination and confession of Christ. Now follows the third point concerning the policies which Pilate used to save Christ, and they are three. First, when he heard that "Christ was of Galilee" [Luke 23:7], he took occasion to send Him to Herod, thinking thereby to shift his hands of Him and not to shed His blood. In which policy, though he seem unwilling to put Christ to death, yet herein he is a most unjust judge; for, having given testimony of Christ that He is innocent, he ought to have acquitted Him and not have sent Him to Herod for further judgment. In Herod's dealing with Christ, we may observe these points. The first, that he is wonderfully glad of His coming. Why so? The text says, because "he was desirous to see him of a long season, because he had heard many things of him, and trusted to have seen some sign done by him" (v. 8). Here mark how he rejoiced not in Christ because He was Christ— that is, his Messiah and Redeemer—but because He wrought miracles, signs, and wonders. And so it is among us at this day. It is a rare thing to find a man that loves Christ because He is Christ. Some love Christ for honor; some for wealth; and others for praise—that is, because they get honor, wealth, and praise by confessing His name. Again, many profess Christ only because it is the law and custom of their nation. But we must learn to be of this mind: to love Christ because He is Christ, even for Himself—not for any other sinister respect. And we must rejoice in Christ even for Himself, though we never have profit nor pleasure neither honor nor wealth by Him. And if we love Him for wealth or pleasure or for any other end but for Himself alone, when these things are taken away, then we shall utterly forsake Christ in like manner. The second point is that Herod desires Christ to work a miracle. He can be content to see the works of Christ, but he cannot abide to hear His word and to bear His yoke. Like to him are many in these days, which gladly desire to hear the gospel of Christ preached only because they would hear speech of some strange things, laying aside all care and conscience to obey that which they hear. Yea, many in England delight to read the strange histories of the Bible and therefore can rehearse the most part of it (and it were to be wished that all could do the like). Yet come to the practice of it, the same persons are commonly found as bad in life and conversation, yea, rather worse than others. Let us therefore labor that with our knowledge we may join obedience and practice with our learning and as well to be affected with the word of Christ as with His works. The third point is that Herod derides Christ and sends Him away clothed in a white garment. This is that Herod whom Christ called a fox, who also when he heard John [the] Baptist preach did many things and heard him gladly (13:32). How then comes Herod to this outrage of wickedness, thus to abuse Christ? *Answer.* We must know that although Herod at the first heard John preach, yet withal he followed his own affections and sought how to fulfill the lusts of his flesh. For when John told him that it was not lawful for him to have his brother Philip's wife, he cast him in prison and afterward cut off his head for it—after which offence he is grown to this height of impiety that he now despises Christ and cannot abide to hear Him. Where we learn that as we are willing to hear God's word preached, so withal we must take heed that we practice no manner of sin but make conscience of everything that may displease God. You may, I grant, be one that fears and favors John [the] Baptist for a time, wallowing in your old sins. But after a while, yielding to the swing of your corrupt heart, you will neither hear John nor Christ Himself but hate and despise them both. This is the cause why some which have been professors of religion heretofore and have had great measure of knowledge are now become very loose persons and cannot abide to hear the word preached unto them. The reason is because they could not abide to leave their sins. Therefore, that we may begin in the Spirit and not end in the flesh, let everyone that calls on the name of the Lord depart from iniquity.

Now follows the second policy of Pilate. For when he saw the first would not prevail, then he took a new course; for he took Jesus into the common hall and scourged Him. And the soldiers platted a crown of thorns and put it on His head, and they put on Him a purple garment and said, "Hail, King of the Jews," and smote Him with their rods [John 19:2–3]. And thus he brought Him forth before the Jews, persuading himself that when they saw Him so abased and so ignominiously abused, they would be content therewith and exact no greater punishment at his hands, thinking thus to have pacified the rage of the Jews and so to have delivered Christ from death by inflicting upon Him some lesser punishment. This policy is as it were a looking glass in which we may behold of what nature and condition all plots and policies of men are which are devised and practiced without the direction of God's Word. In it we may observe two things. The first is the ground thereof, which is a most silly, simple, or rather senseless argument. For he reasons thus, "I find no fault in this man; therefore I will chastise him, and let him go" [Luke 23:14–16]. A man would hardly have thought that one, having but common sense, would have made such a reason, much less a great judge sitting in the room of God. But in him we may behold and see the ground of all human policy, which is besides the word of God—namely, the foolish and blind reason of men. The second thing to be considered is the proceeding and issue of this policy. Pilate must either whip Christ, being innocent, or put Him to death—which are both sins and great offences. Now he makes choice of the lesser, which is to whip Him, and is persuaded that he ought to do so—whereas of two sins or evils, a man ought to do neither. And in doing this, Pilate begins to make a breach in his conscience; and that is the fruit that all politics reap of their devices which proceed by the light of their own reason without the Word of God. By this example we are admonished of two things: first, that before we enterprise any business, we must rectify our judgments by God's Word. David was a most wise king and no doubt had withal a grave and wise counsel, but yet he preferred the Word of God before all, saying, "Thy testimonies are my counselors" (Ps. 119:24). Secondly, in our proceedings we must keep an upright, pure, and unblamable conscience, as Paul exhorts Timothy "to have the mystery of faith in a pure conscience" [1 Tim. 3:9], giving us thereby to understand that a good conscience is as it were a chest or cupboard in which we are to keep and lock up our religion and all other graces of God as the most precious jewels that can be, and that if we suffer this chest to be broken up, all our riches and jewels are gone.

But let us yet view the dealing of Pilate more particularly. He whips Christ, puts on Him a purple garment, puts a reed in His hand, sets a crown of thorns upon His head, and causes the soldiers to mock Him and spit in His face. Now in this that Christ, standing in our room, was thus shamefully abused, we must consider what was due unto every one of us for our sins—namely, shame and reproach in this life and in the life to come endless confusion. And we see the confession of Christ to be true which He made to Pilate, that His "kingdom was not of this world" [John 18:36]. For if it had been so, they would have put a crown of gold upon His head and not a crown of thorns, which nothing at all beseemed an earthly king. And instead of a reed they would have put a scepter into His hand. And instead of buffeting and spitting on Him they would have adored Him and fallen down before Him. Again, whereas Christ, our Head, in this world wore no other crown but one made of thorns, it serves to teach all those that are the members of Christ that they must not look for a crown of glory in this life, because that is reserved for the life to come. And if we would then wear the crown of glory with Christ, we must here in this life wear a crown of thorns as He did; for as Paul says, "If we suffer with Christ, we shall also reign with him" [2 Tim. 2:12]. And that which was fully verified in Christ, the Head, must in some sort be verified in every true member of Christ.

Pilate's third policy was this: when he saw that neither of the two former would prevail, he comes forth unto the Jews and makes an oration to this effect, that now was the feast of the Passover, and that they had a custom that the governor should then deliver unto the people a prisoner whom they would. Therefore, he asked them whether he should let loose unto them Barabbas or Jesus, which is called Christ [Matt. 27:15–18]. This Barabbas was a notable malefactor, that with insurrection had committed murder. And thus Pilate cunningly matches Christ with Barabbas, thinking that the Jews would rather choose Him than Barabbas, being a notorious malefactor, not worthy to live on the face of the earth. And by this means he thought to have delivered Christ from death, though otherwise he accounted Him as a malefactor. The ground of this policy (as we see) is an old custom of the Jews that a prisoner should be let loose at Easter. And it may be the end of this custom was to increase the solemnity of the feast. But whatsoever in truth the end was, the fact itself was but profanation of the time and an abomination before the Lord; for Solomon says, "He that justifieth the wicked, and condemneth the just, even they both are abomination before the Lord" (Prov. 17:15). The like practice takes place with many in these days who think the Lord's Day never well spent unless they may add solemnity thereunto by revel and riot, by frequenting of taverns and alehouses. And furthermore, where Pilate matches Christ, being innocent with Barabbas, and the people prefer him before Christ, having liberty to choose either (Matt. 27:21), it shows that God in His providence had appointed that Christ should not stand in His own room before Pilate, but in our room and stead as a mediator between God and us. And in this fact of the people, we see how sin by degrees takes hold of men, and that speedily. Who would have thought that these Jews, who a little before cried, "Hosanna," and spread their garments before Christ in the way, would ever have preferred a murderer before Him? But it was the doing of the high priests, the scribes, and Pharisees, who did animate and stir them up to this wickedness. And hereupon, when they had yielded first to attack Him and then to accuse Him, they are carried to a higher degree of impiety—namely, to seek His blood. And then, lest He should escape their hands, they plunge themselves deeper yet, preferring a wretched murderer, even seditious Barabbas, before Him. This must teach every one of us to take heed of the beginnings even of the least sins, for the devil is cunning. He will not plunge a man into the greatest sins at the first; but his manner is by little and little to creep into the heart and, having once possession thereof, by steps to bring men to the height of sin, and that with speed. We must therefore in the fear of God prevent sin betimes and at the first motion cut off all occasions hereof. That which Paul says of heresy, comparing it to a canker or gangrene, may be said of all sin [2 Tim. 2:17]. The nature of the gangrene is to run from one joint to another, from the toe to the foot, from the foot to the leg, and from the leg to the thigh, till it have wasted and destroyed the life of the body. So give any sin but an entrance, and it will soon overspread the whole man. And if the devil may be suffered but to put one talon into your heart, he will presently wind himself into you, his head, his body and all. The psalmist says that he is blessed that takes the children of the Babylonians and dashes them against the stones [Ps. 137:9]; and as truly it may be said, blessed is the man that dashes the head of his sins against the ground while they are young, before they get strength to overmaster him.

Thus have we seen the policies of Pilate. Now follows the absolution of Christ; for when Pilate had used many means to deliver Him, and none would prevail, then he absolves Him by giving divers testimonies of His innocency [Matt. 27:23–24]. For he came forth three times and bare witness [Luke 23:14, 22], and last of all he testified the same by washing of his hands [Mark 15:14; John 18:38; 19:4], which rite signifies properly the defiling of the hands before, but as yet Pilate had not defiled his hands, and therefore he used it as a token to show that Christ was innocent and that he would not defile his own hands with innocent blood. There were three causes that moved Pilate to absolve Christ. First, he saw that He was a just man, as St. Matthew notes (27:19–20), and that the high priests and people had delivered Him up of envy, as St. Mark says (15:10). By this it is plain that a very pagan or infidel may in some things go beyond such as be in God's church, having better conscience and dealing more justly than they. Pontius Pilate was a heathen man and a Gentile. The Jews were the church and people of the living God. Yet he sees plainly that Christ was a just man and thereupon is moved to absolve Him, whereas the Jews, which should be men of conscience and religion, seek His death. And thus a very pagan may otherwhiles see more into a matter than they that be reputed of the church. And this must admonish all such as profess the gospel to look unto their proceedings, that they do all things with upright conscience; for if we deal unjustly in our proceedings, we may have neighbors, men of no religion, that will look through us and see the gross hypocrisy of our profession which also would be loath to do those things which we do. The second cause that moved Pilate to absolve Christ was his wife's dream; for when he was set down upon the judgment seat, she sent unto him, saying, "Have thou nothing to do with that just man: for I have suffered many things in a dream by reason of him" (Matt. 27:19). Dreams are of three sorts: natural, rising from the constitution of the body; diabolical, such as come by the suggestion of the devil; divine, which are from God. Some have thought that this dream was of the devil, as though he had labored thereby to hinder the death of Christ and consequently our salvation. But I rather think it was occasioned by the things which she had heard before of Christ, or that it was immediately from God, as the dreams of Pharaoh and Nebuchadnezzar, and served for a further manifestation of Christ's innocency. Here it may be asked whether we may regard our dreams now, as Pilate's wife did, or no? *Answer.* We have the books of the Old and New Testaments to be our direction. As Isaiah says, "To the law and to the testimony" [Isa. 8:20]. They must be our rule and guide. In these days, we must not look to be taught by visions and dreams; yet shall it not be amiss to observe this caveat concerning dreams, that by them we may guess at the constitution of our bodies and oftentimes at the sins whereunto we are inclined. The last motive which caused Pilate to absolve Christ was a speech of the Jews; for they said that Christ ought to die by their law, "because he said he was the Son of God" [John 19:7–8]. And the text says, "When Pilate heard that, he was afraid." Mark how a poor paynim that knew not God's Word at the hearing of the name of the Son of God is stricken with fear. No doubt he shall rise in judgment against many among us that without all fear rend the name of God in pieces by swearing, blaspheming, [and] cursed speaking. But let all those that fear the Lord learn to tremble and be afraid at His blessed name.

Thus much for the causes that moved Pilate to absolve Christ, as also for the second part of Christ's arraignment—namely, His accusation. Now follows the third part, which is His condemnation; and that is twofold. The first, by the ecclesiastical assembly and council of the Jews at Jerusalem in the high priest's hall before Caiaphas. The tenor of his condemnation was this: "He hath blasphemed, what have we any more need of witnesses? he is worthy to die" [Matt. 26:66]. The cause why they say not "he shall die" but "he is worthy to die" [Deut. 17:7–9] is this: the Jews had two jurisdictions—the one ecclesiastical, the other civil—both prescribed and distinctly executed by the commandment of God till the time of the Maccabees in which both jointly together came into the hands of the priests. But afterward about the days of Herod the Great the Roman emperor took away both jurisdictions from the Jews and made their kingdom a province, so as they could do no more but apprehend, accuse, and imprison, as does appear by the example of Saul, who got letters from the high priest to Damascus, that if he found any either man or woman that believed in Christ, he might bring them bound to Jerusalem and imprison them, but kill or condemn they could not [Acts 9:2].

By the fact of this council, we learn sundry points: first, that general councils and the pope himself, sitting judicially in his consistory, may err. If there were any visible church of God at the time of Christ's arraignment upon the face of the whole world, it was no doubt the church of the Jews. For Caiaphas, the high priest, was a figure of Christ; the scribes and Pharisees sat in Moses's chair; and Jerusalem is called by Christ the holy city (Matt. 4:5; 27:53). Yet for all this, that which was foretold is now verified—namely, that the chief cornerstone should be rejected of master builders. For by the general consent of the council at Jerusalem, Christ, the Head of the catholic church and the Redeemer of mankind, is accused of blasphemy and condemned as worthy of death. Wherefore, it is mere dotage of man's brain to avouch that the pope cannot possibly err in giving of definitive sentence in matters either of faith or manners. Neither can the Church of Rome plead privilege, for Jerusalem had as many prerogatives as any people in the world could have [Rom. 9:4].[186]

Again, by this we see there is no reason why we should ascribe to any man or to any ecumenical councils themselves absolute and sovereign power to determine and give judgment in matters of religion, considering they are in danger to be overtaken with notable slips and errors. And therefore the sovereignty of judgment is peculiar to the Son of God, who is the only doctor and lawgiver of the church [Matt. 23:10]. And He puts the same in execution in and by the written Word. As for the speech of the Papists, calling the Scriptures "a dumb judge," it is little to be regarded; for the Scriptures are as it were a letter of the living God, sent from heaven to His church upon earth. And therefore they speak as plainly and as sufficiently unto us of all matters of faith as a man can speak unto his friend by letter, so be it we have the gift of discerning. Yet do we not bar the church of God from all judgment. For the ministerial power of giving judgment both publicly and privately is granted unto it of God, and that is to determine and give sentence of matters in question according to the Word, as the lawyer gives judgment not according as he will but according to the tenor of the law.

Thirdly, we learn that personal succession is no infallible mark of the true faith and of true pastors, unless withal be joined succession in the doctrine of the prophets and apostles. For Caiaphas held his office by succession from Aaron and yet in public assembly condemned the Messiah spoken of by Moses and the prophets. Therefore, the succession of bishops of Rome from Peter is of no moment, unless they can prove that their religion is the religion of Peter, which they can never do.

And thus much of Christ's first condemnation. The second was by Pontius Pilate, who sat in another court as a civil judge. And the tenor of his sentence was that the Jews should take Him and crucify Him [Luke 23:24]. Here we must consider the reasons that moved Pilate to determine thus. The first was the impatience of the Jews. He for his part was loath to defile his hands with innocent blood; but the Jews cried, "His blood be upon us, and our children" [Matt. 27:25],[187] which according to their wish came upon them within [a] few years after, and so remains still unto this day. By which we are taught to take heed of imprecations against ourselves, our children, our servants, or any other creatures; for God hears men's prayers two ways—either in mercy or in His wrath or anger. If you curse yourself or any other, except you turn unto the Lord by speedy repentance, He may hear your prayer in His wrath and verify

186. Originally, "Rom. 9:3."
187. Originally, "Matt. 37:25."

your curse upon you to your utter confusion. The second reason that moved Pilate to condemn Christ was because he feared men more than God; for, being deputy under Tiberius Caesar over the province of Judea, for fear of losing his office and of displeasing the Jews [John 19:12–13] he condemned Christ after he had absolved Him. Whereby we see that it is a grievous sin to fear dust and ashes more than the living God. And therefore St. John says that "the fearful shall have their portion in the burning lake" (Rev. 21:8)—that is, such as are more afraid of men than God. And this sin in Pilate wanted not its[188] just reward; for not long after he lost his deputyship and Caesar's favor and fled to Vienna, where, living in banishment, he killed himself.[189] And thus God meets with them that fear the creature more than the Creator. That we may therefore avoid the heavy hand of God, let us learn to fear God above all, else we shall dishonor God and shame the religion which we profess.

The proper end of Christ's condemnation set down—though not in Pilate's will, yet in God's eternal counsel—was that He might be the cause of absolution at the bar of God's justice unto all those whatsoever they are which shall come to life eternal. For we must still remember that when Christ was condemned by mortal judges, He stood in our place; and in Him were all our sins condemned before God. Therefore, to conclude this point, if this were the end of the counsel of God to have His own Son condemned by Pontius Pilate, a mortal judge, that we might not be condemned but absolved before God's judgment seat, [then] let us all labor to have this absolution sealed up in our hearts by the testimony of God's Spirit. For one day we must come to the bar of God's judgment. And if we have not an absolution by Christ's condemnation at Pilate's earthly bar, let us look for nothing else but the fearful sentence of condemnation at this celestial bar of God's justice to be uttered at the day of the last judgment. If a man should commit such a heinous offence as that he could no otherwise escape death but by the prince's pardon, he neither would nor could be at rest till by one means or other he had obtained the same and had gotten it written and sealed, which done, he would carry it home, lock it up safe and sound, and many times look upon it with great joy and gladness. Well, this is the case of every one of us. By nature we are rebels and traitors against God and have by our sins deserved ten thousand deaths. Now our only stay and refuge is that Christ, the Son of God, was condemned for us; and therefore in Christ we must sue for pardon at God's hands and never rest till we have the assurance thereof sealed up in our hearts and consciences, always remembering that ever after we lead a new life and never commit the like sins against God anymore. It were

---

188. Originally, "his."
189. Euseb. hist. lib. 2. c. 7.

a blessed thing if this would enter into our hearts; but, alas, we are as dead in our sins as a dead carcass is in the grave. The ministers of God may teach this often unto us, and we may also hear the same. But Satan does so possess men's hearts that they seldom or never begin to believe or receive it till it be too late. Everyone can say God is merciful, but that is not enough; for Christ, being most righteous, was condemned, that you, being a wretched sinner, might be saved. And therefore you must labor for yourself to have some testimony of your absolution by Christ's condemnation sealed up in your own conscience, that you may more assuredly say God is and will be merciful unto you.

Having spoken of the whole arraignment of Christ and of His passion in general, now let us proceed to the parts of the passion, which are three: Christ's execution, His burial, and His descending into hell—this being withal remembered, that these three parts are likewise three degrees of Christ's humiliation.

Christ's execution is that part of His passion which He bare upon the cross, expressed in the words of the Creed, "He was crucified and died." In handling of it, we must observe five things: (1) the person that suffered; (2) the place where He suffered; (3) the time when He suffered; (4) the manner how He suffered; (5) the excellency of His passion. For the first, the person that suffered was "Christ the just," as Peter says, "Christ also hath once suffered for sins," the just "for the unjust" [1 Peter 3:18]. And again, "Christ Jesus the just," says St. John, "is the reconciliation for our sins" [1 John 2:1]. And in His execution, we shall have manifest declarations of His righteousness and justice, consisting in two most worthy points. First, when He was upon the cross, and the soldiers were nailing His hands and feet thereunto and racking His body most cruelly, He prayed, "Father, forgive them, they know not what they do" [Luke 23:34].[190] These soldiers were by all likelihood the very same that apprehended Him and brought Him before Caiaphas and from thence to Pontius Pilate and there platted a crown of thorns and set it on His head and buffeted Him and spitefully entreated Him, as we have heard. And yet Christ speaks no word of revenge unto them, but with all patience in the extremity of their malice and injury He prays unto His Father to forgive them. Hence we are taught that when injuries are done unto us, we ought to abstain from all affections of revenge and not so much as manifest the same either in word or deed. It is indeed a hard lesson to learn and practice; but it is our part to endeavor to do it, and not only so, but to be ready for evil, to do good. Yea, even at that instant when other men are doing us wrong, even then (I say) we must be ready, if it be possible, to do them good. When as Christ's enemies were practicing against Him all the treachery they could, even then He performs the work of a mediator and prays for them

---

190. Originally, "Luke 23:35."

unto His Father and seeks their salvation. Again, whereas Christ prays thus, "Father, forgive them," we gather that the most principal thing of all that man ought to seek after in this life is the forgiveness of his sins. Some think that happiness consists in honor; some in wealth; some in pleasure; some in this; some in that—but indeed the thing that we should most labor for is reconciliation with God in Christ, that we may have the free remission of all our sins. Yea, this is blessedness itself, as David says, "Blessed is he whose iniquity is forgiven, and whose sin is covered" [Ps. 32:1]. Here then behold the madness of the men of this world[191] that either seek for this blessing in the last place or not at all.

The second testimony of Christ's righteousness given in the midst of His passion was that He beheld His mother standing by and commended her to the custody of John, His disciple [John 19:26–27]. Whereby He gave an example of most holy obedience unto the fifth commandment, which prescribes honor to father and mother, and this His act shows that the observing of this commandment stands not in outward show and reverence only but in a godly recompence in procuring unto parents all the good we can, both concerning this and a better life. It often falls out that children be as it were Hams to father and mother. Some rail on them; some fight with them. Others see them pine away and starve and not relieve them. But all dutiful children must here learn that as their parents have done many duties unto them and brought them up, so they again must in all reverence perform obedience unto them both in word and deed and when occasion is offered relieve them, yea, in all they can, do good unto them. Again in this we may see what a wretched state is that which the Church of Rome calls the state of perfection—namely, to live apart from the company of men in fasting and praying all the days of a man's life. Hereby the bond of nature is broken, and a man cannot do that duty unto his parents which God's law requires and Christ here Himself practices, nor the duties of a member of Christ which are to be done to the whole church and to the rest of the members thereof.

The place where Christ suffered is called Calvary [Luke 23:33] or Golgotha [Mark 15:22]—that is, the place of dead men's skulls, without the walls of Jerusalem. Concerning the reason of this name, men be of diverse opinions. Some say it was so called because Adam was buried there; and that his skull, being there found, gave the name to the place. And this is the very opinion of some ancient divines that Christ was there crucified where Adam was buried; but because it has no certain ground, I leave it as uncertain.[192] Others think it was called Calvary because the Jews were wont to carry out the bones of the dead

---

191. Originally, "word."

192. Jewish Rabbines. Cypr. lib. de resurrect. August. ser. 17. de temp. Hieron. epist. Paulæ ad Marcellam.

men and there to heap them together, as in times past the manner was in the vaults of sundry churches in this land. And some others think it was called Golgotha or Calvary because thieves and murderers and malefactors were there executed, stoned, burned, whereby it came to pass that many skulls and bones of dead men were found there.

The time when Christ was executed was at the Jews' Passover, when not only the Jews but also many proselytes of many countries and nations were assembled [John 18:28]. And therefore this execution was not in a private corner, but openly in the view of the world. For as he was a savior not to the Jews only but also to the Gentiles, so it was very requisite that His death should be public before all men, both Jews and Gentiles. As for the hour of the day in which He suffered, there is some difficulty in the evangelists; for St. John says that He was condemned about the "sixth hour" [19:14] of the day, and St. Mark says He was crucified the "third hour" [15:25].[193] Hence it may be demanded how both these can stand together. *Answer.* Howsoever the Jew's natural day began at evening, yet the artificial day began at sunrising, and ended at sunsetting; and it was divided two ways. First, into twelve parts called twelve hours, whether the days were longer or shorter. Secondly, into four parts or quarters, and every part contained three hours—as from the first hour to the third, as one part called morning; from the third hour to the sixth, another part called the sixth hour; from the sixth hour to the ninth, the third part called the ninth hour; and from the ninth hour to the twelfth, the fourth part called evening. Now when St. John says Christ was condemned about the sixth hour, it must be understood of the second quarter of the day called the sixth hour; and whereas St. Mark says He was crucified the third hour of the day, he speaks of the lesser hours, twelve whereof made the whole day. And thus they both agree, for the third hour of the day and the beginning of the second quarter follow each other immediately. Again, it may be answered that Christ was condemned at six of the clock after the Roman account,[194] which begins the day at midnight, and crucified at three (which is nine of the clock in the morning with us), after the Jew's account who begin their artificial day, as I said, at the sun rising.

The fourth and last point is the order and whole proceeding of Christ's execution, which may be reduced to four heads: (1) His going to execution; (2) His crucifying; (3) His death; (4) the consequence of His death.[195] Again, in His going to execution we may consider many points.

---

193. Originally, "Mark 15:23."
194. A. Gell noct. att. l. 3. c. 2.
195. Editors note: Each of these points was preceded by "the" (e.g., "the (1)..."), which has been removed in the first three points.

The first, that He is brought out of Jerusalem as a malefactor. For the old and ancient custom of the Jews was to put those whom they judged to be notorious offenders to death without their tents when they wandered in the wilderness and without the walls of Jerusalem, lest they should [in] any way be defiled with their blood [Lev. 21:14; Josh. 7:24; Acts 7:58]. And this fell out by the special providence of God, that that might be fulfilled in Christ which was prefigured in the sacrifices of the Old Testament [Lev. 6:36] when the bodies of beasts were not eaten of the priests but burnt without the camp. Therefore, says the Holy Ghost, "even Jesus that he might sanctify the people with his own blood suffered without the gate" [Heb. 13:12].

Hence may all Christians learn to know their own estate and condition. First, in this world they must look to be accounted "the off-scouring of the earth, and the filth of the world," as the apostle says [1 Cor. 4:13]; and we must all prepare ourselves to bear this estate. They that will be God's children must not look to be better accepted of in the world than Christ was. Secondly, by this every one of us must learn to be content to use this world as strangers and pilgrims, being every day and hour ready to leave the same. For if Christ, the Son of God Himself, was brought out of Jerusalem as not being worthy to have His abode there, then must every Christian man look much more for the like extremity. And therefore it is not for us to have our hearts tied to the world and to seek always to be approved of the same; for that argues that we are not like to Christ. But we must rather do as poor pilgrims in strange countries, and that is only to look for safe conduct through the miseries in this world, having in the mean season our hearts, wills, and affections set on the kingdom which is in heaven. The second thing is that Christ was made to bear His own cross, for so it seems the manner of the Romans was to deal with malefactors. And this must put us in mind of that notable lesson which Christ Himself taught His disciples—namely, that "if any man will be his disciple, he must deny himself, take up his own cross daily, and follow him" [Luke 9:23], where by "the cross" we must understand that portion of affliction which God has allotted to every one of His children. For there is no child of God to whom He has not measured out as it were some bitter cup of misery in this life. And therefore Paul says, "Now rejoice I in my sufferings for you, and fulfill the rest of the sufferings of Christ in my flesh" [Col. 1:24]. By Christ's sufferings, he means not the passion of Christ but the sufferings of the body of Christ—that is, the church whereof Christ is the Head. Moreover, we must suffer as He did, and that daily, because as one day follows another, so one cross comes in the neck of another. And whereas Christ bears the cross that was laid on Him by the hands of the soldiers, it must teach us not to pull crosses upon ourselves but wait till God lay them on us. When that time comes, we must willingly bend our shoulders, stoop down, and take them up, whether they be in body or in soul, and that every day, if it be God's will, so long as we live. And by this shall we most notably resemble our Savior Christ.

Thirdly, when Christ had carried His cross so long till He could carry it no longer, by reason of the faintness of His body, which came by buffets, whippings, and manifold other injuries, then the soldiers, meeting with one Simon of Cyrene, a stranger, made him to bear the cross [Luke 23:26], where we are put in mind that if we faint in the way and be wearied with the burden of our afflictions [Matt. 11:28], God will give good issue and send as it were some Simon of Cyrene to help us and to be our comforter.

The fourth point is that when Christ was carrying His own cross and was now passing on toward Golgotha, certain women met Him and, pitying His case, wept for Him. But Christ answered them and said, "Daughters of Jerusalem, weep not for me, but weep for yourselves, and your children," etc. [Luke 23:28].[196] By this we are first of all taught to pity the state of those that be the children of God, as the apostle exhorts us, saying, "Remember them that are in bonds as though you were bound with them: and them that are in affliction, as though you were afflicted with them" [Heb. 13:3]. In this land by God's especial blessing we have enjoyed the gospel of Christ with peace a long time, whereas other countries and churches are in great distress. Some wallow in palpable ignorance and superstition; others have liberty to enjoy the gospel and want teachers; and some have both the Word and teachers and yet want peace and are in continual persecution. Now when we that have the gospel with peace do hear of these miseries in our neighbor churches, we ought to be moved with compassion toward them as though we ourselves were in the same afflictions. Secondly, where Christ says, "Weep not for me, but for yourselves," He does teach us to take occasion by other men's miseries to bewail our own estate to turn our worldly griefs into godly sorrow for our sins, which causes us rather to weep for our offences than for our friends, although even this may also be done in godly manner. When a man, bleeding at the nose, is brought in danger of his life, the physician lets him bleed in another place, as in the arm, and turns the course of the blood another way to save his life. And so must we turn our worldly sorrows for loss of goods or friends to a godly sorrow for our offences against God; for so St. Paul says, "Godly sorrow causeth repentance unto salvation, not to be repented of: but worldly sorrow causeth death" [2 Cor. 7:10].

The fifth point is that when Christ was brought to the place of execution, they gave Him vinegar to drink, mingled with myrrh and gall [Mark 15:23]. Some say it was to intoxicate His brain and to take away His senses and

---

196. Originally, "Luke 23:27."

memory. If this be true, we may here behold in the Jews a most wicked part, that at the point of death, when they were to take away the life of Christ, they for their parts had no care of His soul. For this is a duty to be observed of all magistrates, that when they are to execute malefactors, they must have a special regard to the good and salvation of their souls. But some think rather that this potion was to shorten and end His torments quickly. Some of us may peradventure think hardly of the Jews for giving so bitter a potion to Christ at the time of His death, but the same does every sinner that repents not. For whensoever we sin, we do as much as temper a cup of gall or the poison of asps and as it were give it God to drink; for so God Himself compares the sin of the wicked Jews to poison, saying, "Their vine is of the vine of Sodom, and of the vines of Gomorrah, their grapes are grapes of gall, their clusters be bitter: their wine is the poison of dragons, and the cruel gall of asps" [Deut. 32:32–33]. And for this cause we ought to think as hardly of ourselves as of the Jews, because so oft as we commit any offence against God, we do as much as mingle rank poison and bring it to Christ to drink. Now afterward, when this cup was given Him, He tasted of it but drank not, because He was willing to suffer all things that His Father had appointed Him to suffer on the cross without any shortening or lessening of His pain.

Thus we see in what manner Christ was brought forth to the place of execution. Now follows His crucifying. Christ in the providence of God was to be crucified for two causes: one, that the figures of the Old Testament might be accomplished and verified. For the heave offering lifted up and shaken from the right hand to the left and the brazen serpent erected upon a pole in the wilderness prefigured the exalting of Christ upon the cross. The second, that we might in conscience be resolved that Christ became under the law and suffered the curse thereof for us and bare in His own body and soul the extremity of the wrath of God for our offences [Gal. 3:13]. And though other kinds of punishments were notes of the curse of God, as stoning and such like, yet was the death of the cross in special manner above the rest accursed, not by the nature of the punishment, not by the opinions of men, not by the civil laws of countries and kingdoms, but by the virtue of a particular commandment of God, foreseeing what manner of death Christ, our Redeemer, should die [Deut. 21:23]. And hereupon among the Jews in all ages this kind of punishment has been branded with special ignominy, as Paul signifies when he says, "He abased himself to the death, even to the death of the cross" [Phil. 2:8]. And it has been allotted as a most grievous punishment to most notorious malefactors [Num. 25:4; 2 Sam. 21:6]. If it be said that the repentant thief upon the cross died the same death with Christ and yet was not accursed, the answer is that in regard of his offences he deserved the curse and was actually accursed, and the sign of this was the death which he suffered, and that in his own confession. But because he repented, his sins were pardoned, and the curse removed. It may further be said that crucifying was not known in Moses's days and therefore not accursed by any special commandment of God in Deuteronomy. *Answer.* Moses indeed speaks nothing in particular of crucifying, yet nevertheless he does include the same under the general. For if everyone which hangs upon a tree be accursed, then he also which is crucified; for crucifying is a particular kind of hanging on a tree. Lastly, it may be alleged that Christ in His death could not be accursed by the law of Moses, because He was no malefactor. *Answer.* Though in regard of Himself He was no sinner, yet as He was our surety He became sin for us and consequently the curse of the law for us, in that the curse every way due unto us by imputation and application was made His.

Furthermore, Christ was crucified not after the manner of the Jews, who used to hang malefactors upon a tree, binding them thereto with cords [Ps. 22:17], and that when they were dead, but after the usual manner of the Romans, His body being partly nailed to the cross and partly in the nailing extremely racked. Otherwise, I see not but that a man might remain many days together alive upon the cross. And here we have occasion to remember[197] that the Papists, who are so devout and zealous toward crucifixes, are far deceived in the making of them. For, first of all, the cross was made of three pieces of wood—one fastened upright in the ground to which the body and back leaned; the second fastened toward the top of the first overthwart to which the hands were nailed; the third fastened toward the bottom of the first on which the feet were set and nailed.[198] Whereas contrariwise popish carvers and painters fasten both the feet of Christ to the first secondly, the feet of Christ were nailed asunder with two distinct nails and not nailed one upon another with one nail alone, as Papists imagine, and that to the very body of the cross. For then the soldiers could not have broken both the legs of the thieves, but only the outmost, because one of them lay upon the other.

Let us now come to the use which may be made of the crucifying of Christ. First of all, here we learn with bitterness to bewail our sins; for Christ was thus cruelly nailed on the cross and there suffered the whole wrath of God, not for any offence that ever He committed, but, being our pledge and surety unto God, He suffered all for us. And therefore just cause have we to mourn for our offences, which brought our Savior Christ to this low estate. If a man should be so far in debt that he could not be freed unless the surety should be cast into prison for his sake, nay, which is more, be cruelly put to death for his debt, it

---

197. Fren. l. 2. c. 42. Aug. l. 50. hom. 3.
198. Author lib. de Passione inter opera. Cypriani.

would make him at his wits' end, and his very heart to bleed. And so is the case with us by reason of our sins. We are God's debtors, yea, bankrupts before Him [Matt. 6:12]. Yet have we gotten a good surety, even the Son of God Himself, who to recover us to our former liberty was crucified for the discharge of our debt. And therefore good cause have we to bewail our estate every day, as by the prophet it is said, "They shall look on him whom they have pierced, they shall lament for him as one mourneth for his own son: they shall be sorry for him as one is sorry for his firstborn" [Zech. 12:10]. Look as the blood followed the nails that were stricken through the blessed hands and feet of Christ, so should the meditation of the cross and passion of our Redeemer be as it were nails and spears to pierce us, that our hearts might bleed for our sins. And we are not to think more hardly of the Jews for crucifying Him than of ourselves, because even by our sins we also crucify Him. These are the very nails which pierce His hands and feet, and these are the spears which pierce through His side. For the loss of a little worldly pelf, oh, how are we grieved! But, seeing our transgressions are the weapons whereby the Son of God was crucified, let us (I say it again and again) learn to be grieved for them above all things and with bleeding and melting hearts bow and buckle under them, as under the cross.

Secondly, Christ says of Himself, "As Moses lift up the serpent in the wilderness, so must the son of man be lifted up" [John 3:14]. The comparison is excellent and worthy the marking. In the wilderness of Arabia, the people of Israel rebelled against God; and thereupon He sent fiery serpents among them, which stung many of them to death. Now, when they repented, Moses was commanded to make a brazen serpent and to set it upon a pole that as many as were stung might look unto it and recover. And if they could but cast a glance of the eye on the brazen serpent when they were stung even to death, they were restored to health and life. Now, every man that lives is in the same case with the Israelites. Satan has stung us at the heart and given us many a deadly wound, if we could feel it. And Christ, who was prefigured by the brazen serpent, was likewise exalted on the cross to confer righteousness and life eternal to every one of us. Therefore, if we will escape eternal death, we must renounce ourselves and lift up the eyes of our faith to Christ crucified and pray for the pardon of our sins, and then shall our hearts and consciences be healed of the wounds and gripes of the devil. And until such time as we have grace to do this, we shall never be cured but still lie wounded with the stings of Satan and bleeding to death even at the very heart, although we feel no pain or grief at all. But some may ask how any man can see Him crucified now after His death? *Answer.* Wheresoever the word of God is preached, there Christ is crucified, as Paul says, "O foolish Galatians, who hath bewitched you, that ye should not obey the truth, to whom before Jesus Christ was described in your sight, and among you crucified?" [Gal. 3:1]—meaning that He was lively preached among them. We need not go to wooden crosses or to golden crucifixes to seek for Him; but where the gospel is preached, thither must we go and there lift up our eyes of faith to Christ as He is revealed unto us in the word, resting on Him and His merits with all our hearts, and with a godly sorrow confess and bewail our sins, craving at His hands mercy and pardon for the same. For till such time as we do this, we are grievously stung by Satan and are every moment even at death's door. And if we can thus behold Christ by faith, the benefits which come hereby shall be great; for as Paul says, "The old man"—that is, the corruption of our nature and the body of sin that reigns in us—"shall be crucified with him" [Rom. 6:6]. For when Christ was nailed on the cross, all our sins were laid upon Him. Therefore, if you do unfeignedly believe, all your sins are crucified with Him, and the corruption of your nature languishes and dies, as He languished and died upon the cross.

Thirdly, we must learn to imitate Christ. As He suffered Himself to be nailed to the cross for our sins, so answerably must every one of us learn to crucify our flesh and the corruption of our nature and the wickedness of our own hearts, as Paul says, "They that are Christ's, have crucified the flesh with the lusts and affections thereof" [Gal. 5:24]. And this we shall do, if for our sins past we wail and mourn with bitterness and prevent the sins to come into which we may fall by reason of the corruption of our natures by using all good means, as prayer, fasting, and the word of God preached, and by flying all occasions of offence. We are not to destroy our bodies or to kill ourselves, but to kill and crucify sin that lives in us and to mortify the corruption of our nature that rebels against the Spirit. Christianity stands not in this: to hear the word of God and outwardly to profess the same, and in the mean season still to live in our sins and to pamper our own rebellious flesh. But it teaches us always to have in readiness some spear or other to wound sin and the sword of the Spirit to cut down corruption in us, that thereby we may show ourselves to be lively followers of Christ indeed.

Fourthly, by this we may learn that the wrath of God against sin is wonderful great, because His own Son, bearing our person and being in our place, was not only crucified and racked most cruelly, but also bare the whole wrath of God in His soul. And therefore we must leave off to make so little account of sin as commonly we do.

Fifthly, whereas the person crucified was the Son of God, it shows that the love of God which He bare unto us in our redemption is endless. Like a sea without a bank or bottom, it cannot be searched into, and if we shall not acknowledge it to be so, our condemnation will be the greater.

Sixthly, in this that Christ bare the curse of the law upon the cross, we learn that those that be the children of God, when they suffer any judgment, cross, or calamity either in body or in mind or both, do not bear them as the curses of God but as the chastisements of a loving father. For it does not stand with the justice of God to punish one fault twice. And therefore, when any man that puts his whole confidence in God shall either in his own person, in his good name, or in his goods feel the heavy hand of God, God does not as a judge curse him but as a father correct him. Here then is condemned the opinion of the Church of Rome, which holds that we by our sufferings do in some part satisfy the justice of God. But this cannot stand, because Christ did make a perfect satisfaction to the justice of His Father for all punishment. And therefore satisfaction to God made by man for temporal punishment is needless and much derogates from Christ's passion.

In the crucifying of Christ, two things specially must be considered: the manner of the doing of it and His continuance alive upon the cross. Touching the manner, the Spirit of God has noted two things. The first, that Christ was crucified between two thieves, the one upon His left hand, the other upon His right. In which action is verified the saying of the prophet Isaiah, "He was numbered among the wicked" [Isa. 53:12]. And the Jews for their parts do hereby testify that they esteemed Him to be not some common wicked man, but even the captain and ringleader of all thieves and malefactors whatsoever. Now whereas Christ, standing upon the cross in our room and stead, is reputed the head and prince of all sinners, it serves to teach every one of us that believe in Him to judge ourselves most vile and miserable sinners and to say of ourselves with Paul that we are "the chief of all sinners" [1 Tim. 1:15]. The second thing is that Christ was crucified naked because He was stripped of His garments by the soldiers when He was to be crucified. The causes why He suffered naked are these.

First, Adam by His fall brought upon all mankind death both of body and soul and also the curses of God which befall man in this life, among which this was one, that the nakedness of the body should be ignominious.[199] And hereupon when Adam had sinned and saw himself naked, he fled from the presence of God and hid himself even for very shame [Gen. 3:7–8]. Christ therefore was stripped of His garments and suffered naked, that He might bear all the punishment and ignominy that was due unto man for sin.

Secondly, this came to pass by the goodness of God that we might have a remedy for our spiritual nakedness, which is when a man has his sins lying open before God's eyes, and by reason thereof he himself lies open to all God's

---

199. This paragraph break is not in the original, as the additional two following.

judgments. Hereof Christ speaks to the angel of Laodicea, saying, "Thou sayest, I am rich, and increased with goods, and have need of nothing, and knowest not how thou art wretched, miserable, blind, and naked" [Rev. 3:17]. So, when the Israelites had committed idolatry by the golden calf, Moses tells them that "they were naked" [Ex. 32:25] not only because they had spoiled themselves of their earrings, but especially because they were destitute of God's favor and lay open and naked to all His judgments for that sin. And Solomon says, "Where there is no vision, there the people are made naked" [Prov. 29:18]—that is, their sins lie open before God. And by reason thereof they themselves are subject to His wrath and indignation. Now Christ was crucified naked that He might take away from us this spiritual nakedness and also give unto us meet garments to clothe us withal in the presence of God—called "white raiment" [Rev. 3:18], as Christ says, "I counsel thee to buy of me white raiment, that thou mayst be clothed, and that thy filthy nakedness do not appear," and "long white robes dipped in the blood of the Lamb" [7:14], which serve to hide the nakedness of our souls. What these garments are the apostle shows when he says, "All that are baptized into Christ, have put on Christ" [Gal. 3:27]. And, "Put on the new man, which after God is created in righteousness, and true holiness" [Eph. 4:24]. Our nakedness makes us more vile in the sight of God than the most loathsome creature that is can be unto us, until we have put on the righteousness of Christ to cover the deformity of our souls, that we may appear holy and without spot before God.

Thirdly, Paul says, "We know if our earthly house of this tabernacle be destroyed, we have a building given of God, etc. For therefore we sigh, desiring to be clothed with our house which is from heaven, because if we be clothed we shall not be found naked" [2 Cor. 5:1–3]. Where it is like[ly] that the apostle alludes to the nakedness of Adam after his fall and therefore gives us another reason why Christ was crucified naked—namely, that after this life He might clothe all His members with eternal glory.

If this be so that a part of our rejoicing stands in the glorious nakedness of Christ crucified, there is no reason why we should be puffed up with the vanity of our apparel. It should rather be an occasion to make us ashamed, than to make us proud. The thief may as well brag of the brand in his hand or of the fetters on his heels as we may of our attire, because it is but the covering of our shame and therefore should put us in mind of our sin and shameful nakedness.

The abode of Christ upon the cross was about the space of six hours.[200] For the death of the cross was no sudden but a lingering death.[201] And in this

---

200. August. ser. 119. de tempore.
201. Producta mors.

space of time there fell out five notable events. The first, that the soldiers, having stripped Christ of His garments, divided them into four parts and cast lots for His coat [Mark 15:24], because it was woven without seam. And by this appears the great love of Christ to man, who was not only content to suffer but also to lose all that ever He had, even to the garments on His back, to redeem us, teaching us answerably that if it please God to call us to any trial hereafter, we must be content to part with all for His sake, that we may win Him. Again, in these soldiers we may behold a picture of this world. When they had nailed Christ to the cross, they will not lose so much as His garments; but they come and divide them and cast lots for them. As for Christ Himself, the Savior and Redeemer of mankind, they regard Him not. And thus fares the world. It is a hard thing to find a man to accept of Christ, because He is Christ, his Redeemer. But when gain comes by Christ, then He is welcome. Esau, that esteemed nothing of his father's blessing, made great account of his brother's pottage. The Gadarenes made more account of their swine than of Christ; for when they heard that they were drowned, they beseech Him to depart out of their coast. Nay, so bad is this age that such as will be taken to be the special members of Christ do not only with the soldiers strip Christ of His garments, but more than this—they bereave Him of His natures and offices. The Church of Rome by their transubstantiation strip Him of His manhood; and by making other priests after the same order with Him, which do properly forgive sins, strip Him of His priesthood; and of His kingly office by joining with Him a vicar on earth and head of the Catholic church, and that in His presence, whereas all deputyships and commissions cease in the presence of the principal. And when they have done all this, then they further load Him with a number of beggarly ceremonies and so do nothing else but make a fained Christ,[202] instead of the true and alone Messiah.

The second event was that Christ was mocked of all sorts of men. First, they set up the cause written why He was crucified—namely, "This is the king of the Jews" [Matt. 27:37–38]. Then the people that passed by reviled Him, wagging their heads at Him, and said, "Thou that destroyest the temple and buildest it in three days, save thyself," etc. Likewise, the high priests, mocking Him, with the scribes and Pharisees and the elders, said, "He saved others, let him save himself." The same also did one of the thieves that was crucified with Him, cast in His teeth. Behold here the wonderful strange dealing of the Jews. They see an innocent man thus pitifully and grievously racked and nailed to the cross and His blood distilling down from hands and feet, and yet are they without all pity and compassion and do make but a mock and a scoff at Him. And in this we may plainly see how dangerous and fearful their case is who are wholly

---

202. Fictitium Christum.

given up to the hardness of their own hearts. And we are further admonished to take heed how we give ourselves to jesting or mocking of others. And if any think it to be a light sin, let them consider what befell the Jews for mocking Christ. The hand of God was upon them within a while after, and so remains to this day. Little children wickedly brought up, when they saw Elisha, the man of God, coming, they mocked him and said, "Come up thou bald pate, come up thou bald pate" (2 King 2:23–24). But Elisha looked back on them and cursed them in the name of the Lord, and two wild bears came out of the forest and did tear in pieces two and forty of them. Julian, once a Christian emperor but after an apostate, did nothing else but mock Christ and His doctrine and made jests of sundry places of Scripture, but, being in fight against the Persians, was wounded with a dart (no man knowing how) and died scoffing and blaspheming. And suchlike are the judgments of God which befall mockers and scorners. Let us therefore in the fear of God learn to eschew and avoid this sin.

Furthermore, if we shall indifferently consider all the mocks and scornings of the Jews, we shall find that they cannot truly convince Him of the least sin, which serves to clear Christ and to prove that He was a most innocent man in whose ways was no wickedness and in whose mouth was found no guile. And therefore He was fitted to stand in our room and suffer for us, which were most vile and sinful. And here by the way a question offers itself to be scanned. St. Matthew says, "The thieves which were crucified with him cast the same in his teeth," which the scribes and Pharisees did [Matt. 27:44]. St. Luke says that one of the thieves mocked Him [Luke 23:39]. Now it may be demanded how both these can be true. *Answer.* Some reconcile the places thus: that the Scripture, speaking generally of anything, by a figure does attribute that to the whole which is proper to some part only,[203] and so here does ascribe that to both the thieves which agrees but to one. Others answer it thus: that at the first both of the evildoers did mock Christ, and of that time speaks Matthew; but afterward one of them was miraculously converted. Then the other alone mocked Him, and of that time speaks St. Luke. And this I rather take to be the truth. But what was the behavior of Christ, when He was thus laded with reproach? In wonderful patience, He replies not but puts up all in silence. Where we are taught that when a man shall rail on us wrongfully we must not return rebuke for rebuke nor taunt for taunt, but we must either be silent or else speak no more than shall serve for our just defense. This was the practice of the Israelites by the appointment of Hezekiah, when Rabshakeh reviled the Jews and blasphemed the name of God. The people held their peace and answered him not a word, for the king's commandment was, "Answer him not" [2 Kings 18:36]. So Hannah,

---

203. Synecdoche.

being troubled in mind, prayed unto the Lord. And Eli marked her mouth; for she spoke in her heart, and her lips did move only, but her voice was not heard. Therefore, Eli thought she had been drunken and said, "How long wilt thou be drunken? Put away thy drunkenness from thee." Such a speech would have moved many a one to very hard words. But she said, "Nay, my Lord, but I am a woman troubled in spirit, I have drunk neither wine nor strong drink: but I have poured out my soul before the Lord" [1 Sam. 1:15].[204] This is a hard lesson for men to learn; but we must endeavor ourselves to practice it, if we will be followers of Christ, and overcome evil with good.

The third thing that fell out in the time of Christ's crucifying was the pitiful complaint in which He cried with a loud voice, "Eli, Eli, lama sabachthani" (Matt. 27:46)—that is, "My God, my God, why hast thou forsaken me?" In the opening of this complaint, many points must be scanned.

The first is, what was the cause that moved Christ to complain?[205] *Answer.* It was not any impatience or discontentation of mind or any despair or any dissembling, as some would have it. But it was an apprehension and a feeling of the whole wrath of God, which seized upon Him both in body and soul.

The second, what was the thing whereof He does complain? *Answer.* That He is forsaken of God the Father. And from this point arises another question. How Christ, being God, can be forsaken of God? For the Father, the Son, and the Holy Ghost are all three but one and the same God. *Answer.* By "God" we must understand God the Father, the first person, according to the common rule: when God is compared with the Son or the Holy Ghost, then the Father is meant by this title "God," as in this place. Not that the Father is more God than the Son, for in dignity all the three persons are equal, but they are distinguished in order only, and the Father is first. And again, whereas Christ complains that He was forsaken, it must be understood in regard of His human nature, not of His Godhead. And Christ's manhood was forsaken, not that His Godhead and manhood were severed—for they were ever joined together from the first moment of the incarnation—but the Godhead of Christ, and so the Godhead of the Father did not show forth His power in the manhood but did as it were lie asleep for a time, that the manhood might suffer. When a man sleeps, the soul is not severed from the body but lies as it were dead and exercises not itself. Even so the Godhead lay still and did not manifest His power in the manhood, and thus the manhood seemed to be forsaken.

The third point is the manner of this complaint. "My God, my God," says He. These words are words of faith. I say not of justifying faith, whereof Christ

---

204. Originally, "1 Sam. 1:14."
205. This paragraph break is not in the original, as the additional four following.

stood not in need; but He had such a faith or hope whereby He did put His confidence in God. The last words, "Why hast thou forsaken me?" seem at the first to be words of distrust. How then (will some say) can these words stand with the former? For faith and distrust are flat contraries. *Answer.* Christ did not utter any speech of distrust, but only make His moan and complaint by reason of the greatness of His punishment and yet still relied Himself on the assistance of His Father.

Hence we learn, first, that religion does not stand in feeling but in faith, which faith we must have in Christ, though we have no feeling at all; for God oftentimes does withdraw His grace and favor from His children that He may teach them to believe in His mercy in Christ then, when they feel nothing less than His mercy. And faith and feeling cannot always stand together, because faith is a subsisting of things which are not seen and the ground of things hoped for; and we must live by faith and not by feeling. Though feeling of God's mercy be a good thing, yet God does not always vouchsafe to give it unto His children. And therefore in the extremity of afflictions and temptations we must always trust and rely on God by faith in Christ, as Christ Himself does when He is as it were plunged into the sea of the wrath of God.

Secondly, here we may see how God deals with His children; for Christ in the sense and feeling of His human nature was forsaken, yet had He sure trust and confidence in God that caused Him to say, "My God, my God." God will oftentimes cast His dear children into huge gulfs of woe and misery where they shall see neither bank nor bottom nor any way to get out. Yet men in this case must not despair but remember still that that which befell Christ, the Head, does also befall His members. Though Christ Himself at His death did bear the wrath of God in such measure as that in the sense and feeling of His human nature He was forsaken, yet for all this He was the Son of God and had the Spirit of His Father, crying, "My God, my God." And therefore, though we be wonderfully afflicted either in body or in mind so as we have no sense or feeling of God's mercy at all, yet must we not despair and think that we are castaways but still labor to trust and rely on God in Christ and build upon Him that we are His children, though we feel nothing but His wrath upon us, against mercy cleaving to His mercy. This was David's practice. "In the day of trouble," says he, "I sought the Lord: my sore ran and ceased not in the night: my soul refused comfort. I did think upon God and was troubled: my soul was full of anguish" (Ps. 77:2–3). And so he continues on, saying, "Will the Lord absent himself forever, and will he show no more favor? hath God forgotten to be merciful?" (vv. 10–12, etc.), but in the end he recovered himself out of this gulf of temptation, saying, "Yet I remember the years of the right hand of the Most High: I remember the work of the Lord, certainly I remember the wonders of old."

Wherefore, this practice of Christ in His passion must then be remembered of us all when God shall humble us either in body or soul or both.

The fourth thing which fell out when Christ was on the cross was this: after Christ knew that all things were performed and that the Scriptures were fulfilled, He said, "I thirst" (John 19:28–30). And then, there standing a vessel full of vinegar, one ran and filled a sponge therewith and put it about a hyssop stalk and put it to His mouth, which, when He had received, He said, "It is finished." The points here to be considered are four. The first, that Christ thirsted. And we must know that this thirst was a part of His passion. And indeed it was no small pain, as we may see by this: when Sisera was overcome by Israel and had fled from his enemies to Jael's tent (Judg. 4:19), he called for a little water to drink, being more troubled with thirst than with the fear of death at the hand of his enemies. And indeed thirst was as grievous to men in the East country as any torment else. And hereupon Samson was more grieved with thirst than with fear of many thousand Philistines (15:18).

Again, whereas Christ complains that He thirsts, it was not for His own sake but for our offences. And therefore answerably we must thirst after Christ and His benefits, "as the dry and thirsty land" [Ps. 143:6] where no water is does after rain. And as "the hart brayeth after the rivers of water" [42:1], so must we say with David, "My soul pants after Thee, O Lord, and the benefits of Thy death."

The second, that a sponge full of vinegar tied upon a hyssop stalk was reached to Christ upon the cross. Now it may be demanded how this could be, considering the stalk of the hyssop is not past a foot long. *Answer.* As the tree of mustard seed with the Jews is far greater and taller than with us, insomuch that the birds of heaven build their nests in it [Matt. 13:36], so it may be that hyssop grows much longer in those countries than with us. Or, as I take it rather, the hyssop stalk was put upon a reed, and by that means the sponge was put to the mouth of Christ.

The third point is that Christ drinks the vinegar offered—but when? Not before all things were finished that were to be done on the cross. And by this He shows His exceeding care for our salvation. He laid aside all things that would turn to His own ease, that He might fully work our redemption and fulfill the will of His Father, who sent Him into the world for that end. The like care must every one of us have to walk dutifully and as it were to go thorough-stitch in our particular callings that God might be glorified by us. When Abraham's servant came to Bethuel to get a wife for Isaac, meat was set before him; but he said, "I will not eat before I have said my message" (Gen. 24:33). So likewise we must first see God's glory procured in our affairs; and then in the second place, if commodity or praise redound to us, we must afterward take it.

The last point is that when Christ had drunk the vinegar, He said, "It is finished." Which words may have a double sense: one, that such things as were figured by the sacrifices of the Old Testament are accomplished; the other, that now upon the cross He had finished His satisfaction to the justice of His Father for man's sin. And this [latter] of the twain I rather think to be His meaning. If it be said that the burial and resurrection and ascension of Christ, etc., which are necessary to man's redemption, were not yet begun, the answer is that the works of Christ's priesthood which follow His death serve not to make any satisfaction to God's justice for sin but only to confirm or apply it after it is made and accomplished on the cross. And if this be so, that Christ in His own person accomplished the work of redemption and made a full and perfect satisfaction for us, as these words import, "It is finished," then human satisfaction to God's justice for sin are altogether superfluous.

The fifth event that fell out when Christ was upon the cross was that He cried with a loud voice and said, "Father, into thy hand I lay down my spirit" (Luke 23:46)[206]—that is, "I commend my soul, as being the most precious thing which I have in this world, into Thy custody, who art a most faithful keeper thereof." These words are taken by Christ out of the Psalms; for when David was in danger of his life by reason of Saul and had no friend to trust, he makes choice of God to be his keeper and said, "Into thy hands, O Lord, do I commend my spirit" (Ps. 31:5). Now our Savior Christ, being in the like distress both by reason of the Jews, who every way sought His final destruction and confusion, and especially because He felt the full wrath of God seizing upon Him, does make choice of David's words and apply them to Himself in His distress. And by His example we are taught not only to read the general history of the Bible but also to observe the things commanded and forbidden and to apply the same unto ourselves and to our particular estates and dealings whatsoever. Thus, the prophet David says, "In the roll of the book it is written of me, that I should do thy will, O my God" (40:7). How can this be? For no part of Scripture penned before the days of David says thus of him. True indeed; but, as I take it, David's meaning is that he read the Book of the Law and found general precepts and commandments given to kings and princes that they should keep all the ordinances and commandments of God, which he, being a king, applies particularly to his own person and thereupon says, "In the volume of the book it is written of me," etc. And this duty is well practiced by the people of God at this day; for the Psalms of David were penned according to the estate of the church in his time. And in these days the church of God does sing the

---

206. Originally, "Luke 23:49."

same with the same spirit that David did and does apply their several estates and conditions.

Now in that Christ commends His soul into the hands of His Father, He does it to testify that He died not by constraint but willingly. And by His own practice He does teach us to do the like—namely, to give up our own souls into the hands of God. And because this duty is of some difficulty, we must observe three motives or preparatives which may induce us to the better doing of it.

The first is to consider that God the Father of Christ is the Creator of our souls, and therefore He is called the "father of spirits."[207] And if He be a creator of them, then is He also a faithful preserver of them; for sure it is that God will preserve His own workmanship. Who is or can be so careful for the ornament and preservation of any work as the craftmaster? And shall not God be more careful than man? Wherefore, St. Peter exhorts us "to commit our souls unto God, as unto a faithful Creator" [1 Peter 4:19].

The second motive is this: we must look to be resolved in our consciences that God the Father of Christ is our Father. Every man for himself must labor to have the assurance of the pardon of his own sins and that the corruption of his soul be washed away in the blood of Christ, that he may say, "I am justified, sanctified, and adopted by Christ." And when any man can say thus, he shall be most desirous and willing to commit his soul into the hands of God. This was the reason which moved Christ to lay down His soul into the hands of God, because He is His Father.

The third motive or preparative is a continual experience and observation of God's love and favor toward us in keeping and preserving him, as appears by David's example, "Into thy hands," says he, "I commend my soul: for thou hast redeemed me, O thou God of truth" [Ps. 31:5].

The time when we are specially to commend our souls into the hands of God is, first of all, in the time of any affliction or danger. This was the time when David commended His soul into the hands of God in the psalm before named. We know that in any common danger or peril, as the sacking of a city or burning of a house, if a man have any precious jewel therein, he will first fetch that out and make choice of a faithful friend to whose custody he will commit the same. Even so, in common perils and dangers we must always remember to commit our souls as a most precious jewel into the hands of God, who is a faithful creator. Another more special and necessary time of practicing this duty is the hour of death, as here Christ does and Stephen, who when the Jews stoned him to death called on God and said, "Lord Jesus, receive my spirit" (Acts 7:59). And as this duty is very requisite and necessary at all times, so most

---

207. This paragraph break is not in the original, as the additional one following.

especially in the hour of death, because the danger is great by reason that Satan will then chiefly assault us, and the guilt of sin will especially then wound the conscience. Lastly, at all times we must commit our souls into God's hands; for though we be not always in affliction, yet we are always in great danger. And when a man lies down to rest, he knows not whether he shall rise again or no. And when he arises, he knows not whether he shall lie down again. Yea, at this very hour we know not what will befall the next.

And great are the comforts which arise by the practice of this duty. When David was in great danger of his life, and his own people would have stoned him because their hearts were vexed for their sons and daughters, which the Amalekites had taken, it is said "he comforted himself in the Lord his God" (1 Sam. 30:6). And the practice of Paul in this case is most excellent: "For the which cause," says he, "I suffer those things, but I am not ashamed: for I know whom I have believed, and am persuaded that he is able to keep that which I have committed unto him against that day" (2 Tim. 1:12). This worthy servant of God had committed his life and soul into God's hand; and therefore he says, "In all my sufferings I am not ashamed," where we see that if a man have grace in his lifetime to commit his soul into God's hand, it will make him bold even at the point of death. And this must be a motive to cause every man daily and hourly to lay down his soul into the hands of God, although by the course of nature he may live twenty or forty years longer. But howsoever this duty be both necessary and comfortable, yet few there be that practice the same. Men that have children are very careful and diligent to bring them up under some man's tuition. And if they have cattle, sheep, or oxen, they provide keepers to tend them; but in the mean season for their own souls they have no care. They may sink or swim or do what they will. This shows the wonderful blindness or rather madness of them in the world that have more care for their cattle than for their own souls. But as Christ has taught us by His example, so let every one of us in the fear of God learn to commit our souls into the hand of God.

Again, in that Christ lays down His own soul and withal the souls of all the faithful into the hands of the Father, we further learn three things. The first, that the soul of man does not vanish away as the souls of beasts and other creatures. There is great difference between them; for when the beast dies, his soul dies also; but the soul of man is immortal. The consideration whereof must move every man above all things in this world to be careful for his soul. If it were to vanish away at the day of death as the souls of beasts do, the neglect thereof were no great matter. But, seeing it must live forever either in eternal joy or else in endless pains and torments, it stands us upon every man for himself so to provide for his soul in this life that at the day of death when it shall depart from his body it may live in eternal joy and happiness. The second, that there is an especial and particular providence of God, because the particular soul of Christ is committed into the hands of His Father, and so answerably the souls of every one of the faithful are. The third, that everyone which believes himself to be a member of Christ must be willing to die when God shall call him thereunto. For when we die in Christ, the body is but laid asleep, and the soul is received into the hands of a most loving God and merciful father, as the soul of Christ was.

Lastly, whereas Christ, surrendering His soul into His Father's hands, calls it a spirit, we note that the soul of man is a spirit—that is, a spiritual, invisible, simple essence without composition, created as the angels of God are.[208] The question whether the soul of a child come from the soul of the parents, as the body does come from their bodies, may easily be resolved. For the soul of man, being a spirit, cannot beget another spirit, as the angels, being spiritual, do not beget angels; for one spirit begets not another. Nay, which is more, one simple element begets not another, as the water begets not water, nor air begets air. And therefore much less can one soul beget another. Again, if the soul of the child come from the soul of the parents, then there is a propagation of the whole soul of the parent or of some part thereof. If it be said that the whole soul of the parents is propagated, then the parents should want their own souls and could not live. If it be said that a part of the parent's soul is propagated, I answer that the soul, being a spirit or a simple substance, cannot be parted. And therefore it is the safest to conclude that the body indeed is of the body of the parents and that the soul of man, while the body is in making, is created of nothing; and for this very cause God is called the "father of spirits" [Heb. 12:9].

Thus much of the crucifying of Christ. Now follows His death. For, having laid down His soul into the hands of His Father, the Holy Ghost says, "He gave up the ghost" (Luke 23:46), to give us to understand that His death was no phantastical but a real death, in that His body and soul were severed as truly as when any of us die. In treating of Christ's death, we must consider many points. The first, that it was needful that He should die, and that for two causes. First, to satisfy God's justice; for sin is so odious a thing in God's sight that He will punish it with an extreme punishment. Therefore, Christ, standing in our room, must not only suffer the miseries of this life but also die on the cross, that the very extremity of punishment which we should have borne might be laid on Him, and so we in Christ might fully satisfy God's justice, for the "wages of sin is death" [Rom. 6:23]. Secondly, Christ died that He might fulfill the truth of God's word, which had said that man for eating the forbidden fruit "should die the death" [Gen. 2:17]. The properties of Christ's death are two: the first,

---

208. This paragraph break is not in the original.

that it was a voluntary and willing death; the second, that it was a cursed death. For the first, whereas I say Christ's death was voluntary, I mean that Christ died willingly and of His own free accord gave up Himself to suffer upon the cross. Howsoever the Jews did arraign and condemn and crucify Him, yet if He had not willed His own death and of His free accord given Himself to die, [then] not the Jews nor all the whole world could ever have taken away His life from Him. He died not by constraint or compulsion, but most willingly. And therefore He says, "No man taketh my life from me, but I," says He, "lay it down of myself: I have power to lay it down, and have power to take it again" (John 10:18). And our Savior Christ gave evident tokens hereof in His death, for "then Jesus cried with a loud voice, and gave up the ghost" [Matt. 27:50; Luke 23:46; Isa. 38:14]. Ordinarily, men that die on the cross languish away by little and little. And before they come to yield up their lives they lose their speech and only rattle or make a noise in the throat. But Christ at that very instant when He was to give up the ghost cried with a loud voice, which shows plainly that He in His death was more than a conqueror over death. And therefore to give all men a token of His power and to show that He died voluntarily it pleased Him to cry with a loud voice, and this made the centurion to say that He was the Son of God [Matt. 27:54].[209] Again, Christ died not as other men do, because they first give up the ghost and then lay their heads aside. But He in token that His death was voluntary first lays His head aside after the manner of a dead man and then afterward gives up the ghost [John 19:30]. Lastly, Christ died sooner than men are wont to do upon the cross, and this was the cause that made Pilate wonder that He was so soon dead [Mark 15:44]. Now, this came to pass not because He was loath to suffer the extremity of death, but because He would make it manifest to all men that He had power to die or not to die. And indeed this is our comfort, that Christ died not for us by constraint but willingly of His own accord.

And as Christ's death was voluntary, so was it also an accursed death; and therefore it is called the death of the cross. And it contains the first and the second death. The first is the separation of the body from the soul; the second is the separation of body and soul from God. And both were in Christ.[210] For besides the bodily death He did in soul apprehend the wrath of God due to man's sin, and that made him cry, "My God, my God, why hast thou forsaken me?"

And here we must not omit a necessary point—namely, how far forth Christ suffered death. *Answer.* Some think that He suffered only a bodily death and such pains as follow the dissolution of nature. But they, no doubt, come too

---

209. Originally, "Matt. 27:39."
210. To signify this point, the Creed says that He was crucified and also died.

short; for why should Christ have feared death so greatly, if it had been nothing but the dissolution of nature? Some again think that He died not only the first but also the second death. But it may be they go too far; for if to die the first death be to suffer a total separation of body and soul, then also to die the second death is wholly and every way to be severed from all favor of God and at the least for a time to be oppressed of the same death as the damned are. Now this never befell Christ, no, not in the midst of His sufferings, considering that even then He was able to call God His God. Therefore, the safest is to follow the mean—namely, that Christ died the first death in that His body and soul were really and wholly severed, yet without suffering any corruption in his body, which is the effect and fruit of the same; and that withal He further suffered the extreme horrors and pangs of the second death, not dying the same death nor being forsaken of God more than in His own apprehension or feeling. For in the very midst of His sufferings the Father was well pleased with Him. And this which I say does not any whit lessen the sufficiency of the merit of Christ; for whereas He suffered truly the very wrath of God and the very torments of the damned in His soul, it is as much as if all the men in the world had died the second death and had been wholly cut off from God forever and ever. And no doubt Christ died the first death, only suffering the pangs of the second, that the first death might be an entrance not to the second death, which is eternal damnation, but a passage to life eternal.

The benefits and comforts which arise by the death of Christ are especially four. The first is the change of our natural death. I say not the taking of it away, for we must all die. But whereas by nature death is a curse of God upon man for eating the forbidden fruit, by the death of Christ it is changed from a curse into a blessing and is made as it were a middle way and entrance to convey men out of this world into the kingdom of glory in heaven. And therefore it is said Christ by His death "hath delivered them from the fear of death, which all the days of their lives were subject to bondage" (Heb. 2:15). A man that is to encounter with a scorpion, if he know that he has a sting, he may be dismayed. But, being assured that the sting is taken away, he need not fear to encounter therewith. Now death in its[211] own nature considered is this scorpion armed with a sting; but Christ our Savior by His death has pulled out the sting of our death and on the cross triumphantly says, "O death where is thy sting! O grave where is thy victory!" (1 Cor. 15:55). And therefore even then when we feel the pangs of death approach, we should not fear but conceive hope, considering that our death is altered and changed by the virtue of the death of Christ.

---

211. Originally, "his."

Secondly, the death of Christ has quite taken away the second death from those that are in Christ, as Paul says, "There is no condemnation to them which are in Christ Jesus, which walk not after the flesh, but after the spirit" (Rom. 8:1).[212]

Thirdly, the death of Christ is a means to ratify His last will and testament. "For this cause was Christ the Mediator of the New Testament, that through death (which was for the redemption of the transgressions which were in the former testament) they which were called might receive the promise of the eternal inheritance. For where a testament is, there must be the death of him that made the testament: for the testament is confirmed when men are dead: for it is yet of no force so long as he is alive that made it" [Heb. 9:15–17]. And therefore the death of Christ does make His last will and testament, which is the covenant of grace, authentical unto us.

Fourthly, the death of Christ does serve to abolish the original corruption of our sinful hearts. As a strong corrosive laid to a sore eats out all the rotten and dead flesh, even so Christ's death, being applied to the heart of a penitent sinner by faith, weakens and consumes the sin that cleaves so fast unto our natures and dwells within us. Some will say, "How can Christ's death, which now is not, because it is long ago past and ended, kill sin in us now?" *Answer.* Indeed, if we regard the act of Christ's death, it is past; but the virtue and power thereof endures forever. And the power of Christ's death is nothing else but the power of His Godhead, which enabled Him in His death to overcome hell, the grave, death, and condemnation and to disburden Himself of our sins. Now when we have grace to deny ourselves and to put our trust in Christ and by faith are joined to Him, then as Christ Himself by the power of His Godhead overcame death, hell, and damnation in Himself, so shall we by the same power of His Godhead kill and crucify sin and corruption in ourselves. Therefore, seeing we reap such benefit by the death of Christ, if we will show ourselves to be Christians, let us rejoice in the death of Christ. And if the question be, "What is the chiefest thing wherein we rejoice in this world?" we may answer: the very cross of Christ, yea, the very least drop of His blood.

The duties to be learned by the death of Christ are two. The first concerns all ignorant and impenitent sinners. Such men, whatsoever they be, by the death of Christ upon the cross must be moved to turn from their sins. And if the consideration hereof will not move them, nothing in the world will. By nature, every man is a vassal of sin and a bondslave of Satan. The devil reigns and rules in all men by nature, and we ourselves can do nothing but serve and obey him. Nay, which is more, we live under the fearful curse of God for the

---

212. This paragraph break is not in the original, as the additional two following.

least sin. Well now, see the love of the Son of God, that gave Himself willingly to death upon the cross for you that He might free you from this most fearful bondage. Wherefore, let all those that live in sin and ignorance reason thus with themselves: has Christ, the Son of God, done this for us, and shall we yet live in our sins? Has He set open as it were the very gates of hell, and shall we yet lie weltering in our damnable ways and in the shadow of death? In the fear of God, let the death of Christ be a means to turn us to Christ. If it cannot move us, let us be resolved that our case is dangerous. To go further in this point, every one of us is by nature a sick man, wounded at the very heart by Satan. Though we feel it not, yet we are deadly sick. And behold, Christ is the good physician of the soul; and none in heaven or earth, neither saint, angel, nor man can heal this our spiritual wound, but He alone, who, though He were equal with the Father, yet He came down from His bosom and became man and lived here many years in misery and contempt. And when no herb nor plaster could cure this our deadly wound or desperate sickness, He was content to make a plaster with His own blood. The pain He took in making it caused Him to sweat water and blood. Nay, the making of it for us cost Him His life, in that He was content by His own death to free us from death—which, if it be true, as it is most true, then woeful and wretched is our case if we will still live in sin and will not use means to lay this plaster to our hearts. And after this plaster is applied to the soul, we should do as a man that has been grievously sick, who when he is on the mending hand gets strength by little and little. And so should we become new creatures, going on from grace to grace, and show the same by living godly, righteously, and soberly, that the world may see that we are cured of our spiritual disease. O happy, yea, thrice happy are they that have grace from God to do this.

The second duty concerns them which are repentant sinners.[213] Has Christ given Himself for you, and is your conscience settled in this? Then, [first,] you must answerably bear this mind, that if your life would serve for the glory of God and the good of the church, you would then give it most willingly if you be called thereto. Secondly, if Christ for your good has given His life, then you must in like manner be content to die for your brethren in Christ if need be. "He," says St. John, "laid down his life for us, therefore we ought to lay down our lives for our brethren" (1 John 3:16). Thirdly, if Christ was content to shed His own heart blood not for Himself but for the sins of every one of us, then we must be thus affected, that rather than by sinning we would willingly offend God, we should be content to have our own blood shed. Yea, if these two things were put to our choice, either to do that which might displease God or else to

---

213. This paragraph break is not in the original.

suffer death, we must rather die than do the same. Of this mind have been all the martyrs of God, who rather than they would yield to idolatry were content to suffer most bitter torments and cruel death. Yea, every good Christian is so affected that he had rather choose to die than to live, not moved by impatience in respect of the miseries of this life, but because he would cease to offend so loving a father. To sin is meat and drink to the world; but to a touched and repentant heart there is no torment so grievous as this is, to sin against God, if once he be persuaded that Christ died for him.

Thus much for Christ's death. Now follow those things which befell Christ when He was newly dead, and they are two especially. The first, that His legs were not broken as the legs of the two thieves were. Of the first, St. John renders a reason—namely, that the Scripture might be fulfilled, which says, "Not a bone of him shall be broken" [John 19:36; Ex. 12:46], which words were spoken by Moses of the paschal lamb and are here applied to Christ as being typically figured thereby. And hence we observe these two things. First, that Christ crucified is the true paschal lamb, as St. Paul says, "Christ our passover is sacrificed" [1 Cor. 5:7], and St. John says, "Behold the Lamb of God" [John 1:29], distinguishing Him thereby from the typical lamb. In this that Christ crucified is the true paschal lamb, the child of God has wonderful matter of comfort. The Israelites did eat the Passover in Egypt and sprinkled the blood of the lamb on the posts of their doors, that when the angel of God came to destroy the firstborn of man and beast and saw the blood upon their houses he might pass over them, that the plague should not be upon them to destruction [Ex. 12:23]. So likewise, if you do feed on the Lamb of God and by a lively faith sprinkle the door of your heart with His blood, the judgment of God in this life and the terrible curse of death with the fearful sentence of condemnation at the day of judgment and all punishments due unto your sins shall pass over you and not so much as touch you. And whereas the legs of our Savior Christ were not broken by the soldiers, who sought by all means possible to work against Him all the mischief they could, we may note that the enemies of Christ and His church, let them intend to show never so much malice against Him, they cannot go beyond that liberty which God gives them. They can do no more for their lives than that which God wills. The Medes and Persians are called the "Lord's sanctified ones" [Isa. 13:3], [and] Cyrus is called "the man of God's counsel" [46:11], because whatsoever they intended against the people of God, yet in all their proceedings they did nothing but that which God had determined before to be done. And when Sennacherib came against the Jews as a wild beast out of his den, the Lord tells Hezekiah concerning Assyria that He will put "his hook in his nostrils, and his bridle in his lips, and bring him back again the same way that he came" [37:29]—that is, He will so rule him that he shall not do the least hurt unto the Jews more than God will. This is a matter of great comfort to God's church oppressed with manifold enemies, Papists, Jews, Turks, and all infidels, maliciously bent against it for Christ's sake. For though they intend and practice mischief, yet more than God's will and counsel is they cannot do, because He has His ring in their nostrils and His bridle in their lips to rule them as He lists.

The second thing which fell out immediately upon the death of Christ is that the soldiers pierced His side with a spear, and thence issued water and blood. The use which arises of this point is twofold. First, it serves to prove that Christ died truly and not in show or a feigned death; for there is about the heart a film or skin like unto a purse,[214] wherein is contained clear water to cool the heat of the heart. And therefore, when water and blood issued out after piercing of the side, it is very likely that that very skin[215] was pierced; for else in reason we cannot conjecture whence this water should come. St. John, an eyewitness of this thing, being about to prove that Jesus, the son of Mary, was the true Messiah, brings in six witnesses: three in heaven, "the Father, the word, and the Holy Ghost" [1 John 5:7–8]; and three in earth, "the water, the Spirit, and the blood"—where no doubt he alludes to the water and blood that issued out of the side of Christ. By "Spirit," we may understand the efficacy and operation of God's Spirit, making men to bring forth the fruits of the same, as love, peace, joy, etc. And the second witness—namely, water—has relation to the water that came forth of Christ's side, which signifies the inward washing away of sin and the purging of the heart by Christ's blood, which also is and was signified by the outward washing of the body with water in baptism. The third witness he calls blood, alluding to the blood that issued out of Christ's side, whereby is signified the expiation or satisfaction made to God's justice for man's sin. The same use had the ceremonial sprinkling in the Old Testament, typically signifying the sprinkling of Christ's blood. Now these three witnesses are not to be sought for in heaven, but every Christian man must search for them in his own heart and conscience; and there shall he find them in some measure. And this water and blood, flowing out of the side of Christ, being now dead, signifies that He is our justification and sanctification even after His death, and that out of His death springs our life. And therefore, as Eve was made of a rib taken out of the side of Adam, so springs the church out of the blood that flows out of the side of the second Adam.

Having thus entreated of Christ's execution, let us now come to the last point—namely, the excellency of Christ's passion, consisting in these two

214. Columb. de re Anat. l. 7.
215. Pericardium.

points: (1) a sacrifice; (2) a triumph. For the first, when Christ died, He offered a propitiatory and real sacrifice to His Father; and herein His death and passion differs from the sufferings and deaths of all men whatsoever. In this sacrifice, we must consider four things: (1) who was the priest; (2) what was the sacrifice; (3) what was the altar; (4) the time wherein this sacrifice was offered.

The priest was Christ Himself, as the author of the epistle to the Hebrews proves at large [in] Hebrews from the third chapter to the ninth.[216] And of Him we are to consider these four points. The first, what is the office of Christ's priesthood? *Answer.* The office of Christ's priesthood stands in three things. (1) To teach doctrine. And therefore He is called the "high priest of our profession" [3:1]—that is, of the gospel which we profess—because He is the author and doctor of the same. (2) To offer up Himself unto His Father in the behalf of man for the appeasing of His wrath for sin. (3) To make request or intercession to God the Father, that He would accept the sacrifice which He offered on the cross for us.

The second point is, according to which nature He was a priest, whether in His manhood, or in His Godhead, or both together?[217] *Answer.* The office of His priesthood is performed by Him according to both His natures. And therefore He is a priest not as the Papists would have Him, according to His manhood only, but as He is both God and man. For as He is a mediator, so is He a priest. But Christ is a mediator according to both natures, each nature doing that which is peculiar to it and conferring something to the work of redemption. And therefore He is a priest as He is both God and man.

The third point, after what order He is a priest? *Answer.* The Scripture mentions two orders of priests: the order of Levi and the order of Melchizedek. Christ was not a priest after the order of Aaron, and yet notwithstanding in that priesthood were many notable rites whereby the priesthood of our Savior Christ was resembled. And we may note five especially.

First, in the anointing of the high priest, as of Aaron and his sons after him, oil was poured on his head [Ex. 29:7], and it ran down to the very edge of his garments [Ps. 133:2], whereby was signified that Christ, the true High Priest, was anointed "with the oil of gladness above his fellows" [45:7]—that is, that His manhood was filled with the gifts and graces of God, both in measure, number, and degree above all men and angels.

Secondly, the sumptuous and glorious apparel which the high priest put on when he came into the sanctuary [Ex. 28:2] was a sign of the rich and glorious

---

216. This paragraph break is not in the original.
217. This paragraph break is not in the original, as the additional six following.

robe of Christ's righteousness, which is the purity and integrity of His human nature and of His life.

Thirdly, the special parts of the high priest's attire were, first, the ephod, the two shoulders whereof had two onyx stones whereon were engraven the names of the twelve tribes of Israel [28:12]—six names on the one stone, and six on the other—as stones of remembrance of the children of Israel to Godward; secondly, the breastplate of judgment [v. 15, 21], like the work of the ephod, wherein were set twelve stones according to the names of the children of Israel, graven as signets every one after his name. Now by these two ornaments were figured two things in Christ. By the first, that He carries all the elect on His shoulders and supports them by His Spirit so long as they are in the world against the world, the flesh and the devil. By the second, that Christ our High Priest, being now in His sanctuary in heaven, has in memory all the elect; and their very names are written as it were in tables of gold before His face, and He has an especial love unto them and care over them. Upon this ground the church in the Canticles prays on this manner: "Set me as a seal on thy heart, and as a signet upon thy arm" [Song 8:6]. And indeed this is a matter of comfort unto us all, that Christ has our several names written in precious stones before His face, though He be now in heaven and we on earth; and that the particular estate of every one of us is both known and regarded of Him.

[Fourthly], again, God gave to Moses the Urim and Thummim, which was put on the breastplate of the high priest [Ex. 28:30] when he was to ask counsel from God of things unknown before the mercy seat, whence God gave answer. What the Urim and Thummim was, it is not known. And it is like[ly] it was not made by any art of man but given by God. And how it was used we cannot tell, but yet the signification of the words affords matter of meditation. "Urim" signifies lights, and "Thummim" signifies perfections. And by this a further matter was prefigured in Christ, who has the perfect Urim and Thummim in His breast, first, because in Him are hid all the treasures of wisdom and knowledge [Col. 2:3]; secondly, because He reveals to His church out of His Word such things as none can know but the children of God—as David says, "The secret of the Lord is revealed to them that fear him" [Ps. 25:14]. And for this cause the Spirit of Christ is called "the spirit of wisdom and revelation" [Eph. 1:17] and "the spirit of God; whereby we know the things that are given unto us of God" [1 Cor. 2:12]—as, namely, our election, vocation, justification, and sanctification in this life and our eternal glorification after this life. Yea, to every member of Christ within His church He gives a special spirit of revelation out of the Word, whereby He may know that God the Father is his Father; the Son the Redeemer, his Redeemer; and the Holy Ghost, his Sanctifier and Comforter.

Lastly, the high priest had a plate on his forehead, and therein was engraven "the holiness of Jehovah" [Ex. 28:36]. This signified the holiness of Christ; for as He is God He is holiness itself, and as He is man He is most holy, being sanctified by the Holy Ghost for this end, that He might cover our sins and unrighteousness with His righteousness and holy obedience.

The second order of priesthood is the order of Melchizedek, of which order Christ was, as David says, "Thou art a priest forever after the order of Melchizedek" [Hebrews 7], and that in two special respects. (1) Melchizedek was both a priest and a king; so was Christ. (2) Melchizedek had neither father nor mother, because his history is set down with mention of neither. So likewise Christ as He is God had no mother, and as He is man He had no father. The Papists avouch Christ to be a priest of this order in a new respect, in that as Melchizedek offered bread and wine when Abraham came from the slaughter of the kings [Gen. 14:18], so (say they) Christ in His last supper did offer His own body and blood under the forms of bread and wine. But this is a frivolous device of theirs; for if we read Hebrews 7, where this point is handled, there is no comparison at all made of their two sacrifices. But the resemblances before named are set down in which person is compared with person. Again, it is not said in Genesis that Melchizedek offered sacrifice, but that he brought forth bread and wine and made a feast to Abraham and his company. And if Christ should be of the order of Melchizedek in regard of the offering of bread and wine, yet would this make much against the Papists.[218] For Melchizedek brought forth true bread and true wine, but in the sacrifice of the mass there is no true bread nor true wine, but (as they say) the real body and blood of Christ under the form of bread and wine.

The fourth point is, whether there be any more real priests of the New Testament besides Christ, or no? *Answer.* In the Old Testament, there were many priests, one following another in continual succession; but of the New Testament there is one only real priest, Christ Jesus, God and man, and no more, as the author of the Hebrews says, because "he endureth forever, he hath an everlasting priesthood" [Heb. 7:24]. And the word translated "everlasting" signifies such a priesthood which cannot pass from Him to any other, as the priesthood of Aaron did. And therefore the priesthood of Christ is so tied to His own person that none can have the same but He—neither man nor angel nor any other creature, no, not the Father nor the Holy Ghost. But the factors of the Church of Rome will say that Christ may have men to be His deputies in His stead to offer sacrifice. *Answer.* We must consider Christ two ways: (1) as He is God; (2) as He is mediator. As He is God with the Father and with the Holy Ghost,

---

218. Protulit, non obtulit. (He brought forth, not offered.)

He has kings and magistrates to be His deputies on earth. And therefore they are called "elohim" [Psalm 82]—that is, "gods." But as He is Mediator and so consequently a priest and a king, He has neither deputy nor viceregent neither king to rule in His stead over His church nor priests to offer sacrifice for Him. Nay, He has no prophet to be His deputy, as He is the doctor of the church. And therefore He says to His disciples [to] be not called doctors, "for one is your doctor" [Matt. 23:10].[219] Indeed, He has His ministers to teach men His will, but a deputy to offer sacrifice in His stead He has not. And therefore we may with good conscience abhor the massing priesthood of the Church of Rome as a thing fetched from the bottom of hell, and the massing priests as instruments of Satan, holding this for a very truth, that we have but one only priest, even Christ Himself, God and man. Indeed, all Christians are priests to offer up spiritual sacrifice, but it is the property of Christ alone to offer an outward and real sacrifice unto God now in the New Testament.

Thus much of the first point, who is the priest. The second follows, what is the sacrifice. *Answer.* The sacrifice is Christ as He is man, or the manhood of Christ crucified. As the priest is both God and man, so the sacrifice is man, not God.[220] So it is said we are "sanctified by the offering of the body of Jesus Christ" [Heb. 10:10]. Touching this sacrifice, sundry questions are to be scanned.

The first, what kind of sacrifice it was?[221] *Answer.* In the Old Testament, there were two kinds of sacrifices: one, propitiatory, which served to satisfy for sin; the other, eucharistical, for praise and thanksgiving. Now the sacrifice of Christ was a sacrifice propitiatory, especially prefigured by the typical sacrifice called the whole burnt offering [Gen. 8:20; Job 1:5];[222] for it was all consumed to ashes upon the altar and turned into smoke. So the fire of God's wrath did seize upon Christ on the cross and did consume Him as it were to nothing to make us something. Secondly, when Noah offered a whole burnt offering after the flood, it is said God "smelled a savor of rest" [Gen. 8:21], not because He was delighted with the smell of the sacrifice, but because He approved his faith in Christ. And hereby was figured that Christ upon the cross was an offering and a "sacrifice of a sweet smelling savor unto God" [Eph. 5:2], because God was well pleased therewith. Now whereas Christ was content wholly to offer up Himself to appease the wrath of His Father for us, it must teach us to give our bodies and souls as holy, living, and acceptable sacrifices, wholly dedicating them to the service of God.

---

219. Originally, "Mark 23:10."
220. Or the Godhead.
221. This paragraph break is not in the original.
222. Originally, "Job 1:8."

The second question is, how oft Christ offered Himself? *Answer.* Once only and no more. This must be held as a principle of divinity: "which once offering hath he consecrated forever, them that are sanctified" [Heb. 10:14]. And again, "Christ was once offered to take away the sins of many" [9:28]. And it serves to overthrow the abominable sacrifice of the mass in which the true body and blood of Christ is offered under the forms of bread and wine really and substantially (as they say) for the remission of the sins of the quick and the dead, and that continually. But if this unbloody sacrifice of Christ be good, then is it either the continuing of that which was begun on the cross by Christ Himself or the iteration of it by the mass priest. Now let Papists choose whether of these two they will. If they say it is the continuing of the sacrifice of Christ, then they speak outrageous blasphemy; for it is in effect to say that Christ's sacrifice was not perfect but only begun on the cross and must be accomplished by the mass priest to the end of the world. If they affirm the second, that it is an iteration of Christ's sacrifice, then also they speak blasphemy; for hereby they make it also an imperfect sacrifice, because it is repeated and iterated. For upon this ground does the author to the Hebrews prove that the sacrifices of the Old Testament were imperfect—because they were daily offered. And whereas they say there be two kinds of sacrifices—one bloody once only offered upon the cross; the other unbloody, which is daily offered—I answer that this distinction has no ground out of God's Word. Neither was it known to the Holy Ghost, who says that without "blood there is no remission of sins" [v. 22].

The third question is, what is the fruit of this sacrifice? *Answer.* The whole effect thereof is contained in these four things. (1) The oblation of Christ purges the believer from all his sins, whether they be original or actual. So it is said, "If we walk in the light, we have fellowship one with another: and the blood of Jesus Christ his son purges us from all sin" [1 John 1:7], whether they be sins of omission in regard of our duties or of commission in doing evil. (2) The oblation serves for the justifying of a sinner before God, as Paul says, "We are justified by his blood, and are reconciled to God by his death" [Rom. 5:10]—this being here remembered, that in the passion of Christ we include His legal obedience, whereby He fulfilled the law for us. (3) The oblation of Christ serves to purge men's consciences from dead works. "How much more then shall the blood of Christ, which through the eternal Spirit offered himself without spot to God, purge your consciences from dead works to serve the living God?" [Heb. 9:14]. (4) The oblation of Christ procures us liberty to enter into heaven. "By the blood of Christ Jesus we may be bold to enter into the holy place, by the new and living way which he hath prepared for us through the veil, that is, his flesh" [10:20]. By our sins there is a partition wall made between God and us; but Christ by offering Himself upon the cross has beaten down this wall, opened heaven, and as it were trained the way with His own blood whereby we may enter into the kingdom of God and without the which we cannot enter in at all.

The last question is, how this sacrifice may be applied to us? *Answer.* The means of applying this sacrifice be two: (1) the hand of God, which offers; (2) the hand of the believer, that receives the sacrifice offered. The hand of God whereby He offers unto us this benefit is the preaching of the word and the administration of the sacraments, baptism and the Lord's Supper. And where-soever these His holy ordinances are rightly administered and put in practice, there the Lord puts forth His hand unto us and offers most freely the virtue and benefit of the death of Christ. And then in the next place comes the hand of the believer, which is faith in the heart, which when God offers does apprehend and receive the thing offered and make it ours.

The third thing to be spoken of is the altar whereon Christ offered Himself. The altar was not the cross, but rather the Godhead of Christ. He was both the priest, the sacrifice, and the altar: the sacrifice, as He is man; the priest, as He is both God and man; the altar, as He is God. The property of an altar is to sanctify the sacrifice, as Christ says, "Ye fools and blind, whether is greater, the offering, or the altar that sanctifieth the offering?" [Matt. 23:19].[223] Now Christ as He is God sanctifies Himself as He was man, and "therefore," says He, "for their sakes sanctify I myself" [John 17:19], by doing two things: (1) by setting apart the manhood to be a sacrifice unto His Father for our sins; (2) by giving to this sacrifice merit or efficacy to deserve at God's hands remission of our sins. The manhood of Christ without the Godhead has no virtue nor efficacy in itself to be a meritorious sacrifice, and therefore the dignity and excellency which it has is derived thence. As for the chalky and stony altars of the Church of Rome, they are nothing else but the toys of man's brain. Christ Himself is the only real altar of the New Testament. And instead of altars which were under the law we have now the Lord's Table whereon we celebrate the sacrament of His body and blood to show forth His death till He come.

The fourth point is concerning the time of Christ's oblation, which He Himself calls the acceptable year of the Lord [Luke 4:19], alluding unto another year under the law called the year of jubilee, which was every fifty years among the Jews, in which at the sound of a trumpet all that had let or sold their pos-sessions received them again. All that were bondmen were then set at liberty [Lev. 25:10]. This jubilee was but a figure of that perfect deliverance which was to be obtained by Christ's passion, which was not a temporary deliverance for every fifty year but an eternal freedom from the bondage of sin, hell, death, and condemnation. And the preaching of the word is the trumpet sounded

---

223. Originally, "Matt. 23:9."

which proclaims unto us freedom from the kingdom of darkness and invites us to come and dwell in perfect peace with Christ Himself. Well, if the year of perpetual jubilee be now come, in what a wretched estate are all our loose and blind people that esteem nothing of that liberty which is offered to them but choose rather to live in their sins and in bondage under Satan and condemnation, than to be at freedom in Christ?

Now follow the uses which are to be made of the sacrifice of Christ. The prophet Haggai says that the second temple built by Zerubbabel was nothing in beauty unto the first which was built by Solomon [Hag. 2:3].[224] And the reason is plain, for (as the Jews write) it wanted five things which the first temple had: (1) the appearing of the presence of God at the mercy seat between the two cherubim; (2) the Urim and Thummim on the breastplate of the high priest; (3) the inspiration of the Holy Ghost upon extraordinary prophets; (4) the ark of the covenant, for that was lost in the captivity; (5) fire from heaven to burn the sacrifices. Yet for all this, the prophet afterward says, "The glory of the last house, shall be greater than the first" [Hag. 2:9].[225] Now it may be demanded how both these sayings can stand together. *Answer.* We are to know that the second temple was standing in the time when Christ was crucified for our sins. And it was the sacrifice of Christ which gave glory and dignity to the second temple, though otherwise for building and outward ornaments it was far inferior to the first. And by this we are taught that if we would bring glory unto our own selves, unto our houses and kindred, either before God or before men, we must labor to be partakers of the sacrifice of Christ and the sprinkling of His blood to purge our hearts. This is the thing that brings renown both to place and person, how base soever we be in the eyes of the world.

Secondly, all oblations and meat offerings were sprinkled with salt, and every sacrifice of propitiation which was to be burned to ashes was first salted; and hereby two things are signified [Lev. 2:13; Ezek. 16:4; 43:24].[226] The first, that every one of us ourselves are loathsome or vile in the sight of God, like unto stinking carrion or raw flesh kept long unpowdered. A dead and rotten carcass is loathsome unto us, but we ourselves are a thousand times more loathsome unto God. The second, that we are as it were salted and made savory and acceptable to God by the virtue of the sacrifice of Christ upon the cross. Our duty then is to labor that we may feel in ourselves the biting and sharpness of the oblation of Christ to waste and consume the superfluities of sin and the corruptions of our nature. And we must withal endeavor that the whole course of our lives and our speech itself be gracious and powdered with salt, lest God at

---

224. Originally, "Hag. 2:4."
225. Originally, "Hag. 2:10."
226. This paragraph break is not in the original, as the additional three following..

length spew us out of His mouth. To this end has God appointed His ministers to be the salt of the earth, that by their ministry they might apply the death of Christ and season the people [Matt. 5:13; Col. 4:6]. And it has pleased God to besprinkle this land with more plenty of this salt than has been heretofore. But, alas, small is the number of them that give any relish of their good seasoning. The more lamentable is their case. For as flesh that cannot be seasoned with salt putrefies, so men that cannot be sweetened and changed by the sacrifice of Christ do rot and perish in their sins. The waters that issued from under the threshold of the sanctuary, when they came into the Dead Sea[227] [Ezek. 47:8, 11], the waters thereof were wholesome, but miry places and marshes, which could not be seasoned, were made salt pits. Now, these waters are the preaching of the gospel of Christ, which, flowing through all the parts of this isle, if it do not season and change our nation, it shall make it as places of nettles and salt pits and at length be an occasion of the eternal curse of God.

Thirdly, Christ's priesthood serves to make every one of us also to be priests. And, being priests, we must likewise have our sacrifice and our altar. Our sacrifice is the "clean offering" [Mal. 1:11],[228] which is the lifting up of "pure hands" [1 Tim. 1:8] to God without wrath or doubting in our prayers, also our body and souls, our hearts and affections, the works of our lives and the works of our callings—all which must be dedicated to the service of God for His glory and the good of His church. The altar whereon we must offer our sacrifice is Christ our Redeemer, both God and man, because by the virtue of His death, as with sweet odors, He perfumes all our obedience and makes it acceptable to God [Heb. 13:10; Rev. 8:3]. The ministers of the gospel are also in this manner priests, as Paul insinuates when he calls the Gentiles his "offering unto God" [Rom. 15:16]. And the preaching of the word is as it were a sacrificing knife whereby the old Adam must be killed in us, and we made a holy and acceptable sweet smelling oblation unto God, sanctified by the Holy Ghost. Therefore, everyone that hears God's word preached and taught must endeavor that by the profitable hearing thereof his sins and whole nature may be subdued and killed, as the beast was slain and sacrificed upon the altar by the hand of the Levite.

Lastly, the exhortation of the Holy Ghost must here be considered. "Seeing," says He, "we have an high priest, which is over the house of God, let us draw near with a true heart in assurance of faith, sprinkled in our hearts from an evil conscience, and washed in our bodies with pure water" [Heb. 10:21–22]. The meaning of the words is this: that if Christ have offered such a sacrifice of such a value and price, which procures pardon of sin, justification, sanctification, and

---

227. Mare mortuum.
228. Originally, "Mal. 1:12."

redemption, then we must labor to be partakers of it, to have our bodies and souls purified and cleansed by His blood and sanctified throughout by the Holy Ghost, that thereby we may be made fit to do sacrifice acceptable to God in Christ. This is the use which the apostle makes of the doctrine of Christ's priesthood in that place which also every man should apply unto himself; for why should we live in our sins and wicked ways, every hour incurring the danger of God's judgments, seeing Christ has offered such a sacrifice whereby we may be purged and cleansed and at length freed from all woe and misery?

Thus much of Christ's sacrifice. Now follows His triumph upon the cross. That Christ did triumph when He was upon the cross, it is plainly set down by the apostle Paul where he says, "That putting out the handwriting of ordinances that was against us, which was contrary to us, he even took it out of the way, and fastened it upon the cross, and hath spoiled the principalities and powers, and hath made show of them openly, and hath triumphed over them in the same cross" (Col. 2:14–15). This triumph is set forth by signs and testimonies of two sorts: (1) by signs of His glory and majesty; (2) by signs of His victory on the cross.

The signs of His glory and majesty are principally seven. The first is the title set over His head upon the cross, "Jesus of Nazareth, king of the Jews" (John 19:19).[229] The end why titles were set over the heads of malefactors was that the beholders might know the cause of the punishment and be admonished to take heed of like offences and be stirred up to a dislike of the parties executed for their offences. And therefore no doubt Pilate wrote the title of Christ for the aggravating of His cause, and that with his own hand. Yet mark the strange event that followed; for when Pilate was about to write the superscription, God did so govern and overrule both his heart and hand that instead of noting some crime he sets down a most glorious and worthy title, calling Him, "Jesus of Nazareth, king of the Jews," which words contain the very sum and pith of the whole gospel of Christ, delivered by the patriarchs and prophets from age to age. We must not think that Pilate did this of any good mind or upon any love or favor that he bare to Christ, but only as he was guided and overruled by the power of God for the advancement of the honor and glory of Christ. The like did Caiaphas, who, though a sworn enemy to Christ, yet he uttered a prophecy of Him, saying that it was necessary that one "should die for the people" (11:50)—not that he had any intent to prophesy, but because the Lord used him as an instrument to publish His truth. And when Balaam for the wages of unrighteousness would have cursed the Lord's people, for his life he could not. Nay, all his cursings were turned into blessings. By this then it appears that it

---

229. Originally, "John 19:18."

is not possible for any man, do what he can, to stop the course of the gospel of Christ. Nay, as we see, God can raise up the wicked sometimes to spread abroad and to publish the truth, though they themselves intend the contrary. Furthermore, let us mark that when the Jews did most of all intend to bring disgrace and ignominy upon our Savior Christ, then did they most of all extol and magnify His name. They could not for their lives have given Him a more renowned title than this, that He was king of the Jews. And the same is the case of all the members of Christ; for let a man walk in a good conscience before God and man, he shall find this to be true, that when he is most disgraced in the world, then commonly he is most honored with God and men.

Further, Pilate wrote this superscription in three languages: Hebrew, Greek, and Latin. And no doubt the end thereof in the providence of God was that the passion of Christ, as also the publishing of His kingdom and gospel, might be spread over the whole world. This shows the malice of the Church of Rome, which will not suffer the Word of God to be published but in the Latin tongue, lest the people should be entangled in errors.

Again, when Pilate had thus written the superscription, the high priests and Pharisees, offended thereat, came to Pilate, willing him to change the title, saying, "Write not the king of the Jews, but that he said, I am the king of the Jews." But Pilate answered them again, "That which I have written, I have written." Though Pilate had been overruled before to condemn Christ to death against his own conscience, yet will he not in any wise condescend to change the superscription. How comes this to pass? Surely, as he was ruled by the hand of God in penning it, so by the same hand of God was he confirmed in not changing it. Hence, we learn sundry instructions. First, that no man in the world, let him endeavor himself to the uttermost of his power, is able to stop the course of the kingdom of God. It stands firm and sure, and all the world is not able to prevail against it. Secondly, whereas Pilate, being but a heathen man, was thus constant that he will not have his writing changed, we may note how permanent and unchangeable the writings of the holy Word of God are. They are not the words of heathen men but were spoken by the mouth of the prophets and apostles, as God gave them utterance. The Book of Scripture therefore is much more immutable, so as no creature shall be able to change the least part of it till it be fulfilled. Thirdly, by Pilate's constancy we learn to be constant in the practice and professions of the religion of Christ. This is a necessary lesson for these days, wherein men's professions do fleet [away] like water and go and come with the tide—many zealous professors today, but tomorrow as cold as water. And the complaint of the Lord touching times past agrees to our days: "O Ephraim, what shall I say to thee? thy righteousness is like the morning dew" (Hosea 6:4).

The second is the conversion of the thief, a most worthy argument of the Godhead of Christ. For by it when He was upon the cross and in the very midst of His passion, He gives unto all the world a lively and notable experience of the virtue and power of His death, so as His very enemies might not only behold the passion itself but also at the same time acknowledge the admirable efficacy thereof. And therefore with the passion of Christ we must join the conversion of the thief, which is as it were a crystal glass wherein we may sensibly behold the endless merit and virtue of the obedience of Christ to His Father, even to the death of the cross. And therefore I will briefly touch the special instructions which are to be learned by it.

First, let us mark that both the thieves in every respect were equal, both wicked and lewd livers, and for their notorious faults both attacked, condemned, and executed both on the cross at the same time with Christ.[230] Yet for all this, the one repenting was saved; the other was not. And in their two examples we see the state of the whole world, whereof one part is chosen to life eternal and thereupon attains to faith and repentance in this life. The rest are rejected in the eternal counsel of God for just causes unknown to Himself, and such, being left to themselves, never repent at all.

Secondly, we are taught hereby that the whole work of our conversion and salvation must be ascribed wholly to the mere mercy of God. Of those two thieves, the one was as deeply plunged in wickedness as the other; and yet the one is saved, the other condemned. The like was in Jacob and Esau [Rom. 9:13][231]—both born at one time and of the same parents and neither of them had done good nor evil when they were born. Yet one was then loved; the other was hated. Yea, if we regard outward prerogatives, Esau was the firstborn and yet was refused [Gen. 35:13].

Furthermore, the thief on the cross declares his conversion by manifest signs and fruits of repentance, as appears by the words which he spoke to his fellow: "Fearest thou not God, seeing thou art in the same condemnation?" [Luke 23:40]. Though hands and feet were fast nailed on the cross, yet heart and tongue are at liberty to give some tokens of his true repentance. The people of this our land hear the word, but for the most part are without either profit in knowledge or amendment of life. Yet for all this they persuade themselves that they have good hearts and good meanings, though they cannot bear it away and utter it so well as others. But, alas, poor souls. They are deluded by Satan, for a man that is converted cannot but express his conversion and bring forth the fruit thereof. And therefore our Savior Christ says, "If a man believe in me,

230. This paragraph break is not in the original, as the additional one following.
231. Originally, "Rom. 9:14."

out of his belly shall flow rivers of water of life" [John 7:38]. The grace (as Elihu says) of God is like "new wine" [Job 32:19] in a vessel which must have a vent. And therefore he that shows no tokens of God's grace in this life is not as yet converted, let him think and say of himself what he will. Can a man have life and never move nor take breath? And can he that brings forth no fruit of conversion live unto God? Well, let us now see what were the fruits of this thief's repentance. They may be reduced to four heads.

First, he rebukes his fellow for mocking Christ, endeavoring thereby to bring him to the same condition with himself, if it were possible.[232] Whereby he discovers unto us the property of a true repentant sinner, which is to labor and strive so much as in him lies to bring all men to the same state that he is in. Thus, David, having tried the great love and favor of God toward himself, breaks forth and says, "Come children, hearken unto me, and I will teach you the fear of the Lord" [Ps. 34:11], showing his desire that the same benefits which it had pleased God to bestow on him might also in like manner be conveyed to others. Therefore, it is a great shame to see men professing religion carried away with every company and with the vanities and fashions of the world, whereas they should rather draw even the worst men that be to the fellowship of those graces of God which they have received. That which the Lord spoke to the prophet Jeremiah must be applied to all men: "Let them return unto thee, but return not thou unto them" [Jer. 15:19]. In instruments of music, the string out of tune must be set up to the rest that be in tune, and not the rest to it.

Again, in that he checks his fellow, it shows that those which be touched for their own sins are also grieved when they see other men sin and offend God. But to go further in this point, let us diligently and carefully mark the matter of his reproof: "Fearest thou not God, seeing thou art in the same condemnation?" In which words he rips up his lewdness even to the quick and gives him a worthy item, telling him that the cause of all their former wickedness had been the want of the fear of God. And this point must every one of us mark with great diligence. For if we enter into our hearts and make a thorough search, we shall find that this is the root and foundation of all our offences. We miserable men for the most part have not grace to consider that we are always before God and to quake and tremble at the consideration of His presence, and this makes us so often to offend God in our lives as we do. Abraham, coming before Abimelech, shifting for himself, said that Sarah was his sister and, being demanded why he did so, answered, "Because he thought the fear of God was not in that place" [Gen. 20:11], insinuating that he which wants the fear of God will not make conscience of any sin whatsoever. Would we then even from the bottom

---

232. This paragraph break is not in the original.

of our hearts turn to God and become new creatures? Then let us learn to fear God, which is nothing else but this: when a man is persuaded in his own heart and conscience that wheresoever he be he is in the presence and sight of God and by reason thereof is afraid to sin. This we must have fully settled in our hearts, if we desire to learn but the first lesson of true wisdom. But what reason uses the thief to draw his fellow to the fear of God? "Thou art," says he, "in the same condemnation"—that is, "By your sins and manifold transgressions you have deserved death, and it is now most justly inflicted upon you. Will you not yet fear God?" Where we are taught that temporal punishments and crosses ought to be a means to work in us the fear of God, for that is one end why they are sent of God. "It is good for me," says David, "that I have been chastised, that I may learn thy statutes" [Ps. 119:71].[233] And Paul says, "When we are chastised, we are nurtured of the Lord" [1 Cor. 11:32].[234] And the Jews are taught by the prophet Micah to say, "I will bear the wrath of the Lord, because I have sinned against him" [Mic. 7:9].

The second fruit of his conversion is that he condemns himself and his fellow for their sins, saying, "Indeed we are righteously here, for we receive things worthy for that we have done"—that is, "We have wonderfully sinned against God's majesty and against our brethren. And therefore this grievous punishment which we bear is most just and due unto us." This fruit of repentance springs and grows very thin among us, for few there be which do seriously condemn themselves for their own sins. The manner of men is to condemn others and to cry out that the world was never so bad; but bring them home to themselves, and you shall find that they have many excuses and defenses as plaster work to cast over their foul and filthy sins. And if they be urged to speak against themselves, the worst will be thus: "God help us. We are all sinners, even the best of us." But certain it is that he which is thoroughly touched in conscience for his sins both can and will speak more against himself for his manifold offences than all the world besides. Thus, Paul when he was converted called himself "the chief of all sinners" [1 Tim. 1:15]. And the prodigal child confessed that he had sinned against heaven and against his father and was not worthy to be called his child.

The third fruit of his conversion is that he excuses our Savior Christ and gives testimony of His innocency, saying, "But this man hath done nothing amiss." Mark here, Pilate condemned Christ; Herod mocked Him; all the learned scribes and Pharisees condemned Him; and the people cry, "Away with Him. Let Him be crucified." And among His own disciples, Peter denied Him,

---

233. Originally, "Ps. 119:17."
234. Originally, "1 Cor. 11:33."

and the rest ran away. There remains only this poor silly wretch upon the cross to give testimony of Christ's innocency, whereby we learn that God chooses the simple ones of this world to overthrow the wisdom of the wise. And therefore we must take heed that we be not offended at the gospel of Christ, by reason that for the most part simple and mean men in the world embrace it. Nay, mark further, this one thief, being converted, had a better judgment in matters concerning God's kingdom than the whole body of the Jews. And by this also students may learn that if they desire to have in themselves upright judgments in matters of religion, first of all, they must become repentant sinners. And though a man have never so much learning, yet if he be carried away with his own blind affections and lusts, they will corrupt and darken his judgment. Men which work in mines and coal pits under the earth are troubled with nothing so much as with damps, which make their candle burn dark and sometimes puts it quite out. Now every man's sins are the damps of his heart, which when they take place do dim the light of his judgment and cast a mist over the mind and darken the understanding and reason. And therefore a needful thing it is that men in the first place should provide for their own conversion.

The fourth fruit of his repentance is that he prays for mercy at Christ's hands. "Lord," says he, "remember me when thou comest into thy kingdom," in which prayer we may see what is the property of faith. This thief at this instant heard nothing of Christ but the scornings and mockings of the people, and he saw nothing but a base estate full of ignominy and shame and the cursed death of the cross. Yet nevertheless he now believes in Christ and therefore entreats for salvation at His hand.

Hence we learn that it is one thing to believe in Christ, and another to have feeling and experience, and that even then when we have no sense nor experience we must believe; for "faith is the subsisting of things which are not seen" [Heb. 11:1], and "Abraham above hope did believe under hope" [Rom. 4:18], and Job says, "Though thou kill me yet will I believe in thee" [Job 13:15]. In philosophy, a man begins by experience, after which comes knowledge and belief, as when a man has put his hand to the fire and feels it to be hot. He comes to know thereby that fire burns. But in divinity we must believe though we have no feeling. First comes faith, and after comes sense and feeling. And the ground of our religion stands in this: to believe things neither seen nor felt; to hope above all hope, and without hope; in extremity of affliction to believe that God loves us, when He seems to be our enemy, and to persevere in the same to the end.

The answer which Christ made to his prayer was, "This day shalt thou be with me in paradise" [Luke 23:43]. Whereby He testifies in the midst of His sufferings the power which He had over the souls of men and verifies that gracious promise, "Ask and ye shall receive, seek and ye shall find, knock, and it shall be opened unto you," and withal confutes the popish purgatory. For if any man should have gone to that forged place of torment, then the thief upon the cross, who, repenting at the last gasp, wanted time to make satisfaction for the temporal punishment of his sins. And by this conversion of the thief we may learn that if any of us would turn to God and repent, we must have three things. (1) The knowledge of our own sins. (2) From the bottom of our hearts we must confess and condemn ourselves for them and speak the worst that can be of ourselves in regard of our sins. (3) We must earnestly crave pardon for them and call for mercy at God's hands in Christ, withal reforming our lives for the time to come. If we do, we give tokens of repentance. If not, we may think what we will, but we deceive ourselves and are not truly converted. And here we must be warned to take heed lest we abuse as many do the example of the thief to conclude thereby that we may repent when we will, because the thief on the cross was converted at the last gasp—for there is not a second example like to this in all the whole Bible. It was also extraordinary. Indeed, sundry men are called at the eleventh hour, but it is a most rare thing to find the conversion of a sinner after the eleventh hour and at the point of the twelfth. This mercy God vouchsafed this one thief that he might be a glass in which we might behold the efficacy of Christ's death; but the like is not done to many men, no, not to one of a thousand. Let us rather consider the sin of the other thief who neither by the dealing of his fellow nor by any speech of Christ could be brought to repentance. Let us not therefore defer our repentance to the hour of death, for then we shall have sore enemies against us: the world, the flesh, the devil, and a guilty conscience. And the best way is beforehand to prevent them. And experience shows that if a man defer repentance to the last gasp, often when he would repent he cannot. Let us take Solomon's counsel, "Remember thy Creator in the days of thy youth, before the evil days come" (Eccl. 12:1). If we will not hear the Lord when He calls us, He will not hear us when we call Him.

The third sign was the eclipsing or darkening of the sun from the sixth hour to the ninth. And this eclipse was miraculous. For by the course of nature the sun is never eclipsed, but in the new moon, whereas contrariwise this eclipse was about the time of the Passover, which was always kept at the full moon. Question is made touching the largeness of it. Some, moved by the words of Luke, who says that darkness was upon the whole earth [Luke 23:44], have thought that the eclipse was universal over the whole world. But I rather think that St. Luke's meaning is that it was over the whole region or country of Jewry. For if such a wonder had happened over the whole world, all historiographers, Greek and Latin and astronomers, diligent observers of all eclipses would have made special mention thereof. And though some writers say that it was over the whole earth,[235] and that it was set down in record both by the Romans and Grecians, yet all the writings prove no more but this, that it was over Jewry and Galilee and the countries bordering near unto.

The uses of this miracle are manifold. (1) This darkening of the sun gives a check to the Jews for their crucifying of Christ. They were not ashamed to apprehend, accuse, and condemn Him; yet this glorious creature, the sun, pulls in its[236] beams, being as it were ashamed to behold that which they were not ashamed to do.

(2) It serves to signify the great judgment of God to come upon the Jews.[237] For as when Christ suffered darkness was over all the land of Jewry, and all the world besides had the light of the sun, so shortly after "blindness of mind" [2 Cor. 3:15] was over the whole nation of the Jews, and all the world besides saw the Sun of Righteousness, shining unto them in preaching of the gospel [Mal. 4:1–2].

(3) It serves to advertise us that such as carry themselves toward Christ as the Jews did have nothing else in them but darkness, and that they sit "in the darkness and shadow of death" [Isa. 8:20; Luke 1:79], and therefore not able any whit better to see the way that leads unto life, than he which is cast into a dark dungeon can—who, if they thus remain, shall at length be cast into utter darkness. This being the estate of all them that be forth of Christ, we must labor to be freed from this darkness, that the daystar may rise in our hearts [2 Peter 1:19] and shine upon us and put life into us.

(4) This miraculous and wonderful darkening of the sun does convince the Jews that Christ, whom they crucified, was the Lord of glory and the Savior of the world. And it is very like[ly] that this was the principal end of this miracle. For whereas neither His doctrine nor His former miracles could move them to acknowledge Him for that Messiah, yet this one work of God does as it were strike the nail to the head and stop all their mouths.

(5) Besides this, whereas at the very instant when Christ was about to make satisfaction to the justice of His Father for our sins the sun was thus darkened, it teaches us, first, to think of the passion of Christ not as of a light matter, but as one of the greatest wonders of the world, at the sight whereof the very frame of nature was changed. Secondly, to think of our own sins as the vilest things in the world and that they deserve the intolerable wrath of God, considering that at the time when they were to be abolished the course of nature even in the very heavens is turned upside down.

235. Euseb. Chron. Tertul. Apol. c. 12. Oros. l. 7. c. 4.
236. Originally, "his."
237. This paragraph break is not in the original, as the additional three following.

The fourth sign is the "rending of the veil of the temple from the top to the bottom" [Matt. 27:51]. The temple was divided into two parts: the more inward, into which no man might come but the high priest, and that once a year, and it was called the holy of holies; the other was that where the people came and offered sacrifices unto the Lord. Now that which parted the temple into these two parts was called the veil, and at the time of Christ's passion it was rent from the top to the very bottom. This has divers uses: (1) The holy of holies signified the third heaven, where God shows Himself in glory and majesty unto His saints. And the rending of the veil figures unto us that by the death of Christ, heaven, which was otherwise shut by our sins, is now set open and a way made to enter thereto [Heb. 9:8]. (2) It signifies that by the death of Christ we have without impediment free access to come unto God the Father by earnest prayer in the name of Christ, which is a most unspeakable benefit [John 1:51]. (3) It signifies that by Christ's death an end is put to all ceremonies, to ceremonial worship, and the sacrifices of the Old Testament. And that therefore in the New Testament there remains one only real and outward sacrifice—that is, Christ crucified on the cross. And the whole service and worship of God for outward ceremonies [is] most simple and plain. (4) The temple was the chief and one of the most principal prerogatives that the Jews had. It was their glory that they had such a place wherein they might worship and do service to the true God. And for the temple's sake, God often spared them, and therefore Daniel prays, "O Lord, hear the prayer of thy servant, and his supplication, and cause thy face to shine upon the sanctuary, that lies waste, for the Lord's sake" [Dan. 9:17]. Yet for all this, when they began to crucify the Lord of life, their prerogatives help them not. Nay, they are deprived thereof, and God even with His own hand rends the veil of the temple in sunder, signifying unto them that if they forsake Him, He will also forsake them. And so we may say of the Church of England. No doubt for the gospel's sake we have outward peace and safety and many other blessings and are in account with other nations. Yet if we make no conscience to obey the Word of God, and if we have no love of Christ and His members, God will at length remove His candlestick from us and utterly deprive us of this ornament of the gospel and make our land as odious unto all the world as the land of the Jews is at this day. Let us therefore with all care and diligence show forth our love both to Christ Himself and to His members and adorn the gospel, which we profess, by bringing forth fruits worthy of it.

The fifth sign is the earthquake, whereby hard rocks were cloven asunder. And it serves very fitly to signify further unto us that the sin of the Jews in putting Christ to death was so heavy a burden that the earth could not bear it but tremble thereat [Matt. 27:51], though the Jews themselves made no bones of it. And it is a thing to be wondered at that the earth does not often in these days trembled and quake at the monstrous blasphemies and fearful oaths by the wounds and blood and heart of Christ, whereby His members are rent asunder, and He traitorously crucified again.

Secondly, the earthquake shows unto us the exceeding and wonderful hardness of the hearts of the Jews, and ours also.[238] They crucified Christ and were not touched with any remorse; and we can talk and hear of His death, yea, we can say He was crucified for our sins, and yet we are nothing affected therewith. Our hearts will not rend, when as hard rocks cleave asunder.

Thirdly, the moving of the earth and the rending of the rocks asunder may be a sign unto us of the virtue of the doctrine of the gospel of Christ, which is nothing else but the publishing of the passion of His death, which, being preached, shall shake heaven and earth, sea and land [Hag. 2:7]. It shall move the earthen, hard, and rocky hearts of men and raise up of mere stones and rocks children unto Abraham. But the main use and end of this point is to prove that He that was crucified was the true Messiah, the Son of God, and therefore had the power of heaven and earth and could move all things at His pleasure.

The sixth sign of the power of Christ is that "graves did open and many bodies of the saints which slept arose" [Matt. 27:52–53] and came out of their graves after His resurrection and went into the holy city and appeared unto many. The use of this sign is this: it signifies unto us that Christ by His death upon the cross did vanquish death in the grave and opened it and thereby testified that He was the resurrection and the life, so that it shall not have everlasting dominion over us, but that He will raise us up from death to life and to everlasting glory.

The seventh sign is the testimony of the centurion with his soldiers which stood by to see Christ executed. St. Mark says when he saw that Christ thus crying gave up the ghost, he said, "Truly this was the Son of God" [Mark 15:39]. Thus, we see it is an easy matter for Christ to defend His own cause. Let Judas betray Him, Peter deny Him, and all the rest forsake Him; yet He can, if it so please Him, make the centurion that stands by to see Him executed to testify His innocency. But what was the occasion that moved Him to give so worthy a testimony? St. Matthew says it was fear, and that fear was caused by hearing the loud cry of Christ and by seeing the earthquake and things which were done (Matt. 27:54). And this must put us in mind not to pass by God's judgments, which daily fall out in the world, but take knowledge of them and as it were to fix both our eyes on them. For they are notable means to strike and astonish the rebellious heart of man and to bring it in awe and subjection to God. After that the two first captains with their fifties, commanding the prophet Elijah to come

---

238. This paragraph break is not in the original, as the additional one following.

down to King Ahaziah, were consumed with fire from heaven, the king sent his third captain over fifty with his fifty to fetch him down. But what does he? It is said he fell on his knees before Elijah and besought him, saying, "O man of God, I pray thee let my life and the lives of these fifty servants be precious in thine eyes" [2 Kings 1:13]. But what was the cause why he prayed thus? Surely, he observed what judgments of God fell upon his two former fellow captains. "Behold," says he, "there came down fire from heaven, and devoured the two former captains with their fifties: therefore let my life be precious now in thy sight" [v. 14]. Thus, laying to his own heart and making use of God's judgments, he humbled himself and was spared with his fifty. And Habakkuk says, "When I heard thy voice"—namely, of God's judgments—"rottenness entered into my bones, and I trembled in myself, that I might be safe in the day of the Lord" [Hab. 3:16]. Now what this fear of the centurion was, there is a further question; and it is very like[ly] that it was but a sudden motion or a certain preparative to better things. For he was but a heathen man and had as yet no knowledge of Christ, and whether he repented or not, it is uncertain. And we must not marvel at this, for there are many sudden motions, in show very good, that upon like occasions rise in the hearts of natural men. When God plagued the land of Egypt, then Pharaoh sent for Moses and confessed that "the Lord was righteous, but he and his people were wicked; and desired Moses to pray to God to take away the plague, who did so" (Ex. 9:27, 34). But so soon as the hand of God was stayed, he returned to his old rebellion again. And as a dog that comes out of the water shakes his ears and yet returns into it again, so is the manner of the world. When crosses and calamities befall men, as sickness, loss of friends or goods, then with Ahab they outwardly humble themselves and go softly. They use to frequent that place where the word is preached and God's name called upon. But, alas, common experience shows that those things are but fits arising of uncertain and flittering motions in the heart. For so soon as the cross is removed, they return to their old bias again and become as bad and as backward as ever they were, being like to the tree that lies in the water, which for a while is green but afterward withers. And therefore we for our parts, when any good motions come into our hearts as the beginnings of further grace, we (I say) must not quench them but cherish and preserve them, remembering that the kingdom of heaven is like a "grain of mustard seed" [Matt. 13:31–32], which, when it is sown, is the least of all seeds; but afterward it grows up into a tree, that the fowls of heaven may build their nests in it. And like to this are the first motions of God's Spirit, and therefore they must be cherished and maintained.

And thus much for the seven signs of the power of Christ's Godhead. Now follows the second part of the triumph of Christ, which contains signs of His victory upon the cross, notably expressed by Paul when he says, "And putting out the handwriting of ordinances which was against us, which was contrary to us, he even took it out of the way, and fastened it upon the cross, and has spoiled the principalities and powers, and hath made a show of them openly and hath triumphed openly in the same" (Col. 2:14–15). In which words he alludes to the manner of heathen triumphs; for it was the custom of the heathen princes, when they had gotten the victory over their enemies, first to cause a pillar of stone or some great oak to be cut down and set up in the place of victory, upon which either the names of the chief enemies were set, or their heads were hanged, or words were written in the pillar to testify the victory. This being done, there followed an open show in which first the conqueror prepares for himself a chariot of victory wherein he was himself to ride, and then the chief of his enemies, bound and pinioned, were led openly after him. Now on the same manner upon the cross there was a pitched field. The conqueror on the one side was Christ; His enemies on the other side were the world, the flesh, hell, death, damnation, the devil, and all his angels—all which, banding themselves against Him, were all subdued by Him upon the same cross. And He Himself gave two signs of His triumph: one was a monument of the victory; the other, open show of His conquest. Now, the monument of Christ's victory was the cross itself whereon He nailed the obligation or bill which was against us whereby Satan might have accused and condemned us before God. For we must consider that God the Father is a creditor and we all debtors unto Him. He has a bill of our hands, which is the law, in that it gives testimony against us, first, by the legal washing, which did show and signify that we were altogether defiled and unclean; secondly, by the sacrifices that were daily offered for the propitiation of our sins. Now, Christ was our surety and paid every jot of the debt which we should have paid and, requiring the acquittance, takes the ceremonial law and the curse of the moral law and nails them to the cross.

Furthermore, in the show of conquest, the chariot is the cross likewise; for it was not only a monument of victory, but also a chariot of triumph. And the captives, bound and pinioned, which followed Christ, are the principalities and powers—that is, the devil and his angels, hell, death, and condemnation—all which are as it were taken prisoners; their armor and weapons are taken from them; and they, chained and bound each to other.

The meditation of this point serves to admonish us to abandon all manner of sin and to make conscience of every good duty, if we will aright profess the gospel of Christ; for when we sin, we do as it were pull Christ out of His chariot of triumph and untie Satan's bonds and give him weapons and (as much as we can) make him valiant and strong again. Now, for any man to make Satan and sin valiant and strong against himself, whereas Christ has weakened him and even bruised his head, is no better than to become an enemy to the cross of

Christ [Phil. 3:18]. Again, hereby we are taught to pray unto God, that our blind eyes may be opened, that we may discern aright of the passion of Christ. It is a wonder to see how men are carried away with a liking of vain shows, games, and interludes—how they spend even whole days in beholding them and their money also that they may come to the places where they are. Oh then how exceedingly ought our hearts to be ravished with this most admirable show in which the Son of God Himself rides most gloriously in His chariot of triumph and leads His and our most cursed enemies captive, yea, treads them under His foot! This triumph is set forth unto us in the preaching of the gospel and may be seen of us all freely without money or money-worth. What wretches then shall we be if we suffer our hearts to be filled with earthly delights and in the mean season have little or no desire to behold with the eyes of our mind this goodly spectacle that is to be seen in the passion of Christ that serves to revive and refresh our souls to life eternal?

Thirdly, if Christ when He was most weak and base in the eyes of men did most of all triumph upon the cross, then every one of us must learn to say with the apostle Paul, "God forbid that I should rejoice in anything, but in the cross of Christ Jesus our Lord" [Gal. 6:14]. That we may say this truly, first of all, we must labor to have the benefit of the cross of Christ not only in the remission but also in the mortification of our sins. Secondly, we must not be discomforted but rather rejoice and triumph therein. A Christian man can never have greater honor than to suffer for the gospel of Christ, when God calls him thereunto. And therefore St. Paul sets forth another most glorious show which all those must make that suffer anything for God's cause [1 Cor. 4:9]. They must encounter with the world, the flesh, and the devil and are placed as it were on a theater; and in this conflict the beholders are men and angels, yea, the whole host of heaven and earth. The umpire or judge is God Himself, who will give sentence of victory on their side, and so they shall overcome. We must not hereupon thrust ourselves into danger; but when it shall please God to call us thereunto, we must think ourselves highly honored of Him. As when God sends loss of friends, of substance, or good name, or any other calamity, we must not despair or be over-grieved but rather rejoice and address ourselves, then with our Savior Christ to make a triumph.

Thus much of Christ's triumph and the passion of His cross. Now follows the second degree of His humiliation, in these words, "and buried." Where we must consider these points: (1) why it was needful that Christ should be buried; (2) who was the author of His burial; (3) the manner or preparation to His burial; (4) the place and time where and when He was buried. Of these in order. For the first, the causes are many, but especially four, why Christ was to be buried. (1) That the truth and certainty of His death might be confirmed unto us, and that no man might so much as imagine that His death was a phantastical death or His body a phantastical body; for men use not to bury a living but a dead man, or a man in show but a true man. (2) That His burial might be unto Him a passage from the estate of humiliation to the estate of exaltation, which began in His resurrection. And He could not have risen again, if He had not been first buried. (3) That the outward humiliation in the form of a servant, which He took upon Him, might be continued upon Him to the lowest degree of all. And therefore it was not sufficient that He should be crucified even to death, but, being dead, He must also be buried. (4) Christ was buried that He might not only vanquish death on the cross, but even after the manner of conquerors subdue him at his own home and as it were pluck him out of his own cabin or den.

(2) The authors of Christ's burial were Joseph of Arimathea and Nicodemus, who came to Jesus by night [Matt. 27:57–58, etc.; Mark 15:43]. Now, concerning them and this their fact, there are many things worthy to be considered in this place. First of all, they were disciples of Christ, and the difference between them and the rest is to be considered [John 19:38]. The other disciples, though in number they were but few, yet in the feast before His passion they openly followed Him. But when Christ was to be arraigned, and the persecution of the church of the New Testament began in Him, then Judas betrayed Him, Peter denied Him, and the rest fled away. Yet even at the same instant these two secret disciples of our Savior Christ, Joseph of Arimathea and Nicodemus, take courage to themselves and in time of danger openly profess themselves to be Christ's disciples by an honorable and solemn burial, God no doubt opening their hearts and enabling them to do so. The like is to be seen in all ages since the passion of Christ in the church of God, in which men zealous for the gospel in peace have been timorous in persecution, whereas weak ones have stood out against their enemies even unto death itself. The reason is because God will humble those His servants which are oftentimes endued with great measure of graces and contrariwise exalt and strengthen the weak and feeble. And the same no doubt will be found true among us, if it should please God to send any new trial into the Church of England. This serves to teach us to think charitably of those which are as yet but weak among us and withal in our profession to carry a low sail and to think basely of ourselves and in the whole course of our lives creep a-low by the ground, running on in fear and trembling, because the Lord oftentimes humbles those that be strong and gives courage and strength to weak ones boldly to confess His name.

Secondly, whereas these two disciples have such care of the burial of Christ, we learn that it is our duty to be careful also for the honest and solemn burial of our brethren.[239] The Lord Himself has commanded it, "Thou art dust, and to dust thou shalt return" [Gen. 3:19]. Also, the bodies of men are the good creatures of God. Yea, the bodies of God's children are the temples of the Holy Ghost, and therefore there is good cause why they should be honestly laid in the earth. And it was a curse and judgment of God upon Jehoiakim that "he must not be buried" but "like a dead ass be drawn and cast out of the gates of Jerusalem" [Jer. 22:19]. And so the Lord threatens a curse upon the Moabites, because they did not bury the king of Edom but burnt his bones into lime [Amos 2:1]. And therefore it is a necessary duty [for] one neighbor and friend to look to the honest burial of another. Hence it follows that the practice of Spain and Italy and all the popish countries which is to keep the parts of men's bodies and such like relics of saints unburied that they may be seen of men and worshipped has no warrant. Dust they are, and to dust they ought to be returned.

Furthermore, the properties and virtues of both these men are severally to be considered. And first, to begin with Joseph, he was a senator, a man of great account, authority, and reputation among the Jews [Luke 23:50]. It may seem a strange thing that a man of such account would abase himself so much as to take down the body of Christ from the cross. It might have been a hindrance to him and a disgrace to his estate and calling, as we see in these days—it would be thought a base thing for a knight or lord to come to the place of execution and take down a thief from the hand of the hangman to bury him. But this noble senator Joseph for the love he bare to Christ made no account of his estate and calling, neither did he scorn to take upon him so base an office, considering it was for the honor of Christ. Where we learn that if we truly love Christ, and our hearts be set to believe in Him, we will never refuse to perform the basest service that may be for His honor. Nothing shall hinder us. It is further said that he was "a good man and a just, and also a rich man" [vv. 50–51]. And the first appears in this, that he would neither consent to the counsel nor fact of the Jews in crucifying Christ. It is rare to find the like man in these days.

From this example, we learn these lessons. That a rich man, remaining a rich man, may be a servant of God and also be saved; for riches are the good blessings of God and in themselves do no whit hinder a man in coming to Christ. But some will say [that] Christ Himself says, "It is easier for a cable to go through the eye of a needle, than a rich man to enter into the kingdom of heaven" [Matt. 19:4]. *Answer.* It is to be understood of a rich man so long as he swells with a confidence in his wealth. But we know that if a cable be untwisted and drawn into small threads, it may be drawn through the eye of a needle. So he that is rich, let him deny himself, abase himself, and lay aside all confidence

---

239. This paragraph break is not in the original.

in himself, in his riches, and honor and be as it were made small as a twine thread and with this good senator Joseph become the disciple of Christ—he may enter into the kingdom of heaven. But Christ says in the parable that riches are thorns which choke the grace of God. *Answer.* It is true; they are thorns in that subject or in that man that puts his trust in them, not in their own nature, but by reason of the corruption of man's heart, who makes of them his god.

St. John says further that Joseph was "a disciple" of Christ [John 19:38], but yet a close disciple for fear of the Jews.[240] And this shows that Christ is most ready to receive them that come unto Him, though they come laden with manifold wants. I say not this [so] that any hereby should take boldness to live in their sins, but my meaning is that though men be weak in the faith, yet are they not to be dismayed but to come to Christ, who refuses none that come to Him. "Draw near to God," says St. James, "and he will draw near to you" [James 4:8]. Christ does not forsake any, till they forsake Him first.

Lastly, the Holy Ghost says of him that he waited for the kingdom of God— that is, he did believe in the Messiah to come and therefore did wait daily till the time was come when the Messiah by His death and passion should abolish the kingdom of sin and Satan and establish His own kingdom throughout the whole world. The same is said of Simeon, that he was a good man and feared God and waited for the consolation of Israel. This was the most principal virtue of all that Joseph had and the very root of all his goodness and righteousness, that he waited for the kingdom of God. For it is the property of faith whereby we have confidence in the Messiah to change our nature and to purify the heart and to make it bring forth works of righteousness. There be many among us that can talk of Christ's kingdom and of redemption by Him and yet make no conscience of sin and have little care to live according to the gospel which they profess. And all is because they do not soundly believe in the Messiah, and they wait not for the kingdom of heaven; and therefore there is no change in them. But we for our parts must labor to have this affiance in the Messiah with Joseph and to wait for the second appearance, that thereby we may be made new creatures, having the kingdom of Satan battered and beaten down in us and the kingdom of God erected in our hearts.

Touching Nicodemus, St. John says that "he came to Jesus by night" [John 19:39]. Many men build upon this example that it is lawful to be present at the mass, so be it in the mean season we keep our hearts to God. And indeed such men are like Nicodemus in that they labor to bury Christ as much as they can, though now after His resurrection He should not be buried again. But though Nicodemus durst not openly at the first profess the name of Christ, yet after

---

240. This paragraph break is not in the original, as the additional one following.

His death, when there is most danger, he does. And by this means he reforms his former action.

Thus much of the persons that buried Christ. The third thing to be observed is the manner of Christ's burial, which stands in these four points: first, they take down His body from the cross; secondly, they wind it; thirdly, they lay it in a tomb; fourthly, the tomb is made sure. Of these in order.

First, Joseph takes down the body of Christ from the cross whereon He was executed—but mark in what manner: he does it not on his own head without leave, but he goes to Pilate and begs the body of Christ and craves liberty to take it down, because the disposing of dead bodies was in Pilate's hand, he being deputy at that time.[241] Whereby we learn that in all our dealings and actions (though they have never so good an end) our duty is to proceed as peaceably with all men as may be, as St. James says, "The wisdom that is from above is first pure, then peaceable, gentle," etc. [James 3:17]. Again, this teaches us that in all things which concern the authority of the magistrate and belong unto him by the rule of God's Word, we must attempt to do whatsoever we do by leave. And by this we see what unadvised courses they take that, being private men in this our church, will notwithstanding take upon them to plant churches without the leave of the magistrate, being a Christian prince.

[Secondly], having thus taken the body of Christ down, they go on to wind it.[242] And Joseph for his part brought linen clothes, and Nicodemus a mixture of myrrh and aloes to the quantity of a hundred pounds for the honorable burial of Christ. His winding was on this manner. They wrapped His body hastily in linen clothes [Luke 24:1; John 19:39], sweet odors put thereto. Besides all this, in the Jews' burials there was embalming and washing of the body, but Christ's body was not embalmed or washed[243] because they had no time to do it, for the preparation of the Passover drew near. And whereas these two men bury Christ at their own cost and charges, we are taught to be like affected to the living members of Christ. When they want, we must relieve and comfort them liberally and freely. It may here be demanded, whether men may not be at cost in making funerals, considering even Christ Himself is with much cost buried. *Answer.* The bodies of all dead men are to be buried in seemly and honest manner. And if they be honorable, they may be buried honorably. Yet now there is no cause why men's bodies should be washed, anointed, and embalmed, as the use was among the Jews; for they used embalming as a pledge and sign of the resurrection. But now since Christ's coming we have a more certain pledge

241. This paragraph break is not in the original.
242. This paragraph break is not in the original.
243. P. Ram. Theol. l. 1. c. 14. Seems to be deceived, in that he puts Christ's burial for His embalming, and His descending into hell, for His burial or lying in the grave.

thereof, even the resurrection of Christ Himself [1 Cor. 15:19]. And therefore it is not requisite that we should use embalming and washing as the Jews did. And the clause which is specified in St. Matthew is not to be omitted, that Joseph wrapped Christ's body in "a clean linen cloth" [27:59], whereby we learn that howsoever the strange fashions fetched from Spain and Italy are monstrous and to be abhorred, yet, seeing the body of a man is the creature of God, therefore it must be arrayed in cleanly manner and in "holy comeliness" [Titus 2:3]. Paul requires that the minister of the gospel in all things be seemly or comely, and herein he ought to be a pattern of sobriety unto all men [1 Tim. 3:2].[244]

Thirdly, after they have wound the body of Christ, they "lay it in a tomb" [John 19:42].[245] And, lastly, they "make it sure, closing it up with a stone rolled over the mouth of it" [Matt. 27:60]. Also the Jews request Pilate to seal it that none might presume to open it [v. 66]. Besides, they set a band of soldiers to watch the tomb and to keep it that His body be not stolen away. Many reasons might be alleged of this their dealing, but principally it came to pass by the providence of God, that hereby He might confirm the resurrection of Christ. For whereas the Jews would neither be moved by His doctrine nor by His works and miracles to believe, He causes this to be done that by the certainty of His resurrection He might convince them of hardness of heart and prove that He was the Son of God.

Thus much of the manner of His burial. Now follows the place where Christ was buried. In the place, we are to mark three things. First, that Christ was laid in Joseph's tomb, whereby we may gather the greatness of Christ's poverty, in that He had not so much ground as to make Himself a grave in. And this must be a comfort to the members of Christ that are in poverty. And it teaches them, if they have no more but food and raiment, to be therewith content, knowing that Christ, their Head and King, has consecrated this very estate unto them.

Secondly, the tomb wherein Christ was laid was a new tomb wherein never any man lay before [John 19:41].[246] And it was the special appointment of God's providence that it should be so, because if any man had been buried there aforetime, the malicious Jews would have pleaded that it was not Christ that rose again, but some other.

Thirdly, we must observe that this tomb was in a garden, as the fall of man was in a garden and as the apprehension of Christ in a garden beyond the brook Kidron [Gen. 3:8; John 18:1]. And here we must note the practice of a good man. This garden was the place of Joseph's delight and holy recreation, wherein he used to solace himself in beholding the good creatures of God; yet

---

244. kesmi/oj. 230a
245. This paragraph break is not in the original.
246. This paragraph break is not in the original, as the additional one following.

in the same place does he make his own grave long before he died. Whereby it appears that his recreation was joined with a meditation of his end, and his example must be followed of us. True it is, God has given us His creatures not only for necessity but also for our lawful delight. But yet our duty is to mingle therewith serious meditation and consideration of our last end. It is a brutish part to use the blessings and creatures of God and not at all to be bettered in regard of our last end by a further use thereof.

The time when Christ was buried was the evening, wherein the Sabbath was to begin according to the manner of the Jews, which began their days at sunsetting from evening to evening, according to that in Genesis: "the evening and the morning was the first day." Now, Joseph comes a little before evening and begs the body of Christ and buries it [Matt. 27:57; Luke 23:53], where note that howsoever we are not bound to keep the Sabbath so strictly as the Jews were, yet when we have any business or work to be done of our ordinary calling, we must not take a part of the Lord's Sabbath to do it in, but prevent the time and do it either before as Joseph did or rather after the Sabbath. This is little practiced in the world. Men think if they go to church before and after noon to hear God's word, then all the day after they may do what they list and spend the rest of the time at their own pleasure. But the whole day is the Lord's and therefore must be spent wholly in His service, both by public hearing of the word and also by private reading and meditation on the same.

To conclude the doctrine of Christ's burial, here it may be demanded how He was always after His incarnation both God and man, considering that He was dead and buried and therefore body and soul were sundered, and a dead man seems to be no man. *Answer*. A dead man in his kind is as true a man as a living man; for though body and soul be not united by the bond of life, yet are they united by a relation which the one has to the other in the counsel and good pleasure of God—and that as truly as man and woman remain coupled into one flesh by covenant of marriage, though afterward they be distant a thousand miles asunder. And by virtue of this relation every soul in the day of judgment shall be reunited to his own body, and every body to his own soul. But there is yet a more straight bond between the body and soul of Christ in His death and burial.[247] For as when He was living, His soul was a mean or bond to unite His Godhead and His body together, so when He was dead, His very Godhead was a mean or middle bond to unite the body and soul. And to say otherwise is to dissolve the hypostatical union, by virtue whereof Christ's body and soul, though severed each from other, yet both were still joined to the Godhead of the Son.

247. Damas.

The use and profit which may be made of Christ's burial is twofold. First, it serves to work in us the burial of all our sins. "Know ye not," says Paul, "that all who have been baptized into Christ, have been baptized into his death, and are buried with him by baptism into his death?" [Rom. 6:3]. If any shall demand how any man is buried into the death of Christ, the answer is this: every Christian man and woman are by faith mystically united unto Christ and made all members of one body, whereof Christ is the Head. Now therefore, as Christ by the power of His Godhead when He was dead and buried did overcome the grave and the power of death in His own person, so by the very same power by means of His spiritual conjunction does He work in all His members a spiritual death and burial of sin and natural corruption. When the Israelites were in burying of a man, for fear of the soldiers of the Moabites they cast him for haste into the sepulcher of Elisha [2 Kings 13:21]. Now the dead man, so soon as he was down and had touched the body of Elisha, he revived and stood upon his feet. So let a man that is dead in sin be cast into the grave of Christ—that is, let him by faith but touch Christ dead and buried—it will come to pass by the virtue of Christ's death and burial that he shall be raised from death and bondage of sin to become a new man.

Secondly, the burial of Christ serves to be a sweet perfume of all our graves and burials; for the grave in itself is the house of perdition, but Christ by His burial has as it were consecrated and perfumed all our graves and instead of houses of perdition has made them chambers of rest and sleep, yea, beds of down [Isa. 57:2]. And therefore, howsoever to the eye of man the beholding of a funeral is terrible, yet if we could then remember the burial of Christ and consider how He thereby has changed the nature of the grave, even then it would make us to rejoice.

Lastly, we must imitate Christ's burial in being continually occupied in the spiritual burial of our sins.[248]

Thus much of the burial. Now follows the third and last degree of Christ's humiliation, He "descended into hell." It seems very likely that these words were not placed in the Creed at the first,[249] or (as some think[250]) that they crept in by negligence, because above threescore creeds of the most ancient counsels and fathers want this clause, and among the rest [is] the Nicene Creed. But if the ancient and learned fathers assembled in that counsel had been persuaded or at the least had imagined that these words had been set down at the first by the apostles, no doubt they would not in any wise have left them out. And an ancient writer says directly that these words, "He descended into hell," are not

---

248. This paragraph break is not in the original.
249. P. Viretin. Symb.
250. Erasm. in Colloq.

found in the creed of the Roman church nor used in the churches of the East; and if they be, that then they signify the burial of Christ.[251] And it must not seem strange to any that a word or twain in process of time should creep into the Creed, considering that the original copies of the books of the Old and New Testament have in them sundry varieties of reading[252] and words otherwhiles, which from the margin have crept into the text.[253] Nevertheless, considering that this clause has long continued in the Creed, and that by common consent of the catholic church of God, and it may carry a fit sense and exposition, it is not, as some would have it, to be put forth.

Therefore, that we may come to speak of the meaning of it, we must know that it has four usual expositions, which we will rehearse in order and then make choice of that which shall be thought the fittest. The first is that Christ's soul after the passion upon the cross did really and locally descend into the place of the damned. But this seems not to be true. The reasons are these.

(1) All the evangelists, and among the rest Luke 1:3, intending to make an "exact narration"[254] of the life and death of Christ, has set down at large His passion, death, burial, resurrection, and ascension, and withal they make rehearsal of small circumstances.[255] Therefore, no doubt they would not have omitted Christ's local descent into the place of the damned, if there had been any such thing. And the end why they penned this history was that we might believe that Jesus Christ is the Son of God, and believing we might have life everlasting [John 20:31]. Now there could not have been a greater matter for the confirmation of our faith than this, that Jesus, the son of Mary, who went down to the place of the damned, returned thence to live in happiness forever.

(2) If Christ did go into the place of the damned, then either in soul or in body or in His Godhead. But His Godhead could not descend, because it is everywhere. And His body was in the grave. And as for His soul, it went not to hell, but presently after His death it went to paradise—that is, the third heaven, a place of joy and happiness: "This day shalt thou be with me in paradise" (23:43), which words of Christ must be understood of His manhood or soul and not of His Godhead. For they are an answer to a demand, and therefore unto it they must be suitable. Now the thief, seeing that Christ was first of all crucified and therefore in all likelihood should first of all die, makes his request to this effect: "Lord, Thou shalt shortly enter into Thy kingdom. Remember me then." To which Christ's answer (as the very words import) is

251. Ruff. in exposit. Symb.
252. Varias lectiones, Matt. 27:9.
253. Jeremio for Zacharie.
254. Omnia assequuto.
255. This paragraph break is not in the original, as the additional two following.

thus much: "I shall enter into paradise this day, and there shall you be with Me." Now there is no entrance but in regard of His soul or manhood. For the Godhead, which is at all times in all places, cannot be said properly to enter into a place. Again, when Christ says, "Thou shalt be with me in paradise," He does intimate a resemblance which is between the first and second Adam. The first Adam sinned against God and was presently cast forth out of paradise. Christ, the second Adam, having made a satisfaction for sin, must immediately enter into paradise. Now to say that Christ in soul descended locally into hell is to abolish this analogy between the first and second Adam.

(3) Ancient councils in their confessions and creeds, omitting this clause, show that they did not acknowledge any real descent and that the true meaning of those words, "he descended," was sufficiently included in some of the former articles. And that may appear because when they set down it, they omit some of the former—as Athanasius in his creed, setting down these words, "he descended," etc., omits the "burial," putting them both for one as he expounds himself elsewhere.[256] Now let us see the reasons which may be alleged to the contrary.

Objection 1. "The Son of man shall be three days and three nights in the earth" (Matt. 12:40)—that is, in hell. *Answer 1.* This exposition is directly against the scope of the place, for the Pharisees desired "to see a sign"—that is, some sensible and manifest miracle. And hereunto Christ answers that He will give them the sign of Jonah, which cannot be the descent of His soul into the place of the damned, because it was insensible, but rather His burial and after it His manifest and glorious resurrection. *[Answer] 2.* The heart of the earth may as well signify the grave, as the center of the earth. For thus Tyrus, bordering upon the sea, is said to be in the "heart of the sea"[257] [Ezek. 27:4].[258] *[Answer] 3.* This exposition takes it for granted that hell is seated in the midst of the earth, whereas the Scriptures reveal unto us no more but this, that hell is in the lower parts. But where these lower parts should be, no man is able to define.

Objection 2. "Thou wilt not leave my soul in hell, neither wilt thou suffer thy holy one to see corruption" (Acts 2:27).[259] *Answer.* These words cannot prove any local descent of Christ's soul. For Peter's drift in alleging of them is to prove the resurrection, and he says expressly that the words must be understood of the resurrection of Christ: "He seeing this before, spake of the resurrection of Christ" (v. 31). What? Namely, these words, "his soul was not left in hell,"

---

256. Lib. de incar. Chri. hom. 1 & 2. in symb.
257. In corde marium.
258. Originally, "Ezek. 17:4."
259. Originally, "Acts 2:37."

etc. Now there is no resurrection of the soul, but of the body only, as the soul cannot be said to fall, but the body. It will be replied that the word yuxh) cannot signify the body, and the word a@dhj, the grave. *Answer.* The first word signifies not only the spiritual part of man, the soul, but also the whole person or the man himself (Rom. 13:1; 1 Cor. 15:40). And the second is as well taken for the grave, as for hell: "Death and a@dhj are cast into the lake of fire (Rev. 20:14). Now we cannot say that hell is cast into hell, but the grave into hell. And the very same word in this text must needs have this sense. For Peter makes an opposition between the grave into which David is shut up and the hell out of which Christ was delivered ([Acts 2:]29, 31). Again, it will be said that in this text there be two distinct parts: the first, of the souls coming forth of hell, in these words, "Thou wilt not leave my soul in hell"; the second, of the bodies rising out of the grave, in the next words, "Neither wilt thou suffer my flesh to see corruption."[260] *Answer.* It is not so. For flesh in this place signifies not the body alone, but the human nature of Christ, as appears (v. 30), unless we shall say that one and the same word in the same sentence is taken two ways. And the words rather carry this sense: "Thou wilt not suffer me to continue long in the grave. Nay, which is more, in the time of my continuance there, Thou wilt not suffer me so much as to feel any corruption, because I am Thy holy one."

Objection 3. "Christ was quickened in spirit, by the which spirit he went and preached to the spirits which are in prison" (1 Peter 3:19). *Answer.* The place is not for this purpose. For by "spirit" is not meant the soul of Christ, but the Godhead, which in the ministry of Noah preached repentance to the old world. And I think that Peter in this place alludes to another place in Genesis 6:3, where the Lord says, "My spirit shall not always strive with man, because he is but flesh." And if the spirit do signify the soul, then Christ was quickened either by His soul or in His soul. But neither is true. For the first, it cannot be said that Christ was quickened by His soul, because it did not join itself to the body; but the Godhead joined them both. Neither was He quickened in soul, for His soul died not. It could not die the first death, which belongs to the body; and it did not die the second death, which is a total separation from God. Only it suffered the sorrows of the second death, which is the apprehension of the wrath of God, as a man may feel the pangs of the first death and yet not die the first death but live. Again, it is to no end that Christ's soul should go to hell to preach—consider that it was never heard of that one soul should preach to another, especially in hell, where all are condemned and in conscience convicted of their just damnation and where there is no hope of repentance or redemption. It will be answered that this preaching is only real or experimental,

---

260. Bellar. quæst. de descen.

because Christ shows Himself there to convince the unbelief of His enemies. But this is flat against reason. For when a man is justly condemned by God and therefore sufficiently convicted, what need the Judge Himself come to the place of execution to convict him?[261] And it is flat against the text, for the preaching that is spoken of here is that which is performed by men in the ministry of the word, as Peter expounds himself, "To this purpose was the gospel preached unto the dead, that they might be condemned according to men in the flesh, that they might live according to God in the Spirit" (1 Peter 4:6). Lastly, there is no reason why Christ should rather preach and show Himself in hell to them that were disobedient in the days of Noah, than to the rest of the damned.

And this is the first exposition. The second follows. "He descended into hell"—that is, Christ descended into the grave or was buried. This exposition is agreeable to the truth, yet is it not meet or convenient. For the clause next before, "he was buried," contained this point. And therefore if the next words following yield the same sense, there must be a vain and needless repetition of one and the same thing twice, which is not in any wise to be allowed in so short a creed as this. If it be said that these words are an exposition of the former, the answer is that then they should be more plain than the former. For when one sentence expounds another, the latter must always be the plainer. But of these two sentences, "he was buried," "he descended into hell," the first is very plain and easy, but the latter very obscure and hard. And therefore it can be no exposition thereof, and for this cause this exposition neither, is it to be received.

Thirdly, others there be which expound it thus: "he descended into hell"—that is, Christ Jesus when He was dying upon the cross felt and suffered the pangs of hell and the full wrath of God seizing upon His soul. This exposition has warrant in God's Word, where hell often signifies the sorrows and pains of hell, as Hannah in her song unto the Lord says, "The Lord killeth and maketh alive, he brings down to hell and raiseth up" [1 Sam. 2:6]—that is, He makes men feel woe and misery in their souls, even the pangs of hell, and after restores them. And David says, "The sorrows of death compassed me, and the terrors of hell laid hold on me" [Ps. 18:5]. This is a usual exposition received of the church, and they which expound this article thus give this reason thereof. The former words, "was crucified, dead, and buried," do contain (say they) the outward sufferings of Christ. Now, because He suffered not only outwardly in body but also inwardly in soul, therefore these words, "he descended into hell," do set forth unto us His inward sufferings in soul when He felt upon the cross the full wrath of God upon Him. This exposition is good and true, and whosoever will

---

261. After just execution conviction is needless.

may receive it. Yet nevertheless it seems not so fitly to agree with the order of the former articles.

For these words, "was crucified dead and buried," must not be understood of any ordinary death, but of a cursed death in which Christ suffered the full wrath of God, even the pangs of hell both in soul and body. Seeing then this exposition is contained in the former words, it cannot fitly stand with the order of this short creed, unless there should be a distinct article of things repeated before.

But let us come to the fourth exposition. "He descended into hell"—that is, when He was dead and buried, He was held captive in the grave and lay in bondage under death for the space of three days. This exposition also may be gathered forth of the Scriptures. St. Peter says, "God hath raised him up"— speaking of Christ—"and loosed the sorrows of death, because it was impossible that he should be holden of it" [Acts 2:24]. Where we may see that between the death and resurrection of Christ there is placed a third matter which is not mentioned in any clause of the Apostles' Creed save in this, and that is His bondage under death, which comes in between His death and rising again. And the words themselves do most fitly bear this sense, as the speech of Jacob shows, "I will go down into hell,[262] unto my son mourning" [Gen. 37:35]. And this exposition does also best agree with the order of the Creed. First, He was crucified and died; secondly, He was buried; thirdly, laid in the grave and was therein held in captivity and bondage under death. And these three degrees of Christ's humiliation are most fitly correspondent to the three degrees of His exaltation. The first degree of exaltation, "he rose again the third day," answering to the first degree of His humiliation, "he died." The second degree of His exaltation, "he ascended into heaven," answering to going down into the grave, "was buried." And, thirdly, His "sitting at the right hand of God"—which is the highest degree of His exaltation—answering to the lowest degree of His humiliation, "he descended into hell." These two last expositions are commonly received, and we may indifferently make choice of either. But the last (as I take it) is most agreeable to the order and words of the Creed.

Thus much for the meaning of the words. Now follow the uses. And, first of all, Christ's descending into hell—teaching every one of us that profess the name of Christ that if it shall please God to afflict us either in body or in mind or in both, though it be in most grievous and tedious manner, yet must we not think it strange. For if Christ upon the cross not only suffered the pangs of hell, but after He was dead, death takes Him and as it were carries Him into his den or cabin and there triumphs over Him, holding Him in captivity and bondage,

---

262. Or the grave.

and yet for all this was He the Son of God. And therefore, when God's hand is heavy upon us any way, we are not to despair but rather think it is the good pleasure of God to frame and fashion us that we may become like unto Christ Jesus as good children of God. David, a man after God's own heart, was by Samuel anointed king over Israel; but withal God raised up Saul to persecute him as the fowler hunts the partridge in the mountains, insomuch that David said there was but one step between him and death. So likewise Job, a just man and one that feared God with all his heart—yet how heavily did God lay His hand upon him? His goods and cattle were all taken away, and his children slain, and his body stricken by Satan with loathsome boils from the sole of his foot to the crown of his head, so as he was fain to take a potsherd and scrape himself, sitting among the ashes [Job 2:8–9]. And Jonah, the servant and prophet of the most high God, when he was called to preach to Nineveh, because he refused for fear of that great city, God met with him, and he must be cast into the sea and there be swallowed up of a whale, that so He might chastise him. And thus does He deal with His own servants to make them conformable to Christ. And further, when it pleases God to lay His hand upon our souls and make us have a troubled and distressed conscience, so as we do as it were struggle with God's wrath as for life and death and can find nothing but His indignation seizing upon our souls, which is the most grievous and perplexed estate that any man can be in—in this case, howsoever we cannot discern or see any hope or comfort in ourselves, we must not think it strange nor quite despair of His mercy. For the Son of God Himself descended into hell, and death carried Him captive and triumphed over Him in the grave. And therefore, though God seem to be our utter enemy, yet we must not despair of His help. In divers psalms we read how David was not only persecuted outwardly of his enemies, but even his soul and conscience were perplexed for his sins so as his very "bones were consumed within him, and his moisture was turned into the drought in summer" [Ps. 32:3–4]. This caused Job to cry out that "arrows of God were within him, and the venom thereof did drink up his spirit, the terrors of God did fight against him, and the grief of his soul was as weighty as the sand of the sea" [Job 6:4], by reason whereof he says that "the Lord did make him a mark and a butt to shoot at." And therefore, when God shall thus afflict us either in body or in soul or in both, we must not always think that it is the wrathful hand of the Lord that begins to bring us to utter condemnation for our sins, but rather His fatherly work to kill sin in us and to make us grow in humility, that so we may become like unto Christ Jesus.

Secondly, whereas Christ for our sakes was thus abased even unto the lowest degree of humiliation that can be, it is an example for us to imitate, as Christ

Himself prescribes: "Learn of me, that I am meek and lowly" [Matt. 11:29].[263] And that we may be the better to do this, we must learn to become nothing in ourselves, that we may be all in all forth of ourselves in Christ. We must loathe and think as basely of ourselves as possibly may be in regard of our sins. Christ Jesus upon the cross was content for our sake to become "a worm and no man," as David says [Ps. 22:6], which did chiefly appear in this lowest degree of His of His humiliation, when as death did as it were tread on Him in his den. And the same mind must likewise be in us which was in Him. The liking that we have of ourselves must be mere nothing, but all our love and liking must be forth of ourselves in the death and blood of Christ.

And thus much of this clause, as also of the state of Christ's humiliation. Now follows His second estate, which is His exaltation into glory, set down in these words, "the third day he rose again from the dead," etc. And of it we are first to speak in general, then in particular according to the several degrees thereof. In general, the exaltation of Christ is that glorious or happy estate into which Christ entered after He had wrought the work of our redemption upon the cross. And He was exalted according to both natures, in regard of His God-head and also of His manhood.

The exaltation of the Godhead of Christ was the manifestation of the Godhead in the manhood.[264] Some will peradventure demand how Christ's Godhead can be exalted, seeing it admits no alteration at all. *Answer.* In itself it cannot be exalted; yet, being considered as it is joined with the manhood into one person, in this respect it may be said to be exalted. And therefore I say the exaltation of Christ's Godhead is the manifestation of the glory thereof in the manhood. For though Christ from His incarnation was both God and man, and His Godhead all that time dwelt in His manhood, yet from His birth unto His death the same Godhead did little show itself and in that time of His suffering did as it were lie hid under the veil of His flesh, as the soul does in the body when a man is sleeping, that thereby in His human nature He might suffer the curse of the law and accomplish the work of redemption for us in the low and base estate of a servant. But after this work was finished, He began by degrees to make manifest the power of His Godhead in His manhood. And in this respect His Godhead may be said to be exalted.

The exaltation of Christ's humanity stood in two things. The first, that He laid down all the infirmities of man's nature, which He carried about Him so long as He was in the state of a servant, in that He ceased to be weary, hungry, thirsty, etc. Here it may be demanded whether the wounds and scars remain

---

263. This paragraph break is not in the original.
264. This paragraph break is not in the original, as the additional one following.

in the body of Christ now after it is glorified. *Answer.* Some think that they remain as testimonies of that victory which Christ obtained of His and our enemies, and that they are no deformity to the glorious body of the Lord but are themselves also in Him in some unspeakable manner glorified.[265] But indeed it rather seems to be a truth to say that they are quite abolished, because they were a part of that ignominious and base estate in which our Savior was upon the cross, which after His entrance into glory He laid aside. And if it may be thought that the wounds in the hands and feet of Christ remain to be seen even to the last judgment, why may we not in the same manner think that the veins of His body remain emptied of their blood because it was shed upon the cross?

The second thing required in the exaltation of Christ's manhood is that both His body and soul were beautified and adorned with all qualities of glory. His mind was enriched with as much knowledge and understanding as can possibly befall any creature and more in measure than all men and angels have. And the same is to be said of the graces of the spirit in His will and affections. His body also was incorruptible, and it was made a shining body, a resemblance whereof some of His disciples saw in the Mount [of Transfiguration]. And it was endued with agility to move as well upward as downward, as may appear by the ascension of His body into heaven, which was not caused by constraint or by any violent motion but by a property agreeing to all bodies glorified. Yet in the exaltation of Christ's manhood we must remember two caveats. First, that He did never lay aside the essential properties of a true body, as length, breadth, thickness, visibility, locality, which is to be in one place at once and no more, but keeps all these still, because they serve for the being of His body. Secondly, we must remember that the gifts of glory in Christ's body are not infinite but finite; for His human nature, being but a creature and therefore finite, could not receive infinite graces and gifts of glory. And hence it is more than manifest that the opinion of those men is false which hold that Christ's body glorified is omnipotent and infinite, every way able to do whatsoever He will—for this is to make a creature to be the Creator.

Thus much of Christ's exaltation in general. Now let us come to the degrees thereof, as they are noted in the Creed, which are in number three: (1) "he rose again the third day"; (2) "he ascended into heaven"; (3) "he sitteth at the right hand of God the Father Almighty."

In the handling of Christ's resurrection, we must consider these points: (1) why Christ ought to rise again; (2) the manner of His rising; (3) the time when He rose; (4) the proofs of His resurrection; (5) the uses thereof.[266] For the

---

265. Olev. l. de subst. foed and Th. Beza.
266. This paragraph break is not in the original.

first, it was necessary that Christ should rise again, and that for three especial causes. First, that hereby He might show to all the people of God that He had fully overcome death. For also, if Christ had not risen, how should we have been persuaded in our consciences that He had made a full and perfect satisfaction for us? Nay rather, we should have reasoned thus: Christ is not risen, and therefore He has not overcome death, but death overcame Him. Secondly, Christ, which died, was the Son of God; therefore, the author of life itself. And for this cause it was neither meet nor possible for Him to be holden of death, but He must needs rise from death to life. Thirdly, Christ's priesthood has two parts: one, to make satisfaction for sin by His one only sacrifice upon the cross; the other, to apply the virtue of this sacrifice unto every believer. Now He offered the sacrifice for sin upon the cross before the last pang of His death and in dying satisfied the justice of God, and therefore, being dead, must needs rise again to perform the second part of His priesthood—namely, to apply the virtue thereof unto all that shall truly believe in Him and to make intercession in heaven unto His Father for us here on earth. And thus much of the first point.

Now, to come to the manner of Christ's resurrection, five things are to be considered in it. The first, that Christ rose again not as every private man does but as a public person, representing all men that are to come to life eternal. For as in His passion, so also in His resurrection He stood in our room and place. And therefore, when He rose from death, we all, yea, the whole church rose in Him and together with Him [Eph. 2:6]. And this point not considered, we do not conceive aright of Christ's resurrection, neither can we reap sound comfort by it.

The second is that Christ Himself and no other for Him did by His own power raise Himself to life. This was the thing that He meant when He said, "Destroy this temple, and in three days I will build it again" (John 2:19); and more plainly, "I have," says He, "power to lay down my life, and I have power to take it again" (10:18). From whence we learn divers instructions. First, whereas Christ raises Himself from death to life, it serves to prove that He was not only man but also true God. For the body, being dead, could not bring again the soul and join itself unto the same and make itself alive again. Neither yet the soul that is departed from the body can return again and quicken the body. And therefore there was some other nature in Christ—namely, His Godhead—which did reunite soul and body together and thereby quicken the manhood. Secondly, if Christ give life to Himself, being dead in the grave, then much more, now being alive in heaven glorified, is He able to raise up His members from death to life. We are all by nature even stark dead in sin, as the dead body rotten in the grave. And therefore our duty is to come to Christ our Lord by humble prayer, earnestly entreating Him that He would raise us up every day more and more from the grave of our sins to newness of life. He can of men dead in their sins make us alive unto Himself to live in righteousness and true holiness all the days of our life.

The third thing is that Christ rose again with an earthquake. And this serves to prove that He lost nothing of His power by death, but still remained the absolute Lord and King of heaven and earth, to whom therefore the earth under His feet trembling does Him homage. This also proves unto us that Christ, which lay dead in the grave, did raise Himself again by His own almighty power. Lastly, it serves to convince the keepers of the grave, the women which came to embalm Him, and the disciples which came to the sepulcher and would not yet believe that He was risen again. But how came this earthquake? *Answer.* St. Matthew says there was a great earthquake. For "the angel of the Lord descended from heaven," etc. (Matt. 28:2). This shows that the power of angels is great, in that they can move and stir the earth. Three angels destroyed Sodom and Gomorrah [Gen. 19:1, 13]. An angel destroyed all the firstborn of Egypt in one night [Ex. 12:29]. In the host of Sennacherib, one angel slew in one night a hundred fourscore and five thousand men [2 Kings 19:35]. Of like power is the devil himself to shake the earth and to destroy us all, but that God of His goodness limits and restrains him of his liberty. Well, if one angel be able to shake the earth, what then will Christ Himself do when He shall come to judgment the second time with many thousand thousands of angels? Oh, how terrible and fearful will His coming be! Not without cause says the Holy Ghost that the wicked at that day shall cry out, wishing hills to fall upon them and the mountains to cover them for fear of that great and terrible day of the Lord.

The fourth thing is that an angel ministered to Christ, being to rise again, in that he came to the grave and rolled away the stone and sat upon it. Where observe, first, how the angels of God minister unto Christ, though dead and buried, whereby they acknowledge that His power, majesty, and authority is not included within the bounds of the earth but extends itself even to the heavens themselves and the hosts thereof, and that according to His humanity. Wicked men for their parts labored to close Him up in the earth as the basest of all creatures; but the angels of heaven most readily accept Him as their sovereign Lord and King, as in like manner they did in His temptation in the wilderness and in His agony in the garden [Matt. 4:11; Luke 22:43]. Secondly, that the opinion of the Papists and others which think that the body of Christ went through the gravestone when He rose again is without warrant. For the end no doubt why the angel rolled away the stone was that Christ might come forth. And indeed it is against the order of nature that one body should pass through another without corruption or alteration of either, considering that every body occupies a place, and two bodies at the same instant cannot be in one proper place.

Furthermore it is said that when the angel sat on the stone, "his countenance was like lightning, and his raiment as white as snow" (Matt. 28:3–4). And this served to show what was the glory of Christ Himself. For if the servant and minister be so glorious, then endless is the glory of the Lord and Master Himself. Lastly, it is said that for fear of the angel the watchmen were astonished and became as dead men, which teaches us that what God would have come to pass, all the world can never hinder. For though the Jews had closed up the grave with a stone and set a band of soldiers to watch, lest Christ should by any means be taken away, yet all this avails nothing. By an angel from heaven the seal is broken, the stone is removed, and the watchmen are at their wits' ends. And this came to pass by the providence of God, that after the watchmen had testified these things to the Jews, they might at length be convicted that Christ, whom they crucified, was the Messiah.

The fifth and last point is that Christ rose not alone but accompanied with others, as St. Matthew says that "the graves opened, and many bodies of the saints which slept, arose, and came out of the graves, and went into the city, and appeared unto many after Christ's resurrection" (27:52–53). And this came to pass that the church of God might know and consider that there is a reviving and quickening virtue in the resurrection of Christ, whereby He is able not only to raise our dead bodies unto life but also when we are dead in sin to raise us up to newness of life. And in this very point stands a main difference between the resurrection of Christ and the resurrection of any other man. For the resurrection of Peter nothing avails to the raising of David or Paul. But Christ's resurrection avails for all that have believed in Him. By the very same power whereby He raised Himself He raises all His members, and therefore He is called a "quickening spirit." And let us mark the order observed in rising.

First, Christ rises, and then the saints after Him.[267] And this came to pass to verify the Scripture, which says that "Christ is the firstborn of the dead" [Col. 1:18]. Now, He is the firstborn of the dead in that He has this dignity and privilege to rise to eternal life the first of all men. It is true indeed that Lazarus and sundry other in time rose before Christ, but yet they rose to live a mortal life and to die again. Christ, He is the first of all that rose to life everlasting and to glory—never any rose before Christ in this manner.

And the persons that rose with Christ are to be noted. They were the saints of God, not wicked men, whereby we are put in mind that the elect children of God only are partakers of Christ's resurrection. Indeed, both good and bad rise again, but there is great difference in their rising; for the godly rise by the virtue of Christ's resurrection, and that to eternal glory, but the ungodly rise by

---

267. This paragraph break is not in the original, as the additional one following.

the virtue of Christ not as He is a redeemer, but as He is a terrible judge and is to execute justice on them. And they rise again for this end, that besides the first death of the body, they might suffer the second death, which is the pouring forth of God's wrath upon body and soul eternally. This difference is proved unto us by that which Paul says, "Christ is the firstfruits of them that sleep" [1 Cor. 15:20]. Among the Jews, such as had cornfields gathered some little quantity thereof before they reaped the rest and offered the same unto God, signifying thereby that they acknowledged Him to be the author and giver of all increase. And this offering was also an assurance unto the owner of the blessing of God upon the rest; and this, being but one handful, did sanctify the whole crop. Now, Christ to the dead is as the firstfruits to the rest of the corn, because His resurrection is a pledge and an assurance of the resurrection of the faithful. When a man is cast into the sea, and all his body is under the water, there is nothing to be looked for but present death. But if he carry his head above the water, there is good hope of a recovery. Christ Himself is risen as a pledge that all the just shall rise again. He is the Head unto His church, and therefore all His members must needs follow in their time. It may be demanded what became of the saints that rose again after Christ's resurrection. *Answer.* Some think they died again; but, seeing they rose for this end to manifest the quickening virtue of Christ's resurrection, it is as like[ly] that they were also glorified with Christ and ascended with Him to heaven.

Thus much of the manner of Christ's resurrection. Now follows the time when He rose again, and that is specified in the Creed, "the third day he rose again." Thus says our Savior Christ unto the Pharisees, "As Jonas was three days and three nights in the whale's belly: so shall the Son of Man be three days and three nights in the heart of the earth" (Matt. 12:39). And though Christ was but one day and two pieces of two days in the grave (for He was buried in the evening before the Sabbath and rose in the morning the next day after the Sabbath), yet is this sufficient to verify the saying of Christ.[268] For if the analogy had stood in three whole days, then Christ should have risen the fourth day. And it was the pleasure of God that He should lie thus long in the grave, that it might be known that He was thoroughly dead; and He continued no longer, that He might not in His body see corruption. Again, it is said that Christ rose again in the end of the Sabbath, when the first day of the week began to dawn [28:1]. And this very time must be considered as the real beginning of the new spiritual world in which we are made the sons of God. And as in the first day of the first world light was commanded to shine out of darkness upon the deeps, so in the first day of this new world the Sun of Righteousness rises and gives

---

268. His abode in the grave was about 38 hours.

light to them that sit in darkness and dispels the darkness that was under the Old Testament. And here let us mark the reason why the Sabbath Day was changed. For the first day of the week, which was the day following the Jews' Sabbath, is our Sabbath Day, which day we keep holy in memory of the glorious resurrection of Christ. And therefore it is called the Lord's Day [Rev. 1:10]. And it may not unfitly be termed "Sunday,"[269] though the name came first from the heathen, because on this day the blessed Sun of Righteousness rose from death to life.

Let us now in the next place proceed to the proofs of Christ's resurrection, which are diligently to be observed because it is one of the most principal points of our religion. For as the apostle says, "He died for our sins, and rose again for our justification" (Rom. 4:25); and again, "If Christ be not risen, then is our preaching vain, and your faith is also vain" (1 Cor. 15:14). The proofs are of two sorts: first, Christ's appearances unto men; secondly, the testimonies of men. Christ's appearances were either on the first day or on the days following. The appearances of Christ the same day He rose again are five. And first of all early in the morning He appeared to Mary Magdalene (Mark 16:9). In this appearance, divers things are to be considered.

The first, of what note and quality the party was to whom Christ appeared.[270] *Answer.* Mary Magdalene was one that had been possessed with seven devils but was delivered and became a repentant sinner and stood by when Christ suffered and came with sweet odors when He was dead to embalm Him. And therefore to her is granted this prerogative, that she should be the first that should testify His resurrection unto men. And hence we learn that Christ is ready and willing to receive most miserable, wretched sinners, even such as have been vassals and bondslaves of the devil, if they will come to Him. Any man would think it a fearful case to be thus possessed with devils, as Mary was. But let all those that live in ignorance and by reason thereof live in sin without repentance know this, that their case is a thousand times worse than Mary Magdalene's was. For what is an impenitent sinner? Surely, nothing else but the castle and hold of the devil, both in body and soul. For look as a captain that has taken some hold or skonse does rule and govern all therein and disposes it at his will and pleasure, even so it is with all blind and impenitent sinners. Not one devil alone but even legions of devils possess them and rule their hearts. And therefore, howsoever they may soothe themselves and say all is well, for God is merciful, yet their case is far worse than Mary's was. Now then, would any be freed from this fearful bondage? Let them learn of Mary Magdalene to

---

269. Hierom.
270. This paragraph break is not in the original.

follow Christ and to seek unto Him; and then, albeit the devil and all his angels possess their hearts, yet Christ, being the strong man, will come and cast them all out and dwell there Himself.

The second is what Christ in His appearance said to Mary. *Answer.* He said, "Touch me not, for I am not yet ascended to my Father" (John 20:17). Mary no doubt was glad to see Christ and therefore looked to have conversed as familiarly with Him as she was wont before His death. But He forbids her to touch Him—that is, not to look to enjoy His corporal presence as before but rather to seek for His spiritual presence by faith, considering He was shortly to ascend to His Father. For this cause when He appeared to His disciples, He stayed not long with them at any time, but only to manifest Himself unto them, thereby to prove the certainty of His resurrection. This prohibition shows, first of all, that it is but a fond thing to delight in the outward picture and portraiture of Christ, as the Jesuits do, who stand much upon His outward form and lineaments. Secondly, it overthrows the popish crucifixes and all the carved and molten images of Christ, wherein the Papists worship Him. For corporal presence is not now required; therefore, spiritual worship only must be given unto Him. Thirdly, it overthrows the real presence of Christ in the Sacrament. Many are of mind that they cannot receive Christ, except they eat and drink His body and blood corporally. But it is not much material whether we touch Him with the bodily hand or no, so be it we apprehend Him spiritually by faith. Lastly, as we must not have earthly considerations of Christ, so must we on the contrary labor for the spiritual hand of faith, which may reach up itself to heaven and there lay hold on Him. This is the very thing which Christ insinuates to Mary in saying, "Touch me not." And St. Paul says, "Henceforth know we no man after the flesh, yea though we had known Christ after the flesh, yet now we know him no more" (2 Cor. 5:16–17)—that is, we know Him no more as a man living among us. And therefore he adds, "If any man be in Christ, he is a new creature," and this new creation is not by the bodily presence of Christ but by the apprehension of faith.

The second appearance was to Mary Magdalene and to the other Mary, as they were going from the grave to tell His disciples, at which time Christ meets them and bids them go tell His brethren that He is risen again [Matt. 28:9–10]. And whereas Christ sends women to His disciples, He purposed hereby to check them for their unbelief. For these women forsook Him not at His death but stood by and saw Him suffer, and when He was buried they came to embalm Him. But all this while, what became of His disciples? Surely, Peter denied Him, and all the rest fled away, even James and John, the sons of thunder, save that John stood aloof to behold His death. Hereupon Christ to make them ashamed of their fault sends these women unto them to publish that unto them which they by their calling ought above other[s] to have published.

Secondly, this teaches that whereas Christ builds His kingdom and publishes His gospel by apostles, evangelists, pastors, teachers, He can if it so please Him perform the same by other means.[271] In this His second appearance, He used weak and unlearned[272] women to publish His resurrection and thereby shows that He is not bound to the ordinary means, which now He uses.

Thirdly, He sent them to His disciples to show that howsoever they had dealt unfaithfully with Him by forsaking Him and denying Him, yet He had not quite forsaken them; but if they would repent and believe, He would receive them into His love and favor again. And therefore [He] calls them His brethren, saying, "Go and tell my brethren." This teaches us a good lesson that, howsoever our sins past are to humble us in regard of ourselves, yet must they not cut off or dismay us from seeking to Christ. Yea, even then when we are laden with the burden of them, we must come unto Him, and He will ease us (Mark 16:7).

Fourthly, whereas unlearned[273] women are sent to teach Christ's disciples, which were scholars brought up in His own school, we are admonished that superiority in place and calling must not hinder us sometimes to hear and to be taught of our inferiors. Job says he never refused the counsel of his servant (Job 31:13), and Naaman the Syrian obeyed the counsel of an unlearned[274] maid which advised him to go to the prophet of the Lord in Samaria to be cured of his leprosy. And when he had been with the prophet, he obeyed the counsel of his servants that persuaded him to do all the prophet had said, "Wash and be clean" [2 Kings 5:3, 13].

Now after that the women are come to the disciples and make relation of Christ's resurrection, the text says, "Their words seemed as feigned things unto them, neither believed they them" (Luke 24:11). Hence we learn two things. The first, that men of themselves cannot believe the doctrine of Christian religion. It is a hard matter for a man to believe sundry things in the work of creation. The temporal deliverance of the children of Israel seemed to them "as a dream" [Ps. 126:1]; and the resurrection of Christ even to Christ's own disciples seemed "a feigned thing." The second, that it is a hard thing truly and unfeignedly to believe the points of religion. Disciples brought up in the school of Christ and often catechized in this very point of Christ's resurrection, yet dull are they to believe it. This confutes and condemns our carnal gospellers, that make it the lightest and easiest thing that can be to believe in Christ. And therefore

---

271. This paragraph break is not in the original, as the additional two following.
272. Originally, "silly."
273. Originally, "silly."
274. Originally, "silly."

they say their faith is so strong that they would not for all the world doubt of God's mercy, whereas indeed they are deceived and have no faith at all, but blind presumption.

The third appearance was on this manner: as two of Christ's disciples were going from Jerusalem to Emmaus about threescore furlongs and talked together of all the things that were done, Jesus drew near and talked with them, but their eyes were holden that they could not know Him [Luke 24:13, 15]. And as they went He communed with them and proved out of the Scripture His resurrection, expounding unto them all things that were written of Him. Then, they made Him stay with them, and their eyes were opened, and they knew Him by breaking of bread; but He was taken out of their sight. In this notable appearance, we may observe these four points.

The first, that Christ held their eyes that they could not know Him.[275] They saw a man indeed, but who He was they could not tell. By this it is more than manifest that the use of our outward senses, as seeing, feeling, smelling, etc., is supplied unto us continually by the power of Christ; and therefore even in these things we must acknowledge the continual goodness of God. Now if one man cannot so much as discern another but by the blessing of Christ, then shall we never be able to discern the way of life from the way of death without Him. And therefore we must pray unto God that He would give us His Holy Spirit to enlighten the eyes of our understanding whereby we may be able to see and know the way that leads unto life and also to walk in the same.

The second, that as Christ was in expounding the Scriptures unto them, "their hearts burned within them" [v. 32]. By this we learn that howsoever the ministers of God publish the gospel to the outward ears of men, yet it is the proper work of Christ alone to touch and enflame the heart by the fire of His Holy Spirit and to quicken and raise men up to the life of righteousness and true holiness. It is He only that "baptizeth with the Holy Ghost and with fire" [3:16]. And it further admonishes us that we should hear the word preached from the mouth of God's ministers with burning and melting heart; but, alas, the ordinary practice is flat contrary. Men's eyes are drowsy and heavy; and their hearts, dead and frozen within them. And that is the cause why after much teaching there follows but little profit.

The third thing is that Christ did "eat with the two disciples, and was known of them in breaking bread" [24:30–31]. It is very like[ly] that our Savior Christ did in some special manner bless the bread which He broke, whereby His disciples discerned Him from others. And in like manner we must by blessing our meats and drinks distinguish ourselves, though not from such as are the servants

---

275. This paragraph break is not in the original.

of God, yet from all ungodly and careless men. Many, being silent themselves, do make their children to give thanks and to bless their meats. And indeed it is a commendable thing if it be done sometimes to nurture the child. But for men to disburden themselves wholly of this duty is a fault. And it is a shame that that mouth which opens itself to receive the good creatures of God should never open itself to bless and praise God for the same. Therefore, in this action of eating and drinking, let us show ourselves followers of Christ, that as by blessing the same He was known from all other, so we may also hereby distinguish ourselves from the profane and wicked of this world. Otherwise, what difference shall there be between us and the very hog that eats mast on the ground, but never looks up to the tree from whence it falls? And as Christ revealed Himself unto His disciples at that time when they caused Him to eat meat with them, so let us suffer Christ to be our guest, and let us entertain Him in His members; and no doubt He will bless us and withal reveal Himself unto us.

The fourth thing is that, having eaten, He is "taken out of their sight" [v. 31].[276] And this came to pass not because the body of Christ became spiritual, but because either He held their eyes as before, or He departed with celerity and speed according to the properties of a body glorified.

The fourth appearance of Christ was to Peter alone, mentioned only by St. Paul, "He was seen of Cephas" (1 Cor. 15:5).

The fifth appearance was to all the disciples together, save Thomas (John 20:19). In it we must consider three things, which are all effectual arguments to prove Christ's resurrection. The first, that He came and stood in the midst among them, the doors being shut. Now it may be demanded, how this could be. *Answer.* The Papists say, his body was glorified and so passed through the door; but (as I have said) it is against the nature of a body, that one should pass through another, as heat does through a piece of iron, both bodies remaining entire and sound. Therefore, we may rather think that whereas Christ came in, when the doors were shut, it was either because by His mighty power He caused the doors to give place, the disciples not knowing how, or else because He altered the very substance of the doors, that His body might pass through, as He thickened the waters to carry His body when He walked upon the sea. Now if this be true, as very like[ly] it is, that these dumb creatures gave place to Christ and became pliable unto His commandment, then much more ought we to carry our hearts conformable and pliant to the will of our Lord Jesus in all His commandments.

The second point is that when as the disciples thought Christ to have been a spirit, He to prove the truth of His manhood showed unto them His hands

---

276. This paragraph break is not in the original.

and feet and the wound in His side and calls for meat and eats among them.[277] But it may be asked how this could be, considering that a glorified body has no blemish nor needs to eat but is supported by God without meat. For if this be true in our bodies when they shall be glorified, then much more was it true in Christ. *Answer.* True it is; a glorified body has no blemishes. But our Savior Christ had not yet entered into the fullness of His glory. If He had been fully glorified, He could not so sensibly and plainly have made manifest the truth of His resurrection unto His disciples. And therefore for their sakes and ours He is content after His entrance into glory still to retain in His body some remnants of the ignominies and blemishes, which, if it had pleased Him, He might have laid aside. He is also content to eat not for need but to prove that His body was not a body in show, but a true body. This teaches us two lessons. First, if Christ for our good and comfort be content to retain these ignominious blemishes, then answerably every one of us must as good followers of Christ refer the works of our callings to the good of others, as Paul says, "He was free from all men, yet he was content to become all things unto all men, that by all means he might win the more" [1 Cor. 9:19]. Secondly, we learn that for the good of our neighbor and for the maintaining of love and charity we must be content to yield from our own right, as in this place our Savior Christ yields of His own glory for the good of His church.

The third point is that He then gave the disciples their apostolical commission, saying, "Go and teach all nations" [Matt. 28:19], of which three points are to be considered. The first, to whom it is given. *Answer.* To them all, as well to one as to another, and not to Peter only. And this overthrows the fond and forged opinions of the Papists concerning Peter's supremacy. If his calling had been above the rest, then he should have had a special commission above the rest. But one and the same commission is given alike to all.

The second, that with the commission He gives His Spirit; for whom He appoints to publish His will and word, them He furnishes with sufficient gifts of His Holy Spirit to discharge that great function.[278] And therefore it is a defect that any are set apart to be ministers of the gospel of Christ which have not received the spirit of knowledge, the spirit of wisdom, and the spirit of prophecy in some measure.

The third point is that in conferring of His Spirit He uses an outward sign; for the text says, "He breathed on them, and said, receive the Holy Ghost" (John 20:22). The reasons hereof may be these. First, when God created Adam and put into him a living soul, it is said, "He breathed in his face" (Gen. 2:7). And

---

277. This paragraph break is not in the original.
278. This paragraph break is not in the original, as the additional one following.

so our Savior Christ in giving unto His disciples the Holy Ghost does the same to show unto them that the same person that gives life gives grace, and also to signify unto them that, being to send them over all the world to preach His gospel, He was as it were to make a second creation of man by renewing the image of God in him which he had lost by the fall of Adam. Again, He breathed on them in giving His Spirit to put them in mind that their preaching of the gospel could not be effectual in the hearts of their hearers before the Lord does breathe into them His Spirit and thereby draw them to believe. And therefore the spouse of Christ desires the Lord "to send forth his north and south wind to blow on her garden, that the spices thereof might flow out" (Song 4:16). The garden is the church of God, which desires Christ to comfort her and to pour out the graces of His Spirit on her, that the people of God, which are the herbs and trees of righteousness, may bring forth sweet spices, whose fruit may be for meat, and their leaves for medicines.

Thus much for the five appearances of Christ the same day He rose again. Now follow the rest of His appearances, which were in the forty days following, which are in number six. The first is mentioned by St. John in these words, "Eight days after when the disciples were within, and Thomas with them, came Jesus when the doors were shut, and stood in the middle of them, and said, Peace be unto you" (John 20:26). In it we must consider two things: (1) the occasion thereof; (2) the dealing of Christ.

The occasion was this: after Christ had appeared unto the other disciples in Thomas's absence, they told him that they had seen the Lord.[279] But he made answer, "Except I see in his body the print of the nails, and put mine hand into his side, I will not believe." Now eight days after, our Savior Christ appeared again unto all His disciples especially for the curing of Thomas's unbelief, which was no small sin, considering it contains in it three great sins. The first is blindness of mind, for he had been a hearer of our Savior Christ a long time and had been instructed touching the resurrection divers times. He was also with Christ and saw Him when He raised Lazarus and had seen or at leastwise had heard the miracles which He did and also had heard all the disciples say that they had seen the Lord, and yet will it not sink into his head. The second is deadness of heart. When our Savior Christ went to raise Lazarus, that was dead, Thomas spoke very confidently to his fellow disciples and said, "Let us go, that we may die with him" (11:16). Yet when Christ was crucified, he fled away and is the longest from Christ after His resurrection; and when he is certainly told thereof, he will not acknowledge it or yield unto it. The third is willfulness; for when the disciples told him that they had seen the Lord, he said flatly that

---

279. This paragraph break is not in the original.

unless he saw in His hands the print of the nails he would not believe. And that which is worse than all this, he continued eight days in this willful mind. Now, in this exceeding measure of unbelief in Thomas, any man, even he that has the most grace, may see what a mass of unbelief is in himself, and what willfulness and untowardness to any good thing, insomuch that we may truly say with David, "Lord, what is man that thou so regardest him?" [Ps. 8:4]. And if such measure of unbelief was in such men, as the disciples were, then we may assure ourselves that it does much more exceed in the common professors of religion in these days, let them protest to the contrary what they will.

Now the cause of his unbelief was this: he makes a law to himself that he will see and feel, or else he will not believe. But this is flat against the nature of faith, which consists neither in seeing nor feeling. Indeed, in things natural a man must first have experience in seeing and feeling, and then belief. But it is contrary in divinity. A man must first have faith and belief, and then comes experience afterward. But Thomas, having not learned this, does overshoot himself; and herein also many deceive themselves which think they have no faith because they have no feeling. For the chiefest feeling that we must have in this life must be the feeling of our sins and the miseries of this life. And though we have no other feeling at all, yet we must not therefore cease to believe.

In Christ's dealing with Thomas, we may consider three actions. The first, that He speaks to Thomas alone and answers him accordingly to the very words which he had spoken of Him in His absence, and that word for word [John 20:27]. And by this He labored to overthrow his unbelief and to convince him that, being absent, He knew what he spoke. And by this we learn that though we want the bodily presence of Christ, He being now in heaven, yet He knows well what we say and if need were could repeat all our sayings word by word. And if it were not so, how could it be true that we must give an account of every idle word? Now, this must teach us to look that our speech be gracious according to the rule of God's holy Word. Secondly, this must make us willing and ready to direct our prayers to Christ, considering He knows what we pray for and hears every word we speak.

The second action is that Christ condescends to Thomas and gives him liberty to feel the print of the nails and to put his finger into His side.[280] He might have rejected Thomas for his willfulness, yet to help his unbelief He yields unto his weakness. This shows that Christ is most compassionate to all those that unfeignedly repent them of their sins and cleave unto Him, although they do it laden with manifold wants. David says that the Lord has compassion on them that fear Him as a father has compassion on his children; and he adds the

---

280. This paragraph break is not in the original, as the additional one following.

reason, "For he knows of what we are made" [Ps. 103:13]. And the prophet Isaiah, "He will not break the bruised reed, and smoking flax he will not quench" [Isa. 42:3]. When a child is very sick, insomuch that it casts up all the meat which it takes, the mother will not be offended thereat, but rather pity it. Now, our Savior Christ is ten thousand times more merciful to them that believe in Him than any mother is or can be.

The third action is that when Thomas had seen and felt the wounds, Christ revived his faith, whereupon he brake forth and said, "My Lord, and my God" [John 20:28]. In which words he does most notably bewail his blindness and unbelief; and as a fire that has been smothered, so does his faith burst forth and show itself. And in this example of Thomas we may see the estate of God's people in this life. First, God gives them faith; yet afterward for a time He does (as it were) hide the same in some corner of their hearts, so as they have no feeling thereof but think themselves to be void of all grace. And this He does for no other end but to humble them, and yet again after all this the first grace is further renewed and revived. Thus dealt the Lord with David and Solomon (for whereas he was a penman of Scripture and therefore a holy man of God, we may not think that he was wholly forsaken), with Peter, and in this place with Thomas. And the experience of this shall every servant of God find in himself.

The second appearance of Christ was to seven of His disciples as they went on fishing [21:1, 6], in which He gives three testimonies of His Godhead and that by death His power was nothing diminished. The first, that when the disciples had fished all night and caught nothing, afterward by His direction they catch fish in abundance, and that presently. This teaches us that Christ is a sovereign lord over all creatures and has the disposing of them in His own hands; and that if good success follow not when men are painful to their callings, it is because God will prepare and make them fit for a further blessing. Christ comes in the morning and gives His disciples a great draught of fish. Yet before this can be, they must labor all night in vain. Joseph must be made ruler over all Egypt, but first he must be cast into a dungeon where he can see no sun nor light to prepare him to that honor. And David must be king over Israel, but the Lord will first prepare him hereunto by raising up Saul to persecute him. Therefore, when God sends any hindrances unto us in our callings, we must not despair nor be discouraged; for they are the means whereby God makes us fit to receive greater blessings at His hands either in this life or in the life to come. The second is that the net was unbroken, though it had in it great fishes to the number of a hundred fifty three. The third, that when the disciples came to land, they saw hot coals and fish laid thereon and bread. Now some may ask, whence was this food? *Answer*. The same Lord that was able to provide a whale to swallow up Jonah and so to save him, and He that was able to provide a fish for Peter's angle with a piece of twenty pence in his mouth, and to make a little bread and few fishes to feed so many thousands in the wilderness—the same also does of Himself provide bread and fishes for His disciples. This teaches us that not only the blessing but also this very having of meat, drink, apparel is from Christ. And hereupon all states of men, even the kings of the earth are taught to pray that God would give them their daily bread. Again, when we sit down to eat and drink, this must put us in mind that we are the guests of Christ Himself. Our food which we have comes of His mere gift, and He it is that entertains us if we could see it. And for this cause we must soberly and with great reverence in fear and trembling use all God's creatures as in His presence. And when we eat and drink, we must always look that all our speech be such as may beseem the guests of our Lord and Savior Jesus Christ. Usually, the practice of men is far otherwise; for in feasting many take liberty to surfeit and to be drunk, to swear, and to blaspheme. But if we serve the Lord, let us remember whose guests we are and who is our entertainer and so behave ourselves as being in His presence, that all our actions and words may tend to His glory.

The third appearance was to James, as St. Paul records [1 Cor. 15:7], although the same be not mentioned in any of the evangelists.

The fourth was to all His disciples in a mountain, whither He had appointed them to come [Matt. 28:16].

The fifth and last appearance was in the Mount of Olives when He ascended into heaven [Acts 1:12]. Of these three last appearances, because the Holy Ghost has only mentioned them, I omit to speak; and with the repeating of them I let them pass.

Thus much of the appearances of Christ after His resurrection. The witnesses thereof are of three sorts: (1) angels; (2) women that came to the grave to embalm Him; (3) Christ's own disciples, who did publish and preach the same according as they had seen and heard of our Savior Christ. And of these likewise I omit to speak, because there is not any special thing mentioned of them by the evangelists.

Now follow the uses, which are twofold: some respect Christ and some respect ourselves. Uses which concern Christ are three. (1) Whereas Christ Jesus, being stark dead, rose again to life by His own power, it serves to prove unto us that He was the Son of God. Thus, Paul, speaking of Christ, says that He was "declared mightily to be the Son of God touching the spirit of sanctification, by the resurrection from the dead" [Rom. 1:4]. And by the mouth of David God said, "Thou art my son, this day have I begotten thee" (Ps. 2:7). Which place must be understood not so much of the eternal generation of Christ before all worlds, as of the manifestation thereof in time after this manner. "This day"—that is, "At this time of Thine own incarnation, but especially at the day of Thy resurrection." "I have begotten thee"—that is, "I have made manifest that Thou art My Son." So is this place expounded by St. Paul in the Acts [13:32–33].

Secondly, Christ's rising from death by His own power proves unto us evidently that He is Lord over all things that are.[281] And this use St. Paul makes hereof, for says he, "Christ therefore died, that he might be Lord both of the dead and of the quick" (Rom. 14:9). And indeed, whereas He rose again on this manner, He did hereby show Himself most plainly to be a mighty prince over the grave, death, hell, and condemnation, and one that had all sufficient power to overcome them.

Thirdly, it proves unto us that He was a perfect priest and that His death and passion was a perfect satisfaction to the justice of God for the sins of mankind. For whereas Christ died, He died for our sins. Now, if He had not fully satisfied for them all (though there had remained but one sin for which He had made no satisfaction), He had not risen again; but death, which came into the world by sin and is strengthened by it, would have held Him in bondage. And therefore, whereas He rose again, it is more than manifest that He has made so full a satisfaction that the merit thereof does and shall countervail the justice of God for all our offences. To this purpose, Paul says, "If Christ be not risen again your faith is vain, and you are yet in your sins" (1 Cor. 15:17)—that is, Christ had not satisfied for your sins, or at least you could not possibly have known that He had made satisfaction for any of them, if He had not risen again.

The uses which concern ourselves are of two sorts: comforts to the children of God and duties that are to be learned and practiced of us all. The comforts are especially three. First, Christ's resurrection serves for the justification of all that believe in Him, even before God the Father—as Paul says, "Christ was given to death for our sins, and is risen again for our justification" (Rom. 4:25), which words have this meaning: when Christ died, we must not consider Him as a private man, as we have shown before, but as one that stood in the stead and room of all the elect. In His death, He bare our sins and suffered all that we should have suffered in our own persons forever; and the guilt of our offences was laid upon Him. And therefore Isaiah says He was numbered "among the wicked" [Isa. 53:12]. Now, in this His rising again, He freed and disburdened Himself not from any sins of His own, because He was without sin, but from the guilt and punishment of our sins imputed unto Him. And hence it comes to pass that all those which put their trust and affiance in the merit of Christ at the very last instant of their believing have their own sins not imputed unto them and His righteousness imputed.

---

281. This paragraph break is not in the original, as the additional one following.

Secondly, the resurrection of Christ serves as a notable means to work inward sanctification, as St. Peter says, "We are regenerate to a lively hope by the resurrection of Jesus Christ from the dead" [1 Peter 1:3]. And St. Paul, "We are then," says he, "buried with him by baptism into his death, that like as Christ was raised up from the dead by the glory of his Father, so we also should walk in newness of life. For if we be grafted with him to the similitude of his death, we shall be also to the similitude of his resurrection" [Rom. 6:4–5]. Which words import thus much, that as Christ by the power of His own Godhead freed His manhood from death and from the guilt of our sins, so does He free those that are knit unto Him by the bond of one Spirit from the corruption of their natures in which they are dead, that they may live unto God. In the natural body, the head is the fountain of all the senses and of motion. And therefore by sundry nerves dispersed through the body the power of moving and of sense is derived even to the least parts, so as the hands and feet move by means of that power which comes from the head. And so it is in the spiritual body of Christ—namely, the church. He is the Head and the fountain of life, and therefore He conveys spiritual life to every one of His members. And that very power of His Godhead whereby He raised up Himself when He was dead He conveys from Himself to His members and thereby raises them up from the death of sin to newness of life. And look as in a perfect body when the head has sense and motion the hand that is of the same body has also the sense and motion convenient for it, so likewise Christ, being the resurrection and the life, as there is spiritual life in Him, so every member of His shall feel in itself spiritual sense and motion whereby it is raised up from sin and lives unto God. For the better conceiving of this, we must consider two things: the outward means of this spiritual life and the measure of it.

For the means, if we will have common water, we must go to the well.[282] And if we would have water of life, we must go unto Christ, who says, "If any man thirst let him come unto me and drink" [John 7:37]. Now this well of the water of life is very deep, and we have nothing to draw with. Therefore, we must have our pipes and conduits to convey the same unto us, which are the word of God preached and the administration of the sacraments. Christ says, "The dead shall hear the voice of the son of God, and they that hear it shall live" [5:25], where by the "dead" is meant not the dead in the grave but those that are dead in sin. And again, Christ says the words which "I speak are spirit and life" [6:63], because the word of God is the pipe whereby He conveys into our dead hearts spirit and life. As Christ when He raised up dead men did only speak the word, and they were made alive, and at the day of judgment by His very

---

282. This paragraph break is not in the original, as the additional one following.

voice when the trumpet shall blow all that are dead shall rise again—so it is in the first resurrection. They that are dead in their sins at His voice uttered in the ministry of the word shall rise again. To go further, Christ raised three from the dead: Jairus's daughter, newly dead; the widow's son, dead and wound up and lying on the hearse; Lazarus, dead and buried and stinking in the grave. And all this He did by His very voice. So also by the preaching of His word He raises all sorts of sinners, even such as have laid long in their sins as rotting and stinking carrion. The sacraments also are the pipes and conduits whereby God conveys grace into the heart, if they are repaired to—that is, if they be received in unfeigned repentance for all our sins and with a true and lively faith in Christ for the pardon of the same sins. And so, I take it, they be rightly used as flagons of wine which revive the church being sick and fallen into a swoon [Song 2:4].

As for the measure of life derived from Christ, it is but small in this life and given by little and little, as Hosea says, "The Lord hath spoiled us, and he will heal us, he hath wounded us, and he will bind us up." After two days He "will revive us," and in the third He "will raise us up, and we shall live in his sight" [Hos. 6:1–2]. The prophet Ezekiel in a vision is carried into the midst of a field, full of dead bones; and he is caused to prophesy over them and say, "O ye dry bones, hear the word of the Lord" [Ezek. 37:6–10]. At the first, there was a shaking, and the bones came together bone to bone, and their sinews and flesh grew upon them, and upon the flesh grew a skin. Then, he prophesied unto the winds the second time, and they lived and stood upon their feet, for the breath came upon them. And they were an exceeding great army of men. Hereby it signifies not only the state of the Jews after their captivity, but in them the state of the whole church of God. For these temporal deliverances signify further a spiritual deliverance. And we may here see most plainly that God works in the hearts of His children the gifts and graces of regeneration by little and little. First, He gives no more than flesh, sinews, and skin. Then after He gives them further graces of His Spirit, which quickens them and makes them alive unto God. The same also we may see in the "vision of the waters that ran out of the temple" [47:3–5]. First, a man may wade to the ankles, then after to the knees, and so to the loins. Then after the waters grow to a river that cannot be passed over. And so the Lord conveys His graces by little and little, till at the last men have a full measure thereof.

Thirdly, the resurrection of Christ serves as an argument to prove unto us our resurrection at the day of judgment. Paul says, "If the spirit of him that raised up Jesus from the dead, dwell in you, he that raised Christ from the dead, shall also quicken your mortal bodies" [Rom. 8:11]. Some will say that this is no benefit; for all must rise again, as well the wicked, as the godly. *Answer.* True indeed, but yet the wicked rise not again by the same cause that the godly do.

They rise again by the power of Christ, not as He is a savior, but as He is a judge to condemn them. For God had said to Adam, at what time he should eat of the forbidden fruit, he should die the death—meaning a double death, both the first and the second death. Now then, the ungodly rise again that God may inflict upon them the punishment of the second death, which is the reward of sin, that so God's justice may be satisfied. But the godly rise again by the power of Christ, their Head and Redeemer, who raises them up that they may be partakers of the benefit of His death, which is to enjoy both in body and soul the kingdom of heaven, which He has so dearly bought for them.

Thus much for the comforts. Now follow the duties, and they are also three. *Duty 1.*[283] First, as Christ Jesus when He was dead rose again from death to life by His own power, so we by His grace in imitation of Christ must endeavor ourselves to rise up from all our sins both original and actual unto newness of life. This is worthily set down by the apostle, saying, "We are buried by baptism into his death, that as Christ was raised up from the dead by the glory of the Father, so we also should walk in newness of life" [6:4]. And therefore we must endeavor ourselves to show the same power to be in us every day by rising up from our own personal sins to a reformed life. This ought to be remembered of us, because howsoever many hear and know this point, yet very few do practice the same. For (to speak plainly) as dead men buried would never hear though a man should speak never so loud, so undoubtedly among us there be also many living men which are almost in the same case. The ministers of God may cry unto them daily and iterate the same thing a thousand times and tell them that they must rise up from their sins and lead a new life, but they hear no more than the dead carcass that lies in the grave. Indeed, men hear with their outward ears, but they are so far from practicing this duty that many judge it to be a matter of reproach and ignominy. And those which make any conscience of this duty, how they are laden with nicknames and taunts, who knows not? I need not to rehearse them, so odious a thing nowadays is the rising from sin to newness of life. Sound a trumpet in a dead man's ears, he stirs not. And let us cry for amendment of life till breath go out of our bodies, no man almost says, "What have I done?" And for this cause undoubtedly, if it were not for conscience of that duty which men owe unto God, we should have but few ministers in England. For it is the joy of a minister to see the unfeigned conversion of his people, whereas, alas, men generally lie snorting in their corruptions and rather go forward in them still than come to any amendment—such is the wonderful hardness that has possessed the hearts of most men. He which has but half an eye may see this to be true. Oh! How exceeds atheism in all places!

---

283. Originally in the margin, as the additional two duties following.

Contempt of God's worship, profanation of the Sabbath, the whoredoms and fornications, the cruelty and oppression of this age cry to heaven for vengeance. By these and such like sins the world crucifies Christ again. For look as Pilate's soldiers with the wicked Jews took Christ and stripped Him of His garments, buffeted him, and slew Him, so ungodly men by their wicked behavior strip Him of all honor and slay Him again. If an infidel should come among us and yield himself to be of our religion, after he had seen the behavior of men, he would peradventure leave all religion; for he might say, "Surely, it seems this God whom these men worship is not the true God, but a God of licentious liberty." And that which is more, whereas at all times we ought to show ourselves new creatures and to walk worthy of our Savior and Redeemer and therefore also ought to rise out of our sins and to live in righteousness and true holiness, yet we for the most part go on still forward in sin and every day go deeper than other to hellward. This has been heretofore the common practice, but let us now learn after the example of Christ, being quickened and revived by His grace, to endeavor ourselves especially to come out of the grave of sin and learn to make conscience of every bad action. True it is, a Christian man may use the creatures of God for his delight in a moderate and godly manner [1 Cor. 7:22], but Christ never gave liberty to any to live licentiously—for "he that is free, is yet servant unto Christ," as Paul says. And therefore we must not enterprise anything but that which may be a work of some good duty unto God, to which end the apostle says, "Awake thou that sleepest, and stand up from the dead, and Christ shall give thee life" [Eph. 5:14]. If this will not move us, yet let the judgment of God draw us thereunto: "Blessed is he," says the Holy Ghost, "that hath part in the first resurrection: for on such the second death hath no power" [Rev. 20:6], where mention is made of a double death. The first is the separation of soul and body; the second is the eternal condemnation of soul and body in hellfire. Would we now escape the second death after this life? We must then labor in this life to be partakers of the first resurrection, and that on this manner: look what sins we have lived in heretofore, we must endeavor to come out of them all and lead a better life according to all the commandments of God. But if it be so that you will have no care of your own souls, [then] go on hardly to your own peril, and so you shall be sure to enter into the second death, which is eternal damnation.

[Duty] 2. Secondly, we are taught by the example of St. Paul to labor above all things "to know Christ, and the virtue of his resurrection" [Phil. 3:10]. And this we shall do when we can say by experience that our hearts are not content with a drowsy profession of religion, but that we feel the same power of Christ whereby He raised up Himself from death to life to be effectual and powerful in us to work in our hearts a conversion from all our sins wherein we have lain dead to newness of life, with care to live godly in Christ Jesus. And that we may further attain to all this, we must come to hear the word of God preached and taught with fear and trembling. Having heard the word, we must meditate therein and pray unto God not only publicly but privately also, entreating Him that He would reach forth His hand and pull us out of the grave of sin wherein we have lain dead so long. And in so doing, the Lord of His mercy according as He has promised will send His Spirit of grace into our hearts to work in us an inward sense and feeling of the virtue of Christ's resurrection. So dealt He with the two disciples that were going to Emmaus. They were occupied in the meditation of Christ's death and passion. And whiles they were in hearing of Christ, who conferred with them, He gave them such a measure of His Spirit as made their hearts to burn within them [Luke 24:32]. And Paul prays for the Ephesians that God would enlighten their eyes that they might see and feel in themselves the exceeding greatness of the power of God which He wrought in Christ Jesus when He raised Him from the dead [Eph. 1:19].

[Duty] 3. Thirdly, as St. Paul says, "If we be risen with Christ, then we must seek the things that are above" [Col. 3:1]. But how and by what means can we rise with Christ, seeing we did not die with Him? *Answer.* We rise with Christ thus. The burgess of a town in the Parliament House bears the person of a whole town. And whatsoever he says, that the whole town says; and whatsoever is done to him is also done to all the town. So Christ upon the cross stood in our place and bare our person; and what He suffered, we suffered. And when He died, all the faithful died in Him. And so likewise as He is risen again, so are all the faithful risen in Him. The consideration whereof does teach us that we must not have our hearts wedded to this world. We may use the things of this life, but yet so as though we used them not. For all our love and care must be for things above, and specially we must seek the kingdom of God and His righteousness, peace of conscience, and joy in the Holy Ghost. We must therefore sue for the pardon of sin, for reconciliation to God in Christ, and for sanctification. These are the precious pearls which we must seek; and when we have found them we must sell all that we have to buy them; and, having bought them, we must lay them up in the secret corners of our hearts, valuing and esteeming of them better than all things in the world beside.

Thus much of Christ's resurrection, containing the first degree of Christ's exaltation. Now follows the second, in these words, "He ascended into heaven." In the handling whereof we are to consider these special points: (1) the time of His ascension; (2) the place; (3) the manner; (4) the witnesses; (5) the uses thereof. For the first, the time of Christ's ascension was forty days after His resurrection, when He taught His disciples the things which appertain to the kingdom of God [Acts 1:3]. And this shows that He is a most faithful king over His church, procuring the good thereof. And therefore Isaiah says, "The government is on his shoulders" [Isa. 9:6]. And the apostle says, "He was more faithful in all the house of God, than Moses was" [Heb. 3:5–6]. Hence, we gather that whereas the apostles changed the Sabbath from the seventh day to the eighth, it was no doubt by the counsel and direction of Christ before His ascension. And likewise in that they planted churches and appointed teachers and meet overseers for the guiding instruction hereof, we may resolve ourselves that Christ prescribed the same unto them before His ascension; and for these and such like causes did He ascend no sooner.

Now look what care Christ at His ascension had over His church, the same must all masters of families have over their households when God shall call them out of this world. They must have care not only that their families be well governed while they live, but also that after their death peace, love, and good order may be continued in their posterity. And therefore the prophet Isaiah is sent to Hezekiah, king of Judah, to bid him "set his house in order, for he must die" [Isa. 38:1], signifying that it is the duty of a good master of a family to have care not only for the government of his house while he is alive, but also that it may be well governed when he is dead. The same also must be practiced of God's ministers, a part of whose fidelity is this, that they have not only a care to feed their particular flocks while they are alive, but also that they further provide for the people after their departure, as much as they can. Example whereof we have in Peter, who says, "I will endeavor always that ye may be able also to have remembrance of these things after my departure" [2 Peter 1:15].

The place of Christ's ascension was the "Mount of Olives near Bethany" [Luke 19:29; 24:50; Acts 1:12], and it was the same place from whence Christ went to Jerusalem to be crucified. One place served to be a passage both to pain and torments and also to glory. This shows that the way to the kingdom of heaven is through afflictions. There are many which have God's hand heavy upon them in lingering sicknesses, as the dead palsy and such like, wherein they are fain to lie many years without hope of cure, whereupon their beds, which should be unto them places of rest and ease, are but places of woe and misery. Yet may these men hence have great comfort if they can make a good use of their sicknesses, for the beds whereon they suffer so much torment shall be places from whence they shall pass to joy and happiness. Again, there be many that for the testimony of the truth and for religion's sake suffer imprisonment with many afflictions. Now, if they can use their afflictions well, their prisons shall be Bethanys unto them. Although they be places of bondage, yet God will at length make them places of entrance to liberty. Many a man for the maintaining of faith and good conscience is banished out of his country and is fain to live in a strange place among a people to whom he is unknown. But let him use it well;

for though it be a place of grief for a time, as Bethany was to Christ when He went to suffer, yet God will make it one day to be a passage into heaven.

Thus much of the place of His ascending. The third thing to be considered is the manner of Christ's ascension, and it contains three points. The first, that Christ, being now to ascend, "lift up his hands, and blessed his disciples" [Luke 24:50]. In the Scriptures are mentioned diverse kinds of blessings. The first, when one prays to God for a blessing upon another; and this blessing do kings and princes bestow upon their subjects, and parents on their children. And for this cause children are well taught to ask their fathers' and mothers' blessing, that they may pray to God to bless them. There is another kind of blessing when a man does not only pray for a blessing, but also pronounces it. This did the priests in the Old Testament. And thus Melchizedek when he met Abraham blessed him, saying, "Blessed art thou Abraham of God, the most high possessor of heaven and earth" [Gen. 14:19]. And this was the ordinary duty of the priests, prescribed by God Himself. And therefore the very form of words which they used is set down after this manner: "The Lord bless thee and keep thee, the Lord make his face to shine upon thee," etc. [Num. 6:24–26]. The third kind of blessing is when a man does not only pray to God and pronounce blessing, but by the spirit of prophecy does foretell a particular blessing upon any. Thus, Isaac blessed Jacob and Esau [Gen. 27:28], particularly foretelling both their estates. And Jacob blessed the twelve patriarchs by the same spirit, foretelling them what should befall them many hundred years after [ch. 49]. Now, our Savior Christ did not bless His disciples any of these three ways. And therefore there remains a fourth kind of blessing which He used, and that was after this manner: Christ in blessing His disciples did not only pronounce or foretell a blessing that should come to His disciples, but did confer and give the same unto them. For He is the fountain and author of all blessings. And therefore Paul says that "God the Father has blessed us in all spiritual blessings in Christ" [Eph. 1:3].

Hence we learn, first, that all those which deny themselves and fly to Christ and put their affiance in Him shall be freed from the curse of the law and from the wrath of God due unto them for their sins, whatsoever they are. Secondly, that the curses of men must not discourage us from doing well. For though men curse, yet Christ blesses; and for this cause He says, "Woe be unto you, when all men speak well of you" [Luke 6:26], as if He should say, "Then you want the blessing of God." And we must remember that when men shall curse us for doing our duty, even then the blessing of God shall be upon us, and the curse causeless shall not hurt. And God says to Abraham [that] He will curse them that curse him [Gen. 12:3]. Thirdly, we learn that no witchcraft nor sorcery (which often are done with cursing) shall be able to hurt us. For look where

Christ will bless, there all the devils in hell can never fasten a curse. This is found true by experience. For when Balaam the wizard should have cursed the people of Israel and had assayed to do it many ways, but could not, at length he said, "There is no sorcery against Jacob, nor soothsaying against Israel" [Num. 23:23]. This is a notable comfort to the people of God, that witches and sorcerers, do what they can, shall never be able to hurt them. It may be that their bad practices may annoy men's bodies and goods, yet the Lord will turn all to a blessing upon His servants either in this life or in the life to come.

The second point is that Christ "went apart from his disciples, and ascended upward toward heaven in their sight." For the right understanding of this, sundry special points must be observed. The first, that the lifting up of His body was principally by the mighty power of His Godhead and partly by the supernatural property of a glorified body, which is to move as well upward as downward without constraint or violence. The second, that Christ did go from earth to heaven really and actually, and not in appearance only. The third, that He went visibly in the sight of His disciples. The fourth, that He went locally by changing His place and going from earth to heaven, so as He is no more on earth bodily, as we are now on earth. It may be objected that Christ made a promise "that he would be with his church to the end of the world" [Matt. 28:20]. *Answer.* That promise is to be understood of the presence of His Spirit or Godhead, not of the presence of His manhood. Again, it may be further alleged that if the Godhead be on earth, then must the manhood be there also, because they are both united together. *Answer.* It is not true that of two things conjoined, where the one is, there must the other be also. For the sun itself and the sunbeams are both joined together, yet they are not both in all places together. For the body of the sun is only in the heavens, but the sunbeams are also upon the earth. The argument therefore follows not: Christ's manhood subsists in that person which is everywhere; ergo, His manhood is everywhere.[284] And the reason is because the Son of God subsists not only in His divine nature, but also by it, whereas He does not subsist at all by the manhood, but only in it; for He subsisted before all eternity, when the manhood was not. Nay, rather because the manhood does subsist by the person of the Son, therefore the person extends itself further than the manhood, which is assumed and sustained by it and has His existing thence. For that very thing whereby any other thing either essentially or accidentally is extends itself further than the thing whereby it is, as the human nature whereby Peter is a man extends itself further than to Peter—namely, to all other men—and the whiteness whereby the snow is white extends itself further than to that snow which a man holds in his hand.

---

284. Vide Th. contra. Gent. lib. 4. c. 49.

The third point is that in the ascension "a cloud took Christ from the sight of his disciples" [Acts 1:9]. And whereas He caused a cloud to come between their sight and Himself, it signified unto them that they must now be contented with that which they had seen and not to seek to know further what became of Him afterward. And the same thing is taught unto us also. We must content ourselves with that which God has revealed in His Word, and seek no further, specially in things which concern God. For the like end in the giving of the law in Sinai, God appeared in a cloud [Ex. 19:9]. And when He did manifest His glory in the temple which Solomon made, a thick cloud filled the same [1 Kings 8:10–11].

The fourth point to be considered is concerning the witnesses of His ascension, which were His own disciples in the Mount of Olives at Bethany, and none but they [Luke 24:50; Acts 1:9]. Now it may be demanded why He would not have all the whole nation of the Jews to see Him ascend, that so they might know that He was risen again and believe in Him. *Answer.* The reason may be this: it was His good pleasure that the points of faith and religion whereof this article is one should rather be learned by hearing than by seeing. Indeed, Christ's own disciples were taught the same by sight that they might the better teach others which should not see, whereas now the ordinary means to come by faith is hearing.

The uses to be made of Christ's ascension are of two sorts: some are comforts to God's church and people and some are duties. The comforts are especially four. The first is this: Christ Jesus did ascend up to heaven "to lead captivity captive" [Eph. 4:8]—a most worthy benefit. By "captivity" is meant sin and Satan, which did and do lead men captive into perdition; secondly, death and the grave, which held Him captive and in bondage for the space of three days. And He leads them all captive two ways: first in Himself, in that He began His triumph upon the cross, as I have showed, and continued the same till His very ascension; secondly, in all His members, because by His mighty power, being now ascended, He does subdue and weaken the power of sin and Satan [Rom. 16:20], which He manifests every day by killing the corruption of their natures and the rebellion of their flesh. But it may be demanded how Christ does lead His enemies captive, considering the devil reigns everywhere and the world and death and hell. *Answer.* Christ's victory over His and our enemies has five degrees. First, it is ordained by God; secondly, it is foretold; thirdly, it is wrought; fourthly, it is applied; lastly, it is accomplished. The ordaining of it was before all worlds. The foretelling of it was in all the ages of the Old Testament. The working of it was upon the cross, and afterward. The applying has been since the beginning of the world more or less. And it is only in part in this life that while Christ is bruising of the head of Satan, he again may bruise His heal. The accomplishment shall not be before the last judgment.

From this great benefit bestowed on God's church there are many duties to be learned. First, here is an instruction for all ignorant persons and impenitent sinners, which abound among us in every place, whosoever they be, that live in the blindness of their minds and hardness of their hearts. They must know this, that they are captives and bondslaves of sin and Satan, of hell, death, and condemnation. And let no man flatter himself of what state or degree soever he be. For it is God's truth, if he have not repented of all his sins, he as yet is no better than a servant or a vassal, yea, a very drudge of the devil. Now then, what will you do in this case? The best thing is to lay to your heart this benefit of Christ. He is ascended up to heaven to lead captive and to vanquish the devil and all his angels, under whom you lie bound, and that not only in Himself, but in His members. Now then, if you will become a true member of Christ, He will free you from this bondage. Therefore, take heed how you continue longer in your old sins and in your gross ignorance. And, seeing Christ has made a way to liberty, let us seek to come out of this spiritual bondage. He is ascended for this end and purpose to free us from it. Therefore, if we refuse this benefit, our state will be the more damnable. A man lies bound hand and foot in a dark dungeon, and the keeper comes and sets open the prison door and takes off his bolts and bids him come out. If he refuse and say that he is well, may it not be thought that he is a madman? And will any be sorry for his case? No, surely. Well, this is the state of all impenitent sinners. They lie fast fettered and bound under the power of sin and Satan, and Christ it is who is ascended into heaven to unloose them of this bondage. He has set open the prison door and has unlocked our fetters. If we refuse to come out and lie still in our sins, there remains nothing for us but everlasting thraldom. Let us therefore in the fear of God, if we have care of our own souls, receive and embrace this benefit which redounds unto us by Christ's ascension.

Secondly, in that Christ is ascended to heaven to lead captive sin and Satan, here is a good consolation for all those that are afflicted in conscience for their sins. There is no man in this case but he has great cause to fear, yet must he not be discouraged. For Christ by His ascension like a noble captain has taken sin and Satan prisoner and has pinioned them fast, so as all the power they have is in Christ's hand. And therefore for this cause, although they are suffered to exercise and afflict us, yet by His grace they shall never be able to prevail against us. Therefore, we may safely cast our care upon God and not fear overmuch.

Hence also we may learn a third duty. There is no man that knows what sin means and what the blood of Christ means, but in regard of the corruption of his own nature he will say with Paul that he is sold under sin [Rom. 7:14] and in regard thereof will cry out with him also, "O wretched man that I am, who shall deliver me from this body of death?" [v. 24]. Yea, it will make his heart to bleed within him. Now, what shall he do in this case? Surely, let him remember the end of Christ's ascension, which is to vanquish and subdue the rebellion of his nature, and labor to feel the benefit thereof. And then he shall no doubt find that Christ will "dissolve in him the works of the devil" [1 John 3:8], and "tread Satan under his feet" [Rom. 16:20]. And thus also those that feel in themselves the law of their members, rebelling against the law of their mind, must come to Christ, and He will help and free them.

The second benefit of Christ's ascension is that He ascended up to heaven to bestow gifts upon His church, as it is said in the place before mentioned. "He ascended up on high," etc. "He gave gifts unto men" [Eph. 4:8]—that is, the gift of the knowledge of God's Word, the gift of preaching and prophecy, and all other gifts needful for the good of His church. The consideration of this, that Christ, who is the fountain of grace and in whom are hid all the treasures of wisdom and knowledge, should be mindful of us and vouchsafe such special favor to His church, must cause every one of us who has received any gift of God (as there is no man but he has received his portion) to be humbled in his own eyes for the same. There is no cause why we should be proud of our gifts, seeing we have nothing but that which we have received. For to this end Christ ascended: to give gifts unto men. And therefore our gifts, whatsoever they be, are not our own, but we had them from Christ, and we are stewards of them awhile for the good of others. The more the Lord gives to man, the more He requires at his hands. And as for such as having good gifts abuse the same, their sin is the more grievous, and their danger the greater. Men of great gifts, unless they use them aright with humbled hearts, shall want God's blessing upon them. For He gives grace to the humble. The high hills after much tillage are often barren, whereas the low valleys by streams of water passing through them are very fruitful. And the gifts of God joined with a swelling heart are fruitless, but joined with love and the grace of humility they edify.

Secondly, if Christ ascend up to heaven to give gifts unto men, here we may see how many a man and woman in these our days are overseen, in that they plead ignorance and say that they hope God will have them excused for it, seeing that they are not learned. They have dull wits, and it is not possible to teach them now. They are past learning. And hereupon they presume they may live in gross ignorance, as blind almost in religion as when they were first born. But mark, I pray you, who is it that is ascended up into heaven—namely, Christ Jesus our Lord, who made you of nothing. Now, was He able to give you a being when you were not, and is He not likewise able to put knowledge into your soul, if so be you will use the means which He has appointed? And the rather, seeing He is ascended for that end? But if you will not use the means to come to knowledge, your case is desperate, and you are the cause of your own condemnation, and you bring confusion upon your own head. Therefore, let ignorant men labor for knowledge of God's Word. Ignorance shall excuse none. It will not stand for payment at the day of judgment. Christ is ascended to this end to teach the ignorant, to give knowledge and wisdom unto the simple, and to give gifts of prophecy unto His ministers that they may teach His people. Therefore, I say again, let such as be ignorant use the means diligently, and God will give the blessing. Thirdly, whereas it is thought to be a thing not possible to furnish a whole church with preaching ministers, it seems to be otherwise. For wherefore did Christ ascend to heaven? Was it not to give gifts unto His church? What, is Christ's hand now shortened? Undoubtedly, we may resolve ourselves that Christ bestowed gifts sufficient upon men in the church, but it is for our sins that they are not employed. The fountains of learning, the universities, though they are not dammed up, yet they stream not abroad as they might. Many there be in them endued with worthy gifts for the building of the church, but the covetousness of men hinders the comfortable entrance which otherwise might be. Lastly, seeing Christ ascended to give gifts needful for His church, as the gift of teaching, the gift of prophecy, the gift of tongues, of wisdom, and knowledge, the duty of every man is especially of those that live in the schools of learning to labor by all means to increase, cherish, and preserve their gifts and, as Paul exhorts Timothy, to "stir up the gift of God" [2 Tim. 1:6][285]—that is, as men preserve the fire by blowing it, so by our diligence we must kindle and revive the gifts and graces of God bestowed on us. Christ has done His part, and there is nothing required but our pains and fidelity.

The third benefit that comes by Christ's ascension is that He ascended to prepare a place for all that should believe in Him. "In my Father's house," says Christ, "are many dwelling places, if it were not so, I would have told you, I go to prepare a place for you" [John 14:2]. For by the sin of Adam our entrance into heaven was taken away. If Adam by his fall did exclude himself from the earthly paradise, then how much more did he exclude himself from heaven [Gen. 3:24]? And therefore all mankind, sinning in him, was likewise deprived of heaven. The people of Israel, being in woe and misery, cried out that they had sinned, and therefore "the Lord had covered himself with a cloud, that their prayers could not pass through" [Lam. 3:44]. And Isaiah says that our sins "are a wall betwixt God and us" [Isa. 59:2]. And St. John, that "no unclean thing must enter into the heavenly Jerusalem" [Rev. 21:27]. Now, seeing we have shut ourselves out of heaven by our sins, it was requisite that Christ Jesus our Savior should go before us to prepare a place and to make ready a way for us. For He is King over all. He has the keys of heaven; He opens and no man shuts. And therefore

---

285. Originally, "1 Tim. 1:6."

it is in His power to let us in, though we have shut ourselves out. But some may say, if this be the end of His ascension to prepare a place in heaven, then belike such as died before the coming of Christ were not in heaven. *Answer.* As there are two degrees of glory, one incomplete and the other complete or perfect (for the faithful departed are in glory but in part, and there remains fullness of glory for such then at the day of judgment, when soul and body shall be both glorified together), so answerably there are two degrees of preparation of places in heaven. The places of glory were in part prepared for the faithful from the beginning of the world, but the full preparation is made by Christ's ascension. And of this last preparation is the place of John to be understood.

The use of this doctrine is very profitable. First, it overthrows the fond doctrine of the Church of Rome, which teaches that Christ by His death did merit our justification, and that we, being once justified, do further merit salvation and purchase for ourselves a place in heaven. But this is as it were to make a partition between Christ and us in the work of our redemption, whereas in truth not only the beginning and continuance of our salvation but also the accomplishment thereof in our vocation, justification, sanctification, glorification is wholly and only to be ascribed to the mere merit of Christ. And therefore, having redeemed us on earth, He also ascends to prepare a place in heaven for us.

Secondly, this serves to condemn the fearful, lamentable, and desperate security of these our days. Great is the love of Christ in that He was content to suffer the pangs of hell to bring us out of hell and withal to go to heaven to prepare a place for us there. And yet who is it that cares for the place or makes any account thereof? Who forsakes this world and seeks unto Christ for it? And, further, lest any man should say, "Alas, I know not the way," therefore Christ before He ascended made "a new and living way" with His own blood, as the apostle speaks. And to take away all excuses from men, He has set marks and bounds in this way and has placed guides in it—namely, His ministers—to show all the passengers a straight and ready course into the kingdom of heaven. And though Christ have done all this for us, yet the blindness and security of men is such that none almost walks in this way nor cares to come into this mansion place; but instead of this they walk in byways according to the lusts of their own flesh. When they are commanded to go eastward to Jerusalem, they turn westward another way. When they are commanded to go on forward to heaven, they turn again backward and go straight to hell. Men run on all the days of their lives in the broad way that leads to destruction and never so much as once make inquiry for a resting place in heaven; but when the hour of death comes, then they call for the guide, whereas all their lives before they have run out of the way many thousand miles. But then, alas, it is too late, unless it be the unspeakable mercy of God. For they have wandered so far astray that in so short a space they cannot be able to come into the right way again. Yet generally, this [is] the state of most among us, whose security is so much the more grievous and fearful because Christ has done all that heart can wish. There is nothing else required, but only that by His grace we should walk in the way. There was never any that knew the state of the people in these days but he will grant that this is most true which I say. Besides, as by this we are brought to a sight of the desperate security of this age, so we may further learn our own duties. Is Christ gone to heaven beforehand to prepare a place for you? Then practice that which Paul teaches. Have your conversation "in heaven" [Phil. 3:20]. The words which he uses are very significant, and the meaning of them is: you are free denizens of the city of God; and therefore as free men in God's house let all your cares and duties, all your affairs and doings be in heaven. In the world, if a man make purchase of a house, his heart is always there. There he pulls down and builds again. There he makes him orchards and gardens. There he means to live and die. Christ Jesus has bought the kingdom of heaven for us (the most blessed purchase that ever was) and has paid the dearest price for it that ever was paid, even His own precious blood. And in this city He has prepared for us a dwelling place and made us free denizens of it. Therefore, all our joy and all our affairs ought to be there. It will be said, how shall a man upon earth have his conversation in heaven? *Answer*. We must converse in heaven not in body but in heart. And therefore, though our bodies be on earth, yet our heart's joy and comfort and all our meditation must be in heaven. Thus must we behave ourselves like good free men in God's house. It must be far from us to have our joy and our hearts set on the things of this world.

Thirdly, the consideration of this, that Christ Jesus has prepared a place for us in heaven and also has trained the way with His own blood, must make every one of us "to strive to enter in at the strait gate," as our Savior Christ counsels us (Luke 13:24), and that as wrestlers do, which strive for life and death. Within this gate is a dwelling place of happiness ready for us. If a man were assured that there were made for him a great purchase in Spain or Turkey, so as if he would but come thither, he might enjoy it, would he not adventure the dangers of the sea and of his enemies also, if need were, that he might come to his own? Well, behold, Christ Jesus has made a purchase for us in heaven, and there is nothing required of us but that we will come and enjoy it. Why then should men refuse any pains or fear in the way? Nay, we must strive to get in. It may be we shall be pinched in the entrance, for the gate is strait and low. We must be feign to leave our wealth behind us and the pleasures of this life; and enter we must, though we should be constrained to leave our flesh behind us, for the purchase that is made is worth ten thousand worlds. And besides, if we lose it by fainting in the way, our purchase shall be the blackness of darkness forever with the devil and all his angels—who therefore would not strive, though he lost his life in the gate? The urging of this point is needful in these days. There is striving enough for worldly preferment, but a man almost must go alone in the straight way that leads to heaven, he shall have none to bear him company. And where are they that strive to enter? Where is the violence offered to the kingdom of heaven? Where be the violent which should take it to themselves, as in the days of John [the] Baptist (Matt. 11:12)?

Fourthly, if Christ have prepared a place for us in heaven, then we are in this world as pilgrims and strangers and therefore must learn the counsel of St. Peter: "As strangers and pilgrims abstain from fleshly lusts, which fight against the soul" (1 Peter 2:11). He that does esteem himself as a pilgrim is not to entangle himself with the affairs of this world nor put in practice the behavior thereof, but to behave himself as a free man of heaven, as strangers use to live in foreign countries according to the fashion of their own. And therefore in thought, word, and deed, in life and conversation he must so carry himself as thereby he may appear to all the world of what country he is. An ancient divine, speaking of such as had curled and embroidered hair,[286] bids them consider whether they must go to heaven with such hair or no. And whereas they adorned themselves with winkles made of other women's hair, he asks them whether it may not be the hair of a damned person or no. If it may be, he further demanded, how it may beseem them to wear it which profess themselves to be the sons and daughters of God. The like may be said of all other sins. They that be of God's house must behave themselves as free men there. And when God has made us free, it does not beseem us to make ourselves bondmen of sin and Satan and of this world.

Fifthly, seeing Christ went to heaven to prepare a place for all that believe in Him, here is a good duty for parents. Many of them are very careful to prefer their children to great places and noblemen's houses, and they are not to be blamed therefore. But if they would indeed be good parents to their children, they should first endeavor themselves to get rooms for them in heaven. They that do this are good parents indeed. Some will say, how shall we get this preferment for them? *Answer.* God has two houses: His church and the kingdom of heaven. The church is His house of grace; heaven is His house of glory. Now if you would bring your child to a place in the house of glory, then you are first of all to get him a place in the house of grace, bringing him up so in the fear of God that both in life and conversation he may show himself to be a member of the church. And then assure yourself that after this life he shall be removed to

---

286. Tertul. l. de habit. mul.

the second house of God, which is the house of glory, and there be a free man forever in the kingdom of heaven. And if you shall thus provide for your child, you shall not leave him as an orphan when you die; but he shall have God for his Father, and Christ for his Brother, and the Holy Ghost his Comforter. And therefore, first of all and above all, remember to make your child a member of God's church. Let the example of David excite all parents hereunto. "I had rather," says he, "be a door keeper in the house of God, than to dwell in the tabernacle of wickedness. For a day in thy courts is better than a thousand elsewhere" (Ps. 84:10).[287]

Lastly, hence we may find remedy against the tediousness of sickness and fear of death. You which fear death, remember that Christ is gone to heaven to prepare a place for your body, where it must be glorified and live forever with the blessed Trinity and all the saints and angels, though for a while it lie dead and rot in the grave. Remember this also, you which continue in any lingering sickness: Christ Jesus has prepared a place for you wherein you shall rest in joy and bliss without all pain or faintness.

The fourth benefit is that Christ ascended up to heaven "to send the comforter unto his church." This was a special end of His ascension, as appears by Christ's own words. "It is," says He, "expedient that I go away, for if I go not, the comforter will not come: but if I depart, I will send him unto you" (John 16:7). And again, "I will pray unto the Father, and he shall give you another comforter, which shall abide with you forever, even the spirit of truth" (14:16). But some will say, how can Christ send His Spirit unto His church, for the person sending and the person sent are unequal, whereas all three persons in [the] Trinity are equal, none greater or lesser than another, none inferior or superior to other? *Answer.* It is true indeed; but we must know that the action of sending in the Trinity makes not the persons unequal but only shows a distinction and order among equals. The Father sends the Son; the Father and the Son both send the Holy Ghost. Yet the Father is not above the Son, neither the Father or the Son above the Holy Ghost; but all are equal in degree, though in regard of order one is before another. And it stands with reason, for two men that are equal in degree may upon mutual consent one send another. But it may be further demanded, how the Holy Ghost can be sent, which is everywhere? *Answer.* The Holy Ghost indeed is everywhere. Therefore, He is sent not so much in regard of the presence of His essence or substance as of His operation whereby He renews and guides the members of Christ.

Now then, this being so, here, first, we have occasion to consider the misery of the world. When a man is troubled in his mind (as no ungodly man,

---

287. Originally, "Ps. 48:10."

but sometimes he feels the terror of conscience for his sins), then he labors to remove it by merry company and pleasant books, whereas Christ at His ascension sent His Holy Spirit to be the comforter of His church. And therefore when we are troubled in conscience for our sins, we should not seek ease by such slender means but rather seek for the help and comfort of the Holy Ghost and labor to have our sins washed away and our hearts purified and cleansed by the blood of Christ. As for wine and mirth and such like means of comfort, neither at the day of death nor at the day of judgment shall they stand us in stead or be able to comfort us. Again, when crosses and calamities fall, the counsel of the minister is not sought for, but the help of such as are called cunning men and cunning women, that is, of charmers, enchanters, and figure casters—a bad practice. Christ at His ascension sent His Holy Spirit unto His church and people to be their guide and comforter in their calamities and miseries. And therefore, when any man is in distress, he should have recourse to the right means of comfort—namely, the word and sacraments—and there he should find the assistance of the Holy Ghost. Thus, the prophet Isaiah informs the Jews. When they shall say unto you, inquire at them which have a spirit of divination and at the soothsayers which whisper and murmur, "Should not a people inquire at their God, from the living to the dead? To the law, and to the testimony" [Isa. 8:19]. Rebecca, when the two twins strove in her womb, what did she? The text says she sent to "ask the Lord" [Gen. 25:22]. Yet commonly the men of these days leave God and seek to the instruments of the devil. To go yet further, God uses for sundry causes most of all to afflict His dearest children. "Judgment," says Peter, "begins at God's house" [1 Peter 4:17]. St. Luke says that a certain woman was "bound of Satan eighteen years" [Luke 13:16]—but what was she? "A daughter of Abraham"—that is, a child of God. When the like condition shall befall any of us, let us remember the end why Christ ascended up to heaven. And let us pray unto God that He will give us His Spirit, that thereby we may be eased and delivered or else enabled to persevere and continue in patience. And this is the true way and means to lighten and ease the burden of all afflictions. And for this cause Paul prays that the Colossians might be "strengthened with all might, through his glorious power, unto all patience and long-sufferance with joyfulness" [Col. 1:11]. For to whomsoever God gives grace to believe, to them also He gives power to suffer affliction by the inward work of His Spirit. Secondly, if Christ have sent unto His church the Holy Spirit to be our Comforter, our duty is to prepare our bodies and souls to be fit temples and houses for so worthy a guest. If a man were certified that a prince would come to his house, he would dress it up and have all things in as good order as might be. And shall we not much more endeavor to purify and cleanse our souls and bodies from all sin, that they may be fit temples for the entertainment of the Holy Ghost, whom Christ Jesus had sent to be our Comforter? The Shunammite was careful to entertain the man of God Elisha; for she said to her husband, "Let us make him a little chamber I pray thee, with walls, and let us set him there a bed and a stool, a table and a candlestick" [2 Kings 4:10]. Now, how much more careful ought we to be to entertain God Himself, who is content to come and dwell with us? And therefore we must adorn our bodies and souls with grace, that He may lodge and sup and dine with us as He has promised. But on the contrary, if we defile our bodies with sin, we banish the Holy Ghost out of our hearts and invite the devil to come and dwell with us. For the more a man defiles his body, the fitter and cleaner it is for him. And to conclude this point, let us remember that saying which is used of some,[288] that Christ when He went hence gave us His pawn—namely, His Spirit—to assure us that He would come to us again. And also He took with Him our pawn—namely, His flesh—to assure us further that we should ascend up to Him.

Thus much for the benefits of Christ's ascension. Now follow the duties whereunto we are moved, and they are two. First, we must be here admonished to renounce the ubiquity and the error of the real and essential presence of the body of Christ in the sacrament of the Lord's Supper as flatly oppugning this article of Christ's ascension into heaven. For it is flat against the nature of a true body to subsist in many places at once. Secondly, as the apostles then did when they saw Christ ascending up into heaven, so must we do also: while He was present with them, they gave Him honor; but when they saw Him ascending, they "adored him" [Luke 24:42] with far greater reverence. And so must we now for the same cause bow the knees of our hearts unto Him.

Thus much of the second degree of the exaltation of Christ. Now follows the third, in these words: "and sitteth at the right hand of God the Father Almighty." In the handling whereof, we are first to show the meaning of the words; secondly, the comforts and benefits that redound to God's church; thirdly, the duties that we are moved unto.

For the meaning of the words, if we speak properly, God has neither right hand nor left.[289] Neither can He be said to sit or stand, for God is not a body but a spirit. The words therefore contain a borrowed speech from earthly kings and potentates, whose manner and custom has been to place such persons at their right hands whom they purpose to advance to any special office or dignity. So, King Solomon when his "mother" [1 Kings 2:19] came to speak with him rose up from his throne and met her and caused "a seat to be set at his own right hand" and set her upon it—in token, no doubt, of honor which he gave

---

288. Tertull.
289. This paragraph break is not in the original.

unto her. To the same purpose, David says, "Upon thy right hand did stand the queen in a vesture of gold" [Ps. 45:9]. And the sons of Zebedee made suit to Christ that "one of them might sit at his right hand, and the other at his left in his kingdom" [Mark 10:37]. Now, their request was to have the two special and principal dignities of His kingdom. Thus, we see it is manifest that the sitting at the right hand of an earthly prince signifies advancement into authority and honor, and therefore the same phrase of speech applied to Christ signifies two things. First, His full and manifest exaltation in dignity, honor, and glory. And in this sense it is said that "to him is given a name that is above all names, that at the name of Jesus every knee shall bow" [Phil. 2:9]. Secondly, it signifies His full and manifest exaltation into the authority and government of His kingdom, which spreads itself over heaven and earth. So David says, "The Lord said unto my Lord, Sit thou at my right hand until I make thine enemies thy footstool" (Ps. 110:1). Which place being alleged by St. Paul, repeating the words but changing the phrase, is thus set down: "He shall reign till he have put all his enemies under his feet" (1 Cor. 15:25). And to speak in brief, the scope of the words is to show that Christ, God and man, after His ascension is advanced to such an estate in which He has fullness of glory, power, majesty, and authority in the presence of His Father and all the saints and holy angels.

Furthermore, in the words three circumstances must be observed. The first is the place where Christ is thus advanced, noted in the former article: "he ascended into heaven, and sits"—namely, in heaven—"at the right hand of God." The place then where Christ Jesus in both His natures as He is God and also man does rule in full glory, power, and majesty is heaven itself. To which effect Paul says, "God raised Christ from the dead, and put him at his right hand in the heavenly places" (Eph. 1:20). And in the epistle to the Hebrews it is said He sits "at the right hand of the majesty in highest places" [1:3]. This point well considered serves to discover the oversight of sundry divines which hold and teach that to sit at the right hand of God is to be everywhere in all places and not in heaven only, that they might hereby lay a foundation for the ubiquity of Christ's manhood, which nevertheless the heavens must contain till the time that all things be restored.

The second circumstance is the time when Christ began to sit at the right hand of God the Father, which is to be gathered by the order of the articles.[290] For, first, Christ died and was buried. Then He rose again and ascended into heaven, and after His ascension He is said to sit at the right hand of His Father. This order is also noted unto us by St. Paul: "Who shall condemn?" says he, "It is Christ which is dead, yea or rather risen again, who is also at the right

---

290. This paragraph break is not in the original, as the additional one following.

hand of God" [Rom. 8:34]. And St. Mark says when Christ was risen again He appeared to His disciples, and after He had "spoken unto them, he was received into heaven, and set at the right hand of God" [16:19]. But it may be demanded how this can stand with truth, that Christ should not begin to sit at the right hand of His Father before the ascension, considering He is one God with the Father and therefore an absolute and sovereign king from all eternity? *Answer.* As Christ is God or the Word of the Father, He is coequal and coeternal with Him in the regiment of His kingdom and has neither beginning, middle, nor ending thereof. Yet as Christ is God incarnate, and in one person God-man or man-God, He began after His ascension and not before to sit at the right hand of His Father and as St. Peter says "was made Lord" [Acts 2:36], partly because as He was God He did then manifest Himself to be that which indeed He was before—namely, God and Lord of heaven and earth—and partly because as He was man He received dominion or lordship from the Father, which He had not before, and thereby was even in His manhood exalted to be King of heaven and earth. And in this sense Christ says of Himself, "All power is given to me in heaven and earth" [Matt. 28:18].

The third circumstance is concerning the person at whose right hand Christ sits, noted in the words of the article, of "God the Father Almighty," whereby is signified that He receives all the honor, power, and glory of His kingdom from His Father, as he that is set at the right hand of a prince receives the honor and authority which he has from the prince. Now if it be alleged that by this means Christ shall be inferior to His Father, because he which receives honor of another is inferior to him of whom he receives it, the answer is that in Christ we must consider His person and His office. In respect of His person, as He is the eternal Son of God, He is equal to the Father and is not here said to sit at His right hand. Yet in respect of the office which He bears—namely, as He is a mediator, and as He is man—He is inferior to the Father and receives His kingdom from Him. As He is God, He is our King and Head and has no head more than the Father [1 Cor. 11:3]. As He is Mediator, He is also our Head, yet so as He is under the Father as being His Head. And we must not think it strange that one and the same thing should be both equal and inferior to another, diverse respects considered.

Now in that Christ's placing at the right hand of His Father argues inferiority between the Father and Him, hence we learn that they are deceived which from this article gather that in the glorification of Christ there is a transfusion of the proprieties of the Godhead, as omnipotency, omnipresence, etc., into His manhood. For this is to abolish all inferiority and to make an equality between the creature and the Creator.

And whereas again the word "almighty" is repeated, it is done upon special reason: because Christ sitting at the right hand of God does presuppose omnipotency. For in vain were all power in heaven and earth given to Him, unless He were omnipotent as the Father to execute the same. And therefore the song of the elders was on this manner, "Worthy is the Lamb that was killed to receive power and riches, and wisdom, and strength, and honor, and glory, and praise" (Rev. 5:12).

The benefits which redound unto us by Christ's sitting at the right hand of God are two: one concerns His priesthood; the other, His kingly office. The benefit arising from His priesthood is His intercession for us; for this is one of the ends why Christ is now exalted in glory and sits at the right hand of His Father—namely, to make request in the behalf of all that come unto Him, as Paul says, "Christ is risen again, and sitteth at the right hand of God, and maketh request for us" [Rom. 8:34].

Now that we may rightly understand what His intercession is, we are to consider these points: first, to whom it is made; secondly, in what manner; thirdly, whether it be made by Christ alone or no; fourthly, what be the fruits and benefits thereof; fifthly, the duties whereunto we are moved thereby. For the first, intercession is to make suit, request, or entreaty in someone's behalf to another; and this is done by Christ for us unto God, as Paul says, "There is one God, and one mediator between God and man; which is the man Christ Jesus" [1 Tim. 2:5]. Here at the very first arises a difficulty, for in every intercession there be three parties: the person offended; the person offending; the intercessor, distinct from them both. Now if Christ, the Son of God, make intercession to God for man, then He makes intercession to Himself, because He is true God—which cannot be. How then shall Christ be a mediator? *Answer.* This point has so troubled the Church of Rome that for the resolving of it they have devised an error, avouching that Christ is Mediator only as He is man, not as He is God, which is untrue. For as both natures do concur in the work of satisfaction, so likewise do they both concur in the work of intercession. And therefore a more meet and convenient answer is this: Christ Jesus, God-man, in both natures is directly our Mediator to the first person, the Father, as St. John says, "If any man sin, we have an advocate with the Father, Jesus Christ the just" [1 John 2:1]. And thus we have three persons in the work of intercession really distinguished. The party offended is God the Father; the party offending is man; and, thirdly, the intercessor distinct from them both is Christ, the second person in [the] Trinity. For howsoever in Godhead He and the Father be one, yet in person they are really distinguished. And He as it were in the middle between the Father and us; for the Father is God and not man; we that believe in Christ are men, not God; Christ Himself, both man and God. It may be further replied that this answer will not stand, because not only the Father is offended, but also the Son and the Holy Ghost. And therefore there must be a mediator to them also. *Answer.* The intercession of Christ is directed to the Father, the first person, immediately. Now the Father, the Son, and the Holy Ghost have all one indivisible essence and by consequent one and the same will, whereupon the Father being appeased by Christ's intercession, the Son and the Holy Ghost are also appeased with Him and in Him. Thus then, intercession is made to the whole Trinity, but yet immediately and directly to the first person, and in Him to the rest.

The second point to be considered is the manner of His intercession unto His Father. We must not imagine that Christ now in heaven kneels down on His knees and utters words and puts up a supplication for all the faithful to God the Father, for that is not beseeming the majesty of Him that sits at the right hand of God. But the manner of His intercession is thus to be conceived: when one is to speak to an earthly prince in the behalf of another, first of all, he must come into the presence of the king and, secondly, make his request. And both these Christ performs for us unto God.

For the first, after His ascension He entered into heaven, where He did present unto His Father, first of all, His own person in two natures; secondly, the invaluable merits of His death and passion, in which He was well pleased.[291] And we must further understand that as on the cross He stood in our room, so in heaven He now appears as a public person in our stead, representing all the elect that shall believe in Him, as the Holy Ghost says, "Christ Jesus ascended up into heaven, to appear in the sight of God for us" [Heb. 9:24].

And for the second, Christ makes request for us in that He wills according to both His natures and desires as He is man that the Father would accept His satisfaction in the behalf of all that are given unto Him. And that He makes request on this manner, I prove it thus: look what was His request in our behalf when He was here upon earth, the same for substance it continues still in heaven. But here on earth the substance of His request was that He willed and desired that His Father would be well pleased with us for His merits, as appears by His prayer in St. John, "Father, I will that those which thou hast given me be with me even where I am, that they may behold my glory which thou hast given me: for thou lovedst me before the foundation of the world" [17:24]. Therefore, He still continues to make request for us by willing and desiring that His Father would accept His merits in our behalf. If it be alleged that Christ in this solemn prayer used speech and prostration of His body, the answer is that these actions were no essential parts of His prayer. The prostrating of His body served only as

---

291. This paragraph break is not in the original, as the additional two following.

a token of submission to God, as Christ was a creature; and the speech which He used served only to utter and express His request.

Furthermore, a difference here must be marked between Christ's passion and His intercession. The passion serves for the working and causing of a satisfaction to God's justice for us; and it is as it were the tempering of the plaster. The intercession goes further, for it applies the satisfaction made and lay as the salve to the very sore. And therefore Christ makes request not only for the elect generally, but for particular men, as Paul, James, John, and that particularly, as He testifies of Himself, saying, "I have prayed for thee Peter, that thy faith fail not" [Luke 22:32]. If any shall say that Christ's willing and desiring of a thing cannot be a request or intercession, the answer is that in virtue and efficacy it countervails all the prayers in the world. For whatsoever Christ wills, the same also the Father, being well pleased with Him, wills. And therefore whatsoever Christ as a mediator wills for us at the hands of His Father in effect or substance is a request or prayer.

The third point is that Christ alone and none with Him makes intercession for us. And this I prove by induction of particulars. First of all, this office appertains not to the angels. They are indeed ministering spirits for the good of God's chosen. They rejoice when a sinner is converted, and when he dies they are ready to carry his soul into Abraham's bosom. And God otherwhiles uses them as the messengers to reveal His will. Thus, the angel Gabriel brings a message to Zachar[iah] the priest [1:13] that God had heard his prayer. But it is not once said in all the Scriptures that they make intercession to God for us.

As for the saints departed, they cannot make intercession for us because they know not our particular estates here on earth, neither can they hear our requests.[292] And therefore, if we should pray to them to pray for us, we should substitute them into the room of God, because we ascribe that to them which is proper to Him—namely, the searching of the heart and the knowledge of all things done upon earth, though withal we should say that they do this not by themselves but of God.

As for the faithful here on earth, indeed they have warrant, yea, commandment to pray one for another. Yet can they not make intercession for us. For, first, he that makes intercession must bring something of his own that may be of value and price with God to procure the grant of his request. Secondly, he must do it in his own name. But the faithful on earth make request to God one for another, not in their own names nor for their own merits, but in the name and for the merits of Christ. It is a prerogative belonging to Christ alone to make a request in His own name and for His own merits. We therefore conclude that

---

292. This paragraph break is not in the original, as the additional one following.

the work of intercession is the sole work of Christ, God and man, not belonging to any creature besides in heaven or in earth. And whereas the Papists cannot content themselves with His intercession alone as being most sufficient, it argues plainly that they doubt either of His power or of His will, whereupon their prayers turn to sin [James 1:6].

The fruits and benefits of Christ's intercession are these. First, by means of it we are assured that those which are repentant sinners shall stand and appear righteous before God forever. At what time soever Christ, being now in heaven and there presenting Himself and His merits before His Father, shows Himself desirous and willing, and they, whosoever they are, being sinners, should be accepted of God for the same, even then immediately at that very instant this His will is done, and they are accepted as righteous before God indeed. When a man looks upon things directly through the air, they appear in their proper forms and colors as they are; but if they be looked upon through a green glass, they all appear green. So likewise, if God behold us as we are in ourselves, we appear as vile and damnable sinners. But if He look upon us as we are presented before His throne in heaven in the person of our Mediator Christ Jesus, willing that we should be approved for His merits, then we appear without all spot and wrinkle before Him. And this is the use Paul makes hereof. "It is God," says he, "that justifies"—and the reason is rendered: "for it is Christ that is dead, yea or rather which is risen again, who is also at the right hand of God, and makes request for us" [Rom. 8:34].

Secondly, Christ's intercession serves to preserve all repentant sinners in the estate of grace that, being once justified and sanctified, they may so continue to the end. For when any servant of God is overtaken by the corruption of his own nature and falls into any particular sin, then Christ's intercession is made as a blessed hand to apply the salve of His death to that particular sore. For He continually appears before God and shows Himself to be willing that God the Father should accept His one only sacrifice for the daily and particular sins of this or that particular man; and this is done that a man, being justified before God, may not fall away quite from grace but for every particular sin may be humbled and receive pardon. If this were not so, our estate should be most miserable, considering that for every sin committed by us after our repentance, we deserve to be cast out of the favor of God.

Thirdly, Christ's intercession serves to make our good works acceptable to God. For even in the best works that a man can do, there are two wants. First, they are good only in part. Secondly, they are mingled with sin. For as a man is partly spirit or grace and partly flesh, so are his works partly gracious and partly fleshly. And because grace is only begun in this life, therefore all the works of grace in this life are sinful and imperfect. Now by Christ's intercession His satisfaction is applied to our persons, and by consequent the defect of our works is covered and removed, and they are approved of God the Father. In a vision, St. John saw an angel standing before the altar with a golden censer full of sweet odors to offer up with the prayers of the saints upon the same [Rev. 8:3]. And this signifies that Christ presents our works before the throne of God and by His intercession sanctifies them, that they may be acceptable to God. And therefore we must remember that when we do anything that is accepted of God, it is not for our sakes but by reason of the value and vigor of Christ's merit.

Fourthly, the intercession of Christ made in heaven breeds and causes in the hearts of men upon earth that believe another intercession of the Spirit, as St. Paul says, "He giveth us his spirit, which helpeth our infirmities, and maketh request for us with sighs, which cannot be expressed, but he which searcheth the heart, knoweth what is the meaning of the spirit, for he maketh request for the saints, according to the will of God" [Rom. 8:26]. Now the Spirit is said to make request in that it stirs and moves every contrite heart to pray with sighs and groans unspeakable to God for things needful, and this grace is a fruit derived from the intercession of Christ in heaven by the operation of the Spirit. For as the sun, though the body of it abide in the heavens, yet the beams of it descend to us that are on the earth, so the intercession of Christ made in heaven is tied as it were to His person alone, yet the groans and desires of the touched heart, as the beams thereof, are here on earth among the faithful. And therefore, if we desire to know whether Christ make intercession for us or no, we need not to ascend up into the heavens to learn the truth; but we must descend into our own hearts and look whether Christ have given us His Spirit, which makes us cry unto God and make request to Him with groans and sighs that cannot be expressed. And if we find this in our hearts, it is an evident and infallible sign that Christ continually makes intercession for us in heaven. He that would know whether the sun shine in the firmament must not climb up into the clouds to look, but search for the beams thereof upon the earth, which when he sees he may conclude that the sun shines in the firmament. And if we would know whether Christ in heaven makes intercession for us, let us ransack our own consciences, and there make search whether we feel the Spirit of Christ crying in us, "Abba, Father." As for those that never feel this work of God's Spirit in them, their case is miserable, whatsoever they be. For Christ as yet makes no intercession for them, considering these two always go together, His intercession in heaven and the work of His Spirit in the hearts of men, moving them to bewail their own sins with sighs and groans that cannot be expressed and to cry and to pray unto God for grace. And therefore all such, whether they be young or old, that never could pray but mumble up a few words for fashion's sake cannot assure themselves to have any part in Christ's intercession in heaven.

The duties to be learned hence are these. First, whereas Christ makes intercession for us, it teaches all men to be most careful to love and like this blessed Mediator and to be ready and willing to become His servants and disciples, and that not for form and fashion sake only but in all truth and sincerity of heart. For He ascended to heaven and there sits at the right hand of His Father to make request for us, that we might be delivered from hell and come to eternal life. Wicked Haman procured letters from Ahasuerus for the destruction of all the Jews, men, women, and children, in his dominions. This done, Esther the queen makes request to the king that her people might be saved and the letters of Haman revoked. She obtains her request, and freedom was given, and contrary letters of joyful deliverance were sent in posthaste to all provinces where the Jews were. Whereupon arose a wonderful joy and gladness among the Jews, and it is said that "thereupon many of the people of the land became Jews" [Esth. 8:17]. Well now, behold a greater matter among us than this; for there is the handwriting of condemnation, the law; and therein the sentence of a double death, of body and soul; and Satan, as wicked Haman, accuses us and seeks by all means our condemnation. But yet, behold, not any earthly Esther, but Christ Jesus, the Son of God, is come down from heaven and has taken away this handwriting of condemnation and cancelled it upon the cross and is now ascended into heaven and there sits at the right hand of His Father and makes request for us; and in Him His Father is well pleased and yields to His request in our behalf. Now then, what must we do in this case? Surely, look as the Persians became Jews when they heard of their safety, so we in life and conversation must become Christians, turn to Christ, embrace His doctrine, and practice the same unfeignedly. And we must not content ourselves with a formal profession of religion, but search our own hearts and fly unto Christ for the pardon of our sins, and that earnestly, as for life and death, as the thief does at the bar when the judge is giving sentence against him. When we shall thus humble ourselves, then Christ Jesus, that sits at the right hand of God, will plead our cause and be our attorney unto His Father; and His Father again will accept of His request in our behalf. Then shall we of Persians become Jews and of the children of this world become the sons of God.

Secondly, when we pray to God, we must not do as the blind world does—as it were, rush upon God in praying to Him without consideration had to the Mediator between us and Him.[293] But we always must direct our prayers to God in the name of Christ, for He is advanced to power and glory in heaven

---

293. This paragraph break is not in the original.

that He might be a fit patron for us, who might prefer and present our prayers to God the Father, that thereby they might be accepted [John 16:26], and we might obtain our request. So likewise we must give thanks to God in the name of Christ, for in Him and for His sake God does bestow on us His blessings.

Thus much of Christ's intercession. The other benefit which concerns Christ's kingly office is that He "sits at the right hand of his Father" for the administration of that special kingdom which is committed to Him. I say special, because He is our King, not only by right of creation, governing all things created, together with the Father and the Holy Ghost, but also more specially by the right of redemption in respect of another kingdom not of this world but eternal and spiritual, respecting the very conscience of man. In the administration whereof He has absolute power to command and forbid, to condemn and absolve, and therefore has the keys of heaven and hell to open and shut, which power no creature besides, no, not the angels in heaven can have. For the better understanding of this which I say, we are to consider, first, the dealing of Christ toward His own church; secondly, His dealing in respect of His enemies. And His dealing toward His own church stands in four things.

The first is the collecting or gathering of it.[294] And this is a special end of His sitting at the right hand of His Father. Christ said to His disciples, "I have chosen you out of this world" [15:19]. And the same may truly be said of all the elect, that Christ in His good time will gather them all to Himself, that they may be a peculiar people to God. And this action of His in collecting the church is nothing else but a translation of those whom He has ordained to life everlasting out of the kingdom of darkness, in which they have served sin and Satan, into His own kingdom of grace, that they may be ruled and guided by Him eternally. And this He does two ways.

First, by preaching of the word, for it is a powerful outward means whereby He singles and sorts His own servants from the blind and wicked world, as Paul says, "He gave some to be apostles, and some prophets, and some evangelists, and some pastors and teachers, for the gathering together of the saints" [Eph. 4:11–12]. And hence, we learn two things. The first, that every minister of God's word and everyone that intends to take upon him that calling must propound unto himself principally this end: to single out man from man and gather out of this world such as belong to the church of Christ and, as Jeremiah says, to "separate the precious from the vile" [Jer. 15:19]. The second, that all those which will be good hearers of God's word must show themselves so far forth conformable unto it that it may gather them out of the world and that it may work a change in them and make them the servants of Christ. And if the

---

294. This paragraph break is not in the original, as the additional one following.

preaching of the word does not work this good in our hearts, then the end will be a separation from the presence of God. Christ, when He came near Jerusalem and considered their rebellion whereby they refused to be gathered unto Him, wept over it and said, "O Jerusalem, Jerusalem, thou which stonest the prophets, and killest them that are sent unto thee, how often would I have gathered thy children together as the hen gathers her chickens under her wings, and thou wouldest not!" [Matt. 23:37]. And by this He teaches that if the preaching of the word turn not us to Christ, it turns to our destruction.

The other means of gathering the church, and that more principal, is the inward operation of the Spirit, whereby the mind is enlightened, the heart is mollified, and the whole man is converted to God. And this ordinarily is joined with the ministry or preaching of the word, as appears by the example of Lydia. St. Luke says God opened her heart "to be attentive to the doctrine of the apostles" [Acts 16:14]. And by the example of Paul, when Christ says, "Saul, Saul, why persecutest thou me?" [9:4], at this very speech he is converted and says, "Who art thou, Lord? what wilt thou that I do?" [vv. 5–6]. And this is manifest also by experience. There is nothing in the world more contrary to the nature of man than the preaching of the word; for it is the wisdom of God, to which the flesh is enmity. Here then it may be demanded how it can be in force to turn any man to God. *Answer.* The word preached is the scepter of Christ's kingdom, which against the nature of man by the operation of the Holy Ghost joined therewith does bend and bow the heart, will, and affections of man to the will of Christ.

The second work of Christ is after the church is gathered to guide it in the way to life everlasting. He is the Shepherd of His church, which guides His sheep in and out. And therefore Paul says, "They that are Christ's, are guided by his spirit" [Rom. 8:14]. And by Isaiah the Lord says those His servants which are turned from idolatry, He will guide in the way and "their ears shall hear a voice behind them, saying, This is the way, walk in it, when thou turnest to the right hand and to the left" [Isa. 30:21]. Which voice is nothing else but the voice of the Holy Ghost in the mouth of the ministers, directing them in the ways of God. The children of Israel were traveling from Egypt to the land of Canaan full forty years, whereas they might have gone the journey in forty days. Their way was through the wilderness of Arabia. Their guides were "a pillar of cloud by day, and a pillar of fire by night." The manner of their journey was this: "when the pillar moved, they moved: when the pillar stood still, they stood still" [Ex. 40:36–37]. And so long as the pillar either moved or stood still, they likewise moved or stood still. And by all this a further matter—namely, the regiment of Christ over His church—was signified. Every one of us are as passengers and travelers, not to any earthly Canaan, but to the heavenly Jerusalem.

And in this journey we are to pass through the wild and desert wilderness of this world. Our guide is Christ Himself [Isa. 4:5], figured by the pillar of fire and the cloud, because by His word and Spirit He shows us how far we may go in every action and where we must stand, and He goes before us as our guide to life everlasting.

The third work of Christ is to exercise His church unto spiritual obedience by manifold troubles, crosses, temptations, and afflictions in this world, as earthly kings use to train and exercise their subjects. When our Savior Christ was with His disciples in a ship, there arose a great tempest upon the sea, so as the ship was almost covered with waves. But He was asleep, and His disciples came and awoke Him, saying, "Save us master, we perish" [Matt. 8:24]. Behold here a lively picture of the dealing of Christ with His servants in this life. His manner is to place them upon the sea of this world and to raise up against them bleak storms of contrary winds by their enemies, the flesh, the devil, the world. And further, in the midst of all these dangers He for His own part makes as though He lay asleep for a time, that He may the better make trial of their patience, faith, and obedience. And the ends for which He uses this spiritual exercise are these. The first, to make all His subjects to humble themselves and as it were to go crooked and buckle under their offences committed against His majesty in times past. Thus, Job after the Lord had long afflicted him and laid His hand sore upon him, says, "Behold I am vile" [Job 39:37], and again, "I abhor myself and repent in dust and ashes" [42:6]. In the same manner, we, being His subjects and people, must look to be exercised with temptations and afflictions which shall make us bend and bow for our sins past, as the old man goes crooked and doubles to the earth by reason of age. The second is to prevent sins in the time to come. A father when he sees his child too bold and venturous about fire and water takes it and holds it over the fire or over the water, as though he would burn or drown it, whereas his purpose indeed is nothing else but to prevent danger in time to come. In like manner, Christ's subjects are bold to sin by nature; and therefore to prevent a mischief He does exercise them with affliction and seems for a season as though He would quite forsake His church, but His meaning is only to prevent offences in time to come. The third end is to continue His subjects in obedience unto His commandments. So the Lord says, when He would bring His church from idolatry, "Behold, I will stop thy way with thorns, and make an hedge, that she shall not find her paths" [Hos. 2:6]. The Holy Ghost here borrows a comparison from beasts, which going in the way see green pastures and desire to enter in and therefore go to the hedge but, feeling the sharpness of the thorns, dare not adventure to go in. So God's people, like unto wild beasts in respect of sin, viewing the green pastures of this world, which are the pleasures thereof, are greatly affected therewith. And if it were not for sharpness of crosses and temptations, which are God's spiritual hedge by which He keeps them in, they would range out of the way and rush into sin as the horse into the battle.

The fourth and last work of Christ in respect of His church is that He sits at the right hand of His Father to defend the same against the rage of all enemies whatsoever they are; and this He does two ways. First, by giving to His servants sufficient strength to bear all the assaults of their enemies, the world, the flesh, and the devil. For Paul says those to whom the Lord has given the gift of faith, to them also He has given this gift to suffer afflictions [Phil. 1:29]. And the same apostle also prays for the Colossians that "they may be strengthened with all might through his glorious power unto all patience and longsuffering with joyfulness" [Col. 1:11] The evidence hereof we may more plainly see in the most constant deaths of the martyrs of Christ, recorded both in the Word of God and in the church histories. It is wonderful to see their courage and constancy. For at such times as they have been brought to execution, they refused to be bound or chained, willingly suffering most cruel torments without shrinking or fear, such courage and strength the Lord gave them to withstand the violent rage of all their adversaries.

Secondly, He defends His church by limiting the power and rage of all enemies. And hence it is that although the power of the church of God on earth be weak and slender in itself, and contrariwise the power of the devil exceeding great, yet can he not so much as touch the people of God. And he more prevails by inward suggestions and temptations than by outward violence. And if it were not that the power of Christ does bridle his rage, there could be no abode for the church of Christ in this world.

Thus, we have seen what are the works of Christ in governing His church; and we for our parts that profess ourselves to be members thereof must show ourselves to be so indeed by an experience of these works of His in our own hearts. And we must suffer Him to gather us under His own wing and to guide us by His word and Spirit. And we are to acquaint ourselves with those spiritual exercises, whereby His good pleasure is to nurture us to all obedience. Lastly, we must depend on His aid and protection in all estates. And seeing we in this land have had peace and rest with the gospel of Christ among us a long time, by God's especial goodness we must now after these days of peace look for days of tribulation. We must not imagine that our ease and liberty will continue always. For look as the day and night do one follow another, so likewise in the administration of the church here upon earth Christ suffers a continual intercourse between peace and persecution. Thus, He has done from the beginning hitherto, and we may resolve ourselves that so it will continue till the end. And therefore it shall be good for us in these days of peace to prepare ourselves for troubles and afflictions; and when troubles come, we must still remember the fourth work of Christ in the government of His church—namely, that in all dangers He will defend us against the rage of our enemies, as well by giving us power and strength to bear with patience and joy whatsoever shall be laid upon us, as also bridle the rage of the world, the flesh, and the devil, so as they shall not be able to exercise their power and malice to the full against us.

Thus much of the dealing of Christ toward His own church and people. Now follows the second point—namely, His dealing toward His enemies. And here by enemies I understand all creatures, but especially men, which as they are by nature enemies to Christ and His kingdom, so they persevere in the same enmity unto the end. Now His dealing toward them is in His good time to work their confusion, as He Himself says: "These mine enemies that would not that I should reign over them, bring them hither, and slay them before me" [Luke 19:27]. And David says, "The Lord will bruise his enemies with a rod of iron, and break them in pieces like a potter's vessel" [Ps. 2:9]. And again, "I will make thine enemies thy footstool" [110:1]. As Joshua dealt with the five kings that were hid in the cave—he first makes a slaughter of their armies; then he brings them forth and makes the people to set their feet on their necks and to hang them on five trees [Josh. 10:24]—so Christ deals with His enemies. He treads them under His feet and makes a slaughter not so much of their bodies as of their souls. And this the church of God finds to be true by experience, as well as it finds the love of Christ toward itself.

Now He confounds His enemies two ways. The first is by hardness of heart, which arises when God withdraws His grace from man and leaves him to himself, so as he goes on forward from sin to sin and never repents to the last gasp. And we must esteem of it as a most fearful and terrible judgment of God; for when the heart is possessed therewith, it becomes so flinty and rebellious that a man will never relent or turn to God. This is manifest in Pharaoh; for though God sent most grievous plagues both upon him and all the land of Egypt, yet would he not submit himself, save only for a fit, while the hand of God was upon him—for after he returned to the former obstinance, in which he continued till he was drowned in the sea. And this judgment of God is the more fearful, because when a man is in the midst of all his misery, he feels no misery. And as in some kind of sickness a man may die languishing, so where hardness of heart reigns wholly and finally, a man may descend to the pit of hell triumphing and rejoicing. And to come near to ourselves, it is to be feared lest this judgment of all judgments be among us in these our days. For where is any turning to God by repentance? Still men go forward in sin without remorse. We have had the word preached among us a long time, but it takes no place in men's hearts. They are not softened with the hammer of God's word. Nay, they are like the smith's stithy or anvil, which the more it is beat with the hammer, the harder it is. But in the fear of God, let us seek to be changed and take heed. The deceitfulness of sin is wonderful. Let us not be carried away with an overweaning of ourselves. A man may have good gifts of God, as the gift of knowledge, the gift of prophecy, the gift of conceiving a prayer (I say not of praying truly), and hereupon think himself in good case—and yet for all this have nothing but an impenitent and flinty heart. For this cause, it stands every man upon to look unto it, lest this judgment of God take hold on him. And that we may avoid the same, we must labor for two things: (1) to feel the heavy burden of our sins and to be touched in conscience for them, even as we are troubled in our bodies with the aches and pains thereof. This is a token of grace. (2) We must labor to feel in our souls the want of Christ. We say indeed that we feel it, but it is a very great matter to have a heart that does open itself and as it were gape after Christ, as the dry and thirsty land where no water is. Though we have knowledge and learning never so much and many other gifts of God, yet if we have not broken hearts that feel the burden of our sins and the want of Christ, and that we stand in need of every drop of His blood for the washing away of all these our sins, our case is miserable. And the rather, we must prevent this hardness of heart, because Christ Jesus in heaven sits at the right hand of His Father in full power and authority to kill and confound all those that be His enemies and will not submit themselves to bear His yoke.

The second way is by final desperation. I say "final," because all kind of desperation is not evil. For when a man despairs of himself and of his own power in the matter of his salvation, it tends to his eternal comfort. But final desperation is when a man utterly despairs of pardon of his own sins and of life everlasting. Examples hereof we have in Saul, that slew himself, and in Ahithophel and Judas, that hanged themselves. This sin is caused thus. So many sins as a man commits without repentance, so many most bloody wounds he gives unto his own soul. And either in death or life God makes him feel the smart and the huge weight of them all, whereby the soul sinks down to the gulf of despair without recovery. God said to Cain, "If you do amiss, sin lies at the door" [Gen. 4:7]. Where He uses a borrowed speech from wild beasts, who so long as they are sleeping stir not; but, being awaked, they fly in a man's face and rend out his throat. In like manner, the sins which you commit lie at the door of your heart, though you feel them not. And if you do not prevent the danger by speedy repentance, God will make you to feel them once before you die and raise up such terrors in your conscience that you shall think yourself to be in hell before you are in hell. And therefore it is good for every man to take heed how he continues an enemy to Christ. The best course is to turn betime from our sins and become the friends of Christ, that so we may escape these fearful judgments.

And whereas Christ in this manner governs all things in heaven and earth, we are bound to perform unto Him three duties: reverence, obedience, thankfulness. For the first, Paul says, "God hath exalted him and given him a name above all names, that at the name of Jesus"—which name is His exaltation in heaven in full power and glory—"should every knee bow" (Phil. 2:10). We dare not so much as speak of an earthly king irreverently. What reverence then do we owe unto Christ, the King of heaven and earth? David's heart was touched in that he had cut off but the lap of Saul's garment, when he might have slain him, because he was the Lord's anointed (1 Sam. 24:6). Oh then, how much more ought our hearts to be touched, if we shall in the least measure dishonor Christ Jesus, our Lord and King?

Secondly, we are here taught to perform obedience unto Him and do Him all the homage we can.[295] The master of his family in all his lawful commandments must be obeyed. Now, the church of Christ is a family, and we are members thereof. Therefore, we must yield obedience to Him in all things, for all His commandments are just. When Saul was chosen king over Israel, "certain men which feared God, whose hearts God had touched, followed him to Gibeah, and brought him presents; but the wicked despised him" (10:26–27). The same is much more to be verified in us toward Christ our Lord. We must have our hearts touched with desire to perform obedience unto Him. If not, we are men of Belial that despise Him. If this obedience were put in practice, the gospel would have better success in the hearts of the people, and the Lord's Sabbath would be better kept, and men would bear greater love both to God and to their neighbors than now they do.

The third duty which we owe unto Him is thankfulness for the endless care which He shows in the governing and preserving of us. When David waxed old and had made Solomon, his son, king in his stead, all the people shouted and cried, "God save King Solomon, God save King Solomon, so as the earth rang again" (1 Kings 1:39–40). Shall the people of Israel thus rejoice at the crowning of Solomon, and shall not we much more rejoice when as Christ Jesus is placed in heaven at the right hand of His Father and has the everlasting scepter of His kingdom put into His hand? And we are to show this thankfulness unto Him by doing anything in this world that may tend to His honor and glory, though it be with the adventure of our lives. When David desired to drink of the water of the well of Bethlehem, "three of his mighty men went and brake into the host of the Philistines, and brought him water" (2 Sam. 23:15–16). Thus, they ventured their

---

295. This paragraph break is not in the original, as the additional one following.

lives for David's sake. And shall not we much more willingly venture our lives to do Christ service in token of thankfulness for His continual preserving of us?

Thus much of the highest degree of Christ's exaltation in His kingdom. Now follows the last point to be believed concerning Christ, in these words: "from thence he shall come to judge the quick and the dead." And they contain a proof or a particular declaration of the former article. For as on earth those that are set at the right hand of kings do execute justice in courts or assizes for the maintenance of the state and peace of the kingdom, so Christ Jesus, sitting at the right hand of His Father—that is, being made sovereign Lord of all things both in heaven and earth—is to hold a court of assizes in which He shall come to judge both the quick and the dead.

Now in handling the last judgment, we are to consider these points: (1) whether there shall be a judgment or not; (2) the time of it; (3) the signs thereof; (4) the manner of it; (5) the use which is to be made thereof. Of these in order.

For the first point, whether there shall be a judgment or not?[296] The question is needful, for as St. Peter says, "There shall come in the last days mockers, which shall walk after their lusts, and say, where is the promise of his coming" (2 Peter 3:3)—which days are now. The answer to this question is set down in this article, in which we profess that the coming of Christ to the last judgment is a point of religion specially to be held and avouched. The reasons to prove it are principally two: first, the testimony of God Himself in the books of the Old and New Testament, which afford unto us plentiful proofs touching the last judgment, so as he which will but lightly read the same shall not need to doubt thereof. The second reason is taken from the justice and goodness of God, the property whereof is to punish wicked and ungodly men and to honor and reward the godly. But in this world the godly man is most of all in misery (for judgment begins at God's house), and the ungodly have their heart's ease. Wicked Dives had the world at will, but poor Lazarus is hunger-bitten, full of sores, and miserable every way. This being so, it remains that after this life there must needs be a judgment and a second coming of Christ, when the godly must receive fullness of joy and glory and the ungodly fullness of woe and misery. This second reason may stop the mouths of all gainsayers in the world whatsoever. But it may be objected that the whole world stands either of believers or unbelievers and that there is no last judgment for either of these; for the believer, as Christ says, has everlasting life "and shall not come into judgment" (John 5:24), and the unbeliever is "condemned already" (3:18) and therefore needs no further judgment. *Answer.* Where it is said [that] he that

---

296. This paragraph break is not in the original.

believes shall not come into judgment, it must be understood of the judgment of condemnation and not of the judgment of absolution. And he that believes not is condemned already in effect and substance three ways: (1) in the counsel of God, who did foresee and appoint his condemnation as it is a punishment of sin and execution of His justice. (2) In the Word of God, where he has his condemnation set down. (3) He is condemned in his own conscience; for every ungodly man's conscience is a judge unto himself, which does every hour condemn him, and it is a forerunner of the last judgment. And notwithstanding all this, there may remain a second judgment, which is a manifestation and finishing of that which was begun in the world. And therefore the meaning of that place is this: he that believes not is already judged in part, but so as the full manifestation thereof shall be at the second coming of Christ.

The second circumstance is the time of this judgment, in handling whereof, first, let us see what is the judgment of men; secondly, what is the truth. For the first, two opinions touching this time take place. The first is that the second coming of Christ shall be about six thousand years from the beginning of the world, and for the elect's sake some of these days must be shortened. And now since the beginning of the world are passed five thousand and almost six hundred years, so as there remains but some four hundred. The grounds of this opinion are these. First, the testimony of Elias, "Two thousand years before the law; two thousand years under the law; and two thousand years under Christ. And for the elect's sake, some of these years shall be shortened." *Answer.* This was not the sentence of Elias the Tishbite, but of another Elias which was a Jew, no prophet. And whereas he says, two thousand years before the law, and two thousand years under the law, he fails. For from the giving of the law to the coming of Christ was about one thousand and five hundred years, and from the law to the creation above two thousand. Now if Elias cannot set down a just number for the time past, which a mean man may do, what shall we think that he can do for the time to come? And if he deceive us in that which is more easy to find, how shall we trust him in things that be harder?

The second reason is this: how long God was in creating the world, so long He shall be in governing the same.[297] But He was six days in creating the world, and in the seventh He rested. And so proportionally He shall be six thousand years in governing the world—every day answering to a thousand years, as Peter says, "A thousand years are but as one day with God" (2 Peter 3:8), and then shall the end be. *Answer.* This reason likewise has no ground in God's Word. As for that place of Peter, the meaning is that innumerable years are but as a short time with God, and we may as well say two thousand or ten thousand

---

297. This paragraph break is not in the original.

years are but as one day with God. For Peter meant not to speak anything distinctly of a thousand years, but of a long time (a certain number put for an uncertain).

Thirdly, it is alleged that within six thousand years from the creation of the world shall appear in the heavens strange conjunctions and positions of the stars, which signify nothing else but the subversion of the state of the world. Nay, some have noted that the end thereof should have been AD 1588.[298] Their writings are manifest, but we find by experience that this opinion is false and frivolous, and their grounds be as frivolous. For no man can gather by the ordinary change of the heavens the extraordinary change of the whole world.

The second opinion is that the end of the world shall be three years and a half after the revealing of antichrist. And it is gathered out of places in Daniel and the Revelation, abused. Where a time and times and half a time signify not three years and a half, but a short time. And therefore to take the words properly is far from the meaning of the Holy Ghost. For mark, if the end shall be three years and a half after the revealing of antichrist, then may any man know aforehand the particular month wherein the end of the world should be, which is not possible.

Now the truth which may be avouched against all is this, that no man can know or set down or conjecture the day, the week, the month, the year, or the age wherein the second coming of Christ and the last judgment shall be. For Christ Himself says, "Of that day and hour knows no man, no not the angels in heaven, but God only" (Matt. 24:36). Nay, Christ Himself as He is man knew it not. And when the disciples asked Christ at His ascension whether He would restore the kingdom unto Israel, He answered, "It is not for you to know the times and seasons, which the Father hath put in his own power" (Acts 1:7). And Paul says, "Of the times and seasons, brethren, you have not need that I write unto you. For you yourselves know perfectly, that the day of the Lord shall come, even as a thief in the night" (1 Thess. 5:2). Now we know that a man that keeps his house cannot conjecture or imagine when a thief will come, and therefore no man can set down the particular time or age when Christ shall come to judgment. This must we hold steadfastly; and if we read the contrary in the writings of men, we are not to believe their sayings but account of them as the devices of men, which have no ground in God's Word.

To come to the third point—namely, the signs of the last judgment—they are of two sorts: some go before the coming of Christ, and some are joined with it. The signs that go before are in number seven, recorded distinctly by the Holy Ghost. The first is the preaching of the gospel through the whole world. So

---

298. Originally, "In the year of our Lord, a thousand five hundred eighty eight."

our Savior Christ says, "This gospel of the kingdom must be preached through the whole world for a witness unto all nations, and then shall the end come" (Matt. 24:14). Which place must thus be understood, not that the gospel must be preached to the whole world at any one time—for that (as I take it) was never yet seen, neither shall be—but that it shall be published distinctly and successively at several times. And thus understanding the words of Christ, if we consider the time since the apostles' days, we shall find this to be true, that the gospel has been preached to all the world. And therefore the first sign of Christ's coming is already past and accomplished.

The second sign of His coming is the revealing of antichrist, as Paul says, "The day of Christ shall not come before there be a departure first, and that man of sin be disclosed, even the son of perdition, which is antichrist" (2 Thess. 2:3). Concerning this sign, in AD 602,[299] Gregory, the first pope of Rome, avouched this solemnly as a manifest truth, that whosoever did take to himself the name of "universal bishop," the same was antichrist. Now five years after, Boniface, succeeding him, was by Phocas the emperor entitled the "Universal Bishop, Pastor of the Catholic Church"[300] in AD 607,[301] and of all popes he was the first known antichrist. And since him all his successors have taken unto them the same title of Universal and Catholic Bishop, whereby it does plainly appear that at Rome has been and is the antichrist. And this sign is also past.

The third is a general departing of most men from the faith. For it is said in the place before named, "Let no man deceive you, for the day of Christ shall not come except there be a departing first" (v. 3). General departure has been in former ages. When Arius spread his heresy, it took such place that the whole world almost became an Arian. And during the space of nine hundred years from the time of Boniface, the popish heresy spread itself over the whole earth, and the faithful servants of God were but as a handful of wheat in a mountain of chaff, which can scarce be discerned. This sign is in part already past; nevertheless, it shall continue to the end, because men shall continually depart from the faith. And the nearer the end of the world is, the more Satan rages and seeks to bring men into his kingdom. Therefore, it stands us in hand to labor for the knowledge of true religion and, having learned it, most heartily to love the same.

The fourth sign is a general corruption in manners. This point the apostle sets down at large, saying, "Toward the latter days shall come perilous times, wherein men shall be lovers of themselves, covetous, boasters, proud, cursed speakers, disobedient to parents, unthankful, unholy, and without natural

---

299. Originally, "the year of our Lord 602."
300. Boniface and Phocas.
301. Originally, "the year of our Lord 607."

affection, truce-breakers, false accusers, intemperate, fierce, despisers of them which are good, traitors, heady, high-minded, lovers of pleasures more than lovers of God," etc. (2 Tim. 3:1). This general corruption in the manners of men is noted by our Savior Christ, when He says, "When he cometh he shall scarce find faith upon the earth" (Luke 18:8). This sign has been in former ages and is no doubt at this day in the world. For it is hard to find a man that walks justly, soberly, and faithfully, doing the duties of his calling to God and man.

The fifth sign of Christ's coming stands in terrible and grievous calamities, for Christ's disciples asking Him a sign of His coming and of the end of the world, He says, "There shall be wars and rumors of wars, nation shall rise against nation, and realm against realm: and there shall be pestilence and famine, and earthquakes in diverse places, and men shall be at their wits' end" (Matt. 24:6–7). These have been in former ages. In the first three hundred years after Christ were ten more fearful persecutions; and since in Europe the church of God has been wonderfully persecuted by the antichrist of Rome in the hundred years last past.

The sixth sign is an exceeding deadness of heart, so as neither judgments from heaven nor the preaching of the word shall move the hearts of men. So Christ says it shall be in the coming of the Son of man, as it was in the days of Noah, and in the days of Sodom. "They knew nothing till the flood came, and fire from heaven destroyed them all" [Luke 17:16, 29]. This sign undoubtedly is manifest in these our days, howsoever it has been also in former times. For where are any almost that are moved with God's judgments or touched at the preaching of the word? Nay, rather men harden their hearts and become secure and careless. The small fruit that the word of God brings forth in the lives of men shows this to be most true.

The seventh and last sign set down by the apostle Paul is that there shall be a calling of the Jews before the Lord come to judgment (Rom. 11:25). But of the time when this calling shall be, of the manner how, or the number of them that shall be called there is no mention made in the Word of God. Now it is likely that this sign is yet to come.

These are the signs that go before the coming of Christ, all which are almost past, and therefore the end cannot be far off. Now follows the sign that is joined with the coming of Christ called the "sign of the Son of Man." What this sign is, we find not in the Scriptures. Some think it to be the sign of the cross, but that is frivolous. Some, the glory and majesty of Christ, which shall be made manifest in His appearance, which seems to be otherwise by the very words of Christ: "Then," says He, "shall appear the sign of the Son of Man," etc., and then "they shall see him come in the clouds of heaven with power and great glory"—where He distinguishes the one from the other [Matt. 24:30]. But I rather conjecture it to be the burning of heaven and earth with fire at the very instant of Christ's coming, mentioned by Peter [2 Peter 3:10]. We must not here dispute whence this fire shall come or how it shall be kindled, for that the Word of God has concealed; and where God has no mouth to speak, there we must have no ear to hear.

The uses to be made hereof are these. When St. Peter had set down the change that shall be at the coming of Christ, and that heaven and earth must be purged with fire, he makes this use thereof: "Seeing all things must be dissolved, what manner of men ought we to be in holy conversation and godliness?" [3:11]. And the reason is good. For if heaven and earth must be changed and purged at Christ's coming, then much more ought we to be changed and put off the old man of sin and to become new creatures created after the image of God in righteousness and true holiness. If the brute creatures must be renewed by fire, then much more are we to labor that the heat of God's Spirit may burn up sin and corruption in us and so change us that we may be ready for Him against His coming, else heaven and earth itself shall stand in judgment against us to our condemnation.

Secondly, the consideration of this, that the world shall be consumed with fire, teaches us moderation and sobriety in the use of God's creatures, as in costly building, gorgeous attire, and such like.[302] What madness is this to bestow all that we have on such things, as at the day of judgment shall be consumed with fire? For look whatsoever abuse shall come to God's creatures by our folly, the same shall then be abolished.

Thirdly, we must consider that the cause why heaven and earth must be consumed with fire is man's sin, by means whereof they are made subject to vanity and corruption. Here then we have just occasion to acknowledge the greatness and wretchedness of our sins. If any of us had but seen the Jews' leprosy, it would have made us to wonder; for the contagion thereof did infect not only the whole man but his garments also that were about him and sometimes the walls of his house [Lev. 13:2, 47; 14:34]. But howsoever we cannot see that leprosy among us, yet we may see a worse. For the leprosy of our sins does not only infect our garments and the things about us with our bodies, but even the high heavens and the earth are stained with the contagion thereof and are made subject to vanity and corruption. Yea, by sin in us the most glorious creatures in them, as the sun, moon, and stars, are become subject to vanity. Oh then, how wretched is the heart of man that makes no bones of sin, which is the most noisome thing in all the world, the stink whereof has infected both heaven and earth! If we could consider this, we would not be so slack in humbling

---

302. This paragraph break is not in the original, as the additional one following.

ourselves for the same as we are. We cannot abide to look on a poor lazar[303] full of blains and sores; but if we would see our sins in their right colors, they would make us seem unto ourselves ten thousand times more ugly than any lazar man can be. The contagion thereof is so great and noisome that the very heavens, which are many thousand miles distant from us, are infected therewith. Yet here we are to know that this fire shall not consume the substance of heaven and earth, but only change the quality and abolish the corruption, which our sins have brought upon them.

The fourth point to be considered is the manner of the last judgment, in which we may observe two things: (1) who shall be judge; (2) the proceeding of this judge. The first is expressed in this article: "from thence he shall come to judge." "He"—that is, Christ Jesus, the second person in [the] Trinity. For the Father has committed all judgment unto Him. It is indeed an action common to all the three persons in [the] Trinity, but yet the execution thereof appertains unto the Son. The Father indeed does judge the world, but yet by the Son. But some may object that the "apostles shall sit on twelve thrones, and judge the twelve tribes of Israel" [Matt. 19:28]. And St. Paul says, "The saints shall judge the world" (1 Cor. 6:2). How then is this true, that Christ is the only Judge of the world? *Answer.* The authority of judgment and giving sentence at the last day is proper to Christ alone and does not belong either to the apostles or to the saints, and they shall judge at the last day only as witnesses and approvers of Christ's judgment. At the great day of assize, besides the Judge, the justices on the bench are also in a manner judges, not that they give sentence, but because by their presence they approve and witness the equity of the sentence of the Judge. So, the definitive sentence does belong to Christ, and the apostles and saints do nothing but approve and, being present, give assent to His righteous sentence.

The whole proceeding of the last judgment may be reduced to seven points or heads. The first is the coming of the Judge in the clouds. Here at the first may be demanded why Christ holds the last judgment rather on earth than in heaven? *Answer.* He does it for two causes. One, the creature to be judged has sinned here upon earth; and He proceeds after the manner of earthly judges, who hold their sessions and assizes there where trespasses are commonly committed. The second, because the devil and his angels are to be judged, and it is a part of their punishment to be cast out of heaven. For no unclean thing may come into His heavenly Jerusalem, and therefore they now remain in the lower parts of the world and there must be judged. Furthermore, the second coming of Christ is sudden, as the coming of a thief in the night. He will come when the world thinks not of Him, as the snare does on the bird [Luke 21:35]. The

---

303. *Lazer*: leper.

consideration whereof must teach us the same duties which our Savior Christ taught the men of His time.

First, He teaches them what they must not do; for He, knowing all things, knew also the disposition of man's heart.[304] And therefore He says, "Take heed to yourselves lest at any time your hearts be oppressed with surfeiting and drunkenness, and the cares of this life, lest that day come upon you unawares" [v. 34]. For these sins benumb the heart and steal away all grace. This exhortation in these our days is most needful. For men's hearts are like the smith's stithy. The more they are beaten with the hammer of God's word, the harder they are.

Secondly, He teaches them what they must do. "Watch therefore," says He, "and pray continually: that ye may be counted worthy to escape all these things that shall come to pass, and that ye may stand before the Son of man" [v. 36]. But you will say, how may we be found worthy to stand before Christ at that day? *Answer.* Do but this one thing: for your lives past be humbled before God and come unto Him by true, hearty, and unfeigned repentance; be changed and become new creatures; pray unto Him earnestly for the pardon of your sins in Christ and pray continually that God will turn your hearts from your old sins every day more and more. And then, come the judgment when it will, you shall be found worthy to stand before Christ at His coming. The repentant sinner is he that shall find favor in the sight of God at that day. The consideration hereof may move us to change our lives. Those which were never yet humbled for their sins, let them now begin; and those which have already begun, let them go forward and continue.

But the devil will cry in the hearts of some men that this exhortation is as yet needless, for the day of judgment is not near, because all the signs are not yet passed. *Answer.* Suppose the day of judgment be far off; yet the day of death cannot be so, for the common saying is true, "Today a man, tomorrow none." Now look as death leaves you, so shall the day of judgment find you. Impenitent Cain died long since, and yet the day of judgment when it comes shall find him impenitent still. The same thing may be said of Saul, Ahithophel, and Judas. They died desperately and impenitent, and the Lord shall find them so at His coming. So will it be with you, whatsoever you are that repents not. Death may come upon you, the next day or the next hour. Therefore, watch and pray. Prepare yourself against the day of death, that at the day of judgment you may be found worthy to obtain favor in the sight of the Lord. Security does overwhelm the world; but let us for our parts learn to prepare ourselves daily, for if the day of death do leave you unworthy, then the Lord Jesus at His coming shall find you unworthy. And the devil shall stand before you and accuse you; your

---

304. This paragraph break is not in the original, as the additional two following.

conscience shall condemn you; and hell shall be ready to swallow you up. If this admonition take no place in your heart, then at the day of judgment it shall stand against you and be a bill of indictment to your further condemnation.

The second point follows, that Christ after that He is come in the clouds shall "sit in a throne of glory" [Matt. 25:31] as the sovereign Judge of heaven and earth, after the manner of earthly kings, who when they will show themselves unto their subjects in majesty, power, and glory used to ascend into the thrones of their kingdoms and there to show themselves and appear in state unto all the people. Now what this throne is and how Christ sits in the same, the Scripture has not revealed, and therefore I will not stand to search. Yet here must we further mark that this appearance of His in endless glory and majesty shall be more terrible and dreadful to the ungodly. And therefore in Daniel His throne is said to be like "a flame of fire" [Dan. 7:9], and at the very sight thereof men shall desire the mountains to fall upon them and the hills to cover them.

The third point is the "citing of all men and of the angels before his majesty in that day," there to answer for themselves. This citing shall be done by the voice of Christ, as He Himself says, "In that day all that are in the graves shall hear his voice, and they shall come forth" [John 5:28]. And here we are to consider two things: (1) the power of His voice; (2) the minister whereby it shall be uttered.

For the first, no doubt the power of His voice shall be unspeakable.[305] And therefore it is compared to a trumpet [Matt. 24:31], the loudest and shrillest of all musical instruments; and to the cry of the mariners, whose manner has been in the doing of any business with all their strength at one instant to make a common shout [1 Thess. 4:16]. And sensible experience shall manifest the force thereof. For it shall cause all the dead even from the beginning of the world to rise again, though they have lain rotten in the earth many thousand years. And all unclean spirits shall be forced and compelled, will they, nill they, to come before Christ, who shall be unto them a most fearful and terrible judge. Neither man nor angel shall be able to absent or hide himself. All without exception must appear, as well high as low, rich as poor. None shall be able to withdraw themselves, no, not the mighty monarchs of the earth.

Furthermore, this voice shall be uttered by angels. As in the church Christ uses men as His ministers by whom He speaks unto His people, so the last day He shall use the ministry of angels, whom He shall send forth into the four winds to gather His elect together [Matt. 24:31]. And therefore it is likely that this voice shall be uttered by them. And by this which has been said we must be moved to make conscience of all sin, for there is no avoiding of this

---

305. This paragraph break is not in the original.

judgment. We cannot absent ourselves; no excuse will serve the turn. Even the most rebellious of all creatures, whether man or angel, shall be forced to appear. And therefore it stands us in hand, while we have time in this life, to look unto our estates and to practice the duties of Christianity, that when we shall be cited before His glorious majesty at the last day, we may be cleared and absolved.

The fourth point is the separation of the sheep from the goats, the good from the bad (25:32); for when all the kindreds of the earth and all unclean spirits shall stand before Christ, sitting in the throne of His glory, then as a good shepherd He shall separate them one from another, the righteous from the wicked and the elect from the reprobate. He which knows the hearts of all men knows also how to do this, and He will do it. This full and final separation is reserved to Christ and shall not be accomplished till the last day. For so it is in the parable that "the tares must grow with the wheat until harvest, and the reapers must separate them, and gather the wheat into the barn, but the tares must be burnt with unquenchable fire" [13:30]. By the consideration of this one point, we learn divers things.

First, that in the church of God in this world, good and bad are mingled together, elect and reprobate.[306] And we are not to imagine any perfection of the church of God upon earth, as many have dreamed, which when they could not find, they have therefore forsaken all assemblies. I confess indeed that the preaching of the word is the Lord's fan whereby He cleanses His church in part, but yet the finishing of this work shall not be before the last judgment. For when the ministers of God have done all that they can, yet shall the wicked be mingled with the godly. Therefore, the church is compared to a barn floor, where is both wheat and chaff, and a cornfield, where is both tares and good corn, and a draw net, wherein is both good fish and bad.

Secondly, whereas this separation must not be before the end of the world, hence we learn the estate of God's church in this life. It is like a flock of sheep mingled with goats, and therefore the condition of God's people in this world is to be troubled many ways by those with whom they live. For "goats use to strike the sheep, to annoy their pasture, and to make their water muddy that they cannot drink of it" [Ezek. 34:18]. And therefore we must prepare ourselves to bear all annoyances, crosses, and calamities that shall befall us in this world by the wicked ones among whom we live.

Thirdly, we are taught that goats and the sheep be very [a]like and feed in one pasture and lie both in one fold all their lifetime. Yet Christ can and will sever them asunder at the last day. Therefore, considering as we are born of Adam, we have the nature of the goat, yea, of the wild beast, and not of the

---

306. This paragraph break is not in the original, as the additional two following.

sheep. It stands us in hand to lay aside our goatish conditions and to take unto us the properties of the sheep of Christ, which He expresses in these words: "My sheep," says He, "hear my voice, I know them, and they follow me" (John 10:27). And the properties are three: to know Him, to be known of Him, and to follow Him—namely, in obedience. And he that finds them all in himself wears the brand and mark of the true sheep of Christ; but contrariwise, they that make profession of Christ and yet therewithal join not obedience, howsoever the world may account of them, they are but goats and no sheep. Let us therefore with the knowledge of Christ join obedience to His word, that when the day shall come that the goats must be separated from the sheep, we may be found to be in the number of the true sheep of Christ. We may deceive men both in life and death and bear them in hand that we are sheep; but when the judgment shall come, we cannot deceive Christ. He it is that formed us. He knows our hearts and therefore can easily discern what we are.

The fifth thing is the trial of every man's particular cause, a point especially to be considered. For as at the bar of an earthly judge the malefactor is brought out of prison and set before the judge and there examined, even so in that great day shall every man without exception be brought before the Lord to be tried. But how shall this trial be made? *Answer.* By works, as the apostle says, "We must all appear before the judgment seat of Christ, that every man may receive the things which are done in his body according to that he hath done, whether it be good or evil" (2 Cor. 5:10). And the reason is because works are the outward signs of inward grace and holiness. And though we be justified by faith alone without works, yet may we be judged both by faith and works. For the last judgment does not serve to make men just that are unjust, but only to manifest them to be just indeed which are just before and in this life truly justified. The consideration of this very point should move us all to repent us of our sins past and to reform ourselves throughout and to be plentiful in all good works. And undoubtedly if we seriously think upon it, it will hold us more straitly to all good duties than if with the Papists we held justification by works.

God's Three Books[307]
Furthermore, in this trial two things must be scanned: (1) how all men's works shall be made manifest; (2) by what means they shall be examined. Of the manifestation of every man's works St. John speaks: "And I saw," says he, "the dead both great and small stand before God, and the books were opened: and another book was opened, which is the book of life, and the dead were judged of those things which were written in the book according to their works" (Rev.

---
307. Originally in the margin.

20:12). God is said to have books not properly, but because all things are as certain and manifest to Him as if He had His registers in heaven to keep rolls and records of them. His books are three: the book of providence, the book of judgment, the book of life. (1)[308] The book of His providence is the knowledge of all particular things past, present, or to come. Of this the psalmist speaks, "Thine eyes did see me when I was without form: for in thy book were all things written, which in continuance were fashioned, when there was none of them before" (139:16). (2) The book of judgment is that whereby He gives judgment, and it is twofold. The first is God's knowledge or prescience in which all the affairs of men, their thoughts, words, and deeds, are as certainly known and set down as if they were put in books of record. We may forget our sins, but God keeps them in a register. He knows them, every one. The second book is every man's particular conscience, which also brings to remembrance and testifies what men have done and what they have not done. (3) The book of life is nothing else but the decree of God's election in which God has set down who be ordained to life eternal.

Now the opening of these books is a thing wherein the endless power of God shall most notably show itself. For when we shall stand before the judgment seat of Christ, He then, knowing all things in His eternal counsel, shall reveal unto every man His own particular sins, whether they were in thought, word, or deed. And then also by His mighty power, He shall so touch men's consciences that they shall afresh remember what they have done. Now indeed, the wicked man's conscience is shut up as a closed book. But then it shall be so touched and as it were opened, that he shall plainly see and remember all the particular offences which at any time he has committed, and his very conscience shall be as good as a thousand witnesses, whereupon he shall accuse and utterly condemn himself. The consideration of this ought to terrify all those that live in their sins; for howsoever they may hide and cover them from the world, yet at the last day God will be sure to reveal them all.

Now after that men's works are made manifest, they must further be tried whether they be good or evil. And that shall be done on this manner. They that never heard of Christ must be tried by the law of nature, which serves to make them inexcusable before God. As for those that live in the church, they shall be tried by the law and the gospel, as Paul says, "As many as have sinned in the law, shall be judged by the law" (Rom. 2:12). And again, "At the day of judgment God shall judge the secrets of our hearts according to his gospel" (v. 16). And Hebrews 11:7: "By faith Noah builded an ark, whereby he condemned the old world." Then we must in the fear of God hear His word preached and taught

---

308. Originally in the margin, as the additional two books following.

with all reverence and make conscience to profit by it. For otherwise in the day of judgment when all our works shall be tried by it the same word of God shall be a bill of indictment and the fearful sentence of condemnation against us. Therefore, let us be humbled by the doctrine of the law and willingly embrace the sweet promises of the gospel, considering it is the only touchstone whereby all our words, thoughts, and works must be examined.

The sixth point in the proceeding of the last judgment is the giving of sentence, which is twofold: the sentence of absolution and the sentence of condemnation, both which are to be observed diligently that we may receive profit thereby. And, first of all, Christ shall begin His judgment with the sentence of absolution, which shows that He is ready to show mercy and slow to wrath. In this sentence, we are to consider four points: (1) a calling of the elect to the kingdom of heaven; (2) the reason thereof; (3) a reply of the elect; (4) the answer of Christ to them again.

The calling of the elect is set down in these words: "Come ye blessed of my Father, inherit the kingdom prepared for you from the beginning of the world" [Matt. 25:34].[309] And the words are to be observed one by one. "Come ye blessed." Though Christ now sit in glory and majesty in judgment, yet He ceases not to show His tender affection of love unto His chosen. And this overthrows the opinion of the Church of Rome, which would have us rather to come unto Christ by the intercession of saints than by ourselves immediately, because He is now exalted in glory and majesty. But mark, when He was here on earth, He said, "Come unto me all you that are heavy laden, and I will ease you" [11:28]. And when He shall be most glorious in majesty and power at the day of judgment, He will then also say, "Come ye blessed of my Father," and therefore we may resolve ourselves that it is His will now that we should come unto Him without any intercession of saints. "Ye blessed of my Father." The elect are here called the blessed of God because their righteousness, salvation, and all that they have springs of the mere blessing of God. Nothing therefore must be ascribed to the work of man. "Inherit"—that is, "receive as your inheritance." Therefore, the kingdom of heaven is God's mere gift. A father gives no inheritance unto his son of merit, but of his free gift, whereupon it follows that no man can merit the kingdom of heaven by his works. "The kingdom"—that is, the eternal estate of glory and happiness in heaven. Therefore, in this life we must so use the world as though we used it not. All that we have here is but vain and transitory, and all our study and endeavor must be to come to the kingdom of heaven. "Prepared"—here note the unspeakable care of God for the faithful. Had He such care to provide a kingdom for His children before they

---

309. This paragraph break is not in the original.

were? Then we may assure ourselves He will have greater care over them now when they have a being. "For you"—that is, for the elect and faithful. Hence it appears that there is no universal election, whereby (as some suppose) God decrees that all and every man shall be saved. Indeed, if He had said, "Come ye blessed of my Father, inherit the kingdom prepared for all, but received of you," it had been something; but He says only, "prepared for you." And therefore all were not chosen to salvation.

The reason of this calling is taken from works, as from signs, in these words: "for I was hungry and ye gave me meat," etc. When He says, "for I was hungry," He means His poor and distressed members upon earth. And thereby He signifies unto us that the miseries of His servants are His own miseries. Thus, the Lord says in Zechariah, "He which toucheth you, toucheth the apple of mine eye" [Zech. 2:8]. And when Saul was going to persecute them in Damascus and elsewhere that called on the name of Christ, He cried from heaven, "Saul, Saul, why persecutest thou me?" [Acts 9:4]. And this is a notable comfort to God's church and people, that "they have an high priest who is touched with the feeling of their infirmities" [Heb. 4:15]. And if He account our miseries His own miseries, then no doubt He will pity our estate and make us able to bear the worst. "And ye gave me meat." Here we note that the principal works of men are those which are done to the poor members of Christ. We are indeed to help all, inasmuch as they are our very flesh and the creatures of God. But the rule of St. Paul must be remembered, "Do good to all, but especially to those that are of the household of faith" [Gal. 6:10]. Many are of mind that the best works are to build churches and monasteries, but Christ tells us here that the best work of all is to relieve those that be the living members of His mystical body.

The third point is the reply of the saints to Christ again, in these words: "Lord, when saw we thee an hungred, and fed thee," etc. [Matt. 25:37]. They do not deny that which Christ avouched, but do, as I take it, standing before the tribunal seat of God, humble themselves, having still an after consideration of the infirmities and offences of their lives past. Here, note then that it is a satanical practice for a man to brag of works and to stand upon them in the matter of justification before God. And we must rather do as the saints of God do: abase ourselves in regard of our sins past.

The last point is the answer of Christ to them again, in these words: "Verily, I say unto you, inasmuch as ye did it to the least of these my brethren, ye did it to me" [v. 40]. A most notable sentence, and it serves to teach us how we should behave ourselves in doing works of mercy, which are duties to be performed in this life. We are not to do them of any sinister respect, as for praise of men or commodity; but we must propound unto ourselves the party to whom we do any good and in him look on Christ and so do it as unto Christ and for Christ's sake only. And this is a good work indeed. Christ says, "Whosoever shall give a cup of cold water to a disciple in the name of a disciple, shall not lose his reward" [10:42]. It is but a small gift, but yet the manner of doing it—namely, in the name of a disciple, that is, in respect that he is a member of Christ—does make it an excellent work of mercy. It is a special mark of a child of God to show mercy on a Christian, because he is a Christian. If any would know whether he be a Christian or no, let him search himself whether he love a man and can do good unto him, because he is a child of God and a member of Christ. For this is a plain argument that he also is the child of God. Many can love because they are loved again; but to love for Christ's sake is a work of Christ in us and a special gift of God.

The sentence of condemnation follows in the second place, and it contains four points: (1) the rejection of the ungodly; (2) the reason of their rejection; (3) the defense which the wicked make for themselves; [4] lastly, the answer of Christ to them again. The rejection of the wicked is uttered by a terrible sentence, "Away from me ye cursed into hellfire" [25:41]. The use hereof in general is twofold.

First, it serves to awake and excite all men and women in the world, whosoever they be that shall hear it, to look unto their own estates.[310] It is wonderful to see what great security reigns everywhere in these our days. Men go on in sin from day to day and from year to year without repentance, nothing at all fearing the sentence of condemnation at the last day—like unto many which for the obtaining of other men's goods are neither by the fear of arraignment or imprisonment kept in good order. The occasions of security are twofold: (1) the prosperity of the wicked, who of all men live at most ease without trouble, either in body or in mind; (2) God's patience and longsuffering. As Solomon says, "Because sentence against an evil work is not executed speedily, therefore the hearts of the children of men are fully set in them to do evil" [Eccl. 8:11]. But to awake all those which live in their security, they must remember that howsoever the Lord God does now defer His judgment, yet there is a day wherein He will no way show mercy and longsuffering, when they shall hear this fearful sentence of condemnation pronounced against them, "Away from me, ye cursed."

The second use is to the godly. It serves to nurture them and to keep them in awe before God, and no doubt this was a principal cause why this sentence was here penned by the Holy Ghost. A wise master of a family will check his servant and, if the cause require, correct him in his child's presence, that the child itself may learn thereby to fear and stand in awe of his father. So Christ,

---

310. This paragraph break is not in the original, as the additional four following.

the most careful and wise governor of His church, has set down this sentence of condemnation against the wicked, that the children of God in this world, whensoever they shall hear or read the same, might be moved thereby to stand in fear of God and more dutifully perform obedience unto His commandments.

"Away from me." Here we may learn what a blessed thing it is for a man to have true fellowship with Christ in this world. For in the day of judgment the punishment of the wicked is to be cut off from Him and driven away from His presence. Now, he that would have fellowship with God after this life and escape that punishment must seek to have it in this life, and he that will not seek to have fellowship with Him in this life shall never have it after in the day of judgment. Again, let us mark that it is nothing to draw near unto Christ with our lips, if the heart be not with Him; for such as come near with the lip and keep aloof in the heart shall hear the sentence pronounced, "Away from me ye cursed," and shall be severed as far from Christ as hell from heaven. Therefore, let us not content ourselves with formal profession but open the doors of our hearts that the King of Glory may come in.

"Ye cursed." They are cursed who are born in sin and live in their sins and all the days of their lives so persevere to the last gasp without seeking recovery. Whosoever he be that is in this estate, the curse of God hangs over his head and will so do till he get reconciliation with God in Christ. This being so, above all things in this world we must labor to be at peace with God and never cease nor be quiet with ourselves till we have the same wrought and sealed in our hearts. For before such a time as we be in God's favor, His fearful curse hangs over our heads. And if we so persevere without repentance, the day will come when we shall hear this fearful sentence pronounced against us, "Away from me ye cursed into hellfire." What hellfire is we must not curiously search, but rather give our whole endeavor to learn how we may avoid it—as when a man's house is on fire his care must be not to search how it came, but rather how to quench it. Yet we are to know thus much, that by "hellfire" is not meant any bodily flame, but it signifies the seizing of the fearful and terrible wrath of God both on body and soul forever. For howsoever the body be subject to burning with bodily fire, yet the soul, being spiritual, cannot burn. And therefore hellfire is not a material fire, but a grievous torment fitly resembled thereby.

"Prepared for the devil and his angels." There is in every man's heart by nature this corruption, whereby when he sins, he thinks that there is no danger, but all is well, having, as Isaiah says, made a "covenant with hell" [28:15]. But here consider that although the devil was once an angel of light, yet when he had sinned, he could not escape hell. It was prepared even for him. How then shall ungodly men, which are not half so wily, think to escape?

Now follows the reason of their rejection, in these words: "for I was an hungered, and ye gave me no meat," etc. [Matt. 25:42–43]. Hence we learn these two points. (1) That all man's religion and serving of God is in vain, if so be he show no compassion toward the poor members of Christ in feeding, clothing, lodging, and visiting of them. For we must think that many of those against whom this reason shall be brought did know religion and profess the same. Yea, they prophesied in the name of Christ and called on Him, saying, "Lord, Lord"; and yet the sentence of condemnation goes against them because they show no compassion toward the members of Christ. And therefore it is a principal virtue and a special note of a Christian to show the bowels of compassion toward His needy brethren.

Here again we note that it is not sufficient for us to abstain from evil, but we must also do good.[311] For it is not said, "I was an hungered and ye took from me," but, "When I was hungry ye gave me no meat." They are not charged with doing evil, but for not doing good. St. John says, "The axe is laid to the root of the tree," and the reason follows, not because the tree bare evil fruit, but because it bare not good fruit. Therefore, it must be cast into the fire. This condemns a bad opinion of all worldly men, who think that all is well, and that God will be merciful unto them, because they do no harm. Thus, we see how the devil blinds the eyes of men; for it will not stand for payment at the day of judgment to say, "I have hurt no man," unless we further do all the good we can.

The third point is the defense which impenitent sinners make for themselves, in these words, "Lord, when saw we thee an hungered, or thirsty, or naked, or in prison, or sick, and did not minister unto thee?" [25:44]. Thus, in their own defense, that which Christ says they gainsay and justify themselves. Here, mark the nature of all impenitent sinners, which is to soothe and flatter themselves in sin and to maintain their own righteousness, like to the proud Pharisee in his prayer, who bragged of his goodness and said, "Lord, I thank thee, that I am not as other men are, extortioners," etc. [Luke 18:11]. And in the very same manner ignorant persons of all sorts among us justify themselves in their strong faith and brag of their zeal of God's glory and of their love to their brethren and yet indeed show no signs thereof. And truly we are not to marvel when we see such persons to justify themselves before men, whereas they shall not be ashamed to do it at the day of judgment before the Lord Jesus Himself.

The last point is Christ's answer to them again, in these words: "Verily I say unto you, inasmuch as ye did it not to one of the least of these, ye did it not to me" [Matt. 25:45].[312] This sentence being repeated again does teach us

---

311. This paragraph break is not in the original.
312. This paragraph break is not in the original.

the lesson which we learned before, that when we are to show compassion to any man, especially if he be a member of God's church, we must not consider his outward estate or his baseness in that he wants food or raiment, but behold Christ in him, not respecting him as a man but as a member of Christ. This it is that must move us to compassion and cause us to make a supply of his wants more than any respect in the world besides. And surely, when Christ in His members comes to our doors and complains that He is hungry and sick and naked, if our bowels yearn not toward Him, there is not so much as a spark of the love of God in us.

The seventh point in the proceeding of the last judgment is the retribution or reward, in these words: "and they shall go into everlasting pain, and the righteous into life eternal" [v. 46]. How do the wicked enter into hell, and the godly into heaven? *Answer.* By the powerful and commanding voice of Christ, which is of that force that neither the greatest rebel that ever was among men nor all the devils in hell shall be able to withstand it. And seeing that after the day of judgment we must remain forever either in heaven or in hell, we are to look about us and to take heed unto our hearts. Indeed, if the time were but a thousand or two thousand years, then with more reason men might take liberty to themselves; but, seeing it is without end, we must be more careful through the whole course of our lives so to live and behave ourselves that when the day of judgment shall come we may avoid that fearful sentence of everlasting woe and condemnation which shall be pronounced against the wicked. And whereas all wicked men shall go to hell at Christ's commandment, it teaches us willingly to obey the voice of Christ in the ministry of the word. For if we rebel against His voice in the word, when in the day of judgment sentence shall be pronounced against us, we shall hear another voice, at the giving whereof we must obey whether we will or no and thereupon go to everlasting pain, whither we would not. Let us therefore in time deny ourselves for our sins past and only rely upon Christ Jesus for the free remission of them all and for the time to come lead a new reformed life.

Thus much of the order of Christ's proceeding at the day of judgment. Now follow the uses thereof, which are either comforts to God's church or duties for all men. The first comfort or benefit is this, that the same person which died for us upon the cross to work our redemption must also be our Judge. And hence we reap two special comforts. (1) The people of God shall hereby enjoy full redemption from all miseries and calamities which they had in this life. So Christ Himself, speaking of the signs of the end of the world, says to His disciples, "When you see these things, lift up your heads: for your redemption draws near" [Luke 21:28]. Then He shall wipe all tears from their eyes. [2] Secondly, we shall hereby have a final deliverance from all sin. Now, what a joyful thing it is to be freed from sin may plainly appear by the cry of St. Paul: "O wretched man that I am, who shall deliver me from this body of death?" [Rom. 7:24]. And certain it is that he which knows what sin is and seriously repents him of the same would wish with all his heart to be out of this world, that he might leave off to sin and thereby cease to displease God.

The second comfort is this: the godly in this world have many enemies. They are reviled, slandered, and oftentimes put to death. Well, Christ Jesus at the day of judgment will take every man's cause into His own hand. He will then hear the complaint of the godly, howsoever in this world they found no remedy; and then He will revenge their blood that is shed upon the earth according to their prayer [Rev. 6:10]. This comfort is to be considered especially of all those that are any way persecuted or molested by the wicked of this world.

Now follow the duties to be learned of every one of us, and they are divers. First, the consideration of the last judgment serves to teach all ignorant persons and impenitent sinners repentance and humiliation for their sins and to move them with speed to seek unto Christ for the pardon of the same. When Paul preached to the Athenians, he willed them to repent upon this ground and reason: "because, the Lord has appointed a day wherein he will judge the world in righteousness" [Acts 17:31]. To speak plainly, we can be content to hear the word of God and to honor Him with our lips, yet for the most part all is done but for fashion's sake; but still we live in our old sins, [and] our hearts are not turned. But in the fear of God let us bethink ourselves of the time when we shall come before the Judge of heaven and earth and have all our sins laid open, and we must answer for them all. This is the point which the Holy Ghost uses as a reason to move men unto repentance, and assuredly if this will not move us, there is nothing in the world will.

Secondly, to this purpose Paul says, "If we would judge ourselves, we should not be judged" (1 Cor. 11:31).[313] Would you then escape the judgment of Christ at the last day? Then in this life judge yourself. Now, a man in judging of himself must perform four things. (1) He must examine himself of his own sins. (2) He must confess them before the Lord. (3) He must condemn himself and as a judge upon the bench give sentence against himself. [4] Lastly, he must plead pardon and cry unto God as for life and death for the remission of all his sins. And he that does this unfeignedly shall never be judged of the Lord at the last day; but if we slack and neglect this duty in this life, then undoubtedly there remains nothing but eternal woe in the world to come.

Thirdly, by this we may learn one not to judge or condemn another, as Paul says, "Judge nothing before the time, until the Lord come, who will lighten all

---

313. This paragraph break is not in the original.

things that are in darkness, and make the counsels of the hearts manifest" (4:5). And Christ says, "Judgment is mine: and judge not, and ye shall not be judged" (Luke 6:37). And again Paul says to the Romans, "Why dost thou judge thy brother? for we must all appear before the judgment seat of Christ" [14:10]. But some will ask, how does one judge another? *Answer.* Thus: (1) when a man does well, to say of him that he does evil; (2) when a man does evil, then to make it worse; (3) when a thing is doubtful, to take it in the worst part. And by any of these three ways we are not to judge either of men's persons or of their actions.

Fourthly, we must endeavor ourselves to keep a good conscience before God and before all men. This is the practice of St. Paul, who in consideration and "hope of a resurrection unto judgment, as well of the just as of the unjust, endeavored himself to have always a clear conscience both toward God, and toward men" [Acts 24:15–16]. His example is worthy our marking and imitation, for few there be that upon this occasion make any conscience either of duty to God or to their brethren.

Fifthly, the last judgment must stir us up to a reverent fear of God and cause us to glorify Him—as the angel says in the Revelation, "Fear God, and give glory to him: for the hour of his judgment is come" [14:7]. And doubtless, if anything in the world will move a man to fear the Lord, it is this, to remember the fearful and terrible day of judgment.

Now, having spoken hitherto of the first person, the Father, and also of the Son, it follows in the next place to speak of the third person, in these words, "I believe in the Holy Ghost." In which we may consider two things: the title of the person and the action of faith, repeated from the beginning.

The title is, "Holy Ghost," or "Spirit."[314] It may here be demanded how this title can be fit to express the third person, which seems to be common to the rest; for the Father is holy, and the Son is holy; again, the Father is a spirit, and the Son is a spirit. *Answer.* Indeed, the Father and the Son are as well to be termed holy in respect of their natures as the third person; for all three, subsisting in one and the same Godhead, are consequently holy by one and the same holiness. But the third person is called holy, because besides the holiness of nature His office is to sanctify the church of God. Now, if it be said that sanctification is a work of the whole Trinity, the answer is that although it be so, yet the work of sanctification agrees to the Holy Ghost in special manner. The Father sanctifies by the Son and by the Holy Ghost. The Son sanctifies from the Father and by the Holy Ghost. The Holy Ghost sanctifies from the Father and from the Son by Himself immediately. And in this respect is the third person termed holy. Again, the third person is termed a spirit not only because His nature is

---

314. This paragraph break is not in the original.

spiritual (for in that respect the Father is a spirit, and the Son is a spirit), but because He is spired or breathed from the Father and from the Son, in that He proceeds from them both. Thus, we see there is a special cause why the third person is called the Holy Ghost.

Now, the action of faith which concerns the third person is to believe in Him. Which is (1) to acknowledge the Holy Ghost as He has revealed Himself in the Word; (2) in special to believe that He is my Sanctifier and Comforter; (3) to put all the confidence of my heart in Him for that cause. In these words are comprised four points of doctrine which are to be believed concerning the Holy Ghost.

The first, that He is very God.[315] For we are not to put affiance or confidence in any but in God alone. And no doubt the penners of the Creed, in that they prefixed these words, "I believe in," before the article of the third person meant thereby to signify that He is true God, equal with the Father and the Son, according to the tenor of the Scriptures themselves. Peter says to Ananias, "Why hath Satan filled thine heart that thou shouldest lie unto the Holy Ghost?"; and, continuing the same speech, he changes the term only and says, "Thou hast not lied unto men, but unto God" [Acts 5:3–4]—whereby he insinuates that the Holy Ghost is very God. In the vision of the prophet Isaiah, the words by him set down are thus: "I heard the voice of Jehovah, saying, Whom shall I send, etc., and he said, Go and say to this people: Ye shall hear indeed; but yet ye shall not understand" [Isa. 6:8–9]. But Paul, quoting the same place, spoke on this manner: "Well spake the Holy Ghost by Isaiah the prophet, saying, Go unto this people and say unto them," etc. [Acts 28:25–26]. Now these places, being compared together, make it plain that the title of Jehovah agrees to the Holy Ghost. But yet the enemies of this truth, which think that the Holy Ghost is nothing else but the action or operation of God, object out of the Scriptures to the contrary.

(1) God knows the Son. The Holy Ghost knows not the Son, "for none knows the Son but the Father" [Matt. 11:27]. Ergo, the Holy Ghost is not God. *Answer.* That place excludes no person in [the] Trinity, but only creatures and false gods. And the meaning is this: none—that is, no creature or idol god—knows the Son of God, but the Father. And the opposition is made to exclude creatures, not to exclude the Holy Ghost.

[2] Again they object that the Holy Ghost makes request for us with groans and sighs that cannot be uttered [Rom. 8:16]. Therefore, say they, the Holy Ghost is not God but rather a gift of God. For He that is true God cannot pray, groan, or sigh. *Answer.* Paul's meaning is thereby to signify that the Holy Ghost

---

315. This paragraph break is not in the original, as the additional four following.

causes us to make requests and stirs up our hearts to groan and sigh to God; for he said before, "We have received the spirit of adoption, whereby we cry Abba, father" [v. 15].

[3] Yet further, they object the words of the angel Gabriel to the Virgin Mary, saying, "The virtue of the most high hath overshadowed thee" [Luke 1:35]. And hence they gather that if the Holy Ghost be the virtue of God, then He is not God indeed. *Answer*. As Christ is called the Word of God, not a word made of letters or syllables, but a substantial Word—that is, being forever of the same substance with the Father—so in this place the Holy Ghost is called the virtue of the Most High not because He is a created quality, but because He is the substantial virtue of the Father and the Son and therefore God equal with them both.

[5] Furthermore, they allege that neither the Scriptures nor the practice of the primitive church does warrant us to pray to the Holy Ghost. *Answer*. It is not true; for whensoever we direct our prayers to any one of the three persons, in Him we pray to them all. Besides, we have example of prayer made to the Holy Ghost in the Word of God. For Paul says to the Corinthians, "The grace of our Lord Jesus Christ, the love of God the Father, and the fellowship of the Holy Ghost be with you all" [2 Cor. 13:14]. And the words are as if St. Paul had said thus: "O Father, let Thy love; O Son, let Thy grace; O Holy Ghost, let Thy fellowship be with them all." And therefore this first doctrine is true and as well to be believed as any other, that the Holy Ghost is God.

The second point is that the Holy Ghost is a distinct person from the Father and the Son. Hereupon the articles touching the three persons are thus distinguished: I believe in the Father; I believe in the Son; I believe in the Holy Ghost. This point also is consonant to the Scriptures, which make the same distinction. In the baptism of Christ, the Father utters a voice from heaven, saying, "This is my beloved Son, in whom I am well pleased" [Matt. 3:17], and not the Son or the Holy Ghost. Secondly, the Son stood in the water and was baptized by John, and not the Father or the Holy Ghost. Thirdly, the Holy Ghost descended from heaven upon Christ in the form of a dove—and not the Father or the Son, but the Holy Ghost alone. Christ in His commission unto His disciples says, "Go teach all nations baptizing them in the name of the Father, the Son, and the Holy Ghost" (28:19). Now if the Holy Ghost had been the same person either with the Father or with the Son, then it had been sufficient to have named the Father and the Son only. And the distinction of the third person from the rest may be conceived by this, that the Holy Ghost is the Holy Ghost and not the Father or the Son.

The third point to be believed is that the Holy Ghost proceeds from the Father and the Son. For a further proof hereof, consider these places. Paul says,

"Ye are not in the flesh, but in the spirit: for the spirit of God dwells in you. But if any man have not the spirit of Christ, he is not his" (Rom. 8:9). And again, "Because you are sons, God hath sent forth the spirit of the Son into your hearts" (Gal. 4:6). Where we may observe that the Holy Ghost is the Spirit both of the Father and of the Son. Now the Holy Ghost is called the Spirit of the Father not only because He is sent of Him, but because He proceeds from the Father—as Christ says to His disciples, "When the comforter will come, whom I shall send unto you from the Father, even the spirit of truth which proceeds of the Father, he shall testify of me" [John 15:26]. And therefore likewise He is the Spirit of the Son not only because He is sent of the Son, but also because He proceeds from Him. Again, in the Trinity, the person sending does communicate His whole essence and substance to the person sent—as the Father, sending the Son, does communicate His essence and substance to the Son, for sending does presuppose a communication of essence. Now, the Father and the Son send the Holy Ghost. Therefore, both of them communicate their substance and essence unto the same person. Thirdly, Christ says, "The Holy Ghost hath received of mine which he shall show unto you" [16:14]—namely, knowledge and truth to be revealed unto His church. Where we may reason thus: the person receiving knowledge from another receives essence also. The Holy Ghost receives truth and knowledge from Christ to be revealed unto the church. And therefore, first of all, He has received substance and essence from the Son. But some peradventure will say, where is it written in all the Bible in express words that the Holy Ghost proceeds from the Son as He proceeds from the Father? *Answer.* The Scripture says not so much in plain terms, yet we must know that that which is gathered from thence by just consequence is no less the truth of God than that which is expressed in words. Hereupon all churches save those in Greece with one consent acknowledge the truth of this point.

The fourth and last point is that the Holy Ghost is equal to the Father and the Son. And this we are taught to acknowledge in the Creed, in that we do as well believe in the Holy Ghost as in the Father and the Son. And though the Holy Ghost be sent of the Father and the Son, yet (as I have said before) that argues no inequality (for one equal may send another by consent) but order only, whereby the Holy Ghost is last of all the three persons. Again, in that the Holy Ghost receives from the Son, it proves no inferiority, because He receives from the Son whatsoever He receives by nature and not by grace. And He receives not a part but all that the Son has, saving the property of His person.

Now follow the benefits which are given by the Holy Ghost, and they are of two sorts: some are common to all creatures, and some are proper to men. The benefit of the Holy Ghost common to all creatures is the work of creation and preservation. For all things were created and made and afterward preserved by the Holy Ghost. So Elihu says, "The spirit of God hath made me" (Job 33:4). And Moses says, "In the beginning the spirit moved upon the waters" (Gen. 1:2). The phrase is borrowed from a bird, who in hatching of her young ones sits upon the eggs, moves herself upon them, and heats them. And so likewise the Holy Ghost in the beginning did by His own power cherish and preserve the mass or lump whereof all things were made and caused it to bring forth the creatures. This being evident that the Holy Ghost has a stroke in the work of creation and preservation, we must unfeignedly acknowledge that we were first created and since that time continually preserved by the benefit even of the third person.

The benefits proper unto men are of two sorts: some are common to all men both good and bad, and some proper to the elect and faithful. The benefits common to all men are divers. (1) The gift of practicing a particular calling. As in the body several members have several uses, so in every society several men have several offices and callings; and the gifts whereby they are enabled to perform the duties thereof are from the Holy Ghost. When Gideon became a valiant captain to deliver the Israelites, it is said he "was clothed with the spirit" (Judg. 6:34). Bezaleel and Aholiab, being set apart to build the tabernacle, were filled with the Spirit of God in wisdom and understanding and in all workmanship to find out curious works, to work in gold and in silver and in brass, also in the art to set stones and to carve in timber, etc. [Ex. 31:3]. By this it is manifest that the skill of any handicraft is not in the power of man, but comes by the Holy Ghost. And by this we are taught to use all those gifts well whereby we are enabled to discharge our particular callings, that they may serve for the glory of God and the good of His church. And those that in their callings use fraud and deceit or else live inordinately do most unthankfully abuse the gifts of God and dishonor the Spirit of God, the author of their gifts, for which thing they must give an account one day.

The second gift common to all is illumination, whereby a man is enabled to understand the will of God in His Word [Heb. 6:4]. The "Jews in the reading of the Old Testament had a veil over their hearts," and the like have all men by nature, to whom the Word of God is foolishness. "Paul at his conversion was smitten blind, and scales were upon his eyes" (Acts 9:17–18)—the like also be over the eyes of our minds, and they must fall away before we can understand the will of God. Now, it is the work of the Holy Ghost to remove these scales and films from our eyes. And for this very cause He is called the anointing and eye salve; for as it does clear the eyes and take away the dimness of them [1 John 2:20; Rev. 3:18], so does the Holy Ghost take away blindness from our minds that we may see into the truth of God's Word. This being a common gift and received both of good and bad, it stands us in hand not to content ourselves with the bare knowledge of the Word, but therewithal we must join obedience and make conscience thereof; or else that will befall us which Christ foretold, that he which knows his master's will and does it not shall be beaten with many stripes [Luke 12:47].

The third gift of the Holy Ghost is the gift of prophecy, whereby a man is made able to interpret and expound the Scriptures [1 Cor. 12:10]. Now, albeit this gift be very excellent and not given to every man, yet is it common both to good and bad. For in the day of judgment when men shall come to Christ and say, "Master, we have prophesied in thy name," He shall answer again, "I never knew you, depart from me ye workers of iniquity" [Matt. 7:22–23]. Hereupon those that are in the calling of the ministry and have received the gift of prophecy must not here withal be puffed up. For if they be not as well doers of God's will as teachers, their gifts will turn to their further condemnation. As the carpenters that built Noah's ark when the flood came were drowned because they would not obey Noah's preaching, so those that have the gift of prophecy and are builders in God's house—if they build not themselves as well as others, for all their preaching, at the day of judgment they shall be condemned. And therefore it stands them in hand not to content themselves with this, that they know and teach others God's will, but they themselves must be the first doers of the same.

The fourth common gift of the Holy Ghost is ability to bridle and restrain for some affections so as they shall not break out into outrageous behavior. Haman, a wicked man and an enemy to God's church, when he saw Mordecai the Jew sitting in the king's gate and that he would not stand up to move unto him, he was full of indignation. Nevertheless, the text says that "he refrained himself" (Esth. 5:10). And when Abimelech, a heathen king, had taken Sarah, Abraham's wife, God said unto him, "I know that thou didst this with an upright heart" [Gen. 20:6]. And the text adds further, "I have kept thee that thou shouldest not sin against me." And thus the Lord gives to men as yet without the Spirit of sanctification this gift to bridle themselves, so as in outward action they shall not practice this or that sin. For why did not Abimelech commit adultery? Surely, because God kept him from it. Again, in the histories of the heathen we may read of many that were just, liberal, meek, continent, etc., and that by a general operation of the Holy Ghost, that represses the corruption of nature for the common good. Here then, if any man ask how it comes to pass that some men are more modest and civil than others, seeing all men by nature are equally wicked, the answer may be, not as the common saying is—because some are of better nature than others (for all the sons of Adam are equal in regard of nature; the child newborn in that respect is as wicked as the oldest man that ever lived)—but the reason is because God gives this common gift of restraining the affections more to some than to others. This must be considered of us all. For a man may have the Spirit of God to bridle many sins and yet never have the Spirit to mortify the same and to make him a new creature. And this being so, we must take heed that we deceive not ourselves. For it is not sufficient for a man to live in outward civility and to keep in some of his affections upon some occasion (for a wicked man may do), but we must further labor to feel in ourselves the Spirit of God not only bridling sin in us but also mortifying and killing the same. Indeed, both of them are the good gifts of God's Spirit, but yet the mortification of sin is the chiefest, being an effectual sign of grace and proper to the elect.

The fifth grace and gift of the Holy Ghost is to hear and receive the word of God with joy. In the parable of the sower, one kind of bad ground are they "which when they have heard, receive the word with joy" [Luke 8:13]; and this is that which the author of the Hebrews calls "the tasting of the good word of God, and of the power of the world to come" [6:5]. We know that there is great difference between tasting of meat and eating of it. They that sit down at the table do both taste and eat, but they that dress the meat do only see and taste thereof. So it is at the Lord's Table. Many there be that have this gift truly both to taste and eat of the body and blood of Christ offered in the word and sacraments. And some again do only taste and feel the sweetness of them and rejoice therein, but yet are not indeed partakers thereof. Now if this be so, then all those which hear the word of God must take heed how they hear and labor to find these two things in themselves by hearing: (1) that in heart and conscience they be thoroughly touched and humbled for their sins; (2) that they be certainly assured of the favor and love of God in Christ and that the sweet promises of the gospel do belong to them. And in consideration hereof they must make a conscience of all sin both in thought, word, and deed through the whole course of their lives. And this kind of hearing brings that joy which vanishes not away.

Thus much of the benefits of the Holy Ghost common to all men both good and bad. Now follow such as are proper to the elect, all which may be reduced unto one—namely, the inhabitation of the Spirit, whereby the elect are the temples of the Holy Ghost, who is said "to dwell in men" [Rom. 8:9; 1 Cor. 3:16] not in respect of substance (for the whole nature of the Holy Ghost cannot be comprised in the body or soul of man), but in respect of a particular operation. And this dwelling stands in two things. The first, that the Holy Ghost does abide in them not for a time only but forever, for the word "dwelling" notes perpetuity. Secondly, that the Holy Ghost has the full disposition of the heart, as when a man comes to dwell in a house whereof he is lord he has liberty to govern it after his own will. Now, this disposition of the hearts of the faithful by the Holy Ghost stands in five special and notable gifts, every one worthy our observation.

The first is a certain knowledge of a man's own reconciliation to God in Christ as it is said in Isaiah 53:11: "by his knowledge my righteous servant shall justify many." And Christ says, "This is life eternal, that they know thee to be the only very God, and whom thou hast sent, Jesus Christ" (John 17:3). This knowledge is not general, for then the devils might be saved; but it is particular, whereby a man knows God the Father to be his Father and Christ the Redeemer to be his Redeemer, and the Holy Ghost to be his Sanctifier and Comforter. And it is a special work of the Holy Ghost, as Paul says, "The spirit of God beareth witness to our spirits, that we are the children of God" (Rom. 8:16); and, "We have received the spirit which is of God, that we might know the things that are given unto us of God" (1 Cor. 2:12).

The second gift is regeneration, whereby a man of a limb of the devil is made a member of Christ, and of a child of Satan (whom every one of us by nature do as lively resemble as any man does his own parent) is made the child of God. "Except a man," says our Savior Christ, "be born again by water and the spirit, he cannot enter into the kingdom of heaven" (John 3:5). John [the] Baptist in saying that Christ baptized with the Holy Ghost and fire compares the Spirit of God to fire and water [Matt. 3:11]. To fire, for two causes. (1) As it is the nature of fire to warm the body that is benumbed and frozen with cold, so when a man is benumbed and frozen in sin, yea, when he is even stark dead in sin, it is the property of the Holy Ghost to warm and quicken his heart and to revive him. (2) Fire does purge and eat out the dross from the good metal. Now, there is no dross nor canker that has so deeply eaten into any metal as sin into the nature of man. Therefore, the Holy Ghost is as a fire to purge and eat out the hidden corruptions of sin out of the rebellious heart of man. Again, the Holy Ghost is compared to clear water for two causes. (1) Man by nature is as dry wood without sap, and the property of the Holy Ghost is as water to supple and to put sap of grace into the dead and rotten heart of man. (2) The property of water is to cleanse and purify the filth of the body. Even so the Holy Ghost does spiritually wash away our sins, which are the filth of our nature. And this is the second benefit of the Holy Ghost.

By this we are taught that he which would enter into the kingdom of God and have the Holy Ghost to dwell in him must labor to feel the work of regeneration by the same Spirit.[316] And if a man would know whether he has this work wrought in him or no, let him mark what St. Paul says, "They that are of the spirit, savor the things of the spirit: but they that live after the flesh, savor

---

316. This paragraph break is not in the original.

the things of the flesh" (Rom. 8:5). If therefore a man have his heart continually affected with that which is truly good either more or less, it is a certain token that his wicked nature is changed, and he regenerate. But contrariwise, if his heart be always set on the pleasures of sin and the things of this world, he may justly suspect himself that he is not regenerated. As, for example, if a man have all his mind set upon drinking and gulling in of wine and strong drink, having little delight or pleasure in anything else, it argues a carnal mind and unregenerate, because it affects the things of the flesh; and so of the rest. And, on the contrary, he that has his mind affected with a desire to do the will of God in practicing the works of charity and religion—he, I say, has a spiritual and a renewed heart and is regenerate by the Holy Ghost.

The third work of the Holy Ghost is to govern the hearts of the elect. This may be called spiritual regiment. A man that dwells in a house of his own orders and governs it according to his own will. Even so the Holy Ghost governs all them in whom He dwells, as Paul says, "They that are the sons of God, are led by his spirit" (v. 14)—a most notable benefit; for look where the Holy Ghost dwells, there He will be Lord, governing both heart, mind, will, and affections, and that two ways: (1) by repressing all bad motions unto sin, arising either from the corruption of man's nature, from the world, or from the devil; (2) by stirring up good affections and motions upon every occasion. So it is said, "The flesh"—that is, the corruption of man's nature—"lusteth against the spirit: and the spirit"—that is, grace in the heart—"lusteth against the flesh" (Gal. 5:17), and that after a double sort: first, by laboring to overmaster and keep down the motions thereof; secondly, by stirring up good motions and inclinations to piety and religion. In Isaiah, the Holy Ghost has most excellent titles: the Spirit of the Lord (Isa. 11:2); the Spirit of wisdom and understanding; the Spirit of counsel and of strength; the Spirit of knowledge and of the fear of the Lord. Now, He is so called because He stirs up good motions in the godly of wisdom, of knowledge, of strength, of understanding, of counsel, and of the fear of the Lord. And St. Paul says that the fruits of the Spirit are "joy, peace, love, longsuffering, gentleness, goodness, faith, meekness, temperance," etc. [Gal. 5:22]—all which are so termed because where the Holy Ghost rules, there He engenders these good gifts and motions of grace. But among all the inward motions of the Spirit, the most principal are these:

(1) An utter disliking of sin, because it is sin.[317] And that is when a man has an eye not so much to another man's sins as to his own and, seeing them, is truly sorrowful for them and dislikes them and himself for them, not so much because there is a place of torment or a day of judgment to come, wherein he

---

317. This paragraph break is not in the original, as the additional two following.

must answer to God for them all, but as if there were no hell or judgment—because God is displeased by them, who has been unto him a most loving and merciful father in redeeming him by Christ.

[2] The second is a hungering desire above all things in this world to be at unity with God in Christ for the same sins. This is a motion of the Holy Ghost, which no man can have but he in whom the Holy Ghost does dwell.

[3] The third, the gift of hearty prayer. For this cause the Holy Ghost is called the "spirit of supplications" [Zech. 12:10], because it stirs up the heart and makes it fit to pray. And therefore Paul says that "the spirit of God helpeth our infirmities: for we know not what to pray, as we ought, but the same spirit itself maketh request for us with sighs which cannot be expressed" [Rom. 8:26]. This is an ordinary work of the Holy Ghost in all that believe, and he that would know whether he have the Spirit dwelling truly in his heart shall know it by this: a mother carries her child in her arms; if it cry for the dug[318] and suck the same, it is alive. Being observed many days together, if it neither cry nor stir, it is dead. In like manner, it is an infallible note of a true child of God to cry out to his Father in heaven by prayer. But he that never cries nor feels himself stirred up to make his moan to God is in a miserable case, and he may well be thought to be but a dead child. And therefore let us learn in prayer unfeignedly to pour out our souls before God, considering it is a special gift of the Holy Ghost bestowed on the children of God.

The fourth work of the Holy Ghost in the heart of the elect is comfort in distress; and therefore our Savior Christ calls Him the "Comforter whom he will send" (John 15:26), and in the psalm He is called "the oil of gladness" (45:7), because He makes glad the heart of man in trouble and distress. There be two things that fill the heart full of endless grief. The first, outward calamities, as when a man is in any danger of death, when he loses his goods, his good name, his friends, and such like. The second is a troubled conscience, whereof Solomon says, "A troubled spirit, who can bear it?" (Prov. 18:14). And of all other it is the most heavy and grievous cross that can be. When as the hand of God was heavy upon Job, this was the sorest of his afflictions; and therefore he cries out that "the arrows of the Almighty did stick in his soul" (Job 6:4). Now what is the comfort in this case? *Answer.* In the midst of all our distresses, the Holy Ghost is present with us to make us rejoice and to fill us with comforts (that no tongue can express) out of the Word of God, and specially the promises thereof. And hereupon the ungodly man when afflictions befall him is ready to make away himself, because he wants the comfort of the Holy Ghost.

318. *Dug*: breast.

The last benefit wrought in the hearts of the elect is the strengthening of them to do the weightiest duties of their callings. And hence the Holy Ghost is called "the spirit of strength" (Isa. 11:2). There be divers things to be done of a Christian man that are far beyond the reach of his power, as, first, when he sees his own sins and is truly humbled for them, then to lift up the hand of faith to heaven and thereby to catch hold on the mercy of God in Christ is the hardest thing in the whole world. And this do all those which know what it is to believe. Secondly, it is as hard a thing in the time of temptation to resist temptation as for dry wood to resist the fire when it begins to burn. Thirdly, when a man is put to his choice either to lose his life, goods, friends, and all that he has, or else to forsake religion—even then, to forsake all and to stick unto Christ is a matter of as great a difficulty as any of the former. Fourthly, when a man wants the ordinary means of God's providence, as meat, drink, and clothing, then at the very instant to acknowledge God's providence, to rejoice in it, and to rely thereon is as much as if a man should shake the whole earth. It is against our wicked nature to trust God, unless He first lay down some pawn of His love and mercy to us. How then, will some say, shall anyone be able to do these things? *Answer.* The Holy Ghost is the Spirit of strength, and by Him we do all things, as Paul says, "I am able to do all things through the help of Christ which strengtheneth me" [Phil. 4:13].

Concerning these gifts of the Holy Ghost, two questions may be moved. First, what is the measure of grace in this life? *Answer.* Small, in respect. In this world we receive, as Paul says, not the tenth but the "firstfruits of God's spirit" (Rom. 8:23) and the "earnest of the spirit" (2 Cor. 1:22). Now the firstfruits properly are but as a handful or twain of corn to a whole cornfield containing many acres and furlongs of ground. And the earnest in a bargain it may be is but a penny laid down for the paying of twenty thousand pounds. The second question is, whether the graces of the Holy Ghost may be wholly lost or not? *Answer.* The common gifts of the Spirit may be lost and extinguished; but the gifts proper to the elect cannot. Indeed, they may be diminished and covered as coals under ashes and as the sap in the root of the tree in the winter season, not appearing at all in the branches; and the feeling of them may be lost. But they cannot either finally or totally be lost. It is true that God does forsake His children; but that is only in part, as He "left Hezekiah to prove and try what was in his heart" (2 Chron. 32:31). A mother that loves her child most tenderly sets it down in the floor, lets it stand and fall and break the face, and all this while she hides herself, not because her purpose is to leave her child quite or to make it hurt itself, but that when she takes it up again, it may love her the better. So deals the Holy Ghost with men to make them know their weakness and frailty.

He hides Himself as it were in some corner of the heart for a season, that they may the more earnestly hunger after grace, the want whereof they feel.

The use of this article whereby we confess that we believe in the Holy Ghost is manifold. First, considering that all the gifts which any man has, whether they be gifts of knowledge in the Word of God or of human learning or any gifts whereby men are enabled to practice their trades or handicrafts, do come not from ourselves, but from the Holy Ghost, we are taught this duty: look what gifts soever we for our parts have received of the Spirit of God, we must use them so as they may ever serve for the glory of God and good of our brethren and not to the practicing and setting forth of any manner of sin and by consequent to the service of the devil. For that is as if a man, receiving riches and revenues of his prince, should straightway go to the prince's enemy and employ them for his benefit—which were a point of exceeding treachery.

Furthermore, in every place the greater part of men are blind and ignorant persons both young and old; and aged folks, as they are ignorant themselves, so they muzzle up their youth in ignorance. Confer with them; you shall find that they can say nothing but that which may be learned by common talk, as that there is a God, and that this God must be worshipped. But ask them further of the means of their salvation and of their duties to God and man, and they will answer you that they are not book-learned. Tell them further that the ordinary means to bring men to knowledge is the preaching of the word, which if they will not use, they shall be inexcusable—they will say, "Alas, we are dull of memory and cannot learn." Well, for all this, you say you believe in the Holy Ghost, and He is your schoolmaster to teach you. Though your capacity be dull, yet He is able to open your understanding; for as there is outward teaching by the minister, so the work of the Holy Ghost is joined withal to enlighten the conceit of the mind, that they which hear the word with reverence may profit thereby and get knowledge. But if for all this men will not learn but remain ignorant still, then let them mark the example of the sons of Eli. He in some part did rebuke them for their wickedness, but yet they would not obey. And the reason is there set down, "because the Lord would destroy them" (1 Sam. 2:25). In the same manner, howsoever we may not judge of any man's person, yet this may be said, that if men refuse to hear the word of God when they may, or if in hearing they will not obey, it is a fearful sign that God will at length destroy them. When a trumpet is sounded in a man's ear, and he lies still, not stirring at all, he is certainly dead. And surely, when the trumpet of the gospel is sounded in the ears of our hearts, if we awake not out of our sins to newness of life, we are no better than dead men before God. Wherefore, the case being thus dangerous, and the punishment so great, let us labor in time for the knowledge of God's will and prevent God's judgments before they light upon us.

Thirdly, as the apostle says, "If we live in the spirit, we must walk in the spirit" (Gal. 5:25)—that is, if we be dead unto sin by the power of the Holy Ghost and be raised up to newness of life, then we must walk in the Spirit. Now to walk in the Spirit is to lead our lives in showing forth the fruits of the Spirit. In Isaiah, the Holy Ghost is compared unto "water poured forth on the dry land, which maketh their seed to grow like the willows by the rivers of waters" (Isa. 44:3–4). Wherefore, those that have the gifts of the Spirit must be trees of righteousness, bringing forth the fruits of the Spirit, which (as they are set down by Paul) are principally nine [Gal. 5:22–23].

The first fruit is love, which respects both God and man. Love unto God is an inward and spiritual motion in the heart whereby God is loved absolutely for Himself. This love shows itself in two things: (1) when a man's heart is set and disposed to seek the honor and glory of God in all things; (2) when a man by all means strives and endeavors himself to please God in everything, counting it a most miserable estate to live in the displeasure of God. And the heart that is thus affected can have no greater torment than to fall into sin, whereby God is offended, and His displeasure provoked. By these two signs, a man may know whether he love God or no, and by them also must he testify his love. Now, our love to man is a fruit of this love of God, for God is to be loved for Himself, [and] man is loved for God. This love must not be in show only, but in deed and action. St. John bids us not to love in word and tongue only, but in deed and truth (1 John 3:18). Brotherly love does always lie hid; but when an occasion is offered, it does break forth into action. It is like fire, which though for a time it be smothered, yet at length it breaks forth into a flame. And so much love a man shows to his neighbor as he has; and where none is showed, none is.

The second fruit is joy, when a man is glad at the good of his neighbor as at his own good; and this is a special work of the Holy Ghost. For the nature of man is to pine away and to grieve at the good of another, and contrariwise it is a work of grace to rejoice thereat. Paul says, "Rejoice with them that rejoice" (Rom. 12:15). And this was the holy practice of the friends and neighbors of Zachariah and Elizabeth—when John [the] Baptist was born, "they came and rejoiced with them."

The third fruit of the Spirit is peace. Of this Paul speaks most excellently, saying, "If it be possible, as much as in you is, have peace with all men" (v. 18). It is nothing else but concord which must be kept in a holy manner with all men, both good and bad, so far forth as can be. Isaiah the prophet, speaking of the fruits of the gospel, says, "The wolf shall dwell with the lamb, and the leopard with the kid," etc. (Isa. 11:6). Where note that in the kingdom of Christ, when a man is called into the state of grace, howsoever by nature he be as a wolf, as a leopard, as a lion, or as a bear, yet he shall then lay away his cruel nature and become gentle and live peaceably with all men. Now, for the practicing of this peace, there are three duties especially to be learned and performed.

(1) Rather than peace should be broken, a man must yield of his own right.[319] When publicans came to our Savior Christ for tribute, He had a lawful excuse; for howsoever He lived in low estate among men, yet He was the right heir to the kingdom and therefore was free. Nevertheless, He stood not on His privilege but called Peter, saying, "Lest we offend them go to the sea and cast in an angle and take the first fish that cometh up: and when thou hast opened his mouth, thou shalt find a piece of twenty pence: take it and give it to them for thee and me" (Matt. 17:26–27). Here we see that our Savior Christ, rather than He would break the common peace, yields of His own right; and so we must do if we will be good followers of Him.

[2] Secondly, when any man shall sin either in word or in deed, specially if it be upon infirmity, we must avoid bitter invectives and mildly tell him of his fault and in all meekness and love labor for his amendment. So Paul teaches us, saying, "If any man be fallen into any fault by occasion, restore such an one with the spirit of meekness, considering thyself, lest thou be also tempted, etc. Bear ye one another's burden" (Gal. 6:1–2).

[3] Thirdly, every man within the compass of his calling must be a peacemaker between them that are at variance. This is a special duty of godliness and Christianity, and therefore our Savior Christ does highly commend such and pronounces His blessing upon them, that "they shall be called the children of God" [Matt. 5:9].

The fourth fruit of the Spirit is longsuffering, and it stands in two points: (1) when a man defers his anger and is hardly brought to it; (2) being angry does yet[320] moderate the same and stay the hotness of that affection. For the first, to bridle anger, it is a special work of the Holy Ghost, and the means to attain unto it are these. (1) Not to take notice of the injuries and wrongs done unto us, if they be not of great moment, but to let them pass, as not knowing them. Solomon says, "It is a man's discretion to defer his anger" (Prov. 19:11). Now how is that done? It is added in the next words, "It is the glory of a man to pass by infirmity"—that is, when a man shall overshoot himself either in word or deed to let it pass either wholly or till a time convenient, as though we knew not of it. [2] The second way to defer and bridle anger is when a man has injured us either in word or deed to think with ourselves that we have injured others in the same manner; and for this cause Solomon says, "Give not thine heart to all that men speak, lest thou hear thy servant cursing thee: for

---

319. This paragraph break is not in the original, as the additional two following.
320. Originally, "not."

oftentimes thine heart also knoweth that thou hast cursed others" (Eccl. 7:21–24). A man must not listen to every man's words at all times; but he is to think that he has spoken or done the same unto other men, and that now the Lord meets with him by the like, as it is said, "With what measure ye mete, it shall be measured to you again" (Matt. 7:2). This is a thing which few consider. Evil men desire good report and would have all men speak well of them, whereas they can speak well of none. But indeed they must begin to speak well of others before others speak well of them. Thirdly, a man must consider how God deals with him. For so often as he sins he provokes God to cast him away and to confound him eternally, yet the Lord is merciful and longsuffering. Even so, when men do offend and injure us, we must do as God does: not be angry, but fight against our affections, endeavoring to become patient and longsuffering as God is with us.

The second property of longsuffering is to keep the affection of anger in moderation and compass.[321] It is not always a sin to be angry, and therefore it is said of Christ (in whom was no blemish of sin) that "he was angry" [Mark 3:5]. Yet we must look that our anger be moderate, not continuing overlong, as Paul says, "Let not the sun go down upon your wrath" [Eph. 4:26].

The fifth fruit of the Spirit is gentleness, whereby a man behaves and shows himself friendly and courteous to every man, as Paul says to Titus, "Put them in remembrance that they speak evil of no man, that they be no fighters, but soft, showing all meekness unto all men, whether they be good or bad" (Titus 3:2). This gentleness stands in these points: (1) to speak to every man friendly and lovingly; (2) to salute friendly and courteously; (3) to be ready upon every occasion to give reverence and honor to every man in his place. It is made a question of some whether a man is to salute and speak unto them that are known to be lewd and wicked men. But here we see what our duty is, in that we are taught to be courteous to all men both good and bad, yet so as we approve not of their sins—as for that which St. John says of false prophets, "Receive them not, neither bid them godspeed" (2 John 10), it is to be understood of giving an outward approbation to false teachers.

The sixth fruit is goodness, which is when a man is ready to do good and become serviceable in his calling to all men at all times upon all occasions. This was to be seen in that holy man Job. He says that "he was eyes to the blind, and feet to the lame, a father unto the poor, and when he knew not the cause, he sought it out" (Job 29:15–16). And St. Paul showed this fruit most notably after his conversion, for he says that "he was made all things to all men that he might save some" (1 Cor. 9:22). He was content to undergo anything for the good of

---

321. This paragraph break is not in the original.

any man. And as we have heard, the godly are trees of righteousness, bearing fruit not for themselves but for others; and therefore Paul in the epistle to the Galatians gives this rule, "Do service one to another in love." In these days, it is hard to find these duties performed in any place. For both practice and proverb is commonly this, "Every man for himself, and God for us all." But it is a graceless saying, and the contrary must be practiced of all that desire to be guided by the Spirit.

The seventh fruit is faith. Faith or fidelity stands in these two duties. One, to make conscience of a lie and to speak everything whereof we speak as we think it is, and not to speak one thing and think another. A rare thing it is to find this virtue in the world nowadays. Who is he that makes conscience of a lie? And is not truth banished out of our coasts, considering that for gains and outward commodities men make no bones of glozing[322] and dissembling? But alas, the practice is damnable, and the contrary is the fruit of the Holy Ghost—namely, to speak the truth from the heart. And he that can do this by the testimony of God Himself "shall rest in the mountain of his holiness" [Ps. 15:1–2], even in the kingdom of heaven. The second point wherein fidelity consists is when a man has made a promise that is lawful and good to keep and perform the same. Some think it is a small matter to break promise, but indeed it is a fruit of the flesh, and contrariwise a fruit of the Spirit to perform a lawful promise; and a man's word should be as sure as an obligation. And in conscience a man is bound to keep promise so far forth as he will to whom the promise is made. Indeed, if a man be released of his promise, he is then free. Otherwise, if we promise and do not perform, we do not only crack our credit before men, but also sin before God.

The eighth fruit of the Spirit is meekness, which is a notable grace of God, when a man provoked by injuries does neither intend nor enterprise the requital of the same. And it stands in three duties. The first is to interpret the sayings and doings of other men in better part, as much as possibly may be. The second, when men mistake and misconstrue our sayings and doings, if the matter be of smaller moment, to be silent and patient as Christ was when He was accused before the high priests and Pharisees—this being withal remembered, that if the matter be of weight and moment, we may defend ourselves by soft and mild answers. The third is not to contend in word or deed with any man, but when we are to deal with others to speak our mind and so an end.

The last fruit of the Spirit is temperance, whereby a man bridles his appetite or lust in meat, drink, and apparel. In bridling the lusts, these rules must be observed. (1) Eating and drinking must be joined with continual fasting, after

---

322. *Glozing*: flattering.

this manner: we must not glut ourselves but rather abstain from that which nature desires and, as some use to speak, leave our stomachs craving. (2) A man must so eat and drink as afterward he may the better be enabled for God's worship. Creatures are abused when they make us unfit to serve God. The common fault is on the Sabbath Day men so pamper themselves as that they are made unfit both to hear and learn God's Word and fit for nothing but to slumber and sleep. But, following this rule of temperance, these faults shall be amended. (3) This must be a caveat in our apparel, that we be attired according to our callings in holy comeliness. The Lord has threatened to "visit all those that are clothed in strange apparel" (Zeph. 1:8). And holy comeliness is this: when the apparel is both for fashion and matter so made and worn that it may express and show forth the graces of God in the heart, as sobriety, temperance, gravity, etc., and the beholder may take occasion by the apparel to acknowledge and commend these virtues [Titus 2:3]. But lamentable is the time. Look on men and women in these days, and you may see and read their sins written in great letters on their apparel, as intemperance, pride, and wantonness. Every day new fashions please the world; but indeed that "holy comeliness," which the Holy Ghost does commend to us, is the right fashion when all is done. And these are the nine fruits of the Spirit, which we must put in practice in our lives and conversations.

Fourthly, if we believe in the Holy Ghost and thereupon do persuade ourselves that He will dwell in us, we must daily labor as we are commanded "to keep our vessels in holiness and honor unto the Lord" (1 Thess. 4:4); and the reason is good. If a man be to entertain but an earthly prince or some man of state, he would be sure to have his house in a readiness and all matters in order against his coming, so as everything might be pleasing unto so worthy a guest. Well now, behold, we put our confidence and affiance in the Holy Ghost and do believe that He will come unto us and sanctify us and lodge in our hearts. He is higher than all states in the world whatsoever, and therefore we must look that our bodies and souls be kept in an honorable and holy manner so as they may be fit temples for Him to dwell in. St. Paul bids us "not to grieve the Holy Spirit" (Eph. 4:30), where the Holy Ghost is compared to a guest, and our bodies and souls unto inns. And as men use their guests friendly and courteously, showing unto them all service and duty, so must we do to God's Spirit, which is come to dwell and abide in us, doing nothing in any case which may disquiet or molest Him. Now there is nothing so grievous unto Him as our sins; and therefore we must make conscience of all manner of sin, lest by abusing of ourselves we do cause the Holy Ghost (as it were) with grief to depart from us. When the "ark of the covenant," which was a sign of the presence of God, was in the house of Obed-edom, the text says that "the Lord blessed him and all his house" (2 Sam. 6:11). But when the Holy Ghost dwells in a man's heart, there is more than the ark of the Lord present—even God Himself—and therefore may we look for a greater blessing. Now then, shall we grieve the Holy Ghost by sinning, seeing we reap such benefit by His abode? It is said that our Savior Christ "was angry when he came into the temple at Jerusalem, and saw the abuses therein" (John 2:15). Now shall He be angry for the abuses that are done in a temple of stone and, seeing the temples of our bodies, which are not made of stone, but are spiritual, figured by that earthly temple—seeing them (I say) abused by sin, will He not be much more angry? Yea, we may assure ourselves He cannot abide that. And therefore, if we believe in the Holy Ghost, we must hereupon be moved to keep our bodies and souls pure and clean. And further to persuade us hereunto, we must remember this, that when we pollute our souls and bodies with any manner of sin, we make them even stables and [pig] sties for our wretched enemy, the devil, to harbor in. For when Satan is once cast out, if afterward we fall again to our old sins and looseness of life and so defile our bodies, they are then most clean and neat for him to dwell in, whereupon he will come and bring seven other devils worse than himself; and so a man's last end shall be worse than his beginning. Now, what a fearful thing is this, that the body, which should be a temple for the Holy Ghost, by our sins be made a stable for the devil! Furthermore, St. Paul bids us not to "quench the spirit" [1 Thess. 5:19]. The graces of the Holy Spirit in this life are like sparks of fire, which may soon be quenched with a little water. Now so oft as we sin, we cast water upon the grace of God and as much as we can put out the same. Therefore, it stands us in hand to make conscience of everything wherein we may offend and displease God. And we may assure ourselves that so long as we live and lie in our corruptions and sins, the Holy Ghost will never come and dwell with us. He is a spirit most pure and chaste and therefore must have an undefiled temple to dwell in.

Thus, we have heard what is to be believed concerning the Father, Son, and Holy Ghost. Now, look as we believe in God, distinguished into three persons, so we must remember that when we perform divine worship to Him, we may distinguish the persons, but we are not to sever them. When we pray to the Father, we must not omit the Son or the Holy Ghost, but make our prayers to them all; for as in nature they are one and in person not divided but distinguished, so in all worship we must never confound or sever the persons but distinguish them and worship the Trinity in unity and unity in Trinity—one God in three persons, and three persons in one God.

Hitherto we have entreated of the first part of the Creed concerning God. Now follows the second part thereof concerning the church. And it was added to the former upon special consideration. For the right order of a confession did require[323] that after the Trinity the church should be mentioned, as the house after the owner, the temple after God, and the city after the builder. Again, the Creed is concluded with points of doctrine concerning the church, because whosoever is out of it is also forth of the number of God's children. And he cannot have God for his Father which has not the church for his mother.[324]

Question is made what the words are which are to be supplied in this article, "the holy catholic church"—whether, "I believe," or, "I believe in." And ancient expositors have sufficiently determined the matter. One says, "In these words in which is set forth our faith of the Godhead, it is said, 'In God the Father, in the Son, and in the Holy Ghost.' But in the rest, where the speech is not of the Godhead but of creatures and mysteries, the preposition (in) is not added that it should be, 'in the holy church,' but that we should believe there is a holy church, not as God, but as a company gathered to God. And men should believe that there is remission of sins, not, 'in the remission of sins.' And they should believe the resurrection of the body, not, 'in the resurrection of the body.' Therefore by this preposition the Creator is distinguished from the creatures, and things pertaining to God from things pertaining to men."[325] Another upon these words, "This is the work of God that you believe in Him," says, "If you believe in Him, you believe Him. Not if you believe Him, you believe in Him; for the devils believed God, but did not believe in Him. Again of the apostles, we may say we believe Paul, but we do not believe in Paul; we believe Peter, but we believe not in Peter. For his faith that believes in Him which justifies the ungodly is imputed to him for righteousness."[326]

What is it therefore to believe in Him? By believing, to love and like and as it were to pass into Him and to be incorporated into His members." Now the reasons which some Papists bring to the contrary to prove that we may believe in the creatures and in the church are of no moment. First, they allege the phrase of Scripture: "They believed in God, and in Moses" (Ex. 14:31); "And Achish believed in David" (1 Sam. 27:12); "Believe in the prophets and prosper" (2 Chron. 20:20). *Answer.* The Hebrew phrase in which the servile letter beth is used must not be translated with a preposition that rules an accusative or ablative case, but with a dative on this manner, "Believe Moses, David, the prophets." And it does not import any affiance in the creature, but only a giving of credence one man to another. Secondly, they allege that ancient fathers read the article on this manner, "I believe in the holy catholic church."[327] *Answer.*

---

323. August. in enchir. cap. 59.
324. August. l. 4. cap. 10. de symb. ad Catec.
325. Ruffin. in symb.
326. August. tract. 29. in Job.
327. Epiphan. in Anchor.

Indeed, some have done so; but by this kind of speech they signified no more but this much, that they believed that there was a catholic church.

Thus, having found what words are to be supplied, let us come to the meaning of the article. And that we may proceed in order, let us first of all see what the church is. The church is a peculiar company of men predestinated to life everlasting and made one in Christ. First, I say it is a peculiar company of men, for St. Peter says, "Ye are a chosen generation, a royal priesthood, an holy nation, and a peculiar people" [1 Peter 2:9]. He speaks indeed of the church of God on earth, but his saying may be also extended to the whole church of God, as well in heaven as in earth. Now, because there can be no company unless it have a beginning and cause whereby it is gathered, therefore I add further in the definition "predestinated to life everlasting," noting thereby the ground and cause of the catholic church—namely, God's eternal predestination to life everlasting. And to this purpose our Savior Christ says, "Fear not little flock, for it is your father's will to give you the kingdom" [Luke 12:32], signifying thereby that the first and principal cause of the church is the good pleasure of God, whereby He has before all worlds purposed to advance His elect to eternal salvation. Therefore, one says well, "Only the elect are the church of God."[328] And further, because no company can continue and abide forever unless the members thereof be joined and coupled together by some bond, therefore I add in the last place "made one with Christ." This union makes the church to be the church; and by it the members thereof, whether they be in heaven or in earth, are distinguished from all other companies whatsoever. Now, this conjunction between Christ and the church is avouched by St. Paul when he says, "Christ is the head to the body which is his church" [Col. 1:18], and when he ascribes the name of Christ not only to the person of the Son but to the church itself, as in the epistle to the Galatians, "To Abraham and to his seed were the promises made" [3:16]. He says not "and to his seeds," as speaking of many, but "and unto his seed," as speaking of one, which is Christ—that is, not the Redeemer alone, but also the church redeemed. For Christ as He is man is not the only seed of Abraham. And this definition of the church is almost in so many words set down in the Scriptures, in that it is called the "family of God" [Eph. 3:15], partly in heaven and partly in earth, named of Christ. And also it is called the "heavenly Jerusalem, the mother of us all" [Gal. 4:26] and "the celestial Jerusalem" and the "congregation of the firstborn" [Heb. 12:22–23]. Now, for the better understanding of the nature, estate, and parts of the church, two points among the rest must be considered: the efficient cause thereof, God's predestination; and the form, the mystical union.

328. Bernard in Cant.

In handling the doctrine of predestination, my meaning is only to stand on such points as are revealed in the Word and necessary, tending to edification. And, first, I will show what is the truth and, secondly, the contrary falsehood. In the truth, I consider four things: (1) what predestination is; (2) what is the order of it; (3) what be the parts of it; (4) what is the use.

Predestination may thus be defined: it is a part of the counsel of God whereby He has before all times purposed in Himself to show mercy on some men and to pass by others, showing His justice on them for the manifestation of the glory of His own name. First, I say it is a part of His counsel, because the counsel or decree of God universally extends itself to all things that are. And predestination is God's decree so far forth as it concerns the reasonable creatures, especially men. Now in every purpose or decree of God, three things must be considered: the beginning, the matter, the end.

The beginning is the will of God whereby He wills and appoints the estate of His creatures.[329] And it is the most absolute, supreme, and sovereign cause of all things that are, so far forth as they have being, having nothing either above itself or out of itself to be an impulsive cause to move or incline it. And to say otherwise is to make the will of God to be no will. Indeed, men's wills are moved and disposed by external causes out of themselves, borrowed from the things whereof deliberation is made, because they are to be ruled by equity and reason; and a man's bare will without reason is nothing. Now, God's will is not ruled by another rule of reason or justice, but itself is an absolute rule both of justice and reason. A thing is not first of all reasonable and just and then afterward willed by God, but it is first of all willed by God and thereupon becomes reasonable and just.

The matter of His purpose is a decreed manifestation of two of the most principal attributes of the Godhead, mercy and justice, and that with a limitation or restraint of mercy to some of the creatures and justice to some others, because it was His good will and pleasure. And we are not to imagine that this is a point of cruelty in God, for His very essence or nature is not justice alone or mercy alone, but justice and mercy both together. And therefore to purpose the declaration of them both upon His creatures over whom He is a sovereign lord, and that without other respects, upon His very will and pleasure is no point of injustice.

The supreme end of the counsel of God is the manifestation of His own glory partly in His mercy and partly in His justice. For in common equity, the end which He propounds unto Himself of all His doing must be answerable to His nature, which is majesty and glory and (as I have said) justice and mercy itself.

---

329. This paragraph break is not in the original, as the additional two following.

Romans 9 Opened[330]

And because Paul's disputation [in the] ninth chapter to the Romans gives light and sufficient confirmation to this which I now teach, I will stand a little to open and resolve the same. In the first verse to the sixth, he sets down his grief conceived for his brethren the Jews. And therewithal, that it might not be thought that he spoke of malice, he does only in close and obscure manner insinuate the rejection of that nation. This done, in the sixth verse he answers a secret objection which might be made, on this manner: if the Jews be rejected, then the "word of God is of none effect"—that is, then the covenant made with the forefathers is void. But the covenant cannot be void. Therefore, the Jews are not rejected. The assumption he takes for granted and denies the consequence of the proposition. And the ground of his denial is because there is a distinction between man and man, even among the Jews, whereby some are indeed in the covenant, some not. And this distinction is proved by three examples. The first, in this verse, that of the children of Jacob, the common parent of all the Jews, some are Israel—that is, truly in the covenant as Jacob was—and some are not Israel.

Now, it might be further objected that the Jews are not only the posterity of Jacob but the seed of Abraham in whom all nations of the earth are blessed, and therefore not to be rejected.[331] And to this Paul answers (v. 7), alleging a second example of the distinction between man and man out of the family of Abraham in which some were indeed sons, some were not. For the proof of this, first, he sets down the words of the text in Moses, "In Isaac shall thy seed be called"; and, secondly, makes an exposition of them with a collection on this manner: all they which are the sons of the promise are the seed of Abraham, or, the sons of God. But Isaac is a son of promise and not Ishmael. Therefore, Isaac is the seed of Abraham and heir of the blessing, and not Ishmael. The proposition is in the eighth verse; the assumption, in the ninth verse; the conclusion, in the seventh verse. Here mark (1) how he makes a double seed, one according to the flesh, the other spiritual; and two kinds of sons, one of the flesh, the other the son of the promise, or, the son of God—for he put the one for the other. (2) That the distinction between Isaac and Ishmael whereby one is in the covenant of grace, the other not, stands not in their foreseen faith and unbelief and the fruits of them, but in the purpose and will of God itself. For Isaac is called the child of promise, because by the virtue of it he was born and believed and was adopted the child of God and made heir of the covenant given to Abraham; and therefore consequently the right of adoption befell him by the mere good

---

330. Originally in the margin.
331. This paragraph break is not in the original, as the additional four following.

pleasure of God, which is the first cause of our salvation without respect of anything in the person of Isaac. For what God by His promise brings to pass in time, that He most freely decreed before all times.

Now, considering the Jews might say that Ishmael was rejected because he was born of the handmaid Hagar, whereas they for their parts descend of Abraham and Sarah by Isaac, the lawful son, Paul adds a third example of the distinction between man and man out of the family of Isaac, in which Jacob was a true son and heir of the promise, and Esau was not. Now, the distinction of these two persons is propounded in the tenth verse and confirmed in verses 11–13, in which are set down three things.

(1) The time of this distinction, "ere the children were born" and therefore "when they had neither done good nor evil." And this circumstance is noted to show that God was not moved by any prevision or preconsideration of Jacob's godliness and Esau's profaneness to prefer the one before the other.

(2) The end why the distinction was made at this time and not afterward when they were born is "that the purpose of God which is according to his election might remain sure, not of works, but by him that calleth"—that is, that by this means it might appear that when God receives any man into the covenant of eternal life, it proceeds not of any dignity in the man whom God calls, but from His mercy and alone good pleasure, that His decree of saving the elect might remain firm and sure forever. Hence it is manifest that there is an unchangeable decree of election of some men (for He that takes all and excepts none cannot be said to choose) to salvation, depending upon the alone will of God. And therefore necessarily, by the law of contraries, there is an opposite decree of reprobation; for in that God ordains some to eternal salvation, He testifies thereby that His purpose is to pass by some without showing of mercy.

(3) The author of this distinction is God Himself by His purpose before all times, which purpose He made manifest by testimony given to Rebekah, saying, "The elder shall serve the younger" [Gen. 25:23]—that is, the firstborn and more excellent according to the flesh shall lose his birthright and the blessing of his father and in respect of title to the covenant be subject to the younger. And because this testimony concerning the freedom and servitude of Jacob and Esau might seem insufficient to prove the election of the first and the rejection of the second, therefore Paul adds a second testimony out of Malachi, "I have loved Jacob, and hated Esau" [Mal. 1:2]—that is, "I have purposed to love Jacob and to hate Esau." And these words no doubt are alleged to expound the former place out of Moses and show that the bondage of Esau was joined with the hatred of God and the freedom of Jacob with the love of God as tokens hereof.

Against this received exposition of the former words which I have now propounded, sundry expositions are made. First, that the prerogative of Isaac above Ishmael and Jacob above Esau was only in temporary blessings in that God vouchsafed unto them the right of the land of Canaan. *Answer.* If these places are to be understood of temporal blessings and not spiritual, then the apostle has not fitly alleged the former examples to prove the rejection of the Jews from the covenant. For though it be granted there be a difference between man and man in respect of earthly blessings, yet does it not follow that there shall be the same difference in things concerning the kingdom of heaven. If a father for some cause disinherit one to two of his children, it were absurd thereupon to conclude that he might therefore kill any of the rest. Again, the land of Canaan was not only an earthly inheritance but also a pledge and figure unto our forefathers of a better inheritance in heaven. And therefore the excluding of Ishmael and Esau from the land of Canaan was a sign that they were excluded from the covenant of grace and the right of eternal life.

Some others say that by Jacob and Esau are not meant two persons, but the two nations of the Idumeans and the Israelites.[332] *Answer.* It is a manifest untruth. For it was not possible for two nations to strive in the womb of Rebekah, unless we considered them as they were comprehended under the two heads—to wit, the very persons of Jacob and Esau. And whereas they say that Esau in person never served Jacob, but only in his posterity, the answer is that Jacob's freedom and prerogatives were spiritual and not temporal, which by faith he saw afar off, but enjoyed not. And therefore proportionally Esau was debased to the condition of a servant in respect of his younger brother, not so much in respect of his outward estate and condition as in regard of the covenant made with his ancestors from which he was barred. And though it be granted that by Jacob and Esau two nations and not two persons are to be understood, yet all comes to one head; for the receiving of the nation of the Israelites into the covenant and the excluding of the nation of the Edomites, both descending of Jacob and Esau, serve as well to prove God's eternal election and reprobation, as the receiving and rejecting of one man.

Others say that these words, "I have hated Esau," are thus to be understood: "I have less loved Esau than Jacob." But how then shall we say that Paul has fitly alleged this text to prove the rejection of the Jews from the favor of God and the covenant of grace, considering that of men whereof one is loved more of God, the other less, both may still remain in the covenant.

Lastly, it is alleged that the former exposition makes Ishmael and Esau damned persons. *Answer.* We must leave unto God all secret judgment of particular persons; and yet, nevertheless, Paul does very fitly in their two persons, both descending of Abraham and both circumcised, set forth examples of such

---

332. This paragraph break is not in the original, as the additional two following.

as for all their outward prerogatives are indeed barred from the covenant of life everlasting before God. And again the opposition made by Paul requires that the contrary to that which is spoken of Isaac and Jacob should be said of Ishmael and Esau. And there is nothing spoken of either of them in the Scriptures which argues the disposition of men ordained to eternal life. Ishmael is noted with the brand of a mocker, and Esau of a profane man.

To proceed in the text, because the doctrine of Paul delivered in the former verses might seem strange unto the Romans, therefore in the fourteenth verse he lays down an objection and answers the same. The objection is this: if God put distinction between man and man without respect had to their persons upon His own will and pleasure, then is He unjust. But He is not unjust. Therefore, He makes no such distinction. The answer is, "God forbid." Whereby he denies the consequence of the proposition, on this manner: though God should elect some to salvation and reject some others, and that upon His will, yet were there no injustice with God. The reason of this answer follows in the eighteenth verse: God has absolute power or freedom of will, whereby without being bound to any creature He may and can, first of all, have mercy on whom He will and, secondly, harden whom He will. For the proof of the first, that God has mercy on whom He will, he lays down the testimony of Moses, "I will have mercy on whom I will show mercy, and I will have compassion on him on whom I will have compassion" (v. 15). And in verse 16, [he] makes his collection thence: "that it"—namely, the purpose of God according to election (v. 11)—"is not in him that willeth, or in him that runneth, but in God that showeth mercy." Whereby he teaches that the free election of God in order goes before all things that may in time befall man, and that therefore neither the intentions and endeavors of the mind nor the works of our life, which are the effects of election, can be the impulsive causes to move God to choose us to salvation. The second, that God hardens whom He will, is confirmed and made plain by the testimony of Scripture concerning Pharaoh (v. 17).

In the nineteenth verse, there follows another objection, arising out of the answer to the former, on this manner: if God will have some to be hardened and rejected, and His will cannot be resisted, then with no justice can He punish them that are necessarily subject to His decree. But God will have some to be hardened and rejected, and His will cannot be resisted. Therefore, (says the adversary) with no justice can He punish man that is necessarily subject to His decree. Here, mark that if there had been a universal election of all men, and if men had been elected or rejected according as God did foresee that they would believe or not believe, the occasion of this objection had been cut off.[333] But let us come to Paul's answer. In the twentieth verse, he takes the assumption for granted, that some are rejected because God will, and that the will—that is, the decree of God—cannot be resisted. And [he] only denies the coherence of the proposition, checking the malapert pride of the adversary and showing that the making of this wicked and blasphemous collection against the will of God is as if a man should sue God at the law and bring Him as it were to the bar and plead against Him as His equal, whereas indeed the creature is nothing to the Creator and is absolutely to submit itself to His will in all things. In verse 21, he proceeds to a second answer, showing that God's will is not to be blamed, because by His absolute sovereignty and the right of creation He has power to choose men or to reject or harden them. And where there is right and power to do a thing, the will of the doer is not to be blamed. Now that God has this right and power over His creature, it is proved by a comparison from the less to the greater, on this manner: the potter has power over the clay to make of the same lump one vessel to honor and another to dishonor. Therefore may God much more "make some vessels of mercy, and some vessels of wrath prepared to destruction." The first part of the comparison is verse 21; the second part, verses 22–23. And lest any man should think that God makes vessels of honor and dishonor without sufficient and just cause in Himself, as the potter may do, therefore he sets down ends of the will of God. He makes vessels of dishonor "to show his wrath" and to "make manifest his power." And again, He condemns no man till He have "suffered him with long patience." And He makes vessels of honor that He might "declare the riches of his glory" upon them. Hence it is manifest, first, that the end of predestination is the glory of God, which is to be made manifest partly in His justice and partly in His mercy. Secondly, that men are not elected or refused of God for their foreseen corruptions or virtues; for then Paul would not have said that God made vessels of dishonor, but that, being so already, He left them in their dishonor.

Thus from the sixth verse of this chapter to the twenty-fourth, Paul has described unto us the doctrine of God's eternal predestination, and that by the judgment of divines[334] in all ages.

The order of God's predestination is this: it is the property of the reasonable creatures to conceive one thing after another, whereas God conceives all things at once with one act of understanding; and all things both past and to come are present with Him. And therefore in His eternal counsel He decrees

---

333. A child might answer this objection, if men were elect and refused for their foreseen faith and unbelief.

334. Aug. de Prædest. sanct. Ad Paulinum ep. 79. Enchir. 98-99. ad Sixtum 105. ep. Hieron. Hedibiæ quo Bed. in Rom. and Aquinas, etc.

not one thing after another, but all things at once. Nevertheless, for our understanding's sake, we may distinguish the counsel of God concerning man into two acts or degrees. The first is the purpose of God Himself in which He determines what He will do and the end of all His doings, and that is to create all things, specially man for His own glory, partly by showing on some men His mercy and upon others His justice. The second is another purpose whereby He decrees the execution of the former and lays down means of accomplishing the end thereof. These two acts of the counsel of God are not to be severed in any wise nor confounded, but distinctly considered with some difference. For in the first, God decrees some men to honor by showing His mercy and love on them and some again to dishonor by showing His justice on them, and this man more than that, upon His will and pleasure—and there is no other cause hereof known to us. In the second, known and manifest causes are set down of the execution of the former decree. For no man is actually condemned, yea, God decrees to condemn no man but for his sins, and no man is actually saved but for the merit of Christ. Furthermore, this latter act of the counsel of God must be conceived of us in the second place and not in the first. For evermore the first thing to be intended is the end itself and then afterward the subordinate means and causes whereby the end is accomplished. Again, the second act of God's counsel contains two others, one which sets down the preparation of the means whereby God's predestination begins to come in execution. And they are two: the creation of man righteous after the image of God [and] the voluntary fall of Adam and withal the shutting up of all men under damnation. The other appoints the applying of the several means to the persons of men, that God's decree, which was set down before all times, may in time be fully accomplished, as shall afterward in particular appear.

Predestination has two parts: the decree of election [and] the decree of reprobation, or, no election. This division is plain by that which has been said out of the ninth chapter to the Romans, and it may be further confirmed by other testimonies. Of some it is said that the Lord "knows who are his" [2 Tim. 2:19]; and of some others Christ shall say in the day of judgment, "I never knew you" [Matt. 7:23]. In the Acts, it is said that as many of the Gentiles as were "ordained to life everlasting, believed" [13:48]. And Jude says of false prophets that they were "ordained to condemnation" [v. 4].

In handling of the decree of election, I will consider three things: (1) what election is; (2) the execution thereof; (3) the knowledge of particular election. For the first, God's election is a decree in which according to the good pleasure of His will He has certainly chosen some men to life eternal in Christ for the praise of the glory [of] His grace. This is the same which Paul says to the Ephesians, "God hath chosen us in Christ before the foundation of the world, that we should be holy and without blame before him in love: who hath predestinated us to be adopted through Jesus Christ unto himself, according to the good pleasure of his will" [Eph. 1:4–5]. Now, that we may the better conceive this doctrine, let us come to a consideration of the several points thereof.

First of all, I say election is God's decree.[335] For there is nothing in the world that comes to pass either universally or particularly without the eternal and unchangeable decree of God. And therefore, whereas men are actually chosen and brought to life everlasting, it is because God did purpose with Himself and decree the same before all worlds. Now, touching the decree itself, six things are to be observed.

The first, what was the motive or impulsive cause that moved God to decree the salvation of any man? *Answer.* The good pleasure of God. For Paul says, "He will have mercy on whom he will have mercy" [Rom. 9:18], and, "He hath predestinated us according to the good pleasure of God" [Eph. 1:5]. As for the opinion of them that say that foreseen faith and good works are the cause that moved God to choose men to salvation, it is frivolous. For faith and good works are the fruits and effects of God's election. Paul says, "He hath chosen us"—not because He did foresee that we would become holy, but—"that we might be holy" [v. 4]. And He "hath predestinated us to adoption," which is all one as if he had said He has predestinated us to believe because adoption comes by believing [John 1:12]. Now, if men are elected that they might believe, then are they not elected because they would believe. For it cannot be that one thing should be both the cause and the effect of another.

The second point is that God's election is unchangeable, so as they which are indeed chosen to salvation cannot perish but shall without fail attain to life everlasting. Paul takes it for a conclusion that "the purpose of God according to election must remain firm and sure" [Rom. 9:11]; and again, that "the gifts and calling of God are without repentance" [11:29]. And Samuel says, "The strength of Israel will not lie or repent: For he is not a man that he should repent" [1 Sam. 15:29]. Such as God's nature is, such is His will and counsel. But His nature is unchangeable. "I am Jehovah," says He, "and I change not" [Mal. 3:6]. Therefore, His will likewise and His counsels be unchangeable. And therefore wheresoever the Spirit of God shall testify unto our spirit that we are justified in Christ and chosen to salvation, it must be a means to comfort us and to establish our hearts in the love of God. As for the opinion of them that say the elect may fall from grace and be damned, it is full of hellish discomfort and no doubt from the devil. And the reasons commonly alleged for this purpose are of no moment, as may appear by the scanning of them.

---

335. This paragraph break is not in the original, as the additional one following.

First, they object that the churches of the Ephesians, Thessalonians, and the dispersed Jews are all called elect by the apostles themselves; yet sundry of them afterward fell away [Eph. 1:4; 1 Thess. 1:4; 1 Peter 1:1–2].[336] *Answer.* (1) There are two kinds of judgment to be given of men: the judgment of certainty and the judgment of charity. By the first indeed is given an infallible determination of any man's election; but it belongs unto God principally and properly and to men but in part—namely, so far forth as God shall reveal the estate of one man unto another. Now, the judgment of charity belongs unto all men; and by it, leaving all secret judgments unto God, we are charitably to think that all those that live in the church of God, professing themselves to be members of Christ, are indeed elect to salvation, till God make manifest otherwise. And on this manner and not otherwise do the apostles call whole churches elect. (2) They are called elect of the principal part and not because every member thereof was indeed elect—as it is called a heap of corn though the bigger part be chaff.

Secondly, it is alleged that David prays that his enemies "may be blotted out of the book of life" [Ps. 69:28], which is the election of God, and that Moses [Ex. 32:32] and Paul [Rom. 9:3] did the like against themselves. *Answer.* David's enemies had not their names written in the book of life, but only in the judgment of men. Thus, Judas so long as he was one of the disciples of Christ was accounted as one having his name written in heaven. Now, hence it follows that men's names are blotted out of God's book when it is made clear and manifest unto the world that they were never indeed written there. And where Moses says, "Forgive them this sin: if not, blot me out of thy book," and Paul, "I could wish to be accursed," etc. their meaning was not to signify that men elected to salvation might become reprobates; only they testify their zealous affections that they could be content to be deprived of their own salvation, rather than the whole body of the people should perish, and God lose His glory. As for that which Christ says, "Have I not chosen you twelve, and one of you is a devil?" [John 6:70], it is to be understood not of election to salvation but of election to the office of an apostle, which is temporary and changeable.

The third point is that there is an actual election made in time, being indeed a fruit of God's decree and answerable unto it. And therefore I added in the description these words, "whereby He has chosen some men." All men by nature are sinners and children of wrath, shut up under one and the same estate of condemnation. And actual election is when it pleases God to sever and single out some men above the rest out of this wretched estate of the wicked

---

336. This paragraph break is not in the original, as the additional one following.

world and to bring them to the kingdom of His own Son. Thus, Christ says of His own disciples, "I have chosen you out of the world" [15:19].

The fourth point is the actual or real foundation of God's election, and that is Christ. And therefore we are said to be chosen to salvation in Christ. He must be considered two ways. As He is God, we are predestinated "of him" [Eph. 1:4], even as we are predestinated of the Father and the Holy Ghost. As He is our Mediator, we are predestinated in Him. For when God with Himself had decreed to manifest His glory in saving some men by His mercy, He ordained further the creation of man in His own image, yet so as by his own fall he should enfold himself and all his posterity under damnation. This done, He also decreed that the Word should be incarnate actually to redeem these out of the former misery whom He had ordained to salvation. Christ therefore Himself was first of all predestinated as He was to be our Head and, as Peter says, "ordained before all worlds" [1 Peter 1:20],[337] and we secondly predestinated in Him, because God ordained that the execution of man's election should be in Him. Here, if any demand how we may be assured that Christ in His passion stood in our room and stead, the resolution will be easy, if we consider that He was ordained in the eternal counsel of God to be our surety and pledge and to be a public person to represent all the elect in His obedience and sufferings. And therefore it is that Peter says that He "was delivered by the foreknowledge and determinate counsel of God" [Acts 2:23]; and Paul, that "grace was given unto us through Christ Jesus before the world was" [2 Tim. 1:9].

The fifth point is concerning the number of the elect. And that I express in these words, "has chosen some men to salvation." If God should decree to communicate His glory and His mercy to all and every man, there could be no election; for he that takes all cannot be said to choose. Therefore, Christ says, "Many are called but few are chosen" [Matt. 22:14]. Some make this question: how great the number of the elect is? And the answer may be this, that the elect considered in themselves be innumerable, but considered in comparison to the whole world they are but few. Hence it follows necessarily that saving grace is not universal, but indefinite or particular, unless we will against common reason make the streams more large and plentiful than the very fountain itself. And this must excite us above all things in the world to labor to have fellowship with Christ and to be partakers of the special mercy of God in Him—yea, to have the same sealed up in our hearts. Benefits common to all, as the light of the sun, etc., are not regarded of any. Things common to few, though they be but temporal blessings, are sought for of all. God gives not riches to all men, but to some more, to some less, to some none. And hereupon how do men

---

337. Aug. de præd. sanct. c. 13.

like drudges toil in the world from day to day and from year to year to enrich themselves! Therefore, much more ought men to seek for grace in Christ, considering it is not common to all. We must not content ourselves to say God is merciful, but we must go further and labor for a certificate in the conscience that we may be able to say that God is indeed merciful to us. When the disciples would have known how many should be saved, He, omitting the question, answers thus, "Strive to enter in at the strait gate" [Luke 13:24].

The last point is the end of God's election, and that is "the manifestation of the praise and excellency of the glorious grace of God" (Eph. 1:6).

Thus having seen what election is, let us come to the execution thereof. Of which remember this rule: men predestinated to the end—that is, glory or eternal life—are also predestinated to the subordinate means, whereby they come to eternal life; and these are vocation, justification, sanctification, obedience. For the first, he that is predestinated to salvation is also predestinated to be called, as Paul says, "Whom he hath predestinated, them also he calls" (Rom. 8:30). Secondly, whom God calls, they also were predestinated to believe. Therefore, saving faith is called "the faith of the elect" (Titus 1:1). And in Acts 13:48, "As many as were ordained to life everlasting, believed." Thirdly, whom God has predestinated to life, them He justifies, as Paul says: whom He has "predestinated, them he calleth, and whom he calleth, them he justifieth" (Rom. 8:30). Fourthly, whom He has predestinated to life, them He has predestinated to sanctification and holiness of life, as Peter says that the Jews were elect according "to the foreknowledge of God the Father unto the sanctification of the spirit" (1 Peter 1:2). Lastly, they that are predestinated to life are also predestinated to obedience, as Paul says to the Ephesians, "We are the workmanship of God created in Christ Jesus unto good works, which God hath ordained that we should walk in them" (Eph. 2:10). This rule, being the truth of God, must be observed; for it has special use.

First of all, it serves to stop the mouths of ungodly and profane men.[338] They use to bolster up themselves in their sins by reasoning on this manner: "If I be predestinated to eternal life, I shall be saved whatsoever come of it, how wickedly and lewdly soever I live. I will therefore live as I list and follow the swing of mine own will." But alas, like blind bayards they think they are in the way, when as they rush their heads against the wall and far deceive themselves. For the case stands thus: all men that are ordained to salvation are likewise ordained in the counsel of God to use all the good means whereby they may come to salvation. And therefore all the elect that live in this world shall be called, justified, sanctified, and lead their lives in all good conscience before

---

338. This paragraph break is not in the original, as the additional one following.

God and men. And they that live and continue in their own wicked ways disputing on this manner, "If I be ordained to salvation, I shall not be damned," overshoot themselves and as much as they can plunge themselves headlong into the very pit of hell. And for a man to live and die in his sins, let the world dispute as they will, it is an infallible sign of one ordained to damnation.

Secondly, there be others that think that the preaching of the word, the administration of the sacraments, admonitions, exhortations, laws, good orders, and all such good means are needless, because God's counsels be unchangeable. If a man shall be condemned, nothing shall help; if a man shall be saved, nothing shall hinder. But we must still for our part remember that God does not only ordain the end but also the means whereby the end is compassed, and therefore the very use of all prescribed means is necessary. And for this cause we must be admonished with diligence to labor and use all good means, that we may be called by the ministry of the gospel and justified and sanctified and at length glorified. If a king should give unto one of his subjects a princely palace upon condition that he shall go unto it in the way which he shall prescribe, oh what pains would that man take to know the way and afterward to keep and continue in it. But behold, the kingdom of heaven is the most glorious and royal palace that ever was; and God has bestowed the same on His elect, and He requires nothing at their hands but that they would turn their faces from this world and walk unto it in the way which He has chalked forth unto them in His Word. Therefore, if we would have life everlasting, we must come forth of the broad way which leads to destruction and enter into the strait way that leads to eternal life. We must acquaint ourselves with the guides, which are the ministers of the word, that will cry unto us, "Here is the way, walk ye in it, when ye go to the right hand or to the left" (Isa. 30:21). Vocation, justification, sanctification, repentance, new obedience are the marks of the way, and we must pass by them all. And thus our weary souls, weltering awhile in this wretched world, shall at length be received into eternal joy and happiness.

Touching the knowledge of particular election, two special points are to be scanned: (1) whether a man may know his election; (2) how it may be known. For the first, Papists are of mind that no man can certainly know his own election unless he be certified thereof by some special revelation from God. But the thing is false and erroneous which they say. When the disciples of our Savior Christ returned from preaching and showed what wonders they had done and how devils were subject unto them, the text says they rejoiced greatly. But Christ answered them again, saying, "In this rejoice not, but rather rejoice that your names are written in heaven" (Luke 10:20), whereby He signifies that men may attain to a certain knowledge of their own election, for we cannot neither do we rejoice in things either unknown or uncertain. St. Peter says, "Give all diligence to make your election sure" (2 Peter 1:10). Now, in vain were it to use diligence if the assurance of election could not be any ways compassed without an extraordinary revelation. And Paul says to the Corinthians, "Prove yourselves whether ye be in the faith or not" (2 Cor. 13:5)—where he takes it for granted that he which has faith may know he has faith and therefore may also know his election, because saving faith is an infallible mark of election.

The second point is how any man may come to know his own election. And there be two ways of knowing it. The one is by ascending up as it were into heaven, there to search the counsel of God, and afterward to come down to ourselves. The second, by descending into our own hearts to go up from ourselves as it were by Jacob's ladder to God's eternal counsel. The first way is dangerous and not to be attempted, for the ways of God are unsearchable and past finding out. The second way alone is to be followed, which teaches us by signs and testimonies in ourselves to gather what was the eternal counsel of God concerning our salvation. And these testimonies are two: the testimony of God's Spirit and the testimony of our spirits—as Paul says, "The spirit of God beareth witness together with our spirits, that we are the sons of God" (Rom. 8:16).

Touching the testimony of God's Spirit, two questions may be demanded. The first is by what means the Spirit of God gives a particular testimony in a man's conscience of his adoption. *Answer.* It is not done by any extraordinary revelation or enthusiasm—that is, an ordinary revelation without the Word—but by an application of the promises of the gospel in the form of a practical syllogism, on this manner: whosoever believes in Christ is chosen to life everlasting. This proposition is set down in the Word of God, and this further propounded, opened, and applied to all that be in the church of God by the ministers of the gospel set apart for this end. Now, while the hearers of God's word give themselves to meditate and consider of the same promise, [there] comes the Spirit of God and enlightens the eyes and opens the heart and gives them power both to will to believe and to believe indeed, so as a man shall with freedom of spirit make an assumption and say, "But I believe in Christ. I renounce myself. All my joy and comfort is in Him." Flesh and blood cannot say this; it is the operation of the Holy Ghost. And hence arises the blessed conclusion, which is the testimony of the Spirit: "Therefore, I am the child of God."

The second question is how a man may discern between the illusion of the devil and the testimony of the Spirit. For as there is a certain persuasion of God's favor from God's Spirit, so there be sleights and frauds of the devil whereby he flatters and soothes men in their sins. And there is in all men natural presumption in show like faith, indeed, no faith. And this counterfeit, mock faith is far more common in the world than true faith is. Take a view hereof in our ignorant and careless people. Ask any one of them whether he be certain of his salvation or no. He will without bones-making protest that he is fully persuaded and assured of his salvation in Christ; that if there be but one man in a country to be saved it is he; that he has served God always and done no man hurt; that he has evermore believed; and that he would not for all the world so much as doubt of his salvation. These and such like presumptuous conceits in blind and ignorant persons run for current faith in the world. Now, the true testimony of the Spirit is discerned from natural presumption and all illusions of the devil by two effects and fruits thereof, noted by Paul in that he says that the Spirit makes us cry, "Abba"—that is, "Father" (Rom. 8:16, 26). The first is to pray so earnestly with groans and sighs as though a man would even fill heaven and earth with the cry not of his lips, but of his heart, touched with sense and feeling of his manifold sins and offences. And this indeed is a special and principal note of the spirit of adoption. Now, look upon the loose and careless man that thinks himself so filled with the persuasion of the love and favor of God, you shall find that he very seldom or never prays. And when he does, it is nothing else but a mumbling over the Lord's Prayer, the Creed, and the Ten Commandments for fashion's sake—which argues plainly that the persuasion which he has of God's mercy is of the flesh and not of the Spirit. The second fruit is the affection of a dutiful child to God, a most loving father; and this affection makes a man stand in fear of the majesty of God, wheresoever he is, and to make conscience of every evil way. Now, those that are carried away with presumption, so soon as any occasion is given, they fall straight into sin without mislike or stay, as fire burns with speed when dry wood is laid unto it. In a word, where the testimony of the Spirit is truly wrought, there be many other graces of the Spirit joined therewith, as when one branch in a tree buds, the rest bud also.

The testimony of our spirit is the testimony of the heart and conscience, purified and sanctified in the blood of Christ. And it testifies two ways: by inward tokens in itself; by outward fruits. Inward tokens are certain special graces of God imprinted in the spirit, whereby a man may certainly be assured of his adoption. These tokens are of two sorts. They either respect our sins or God's mercy in Christ. The first are in respect of sins past, present, or to come.

The sign in the spirit which concerns sins past is "godly sorrow" (2 Cor. 7:10), which I may term a beginning and mother-grace of many other gifts and graces of God.[339] It is a kind of grief conceived in [the] heart in respect of God. And the nature of it may the better be conceived if we compare it with the contrary. Worldly sorrow springs of sin, and it is nothing else but the horror of conscience and the apprehension of the wrath of God for the same. Now godly

---

339. This paragraph break is not in the original.

sorrow, it may indeed be occasioned by our sins, but it springs properly from the apprehension of the grace and goodness of God. Worldly sorrow is a grief for sin only in respect of the punishment. Godly sorrow is a lively touch and grief of heart for sin because it is sin, though there were no punishment for it. Now, that no man may deceive himself in judging of this sorrow, the Holy Ghost has set down seven fruits or signs thereof whereby it may be discerned (v. 11). The first is care to leave all our sins. The second is apology, whereby a man is moved and carried to accuse and condemn himself for his sins past, both before God and man. The third is indignation, whereby a man is exceedingly angry with himself for his offences. The fourth is fear, lest he fall into his former sins again. The fifth is desire, whereby he craves strength and assistance that his sins take no hold on him as before. The sixth is zeal in the performance of all good duties contrary to his special sins. The seventh is revenge, whereby he subdues his body, lest it should hereafter be an instrument of sin as it has been in former time. Now when any man shall feel these fruits in himself, he has no doubt the godly sorrow which here we speak of.

The token which is in regard of sins present is the combat between the flesh and the Spirit (Gal. 5:17), proper to them that are regenerate, who are partly flesh and partly spirit. It is not the check of conscience which all men find in themselves both good and bad, so oft as they offend God; but it is a fighting and striving of the mind, will, and affections with themselves, whereby so far forth as they are renewed, they carry the man one way, and as they still remain corrupt, they carry him flat contrary. Men having the disease called "ephialtes" when they are half asleep feel as it were some weighty thing lying upon their breasts and holding them down. Now, lying in this case, they strive with their hands and feet and with all the might they have to raise up themselves and to remove the weight and cannot. Behold here a lively resemblance of this combat. The flesh, which is the inborn corruption of man's nature, lies upon the hearts of the children of God and presses them down, as if it were the very weight of a mountain. Now they according to the measure of grace received strive to raise up themselves from under this burden and to do such things as are acceptable to God, but cannot as they would.

The token that respects sin to come is care to prevent it. That this is the mark of God's children appears by the saying of John, "He that is born of God sins not, but keeps himself, that the wicked one touch him not" (1 John 5:18). And this care shows itself not only in ordering the outward actions, but even in the very thoughts of the heart. For where the gospel is of force, it brings "every thought into captivity to the obedience of Christ" (2 Cor. 10:5), and the apostle's rule is followed: "whatsoever things are true, whatsoever things are honest, etc., think on these things" (Phil. 4:8).

The tokens which concern God's mercy are specially two. The first is when a man feels himself distressed with the burden of his sins, or when he apprehends the heavy displeasure of God in his conscience for them, then further to feel how he stands in need of Christ and withal heartily desire, yea, to hunger and thirst after reconciliation with God in the merit of Christ, and that above all other things in the world. To all such, Christ has made most sweet and comfortable promises, which can appertain to none but to the elect. "If any man thirst, let him come to me and drink: he that believeth in me" [John 7:37], as says the Scripture, "out of his belly shall flow rivers of water of life." "I will give unto him which is athirst, of the well of the water of life freely" (Rev. 21:6). Now if he that thirsts drink of these waters, mark what follows, "Whosoever drinketh of the water that I shall give him, shall never be more athirst: but the water that I shall give him, shall be in him a well of water springing up unto everlasting life" (John 4:14).

The second is a strange affection wrought in the heart by the Spirit of God, whereby a man does so esteem and value and as it were set so high a price on Christ and His righteousness that he accounts even the most precious things that are to be but as dung in regard thereof. This affection was in Paul, and it is expressed in the parable in which after a man has found a treasure he first hides it and then sells all he has and makes a purchase of the field where it is [Matt. 13:43]. Now, every man will say of himself that he is thus affected to Christ and that he more highly esteems the least drop of His blood than all things in the world besides, whereas indeed most men are of Esau's mind—rather desiring the red broth than Isaac's blessing—and of the same affection with the Israelites, which liked better the onions and fleshpots of Egypt than the blessings of God in the land of promise. Therefore, that no man may deceive himself, this affection may be discerned by two signs.

The first is to love and like a Christian man because he is a Christian.[340] For he that does aright esteem of Christ does in like manner esteem of the members of Christ. And of this very point our Savior Christ says, "He that receiveth a prophet in the name of a prophet, shall receive a prophet's reward; and he that receives a righteous man in the name of a righteous man, shall receive the reward of a righteous man" [10:41]. And St. John says, "Hereby we know that we are translated from death to life, because we love the brethren" [1 John 3:14]—that is, such as are members even because they are so.

The second sign of this affection is a love and desire to the coming of Christ, whether it be by death unto any man particularly or by the last judgment universally, and that for this end, that there may be a full participation of

---

340. This paragraph break is not in the original, as the additional one following.

fellowship with Christ. And that this very love is a note of adoption, it appears by that which St. Paul says, that "the crown of righteousness is laid up for all them that love the appearing of Christ" (2 Tim. 4:8).

The outward token of adoption is new obedience, whereby a man endeavors to obey God's commandments in his life and conversation, as St. John says, "Hereby we are sure that we know him, if we keep his commandments" (1 John 2:3). Now, this obedience must not be judged by the rigor of the moral law, for then it should be no token of grace but rather a means of damnation. But it must be esteemed and considered as it is in the acceptation of God, "who spares them that fear him, as a father spares an obedient son" (Mal. 3:17), esteeming things done not by the effect and absolute doing of them, but by the affection of the doer.[341] And yet lest any man should here be deceived, we must know that the obedience, which is an infallible mark of the child of God, must be thus qualified.

First of all, it must not be done unto some few of God's commandments, but unto them all without exception.[342] Herod heard John [the] Baptist willingly and did many things (Mark 6:20); and Judas had excellent things in him, as appears by this, that he was content to leave all and to follow Christ, and he preached the gospel of God's kingdom in Jewry as well as the rest. Yet alas, all this was nothing; for the one could not abide to become obedient to the seventh commandment in leaving his brother Philip's wife, and the other would not leave his covetousness to die for it. Upright and sincere obedience does enlarge itself to all the commandments, as David says, "I shall not be confounded, when I have respect to all thy commandments" (Ps. 119:6). And St. James says, "He which faileth in one law is guilty of all" (James 2:10)—that is, the obedience to many commandments is indeed before God no obedience, but a flat sin, if a man wittingly and willingly carry a purpose to omit any one duty of the law. He that repents of one sin truly does repent of all; and he that lives but in one known sin without repentance, though he pretend never so much reformation of life, indeed repents of no sin.

Secondly, this obedience must extend itself to the whole course of a man's life after his conversion and repentance. We must not judge of a man by an action or two, but by the tenor of his life. Such as the course of a man's life is, such is the man. Though he through the corruption of his nature fail in this or that particular action, yet does it not prejudice his estate before God, so be it he renew his repentance for his several slips and falls, not lying in any sin, and withal from year to year walk unblamable before God and men. St. Paul

---

341. Si quod vis non potes, Deus factum computat. Aug.
342. This paragraph break is not in the original, as the additional two following.

says, "The foundation of God remaineth sure: the Lord knoweth who are his" (2 Tim. 2:19). Now, some might hereupon say, "It is true indeed, God knows who are His. But how may I be assured in myself that I am His?" To this demand, as I take it, Paul answers in the next words: "Let every one that calleth on the name of the Lord depart from iniquity"—that is, let men invocate the name of God, praying seriously for things whereof they stand in need, withal giving thanks and departing from all their former sins; and this shall be unto them an infallible token that they are in the election of God.

Thirdly, in outward obedience is required that it proceed from the whole man (1 Thess. 3:13), as regeneration, which is the cause of it, is through the whole man in body, soul, and spirit. Again, obedience is the fruit of love, and love is from a pure heart, a good conscience, and faith unfeigned.

Thus, we have heard the testimonies and tokens whereby a man may be certified in his conscience that he was chosen to salvation before all worlds. If any desire further resolution in this point, let them meditate upon Psalm 15 and 1 John, being parcels of Scripture penned by the Holy Ghost for this end.

Here some will demand how a man may be assured of his adoption, if he want the testimony of the Spirit to certify him thereof. *Answer.* Fire is known to be no painted but a true fire by two notes: by heat and by the flame. Now, if the case fall out that the fire want a flame, it is still known to be fire by the heat. In like manner, as I have said, there be two witnesses of our adoption: God's Spirit and our spirit. Now, if it fall out that a man feel not the principal, which is the Spirit of adoption, he must then have recourse to the second witness and search out in himself the signs and tokens of the sanctification of his own spirit, by which he may certainly assure himself of his adoption, as we know fire to be fire by the heat, though it want a flame.

Again, it may be demanded on this manner, how if it come to pass that after inquiry we find but few signs of sanctification in ourselves. *Answer.* In this case, we are to have recourse to the least measure of grace, less than which, there is no saving grace; and it stands in two things: a hearty disliking of our sins because they are sins, and a desire of reconciliation with God in Christ for them all. And these are tokens of adoption, if they be soundly wrought in the heart, though all other tokens for the present seem to be wanting. If any shall say that a wicked man has this desire, as Balaam, who desired to die the death of the righteous, the answer is that Balaam indeed desired to die as the righteous man does, but he could not abide to live as the righteous. He desired the end but not the proper subordinate means which tend unto the end, as vocation, justification, sanctification, repentance, etc. The first is the work of nature; the second is the work of grace. Now, I speak not this to make men secure and to content themselves with these small beginnings of grace, but only to show

how any may assure themselves that they are at the least babes in Christ, adding this withal, that they which have no more but these small beginnings must be careful to increase them, because he which goes not forward, goes backward.

Lastly, it may be demanded what a man should do if he want both the testimony of God's Spirit and his own spirit and have no means in the world of assurance? *Answer.* He must not utterly despair, but be resolved of this, that though he want assurance now, yet he may obtain the same hereafter. And such must be advertised to hear the word of God preached and, being outwardly of the church, to receive the sacraments. When we have care to come into the Lord's vineyard and to converse about the winepress, we shall find the sweet juice of heavenly grace pressed forth unto us plentifully by the word and sacraments to the comfort of our consciences concerning God's election. This one mercy, that God by these means in some part reveals His mercy, is unspeakable. When sickness or the day of death comes, the dearest servants of God, it may be, must encounter with the temptations of the devil and wrestle in conscience with the wrath and displeasure of God, as for life and death. And no man knows how terrible these things are, but those which have felt them. Now, when men walk thus through the valley of the shadow of death, unless God should as it were open heaven and stream down unto us in this world some lightsome beams of His love in Christ by the operation of His Spirit, miserable were the case even of the righteous.

Thus much of election. Now follows reprobation, in handling whereof we are to observe three things: (1) what it is; (2) how God does execute this decree; (3) how a man may judge of the same.

For the first, reprobation is God's decree in which because it so pleased Him He has purposed to refuse some men by means of Adam's fall and their own corruptions for the manifestation of His justice. First, I say it is a decree, and that is evident thus: if there be an eternal decree of God whereby He chooses some men, then there must needs be another whereby He does pass by others and refuse them. For election always implies a refusal. Again, what God does in time, that He decreed to do before time—as the case falls out even with men of mean wisdom, who first of all intend with themselves the things to be done and after do them. But God in time refuses some men, as the Scripture testifies, and it appears to be true by the event. Therefore, God before all worlds decreed the rejecting of some men.

Now, in this decree four points are to be considered. The first is the matter or object thereof, which is the thing decreed—namely, the rejection of some men in respect of mercy, or, the manifestation of His justice upon them. This may seem strange to man's reason, but here we must with all submission strike our topsails, for the Word of God says as much in plain terms. The apostle

Jude, speaking of false prophets, says that "they were of old ordained to this damnation" (v. 4). And Paul says in emphatical terms that "God makes vessels of wrath prepared to destruction" (Rom. 9:22), and some "are rejected" [2 Cor. 4:3; 2 Thess. 2:9, 13], whom he opposes to them which are elected to salvation.

The second point is the impulsive cause that moved God to set down this decree concerning His creature, and that was nothing out of Himself but His very will and pleasure. He hardened Pharaoh with final hardness of heart, because He would. And therefore He decreed to do so because He would. And our Savior Christ says, "I thank thee, O Father, Lord of heaven and earth, because thou hast hid these things from the wise and men of understanding, and hast opened them unto babes" [Matt. 11:25]. But upon what cause did God so? It follows in the next words, "It is so, O Father, because thy good pleasure is such" (v. 26). And if it be in the power and liberty of a man to kill an ox or a sheep for his use, to hunt and kill the hare and partridge for his pleasure, then much more without injustice may it be in the will and liberty of the Creator to refuse and forsake His creature for His glory. Nay, it stands more with equity a thousandfold that all the creatures in heaven and earth should jointly serve to set forth the glory and majesty of God the Creator in their eternal destruction, than the striking of a fly or the killing of a flea should serve for the dignity of all men in the world. For all this, it is thought by very many to be very hard to ascribe unto God, who is full of bounty and mercy, such a decree, and that upon His very will. But let us see their reasons.

First of all, they say it is a point of cruelty with God to purpose to create a great part of the world to damnation in hellfire.[343] The answer is that by the virtue of this decree God cannot be said to create any to damnation, but to the manifestation of His justice and glory in His due and deserved damnation; and the doing of this is absolute justice.

Secondly, it is alleged that by this means God shall hate His own creature, and that before it is. But it is an untruth. We must distinguish between God's purpose to hate and actual hating. Now, indeed God before all worlds did purpose to hate some creatures, and that justly so far forth as His hating of them will serve for the manifestation of His justice. But He neither hates them indeed nor loves them before they are, and therefore actual hatred comes not in till after the creation. Whom God has decreed to love, them, when they are once created, He begins to love in Christ with actual love. And whom He has decreed to hate, them, being once created, He hates in Adam with actual hatred.

Thirdly, it is objected that by this doctrine God shall be the author of sin, for he which ordains to the end ordains to the means of the end. But God

---

343. This paragraph is not in the original, as the additional two following.

ordains men to the end—that is, damnation. Therefore, He ordains them to the means thereof—that is, sin. *Answer.* The proposition, being thus understood, "He which ordains a man to an end in the same order and manner ordains him to the means," is false. For one may be ordained to the end simply, the end being simply good, and yet not be simply ordained to the means, because they may be evil in themselves and only good in part—namely, so far forth as they have respect of goodness in the mind of the ordainer. Secondly, the assumption is false; for the supreme end of God's counsel is not damnation but the declaration of His justice in the just destruction of the creature. Neither does God decree man's damnation as it is damnation—that is, the ruin of man and the putting of him forth to perishment—but as it is a real execution of justice. Thirdly, we must make distinction between sin itself and the permission thereof, and between the decree of rejection and actual damnation. Now the permission of sin and not sin itself properly is the subordinate means of the decree of rejection. For when God had decreed to pass by some men, He withal decreed the permission of sin, to which permission men were ordained; and sin itself is no effect, but only the consequent of the decree, yet so as it is not only the antecedent but also the efficient and meritorious cause of actual damnation.

The third point is the real foundation of the execution of this decree in just condemnation, and that is the voluntary fall of Adam and of all his posterity in him, with the fruit thereof, the general corruption of man's nature. For howsoever God has purposed to refuse men because it so pleased Him, yet when His purpose comes to execution, He condemns no man but for His sins. And sin, though it were not in the counsel of God an impulsive cause that moved Him to purpose a declaration of justice and judgment, yet was it a subordinate means of damnation, God in wonderful wisdom ordering and disposing the execution of this decree, so as the whole blame and fault of man's destruction should be in himself. And therefore the Lord in the prophet Hosea says, "One hath destroyed thee, but I will help thee" (13:9)—that is, salvation is of God, and the condemnation of men is from themselves. Now whereas many, depraving our doctrine, say that we ascribe unto God an absolute decree in which He does absolutely ordain men to damnation, they may here be answered. If by "absolute" they understand that which is opposed to conditional, then we hold and avouch that all the eternal decrees of God are simple or absolute and not limited or restrained to this or that condition or respect. If by "absolute" they understand a bare and naked decree without reason or cause, then we deny God's decree to be absolute. For though the causes thereof be not known to us, yet causes there be known to Him, and just they are. Yea, the very will of God itself is cause sufficient, it being the absolute rule of justice. And though men in reason cannot discern the equity and justice of God's will in this point, yet may we not thereupon conclude that therefore it is unjust. The sun may shine clearly, though the blind man see it not. And it is a flat mistaking to imagine that a thing must first of all be just in itself, and then afterward be willed of God. Whereas contrariwise, God must first will a thing before it can be just. The will of God does not depend upon the quality and nature of the thing, but the qualities of things in order of causes follow the will of God. For everything is as God wills it. Lastly, if it be called an absolute decree because it is done without all respect to man's sin, then we still deny it to be absolute. For as God condemns man for sin, so He decreed to condemn him for and by his sin. Yet so as if the question be made, what is the cause why He decrees rather in His justice to condemn this man than that man, no other reason can be rendered but His will.

The last point is the end of God's decree—namely, the manifestation of His justice, as Solomon says, "The Lord hath made things for his own sake, and the wicked for the day of evil" [Prov. 16:4]. And Paul says that God made vessels of wrath "to shew his wrath, and to make his power known" [Rom. 9:22].

Thus, we have seen what reprobation is. Now follows the execution thereof; for that which God decrees before time, in time He executes. And here a special rule to be remembered is this: those which are ordained to just damnation are likewise ordained to be left to themselves in this world in blindness of mind and hardness of heart, so as they neither shall nor will repent of their sins. The truth of this we may see in God's Word. For St. Peter, speaking of the priests and doctors and chief of the people among the Jews, says plainly, "They stumbled at the word, and were disobedient." Why so? The reason is there set down: "because they were ordained to it of old." And so Paul says to the Corinthians that he handled not the Word of God deceitfully, but in the declaration of the truth he approved himself to every man's conscience in the sight of God. Now hereupon it may be said, how then comes it to pass that all receive not the gospel in Corinth? And to this he answers with a terrible sentence: "If," says he, "our gospel be hid, it is hid to them that perish" (2 Cor. 4:3), giving us to understand that God leaves them to themselves in this world whom He purposes to refuse. And the Lord by the prophet Isaiah says of the Jews, "By hearing they shall hear and not understand, and by seeing they shall see and not perceive, lest they should hear with their ears, and see with their eyes, and understand with their hearts, and so turn and be saved" (Isa. 6:9).

The use of this is manifold. First, it serves to overthrow the opinion of carnal men, which reason thus: "If I be ordained to damnation, let me live never so godly and well, I am sure to be damned. Therefore, I will live as I list, for it is not possible for me to alter God's decree." Blasphemous mouths of men make nothing of this and like speeches, and yet they speak flat contraries. For whom God has purposed in His eternal counsel to refuse, them also He has purposed for their sins to leave to the blindness of their minds and hardness of their hearts, so as they neither will nor can live a godly life.

Secondly, this rule does as it were lead us by the hand to the consideration of the fearful estate of many people among us.[344] We have had for the space of thirty years and more the preaching of the gospel of Christ and the more plentifully by reason of the schools of learning. But what has been the issue of it? I doubt not but in many it has been the means of their conversion and salvation. But to speak generally of the greater part, there is little or no fruit to be seen. The most after this long preaching remain as blind, as impenitent, as hardhearted, and as unreformed in their lives as ever they were, though they have heard the Lord calling them to repentance from day to day and from year to year. Well, if this rule be the truth of God, as no doubt it is, then I say plainly that there is a most fearful judgment of God among us. My meaning is not to determine or give sentence of any man's person, of any town, or people, nevertheless this may be avouched, that it is a terrible and dangerous sign of the wrath of God that after this long and daily preaching there is still remaining a general hardness of heart, impenitency, and want of reformation in the lives of men. The smith's stithy, the more it is beaten, the harder it is made; and commonly the hearts of men, the more they are beaten with the hammer of God's word, the more dull, secure, and senseless they are. This being so, it stands every man in hand to look to his own estate. We are careful to fly the infection of the bodily plague. Oh then! How careful should we be to fly the common blindness and hardness of heart which is the very plague of all plagues, a thousandfold worse than all the plagues of Egypt? And it is so much the more fearful, because the more it takes place, the less it is perceived. When a malefactor on the day of assize is brought forth of the jail with great bolts and fetters to come before the judge, as he is going all men pity him and speak comfortably unto him. But why so? Because he is now to be arraigned at the bar of an earthly judge. Now, the case of all impenitent sinners is far more miserable than the case of this man; for they lie fettered in bondage under sin and Satan, and this short life is the way in which they are going every hour to the bar of God's justice, who is the King of kings and Lord of lords, there to be arraigned and to have sentence of condemnation given against them. Now can you pity a man that is before an earthly judge, and will you not be touched with the misery of your own estate, who goes every day to the bar of God's justice, whether you be sleeping or waking, sitting or standing, as a man on the sea in a ship goes continually toward the haven, though he stir not his foot? Begin now at length to lay this point to

---

344. This paragraph break is not in the original, as the additional one following.

your hearts that, so long as you run on in your blind ways without repentance, as much as you can, you make posthaste to hellward. And so long as you continue in these miserable conditions, as St. Peter says, "Your judgment is not far off, and your damnation sleepeth not" (2 Peter 2:3).

Thirdly, seeing those whom God has purposed to refuse shall be left unto themselves and never come to repentance, we are to love and embrace the word of God preached and taught unto us by the ministers of the gospel and withal submitting ourselves unto it and suffering the Lord to humble us thereby, that we may come at length out of the broad way of blindness of mind and hardness of heart, leading to destruction, into the strait way of true repentance and reformation of life, which leads to salvation. For so long as a man lives in this world after the lusts of his own heart, he goes on walking in the very same broad way to hell in which all that are ordained to condemnation walk—and what a fearful thing is it, but for a little while to be a companion in the way of destruction with them that perish. And therefore I say once again, let us all in the fear of God lay His word unto our hearts and hear it with reverence, so as it may be in us the sword of the Spirit to cut down the sins and corruptions of our natures and work in us a reformation of life and true repentance.

The third point concerning the decree of reprobation is the judgment to be given of it.[345] This judgment belongs to God principally and properly, because He knows best what He has determined concerning the estate of every man, and none but He knows who they be which are ordained to due and deserved damnation. And again, He only knows the hearts and wills of men and what grace He has given them, what they are, and what all their sins be, and so does no angel nor creature in the world beside. As for men, it belongs not to them to give judgment of reprobation in themselves or in others, unless God reveal His will unto them and give them the gift of discerning. This gift was bestowed on sundry of the prophets in the Old Testament and in the New Testament on the apostles. David in many psalms makes request for the confusion of his enemies [Psalm 69; 109], not praying only against their sins (which we may do), but even against their persons, which we may not do. No doubt he was guided by God's Spirit and received thence an extraordinary gift to judge of the obstinate malice of his adversaries. And Paul prays against the person of Demetrius, saying, "The Lord reward him according to his doings" [2 Tim. 4:14]. And such kind of prayers were lawful in them because they were carried with pure and upright zeal and had no doubt a special gift whereby they were able to discern of the final estate of their enemies. Again, God sometimes gives this gift of discerning of some men's final impenitency to the church upon earth. I say not, to

---

345. This paragraph break is not in the original.

this or that private person, but to the body of the church or greater part thereof. St. John, writing unto the churches, says, "There is a sin unto death"—that is, against the Holy Ghost—"I say not that thou shouldest pray for it" (1 John 5:16), in which words he takes it for granted that this sin might be discerned by the church in those days. And Paul says, if any man believe not the Lord Jesus, "let him be had in execration, Maranatha" [1 Cor. 16:22]—that is, pronounced accursed to everlasting destruction. Whence it appears that the church has power to pronounce men rejected to everlasting damnation, upon some special occasions, though[346] I dare not say ordinarily and usually. The primitive church with one consent prayed against Julian the Apostate, and the prayers made were not in vain, as appears by the event of his fearful end. As for private and ordinary men, for the tempering and rectifying of their judgment, in this case they must follow two rules. The one is that every member of the church is bound to believe his own election. It is the commandment of God binding the very conscience, "that we should believe in Christ" (1 John 3:23). Now to believe in Christ is not only to put our affiance in Him and to be resolved that we are justified and sanctified and shall be glorified by Him, but also that we are elect to salvation in Him before the beginning of the world, which is the foundation of the rest. Again, if of things that have necessary dependence one upon another we are to believe the one, then we are to believe the other. Now election and adoption are things conjoined, and the one necessarily depends upon the other. For all the elect (as St. Paul says) are predestinated to adoption, and we are to believe our own adoption and therefore also our election. The second rule is that concerning the persons of those that be of the church, we must put in practice the judgment of charity, and that is to esteem of them as of the elect of God, till God make manifest otherwise. By virtue of this rule the ministers of God's word are to publish and preach the gospel to all without exception. It is true indeed there is both wheat and darnell in God's field, chaff and corn in God's barn, fish and dross in God's net, sheep and goats in Christ's fold. But secret judgments belong unto God; and the rule of love, which is to think and wish the best of others, is to be followed of us that profess faith working by love. It may be demanded what we are to judge of them that as yet are enemies of God. *Answer.* Our duty is to suspend our judgment concerning their final estate; for we know not whether God will call them or no, and therefore we must rather pray for their conversion, than for their confusion.

Again, it may be demanded what is to be thought of all our ancestors and forefathers that lived and died in the times when popery took place. *Answer.* We may well hope the best and think that they were saved; for though the

---

346. Sic Chry.

papacy be not the church of God and though the doctrine of popery raze the foundation, yet nevertheless in the very midst of the Roman papacy God has always had a remnant which have in some measure truly served Him. In the Old Testament, when open idolatry took place in all Israel,[347] God said to Elijah, "I have reserved seven thousand to myself, that never bowed knee to Baal" (1 Kings 19:18). And the like is and has been in the general apostasy under antichrist. St. John says that when the woman fled into the wilderness for a time, even then "there was a remnant of her seed which kept the commandments of God, and had the testimony of Jesus Christ" [Rev. 12:17]. And again, when ordinary means of salvation fail, then God can and does make a supply by means extraordinary; and therefore there is no cause why we should say that they were condemned.

Thirdly, it may be demanded, whether the common judgment given of Francis Spira that he is a reprobate be good or no? *Answer.* We may with better warrant say no, than any man say yea. For what gifts of discerning had they which came to visit him in his extremity, and what reasons induced them to give this peremptory judgment? He said himself that he was a reprobate; that is nothing. A sick man's judgment of himself is not to be regarded. Yea, but he despaired—a senseless reason; for so does many a man year by year, and that very often as deeply as ever Spira did. And yet by the good help of the ministry of the word both are and may be recovered. And they which will avouch Spira to be a reprobate must go further and prove two things: that he despaired both wholly and finally, which if they cannot prove, we for our parts must suspend our judgments; and they were much to blame that first published the book.

Lastly, it may be demanded, what is to be thought of them that make very fearful ends in raving and blaspheming? *Answer.* Such strange behaviors are oftentimes the fruits of violent diseases which torment the body and bereave the mind of sense and reason. And therefore, if the persons lived well, we must think the best; for we are not by outward things to judge of the estate of any man. Solomon says that "all things come alike to all, and the same condition to the just, and to the wicked" [Eccl. 9:2].

Thus much of the parts of predestination. Now follows the use thereof; and it concerns partly our judgments, partly our affections, and partly our lives. The uses which concern judgment are three. And, first, by the doctrine of predestination we learn that there cannot be any justification of a sinner before God by his works. For God's election is the cause of justification, because whom God elects to salvation after this life, them He elects to be justified in this life. Now election itself is of grace, and of grace alone, as Paul says, "Election is by

---

347. See Fllyr. Catal. test. verit.

grace, and if it be of grace, it is no more of works: or else were grace no grace" (Rom. 11:6). Therefore, justification is of grace and of grace alone; and I reason thus: the cause of a cause is the cause of all things caused. But grace alone is the cause of predestination, which is the cause of our vocation, justification, sanctification, etc. Grace therefore is also the alone cause of all these. Therefore, the Scriptures ascribe not only the beginning but also the continuance and accomplishment of all our happiness to grace. For, first, as election, so vocation is of grace. Paul says, "God hath called us not according to our works," but "according to his purpose and grace" (2 Tim. 1:9). Again, faith in Christ is of grace. So it is said, "To you it is given to believe in Christ" (Phil. 1:29). Also, the justification of a sinner is of grace. So Paul says plainly to the Romans, "You are justified" freely "by his grace" (3:24). Again, sanctification and the doing of good works is of grace. So it is said, "We are his workmanship created in Christ Jesus unto good works, which God hath ordained that we should walk in them" (Eph. 2:10). Also, perseverance in good works and godliness is of grace. So the Lord says, "I will make an everlasting covenant with them, that I will never turn away from them to do them good, but I will put my fear in their hearts, that they shall not depart from me" (Jer. 32:40). Lastly, life everlasting is of grace. So Paul says, "Life everlasting is the gift of God through Jesus Christ" (Rom. 6:23). Now, they of the Church of Rome teach the flat contrary. They make two justifications: the first, whereby a man of an evil man is made a good man; the second, whereby of a good man he is made better. The first they ascribe to grace, but so as the second is by works.

Secondly, hence we learn that the art of judicial astrology is vain and frivolous.[348] They that practice it do profess themselves to tell of things to come almost whatsoever, and this they do by casting figures; and the special point of their art is to judge of men's nativities. For if they may know but the time of a man's birth, they take upon them to tell the whole course of his life from year to year, from week to week, and from day to day, from the day of his birth to the hour of his death. Yea, that which is more, they profess themselves to tell all things that shall befall men either in body, goods, or good name, and what kind of death they shall die. But that this their practice is not of God but indeed unlawful, it may appear by this: because it stands not with the doctrine of God's predestination. Two twins, begotten of the same parents and born both at one and the same time, by the judgments of astrologists must have both the same life and the same death and be every way alike both in goods and good name. Yet we see the contrary to be true in Jacob and Esau, who were born both of the same parents at one time. For Jacob took Esau by the heel, so as there could not

---

348. This paragraph break is not in the original, as the additional one following.

be much difference between them in time. Yet for all this Esau was a fierce man and wild, given to hunting; but Jacob was mild of nature and lived at home. The one had favor at God's hand and was in the covenant, but God kept back that mercy from the other. Again, in a pitched field are slain a thousand men at one and the same time. Now, if we consider the time of their births, it may be they were born at a thousand sundry times and therefore under so many diverse positions of the heavens and so by the judgment of all astrologers should have all diverse and sundry lives and ends. But we see according to the determination of the counsel of God they have all one and the same end, and therefore this must admonish all those that are brought up in schools of learning to have care to spend their time in better studies. And it teaches those that are fallen into any manner of distress not to have recourse unto these fond figure-casters. For their astrological judgments are false and foolish, as we may see by the two former examples.

Thirdly, the knowledge of God is one of the most special points in Christian religion. And therefore the Lord says, "Let him that rejoiceth, rejoice in this, that he understandeth and knoweth me. For I am the Lord which shew mercy and judgment in the earth" (9:24). And our Savior Christ says, "This is life eternal to know thee, the only very God, and whom thou hast sent Jesus Christ" (John 17:3). Now, God's predestination is a glass wherein we may behold His majesty. For, first, by it we see the wonderful wisdom of God, who in His eternal counsel did foresee and most wisely set down the estate of every man. Secondly, His omnipotency, in that He has power to save and power to refuse whom He will. Thirdly, His justice and mercy both joined together in the execution of election: His mercy, in that He saves those that were utterly lost; His justice, in that He ordained Christ to be a mediator to suffer the curse of the law and to satisfy His justice for the elect. Fourthly, His justice, in the execution of the decree of reprobation; for though He decreed to hold back His mercy from some men because it so pleased Him, yet He condemns no man but for his sins. Now, the consideration of these and the like points bring us to the knowledge of the true God.

The uses which concern our affections are these. First, the doctrine of predestination ministers to all the people of God matter of endless consolation. For considering God's election is unchangeable, therefore they which are predestinated to salvation cannot perish. Though the gates of hell prevail against them so as they be hardly saved, yet shall they certainly be saved. Therefore, our Savior Christ says that in the latter days shall arise false christs and false prophets, which shall show great signs and wonders, "so that if it were possible they should deceive the very elect" (Matt. 24:24). In which words He takes it for granted that the elect of God can never finally fall away. And hereupon He says to His disciples when they rejoiced that the devils were subject to them, "Rather rejoice that your names are written in heaven" (Luke 10:20). And St. Paul, speaking of Hymenaeus and Philetus, which had fallen away from the faith, lest the church should be discouraged by their fall, because they were thought to be worthy men and pillars of the church, he does comfort them from the very ground of election, saying, "The foundation of God remaineth sure, and hath this seal: The Lord knoweth who are his" (2 Tim. 2:19). Where God's election is compared to the foundation of a house, the building whereof may be shaken, but the groundwork stands fast. And therefore Paul says further, "Who shall lay any thing to the charge of God's elect?" (Rom. 8:33). Now then, that we may have comfort in distress and something to stay upon in all our troubles, we in this world are as strangers in a far country. Our passage homeward is over the sea of this world. The ship wherein we sail is the church. And Satan stirs up many blasts of troubles and temptations, and his purpose is to sink the ship or to drive it on the rock. But we must take the anchor of hope and fasten it in heaven upon the foundation of God's election, which, being done, we shall pass in safety and rejoice in the midst of all storms and tempests.

Secondly, whereas God refuses some men and leaves them to themselves, it serves to strike a fear into every one of us whatsoever we be, as St. Paul says in the like case: the Jews being the natural branches "are broken off through unbelief, and thou standest by faith: be not high minded, but fear" (11:20).[349] This indeed was spoken to the Romans, but we must also lay it to our hearts. For what is the best of us, but a lump of clay? And howsoever in God's counsel we are chosen to salvation, yet in ourselves we are all shut up under unbelief and are fit to make vessels of wrath. Our Savior Christ calls Judas a devil, and we know his lewd life and fearful end. Now what are we better than Judas by nature? If we had been in his stead, without the special blessing of God, we should have done as he did. He betrayed Christ; but if God leave us to ourselves, we shall not only betray Him but by our sins even crucify Him a thousand ways. Furthermore, let us bethink ourselves of this, whether there be not some already condemned in hell who in their lives were not more grievous offenders than we. Isaiah called the people of his time a people of Sodom and Gomorrah [Isa. 1:10], giving the Jews then living to understand that they were as bad as the Sodomites and as the people of Gomorrah, on whom the Lord had showed His judgments long before. If this be true, then let us with fear and trembling be thankful to His majesty that He has preserved us hitherto from deserved damnation.

---

349. This paragraph break is not in the original.

The uses which respect our lives and conversations are manifold. First, seeing God has elected some to salvation and has also laid down the means in His holy Word whereby we may come to the knowledge of our particular election, we must therefore as St. Peter counsels us, "Give all diligence to make our election sure" (2 Peter 1:10). In the world, men are careful and painful enough to make assurance of lands and goods to themselves and to their posterity. What a shame is it then for us, that we should be slack in making sure to ourselves the election of God, which is more worth than all the world besides? And if we shall continue to be slack herein, the leases of our lands and houses and all other temporal assurances shall be bills of accusation against us at the day of judgment to condemn us.

Secondly, by this doctrine we are taught to live godly and righteously in this present world, because all those whom God has chosen to salvation He has also appointed to live in newness of life, as St. Paul, "God hath chosen us in Christ before the foundation of the world; that we should be holy and without blame before him" (Eph. 1:4).[350] And again, "We are created in Christ Jesus unto good works, which God hath ordained that we should walk in them" (2:10). And, "God hath chosen you to salvation through sanctification of the spirit and faith of the truth" [2 Thess. 2:13]. The elect are vessels of "honor" [Rom. 9:23; 2 Tim. 2:21], and therefore all those that will be of the number of the elect must carry themselves as vessels of honor. For so long as they live in their sins, they be like vessels of dishonor, employing themselves to the most base service that can be, even to the service of the devil. The sun was ordained to shine in the day and the moon in the night, and that order they keep. Yea, every creature in his kind observes the course appointed unto it by creation, as the grass to grow and trees to bring forth fruit. Now, the elect were ordained to this end, to lead a godly life; and therefore, if we would either persuade ourselves or the world that we are indeed chosen to salvation, we must be plentiful in all good works and make conscience of every evil way. And to do otherwise is as much as to change the order of nature, and as if the sun should cease to shine by day and the moon by night.

Thirdly, when God shall send upon any of us in this world crosses and afflictions either in body or in mind or any way else (as this life is the vale of misery and tears, and judgment must begin at God's house), we must learn to bare them with all submission and contentation of mind. For whom God knew before, them He has "predestinated to be made like unto his son" [Rom. 8:29]. But wherein is this likeness? Paul says, "In the fellowship of his affliction" and in a conformity to His death (Phil. 3:10). And the consideration of this,

---

350. This paragraph break is not in the original, as the additional one following.

that afflictions were ordained for us in the eternal predestination of God, must comfort our hearts and restrain our impatience so oft as we shall go under the burden of them.

Hence, again we learn that they which persuade themselves that they are in the favor of God because they live at ease in wealth and prosperity are far deceived. For St. Paul says, "God suffereth with long patience the vessels of wrath prepared to destruction, to make known his power, and to shew forth his wrath on them" (Rom. 9:22). This being so, no man then by outward blessings ought to plead that he has the love of God. Sheep that go in fat pastures come sooner to the slaughterhouse than those which are kept upon the bare commons. And they which are pampered with wealth of this world sooner forsake God and therefore are sooner forsaken of God than others. Solomon says, "No man knoweth love or hatred" (Eccl. 9:1)—that is, by outward things—for all things come alike to all. The same condition is to the just and to the unjust, to the wicked and good, to the pure and polluted. Lastly, it may be an offence unto us when we consider that the doctrine of the gospel is either not known or else despised and persecuted of the whole world. But we must stay ourselves with this consideration, that nothing comes to pass by chance; that God knows who are His; and there must be some in the world on whom God has in His eternal counsel purposed to manifest His power and justice. Again, ministers of the gospel may be discouraged when after long preaching they see little or no fruit of their labors, the people whom they teach remaining as blind, impenitent, and unreformed as ever they were. But they must also consider that it is the purpose of God to choose some to salvation and to refuse others; and that of the first, some are called sooner, some later; and that the second, being left to themselves, never come to repentance. To this Paul had regard when he said, "If our gospel be hid, it is hid to them that perish" (2 Cor. 4:3). And again, "We are unto God the sweet savor of Christ in them that are saved, and in them that perish" (2:15).

Hitherto I have delivered the truth of this weighty point of religion, which also is the doctrine of the Church of England. Now, it follows that we should consider the falsehood. Sundry divines have devised and in their writings published a new frame or platform of the doctrine of predestination, the effect whereof is this. The nature of God (say they) is infinite love, goodness, and mercy itself. And therefore He propounds unto Himself an end answerable thereunto, and that is the communication of His love and goodness unto all His creatures. Now, for the accomplishing of this supreme and absolute end, He did four things. First, He decreed to create man righteous in His own image. Secondly, He foresaw the fall of man after his creation, yet so as He neither willed nor decreed it. Thirdly, He decreed the universal redemption of all and every man actually by Christ, so be it they will believe in Him. Fourthly, He decreed to call all and every man effectually, so as if they will, they may be saved. This being done, He in His eternal counsel foreseeing who would believe in Christ did thereupon elect them to eternal salvation, and again, foreseeing who would not believe but contemn grace offered, did thereupon also decree to reject them to eternal damnation.

This platform, howsoever it may seem plausible to reason, yet indeed it is nothing else but a device of man's brain, as will appear by sundry defects and errors that be in it. For, first, whereas it is avouched that Adam's fall came by the bare prescience of God without any decree or will of His, it is a flat untruth. The putting of Christ to death was as great a sin as the fall of Adam, nay, in some respects greater. Now that came to pass not only by the foreknowledge of God but also by "his determinate counsel" [Acts 2:23]. And therefore as the church of Jerusalem says, "Herod and Pontius Pilate with the Gentiles, and the people of Israel, gathered themselves together, to do whatsoever thine hand and thy counsel had determined before to be done" (4:28), so may we say that Adam in his fall did nothing but that which the hand of God and His counsel had determined before to be done. And considering the will of God extends itself to the least things that are, even to "sparrows" [Matt. 10:29], whereof none do light upon the ground without our heavenly Father, how can a man in reason imagine that the fall of one of the most principal creatures that are shall fall out altogether without the will and decree of God? And there can be nothing more absurd than to sever the foreknowledge of God from His counsel or decree. For by this means things shall come to pass, God nilling or not knowing or not regarding them.[351] Now if anything come to pass, God nilling it, then that is done which God would not have done; and to say so is to bereave Him of His omnipotency. And if we shall say that things fall out, God not knowing of them, we make Him to be imprudent and deny His omniscience. Lastly, if we shall say that a thing is done, God not regarding it, we bring in an idol of our own brains and stablish the idol god of the Epicureans. But it is objected to the contrary that if God any way decreed and willed the fall of Adam, then He was the author of sin, which once to say is blasphemy. *Answer.* The argument follows not. There be three actions in the will of God. One, whereby He does absolutely will anything and delight in it.[352] And of all such things God Himself is the author. The second is wholly or absolutely to nill a thing.[353] And all things thus nilled cannot possibly come to pass or have the least being in nature. There is also a third action which comes as a mean between the two

351. Nolente, nesciente, non curante.
352. 1. Volendo velle.
353. 2. Nolendo nolle, or penitus nolle.

former, which is remissly or in part both to nill and will a thing,[354] whereby, though God approve not evil as it is evil and therefore does it not, yet He wills the permitting of it to be done by others or the being of it, because in respect of God, that decrees the permitting of evil, it is good that there should be evil. And on this manner and no otherwise God willed the fall of Adam; and therefore in the reason of any indifferent man, though He decreed the fall, yet shall He be free from the blame thereof, which lies wholly upon the doer—these two caveats always remembered: first, that God by His will did not constrain or force the will of Adam to sin or infuse into it any corruption, and that therefore he sinned willingly and freely only by the necessity of immutability[355] and not by the necessity of coaction; secondly, that God willed the fall for a most worthy end, which was to lay down a way tending to the manifestation both of justice and mercy. Again, it is alleged that if God willed Adam's fall, then His will is flat contrary to itself, because He wills that which He had by express commandment forbidden. *Answer.* Indeed, if God should both will and forbid one and the same thing in one and the same respect, there should be a contradiction in God's will; but that God does not. He forbad Adam's fall as it was sin, for so in every commandment sin as it is sin is condemned and punished and yet, because it was in a new respect, a means of manifesting His glory, who is able to bring light out of darkness. Therefore, He willingly decreed the permission of it. Incest as it is sin, it is condemned in the seventh commandment and punished with death; yet as incest was a punishment of David's adultery, God is said to take his wives and "to give them to his son Absalom" (2 Sam. 12:11).

Some again, as it appears by their writings, fear to ascribe unto God so much as a permission of Adam's fall; but no doubt they are deceived. For if these rules be true—that God is omnipotent; that He works all things that are by the counsel of His will and governs them; that He has care and regard over men; that nothing is hid from Him; that He is unchangeable—[then] there must needs be permission of evil. If the devil could not enter so much as into a herd of swine without permission [Mark 5:12], shall we think that he could compass the fall and overthrow of man without permission? Indeed, to permit is not to hinder evil when one may; and with men it is a fault, but not with God, because He is not bound to hinder the evil which He permits.

The second fault is that they make the prescience of man's faith and unbelief to be the impulsive cause of God's decree.[356] For they say that God eternally decrees to save or refuse men because He did foresee that they would believe or not believe. But indeed it is a manifest untruth. Among the causes of all things

---

354. 3. Remisse & velle & nolle, aut nolendo velle.
355. Decretum Dei non tollit libertatem doluntatis, sed ordinat.
356. Or as some speak, a rule according to which He orders His decree.

that are there is an order set down by God Himself, in which order some causes are highest, some lowest, some in the midst. Now the highest cause of all is that which overrules all and is overruled of none; and that is God's will, beyond which there can be no higher cause, for God is placed above all and subject unto none, and this very will of His is the cause of all things that have being. For we must not imagine that a thing first of all exists and then afterward is willed of God; but first of all God wills a thing, and then afterward it comes to have a being. Now, to say that foreseen faith or unbelief are the moving causes whereby God was induced to ordain men either to salvation or just damnation is to undo this divine order of causes and to displace the links, in that God's will is made a secondary or middle cause subordinate to other causes placed above it. Yea, this is to make the will of God to depend upon the quality and condition of the creature, whereas contrariwise all things depend upon God's will. Again, Paul says that God had opened the mystery of His will according to His good pleasure "which he had purposed in himself" (Eph. 1:9), whereby he makes a distinction between the creature and the Creator. Men, when they purpose the doing of anything borrow reasons of their purposes and wills out of themselves from the things to be done, because man's bare will is no sufficient cause to warrant the doing of this or that in this or that manner, unless there be just reason. But God's will is a simple and absolute rule of righteousness, and a thing is good so far forth as God wills it. Therefore, there is no cause why He should go forth of Himself for eternal inducements and reasons of His external counsel. His very will in Himself is a sufficient reason of all His purposes and decrees. And hereupon Paul says that God's "purpose was in himself" to show that there is no dependence of His will upon the creature, and that in ordering and disposing of His decrees He had no reference or respective consideration of the qualities and works of them.

Thirdly, by this doctrine there is fastened upon God want of wisdom, who is wisdom itself; and that is very absurd.[357] A simple man that has in him but a spark of the wisdom of God, first of all, intends with himself the end and event of the business to be done and then afterward the means whereby the end is accomplished. But in this platform God is brought in in the first place to foresee and consider with Himself the means which tend to the end—namely, faith and unbelief of men—and then afterward to determine with Himself what shall be the end and final condition of every man either in life or death, as if a man should purpose with himself to build a house without any consideration of the end why and afterward conceive with himself the particular uses to which he will apply it.

---

357. This paragraph break is not in the original, as the additional three following.

Fourthly, hence it follows that faith shall not only be an instrument but also an efficient cause in the act of justification of a sinner before God. For the cause of a cause is also the cause of a thing caused, but foreseen faith is an impulsive cause whereby God was moved to choose some men to salvation (as it is said). And therefore it is not only an instrument to apprehend Christ's righteousness, but also a cause or means to move God to justify a sinner, because justification proceeds of election, which comes of foreseen faith. Now, this is erroneous by the doctrine of all churches, unless they be popish.

Fifthly, this doctrine takes it for granted that all, both young and old, even infants that die in their infancy, have knowledge of the gospel, because both faith and unbelief in Christ presuppose knowledge of our salvation by Him, considering that neither ordinarily nor extraordinarily men believe or contemn the thing unknown. But how false is this even common experience does show.

Lastly, this platform quite overthrows itself. For whereas all men, equally corrupt in Adam, are effectually both redeemed and called, the difference between man and man stands not in believing or not believing, for all have power to believe, but in this properly: that some are confirmed in faith, some are not. Now when all without exception are indued with grace sufficient for salvation, I demand why some men are confirmed in grace, and others not confirmed; as also of angels, why some confirmed stand, and some not confirmed fell? No other reason can be rendered but the will of God. And to this must all come, strive as long as they will, that of men being in one and the same estate, some are saved, some justly forsaken, because God would. Again, as the foreseeing of faith does presuppose God's giving of faith, unless men will say it is natural, so the foreseeing of faith in some men alone does presuppose the giving of faith to some men alone. But why does not God confer the grace of constant faith to all? No other reason can be rendered, but because He will not. Thus then, those men whose faith was foreseen are saved not because their faith was foreseen, but because God would.

The third fault is that they ascribe unto God a conditional purpose or counsel, whereby He decrees that all men shall be saved, so be it they will believe. For it is every way as much against common sense as if it had been said that God decreed nothing at all concerning man. A conditional sentence determines nothing simply but conditionally, and therefore uncertainly. And when we speak of God, to determine uncertainly is as much as if He had determined nothing at all, especially when the thing determined is in the power of man's will, and in respect of God the decree may come to pass or not come to pass. Men if they might always have their choice desire to determine of all their affairs simply without condition; and when they do otherwise, it is either because they know not the event of things or because things to be done are not in their power. No reason therefore that we should burden God with that, whereof we would dis-burden ourselves. Again, the majesty of God is disgraced in this kind of decree. God for His part would have all men to be saved. Why then are they not? Men will not keep the condition and believe. This is flat to hang God's will upon man's will, to make every man an emperor, and God his underling, and to change the order of nature by subordinating God's will, which is the first cause, to the will of man, which is the second cause, whereas by the very law of nature the first cause should order and dispose the second cause. But for the justifying of a conditional decree it is alleged that there is no eternal hidden decree of God besides the gospel, which is God's predestination revealed. *Answer.* It is an untruth. There be two wills in God: one, whereby He determines what He will do unto us or in us;[358] the other, whereby He determines what we shall do to Him.[359] Now, predestination is the first, whereupon it is commonly defined to be the preparation of the blessing of God whereby they are delivered which are delivered; and the gospel is the second. Again, predestination determines who they are and how many which are to be saved, and hereupon Christ says, "I know whom I have chosen" (John 13:18). But the gospel rather determines what kind of ones and how they must be qualified which are to be saved. Lastly, predestination is God's decree itself; and the gospel is an outward means of the execution of it. And therefore, though the gospel be propounded with a condi-tion, yet the decree of God itself may be simple and absolute.

The fourth defect is the opinion of universal saving grace, appertaining to all and every man, which may fitly be termed the school of universal atheism. For it pulls down the pale of the church and lays it waste as a very common field. It breeds a carelessness in the use of the means of grace, the word and sacraments, when as men shall be persuaded that grace shall be offered to everyone effectually, whether he be of the church or not, at one time or other, wheresoever or howsoever he live—as in the like case, if men should be told that whether they live in the market town or no, there shall be sufficient provi-sion brought them, if they will but receive it and accept of it, who would then come to market?

Universal grace has three parts: universal election; universal redemption; universal vocation. Universal election of all and every man is a witless conceit; for if men universally be appointed to grace without exception, then there is no election or choosing of some out of mankind to grace. And if some alone be appointed to grace, as it must needs be in election, then is not grace universal. And it is flat against the Word of God. For Christ avouches plainly that fewer

358. Quid vult fieri de nobis, or, in nobis.
359. Quid vult fieri a nobis.

be chosen than called, and (as afterward we shall see) all are not called (Matt. 12:14). And He further says that all which are "given unto him" [John 17:2] shall be one with Him and have life everlasting. But all men shall not be one with Him and have life everlasting. And therefore all men are not given to Christ of the Father—that is, ordained to salvation. And the Scripture says that all men's names are not written in the book of life (Rev. 17:14; 20:15), and that the kingdom of heaven was not prepared for all. And whereas men build this their universal election upon the largeness of the promise of the gospel, upon the like ground they might as well make a universal decree of reprobation, whereby God decrees all men to be damned indefinitely upon this condition, if they do not believe. Now if universal reprobation be absurd, as it is indeed, then universal election of all and every man must take part therewith.

As for the universal redemption of all and every man, it is no better than a forgery of man's brain. There shall be many in the day of judgment of whom Christ shall say that He "never knew them" (7:23). Again He says, "He which believeth not, is already judged, and the wrath of God" abides upon "him" (John 3:36). But if all were effectually redeemed and only condemned for not believing in Christ, it should have been said that they are already judged and that the wrath of God not abides but returns upon them. Christ makes no intercession for the world (17:9), and therefore His redemption is not effectual to all men. For the intercession is the means of applying the satisfaction. If it be said that by "the world" is meant only contemners of grace, it appears to be otherwise in that Christ opposes the world to them which "are the Father's" and are "given to Christ" by Him, thereby signifying that by "the world" He means all such as are not the Father's and were never given to Christ. And John 10:17, "He lays down his life for his sheep." Now the sheep have all these brands or marks. They "hear his voice"; they "know him"; they "follow him"; they "shall not perish" [v. 27]. None shall pluck them out of Christ's hands [v. 28]. And these are only such of whom Paul says, "Who shall lay anything to the charge of God's elect: it is God that justifieth, who shall condemn?" (Rom. 8:33). And if this should be true that Christ was crucified and died no less to make satisfaction for the sins of the damned than for the sins of Peter and Paul and the rest of the saints, it follows necessarily that all their sins are forgiven, considering that remission of sin depends inseparably upon satisfaction made to God's justice for sin; and satisfaction does necessarily abolish all fault. We grant that Christ's death is sufficient to save many thousand worlds. We grant again it is every way most effectual in itself; but that it is effectual in or unto the person of every man, that we deny. For if it were thus effectual, then it should be applied to the person of every man, as to Cain, Judas, Nero, Heliogabalus, etc., even as the plaster is laid to the sore, being applied. Christ's righteousness should be imputed for

the justification and sanctification of all and every man. And thus some justified before God and sanctified should after go to hell and be damned, whereas
David, never so much as dreaming of this divinity, says that they are blessed
which have the pardon of their sins (Ps. 32:1); and Paul, that they which are
justified have peace with God (Rom. 5:1).

But let us hear what reasons may be alleged for the universality of redemption. (1) "As I live, saith the Lord, I will not the death of the wicked," but "that
the wicked return from his wicked way" (Ezek. 33:11). *Answer.* The place is to
be understood not simply but in respect. Of the twain, God rather wills the
repentance of the sinner than his death. Again, He wills not death as it is the
destruction of His creature, and so this place may be understood. Yet nevertheless, He wills the same as it is a means of the manifestation of His justice. And
therefore the prophet Isaiah says, "God createth evil" (Isa. 45:7).

(2) "God would have all men to be saved: and come to the acknowledgement of the truth" (1 Tim. 2:4).[360] *Answer.* The place is meant not of the persons
of all particular men, but of the orders and kinds of men. For in the first verse
Paul exhorts Timothy that prayer should be made for all men; and in the second verse, opening his own meaning, he adds these words, "for kings and all
that be in authority"—as though he should say we must pray not only for private men and for the common people, but also for public persons, though they
persecute the gospel. But why? Because in that very order God has His elect,
which shall be saved. And on this manner Paul expounds himself elsewhere,
"There is neither Jew nor Grecian: there is neither bond nor free: there is neither male nor female: for ye are all one in Christ" (Gal. 3:28).

(3) "God hath shut up all in unbelief that he might have mercy on all"
(Rom. 11:32). *Answer.* The word "all" must be understood of all that are to be
saved, both of Jews and Gentiles, as the article added to "all" imports. And
the meaning is that God will save all whom He purposes to save of His mercy
and not of their merit, because all are sinners, as well Jews as Gentiles. Thus,
Paul expounds himself, "The scripture hath concluded all under sin, that the
promise by the faith of Jesus Christ should be given unto them that believe"
(Gal. 3:22). And if we should expound the word "all" for every particular man,
as some would have it, Paul must contradict himself, who said before that God
would have mercy on whom He will have mercy, and whom He will He hardens. And in this very chapter his drift is to prove the rejection of the Jews and
the calling of the Gentiles.

(4) "God so loved the world that he hath given his only begotten Son, that
whosoever believeth in him shall not perish but have everlasting life" (John 3:16);

---

360. This paragraph break is not in the original, as the additional four following.

and, "I will give my flesh for the life of the world" (6:51). *Answer.* By "world" we must not understand every particular man in the world, but the elect among the Jews and Gentiles; for in both these places Christ does overthwart the conceit of the Jews, which thought that they alone were loved of God and not the Gentiles. And how this word is to be understood in the New Testament Paul does fully declare. "If," says he, "the fall of them"—that is, the Jews—"be the riches of the world, and the diminishing of them, the riches of the Gentiles," etc. (Rom. 11:12). And, "If the casting away of them, be the reconciling of the world, what shall the receiving be but life from the dead?" (v. 15). Where by "the world" he understands the body of the Gentiles in the last age of the world. And thus he fully declares his own meaning, when he says to the Corinthians, "God was in Christ reconciling the world unto himself" (2 Cor. 5:18).

(5) "Destroy not him with thy meat for whom Christ died" (Rom. 14:15). "Denying the Lord that bought them, and bring upon themselves swift damnation" (2 Peter 2:1). Therefore, Christ died for them also which are condemned. *Answer.* The reason is not good; for in these and such like places the Scripture speaks of men not as they are indeed before God, but as they are in appearance and profession and as they are in acceptation with men. For so long as a man holds and embraces the Christian faith, so long in the judgment of charity we must esteem him to be one that is redeemed by Christ, though indeed he be not. And this is the meaning of Peter when he says that false prophets deny the Lord that bought them.

(6) In the preaching of the gospel, grace is freely offered not only to the elect but to all men indifferently; and God in offering grace deludes no man. Therefore, Christ's death appertains and belongs to all men indifferently. *Answer.* The preaching of the gospel is an ordinance of God appointed for the gathering together and the accomplishment of the number of the elect. And therefore in the ministry of the word grace and salvation is offered principally and directly to the elect and only by consequent to them which are ordained to just damnation, because they are mingled with the elect in the same societies and because the ministers of God, not knowing His secret counsel, in charity think all to be elect. And though God in offering grace do not confer it to all, yet is there no delusion. For the offering of grace does not only serve for the conversion of a sinner, but also to be an occasion by men's fault of blinding the mind and hardening the heart and taking away excuse in the day of judgment.

To conclude this point, universal redemption of all men, we grant the Scripture says so; and there is a universality among the elect and believers. But universal redemption of all and every man, as well the damned as the elect, and that effectually, we renounce as having neither footing in the Scripture nor in the writing of any ancient and orthodox divine, for many hundred years after Christ's words not depraved and mistaken.

As for the universal vocation, it is of the same kind with the former. Because it is flat against the Word of God in which is set down a distinction of the world from the creation to the days of Christ into two parts: one, the people of God, being received into the covenant; the other (being the greatest part of the world), no people and forth of the covenant. From the beginning of the world to the giving of the law the church was shut up in the families of the patriarchs, and the covenant in the very family of Abraham was restrained to Isaac. And the members of these families for this cause were called the sons of God [Gen. 6:2], and the rest of the world besides being termed as they were indeed—the sons of men. From the giving of the law till Christ, the nation of the Jews, the church of God, and the rest of the world besides, no people of God. And therefore Isaiah calls them "prisoners" and them that "are in darkness" [49:9]; and Hosea, such as are "without mercy" [2:23] and "no people" [1:10]; and Zechariah, such as are "not joined to the Lord" [2:11]; and Paul, such as are "set to walk in their own ways" [Acts 14:16], being "without God" and "without Christ" in the world [Eph. 2:12]. And this distinction between Jew and Gentile stood till the very ascension of Christ. And hereupon when He was to send His disciples to preach, He charged them "not to go into the way of the Gentiles" and "not to enter into the cities of the Samaritans, but rather to go to the lost sheep of the house of Israel" (Matt. 10:5). And when the woman of Canaan made request for her daughter, He gave a denial at the first upon this distinction, saying, "It is not meet to take the children's bread and give it unto dogs," and again, "I am sent but unto the lost sheep of the house of Israel" (15:24, 26). It will be said that this distinction arose of this, that the Gentiles at the first fell away from the covenant and contemned the Messiah. It is true indeed of the first heads of the Gentiles, the sons of Noah; but of their posterity it is false, which in times following did not so much as hear of the covenant and the Messiah. The prophet Isaiah says of Christ, "A nation that knew not thee, shall run unto thee" (55:5). And Paul, speaking to the Athenians, says that the times of this "their ignorance" God regarded not, but "now" admonishes all men everywhere to repent (Acts 17:30). And to the Romans he says that the mystery touching Christ and His benefits "was kept secret" since the world began (Rom. 16:25) and "now" opened and published among all nations (1 Tim. 3:16). And if the Gentiles had but known of the Messiah, why did not their poets and philosophers, who in their writings notoriously abuse the Jews with sundry nicknames,[361] at the least signify the contempt of the Redeemer?

---

361. Apella, Verpus, Recutitus, Sabbatarius, Cultor nubium.

Wherefore, to hold and much more to avouch by writing that all and every one of the heathen were called—it is most absurd. And if it were so, the cannibals and the savage nations of America should have known Christ without preaching, which by the histories of those countries is known to be false.

Again, if the vocation of every man be effectual, then faith must be common to all men either by nature or by grace or both. Now, to say the first—namely, that the power of believing is common to all by nature—is the heresy of the Pelagians. And to say it is common to all by grace is false. "All men have not faith," says Paul (2 Thess. 3:2). Nay, many to whom the gospel is preached do not so much as understand it and give assent unto it, "Satan blinding their minds that the light of the glorious gospel of Christ should not shine unto them" (2 Cor. 4:4). And to say that faith is partly by nature and partly by grace is the condemned heresy of the semi-pelagian, for we cannot so much as think a good thought of ourselves (3:5).

The last defect in the platform is that they ascribe unto God a wrong end of His counsels—namely, the communication of mercy or goodness in eternal happiness. For the absolute and sovereign end of all God's doings must be answerable to His nature, which is not mercy and love alone but also justice itself. And therefore the right end is the manifestation of His glory both in justice and mercy by the express testimony of Scripture. Again, if the communication of His goodness were the highest end of all His counsels, all men without exception should be saved, because God cannot be frustrated of His end and purpose; and if but one man be damned, he is damned either because God will not save him or because He cannot. If they say He will not, then is He changeable; if He cannot, then is He not omnipotent, considering His purpose was to convey happiness to all creatures.

Thus much of the efficient cause of the church—namely, God's predestination—which doctrine could not here be omitted, considering no man can believe himself to be a member of the church unless withal he believe that he is predestinated to life everlasting. Now, we come to the second point—namely, the mystical union, which is the very form of the church wherein all that believe are "made one with Christ" (Gal. 3:28). To the causing of this union, two things are required, a donation or giving of Christ unto man, which is to be made one with Him, and a conjunction between them both. Of the first, the prophet Isaiah says, "Unto us a child is born, and unto us a Son is given" (Isa. 9:6); and Paul, "Who spared not his own Son, but gave him for us all: how shall he not with him give us all things?" (Rom. 8:32). And touching it sundry points must be considered. The first is, what is meant by this giving? *Answer.* It is an action or work of God the Father by the Holy Ghost whereby Christ as Redeemer in the appointed time is really communicated to all ordained to salvation, in such manner that they may truly say that Christ Himself with all His benefits is theirs, both in respect of right thereto and in respect of all fruits redounding thence, and that as truly as any man may say that house and land given him of his ancestors is his own both to possess and to use.

The second point is, what is the very thing given? *Answer.* Whole Christ, God and man, is given, because His humanity without His Godhead or the Godhead without the humanity does not reconcile us to God. Yet in this giving there must be a diverse consideration had of the two natures of Christ; for the communication of the Godhead is merely energetical—that is, only in respect of operation—in that it does make the manhood personally united unto it to be propitiatory for our sins and meritorious of life eternal. And to avouch any communication of the Godhead in respect of essence were to bring in the heresy of the Manichees and to maintain a composition and a commixtion of our natures with the nature of God. Again, in the manhood of Christ we must distinguish between the subject itself, the substance of body and soul, and the blessings in the subject which tend to our salvation. And the communication of the aforesaid manhood is in respect of both, without separation; for no man can receive saving virtue from Christ unless first of all he receive Christ Himself, as no man can have the treasure hid in the field unless he first of all have the field, and no man can be nourished by meat and drink unless first of all he receive the substance of both (John 6:53–54). And this is the cause why not only in the preaching of the word but also in the institution of the Lord's Supper express mention is made not only of Christ's merit but also of His very body and blood, whereby the whole humanity is signified, as appears by that place where it is said that the "word was made flesh" (John 1:14). And though the flesh of itself profit nothing, as St. John says, yet as it is joined to the Godhead of the Son and does subsist in His person it receives thence quickening virtue to revive and renew all those to whom it shall be given. Lastly, among the blessings that are stored up in the manhood of Christ for our salvation, some are given unto us by imputation, as when we are justified by the righteousness, indeed inherent in His manhood but imputed unto us; some by infusion, as when holiness is wrought in our hearts by the Spirit as a fruit of that holiness which is in the manhood of Christ and derived from it, as the light of one candle from another.

The third point is in what manner Christ is given unto us. *Answer.* God the Father gives Christ unto His church not in an earthly or bodily manner, as when a king bestows a gift with his own hand and puts it into the hand of his subject; but the manner is altogether celestial and spiritual, partly because it is brought to pass by the mere divine operation of the Holy Ghost, and partly because in respect of us this gift is received by an instrument which is supernatural—namely, faith, whereby we lay hold on and apply unto ourselves the evangelical promises. And this manner of giving may be conceived thus: a man that never stirred foot out of England holds and enjoys land in Turkey. But how comes it to be his? Thus: the emperor was willing and content to bestow it; and the man for his part was willing to accept and receive it. And by this means that which at the first was the emperor's by mutual consent becomes the man's. In the same manner, God the Father has made an evangelical covenant with His church in which of His mercy He has made a grant of His own Son unto us with righteousness and life everlasting in Him; and we again by His grace accept of this grant and receive the same by faith. And thus by mutual consent according to the tenor of the covenant any repentant sinner may truly say, "Though I now have my abode upon earth, and Christ in respect of His manhood be locally in heaven, yet is He truly mine to have and to enjoy. His body is mine; His blood is mine." As for the giving and receiving of the body and blood of Christ in bodily manner (which the Papists maintain in avouching the real transubstantiation of bread and wine in the sacrament into the body and blood of Christ, and the Lutherans also in teaching that His body and blood is substantially either in or with or under the bread and wine) is an erroneous conceit, flat opposite to sundry points of the Christian faith. For Christ to this very hour retains still the essence and essential properties of a true body; and we believe that really and visibly He ascended into heaven and there abides till His second coming to the last judgment. Who then, having but common reason, would imagine a communication of the body of Christ pent up in the element of bread and conveyed into our bodies by the mouth and stomach?

The fourth point is whether we are not lords of Christ, He being thus given unto us? *Answer.* No, for this donation is not single but mutual. As Christ is given unto us, so we again are given to Christ, as He Himself says, "Those whom thou hast given me, Father, I have kept" (John 17:24). And we are given unto Him that our bodies and souls are made His, not only as He is God, but also as He is our Redeemer; and our sins with the guilt thereof are made His by imputation, and the punishment thereof is wholly laid upon Him. This is all the dowry which the church, being the spouse of Christ, has brought unto Him.

The fifth point is how any man in particular may know that Christ is given unto him of the Father. *Answer.* When God gives Christ to man, He withal gives man grace and power to receive Christ and to apprehend Him with all His benefits; and this we do when we utterly renounce ourselves, this world, and all things therein, bewail our sins past, resting on the death of Christ for the pardon of them all and as it were with both the arms of faith catching hold upon Him in all estates both in life and death. When the heart of any man is truly disposed and inclined to do these and the like things, we may truly say that God has given him grace to receive Christ.

The second thing required to make us one with Christ is the mystical union, which is a conjunction whereby Christ and His church are actually coupled into one mystical body. Now that we may the better conceive the nature of it, sundry questions are to be moved. The first, what kind of conjunction this is? *Answer.* In the Scripture we meet with three kinds of conjunctions. The first is conjunction in nature, when sundry things are coupled by one and the same nature—as the Father, the Son, and the Holy Ghost, being three distinct substances, are all one and therefore joined in one Godhead or divine nature. Now Christ and the believer are not joined in nature, for then they twain should have one body and soul. The second conjunction is in person, when things in nature different so concur together that they make but one person, as the body and soul make one man, and the Godhead of the Son with His manhood make but one Christ, in whom there is a union of distinct natures with unity of person. Now, Christ and a Christian are not joined in person; for Christ is one person, Peter a second person, and Paul a third distinct from them both. And so many men as there be, so many several persons. The third conjunction is in spirit, and this is the conjunction meant in this place, whereby Christ and His church are joined together; for the very same Spirit of God that dwells in the manhood of Christ and fills it with all graces above measure is derived thence and dwells in all the true members of the church and fills them with the like graces in measure. And therefore St. John says, "Hereby we know that we dwell in him, and he in us, because he hath given us of his spirit" [1 John 4:13]. Hence it follows that the bond of this conjunction is one and the same Spirit, descending from Christ, the Head, to all His members, creating also in them the instrument of faith whereby they apprehend Christ and make Him their own.

The second is, what are the things united? *Answer.* Not the body of the believer to the body of Christ, or the soul to His soul, but the whole person of the man to the whole person of Christ—yet in this order: we are first of all and immediately joined to the manhood of Christ, and by the manhood to the Godhead.

The third question is, what is the manner of this conjunction? *Answer.* We must not think that Christ and His church are joined by imagination, as the mind of man and the thing whereof he thinks; or by consent of heart, as one friend is joined with another and as the Jews converted were all of one heart and soul [Acts 2:42]; or by any abode in one place or by touching, as sea and land are both joined together and make one globe; or by any composition or commixtion of substances, as when many ingredients are put together to make one medicine. But this conjunction is altogether spiritual as the former giving was and incomprehensible to man's reason, and therefore we must rather labor to feel it by experience in the heart than to conceive it in the brain. Yet nevertheless it shall not be amiss to consider a resemblance of it in this comparison. Suppose a man, having the parts of his body disjoined far asunder, his head lying in Italy, one arm in Germany, the other in Spain, and his legs with us in England. Suppose further all these parts or quarters have all one soul, extending itself unto them all and quickening each of them severally, as though they were nearly joined together. And though the parts be severed many hundred miles asunder, yet the distance of place does not hinder the conjunction, considering one and the same soul does enlarge itself and give life unto them all. In the same manner, the Head of the mystical body, Christ our Savior, is now in heaven. Some of His members in heaven with Him, and some in earth. And of these, some in England, some in Germany, some in Italy, some in Spain, distant many thousand miles asunder. And the Spirit of God is as it were the soul of this body which gives spiritual life to all the members. Distance of place does not hinder this conjunction, because the Holy Ghost which links all the parts together is infinite.

The benefits which we receive by this mystical union are manifold, for it is the ground of the conveyance of all grace. The first is that by means hereof every Christian as he is a Christian or a man regenerate has his beginning and being in Christ, howsoever as he is a man he has his being and subsisting in himself, as Paul says, "Ye are of God in Christ" (1 Cor. 1:30), and, "Ye are members of his body, of his flesh, and of his bones" (Eph. 5:30). How (will some say) can this be? After this manner: the comparison is taken from our first parents. Eve was made of a rib taken out of Adam's side, he being cast into a slumber. This being done, Adam awakened and said, "This now is bone of my bone, and flesh of my flesh" (Gen. 2:23). Christ was nailed on the cross, and His most precious blood was shed, and out of it arise and spring all true Christians—that is, out of the merit of Christ's death and passion, whereby they become new creatures.

Secondly, everyone that believes in Christ by reason of this union has an unspeakable prerogative; for hereby he is first united to Christ and by reason thereof is also joined to the whole Trinity, the Father, the Son, and the Holy Ghost, and shall have eternal fellowship with them.[362]

Thirdly, sundry men, specially Papists, deride the doctrine of justification by imputed righteousness, thinking it is absurd that a man should be just by that righteousness which is inherent in the person of Christ—as if we would say that one man may live by the soul of another, or be learned by the learning of another. But here we may see that it has sufficient foundation. For there is a most near and straight union between Christ and all that believe in Him. And in this union Christ with all His benefits according to the tenor of the covenant

---

362. This paragraph break is not in the original, as the additional four following.

of grace is made ours really, and therefore we may stand just before God by His righteousness, it being indeed His because it is in Him as in a subject, yet so as it is also ours because it is given unto us of God. Now there is no such union between man and man, and for that cause one man cannot live by the soul of another or be learned by the learning of another.

Fourthly, from this fountain springs our sanctification, whereby we die to sin and are renewed in righteousness and holiness. Worms and flies that have lain dead all winter, if they be laid in the sun in the springtime, begin to revive by virtue thereof. Even so, when we are united to Christ and are (as it were) laid in the beams of this blessed Sun of Righteousness, virtue is derived thence, which warms our benumbed hearts dead in sin and revives us to newness of life, whereby we begin to affect and like good things and put in practice all the duties of religion.

Fifthly, hence we have the protections of God's angels; for they always wait and attend on Christ, and because we are made one with Him, they attend upon us also.

Lastly, by reason of this union with Christ every believer comes to have interest and to recover his title in the creatures of God and to have the holy and lawful use of them all. For we must consider that although Adam, created in the image of God, was made lord over all things in heaven and earth, yet when he fell by eating the forbidden fruit he and in him all mankind lost the title and use of them all. Now therefore, that a man may recover his interest, he must first of all be united and made one with Christ; and then by Christ, who is Lord and King over all, shall he recover that title in the creatures of God which he had by creation and be made lord over them again. But some will say, if this be so, then a Christian man may have and enjoy all creatures at his pleasure and therefore the goods of other men. *Answer.* The reason is not good, for in this life we have no more but right unto the creature[363] and right in it[364]—that is, actual possession—is reserved for the life to come. Therefore, we must content ourselves with our allowed portions given unto us by God, by His grace using them in holy manner, expecting by hope the full fruition of all things till after this life. Again, if all titles to the creatures be recovered by Christ, it may be demanded, whether infidels have any interest to their goods or no? *Answer.* Infidels before men are right lords of all their lands and possessions which they have obtained by lawful means, and in the courts of men they are not to be deprived of them; but before God they are but usurpers, because they hold them not *in capite*— that is, in Christ. Neither have they any holy and right use of them, "for to the

---

363. Jus ad rem.
364. Jus in re.

unclean, all things are unclean" (Titus 1:15). And they must first of all become members of Christ before they can hold and enjoy them aright and use them with good conscience.

The duties which are to be learned of the doctrine of this union are manifold. And, first of all, we are taught to purge our hands and hearts of all our sins and especially to avoid all those sins whereby men's bodies are defiled, as drunkenness, uncleanness, fornication; for they drive away the Spirit of God from His own house and dissolve the bond of the conjunction between Christ and us.

Secondly, we must, every one of us which profess ourselves to be members of Christ, labor to become conformable unto Him in holiness of life and to become new creatures; for this union requires thus much.[365] Let a man take the grafts of a crab tree and set them into good stocks; yet will they not change their sap but bring forth fruit according to their own nature, even sour crabs. But it must not be so with us. We are indeed wild olives and the branches of wild vines; yet, seeing we are persuaded that we are grafted into Christ and made one with Him, we must lay aside our wild and sour nature and take upon us the nature of the true vine, bear good fruit, have good juice in us, and render sweet wine.

Thirdly, we are taught hence to be plentiful in all good works, considering we are joined to Him that is the fountain of grace. And therefore Christ says, "I am the true vine, and my father is the husbandman: every branch that beareth not fruit in me, he taketh away: and every one that beareth fruit, he purgeth it, that it may bear more fruit" (John 15:1). And the prophet Isaiah compares the church of God to a vineyard with a tower and winepress in it [5:7]. And God Himself comes often down unto it "to see the fruits of the valley, to see if the vine bud, and the pomegranates flourish" [Song 6:10]. And further, we must bring forth "fruit with patience" [Luke 8:15]. For the Lord of this vineyard comes with crosses and afflictions, as with a pruning knife in His hand, to pare and to dress us that we may be fit to bring forth fruit, plentiful in duties of piety to God and in duties of love to all men, yea, to our enemies. Christian men are "trees of righteousness growing by the waters of the sanctuary" [Ezek. 47:12]—but what trees? Not like ours; for they are rooted upward in heaven in Christ, and their grains and branches grow downward that they may bear fruit among men.

Hitherto we have heard what the church is. Now to "believe the church" is nothing else but to believe that there is a company of the predestinated made one in Christ, and that withal we are in the number of them.

---

365. This paragraph break is not in the original, as the additional one following.

Before we proceed any further, three rules must be observed touching the church in general. The first, that Christ alone is the Head of the catholic church, and that He neither has nor can have any creature in heaven or earth to be fellow herein [Eph. 2:22]. For the church is His body, and none but He can perform the duty of a head unto it [Col. 2:19], which duty stands in two things. The first is to govern the church by such power and authority whereby He can and does prescribe laws properly binding the conscience of all His members. The second is by grace to quicken and to put spiritual life into them, so as they shall be able to say that they live not, but Christ in them. As for the supremacy of the see of Rome, whereby the pope will needs stand ministerial head to the Catholic Church, it is a satanical forgery. For the headship (as I may term it) of Christ is of that nature or quality that it can admit no deputy, whether we respect the commanding or the quickening power of Christ before named. Nay, Christ needs no vicar or deputy; for He is all-sufficient in Himself and always present with His church, as He Himself testifies, saying, "Where two or three be gathered together in my name, there am I in the midst among them" (Matt. 18:20). And whereas all commissions cease in the presence of him that gives the commission, it is as much pride and arrogancy for the pope to take unto himself the title of the head and universal bishop of the church, as it is for a subject to keep himself in commission in the presence of his king.

The second rule is that there is no salvation out of the church, and that therefore everyone which is to be saved must become a member and a citizen of the catholic and apostolic church; and such as remain forever out of the same perish eternally. Therefore, St. John says, "They went out from us, they were not of us: for if they had been of us, they would have remained with us: but this cometh to pass that it might appear that they are not all of us" [1 John 2:19]. And again, that such as be holy are in the city of God; "but without"— that is, forth of the church—"are dogs, enchanters, whoremongers, adulterers," etc. [Rev. 22:15]. And the ark, out of which all perished, figured the church, out of which all are condemned. And for this cause St. Luke says that "the Lord added to the church from day to day such as should be saved" [Acts 2:47]. And the reason hereof is plain, for without Christ there is no salvation. But out of the militant church there is no Christ nor faith in Christ, and therefore no salvation. Again, forth of the militant church there are no means of salvation—no preaching of the word, no invocation of God's name, no sacraments, and therefore no salvation. For this cause every man must be admonished evermore to join himself to some particular church, being a sound member of the catholic church.

The third rule is that the church which here we believe is only one. As Christ Himself speaks, "My dove is alone, and my undefiled is the only daughter of her mother" [Song 6:9]. And as there is only one God and one Redeemer, one faith, one baptism, and one way of salvation by Christ only, so there is but one church alone.

The catholic church has two parts: the church triumphant in heaven and the church militant on earth.

The triumphant church may thus be described: it is a company of the spirits of just men, triumphing over the flesh, the devil, and the world, praising God. First I say it is a company of the spirits of men, as the Holy Ghost expressly terms it, because the souls only of the godly departed, as of Abraham, Isaac, Jacob, David, etc., are as yet ascended into heaven, and not their bodies [Heb. 12:23]. Furthermore, the properties of this company are two.

The first is to make triumph over their spiritual enemies, the flesh, the devil, the world.[366] For the righteous man, so long as he lives in this world, is in continual combat without truce with all the enemies of his salvation; and by constant faith, obtaining victory in the end of his life, he is translated in glorious and triumphant manner into the kingdom of glory. This was signified to John in a vision in which he saw an "innumerable company of all sorts of nations, kindreds, people and tongues stand before the Lamb, clothed in long white robes, with palms in their hands" [Rev. 7:9], in token that they had been warriors but now by Christ have gotten the victory and are made conquerors.

Their second property is to praise and magnify the name of God, as it follows in the former place: "saying Amen: praise, and glory, and wisdom, and thanks, honor, power and might be unto our God for evermore" [v. 12]. Hence it may be demanded, whether angels be of this triumphant church or no? *Answer.* The blessed angels be in heaven in the presence of God the Father, the Son, and the Holy Ghost; but they are not of the mystical body of Christ, because they are not under Him as He is their Redeemer, considering they cannot be redeemed which never fell. And it cannot be proved that they now stand by the virtue of Christ's redemption. But they are under Him as He is their Lord and King; and by the power of Christ as He is God, and their God, are they confirmed. And therefore, as I take it, we cannot say that angels are members of the mystical body of Christ or of the triumphant church, though indeed they be of the company of the blessed.

The church militant may be thus described: it is the company of the elect or faithful living under the cross, desiring to be removed and to be with Christ. I say not that the militant church is the whole body of the elect, but only that part thereof which lives upon earth. And the infallible mark thereof is that

---

366. This paragraph break is not in the original, as the additional one following.

faith in Christ which is taught and delivered in the writings of the prophets and apostles. And this faith again may be discerned by two marks.

The first is that the members of this company live under the cross and profit by it in all spiritual grace.[367] And therefore it is said that "we must through many afflictions enter into the kingdom of heaven" [Acts 14:22]. And our Savior Christ says, "If any man will come after me, let him deny himself, and take up his cross every day and follow me" [Luke 9:23].

The second mark is a desire to depart hence and to be with Christ, as Paul says, "We love rather to be removed out of this body and to be with Christ" [2 Cor. 5:8]. And again, "I desire to be loosed and to be with Christ, which is best of all" [Phil. 1:23]. Where yet we must remember that the members of Christ do not desire death simply and absolutely, but in two respects: (1) that they might leave off to sin and by [not] sinning leave to displease God; (2) that they might come to enjoy happiness in heaven and to be with Christ.

Touching the general estate of the militant church, two questions are to be considered. The first, how far forth God is present with it, assisting it by His grace. *Answer.* God gives His Spirit unto it in such a measure that, although the gates of hell cannot prevail against it, yet nevertheless it remains still subject to error both in doctrine and manners. For that which is true in every member of the church is also true in the whole. But every member of the militant church is subject to error both in doctrine and manners, because men in this life are but in part enlightened and sanctified and therefore still remain subject to blindness of mind and ignorance and to the rebellion of their wills and affections, whereby it comes to pass that they may easily fail either in judgment or in practice. Again, that which may befall one or two particular churches may likewise befall all the particular churches upon earth, all being in one and the same condition; but this may befall one or two particular churches, to fail either in doctrine or manners. The church of Ephesus failed in "leaving her first love" [Rev. 2:4],[368] whereupon Christ threatens to remove from her the candlestick. And the church of Galatia was "removed to another gospel from him that had called them in the grace of Christ" [Gal. 1:6]. Now, why may not the same things befall twenty, yea, a hundred churches, which befell these twain? Lastly, experience shows this to be true, in that general councils have erred. The Council of Nicaea, being to reform sundry behaviors among the bishops and elders, would with common consent have forbidden marriage unto them, thinking it profitable to be so, unless Paphnutius had better informed them out of the Scriptures. In the Third Council at Carthage, certain books Apocryphal,

---

367. This paragraph break is not in the original, as the additional one following.
368. Originally, "Revelation 4."

as the book of Sirach, Tobias, and the Maccabees, are numbered in the canon and yet were excluded by the Council of Laodicea. And the saying of a divine is received, that "former councils are to be reformed and amended by the later."[369] But Papists, maintaining that the church cannot err, allege the promise of Christ: "Howbeit when he is come which is the spirit of truth, he will lead you into all truth" [John 16:13]. *Answer.* The promise is directed to the apostles, who with their apostolical authority had this privilege granted them that in the teaching and penning of the gospel they should not err; and therefore in the Council at Jerusalem they conclude thus, "It seems good unto us, and to the Holy Ghost" [Acts 15:28]. And if the promise be further extended to all the church, it must be understood with a limitation: that God will give His Spirit unto the members thereof to lead them into all truth, "so far forth as shall be needful their salvation" [1 John 3:24].

The second question is, wherein stands the dignity and excellency of the church? *Answer.* It stands in subjection and obedience unto the will and word of her Spouse and Head, Christ Jesus. And hence it follows that the church is not to challenge unto herself authority over the Scriptures, but only a ministry or ministerial service, whereby she is appointed of God to preserve and keep, to publish and preach them, and to give testimony of them [Acts 20:20, 27]. And for this cause it is called "the pillar and ground of truth" [1 Tim. 3:15]. The Church of Rome, not content with this, says further that the authority of the church in respect of us is above the authority of the Scripture, because (say they) we cannot know Scripture to be Scripture, but by the testimony of the church. But indeed they speak an untruth. For the testimony of men that are subject to error cannot be greater and of more force with us than the testimony of God, who cannot err. Again, the church has her beginning from the Word (for there cannot be a church without faith, and there is no faith without the word, and there is no word out[side] of the Scriptures); and therefore the church in respect of us depends on the Scripture, and not the Scripture on the church. And as the lawyer, which has no further power but to expound the law, is under the law, so the church, which has authority only to publish and expound the Scriptures, cannot authorize them unto us but must submit herself unto them. And whereas it is alleged that "faith comes by hearing" [Rom. 10:17], and this hearing is in respect of the voice of the church, and that therefore faith comes by the voice of the church, the answer is that the place must be understood not of that general faith whereby we are resolved that Scripture is Scripture, but of justifying faith whereby we attain to salvation. And faith comes by hearing the voice of the church not as it is the church's voice, but as it is a ministry or

369. August. bap. l. 2. c. 3.

means to publish the word of God, which is both the cause and object of our believing. Now on the contrary we must hold that as the carpenter knows his rule to be straight not by any other rule applied unto it, but by itself, for casting his eye upon it he presently discerns whether it be straight or no, so we know and are resolved that Scripture is Scripture even by the Scripture itself, though the church say nothing, so be it we have the spirit of discerning when we read, hear, and consider the Scripture. And yet the testimony of the church is not to be despised; for though it breed not a persuasion in us of the certainty of the Scripture, yet it is a very good inducement thereto.

The militant church has many parts. For as the ocean sea which is but one is divided into parts according to the regions and countries against which it lies, as into the English, Spanish, Italian Sea, etc., so the church, dispersed over the face of the whole earth, is divided into other particular churches according as the countries are several in which it is seated, as into the church of England and Ireland, the church of France, the church of Germany, etc.

Again, particular churches are in a twofold estate: sometimes they lie hid in persecution, wanting the public preaching of the word and the administration of the sacraments; and sometimes again they are visible, carrying before the eyes of the world an open profession of the name of Christ—as the moon is sometimes eclipsed, and sometime shines in the full.

In the first estate was the church of Israel in the days of Elijah, when he wished to die because "the people had forsaken the covenant of the Lord, broken down his altars, slain his prophets with the sword, and he was left alone, and they sought to take his life also" [1 Kings 19:14].[370] Behold, a lamentable estate when so worthy a prophet could not find another besides himself that feared God; yet mark what the Lord says unto him, "I have left seven thousand in Israel, even all the knees that have not bowed unto Baal, and every mouth that has not kissed him" [v. 18]. Again, it is said that "Israel had been a long season without the true God, without priest to teach, and without the law" [2 Chron. 15:3]. Neither must this trouble any that God should so far forth forsake His church, for when ordinary means of salvation fail, He then gathers His elect by extraordinary means, as when the children of Israel wandered in the wilderness, wanting both circumcision and the Passover, He made a supply by manna and by the pillar of a cloud. Hence we have direction to answer the Papists, who demand of us where our church was threescore years ago before the days of Luther. We say that then for the space of many hundred years a universal apostasy overspread the whole face of the earth, and that our church

---

370. This paragraph break is not in the original.

then was not visible to the world but lay hid under the chaff of popery. And the truth of this, the records of all ages manifest.

The second estate of the church is when it flourishes and is visible, not that the faith and secret election of men can be seen (for no man can discern these things but by outward signs), but because it is apparent in respect of the outward assemblies gathered to the preaching of the word and the administration of the sacraments for the praise and glory of God and their mutual edification. And the visible church may be thus described: it is a mixed company of men, professing the faith, assembled together by the preaching of the word.

First of all, I call it a mixed company, because in it there be true believers and hypocrites, elect and reprobate, good and bad.[371] The church is the Lord's field in which the enemy sows his tares [Matt. 13:25, 47]. It is the corn floor in which lies wheat and chaff. It is a band of men in which besides those that be of valor and courage there be white-livered soldiers. And it is called a church of the better part—namely, the elect whereof it consists—though they be in number few. As for the ungodly, though they be in the church, yet are they no more parts of it indeed than the superfluous humors in the veins are parts of the body.

But to proceed, how are the members of the visible church qualified and discerned? The answer follows in the definition, "professing the faith." Whereby I mean the profession of that religion which has been taught from the beginning and is now recorded in the writings of the prophets and apostles. And this profession is a sign and mark whereby a man is declared and made manifest to be a member of the church.

Again, because the profession of the faith is otherwhiles true and sincere and otherwhiles only in show, therefore there be also two sorts of members of the visible church: members before God and members before men. A member of the church before God is he that besides the outward profession of the faith has inwardly a pure heart, good conscience, and faith unfeigned, whereby he is indeed a true member of the church. Members before men, whom we may call reputed members, are such as have nothing else but the outward profession, wanting the good conscience and the faith unfeigned. The reason why they are to be esteemed members of us is because we are bound by the rule of charity to think of men as they appear unto us, leaving secret judgment unto God.

I added in the first place that the church is gathered by the word preached to show that the cause whereby it is begun and continued is the word, which for that cause is called the immortal seed [1 Peter 1:23] whereby we are born anew, and milk [1 Cor. 3:2; Heb. 5:13] whereby we are fed and cherished to life

---

371. This paragraph break is not in the original, as the additional one following.

everlasting. And hence it follows necessarily that the preaching of the doctrine of the prophets and apostles, joined with any measure of faith and obedience, is an infallible mark of a true church. Indeed, it is true, there be three things required to the good estate of the church: the preaching of the gospel, the administration of the sacraments, and the due execution of discipline according to the Word. Yet if the two latter be wanting, so be it there be preaching of the word with obedience in the people, there is for substance a true church of God. For it is the banner of Christ displayed under which all that war against the flesh, the devil, the world must rank themselves. As the Lord says by the prophet Isaiah, "I will lift up my hand to the Gentiles, and set up my standard unto the people, and they shall bring their sons in their arms, and their daughters shall be carried upon their shoulders" [Isa. 49:22]. Hence it follows that men which want the preaching of the gospel must either procure the same unto themselves, or, if that cannot be because they live in the midst of idolatrous nations, as in Spain and Italy, it is requisite that they should join themselves to those places where with liberty of conscience they may enjoy this happy blessing. Men are not to have their hearts glued to the honors and riches of this world, but they should be of David's mind and rather desire to be doorkeepers in the house of God than to dwell in the tents of ungodliness. In the Song of Solomon, the spouse of Christ says, "Shew me, O thou whom my soul loveth, where thou feedest, where thou liest at noon: for why should I be as she that turns aside to the flocks of thy companions?" [1:7]. To whom He answers thus: "If thou know not, O thou the fairest among women, get thee forth by the steps of the flock, and feed thy kids by the tents of the shepherds" [v. 8]—that is, in those places where the doctrine of righteousness and life everlasting by the Messiah is published. When the Shunammite's child was dead, she told her husband that she would go to the man of God, to whom he answered thus, "Why wilt thou go to him today? It is neither new moon, nor Sabbath Day" [2 Kings 4:23], whereby it is signified that when teaching was scarce in Israel, the people did resort to the prophets for instruction and consolation. And David says that the people, wheresoever their abode was, "went from strength to strength till they appeared before God in Sion" [Ps. 84:7]. And oftentimes they being proselytes, their abode must needs be out of the precincts of Jewry.

Thus we see what the visible church is. Now further, concerning it, three questions are to be scanned. The first is how we may discern whether particular men and particular churches, holding errors, be found members of the catholic church or no. For the answering of this, we must make a double distinction: one of errors; the other of persons that err. Of errors, some are destroyers of the faith; some only weakeners of it. A destroyer is that which overturns any fundamental point of religion, which is of that nature that, if it be denied, religion itself is overturned—as the denial of the death of Christ and the immortality of the soul, justification by works, and such like. And the sum of these fundamental points is comprised in the Creed of the Apostles and the Decalogue. A weakening error is that the holding whereof does not overturn any point in the foundation of salvation—as the error of free will and sundry such like. This distinction is made by the Holy Ghost, who says expressly that the doctrines of repentance and faith and baptism and laying on of hands and the resurrection and the last judgment "are the foundation" [Gal. 5:1, 3]—namely, of religion. And again, that "Christ is the foundation" [1 Cor. 3:10; Heb. 6:1], and that other doctrines consonant to the Word are as gold and silver laid thereupon.

Secondly, persons erring are of two sorts: some err of weakness, being carried away by others, or of simple ignorance, not yet being convicted and informed concerning the truth; some again err of obstinacy or affected ignorance, which, having been admonished and convicted, still persevere in their forged opinions.[372]

This being said, we now come to the point. If any man or church shall hold an error of the lighter kind, he still remains a member of the church of God and so must be reputed of us—as when a Lutheran shall hold that images are still to be retained in the church, that there is a universal election of all men, etc. For these and such like opinions may be maintained, the foundation of salvation unrazed. This which I say is flatly avouched by Paul. If any man (says he) build on this foundation gold, silver, precious stones, "timber, hay, stubble" [1 Cor. 3:11, 13], his work shall be made manifest by the fire, etc. "And if any man's work burn, he shall lose"—but yet he shall be safe "himself" [v. 15]. And therefore the hay and stubble of men's errors that are besides the foundation on which they are laid do not debar them from being Christians or members of the church. A man breaks down the windows of his house. The house stands. He breaks down the roof or the walls. The house yet stands, though deformed. He pulls up the foundation—the house itself falls and ceases to be a house. Now religion, which we profess, is like a house or building; and some points thereof are like windows, doors, walls, roofs, and some are the very foundation. And the former may be battered, the foundation standing.

Again, if the error be directly or by necessary consequent, even in common sense, against the foundation, consideration must be had whether the church or party errs of weakness or malice. If of weakness, the party is to be esteemed as a member of the catholic church. And thus Paul writes unto the church of Galatia as to a church of God, though by false teachers it had been turned away to another gospel, embraced the fundamental error of justification by

---

372. This paragraph break is not in the original, as the additional two following.

works. But when any man or church shall hold fundamental errors in obstinacy or affected ignorance, we are not then bound to repute them any longer as churches or Christians, but as such to whom condemnation belongs, as Paul shows by the example of Jannes and Jambres. "And as Jannes and Jambres," says he, "withstood Moses, so do these also resist the truth, men of corrupt minds, reprobate concerning the faith" [2 Tim. 3:8]. Yet withal, this caveat must ever be remembered, that we rather condemn the error than the person that errs, because God's mercy is like to a bottomless sea, whereby He works what He will and when He will in the hearts of miserable sinners.

The second question is where at this day we may find such visible churches as are indeed sound members of the catholic church. And for the resolving of it, we are to go through all countries and religions in the world. And first to begin with Turks and Jews, we are not in any wise to acknowledge their assemblies for churches, because they worship not God in Christ, who is the Head of the church.

As for the assemblies of Papists, which have been a great part of the world, if thereby we understand companies of men holding the pope for their head and believing the doctrine established in the Council of Trent, in name they are called churches, but indeed they are no true or sound members of the catholic church. For both in their doctrine and in the worship of God they raze the very foundation of religion, which will appear by these three points.

First of all, they hold justification by works of grace, avouching that they are not only justified before God by the merit of Christ, but also by their own doings.[373] Which opinion flatly overturns justification by Christ. For as Paul says to the Galatians, "If ye be circumcised, Christ profiteth you nothing" [Gal. 5:2]—that is, if you look to be justified by the works of the ceremonial law, you are fallen from Christ. Join circumcision and Christ together in the matter of justification, and you do quite overthrow justification by Christ. Now, if this be true, which is the Word of God, that cannot lie, then we say to the Papists, if you will needs be justified by works of grace, you are fallen from grace.

The second point is that they maintain a daily, real sacrifice of the body of Christ in the Mass for the sins of the quick and dead. And this is also a fundamental heresy. For Christ's sacrifice on the cross must either be a perfect sacrifice or no sacrifice; and if it be often iterated and repeated by the Mass priest, it is not perfect but imperfect.

The third point is that they worship the images of the Trinity and saints departed and their breaden god, which is as vile an abomination as ever was among the Gentiles—all being directly against the true meaning of the second

---

373. This paragraph break is not in the original, as the additional eight following.

commandment and defacing the worship of God in the very substance thereof. Thus then, it appears that the old Church of Rome is changed and is now at this day of a spouse of Christ become an harlot, and therefore no more a church of Christ indeed than the carcass of a dead man that wears a living man's garment is a living man, though he look never so like him. And whereas they plead for themselves that they have succession from the apostles, the answer is that succession of person is nothing without succession of doctrine, which they want, and we see that heretics have succeeded lawful ministers.

Secondly, whereas it is alleged that in the popish assemblies the sacrament of baptism is rightly for substance administered, and that also is a note of a church, three things may be answered. First, that baptism, severed from the preaching of the gospel, is no more a sign of a church than the seal severed from the indenture is of force—and that is, nothing. Circumcision was used in Colchis, yet no church; and among the Samaritans, and yet no people [Hos. 1:9].[374]

Secondly, baptism in the assemblies of the Church of Rome is as the purse of a true man in the hand of a thief, and indeed does no more argue them to be churches than the true man's purse argues the thief to be a true man. For baptism, though it be in their assemblies, yet does it not appertain unto them but unto another hidden church of God, which He has in all ages gathered forth of the midst of them.

Thirdly, though they have the outward baptism, yet they by necessary consequent of doctrine overturn the inward baptism that stands in justification and sanctification. Moreover, whereas it is alleged that they maintain the books of the Old and New Testament penned by the prophets and apostles, the answer is that they do it with adding to the canon and by corrupting the native sense of the Scriptures in the very foundation; and therefore they are but as a lantern that shows light to others and none to itself.

Fourthly, it is further said that they hold the Creed of the apostles and make the same confession of faith that we do. I answer that in show of words they do so indeed, but by necessary consequences in the rest of their doctrine they overturn one of the natures and all the offices of Christ, and therewithal most of the articles of the Creed. And herein they deal as a father that in outward show tenders the body of his child and will not abide the least blemish upon it, and yet by secret conveyances inwardly annoys the heart or the liver and so in truth destroys the same.

Fifthly, it is alleged that antichrist must sit in the temple of God—that is, the church. Therefore say some that desire a union between us and the Papists

---

374. Herodot.

[that] popish assemblies are true churches. But the argument is not good. For it is one thing to be in the church, and another thing to be of it. And antichrist is said to sit in the church not as a member thereof, but as a usurper or as the pirate in the ship of the merchant. And hence it cannot be proved that the assemblies of Papists are churches, but that in them and with them there is mingled another hidden church, in the midst whereof antichrist, the pope, rules, though himself has no part therein.

Lastly, whereas some being no Papists think their churches to be like a body diseased and full of sores and wounds from the head to the foot, and the throat also cut, yet so as life is still remaining, we may better think (their foul errors considered, and their worship of God, which is nothing else but a mixture of Judaism and paganism) that it is a rotten and dead corpse void of spiritual life. And therefore we have severed ourselves from the Church of Rome upon just cause; neither are we schismatics in so doing, but they rather, because the ground and the proper cause of the schism is in them.

As for the assemblies of Anabaptists, Libertines, Antinomies, Tritheists, Arians, Samosatenians—they are no churches of God but conspiracies of monstrous heretics judicially condemned in the primitive church and again by the malice of Satan renewed and revived in this age. The same we are to think and say of the Family of Love.

As for the churches of Germany commonly called the churches of the Lutherans, they are reputed of us as the true churches of God. Though their Augsburg Confession has not satisfied the expectation of other reformed churches, yet have they all the same enemies in matter of religion and do alike confess the Father, the Son, and the Holy Ghost; and of the office of the Mediator, of faith and good works, of the Word, the church, and the magistrate, [we] are all of one judgment. They differ indeed from us in the question of the Sacrament, but it is no sufficient cause to induce us to hold them as no church. For that there is a true or real receiving of the body and blood of Christ in the Lord's Supper, we all agree; and we jointly confess that Christ is there present, so far forth that He does truly feed us with His very body and blood to eternal life. And all the controversy lies in the manner of receiving, we contenting ourselves with that spiritual receiving which is by the hand of faith; they adding there to the corporal, whereby they imagine themselves to receive Christ with the hand and mouth of the body. And though to maintain this their opinion they be constrained to turn the ascension of Christ into a disparition, whereby His body, being visible becomes invisible, yet in the main points we agree that He entered into His kingdom in our name and for us, that we are governed and preserved by His power and might, and that whatsoever good thing we have or do proceeds wholly from the grace of His Spirit. Indeed, the opinion of the ubiquity of the body of Christ revives the condemned heresies of Eutychus and Nestorius, and it overturns by necessary consequent most of the articles of faith; but that was private to some men, as Brentius and others, and was not received of whole churches. And whereas the men were godly and learned, and we are uncertain with what affection and how long they held this error, we rest ourselves in condemning it, leaving the persons to God. Again, popish transubstantiation and Lutheran consubstantiation are both against the truth of the manhood of Christ, yet with great difference. Transubstantiation is flat against an article of faith; for if Christ's body be made of bread, and His blood of wine (which must needs be, if there be a conversion of the one into the other), then was not He conceived and born of the Virgin Mary—for it cannot both be made of baker's bread and of the substance of the Virgin. Again, it abolishes the outward sign in the Lord's Supper, as also the analogy between the sign and the thing signified, and so overturns the Sacrament. But consubstantiation does not so, neither does it overturn the substance of any article of religion but only a main point of philosophy, which is that a body does occupy one only place at once.

Furthermore, the churches of Helvetia and Savoy and the free cities of France and the Low Countries and Scotland are to be reverenced as the true churches of God, as their confessions make manifest. And no less must we think of our own churches in England and Ireland. For we hold, believe, and maintain and preach the true faith—that is, the ancient doctrine of salvation by Christ, taught and published by the prophets and apostles—as the book of the articles of faith agreed upon in open Parliament does fully show. And withal now we are and have been ready to testify this our faith by venturing our lives even in the cause of religion against foreign power, and especially the Spaniard; and hereupon all the churches in Europe give unto us the hand of fellowship. And whereas sundry among us that separate and indeed excommunicate themselves give out that there is no church in England, no ministers, no sacraments, their peremptory asseverations, wanting sufficient ground, are but as paper shot. They allege that our assemblies are full of grievous blots and enormities. *Answer.* The defects and corruptions of churches must be distinguished; and they be either in doctrine or manners. Again, corruptions in doctrine must further be distinguished: some of them are errors indeed, but besides the foundation; and some errors directly against the foundation—and these overturn all religion, whereas the former do not. Now it cannot be showed that in our churches is taught any one error that razes the foundation and consequently annihilates the truth of God's church. Indeed, there is controversy among us touching the point of ecclesiastical regiment, but mark in what manner. We all jointly agree in the substance of the regiment, confessing freely that there must be preaching of the word, administration of the sacraments, according to the institution and the use or the power of the keys in admonitions, suspensions, excommunications. The difference between us is only touching the persons and the manner of putting this government in execution. And therefore men on both parts, though both hold not the truth in this point, yet because both hold Christ the foundation, they still remain brethren and true members of Christ. As for corruptions in manners, they make not a church to be no church, but a bad church. When as the wicked scribes and Pharisees, sitting in Moses' chair [Matt. 23:2], taught the things which he had written, the people are commanded to heed them and to do the things which they say, not doing the things which they do. And whereas it is said that we hold Christ in word and deny Him in deed, that is answered thus: denial of Christ is double—either in judgment or in fact. Denial in judgment joined with obstinacy makes a Christian to be no Christian. Denial in fact, the judgment still remaining sound, makes not a man to be no Christian, but a bad Christian. When the Jews had crucified the Lord of life, they still remained a church (if any upon earth); and, notwithstanding this their fact, the apostles acknowledged that the covenant and the promises still belonged unto them [Acts 2:39–40; Rom. 9:4]. And they never made any separation from their synagogues till such time as they had been sufficiently convicted by the apostolical ministry that Christ was the true Messiah.

Thus, we see where at this day we may find the true church of God. Now I come to the third question, and that is, at what time a man may with good conscience make separation from a church. *Answer.* So long as a church make no separation from Christ, we must make no separation from it. And when it separates from Christ, we may also separate from it. And therefore in two cases there is warrant of separation.

The one is when the worship of God is corrupt in substance.[375] And for this we have a commandment. "Be not," says Paul, "unequally yoked with infidels, for what fellowship hath righteousness with unrighteousness, or what communion hath light with darkness? or what concord hath Christ with Belial? or what part hath the believer with the infidel? or what agreement hath the temple of God with idols? wherefore come out from among them, and separate yourselves, saith the Lord" [2 Cor. 6:14]. And we have a practice of this in the Old Testament. When Jeroboam had set up idols in Israel, then the priests and Levites "came to Judah and Jerusalem to serve the Lord" [2 Chron. 11:14].

The second is when the doctrine of religion is corrupt in substance, as Paul says, "If any man teach otherwise, and consent not to the wholesome words of our Lord Jesus Christ, and to the doctrine which is according to godliness, he

---

375. This paragraph break is not in the original, as the additional one following.

is puffed up: from which separate yourselves" [1 Tim. 6:3, 5]. A practice of this we have in the apostle Paul, who, being in Ephesus in a synagogue of the Jews, spoke boldly for the space of three months, disputing and exhorting to the things which concern the kingdom of God. "But when certain men were hardened and disobeyed, speaking evil of the way of God, he departed from them and separated the disciples of Ephesus" [Acts 19:9]. And the like he did at Rome also. As for the corruptions that be in the manners of men that be of the church, they are no sufficient warrant of separation, unless it be from private company, as we are admonished by the apostle Paul [1 Cor. 5:11] and by David's [Ps. 17:4] and Lot's [2 Peter 2:8] examples. By this which has been said, it appears that the practice of such as make separation from us is very bad and schismatical, considering our churches fail not either in the substance of doctrine or in the substance of the true worship of God.

Now to proceed in the Creed, the church is further set forth by certain properties and prerogatives. The properties or qualities are two: holiness and largeness. That the church is holy, it appears by Peter, which calls it "an holy nation, and a chosen people" [1 Peter 2:9], and by St. John, who calls it "the holy city" [Rev. 11:2]. And it is so called that it may be distinguished from the false church, which is termed in Scriptures "the synagogue of Satan" [2:9; 3:9] and the "malignant church" [Ps. 26:5].

Now, this holiness of the church is nothing else but a created quality in every true member thereof, whereby the image of God, which was lost by the fall of Adam, is again renewed and restored. The author of it is God by His word and Spirit by little and little abolishing the corruption of sin and sanctifying us throughout, as Christ says, "Father sanctify them in thy word, thy word is truth" [John 17:17]. And holiness must be conceived to be in the church on this manner: it is perfect in the church triumphant, and it is only begun in the church militant in this life, and that for special cause—that we might give all glory to God [1 Tim. 1:17]; that we might not be high-minded [Rom. 11:20]; that we might work out our salvation with fear and trembling [Phil. 2:12]; that we might deny ourselves and wholly depend upon God.

Hence, we learn three things. First, that the Church of Rome errs in teaching that a wicked man, yea, such a one as shall never be saved, may be a true member of the catholic church; for in reason, every man should be answerable to the quality and condition of the church whereof he is a member. If it be holy, as it is, he must be holy also. Secondly, we are every one of us, as Paul says to Timothy, to "exercise ourselves unto godliness" [1 Tim. 4:7], making conscience of all our former unholy ways, endeavoring ourselves to please God in the obedience of all His commandments. It is a disgrace to the holy church of God that men, professing themselves to be members of it, should be unholy.

Thirdly, our duty is to eschew the society of atheists, drunkards, fornicators, blasphemers, and all wicked and ungodly persons, as Paul says, "Be no companions of them, and have no fellowship with unprofitable works of darkness" [Eph. 5:7, 11]. And he charges the Thessalonians that if any man among them "walk inordinately, they have no company with him, that he may be ashamed" (2 Thess. 3:14).

The largeness of the church is noted in the word "catholic"—that is, general or universal. And it is so called for three causes. For, first of all, it is general in respect of time, because the church has had a being in all times and ages, ever since the giving of the promise to our first parents in paradise. Secondly, it is general in respect of the persons of men; for it stands of all sorts and degrees of men, high and low, rich and poor, learned and unlearned, etc. Thirdly, it is catholic or universal in respect of place, because it has been gathered from all parts of the earth, specially now in the time of the New Testament, when our Savior Christ says that the "gospel shall be preached in all the world" (Matt. 26:13). To this purpose St. John says in Revelation 7:9, "I beheld, and lo, a great multitude which no man could number, of all nations and kindred and peoples, and tongues, stood before the throne and before the Lamb, clothed with long white robes and palms in their hands."

And the church which we here profess to believe is called catholic[376] that we may distinguish it from particular churches, which are not believed but seen with [the] eye, whereof mention is made often in the Scriptures: "the church in their house" (Rom. 16:5); and, "the churches of Asia" (1 Cor. 16:19); "salute Nymphas and the church in his house" (Col. 4:15); "the church of Jerusalem" (Acts 11:22); "the church at Antioch," (13:1), etc.

That the church is catholic in respect of time, place, person, it ministers matter of endless comfort unto us. For hereby we see that no order, degree, or estate of men are excluded from grace in Christ, unless they will exclude themselves. St. John says, "If any man sin, we have an advocate with the Father, Jesus Christ the righteous" (1 John 2:1). Now it might be answered, "It is true indeed, Christ is an advocate to some men. But He is no advocate to me." St. John therefore says further, "And he is the reconciliation for our sins, and not for our sins only, but for the whole world" (v. 2)—that is, for all believers of what condition or degree soever.

Thus much of the properties of the church. Now follow the prerogatives or benefits which God bestows on it, which are in number four. The first is expressed in these words, "the communion of saints." Where "communion" signifies that fellowship or society that one has with another; and by "saints"

---

376. Catholica. 1. per totum orbeus diffusa. Aug. epist. 150.

we understand not dead men enrolled in the pope's calendar, but all that are sanctified by the blood of Christ, whether they be living or dead, as Paul says, "Unto the church of God which is at Corinth, to them that are sanctified in Jesus Christ, saints by calling" (1 Cor. 1:2). And, "God is the God of peace in all the churches of the saints" (14:33). Now, if we add the clause "I believe" unto these words, the meaning is this: "I confess and acknowledge that there is a spiritual fellowship and society among all the members of Christ, being the faithful servants and children of God; and withal I believe that I am partaker of the same with the rest."

This communion has two parts: fellowship of the members with the Head, and of the members with themselves. The communion of the members with their Head is not outward but altogether spiritual in the conscience. And for the opening of it, we must consider what the church receives of Christ, and what He receives of it. The church receives of Christ four most worthy benefits.

The first, that Christ, our Mediator, God and man, has truly given Himself unto us and is become our lot and portion and withal God the Father and the Holy Spirit in Him, as David says, "Jehovah is the portion of mine inheritance, and of my cup: thou shalt maintain my lot: the lines are fallen unto me in pleasant places: yea I have a fair heritage" [Ps. 16:5].[377] And, "My flesh faileth and my heart also: but God is the strength of my heart, and my portion forever" (73:26).

The second is the right of adoption, whereby all the faithful whether in heaven or earth are actually made the true children of God. The benefit is wonderful, howsoever carnal men esteem not of it. If a man should either by election or birth or any way else be made the son and heir of an earthly prince, he would think himself highly advanced. How highly then are they extolled which are made the sons of God Himself?

The third benefit is a title and right to the righteousness of Christ in His sufferings and His fulfilling of the law. The excellency of it is unspeakable, because it serves to award the greatest temptations of the devil. When the devil replies thus, "You are a transgressor of the law of God. Therefore, you shall be damned," by means of that communion which we have with Christ, we answer again that Christ suffered the curse of the law to free us from due and deserved damnation. And when he further replies that, seeing we never fulfilled the law, we cannot therefore enter into heaven, we answer again that Christ's obedience is a fulfilling of the law for us, and His whole righteousness is ours to make us stand righteous before God.

---

377. This paragraph break is not in the original, as the additional three following.

The fourth benefit is a right to the kingdom of heaven, as Christ, comforting His disciples, says, "Fear not little flock, it is your father's pleasure to give you the kingdom." And hence it is sundry times called "the inheritance" and the "lot of the saints" [Acts 26:18; Eph. 1:18; Col. 1:12].

Furthermore, for the conveyance of these benefits unto us, God has ordained the preaching of the word and the administration of the sacraments, especially the Lord's Supper, and has commanded the solemn and ordinary use of them in the church. And hereupon the Lord's Supper is called the communion. "The cup of blessing," says Paul, "which we bless, is it not the communion of the blood of Christ? and the bread which we break, is it not the communion of the body of Christ?" (1 Cor. 10:16)—that is, a sign and seal of the communion.

Again, the things which Christ receives of us are two: our sins with the punishment thereof made His by application or imputation; and our afflictions with all the miseries of this life, which He accounts His own and therefore does as it were put under His shoulders to bear the burden of them. And this communion between Christ and us is expressed in the Scriptures by that blessed and heavenly bargain in which there is mutual exchange between Christ and us. He imparts unto us "milk and wine without silver or money" to refresh us and "gold tried by the fire" that we may become rich (Isa. 55:1) and "white raiment" that we may be clothed and "eye salve" to anoint our eyes that we may see (Rev. 3:18). And we for our parts return unto Him nothing but blindness and nakedness and poverty and the loathsome burden of all our sins.

The second part of the communion is that which the saints have one with another. And it is either of the living with the living or of the living with the dead. Now the communion of the living stands in three things: (1) in the like affection; (2) in the gifts of the Spirit; (3) in the use of temporal riches.

For the first, communion in affection is whereby all the servants of God are like affected to God, to Christ, to their own sins, and each to other.[378] They are all of one nature and heart alike disposed, though they be not acquainted nor have any external fellowship in the flesh. As in a family children are for the most part one like another and brought up alike, even so it is in God's family which is His church—the members thereof are all alike in heart and affection. And the reason is because they have one Spirit to guide them all, and therefore St. Peter says, "The multitude of them that believed, were of one heart and of one soul, neither any of them said that anything which he possessed was his own, but they had all things common" (Acts 4:32). And the prophet Isaiah, foretelling the unity which should be in the kingdom of Christ, said, "The wolf

---

378. This paragraph break is not in the original.

shall dwell with the lamb, and the leopard shall lie with the kid, and the calf, and the lion, and the fat beast together, and a little child shall lead them. The cow and the bear shall feed, and their young ones shall lie together: and the lion shall eat straw like the bullock. The sucking child shall play upon the hole of the asp, and the weaned child shall put his hand into the cockatrice hole" (Isa. 11:6–7). By these beasts are signified men that be of a wicked and brutish nature, which when they shall be brought into the kingdom of Christ shall lay aside the same and become loving, gentle, courteous, and all of one mind. And St. Peter requires of the church the practice of brotherly love, and that is to carry a tender affection to men not because they are of the same flesh, but because they are joined in the bond of one Spirit with us (2 Peter 1:7). Furthermore, by reason of this, that all the children of God are of one heart, there follows another duty of this communion, whereby they bear one the burdens of another [Gal. 6:2]—and when one member is grieved, all are grieved; when one rejoices, all rejoice, as in the body when one member suffers all suffer.

The second branch of their communion is in the gifts of God's Spirit, as love, hope, fear, etc. And this is shown when one man does employ the graces of God bestowed on him for the good and salvation of another. As a candle spends itself to give light to others, so must God's people spend those gifts which God has given them for the benefit of their brethren. A Christian man, howsoever he be the freest man upon earth, yet is he servant to all men, especially to the church of God [5:13] to do service unto the members of it by love for the good of all. And this good is procured when we convey the graces of God bestowed on us to our brethren. And that is done five ways: (1) by example; (2) by admonition; (3) by exhortation; (4) by consolation; (5) by prayer.

The first, which is good example, we are enjoined by Christ, saying, "Let your light so shine before men, that they may see your good works, and glorify your Father which is in heaven" [Matt. 5:16].[379] And that our hearts might be touched with special care of this duty, the Lord sets afore us His own blessed example, saying, "Be ye holy as I am holy" (Lev. 11:44); and, "Learn of me that I am meek and lowly" (Matt. 11:29). And Paul says, "Be ye followers of me, as I follow Christ" (1 Cor. 11:1). And the higher men are exalted, the more careful ought they to be in giving good example. For let a man of note or estimation do evil, and he shall presently have many followers. Evil example runs from one to another like a leprosy or infection; and this Christ signified when He said that the fig tree planted in the vineyard, "if it bears no fruit, makes all the ground barren" (Luke 13:7).

---

379. This paragraph break is not in the original, as the additional four following.

The second means of communication of the gifts of God unto others is admonition, which is an ordinance of God whereby Christian men are to recover their brethren from their sins. A man by occasion fallen into the water is in danger of his life, and the reaching of the hand by another is the means to save him. Now, every man when he sins does as much as in him lies cast his soul into the very pit of hell, and wholesome admonitions are as the reaching out of the hand to recover him again. But it will peradventure be said, how shall we proceed in admonishing of others? *Answer.* We are to observe three things. The first is to search out whether we that are to reprove be faulty ourselves in the same things or no. First, we must take out the beam that is in our own eye, and so shall we see clearly to pull out the mote in our brother's eye (Matt. 7:5). Secondly, before we reprove we must be sure that the fault is committed. We must not go upon hearsay or likelihoods. And therefore the Holy Ghost says, "Let us consider or observe one another to provoke unto love and good works" (Heb. 10:24). Thirdly, before we reprove, we must in Christian wisdom make choice of time and place; for all times and places serve not to this purpose. And therefore Solomon says, "It is the glory of a man to pass by an offence." Furthermore, in the action of admonishing two things are to be observed: (1) a man must deliver the words of his admonition (so far forth as he can) out of the Word of God, so as the party which is admonished may in the person of man see God Himself to reprove him; (2) his reproof must be made with as much compassion and fellow-feeling of other men's wants as may be. As Paul says, "If any man be fallen by occasion into any fault, ye which are spiritual restore such an one with the spirit of meekness" (Gal. 6:1).[380]

The third way of communicating good things to others is exhortation, and it is a means to excite and stir them on forward which do already walk in the way of godliness. Therefore, the Holy Ghost says, "Exhort one another daily, lest any of you be hardened through the deceitfulness of sin" (Heb. 3:13). But alas, the practice of this duty, as also of the former, is hard to be found among men; for it is usual in families that masters and fathers instead of admonishing their servants and children teach them the practice of sin in swearing, blaspheming, slandering, etc. And as for exhortation, it is not used. Let a man that has the fear of God offend never so little, instead of brotherly exhortation, he shall hear his profession cast in his teeth and his hearing of sermons. This practice is so general that many beginning newly to tread in the steps of godliness are hereby daunted and quite driven back.

The fourth way is consolation, which is a means appointed by God whereby one man should with words of heavenly comfort refresh the souls of others

---

380. As surgeons tenderly set arms and legs in joint.

afflicted with sickness or any other way feeling the hand of God either in body or in mind. And this duty is as little regarded as any of the former. In time of men's sickness, neighbors come in—but what say they? "I am sorry to see you in this case. I hope to see you well again. I would be sorry else," etc. Not one of a hundred can speak a word of comfort to the weary. But we are faulty herein. For with what affection do we believe the communion of saints, when we ourselves are as dry fountains that do scarce convey a drop of refreshing to others?

The last means is prayer, whereby God's church procures blessings for the several members thereof, and they again for the whole. And herein lies a principal point of the communion of saints, which ministers notable comfort to every Christian heart. For hence we may reason thus: "I am indeed a member of the catholic church of God. And therefore, though my own prayers be weak, yet my comfort is this: I know that I am partaker of all the good prayers of all the people of God dispersed over the face of the whole earth, my fellow members, and of all the blessings which God bestows on them." This will make us in all our troubles to say with Elisha, "Fear not, for they that be with us are more than they that be with them" (2 Kings 6:16). When the people of Israel had sinned in worshipping the golden calf, the wrath of the Lord was kindled and made a breach into them, as cannon shot against a wall. But Moses, the servant of God, stood in the breach before the Lord to turn away His wrath lest He should destroy them [Ps. 106:23]. And the prayer of Moses was so effectual that the Lord said, "Let me alone" (Ex. 32:10), as though Moses by prayer had held the hand of God that He could not punish the people. And some think that Stephen's prayer for his enemies when he was stoned was a means of Paul's conversion. And surely, though there were no other reason, yet this were sufficient to move a man to embrace Christian religion, considering that, being a member of the church, he has part in all the prayers of the saints through the world and of the blessings of God that come thereby.

The third part of this communion is in temporal things, as goods and riches, whereby I mean no Anabaptistical communion,[381] but that which was used in the primitive church when they had all things common in respect of use. And some sold their goods and possessions and parted them to all men as everyone had need [Acts 4:34; 2 Cor. 9:1]. And by their example we are taught to be content to employ those goods which God has bestowed on us for the good of our fellow members within the compass of our callings and to our ability and beyond our ability, if need require. Paul says, "Do good to all, but especially to them which are of the household of faith" (Gal. 6:10).

---

381. Spiritual communion does not bar a division of temporal goods.

The communion of the living with the dead stands in two things. The one is that the saints departed in the church triumphant do in general pray for the church militant upon earth, desiring the final deliverance of all their fellow members from all their miseries. And therefore in the Apocalypse they cry on this manner, "How long Lord holy and true! dost not thou judge and avenge our blood on them that dwell on the earth?" [6:10]. I say in general, because they pray not for the particular conditions and persons of men upon earth, considering they neither know nor see nor hear us; neither can they tell what things are done upon earth. The second is that the godly on earth do in heart and affection converse with them in heaven, desiring continually to be dissolved and to be with Christ. Now, whereas the Papists do further enlarge this communion, avouching that the saints in heaven do make intercession to Christ for us and impart their merits unto us, and that we again for that cause are to invoke them and to do unto them religious worship, we dissent from them, being resolved that these things are but inventions of man's brain, wanting warrant out of the Word.

Lastly, to conclude, a question may be demanded, how any one of us may particularly know and be assured in ourselves that we have part in this communion of saints. *Answer.* St. John opens this point to the full when he says, "If we say that we have fellowship with him, and yet walk in darkness, we lie: but if we walk in the light, as he is light, then we have fellowship one with another, and the blood of Christ purges us from all our sins" (1 John 1:6–7). In which words he makes knowledge of God's will joined with obedience to be an infallible mark of one that is in the communion; as, on the contrary, ignorance of God's will or disobedience or both to be tokens of one that has neither fellowship with Christ or with the true members of Christ. And therefore to end this point, if we would have fellowship with Christ, let us learn to know what sin is and to fly from the same as from the bane of our souls and to make conscience of every evil way.

The duties to be learned by the communion of saints are manifold. And, first of all, if we do believe the fellowship which all the faithful have with Christ and with themselves and be resolved that we have part therein, then must we separate and withdraw ourselves from all ungodly and unlawful societies of men in the world whatsoever they be. Unlawful societies are manifold, but I will only touch one, which everywhere annoys religion and hinders greatly this communion of saints; and that is when men join themselves in company to pass away the time in drinking, gaming, etc. Behold, a large fellowship which bears sway in all places. There is almost no town but there is at the least one knot of such companions, and he that will not be combined with such loose mates, he is thought to be a man of no good nature. He is foisted forth of every company.

He is nobody. And if a man will yield to run riot with them in the misspending of his time and goods, he is thought to be the best fellow in the world. But what is done in this society? And how do these cup companions spend their time? Surely, the greatest part of day and night is usually spent in swearing, gaming, drinking, surfeiting, reveling, and railing on the ministers of the word and such as profess religion, to omit the enormities which they procure to themselves hereby. And this behavior spreads itself like a canker over every place, and it defiles both town and country. But we that look for comfort by the communion of saints must not cast in our lot with such a wicked generation but separate ourselves from them. For undoubtedly their society is not of God but of the devil; and they that are of this society cannot be of the holy communion of saints. And surely except the magistrate by the sword or the church by the power of the keys do pull down such fellowship, the holy society of God's church and people must decay. Excommunication is a censure ordained of God for this end, to banish them from this heavenly communion of the members of Christ that live inordinately and have communion with men in the works of darkness.

Secondly, by this we are taught that men professing the same religion must be linked in society and converse together in Christian love, meekness, gentleness, and patience, as St. Paul taught the Philippians, "If there be any fellowship of the spirit, if there be any compassion and mercy, fulfill my joy, that we may be like-minded, having the same love, being of one accord, and of like judgment" [Phil. 2:1–2]. And again, "Keep," says he, "the unity of the spirit in the bond of peace" [Eph. 4:3]. Why? Mark how his reason is fetched from this communion: "because there is one body, one spirit, even as you are called into the hope of your vocation: one Lord, one faith, one hope, one baptism, one God and Father of all, which is above all, and in you all" [vv. 4–6]. And no doubt the same reason made David say, "All my delight is in the saints which be upon earth" (Ps. 16:3).

Thirdly, every Christian man that acknowledges this communion must carry about with him a fellow-feeling—that is, a heart touched with compassion in regard of all the miseries that befall either the whole church or any member thereof, as Christ, our Head, teaches us by His own example when He called to Saul and said, "Saul, Saul, why persecutest thou me?" [Acts 9:4], giving him to understand that He is touched with the abuses to His church, as if they had directly been done to His own person. The prophet Amos reproves the people because they drank wine in bowls and anointed themselves with the chief ointments. But why? Was it not lawful for them to do so? Yes, but the cause for which they were reproved follows. "No man," says he, "is sorry for the afflictions of Joseph" [Amos 6:6]. In the midst of their delights and pleasures, they had no regard of the miseries of the poor church and servants of God elsewhere in affliction, which every man ought to show forth in the practice of all duties of love. And therefore Paul says, "Pray always with all manner of prayers and supplications in the spirit, and watch thereunto with all perseverance and supplications for the saints" [Eph. 6:18]. And he highly commends the Philippians "for communicating to his afflictions" [4:14]. And further he bids Philemon to "comfort Onesimus his bowels in the Lord" [v. 20]. And St. John says, if a man's life would save his neighbor's soul, "he must lay it down" [1 John 3:16], if need require. We have all of us daily occasion to practice this duty toward the afflicted members of God's church in other countries. For howsoever we enjoy the gospel with peace, yet they are under persecution for the same. And so oft as we hear report of this, we should suffer our hearts to be grieved with them and pray to God for them.

We must here be admonished not to seek our own things but to refer the labors of our callings to the common good, especially of the church whereof we are members. As for them that seek for nothing but to maintain their own estate and wealth and therefore in their trades use false weights and measures, the engrossing, corrupting, mingling of wares, glozing, lying, smoothing, swearing, foreswearing, dissembling, griping, oppressing of the poor, etc.—they may plead for themselves what they will, but in truth they never knew yet what the communion of saints meant.

Lastly, considering we are all knit into one mystical body and have mutual fellowship in the same, our duty is to redress the faults of our brethren and to cover them as the hand in the body lays a plaster upon the sore in the foot or in the leg and withal covers it. Love covers the multitude of sins. And when men disgrace their brethren for their wants and blaze them to the world, they do not the duty of fellow members.

Thus much for the first benefit bestowed on the church. The second is forgiveness of sins, which may be thus described: forgiveness of sins is a blessing of God upon His church procured by the death and passion of Christ, whereby God esteems of sin as no sin, or, as not committed. In this description, I have couched five points, which we are severally to consider.

The first, who is the author of forgiveness of sins?[382] *Answer.* God, whose blessing it is; for sin is only committed against God, and the violating of His laws and commandments are properly sins. And the offence done to any man or creature is no more in itself but an offence or injury. Yea, the breach of man's commandment is no sin, unless it do imply withal the breach of God's commandments. Therefore, it is a prerogative belonging to God alone to pardon sin. And when we are taught to say, "Forgive us our trespasses, as we forgive

---

382. This paragraph break is not in the original, as the additional four following.

them that trespass against us" [Luke 11:4], the meaning is not that we forgive sins as they are sins, but only as trespasses—that is, losses, hurts, and damages done unto us by men.

It may be further said God has given this power and commandment to His ministers to forgive sins, saying, "Whose sins ye remit, they are remitted" [John 20:13]. *Answer.* God's ministers do not properly forgive sins, but only in the name of God according to His Word pronounce to a penitent sinner that his sins are pardoned and forgiven of God. And therefore it is a most certain truth that none can forgive sins but God only. It was avouched by the Pharisees and not denied by Christ [Mark 2:7, 9]. Hence it follows that remission of sin, being once granted, remains forever, because God's love unto the elect is unchangeable, and His decree concerning their salvation cannot be altered.

The second point is, to whom remission of sins is given? *Answer.* To the catholic church—that is, to the whole company of men predestinated to salvation, as Isaiah says, "The people that dwell therein"—that is, the church—"shall have their sins forgiven" [Isa. 33:24]. And, "They shall call them the holy people, the redeemed of the Lord: and thou shalt be named, A city sought out, and not forsaken" [62:12]. And if there had been a universal remission of sins to all men, as some do dream, it should not here have been made a peculiar prerogative of the church.

The third point is, what is the means whereby pardon of sin is procured at God's hand? *Answer.* The death and passion of Christ. So Paul says, "Christ died for our sins" (Rom. 4:25)—that is, Christ died to be a payment and satisfaction to God's justice for our sins. And St. John says, "The blood of Jesus Christ his Son cleanseth us from all sin" [1 John 1:7]. And Peter says, "Knowing that ye were not redeemed with corruptible things, as silver and gold from your vain conversation, etc., but with the precious blood of Christ, as of a lamb undefiled and without spot" [1 Peter 1:18–19].

The fourth point is, after what manner sin is forgiven? *Answer.* By an action of God, whereby for the merit of Christ He esteems and accounts sin as no sin, or, as if it had never been committed. Therefore, David says, "Blessed is the man to whom the Lord imputeth no sin" (Ps. 32:2). And in Isaiah 44:22, the Lord says, "I have put away thy transgressions like a cloud, and thy sins as a mist." Now, we know that clouds and mists, which appear for a time, are afterward by the sun utterly dispersed. And King Hezekiah when he would show that the Lord had forgiven him his sins says, "God hath cast them behind his back" [38:17], alluding to the manner of men who when they will not remember or regard a thing do turn their backs upon it. And Micah says that "God doth cast all the sins of his people into the bottom of the sea" [Mic. 7:12], alluding to Pharaoh, whom the Lord drowned in the bottom of the Red Sea. And Christ has taught us to pray thus, "Forgive us our debts, as we forgive our debtors" [Matt. 6:12], in which words is an alluding to creditors, who then forgive debts when they account that which is debt as no debt and cross the book. Hence, it appears that damnable and vile is the opinion of the Church of Rome, which holds that there is a remission of the fault without a remission of the punishment; and here withal fall to the ground the doctrine of human satisfactions and indulgences and purgatory and prayer for the dead built upon this foundation, which are of the same kind.

Moreover, we must remember to add to this clause, "I believe," and then the meaning is this: "I do not only believe that God does give pardon of sin to His church and people (for that the very devils believe), but withal I believe the forgiveness of mine own particular sins." Hence, it appears that it was the judgment of the primitive church that men should believe the forgiveness of their own sins.

By this prerogative we reap endless comfort; for the pardon of sin is a most wonderful blessing, and without it every man is more miserable and wretched than the most vile creature that ever was. We loathe the serpent or the toad; but if a man have not the pardon of his sins, procured by the death and passion of Christ, he is a thousandfold worse than they. For when they die, there is the end of their woe and misery. But when man dies without this benefit, there is the beginning of his. For first in soul till the day of judgment and then both in body and soul forevermore he shall enter into the endless pains and torments of hell, in which if one should continue so many thousand years as there are drops in the ocean sea and then be delivered, it were some ease. But having continued so long (which is an unspeakable length of time), he must remain there as long again, and after that forever and ever without release. And therefore among all the benefits that ever were or can be thought of, this is the greatest and most precious. Among all the burdens that can befall a man, what is the greatest? Some will say sickness; some, ignominy; some, poverty; some, contempt. But indeed among all the heaviest and the greatest is the burden of a man's own sins, lying upon the conscience and pressing it down without any assurance of pardon. David, being a king, had no doubt all that heart could wish; and yet he, laying aside all the royalties and pleasures of his kingdom, says this one thing above all, that "he is a blessed man that is eased of the burden of his sin." A lazar man full of sores is ugly to sight, and we cannot abide to look upon him. But no lazar is so loathsome to us as all sinners are in the sight of God. And therefore David counted him blessed "whose sins are covered" [Ps. 32:1]. It may be, some will say, there is no cause why a man should thus magnify the pardon of sin, considering it is but a common benefit. Thus indeed men may imagine, which never knew what sin meant. But let a man only as it were but with the tip of his finger have a little feeling of the smart of his sins, he shall find his estate so fearful that if the whole world were set before him on the one side and the pardon of his sin on the other side, he would choose the pardon of his sins before ten thousand worlds. Though many drowsy Protestants esteem nothing of it, yet to the touched conscience it is a treasure, which when a man finds he hides it and goes home and sells all that he has and buys it. Therefore, this benefit is most excellent, and for it the members of God's church have great cause to give God thanks without ceasing.

The duties to be learned hence are these. And first of all here comes a common fault of men to be rebuked. Everyone will say that he believes the remission of sins, yet no man almost labors for a true and certain persuasion hereof in his own conscience. And for proof hereof, propound this question to the common Christian: do you persuade yourself that God gives remission of sins unto His church? The answer will be, "I know and believe it." But ask him further: do you believe the pardon of your own sins? And then comes in a blind answer, "I have a good hope to Godward, but I cannot tell. I think no man can say so much, for God says to no man, your sins are pardoned." But this is to speak flat contraries—to say they believe, and they cannot tell. And it bewrays exceeding negligence in matters of salvation. But let them that fear God or love their own soul's health give all diligence to make sure the remission of their own sins, withal avoiding hardness of heart and drowsiness of spirit, the most fearful judgments of God which everywhere take place. The foolish virgins went forth to meet the bridegroom with lamps in their hands as well as the wise, but they never so much as dreamed of the horn of oil till the coming of the bridegroom [Matt. 25:3]. So many men live in the church of God as members thereof, holding up the lamp of glorious profession; but in the mean season they seek only for the things of this life, never casting how they may assure themselves in conscience touching their reconciliation with God, till the day of death come.

Secondly, if we be here bound to believe the pardon of all our sins, then we must every day humble ourselves before God and seek pardon for our daily offences; for He gives grace to the humble or contrite. He fills the hungry with good things, when the rich are sent empty away. When Benhadad, the king of Syria, was discomfited and overcome by the king of Israel, by the counsel of his servants, who told him that the kings of Israel were merciful men, he sent them clothed in sackcloth with ropes about their necks to entreat for peace and favor [1 Kings 20:31]. Now, when the king saw their submission, he made a covenant of peace with him. We by our sins most justly deserve hell, death, and condemnation every day. And therefore it stands us in hand to come into the presence of God and to humble ourselves before Him in sackcloth and ashes, craving and entreating for nothing in the world so much as for the pardon of our sins, and that day by day without ceasing till the Lord give this blessed answer to our conscience, that all our sins are put out of His remembrance. We must not think that God puts grace into men's hearts when they lie snorting upon their elbows and either not use or despise the means. But we must first use the means partly by making confession of our sins to God and partly by crying to heaven for pardon; and then when by His grace we begin to desire grace, He gives further grace.

Lastly, if we believe the pardon of our sins, then we must change the tenor and course of our lives and take heed of breaking God's commandments by doing any of those things whereof our consciences may accuse us and tell us that by them we have displeased God heretofore. A man that for some misdemeanor has been cast into prison and laid there many years, winter and summer, in cold irons—when he obtains liberty, he will often bethink himself of his old misery and take heed forever lest he fall into the same offence again. And he which has seen his own sins and felt the smart of them and withal by God's goodness obtained assurance touching the pardon of them will never wittingly and willingly commit the like sins anymore but in all things change the course of his life. As for such as say that they have the pardon of their sins and yet live in them still, they deceive themselves and have no faith at all.

Proofs of the Resurrection[383]

Thus much for the second benefit which God bestows on His church—namely, remission of sins. Now follows the third in these words: the resurrection of the body. In the handling whereof sundry points must be considered. The first, whether there be a resurrection or no? This question must needs be handled because Epicures and atheists in all ages and at this day some do call this article into question. Now, that there is a resurrection of the body after death, it may be proved by many arguments, whereof I will only touch the principal.

[Proof] 1.[384] The first is taken from the work of redemption.[385] St. John writes that "Christ came to dissolve the works of the devil" [1 John 3:8], which are sin and by sin death. And hence I reason thus: if sin and death are to be dissolved utterly, then the bodies of the faithful which are dead in the grave must needs be made alive. Otherwise, death is not abolished. But sin and death must be utterly abolished. Therefore, there shall be a resurrection.

[Proof] 2. Secondly, God had made a covenant with His church, the tenor whereof is this, "I will be thy God, and thou shalt be my people" [Jer. 31:33].

---

383. Originally in the margin.
384. Originally in the margin, as the additional five proofs following.
385. This paragraph break is not in the original, as the additional five following.

This covenant is not for a day or an age or for a thousand years or ages, but is everlasting and without end, so as God's people may say of God forever, "God is our God." And likewise God will say of His church forevermore, "This people is My people." Now, if God's covenant be everlasting, then all the faithful departed from the beginning of the world must be raised again to life. And if God should leave His people in the grave under death forever, how could they be called the people of God? For He is a God of mercy and of life itself. And therefore, though they abide long in the earth, yet they must at length be revived again. This argument Christ uses against the Sadducees, which denied the resurrection: God is not the God of the dead but of the living; but God is the God of Abraham, Isaac, and Jacob [Matt. 22:32], which are dead—and therefore they must rise again.

[Proof] 3. The third argument must be taken from the tenor of God's justice. It is a special part of God's glory to show forth His mercy on the godly and His justice upon the wicked in rewarding them according to their works, as the apostle says, "God will reward every man according to his works: to them that by continuance in well-doing seek glory, and honor and immortality, life eternal: but unto them that disobey the truth, that be contentious, and obey unrighteousness, shall be indignation and wrath" [Rom. 2:6]. But in this life God rewards not men according to their doings; and therefore Solomon, speaking of the estate of all men in this world, says, "All things come alike to all, and the same condition to the just and unjust, to the good and bad, to the pure and polluted, to him that offers sacrifice, and to him that offers none" [Eccl. 9:2]. Nay, which is more, here the wicked flourish, and the godly are afflicted. The ungodly have hearts' ease and all things at will, whereas the godly are oppressed and overwhelmed with all kind of miseries and are as sheep appointed for the slaughter. It remains therefore that there must needs be a general resurrection of all men after this life, that the righteous may obtain a reward of God's free mercy, and the wicked utter shame and confusion. But some will say it is sufficient that God do this to the soul of every man; the body needs not to rise again. I answer that the ungodly man does not work wickedness only in his soul, but his body also is an instrument thereof. And the godly do not only practice righteousness in their souls, but in their bodies also. The bodies of the wicked are the instruments of sin, and the bodies of the righteous are the weapons of righteousness. And therefore their bodies must rise again, that both in body and soul they may receive a reward, according to that which they have wrought in them.

[Proof 4]. The fourth argument, which is also used by Paul, is this: "Christ himself is risen" [1 Cor. 15:12], and therefore all the faithful shall rise again. For He rose not for Himself as a private man, but in our room and stead and for us. If the Head be risen, then the members also shall rise again; for by the same power whereby Christ raised Himself, He both can and will raise all those that be of His mystical body, He being "the first fruits of them that sleep" [v. 20].

[Proof] 5. The fifth argument is taken from express testimony of Scripture. Job has an excellent place for this purpose: "I am sure," says he, "that my redeemer liveth, and he shall stand the last on the earth, and though after my skin worms destroy this body, yet I shall see God in my flesh, whom I myself shall see, and mine eyes shall behold, and none other for me" [Job 19:25–27]. And St. Paul to the Corinthians avouches and proves this point at large by sundry arguments, which I will not stand to repeat [1 Corinthians 15]—this one remembered: "If," says he, "the dead rise not again, then your faith is vain, our preaching is in vain, and the godly departed are perished" [vv. 14, 18].

[Proof] 6. The sixth argument may be taken from the order of nature, which ministers certain resemblances of the resurrection; which though they be no sufficient proofs, yet may they be inducements to the truth. Both philosophers and also divines have written of the phoenix, that first she is consumed to ashes by the heat of the sun, and that afterward of her ashes arises a young one; and on this manner is her kind preserved. Again, swallows, worms, and flies, which have laid dead in the winter season, in the spring by the virtue of the sun's heat revive again. So likewise men fall in sownes and trances, being for a time without breath or show of life, and yet afterward come again. And (to use Paul's example) before the corn can grow and bear fruit, it must first be cast into the ground and there rot. And if this were not seen by experience, men would not believe it. Again, every present day is as it were dead and buried in the night following, and yet afterward it returns again the next morning. Lastly, we read how the old prophets raised some from death; and our Savior Christ raised Lazarus, among the rest, that had laid four days in the grave and stank. And why then should any think it impossible for God to raise all men to life?

But let us see what reasons may be alleged to the contrary. First, it is alleged that the resurrection of bodies resolved to dust and ashes is against common sense and reason. *Answer.* It is above reason, but not against reason. For impotent and miserable man, as experience shows, can by art even of ashes make the curious workmanship of glass. Why then may we not in reason think that the omnipotent and ever-living God is able to raise men's bodies out of the dust?

Secondly, it is said that men's bodies, being dead, are turned into dust and so are mingled with the bodies of beasts and other creatures, and one man's body with another, and that by reason of this confusion men cannot possibly rise with their own bodies.[386] *Answer.* Howsoever this is impossible with

---

386. This paragraph break is not in the original, as the additional three following.

men, yet it is possible with God. For He that in the beginning was able to create all things of nothing is much more able to make every man's body at the resurrection of his own matter and to distinguish the dust of men's bodies from the dust of beasts, and the dust of one man's body, from another. The goldsmith by his art can sunder diverse metals one from another, and some men out of one metal can draw another. Why then should we think it impossible for the almighty God to do the like?

It may be further objected thus: a man is eaten by a wolf; the wolf is eaten of a lion; the lion, by the fowls of the air; and the fowls of the air, eaten again by men. Again, one man is eaten of another, as it is usual among the cannibals. Now the body of that man which is turned into so many substances, especially into the body of another man, cannot rise again. And if the one does, the other does not. *Answer.* This reason is but a cavil of man's brain; for we must not think that whatsoever enters into the body and is turned into the substance thereof must rise again and become a part of the body at the day of judgment. But every man shall then have so much substance of his own as shall make his body to be entire and perfect, though another man's flesh once eaten be no part thereof.

Again, it is urged that because flesh and blood cannot enter into the kingdom of God, therefore the bodies of men shall not rise again [1 Cor. 15:51]. *Answer.* By "flesh and blood" is not meant the bodies of men simply, but the bodies of men as they are in weakness, without glory, subject to corruption. For flesh and blood in Scripture signifies sometimes the original sin and corruption of nature and sometimes man's nature subject to miseries and infirmities or the body in corruption before it be glorified; and so it must be understood in this place.

Lastly, it is objected that Solomon says, "The condition of the children of men, and the condition of beasts are even as one condition" [Eccl. 3:19]. Now beasts rise not again after this life, and therefore there is no resurrection of men. *Answer.* In that place, Solomon expounds himself. They are like in dying; for so he says, as the one dies, so dies the other. He speaks not of their estate after death.

The second point to be considered is the cause of resurrection. In mankind, we must consider two parts: the elect and reprobate. And they both shall rise again at the day of judgment, but by diverse causes. The godly have one cause of their resurrection, and the ungodly another. The cause why the godly rise again is the resurrection of Christ. Yea, it is the proper cause which procures and effects their resurrection. In the Scripture, Adam and Christ are compared together, and Christ is called the second Adam. These were two roots. The first Adam was the root of all mankind, and he conveys sin and by sin death to all that sprang of him, Christ only excepted. The second Adam, which is the root of all the elect, conveys life both in body and soul to all that are united to Him; and by the virtue of His resurrection they shall rise again after this life. For look as the power of the Godhead of Christ when He was dead in the grave raised His body the third day, so shall the same power of Christ's Godhead convey itself unto all the faithful, which even in death remain united unto Him, and raise them up at the last day. And for that cause Christ is called a "quickening spirit" [1 Cor. 15:45]. Now, the cause why the wicked rise again is not the virtue of Christ's resurrection, but the virtue of God's curse set down in His Word: "In the day that thou shalt eat of the tree of knowledge of good and evil, thou shalt die the death" [Gen. 2:17]—that is, a double death, both of body and soul. And therefore they arise only by the power of Christ as He is a judge, that this sentence may be verified on them, and that they may suffer both in body and soul eternal punishment in hellfire.

Furthermore, St. John sets down the outward means whereby the dead shall be raised—namely, the voice of Christ. "The hour shall come," says he, "in which all that are in the grave shall hear his voice, and they shall come forth" [John 5:28]. For as He created all things by His word, so at the day of judgment by the same voice all shall be raised again. This may be a good reason to move us to hear the ministers of God reverently, for that which they teach is the very word of God. And therefore we are to pray that it may be as effectual in raising us up from the grave of sin in this life as it shall be after this life in raising us from the grave of death unto judgment.

Thirdly, we are to consider what manner of bodies shall rise at the last day. *Answer.* The same bodies for substance. This Job knew well when he said, "I shall see him at the last day in my flesh, whom I myself shall see, and none other for me, with the same eyes" [Job 19:26–27]. Nevertheless, the bodies of the elect shall be altered in quality, being made incorruptible and filled with glory [1 Cor. 15:43].

The last point to be considered is the end why these bodies shall rise again. The principal end which God intends is His own glory in the manifestation of His justice and mercy. Now, at the last day when all men shall be raised to judgment by the voice of Christ—the godly to life, and the wicked to condemnation—there shall be a full manifestation both of His mercy and justice, and therefore by consequent a full manifestation of His glory.

Thus much for the doctrines touching the resurrection. Now follow the uses. First, it serves wonderfully for the comfort of all Christian hearts. David, speaking not only of Christ but also of himself, says most notably, "Mine heart is glad, my tongue rejoiceth, and my flesh also doth rest in hope." Why so? "For," says he, "thou shall not leave my soul in the grave, neither wilt thou suffer thy holy one to see corruption" [Ps. 16:9–10]. Though the days of this life be days of woe and misery, yet the day of the resurrection shall be unto all the children of God a time of rejoicing and felicity; and as Peter says, "It is the time of refreshing" [Acts 3:19]. Whosoever is now a hungered shall then eat and be filled with the fruit of the tree of life. And whosoever is now naked shall be then clothed with the white garment dipped in the blood of the Lamb. And whosoever is now lame[387] shall have all his members restored perfectly. And as this day is joyful to the godly, so on the contrary it is a day of woe and misery to the ungodly—as St. John says, "They that have done evil, shall come forth to the resurrection of condemnation" [John 5:29]. If they might cease to live after this life and die as the beast does, O then it would be well with them; for then they might have an end of their misery. But the wicked must after this life rise again to condemnation, which is the accomplishment of their eternal woe and wretchedness—a rueful and doleful case to consider, and yet is it the state of all unbelieving and unrepentant sinners. If a man were bidden to go to bed that after he had slept and was risen again he might go to execution, it would make his heart to ache within him. Yet this, yea, a thousandfold worse is the estate of all impenitent sinners. They must sleep in the grave for awhile and then rise again, that a second death may be inflicted upon them in body and soul, which is the suffering of the full wrath of God both in body and soul eternally. This being so, let us embrace the good counsel of St. Peter, who says, "Amend your lives and turn, that your sins may be done away when the time of refreshing shall come from the presence of the Lord" [Acts 3:19]. If a man die repentant for his sins, it is a day of refreshing; but if he die in his sins, impenitent and hardhearted, it is a day of eternal horror, desperation, and confusion.

Again, if we believe that our bodies shall rise again after this life and stand before God at the last day of judgment, we must daily enter into a serious consideration of this time and have in mind that one day we must meet the Lord face to face. A traveler comes into an inn, having but a penny in his purse. He sits down and calls for all store of provision and dainties. Now, what is to be thought of him? Surely, in the judgment of all men his behavior betokens folly, or rather madness. But why? Because he spends freely and has no regard to the reckoning which must follow. How foolish then and mad is the practice of every man that lives in his sins, bathing himself in his pleasures in this world, never bethinking how he shall meet God at the last day of judgment and there make reckoning of all his doings? An ancient divine writes of himself that this saying ran in his mind and sounded always in his ears: "Arise, ye dead and

---

387. Aug. in Enchir. c. 91.

come unto judgment."[388] And this ought always to be sounding in our ears, that while we have time we should prepare ourselves to meet God at the last day.

Thirdly, if we believe the resurrection of the body, we are not to weep and mourn immoderately for our friends deceased. Our Savior Christ did weep for Lazarus; and when Stephen was stoned to death, certain men that feared God buried him and made great lamentation for him. And therefore mourning is not condemned, and we must not be as stocks that are bereft of all compassion. Yet remember we must what St. Paul says to the Thessalonians: "I would not, brethren, have you ignorant concerning those which are asleep, that ye sorrow not, as others, which have no hope" [1 Thess. 4:13]. For the godly man properly dies not but lays himself down to take a sleep after his manifold labors in this life, which being ended, he must rise again to joys everlasting. And therefore we must needs moderate and mingle our mourning for the deceased with this and such like comforts.

Fourthly, we are taught hence to labor and strive against the natural fear of death; for if there be a resurrection of our bodies after this life, then death is but a passage or middle way from this life to eternal life. If a beggar should be commanded to put off his old rags that he might be clothed with rich and costly garments, would he be sorry because he should stand naked a while till he were wholly bestripped of his rags? No, surely. Well, thus does God when He calls a man to death. He bids him out of his old rags of sin and corruption and be clothed with the glorious robe of Christ's righteousness; and our abode in the grave is but for a space, while corruption be put off. This is Paul's argument, saying, "We know that when our earthly house of this tabernacle shall be dissolved, we have a building given of God, which is an house not made with hands, but eternal in the heavens" [2 Cor. 5:1].

Fifthly, whereas the godly are subject to manifold afflictions and miseries both in body and mind in this life, here they shall find a sufficient stay to quiet and calm their minds, if they consider that after this short life is ended there will ensue a joyful resurrection. Job in the extremity of all his temptations made this the comfort of his soul, that one day he should rise again in which he should enjoy the glorious presence of his Creator [Job 19:26]. And the Holy Ghost says that the servants of God in the days of Antiochus were wracked and tormented and would not be delivered. Why so? Because "they looked for a better resurrection" [Heb. 11:35].

Lastly, the consideration of this point serves to be a bridle to restrain a man from sin and a spur to make him go forward in all godliness of life and conversation. St. Paul "had hope toward God, that the resurrection of the dead

---

388. Hierome.

should be both of the just and unjust." Now, what did this move him unto? Mark: "Herein," says he—that is, in this respect[389]—"I endeavor myself always to have a clear conscience toward God and toward men" [Acts 24:16]. And let us for our part likewise remember the last judgment, that it may be a means to move us so to behave ourselves in all our actions that we may keep a good conscience before God and before men. And let it also be a bridle unto us to keep us back from all manner of sin. For what is the cause why men daily defile their bodies and souls with so many damnable practices without any remorse of conscience? Surely, they never seriously remember the day of the resurrection after this life wherein they must stand before Christ to give an account of that which they have done in this life, whether it be good or bad.

Thus much of the duties. Now mark, it is further said, "the resurrection of the body." If the body rise, it must first fall. Here then this point is wrapped up as a confessed truth, that all men must die the first death. And yet, considering that the members of the church have the pardon of their sins, which are the cause of death, it may be demanded, why they must die? *Answer.* We are to know that when they die death does not seize upon them as it is in its[390] own nature a curse—for in that respect it was borne of Christ upon the cross, and that for us—but for two other causes, which we must think upon as being special means to make a man willing to die. (1) They must die that original corruption may be utterly abolished; for no man living on earth is perfectly sanctified, and original sin is remaining for special causes to the last moment of this life. Then it is abolished, and not before. (2) The godly die that by death as by a strait gate they may pass from this vale of misery to eternal life. And thus Christ by His death makes death to be no death and turns a curse into a blessing.

And to proceed, it is not here said, "the resurrection of the soul," but "of the body" only. What then (will some say) becomes of the soul? Diverse have thought that the souls then, though they do not die, yet are still kept within the body (being as it were asleep) till the last day. But God's Word says to the contrary. For the souls of the godly lie under the altar and cry, "How long Lord Jesus?" [Rev. 6:10]. Dives in soul did suffer the woe and torments of hell, and Lazarus had joy in Abraham's bosom [Luke 16:23]. Again, some others think that men's souls after this life do pass from one man's body to another. And Herod may seem to have been of this opinion; for when news was brought him of Christ, he said that John [the] Baptist, being beheaded, "was risen again" [Matt. 14:2], thinking that the soul of John [the] Baptist was put into the body of some other man. And for proof hereof, some allege the example of Nebuchadnezzar,

---

389. Or in the mean season.
390. Originally, "his."

who, forsaking the society of men, lived as beasts and did eat grass like a beast. And they imagine that his own soul went out of him and that the soul of a beast entered into the room thereof. But this indeed is a fond conceit; for even then he had the soul of a man when he lived as a beast, being only stricken by the hand of God with an exceeding madness whereby he was bereft of common reason, as does appear by that clause in the text, where it is said that his "understanding" or "knowledge returned to him again" [Dan. 4:33]. Again, some others think that the soul neither dies nor sleeps nor passes out of one body into another, but wanders here on earth among men and oftentimes appears to this or that man. And this is the opinion of some heretics and of the common people, which think that dead men walk. And for proof hereof some allege the practice of the witch of Endor, who is said to make Samuel to appear before Saul. But the truth is it was not Samuel indeed, but only a counterfeit of him. For not all the witches in the world nor all the devils in hell are able to disquiet the souls of the faithful departed, which are in the keeping of the Lord without wandering from place to place. For when men die in the faith, their souls are immediately translated into heaven and there abide till the last judgment. And contrariwise, if men die in their sins, their souls go straight to the place of eternal condemnation and there abide as in a prison, as Peter says. In a word, when the breath goes out of the body, the soul of every man goes straight either to heaven or hell; and there is no third place of abode mentioned in Scripture.

To conclude, the resurrection of the body is expressly mentioned in the Creed to show that there is no resurrection of the soul, which neither dies nor sleeps but is a spiritual and invisible substance, living and abiding forever as well forth of the body as in the same.

Thus much of the third prerogative or benefit. Now follows the fourth and last, in these words: "and life everlasting." To handle this point to the full and to open the nature of it as it deserves is not in the power of man. For both the prophet Isaiah and St. Paul say that "the eye hath not seen, and the ear hath not heard, neither came it into man's heart to think of those things which God hath prepared for those that love him" [1 Cor. 2:9]. Again, Paul when he was rapt into the third heaven says that he "saw things not to be uttered" [2 Cor. 12:4]. Nevertheless, we may in some part describe the same, so far forth as God in this case has revealed His will unto us. Wherefore, in this last prerogative I consider two things: the first is life itself; the second is the continuance of life noted in the word "everlasting."

Life itself is that whereby anything acts, lives, and moves itself, and it is twofold: uncreated or created.[391] Uncreated life is the very Godhead itself

---

391. This paragraph break is not in the original.

whereby God lives absolutely in Himself, from Himself, and by Himself, giving life and being to all things that live and have being. And this life is not meant here because it is not communicable to any creature. Created life is a quality in the creature, and it is again twofold: natural, spiritual. Natural life is that whereby men in this world live by meat and drink and all such means as are ministered by God's providence. Spiritual life is that most happy and blessed estate in which all the elect shall reign with Christ, their Head, in the heavens after this life and after the day of judgment forever and ever. And this alone is the life which in the Creed we confess and believe, and it consists in an immediate conjunction and communion or fellowship with God Himself—as Christ in His solemn prayer to His Father a little before His death signifies: "I pray not for these alone, but for them also which shall believe in me through their word, that they all may be one, as thou, O Father, art in me and I in thee, even that they may be one also in us" [John 17:20–21]. And when St. John in the Revelation says, "Behold the tabernacle of God is with men, he will dwell with them, and they shall be his people, and God himself shall be their God with them" [Rev. 21:3], he shows that the very foundation of that happiness which God has prepared for His servants stands in a society between God and them, whereby God shall dwell with them in heaven, and they again shall there enjoy His glorious presence.

Touching this communion, three points must be considered. The first is in what order men shall have fellowship with God. *Answer.* This communion shall be first of all with Christ as He is man. And by reason that the manhood of Christ is personally united to the Godhead of the Son, it shall also be with Christ as He is God, and consequently with the Father and the Holy Ghost. The reason of this order is because Christ, though He be the author and the fountain of eternal life as He is God, yet He conveys the same unto us only in and by His flesh or manhood. Yet must we not here think that life proceeds from the manhood itself, as from a cause efficient; for the flesh quickens not by any virtue from itself, but by the Word to which it is personally united, it being as it were a pipe eternally to convey life from the Godhead unto us.

The second point is in what things this communion consists. *Answer.* St. Paul opens this point to the very full when he says that after Christ has subdued all things unto Him, then "God shall be all in all" [1 Cor. 15:28]—that is, God Himself immediately shall be all good things that heart can wish to all the elect. But some may say, "What? Is not God all in all unto us even in this life? For whatsoever good things we have, they are all from Him." *Answer.* It is true indeed, God is all in all even in this life. But how? Not immediately, but by outward means, and that also in small measure. For He conveys His goodness and mercy unto us so long as we live on earth partly by His creatures and partly by His word and sacraments. But after this life is ended, all helps and outward means shall cease. Christ shall give up His kingdom, and as He is Mediator shall cease to put in execution the office of a priest, a prophet, or a king. All authority and power shall be abolished; and therefore all callings in the three main estates of the church, the commonwealth, the family shall have an end. There shall be no more magistrate and subject, pastor and people, master and servant, father and son, husband and wife. There shall be no more use of meat, drink, clothing, respiration, physic, sleep. And yet for all this, the condition of men shall be many thousandfold more blessed than ever it was. For the Godhead in the Trinity immediately without all means shall be all things to all the chosen people of God in the kingdom of heaven, world without end. This may seem strange to man's reason, but it is the very flat truth of God's Word. St. John in the description of the heavenly Jerusalem says that there shall be no temple in it. Why? How then shall God be worshipped? Mark what follows: "the Lord God Almighty and the Lamb are the temple of it" [Rev. 21:22]. Whereby it is signified that although now we use the preaching of the word and the administration of the sacraments as means of our fellowship with God; yet when this life is ended they must all cease, God and Christ being instead of all these means unto us. And he adds further, "The city hath no need of the sun, nor of the moon to shine in it." What then, will some say—must there be nothing but darkness? Not so. For the "glory of God doth light it, and the Lamb is the light of it" [v. 23]. Again, he says that in the paradise of God there is "the river of water of life, and tree of life bearing fruit every month" [22:2], and that is Christ. And therefore we shall have no need of meat, drink, apparel, sleep, etc. But Christ Himself, our Head and Redeemer, shall be instead of them all unto us, on whom all the elect shall feed and by whom both in body and soul they shall be preserved evermore. If a man would have glory, the Father, Son, and Holy Ghost shall be his glory. If a man desire wealth and pleasure, God Himself shall be wealth and pleasure unto him, and whatsoever else the heart of man can wish. Hence, it appears that this communion is admirable, and that no tongue can tell nor heart conceive the least part of it.

The third point is touching the benefits or prerogatives that proceed of this communion, and they are in number six. The first is an absolute freedom from all wants. In the mind, there shall be no ignorance, no unbelief, no distrust in God, no ambition, no envy, nor anger, nor carnal lusts, nor terror in conscience, or corrupt affection. In the body, there shall be no sore, no sickness, nor pain; for God shall wipe away all tears from their eyes. Nay, then all defects or wants in body or soul or in both shall be supplied, and the whole man made perfect every way [21:4].

The second is perfect knowledge of God. In this life, the church and all the servants of God know Him but in part. Moses would have seen God's face, but he was permitted to see only His hinder parts; and as Paul says, now we know in part, and darkly, as through a glass [1 Cor. 13:12]. In this life, we can no otherwise discern but as an old man through spectacles. And the creatures, but specially the Word of God and the sacraments, are the spectacles of our mind, wherein we behold His justice, mercy, love, etc.; and without them we can discern little or nothing. Yet after this life when that which is perfect is come, and that which is imperfect is abolished, we shall see God as He is to be seen, not as through a glass, but face to face. And we shall know Him as we are known of His majesty, so far forth as possibly a creature may. God indeed is infinite, and therefore the full knowledge of His majesty can no more be comprehended by the understanding of the creature, which is finite, than the sea by a spoon. Yet nevertheless God shall be known every way of man, so far forth as a creature may know the Creator.

Now upon this that the elect have such fullness of knowledge, it may be demanded whether men shall know one another after this life or no. *Answer.* This question is oftener moved by such as are ignorant than by them that have knowledge, and oftentimes it is tossed in the mouths of them that have little religion in their hearts. And therefore I answer, first, men should rather have care to seek how they may come to heaven than to dispute what they shall do when they are there. The common proverb is true: it is no good counting of chickens, before they be hatched. Secondly, I say that men in heaven shall know each other. Yea, they shall know them which were never known or seen of them before in this life, which may be gathered by proportion out of God's Word. Adam in his innocency knew Eve, whom he had never seen before, and gave her a fit name so soon as she was created. And when our Savior Christ was transfigured in the Mount [of Transfiguration], Peter knew Moses and Elijah, whom before he had never seen [Matt. 17:4]. And therefore it is like[ly] that the elect shall know each other in heaven, where their knowledge and their whole estate shall be fully perfected. But whether they shall know one another after an earthly manner, as to say, "This man was my father; this, mine uncle; this, my teacher," etc., the Word of God says nothing. And therefore I will be silent, and we must be content a while to be ignorant in this point.

The third prerogative of everlasting blessedness is that the elect shall love God with as perfect love as a creature possibly can. The manner of loving God is to love Him for Himself, and the measure is to love Him without measure; and both shall be found in heaven. For the saints of God shall have an actual fruition of God Himself and be as it were swallowed up with a sea of His love and wholly ravished therewith, for which cause, as far as creatures can, they shall love Him again. Again, the love of a thing is according to the knowledge thereof, but in this life God is known of man only in part and therefore is loved only but in part. But after this life, when the elect shall know God fully, they shall love Him without measure. And in this respect love has a prerogative above faith or hope, howsoever in some respects again they go beyond love.

The fourth prerogative is that the saints of God keep a perpetual Sabbath in heaven. In this life, it is kept but every seventh day; and when it is best of all sanctified, it is done but in part. But in heaven every day is a Sabbath, as the Lord says by the prophet Isaiah, "From month to month, and from sabbath to sabbath, all flesh shall come before me" [Isa. 66:23]. And therefore the life to come shall be spent in the perpetual service of God [Heb. 4:9].

Fifthly, the bodies of the elect after this life in the kingdom of heaven shall be like the glorious body of Christ. So Paul says, "Christ Jesus our Lord shall change our vile bodies, that they may be like his glorious body" [Phil. 3:21]. Now, the resemblance between Christ's body and ours stands in these things: as Christ's body is incorruptible, so shall our bodies be void of all corruption; as Christ's body is immortal, so ours in the kingdom of heaven shall never die; as Christ's body is spiritual, so shall ours be made spiritual, as the apostle says, "It is sown a natural body, it is raised a spiritual body" [1 Cor. 15:44]—not because the body shall be changed into a spirit, for it shall remain the same in substance, and that forever, but because it shall be preserved by a spiritual and divine manner. For in this life it is preserved by meat, drink, clothing, sleep, physic, rest, and diet; but after without all these means the life of the body shall be continued, and body and soul kept together by the immediate power of God's Spirit forever and ever. Thus, the body of Christ is now preserved in heaven, and so shall the bodies of all the elect be after the day of judgment. Furthermore, as Christ's body is now a shining body, as does appear by His transfiguration in the Mount, so in all likelihood after the resurrection the bodies of the elect shall be shining and bright, always remaining the same for substance. Lastly, as Christ's body after it rose again from the grave had this property of agility, besides swiftness, to pass from the earth to the third heaven, being in distance many thousand miles from us, and that without violence, so shall the bodies of the saints. For, being glorified, they shall be able as well to ascend upward as to go downward and to move without violence, and that very swiftly.

The sixth and last prerogative is an unspeakable and eternal joy, as David says, "In thy presence is fullness of joy: at thy right hand there are pleasures forevermore" [Ps. 16:11]. It is said that when Solomon was crowned king, the people rejoiced exceedingly [1 Kings 1:40]. If there were such great joy at his coronation which was but an earthly prince, what joy then shall there be when the elect shall see the true Solomon crowned with glory in the kingdom of heaven? It is said that the wise men which came from the East to worship Christ, when they saw the star, standing over the place where the babe was, were exceedingly glad [Matt. 2:10]. How much more shall the elect rejoice, when they shall see Christ not lying in a manger but crowned with immortal glory in the kingdom of heaven? Wherefore, this joy of the elect after this life is most wonderful and cannot be uttered.

The property of life eternal is to be an inheritance which God bestows on them which are made His sons in Christ, who is the only begotten Son of the Father [Rom. 8:17]. Hence, it follows necessarily that in the Scripture it is called a reward, not because it is deserved by our works, as the Church of Rome erroneously teaches, but for two other causes. First, because life eternal is due to all that believe by virtue of Christ's merit. For His righteousness is made ours by imputation; so consequently the merit thereof is also ours. And by it (all personal merits in ourselves utterly excluded) we deserve or merit eternal happiness as a reward, which nevertheless in respect of ourselves is the free and mere gift of God [6:23]. The second is because there is a resemblance between eternal life and a reward. For as a reward is given to a workman after his work is done, so everlasting life is given unto men after the travels and miseries of this life are ended.

The degrees of life are three. The first is in this life, when men, being justified and sanctified, have peace with God. Many imagine that there is no eternal life till after death; but they are deceived, for it begins in this world, as our Savior Christ testifies, saying, "Verily, verily I say unto you, he that hears my words, and believes him that sent me, hath everlasting life, and shall not come into condemnation, but hath passed from death to life" [John 5:24]. This being so, we are hence to learn a good lesson. Considering we look for life everlasting after this life, we must not deceive ourselves, lingering and deferring the time till the last gasp. But we must lay the foundation of life eternal in ourselves in this world and have the earnest thereof laid up in our hearts against the day of death. But how is that done? We must repent us heartily of all our sins and seek to be assured in conscience that God the Father of Christ is our Father, God the Son our Redeemer, and God the Holy Ghost our Comforter—for as Christ says, "This is life eternal, to know thee the only God, and whom thou hast sent Jesus Christ" [John 17:3]. And we must go further yet, endeavoring to say with Paul that we live not, but that Christ lives in us—which, when we can say, we have in us the very seed of eternal life [Gal. 2:20]. The second degree is in the end of this life, when the body, freed from all diseases, pains, and miseries, is laid to rest in the earth, and the soul is received into heaven. The third is after the day of judgment, when body and soul reunited shall be both advanced to eternal glory.

Again, in this third degree of life, there be in all likelihood sundry degrees of glory. Daniel, speaking of the estate of the elect after this life, says, "They that be wise, shall shine as the brightness of the firmament, and they that turn many to righteousness, shall shine as the stars for evermore" [Dan. 12:3]. Now, we know there is difference between the brightness of the firmament and the brightness of the stars. Again, there be degrees of torments in hell, as appears by the saying of Christ, "It shall be easier for Tyre and Sidon in that day, than for this generation" [Matt. 11:22]. And therefore there be proportional degrees of glory. And Paul says, "There is one glory of the sun, another glory of the moon, another glory of the stars: for one star differs from another in glory," so is the resurrection of the dead [1 Cor. 15:41–42]. In which words he applies the differences of excellency that be in the creatures to set forth the differences of glory that shall be in men's bodies after the resurrection. Furthermore (if we may conjecture), it may be the degrees of glory shall be answerable to the diverse measures of gifts and graces bestowed on men in this life and according to the employance of them to the glory of God and edification of the church. And therefore the twelve apostles, who were exceedingly enriched with the gift of the Spirit and were master builders of the church of the New Testament, shall sit on twelve thrones and judge the twelve tribes of Israel. But it may be objected that if there be degrees of glory in heaven, some shall want glory. *Answer.* Not so. Though some have more, and some less, yet all shall have sufficient. Take several vessels, whereof some are bigger, and some less, and cast them all into the sea. Some will receive more water, and some less; and yet all shall be full and no want in any. And so likewise among the saints of God in heaven. Some shall have more glory, some less—and yet all without exception full of glory. And whereas it is alleged that "all the laborers in the vineyard receive each of them a penny equally" [Matt. 20:9–10] for their hire, the answer is that our Savior Christ in the parable intends not to set forth the equality of celestial glory and what shall be the estate of the godly after this life; but the very drift of the parable is to show that they which are called first have no cause to brag or insult over others which as yet are uncalled, considering they may be made equal or be preferred before them.

Thus much of life itself. Now follows the continuance thereof, which the Scriptures have noted in calling it eternal or everlasting. And to this end Paul says that "Christ hath abolished death" [2 Tim. 1:10] and brought not only life but also "immortality to light by the gospel." And this very circumstance serves greatly to commend the happiness of the godly in that after they have made an entrance into it they shall never see term of time or end. Suppose the whole world were a sea, and that every thousand years expired, a bird must carry away or drink up one only drop of it. In process of time, it will come to pass that this sea, though very huge, shall be dried up; but yet many thousand millions of years must be passed before this can be done. Now, if a man should enjoy happiness in heaven only for the space of time in which this sea is drying up, he would think his case most happy and blessed. But behold, the elect shall enjoy the kingdom of heaven not only for that time, but when it is ended they shall enjoy it as long again. And when all is done, they shall be as far from ending of this their joy as they were at the beginning.

Having thus seen what life everlasting is, let us now come to the use of the article. And, first of all, if we believe that there is an eternal happiness, and that the same belongs unto us, then we must use this present world and all the things therein as though we used them not. And whatsoever we do in this world, yet the eyes of our minds must always be cast toward the blessed estate prepared for us in heaven. As a pilgrim in a strange land has always his eyes toward his journey's end and is then grieved when by any means he is out of his way, so must we always have our minds and hearts set on everlasting life and be grieved when we are by any means hindered in the strait way that leads thereunto. We have a notable pattern of this duty set out unto us in the patriarch Abraham, who, being called of God, obeyed to go out into a place which he should afterward receive for inheritance. And he went out, not knowing whither he went, and by faith abode in the land of Canaan "as in a strange country, and as one that dwelt in tents" [Heb. 11:9]. Now, the cause that moved him was life everlasting, for the text says, "He looked for a city having a foundation, whose builder and maker is God" [v. 10]. And we ought every one of us to be little affected to the things of this life, never setting our hearts upon them but using them as a pilgrim does use his staff in the way. So long as it is a help and stay for him in his journey, he is content to carry it in his hand; but so soon as it begins to trouble him, he casts it away.

Secondly, all that profess the gospel of Christ may hence learn to bear with patience the crosses and afflictions which God shall lay on them in this world. It is God's usual manner to begin corrections in His own family upon His own children; and as Peter says, "Judgment begins at God's house" [1 Peter 4:17]. Look as a mother that weans her child lays wormwood or some other bitter thing upon her breast to make the child loathe the milk, so likewise God makes us often feel the miseries and crosses of this life, that our love and liking may be turned from this world and fixed in heaven. As raw flesh is loathsome to the stomach, so is every sinner and unmortified man loathsome unto God, till the Lord by afflictions mortify in him the corruptions of his nature and specially the love of this world. But when a man is afflicted, how shall he be able to endure the cross? Surely, by resolving that the Lord has prepared life everlasting for him. Thus, we read that Moses "by faith when he was come to age, refused to be called the son of Pharaoh's daughter, and chose rather to suffer adversity with the people of God, than to enjoy the pleasures of sin for a season, esteeming the rebuke of Christ greater riches than the treasures of Egypt" [Heb. 11:24–26]. But I pray you, what moved Moses to be of this mind? The reason is added: "because he had respect to the recompence of reward"—that is, he had always a special regard of life everlasting, and that was it that made him content and willing to suffer affliction with the people of God. Here then, behold a notable precedent for us to follow, in which we are taught that the best way to endure afflictions with patience is to have an eye to the recompense of reward. This is it that makes the yoke of Christ easy and lightsome. When it shall please God to bring unto us a cup of afflictions and bid us drink a draught thereof to the bottom, the meditation of life eternal must be as sugar in our pockets to sweeten the cup withal.

Lastly, if this be true that God of His goodness and endless mercy toward mankind has prepared life everlasting, yet not for all men, but for the elect, whose names are written in the book of life, [then] we must above all things in this world seek to be partakers of the same. Let us receive this as from the Lord and lay it to our hearts: whatsoever we do evening and morning, day or night, whether we be young or old, rich or poor, first we must seek for the kingdom of heaven and His righteousness. If this benefit were common to all and not proper to the church, less care might be had. But, seeing it is proper to some alone, for this very cause let all our studies be to obtain the beginnings of life everlasting given in this life. For if we have it not, whosoever we be, it had been better for us that we had never been born, or that we had been born dogs and toads than men—for when they die, there is an end of their misery; but man, if he lose everlasting happiness, has ten thousand millions of years to live in misery and in the torments of hell. And when that time is ended, he is as far from the end of his misery as he was at the beginning. Wherefore, I pray you, let not the devil steal this meditation out of your hearts, but be careful to repent of all your sins and to believe in Christ for the pardon of them all, that by this means you may come to have the pawn and earnest of the Spirit concerning life everlasting, even in this world. What a miserable thing is it that men should live long in this world and not so much as dream of another, till at the last gasp? Let us not suffer Satan thus to abuse and bewitch us; for if we have not eternal life in this world, we will never have it.

Hitherto by God's goodness I have shown the meaning of the Creed. Now to draw to a conclusion, the general uses which are to be made of it follow. And, first of all, we learn by it that the Church of Rome has no cause to condemn us for heretics; for we do truly hold and believe the whole apostolical Symbol or Creed, which is an epitome of the Scriptures and the very key of faith. It will be said that we deny the pope's supremacy, justification by works, purgatory, the sacrifice of the Mass for the sins of the quick and the dead, the invocation and intercession of saints, etc., which are the greatest points of religion. It is true indeed; we deny and renounce them as doctrines of devils, persuading ourselves that if indeed they had been apostolical and the very grounds and pillars of religion, as they are avouched to be, they should in no wise have been left forth of the Creed. For it is an oversight in making a confession of our faith to omit the principal points and rules of faith. It will be further said that in the Creed we believe the church, and so consequently are to believe all these former points which are taught and avouched by the church. But this defense is foolish; for it takes this for granted, that the Church of Rome is the church here meant, which we deny, unless they can prove a particular church to be universal or catholic. Nay, I add further that the principal grounds of popish faith for which they contend with us as for life and death are not mentioned in any other creeds which were made by the churches and councils for many hundred years after Christ.

Secondly, the Creed serves as a storehouse of remedies against all troubles and temptations whatsoever. (1) If a man be grieved for the loss of earthly riches, let him consider that he believes God to be his Creator, who will therefore guide and preserve His own workmanship and by His providence minister all things needful unto it; and that he has not lost the principal blessing of all, in that he has God to be his Father, Christ to be his Redeemer, and the Holy Ghost to be his Comforter; and that, considering he looks for life eternal, he is not to be overmuch careful for this life; and that Christ, being our Lord, will not forsake us, being the servants in His own house, but will provide things needful for us. (2) If any man be grieved in respect of outward disgrace and contempt, let him remember that he believes in Christ crucified, and that therefore he is to rejoice in contempt for righteousness's sake. (3) They which are troubled for the decease of friends are to comfort themselves in the communion of saints and that they have God the Father and Christ and the Holy Ghost for their friends. (4) Against bodily captivity, let men consider that they believe in Christ, their Lord, whose service is perfect liberty. (5) Against the fear of bodily diseases, we must remember the resurrection of the body in which all diseases and infirmities shall be abolished. (6) If a man fear death of the body, let him consider that he believes in Christ, which died upon the cross, who by death has vanquished death. (7) The fear of persecution is restrained, if we call to remembrance that God is a father almighty, not only able but also willing to repress the power of the adversary, so far forth as shall be for the good of His children. (8) Terrors arising of the consideration of the last judgment are allayed by remembrance of this, that Christ shall be our Judge, who is our Redeemer. (9) Fear of damnation is remedied by consideration that Christ died to make satisfaction for us and now sits at the right hand of His Father to make intercession for us, and by the resurrection of the body to life everlasting. (10) Terrors of conscience for sin are repressed if we consider that God is a father, and therefore much in sparing, and that it is a prerogative of the church to have remission of sins.

Trin-uni Deo Gloria.

AN
EXPOSITION
OF THE LORD'S PRAYER
IN THE WAY OF CATECHIZING,
SERVING FOR IGNORANT PEOPLE.

Corrected and amended

Hereunto are adjoined the prayers of Paul,
taken out of his Epistles.

By William Perkins

London,
Printed by John Legatt
1626

TO THE RIGHT HONORABLE EDWARD, LORD RUSSELL, EARL OF BEDFORD: GRACE AND PEACE BE MULTIPLIED.

Right Honorable, if you consider what is one of the chiefest ornaments of this noble state, unto which God has advanced you, it will appear, that there is none more excellent than the spirit of grace and prayer. For what does your heart affect? Would you speak the languages? Behold, by prayer you may speak the most heavenly tongue that ever was [Isa. 19:12; Rom. 15:6], even the language of Canaan. Would you have the valor of knighthood? By prayer you may stand in place where God's hand has made a breach [Ps. 106:23], and do as much as all the chariots and horsemen in a kingdom [2 Kings 2:12]. Would you enjoy God's blessings which you want? By prayer you may (as it were) put your hands into the coffers of God's treasures and enrich yourself [Matt. 7:7]. Do you desire the favor of monarchs and princes? By prayer you may come in presence, and have speech with Jehovah, the King of heaven and earth. Lastly, would you know, whether now living you be dead, that being dead you may live forever? By prayer a man may know, whether he be dead to sin, dead to the world, alive to God, live to Christ, and live eternally.

Prayer then, being so excellent a point of religion, I am emboldened to commend this small treatise to your Honor, not so much for itself, as because it does set out the matter and true manner of invocation of God's holy name. And I hope for your favor in accepting of it, the rather, because I doubt not but your desire is to be answerable to your most honorable and for religion most worthy ancestors, in the care of maintaining and countenancing any good thing that may any way serve for the furthering of the gospel of Christ.

Now Jesus Christ our Lord, and God even the Father, which has loved us and given us everlasting consolation and good hope through grace, establish your Honor in every good word and work to the end.

Your H. to command,
William Perkins

A Brief Exposition upon the Lord's Prayer.

1. The parts	The words	The meaning of the words	Wants to be bewailed	Graces to be desired
The Preface	Our Father.	O Father of Christ, and in Him our Father.	1. Want of reverence. 2. By-thoughts.	1. Love of our brethren. 2. The spirit of adoption.
	Which art in heaven.	Who though Thou be present everywhere, yet dost manifest Thyself to us in majesty and glory from the highest heavens.		3. Fear, trembling, reverence, Eccl. 5.
2. Petition 1	Hallowed be Thy name.	Grant that in all our thoughts, words, and deeds, we may give glory and praise to Thee.	1. Pride of heart. 2. Hardness of heart. 3. Ingratitude. 4. Evil life.	1. Knowledge of God. 2. Zeal of God's glory. 3. A desire of sincerity of life.
Petition 2	Thy kingdom come.	Let not sin and Satan reign and rule in our hearts: but reign those by Thy word and spirit: and so build in us the kingdom of grace, and hasten the kingdom of glory.	1. Bondage under sin and Satan. 2. Want of preaching, and sacraments, etc. 3. Impediments.	1. The kingdom of grace. 2. The prosperity of the Church. 3. The hastening of the Last Judgment.
Petition 3	Thy will be done.	Give grace, that in our lives and callings we may perform obedience to Thy commandments.	1. The rebellion of our natures. 2. the wickedness of the world. 3. Imperfection of obedience.	1. Denying ourselves. 2. Obedience. 3. Patience in affliction. 4. Sincerity.
	In earth, as it is in heaven.	And that sincerely, of us men on earth, as thy Angels and St.s in heaven do it.		

Petition 4	Give us this day our daily bread.	Bestow on us all things needful for this life; yet so as whether they be more or less, we may be content therewith, from time to time resting on Thy providence in all estates.	1. Covetousness. 2. Distrust in God's providence.	1. Contentation. 2. Assiance in God's providence.
Petition 5	And forgive us our debts, as we forgive our debtors.	Accept the passion, obedience, and righteousness of Christ, as a full discharge for our sins, and in Him accept us as righteous for even we that have not so much as a drop of mercy in us, in respect of Thee, are content by Thy grace, to forgive the injuries done unto us, either by friend or foe.	1. The burden of sin.	1. The Spirit of deprecation.
Petition 6	And lead us not into temptation: but deliver, etc.	Thou rulest all things in heaven and earth, power of doing all things is from Thee: glory and praise of them both appertain to Thee.	1. Bondage under sin and Satan.	1. The free spirit.
A reason of the praise of God.	For Thine is the kingdom, etc.			1. A base estimation of ourselves, with a high estimation of God.
3. Testification of faith.	Amen.	As we have asked these things; so we do believe that Thou wilt grant them to us.		Faith in God's promises.

An Exposition of the Lord's Prayer
In the Way of Catechism:
Serving for ignorant people, by W. Perkins

"After this manner therefore pray ye: Our Father," etc.
—Matthew 6:9

The occasion and so also the coherence of these words with the former is this: the evangelist Matthew, setting down the sermons and sayings of our Savior Christ, keeps not this course to propound everything as it was done or spoken; but sometimes he sets down that first which was done last, and that last which was done before, according as the Spirit of God directed him. Which thing is verified in these words where the prayer is mentioned, yet the occasion wherefore our Savior Christ taught His disciples to pray is not here specified. But in St. Luke 11:1, the occasion of these words is evident. For there it is said that the disciples of our Savior, knowing that John taught his disciples to pray, made request to their Master that He would do the same to them likewise.

These few words set before the prayer are a commandment, and it prescribes unto us two duties: the first, to pray; the second, to pray after the manner following. Touching the first point, considering very few among the people know how to pray aright, we must learn what it is to pray.

To make prayer is to put up our request to God according to His Word from a contrite heart in the name of Christ with assurance to be heard.

For the better opening of these words, we are to consider six questions. The first is to whom we are to pray. The answer is to God alone. "How shall they call on him in whom they have not believed?" etc. (Rom. 10:14). Mark how invocation and faith are linked together. And Paul's reason may be framed thus: in whom we put our affiance or belief, to him alone must we pray. But we believe only in God. Therefore, we must only pray to Him. As for saints or angels, they are in no wise to be called upon, because not the least tittle of God's Word prescribes us so to do, because they cannot hear our prayers and discern what are the thoughts and desires of our hearts and because invocation is a part of divine worship and therefore peculiar to God alone.

Objection. What need any man to pray unto God, considering He knows what we want before we ask and is ready and willing to give that which we crave? *Answer.* We pray not for this end, to manifest our case to God, as though He knew it not, to win and procure His favor and good will, but for other weighty ends. First, that we might show our submission and obedience to God, because He has given us a direct commandment to pray, and it must be obeyed. Secondly, that we may by invocation show forth that we do indeed believe and repent, because God has made the promise of remission of sins and of all good blessings to such as do indeed repent and humble themselves under the hand of God and by true faith apprehend and apply the promises of God unto themselves. Thirdly, we pray to God that we may (as our duty is) acknowledge Him to be the fountain, author, and giver of every good thing. Lastly, that we might ease our minds by pouring out our hearts before the Lord; for this end has He made most sweet and comfortable promises (Ps. 37:5; Prov. 16:3).

Objection. What need men use prayer, considering God in His eternal council has certainly determined what shall come to pass? *Answer.* As God determines what things shall come to pass, so He does withal determine the means whereby the same things are effected. Before all worlds, God decreed that men should live upon earth, and He decreed likewise that meat, drink, and clothing should be used that life might be preserved. Now, prayer is one of the most excellent means whereby sundry things are brought to pass. Therefore, God's eternal counsel, touching things to come, does not exclude prayer and like means, but rather includes and implies the same.

The second question is what kind of action prayer is. *Answer.* It is no lip-labor. It is the putting up of a suit unto God, and this action is peculiar to the very heart of a man. "The spirit makes request for us." But how? "With groans in the heart" (Rom. 8:26). "The Lord saith to Moses, Why criest thou?" (Ex. 14:15). Yet there is no mention made that Moses spoke any word at all; the Lord, no doubt, accepted the inward mourning and desire of his heart for a cry (Ps. 12:5).

The third question is, what is the form or rule according to which we are to pray? *Answer.* It is the revealed will and Word of God. A man in humbling his soul before God is not to pray as his affections carry him and for what he list, but all is to be done according to the express Word. So as those things which God has commanded us to ask, we are to ask; and those things which He has not commanded unto us, we are in no wise to pray for. "This is the assurance which we have of him, that if we ask anything according to his will, he heareth us" (1 John 5:14). This then is a special clause to be marked, that men must pray in knowledge, not in ignorance. Here weigh the case of poor ignorant people. They talk much of praying for themselves and others. They imagine that they pray very devoutly to God. But alas, they do nothing less, because they know not what to ask according to God's will. They therefore must learn God's Word and pray according to the same, else it will prove in the end that all their praying was nothing but as mocking and flat dishonor of God.

The fourth question is with what affection a man must pray. *Answer.* Prayer must proceed from a broken and contrite heart. This is the sacrifice which God accepts (Ps. 51:17). When Ahab abased himself, though he did it in hypocrisy, yet God had some respect unto it. "Saith the Lord to Elijah, Seest thou how Ahab is humbled before me?" (1 Kings 21:29). This contrition of heart stands in two things. The first of them is a lively feeling of our own sin, misery, and wretched estate, how that we are compassed about with innumerable enemies, even with the devil and his angels, and within abound even with huge seas of wants and rebellious corruptions, whereby we most grievously displease God and are vile in our own eyes. Being therefore thus beset on every side, we are to be touched with the sense of this our great misery. And he that will pray aright must put on the person and the very affection of a poor, wretched beggar; and certainly not being grieved with the rueful condition in which we are in ourselves, it is not possible for us to pray effectually. "Out of the depths I called upon thee O Lord" (Ps. 130:1)—that is, "When I was in my greatest misery and as it were not far from the gulfs of hell, then I cried to God." "Lord in trouble have they visited thee, they poured out a prayer when thy chastening was upon them" (Isa. 26:16). "I am a woman," says Hannah,[1] "of an hard spirit"—that is, a troubled soul—"and have poured my soul before the Lord" (1 Sam. 1:15). Hence, it appears that the ordinary prayers of most men grievously displease God, seeing they are made for fashion only without any sense and feeling of their miseries. Common men come with the Pharisee in ostentation of their integrity, and they take great pains with their lips, but their hearts wander from the Lord. The second thing required in a contrite heart is a longing desire and hungering after God's graces and benefits whereof we stand in need. It is not sufficient for a man to buckle as it were and to go crooked under his sins and miseries, but also he must have a desire to be eased of them and to be enriched with graces needful.

Thus, Hezekiah, the king, and the prophet Isaiah, the son of Amoz, prayed against Sennacherib and cried unto heaven (2 Chron. 32:20), where we may see what a marvelous desire they had to obtain their request. So also, "The spirit maketh request with groans, so great that they cannot be uttered" (Rom. 8:26), as they are felt. David says that "he desireth after the Lord, as the thirsty land" (Ps. 143.6). Now, we know that the ground parched with heat opens itself in rifts and crannies and gapes toward heaven as though it would devour the clouds for want of moisture, and thus must the heart be disposed to God's grace, till it

---

1. Originally, "Anna."

obtain it. The people of Israel, being in grievous afflictions—how do they pray? "They pour out their souls like water before the face of the Lord" (Lam. 2:19).

The fifth question is in whose name prayer must be made. *Answer.* It must not be made in the name of any creature, but only in the name and mediation of Christ. "If ye ask any thing in my name I will do it" (John 14:14). A man is not to present his prayers to God in any worthiness of his own merits. For what is he, to make the best of himself, what can he make of himself? By nature, he is no better than the very firebrand of hell and of all God's creatures on earth the most outrageous rebel to God and therefore cannot be heard for his own sake. As for saints, they can be no mediators, seeing even they themselves in heaven are accepted of God not for themselves but only for the blessed merits of Christ. "If any man sin," says St. John, "we have an advocate with the Father, Jesus Christ" (1 John 2:1). But how proves he this? It follows then, "and he is the reconciliation for our sins." His reason stands thus: he which must be an advocate must first of all be a reconciliation for us. No saints can be a reconciliation for us. Therefore, no saints can be advocates. Therefore, in this place is manifest another fault of ignorant people. They cry often, "Lord, help me. Lord, have mercy upon me." But in whose name pray they? Poor souls, like blind bayards they rush upon the Lord. They know no mediator in whose name they should present their prayers to Him. Little do they consider with themselves that God is as well a most terrible judge as a merciful father.

The sixth question is whether faith be requisite to prayer or not. *Answer.* Prayer is to be made with faith, whereby a man must have certain assurance to be heard. For he that prays must steadfastly believe that God in Christ will grant his petition. This affiance being wanting, it makes prayer to be no prayer. For how can he pray for anything effectually, who doubts whether he shall obtain it or no?

Wherefore, it is a special point of prayer to be persuaded that God to whom prayer is made not only can but also will grant his request. "Whatsoever ye desire when ye pray, believe that ye shall have it, and it shall be done unto you" (Mark 11:24). Here, we see two things required in prayer: the first, a desire of the good things which we want; the second is faith, whereby we believe that God will grant the things desired. The ground of this faith is reconciliation with God and the assurance thereof. For unless a man be in conscience in some measure persuaded that all his sins are pardoned and that he stands reconciled to God in Christ, he cannot believe any other promises revealed in the Word nor that any of his prayers shall be heard.

Thus much of the definition of prayer. Now let us see what use may be made of this commandment, "pray ye thus." Seeing our Savior commands His disciples and so even us also to pray to God, it is our duty not only to present our prayers to God but also to do it cheerfully and earnestly. "Also brethren I beseech you that ye would strive with me by prayer to God for me" (Rom. 15:30). What is the cause why the Lord does often defer His blessings after our prayers? No cause, but that He might stir us up to be more earnest to cry unto the Lord. When Moses prayed to God in the behalf of the Israelites, the Lord answers, "Let me alone" (Ex. 32:10), as though his prayers did bind the Lord and hinder Him from executing His judgments. Wherefore, this is good advice for all Christian men to continue and to be zealous in prayer. If you be an ignorant man, for shame learn to pray. Seeing it is God's commandment, make conscience of it. We see that there is no man, unless he be desperately wicked, but will make some conscience of killing and stealing. And why is this? Because it is God's commandment, "Thou shalt not kill. Thou shalt not steal."

Well then, this also is God's commandment: to pray. Let this consideration breed in you a conscience of this duty. And although your corrupt nature shall draw you away from it, yet strive to the contrary and know it certainly that the breach of this commandment makes you as well guilty of damnation before God as any other. Furthermore, this must be a motive to prick you forward to this duty, that as God commands us to pray, so also He gives the Spirit of prayer, whereby the commandment is made easy unto us. If the Lord had commanded a thing impossible, then there had been some cause of discouragement. But commanding a thing through the grace of His Spirit very easy and profitable, how much more are we bound to obedience of the same? Again, prayer is the key whereby we open the treasures of God and pull down His mercies upon us. For as the preaching of the word serves to declare and to convey unto us God's graces, so in prayer we come to have a lively feeling of the same in our hearts. And further, this must move us to prayer, seeing in it we have familiarity with God's majesty. It is a high favor for a man to be familiar with a prince. How much more then to be familiar with the King of kings, the mighty Jehovah? This then can be no burden or trouble unto us, being one of the main prerogatives that God bestows on His church. For in the preaching of the word, it pleases God to talk to us. And in prayer God does vouchsafe us this honor: to speak and as it were familiarly to talk with Him—and not as to a fearful judge, but as to a loving and merciful God.

Consider also that prayer is a worthy means of defense not only to us but also to the church and them that are absent. By it Moses stood in the breach which God's wrath had made into the people of Israel and stayed the same. By this Christian men fight as valiant champions against their own corruptions and all other spiritual enemies (Eph. 6:18). Infinite were it to show how many blessings the Lord has bestowed on His servants by prayer. In a word, Luther, whom it pleased God to use as a worthy instrument for the restoring of the gospel, testifies of himself that, having this grace given him to call upon the name of the Lord, he had more revealed unto him of God's truth by prayer than by reading and study.

The second point of the commandment is to pray after the manner propounded in the Lord's Prayer, where it is to be noted that the Lord's Prayer is a direction and as it were sampler to teach us how and in what manner we ought to pray. None is to imagine that we are bound to use these words only and none other. For the meaning of Christ is not to bind us to the word but to the matter and to the manner and to the like affections in praying. If this were not so, the prayers of God's servants set down in the books of the Old and New Testaments should all be faulty, because they are not set down in the very same words with the Lord's Prayer. Nay, this prayer is not set down in the same words altogether by Matthew and Luke.

And whereas sundry men in our church hold it unlawful to use this very form of words as they are set down by our Savior Christ for a prayer, they are far deceived, as will appear by their reasons. First (say they) it is a scripture and therefore not to be used as a prayer. I answer that the same thing may be the scripture of God and also the prayer of man, else the prayers of Moses, David, and Paul, being set down in the Scriptures, cease to be prayers. Again (say they) that in prayer we are to express our wants in particular and the graces which we desire. Now, in these words all things to be prayed for are only in general propounded. I answer that the main wants that are in any man and the principal graces of God to be desired are set down in the petitions of this prayer in particular. Thirdly, they plead that the pattern to make all prayers by should not be used as a prayer. I answer that therefore the rather it may be used as a prayer; and sure it is that ancient and worthy divines have reverenced it as a prayer, choosing rather to use these words than any other.[2] Wherefore, the opinion is full of ignorance and error.

Well, whereas our Savior first gives a commandment to pray and then after gives a direction for the keeping of it, this He does to stir up our dullness and to allure us by all means to the heavenly exercise of prayer. Wherefore, still I say, employ yourselves in prayer fervently and continually; and if you cannot do it, learn to pray. Thus much of the commandment of our Savior Christ. Now follow the words of the prayer.

---

2. As Cyprian Serm, de orat. Dominic. And Tertullian, lib defuga in persequutione. And Augustine Serm. 1, 26, de tempore. [NB, this was originally in the text, not the margin.]

Our Father Which Art, Etc.

These words contain three parts: (1) a preface; (2) the prayer itself, containing six petitions; (3) the testification of faith in the last word, "amen." Which, although it be short, yet it does not contain the smallest point in the prayer. It is (I say) a testification of our faith, whereas the petitions that go before are only testifications of our desires. Now of these three parts in order.

We must consider how our Savior Christ does not set down the petitions abruptly, but He first begins with a solemn preface. Whereby we are taught this lesson, that he which is to pray unto God is first to prepare himself and not boldly without consideration as it were to rush into the presence of God.

If a man be to come before an earthly prince, he will order himself in apparel, gesture, and words that he may do all things in seemliness and dutiful reverence. How much more are men to order themselves when they are to appear before the living God? "Be not rash with thy mouth, and let not thy heart be hasty to utter a thing before the Lord" (Eccl. 5:1). And David "washed his hands in innocency" (Ps. 26:6) before he came to the altar of the Lord to offer sacrifice.

The means whereby men may stir up their dull and heavy hearts and so prepare themselves to prayer are three. The first is to read diligently the Word of God, concerning those matters about which they are to pray. And what then? This will be a means not only to direct him but also to quicken the heart more fervently to deliver his prayer. This is evident by a comparison. The beams of the sun descending heat not before they come to the earth or some solid body where they may reflect, and then by that means the earth and air adjoining is made hot. Even so the Lord sends down unto us His blessed word, even as beams and the goodly sunshine; and thereby He speaks to our hearts. Now, when we make our prayers of that which we have read, God's word is as it were reflected, and our hearts are thereby warmed with the comfortable heat of God's Holy Spirit to pour out our prayers to God more fervently. The second means is to pray to God that He would strengthen us with His Spirit that we might be able to pray as it is practiced (Ps. 143:1). The third means is the consideration of God's most glorious majesty, wherein we are to remember, first, His fatherly goodness and kindness whereby He is willing; and, secondly, His omnipotency, whereby He is able to grant our request. One of these emboldened the leper to pray, "Lord, if thou wilt thou canst make me clean" (Matt. 8:2). Therefore, both together are more effectual.

Now let us come to the preface itself: "Our Father, which art in heaven." It contains a description of the true Jehovah to whom we pray, and that by two arguments: the first is drawn from a relation, "our Father"; the second is taken from the subject or place, "which art in heaven."

Father

1. The Meaning

In the opening of this word or title of God, two questions are to be opened.

Question 1. Whether by this title "Father" is signified the whole Trinity or some one person thereof. *Answer.* Otherwhiles this name is attributed to all the persons in [the] Trinity, or any of them. "Have we not all one father," etc. (Mal. 2:10). "Which was the son of Adam, which was the son of God" (Luke 3:38). And in Isaiah 9:6, Christ is called the Father of eternity, because all that are truly knit to Him and born anew by Him, they are eternally made the sons of God. Again, oftentimes it is given to the first person in [the] Trinity, as in those places where one person is conferred with another. And so in this place principally for some special respects this title agrees to the first person. For, first, He is the Father of Christ as He is the eternal Word of the Father, and that by nature, because He is of the same essence with Him. Secondly, He is the Father of Christ in respect of His manhood, not by nature or adoption, but by personal union, because the human nature does subsist in the person of the Word. Thirdly, He is a father to all the faithful by adoption in Christ.

Question 2. Whether are we to pray to the Son and the Holy Ghost as to the Father? *Answer.* Invocation belongs to all the three persons in [the] Trinity and not only to the Father. Steven prays, "Lord Jesus receive my spirit" (Acts 7:59). "Now God our Father and our Lord Jesus Christ guide our journey unto you" (1 Thess. 3:11). "The grace of our Lord Jesus Christ, the love of God, and the communion of the Holy Ghost be with you" (2 Cor. 13:14). And men are baptized in the name of the Father, the Son, and the Holy Ghost—that is, by calling on the name of the Father, Son, and Holy Ghost.

Some may say this prayer is a perfect platform of all prayers, and yet we are taught to direct our prayers to the Father, not to the Son or Holy Spirit. I answer, the Father, Son, and Holy Ghost are three distinct persons, yet they are not to be severed or divided, because they all subsist in one and the same Godhead or divine nature. And further, in all outward actions, as in the creation and preservation of the world and the salvation of the elect, they are not severed or divided; for they all work together—only they are distinguished in the manner of working. Now, if they be not divided in nature or operation, then they are not to be severed in worship.

And in this place we principally direct our prayers to the Father because He is the first in order, yet so as then we imply the Son and Holy Ghost. For we pray to the Father in the name of the Son by the assurance of the Holy Ghost. And to what person soever the prayer is directed, we must always remember in mind and heart to include the rest.

2. The Uses

The uses of this point are manifold.

(1) First, whereas we are taught to come to God as to a father and therefore in the name of His Son, our Savior Christ, we learn to lay the first ground of all our prayers, which is to hold and maintain the union and the distinction of the three persons in [the] Trinity. This being the lowest and the first foundation of prayer, it is requisite that all which would pray aright should have this knowledge rightly to believe the Trinity and to know how the three persons agree and how they are distinguished and the order of them—how the Father is the first; the Son, the second; and the Holy Ghost, the third; and therefore how the Father is to be called upon in the name of the Son by the Holy Ghost. By this the prayers of God's church and the prayers of heathen men are distinguished, who invoke God as a creator out[side] of the Father, Son, and Holy Ghost. And hence it is manifest that ignorant and silly people which do not so much as dream of the union, distinction, and order of the persons in [the] Trinity make but a cold and slender kind of praying.

(2) Secondly, we may learn hereby that we are not in any wise to invocate saints and angels, but only the true Jehovah. The reason stands thus: this prayer is either a perfect platform for all prayers, or not. To say it were not were an injury to our Savior Christ. To say it is so is also to grant that it does fully set down to whom all prayers are to be made. Now, in these words there is set down no invocation but of God alone. For in prayer to be termed "Our Father" is proper to God: "Thou art our father: though Abraham be ignorant of us, and Israel know us not: yet thou, O Lord, art our father and redeemer" (Isa. 63:16). Papists therefore, that are the great patrons of invocation of saints, in their reformed breviaries and missals deal very fondly; for, first, they pray to Mary that she would pray to Christ for them, and when they have so done, like jugglers they come to Christ and pray unto Him that He would accept Mary's prayers for them.

(3) Thirdly, we learn that there can be no intercessor between God and us, but only Christ. For here we are taught to come to God not as a judge but as to a kind and loving father. Now He is a father to us only by Christ. As for angels and saints and all creatures, they are not able to procure by any means that God should become a father, no, not so much as to one man.

(4) Again, if the God to whom we pray be a father, we must learn to acquaint ourselves with the promises which He has made in His Word to quicken our hearts in all our prayers unto Him and thereby to gather affiance to ourselves and persuasion that He will grant our requests. For this word "Father" implies a readiness and willingness in God to hear and be merciful to our prayers. And a father cannot but must needs make promise of favor to those that be

his children; and therefore it cannot be that he should call to God his Father truly, which has not in his heart this assurance that God will fulfill all His promises made unto him. Promises made to prayer, as these and such like, are to be marked as follow: "If my people, among whom my name is called upon, do humble themselves, and pray and seek my presence, and turn from their wicked ways, then I will hear in heaven, and be merciful unto their sins" (2 Chron. 7:14); "The Lord is with you while ye be with him, and if ye seek him, he will be found of you" (15:2); "Before they call I will answer, and whiles they speak I will hear" (Isa. 65:24); "Ask and it shall be given you, seek and ye shall find, knock and it shall be opened" (Matt. 7:7); "If ye which are evil can give good gifts unto your children, how much more shall your heavenly Father give the Holy Ghost to them that desire him?" (Luke 11:13); "He that is Lord over all, is rich unto all that call on him" (Rom. 10:12); "Draw near unto God, and he will draw near unto you" (James 4:8).

(5) If God be a father who is called upon, then prayer is the note of God's child. St. Luke and St. Paul set out the faithful servants of God by this note: "He hath authority to bind all that call on thy name" (Acts 9:14); "To them that are sanctified by Jesus Christ, saints by calling with all that call on the name of our Lord Jesus Christ" (1 Cor. 1:2). And contrariwise, it is made one of the properties of an atheist never to call on the name of God (Ps. 14:4). And such persons as neither will nor can or use not heartily to pray to God, they may say that they are persuaded there is a God, but in their doings they bear themselves as if there were no God.

(6) He which would pray aright must be like the prodigal child—that is, he must not only confess his sin, saying, "Father I have sinned against heaven, and against thee," etc. [Luke 15:18], but also have a full purpose never after to offend his Father. For how can a child call him father whom he cares not continually to displease through his lewd conditions? He cannot do it; neither can any father delight in such a child. Therefore, in prayer we must call to mind our lewdness and rebellions against our heavenly Father and with the publican in heaviness of soul say, "Lord, be merciful unto me, a sinner." He which can truly do this is a kind child. If we consider ourselves as we are by nature, we are the children of the devil—no child so like his father as we are like him. And in this estate we continually rebel against God, for the devil has all the heart. Our whole joy is to serve and please him. A man that is to pray must think on this and be grieved thereat. And happy, yea, a thousand times happy are they who have grace given them to see their estate and bewail it. And further, it is not sufficient to confess our sins against our merciful Father, but we must set down with ourselves never in such sort to offend Him again and to lead a new life. This point is very profitable for these times. For many there be when any cross and sickness comes on

them will pray and promise repentance and all obedience to God's Word, if it shall please God to deliver them. But this usually is but in hypocrisy; they dissemble with God and man. For when their sickness is past, like a dog that had been in the water, they shake their ears and run straight with all greediness to their former sins. Is this to call God Father? No, he that does this shall not have God to be his Father, but the man that is wounded in his soul for his offences past and carries a purpose in his heart never witting and willingly to offend God again.

(7) Lastly, here we are to observe that he which would pray must be endued with the Spirit of adoption, the actions whereof in the matter of prayer are twofold. The first, to move the heart to cry and call on God as a father. It is no easy thing to pray, for to a man of himself it is as easy to move the whole earth with his hand. How then comes it that we pray? It is a blessed work of the Spirit. "We have received the spirit of adoption whereby we cry, Abba"—that is, "Father" (Rom. 8:15). And, "Likewise the spirit helpeth our infirmities: for we know not what to pray as we ought: but the spirit itself maketh request" (8:26). And the Holy Ghost is called the Spirit "of grace, and of deprecation, and prayers" (Zech. 12:10). Well then, the man that would pray must have God's Spirit to be his schoolmaster to teach him to pray with groans and sighs of the heart; for the words make not the prayer, but the groans and desires of his heart. And a man prays for no more than he desires with the heart; and he which desires nothing prays not at all, but spends lip-labor. The second work of the Spirit is to assure us in our consciences that we are in the state of grace, reconciled to God. "The spirit of adoption beareth witness with our spirits, that we are the children of God" (Rom. 8:16). And this inward certificate of the Spirit in all exercises of invocation is very necessary; for he which wants this assurance, if he be secure and benumbed in his sins, will not and, if he be touched in conscience for them, for his life dares not call God Father. Also this confutes the opinion of the Church of Rome, which teaches that man is to doubt whether he be adopted or no. For how can a man truly call God Father when he doubts whether he be the child of God or no? It is a miserable kind of praying to call God Father and withal to doubt whether He be a father. Indeed, it is true that doubts will often arise, but it is our duty to strive against them and not to yield to them. Yea, but (say they) to be certain of God's mercy is presumption. I answer, if it be presumption, it is a holy presumption, because God has bidden us to call Him Father.

Our Father

1. The Meaning

Thus much of the argument of relation. Now let us proceed. It is further said, "Our Father." And He is so termed because He is the Father of Christ by nature and in Him the Father of every believer, yea, of the whole body of the church.

Question. Whether may it be lawful for us in prayer to say not "our Father," but "my Father"? *Answer.* A Christian may in private prayer say "my Father." This is warranted by the example of our Savior, "O my Father, if it be possible, let this cup pass from me" (Matt. 26:39); and, "My God, my God, why hast thou forsaken me?" (27:46). And Thomas prayed, "My Lord, and my God" (John 20:28). And Paul, "I give thanks to my God," etc. (1 Cor. 1:4). And God's promise is, "Thou shalt call me, my Father" (Jer. 3:19). The meaning of Christ is not to bind us to these words but to teach us that in our prayers we must not have regard to ourselves only but also to our brethren. And therefore when we pray for them in our private prayers, as for ourselves, we put in practice the true meaning of these words.

2. The Uses

When we pray, we must not make request only for ourselves and our own good but for others also as the church and people of God, persuading ourselves that we also are partakers of their prayers. And for the better clearing of this point, let us search who they are for whom we are to pray.

Of men, there be two sorts: some living; some dead. Of these two kinds, the living are to be prayed for, and there is no praying for the dead.

A man that is dead knows what shall be his estate eternally. If he died a wicked person—that is, an unrepentant sinner—his state shall be according in eternal torment. If he died, having repented of his sins, then he shall rest with God in His kingdom. "Blessed are they which die in the Lord, for they rest from their labors, and their works follow them" (Rev. 14:13). "While we have time let us do good to all men" (Gal. 6:10), where we may note that there is a time—namely, after death—when we cannot do good to others.

Again, of the living, some are our enemies and some our friends. Our friends are they which are of the same religion, affection, and disposition. Foes are either private or public. Public foes are either enemies to our country, as tyrants, traitors, etc.; or enemies to our religion, as Jews, Turks, Papists, infidels, atheists. Now, toward all these how ought a man to behave himself in prayer? *Answer.* He is to pray for them all. "Pray for them which hurt you, and persecute you" (Matt. 5:44). "I exhort that prayers, intercessions, etc. be made for all men, for kings," etc. (1 Tim. 2:1). Yet when Paul gave this commandment, we read not that there were any Christian kings, but all infidels. And the Jews are commanded to pray for Babylon, where they were captive: "And seek the prosperity of the city, whither I have caused you to be carried captive, and pray unto the Lord for it" (Jer. 29:7).

Question. How and in what manner are we to pray for our enemies? *Answer.* We are to pray against their sins, counsels, enterprises, but not against their persons. Thus prayed David against Ahithophel, "Lord, I pray thee turn the counsel of Ahithophel to foolishness" (1 Sam. 15:31). And thus did the apostles pray against their persecutors, "O Lord behold their threatenings, and grant unto thy servants with all boldness to speak thy word" (Acts 4:29).

Question. David uses imprecations against his enemies in which he prays for their utter confusion, as Psalm 59 and 109, etc. The like is done by Paul (Gal. 5:12; 2 Tim. 4:14) and Peter (Acts 8:20), though afterward he mitigates his execration. But how could they do it? *Answer.* (1) They were endued with an extraordinary measure of God's Spirit, and hereby they were enabled to discern of their enemies and certainly to judge that their wickedness and malice was incurable and that they should never repent. And the like prayers did the primitive church conceive against Julian the Apostate, because they perceived him to be a malicious and desperate enemy. [2] Secondly, they were endued with a pure zeal and not carried with desire of revenge against their enemies, intending nothing else but the glory of God. Now, for us it is good that we should suspect our zeal, because sinister affections, as hatred, envy, emulation, desire of revenge, will easily mingle themselves therewith.

Question. How far forth may we use those psalms in which David uses imprecations against his enemies? *Answer.* They are to be read and sung with these caveats. (1) We are to use those imprecations indefinitely against the enemies of God and His church; for we may persuade ourselves that always there be some such obstinate enemies, but we must not apply them particularly. [2] Secondly, we must use them (as Augustine says) as certain prophetical sentences of the Holy Ghost, pronouncing the last sentence of destruction upon final, impenitent sinners, which oppose themselves against God's kingdom. (3) They may be used against our spiritual enemies, the flesh, the devil and his angels, and the world.

(2) Furthermore, whereas we are taught to say, "Our Father," this serves to put us in mind that in praying to God we must bring love to men with us. We must all be the children of one Father, lovingly disposed one to another. For how should he call God his Father who will not take the child of God for his brother? "When thou art to offer thy gift unto God, if thy brother hath aught against thee: first be reconciled, and then come and offer thy gift" (Matt. 5:23–24). So also, "The Lord saith, that when they pray unto him he will not hear." Why? "Because their hands are full of blood" (Isa. 1:15). In these times,

many men can be content formally to pray; but yet they will not leave bribing, oppression, deceit, usury, etc. The common song of the world is, every man for himself, and God for us all. This is the common love and care that men have each to other. The prayers of such are abominable, even as "the sacrifice of a dog," as Isaiah 66:3 says. For how can they call God their Father that have no love to their brethren?

(3) Thirdly, hence we may learn that God is no accepter of persons. For this prayer is given to all men of what state or degree so ever. All then, as well poor as rich, unlearned as learned, subjects as ruler, may say, "Our Father." It is not with the Lord as it is with the world, but all are His children that do believe. The poor man has as good interest in God's kingdom and may call God Father as well as the king. Therefore, the weaker sort are to comfort themselves hereby, knowing that God is a father to them as well as to Abraham, David, Peter. And such as are endued with more grace must not therefore swell in pride, because they have not God to be their Father more than their inferiors have.

Which Art in Heaven

1. The Meaning

Question. How may God be said to be in heaven, seeing He is infinite and therefore must needs be everywhere? "The heaven of heavens are not able to contain him" (1 Kings 8:27). *Answer.* God is said to be in heaven, first, because His majesty—that is, His power, wisdom, justice, mercy—is made manifest from thence unto us. "Our God is in heaven, and doth whatsoever he will" (Ps. 115:3). "He that dwelleth in heaven shall laugh them to scorn, and the Lord shall have them in derision" (2:4). Isaiah says, "Thus saith the Lord, Heaven is my throne, and the earth is my footstool" (66:1). Secondly, after this life He will manifest and exhibit the fullness of His glory to His angels and saints in the highest heavens, and that immediately and visibly.

2. The Uses

(1) Hereby we first learn that Romish pilgrimages, whereby men went from place to place to worship God, are vain and foolish. The God to whom we must pray is in heaven. Now, let men travel to what place or country they will, they shall not come the nearer to heaven or nearer to God by traveling, seeing the earth is in every part alike distant from heaven.

(2) Secondly, this overthrows popish idolatry, as worshipping of crosses, crucifixes, roods, etc. used to put men in mind of God and Christ. We are taught to lift up our eyes to heaven, seeing God is there. And how can we do this, as long as our minds and eyes are poring upon an image made by man's art?

(3) Again, we are here admonished to use the action of prayer with as great reverence as possible may be and not to think of God in any earthly manner. Well reasons Solomon, "Be not rash with thy mouth to speak a word before God." Why? "He is in heaven, thou art in earth: therefore let thy words be few" (Eccl. 5:2). This reverence must appear in holiness of all our thoughts and affections and in all comeliness of gesture. And for this cause all wandering by-thoughts and all vain babbling is to be avoided. But how goes the case with us that on the time appointed come to the assemblies to pray? Many by reason of their blindness pray without understanding. Many when they are present at prayer yet have their hearts occupied about other matters, about their goods and worldly business. Such men have no joy or gladness in praying. It is a burden to them. Many come to the assembly for custom only or for fear of punishment. If they might be left free, they could find in their hearts not to pray at all. But let all such men know that this manner of praying is a very grievous sin, nay, greater than mocking of father or mother, killing or stealing; for it is directly against God, [and] the other against men. This sin, because it is against the first table and therefore more hard to be discerned, it is lightly esteemed, and it less troubles the consciences of ignorant men. Yea, as it is indeed, so it is to be esteemed as a disgrace and plain mockery of God's majesty. Wherefore, seeing God is in heaven, away with all drowsy and dead praying. Let us come with reverence in our hearts before the Lord.

(4) Again, we are here to consider that our hearts in prayer must mount up into heaven and there be present with the Lord. "Unto thee O Lord lift I up my soul" (Ps. 25:1). The little child is never well but when it is in the father's lap or under the mother's wing. And the children of God are never in better case than when in affection and spirit they can come into the presence of their heavenly Father and by prayer as it were to creep into His bosom.

(5) And here we must further learn especially to seek for heavenly things and to ask earthly things so far forth as they serve to bring us to an everlasting and immortal inheritance in heaven, to which we are called (1 Peter 1:4).

(6) Lastly, whereas our Father is in heaven, we are to learn that our life on earth is but a pilgrimage and that our desire must be to attain to a better country—namely, heaven itself—and that we must use all means continually to come unto it. In a word, to make an end of the preface, in it is contained a double stay or prop of all our prayers. The one is to believe that God can grant our requests because He is almighty; and thus much is signified when He is said to be in heaven. The second is to believe that God is ready and willing to grant the same, and this we are taught in the title "Father," which serves to put us in mind that God accepts our prayers (John 16:23) and has a care of us in all our

miseries and necessities (Matt. 6:32) and pities us as much as any earthly father can pity his child (Ps. 103:13).

Yet must we not imagine that God will indeed give unto us whatsoever we do upon our own heads fancy and desire. But we must in our prayers have recourse to the promise of God and according to the tenor thereof must we frame and square our petitions. Things promised absolutely, as all graces necessary to salvation, may be asked absolutely; and things promised with condition, as graces less necessary and temporal blessings, are to be asked with condition—namely, so far forth as they shall be for God's glory in us and for our good—except it be so that God promise any temporal blessing absolutely, as He promised issue to Abraham in his old age, the kingdom to David after Saul, a deliverance from captivity in Babylon after seventy years to the Israelites.

Again, the preface serves to stir up love and fear in the hearts of them that are about to pray—love, because they pray to a father; fear, because He is full of majesty in heaven.

Hallowed Be Thy Name

1. The Coherence

Thus much of the preface. Now follow the petitions. They be six in number: the three first concern God; the three last, ourselves. The three former petitions are again divided into two parts: the first concerns God's glory itself; the other two, the means whereby God's glory is manifested and enlarged among men. For God's name is glorified among men when His kingdom does come, and His will is done.

Question. Why is this petition, "Hallowed be thy name," set in the first place? *Answer.* Because God's glory must be preferred before all things, because it is the end of all creatures and of all the counsels of God. "The Lord hath made all things for his own sake: yea, even the wicked for the day of evil" (Prov. 16:4). And from the order of the petitions here arises a worthy instruction—namely, that everyone in all things they take in hand are to propound to themselves and to intend the glory of God. The reason is this: the end which God has appointed to all our doings we are to propound to ourselves. But God has appointed that the highest end of all our doings should be His glory. Therefore, our hearts must be to seek it first of all. That God will have His name glorified by us appears in this, that He punishes those which of obstinacy set themselves to dishonor Him or by negligence did not sanctify Him when they should have done so. Herod, sitting in his royalty, made such an oration that the people cried, "The voice of a God, and not of a man"; and immediately the angel of the Lord smote him, "because he gave not glory to God" (Acts 12:23). And Moses, because he did not sanctify the Lord in the presence of the children of Israel, therefore he came not into the land of promise; yet he did not altogether fail in doing of it. Thus, we may see by these punishments and also by the order of the petitions that it is our duty to prefer the glory of God before all things else.

Question. Whether are we to prefer the glory of God before the salvation of our souls? *Answer.* If the case stand thus, that God's name must be dishonored or our souls condemned, we must account the glory of God more precious than the salvation of our souls. This is manifest in the order of the petitions. The petitions that concern God's glory are first, and the petitions that concern directly our salvation are the fifth and sixth. Whereby we are taught that before God should want any part of His glory, we must let body and soul and all go, that God may have all His glory. This affection had Moses when he said, "Either forgive them, or if thou wilt not, blot my name out of thy book" (Ex. 32:32).

In this petition as also in the rest, we must observe three things: the first is the meaning of the words; the second, the wants which men must learn to bewail; the third, the graces of God which are to be desired.

2. The Meaning

Very few among the people can give the right meaning of the words of this prayer. They pretend that, seeing God knows their good meaning, it is sufficient for them to say the words and to mean well. But faith being one of the grounds of prayer, and there being no faith without knowledge, neither can there be prayer without knowledge. And therefore ignorant men are to learn the right meaning of the words.

Name

Name in this place signifies:

1. God Himself. "He shall build an house to my name" (1 Kings 5:5).
2. His attributes, as His justice, mercy, etc.
3. His works, creatures, and judgments.
4. His word.
5. His honor and praise arising from all these.

For God is known to us by all these, as men are known by their names. And as all a man's praise and glory lies in his name, so all the glory of God in these.

Hallowed

To hallow is to sever or set apart anything from the common use to some proper and peculiar end—as the temple was hallowed, that is, set apart to an holy use; and the priests were sanctified, that is, set apart to the service of God. And all that believe in Christ are sanctified—that is, set apart from sin to serve God.

In like manner, God's name is hallowed when it is put apart from oblivion, contempt, profanation, pollution, blasphemy, and all abuses to a holy, reverent, and honorable use, whether we think, speak of it, or use it any manner of way (Lev. 10:3; Ezek. 38:23).

Question. How can a sinful man hallow God's name, which is pure and holy in itself? *Answer.* We do not here pray that we might make God's name holy, as though we could add something unto it to make it holy, but that we might be means to declare and make manifest to the world by the right usage of it, that it is holy, pure, and honorable. The like phrase is used, "Wisdom is justified by her children" (Matt. 11:19)—that is, acknowledged and declared to be just (Ezek. 38:23).

The scope therefore of the first petition is an earnest desire that we might set forth God's glory, whatsoever become of us. And it may be expressed thus, "O Lord, open our eyes that we may aright know Thee and acknowledge the greatness of Thy power, wisdom, justice, and mercy, which appears in Thy titles, words, creatures, and judgments. And grant that when we use any of these, we may therein honor Thee and use them reverently to Thy glory."

3. The Wants Which Are to Be Bewailed

The wants which we in this place are taught to bewail are specially four. (1) The first is an inward and spiritual pride of our hearts—a sin that none or very few can see in themselves, unless the Lord open their eyes. When our first parents were tempted in paradise, the devil told them they should be as gods, which lesson not only they but we have learned. And we conceive of ourselves as little gods, though to the world we show it not. This hidden pride, when other sins die, it begins to get strength and to show itself and appears in vain thoughts, continually on every occasion ascending in the mind. As may appear in the Pharisee, whose thoughts were these when he prayed thus within himself: "O God I thank thee that I am not as other men, extortioners, unjust, adulterers, or even as this Publican," etc. (Luke 18:11). And as this was in him, so it is in us till God gives grace; for so that men may have praise and glory in the world, they care not for God's glory, though it be defaced. We must therefore learn to discern this hidden corruption and to mourn for it; for it does poison and hinder all good desires of glorifying God, so long as it does or shall prevail in the heart.

(2) Secondly, we are taught here to bewail the hardness of our hearts, whereby we are hindered from knowing God aright and from discerning the glory and majesty of God in His creatures (Mark 6:52). The disciples through the hardness of their hearts could not see God's power in the miracle of feeding many thousands with a few loaves, though themselves were instruments of it, and the food did increase in their hands. Our redemption—what a wonderful

work is it! But how few consider of it or regard it? If we see a man have more with wealth or honor than we have, we straight wonder at him. But, beholding God's creatures, we see nothing in them, because we do not go higher to acknowledge the love, power, wisdom, and justice of the Creator. And this is the cause why God's name is so slenderly honored among men.

(3) The third corruption is our great ingratitude, for the Lord has made heaven and earth and all other creatures to serve man—yet he is the most unthankful of all creatures. Bestow many jewels or a king's ransom on a dead man; he will never return any kindness. So men, being dead in sin, deal with God. Commonly, men are like the swine that run with their groins and eat up the mast but yet never look up to the tree from whence it falls. But the godly are with David to feel this want in themselves and to beseech God to open and as it were to unlock their lips that they may endeavor to be thankful to God (Ps. 51:15).

(4) The fourth is the ungodliness and the innumerable wants that be in our lives, and the sins committed in the world. "Mine eyes," says David, "gush out with rivers of water, because men keep not thy laws" (119:136). The reason is because he which lives in sin reproaches God's name, even as an evil child dishonors his father. Now some will say that this cannot be, because our sins cannot hurt God. True indeed, yet are they a cause of slandering God's name among men; for as we honor Him by our good works, so we dishonor Him by our offences. "Let your light so shine before men, that they may see your good works, and glorify your Father which is in heaven" (Matt. 5:16).

4. Graces to Be Desired

The graces to be desired and to be prayed for at God's hand are three. (1) The first is the knowledge of God—that is, that we might know Him as He has revealed Himself in His Word, works, and creatures. For how shall any glorify God before we know Him? Our knowledge in this life is imperfect (Exodus 33). Moses may not see God's face, but His hinder parts. We may see God as men do through spectacles in His Word, sacraments, and creatures (1 Cor. 13:12). And therefore as Paul prayed for the Colossians that they might increase in the knowledge of God (Col. 1:10), so are we taught to pray for ourselves in this petition.

(2) A desire that the zeal of God's glory may be kindled in our hearts, and that we may be kept from profaning and abusing of His name. "The zeal of thine house hath eaten me up" (Ps. 69:9). "My heart shall utter"—or, "cast up a good matter"—"I will speak in my words of the king" (45:1). Here, the Spirit of God borrows a comparison from men, thus: as he which has somewhat lying heavy in his stomach is never quiet till he have cast it up, even so the care and desire to glorify God's name must lie upon a man's heart as a heavy burden.

And he is not to be at ease and quiet with himself till he be disburdened in sounding forth God's praise. Luther says well that this is *sanctiacipula*—that is, a holy surfeit. And it is no hurt continually to have our hearts overcharged thus.

(3) A desire to lead a godly and upright life before God and men. We see men that in some great calling under honorable personages will so order and behave themselves as they may please and honor their masters. Even so must our lives be well ordered, and we are to labor to walk worthy of the Lord (as Paul speaks) that we may honor our heavenly Father.

Thy Kingdom Come

1. The Coherence

This petition depends on the former most excellently. For in it is laid down the means to procure the first. God's name must be hallowed among men. But how is it done? By the erecting of God's kingdom in the hearts of men. We cannot glorify God until He rule in our hearts by His word and Spirit.

2. The Meaning

Thy

This word does put us in mind that there are two kingdoms: one God's, and that is the kingdom of heaven; the other the devil's, called the kingdom of darkness (Col. 1:13). For when all had sinned in Adam, God laid this punishment on all, that seeing they could not be content to obey their Creator, they should be in bondage under Satan. So that by nature we are all the children of wrath, and the devil holds up the scepter of his kingdom in the hearts of men. This kingdom is spiritual, and the pillars of it are ignorance, error, impiety, and all disobedience to God in which the devil wholly delights, which also are as it were the laws of his kingdom. Blind, ignorant people cannot abide this doctrine that the devil should rule in their hearts. They spit at the naming of him and say that they defy him with all their hearts; but whereas they live in sin and practice it as occasion is offered, though they cannot discern of themselves, yet they make plain proof that they sit in the kingdom of sin and darkness and are flat vassals of Satan and shall so continue till Christ, the strong man, come and bind him and cast him out. And this is the estate of all the children of Adam in themselves. Wherefore, our Savior in this petition teaches us to consider our natural estate and to pray that He would give us His Spirit to set us at liberty in the kingdom of His own Son.

Kingdom

God's kingdom in Scripture is taken two ways. First, generally, and so it signifies that administration by which the Lord governs all things, yea, even the devils themselves. Of which kingdom mention is made in the end of this prayer. And in the Psalm 97:1, "The Lord reigneth, let the earth rejoice." Again, it is taken more specially, and then it signifies the administration of Christ, the Head of the church, in which He frames men by His Word and Spirit to the subjection of the same Word. And so it is taken in this petition.

In a kingdom, there are four things to be noted: (1) there must be a king; (2) there must be subjects; (3) there are laws; (4) [there is] authority.

In this kingdom, Christ is the King. It is He to whom the Father has given all authority in heaven and earth.

In this kingdom, all are not subjects but such as are willing to give free and frank obedience to God's Word or, at the least, though their hearts be not so sound, make an outward profession of it.

The laws of this kingdom are the Word of God in the books of the Old and New Testaments. Therefore, it is called "the kingdom of heaven" (Matt. 13:24); "the gospel of the kingdom" (Mark 1:14); "the rod of his mouth" (Isa. 11:4); "the arm of God" (53:1). As a king by his laws brings his people in order and keeps them in subjection, so Christ by His word and the preaching of it as it were by a mighty arm draws His elect into His kingdom and fashions them to all holy obedience.

The power and authority is that whereby Christ converts effectually those which are to be converted by the inward operation of His Spirit and glorifies Himself in the confusion of the rest.

"Kingdom" being taken thus specially is also twofold. The first is the kingdom of grace, of which mention is made, "The kingdom of God stands not in meat and drink, but in righteousness" (Rom. 14:17)—that is, the assurance of our justification before God in the righteousness of Christ; peace of conscience, which proceeds from this assurance; and joy in the Holy Ghost, which comes from them both. In this kingdom, all men live not, but only those that are subject to Christ, obedient to the laws of His kingdom, and ruled by His authority and are continually taught in His word by His Spirit. But those that refuse to live according to the laws of this King and choose to live at their own liberty are in the kingdom of darkness—that is, sin and Satan.

The second is the kingdom of glory in heaven, which is the blessed estate of all God's people in which God Himself shall be all in all unto them. And the former kingdom of grace is an entrance and preparation to this kingdom of glory.

Come

God's kingdom comes when it takes place and is established and confirmed in men's hearts and made manifest to all the people, the impediments being removed.

Question. This coming implies a stopping. But how should God's kingdom be hindered? *Answer.* "Kingdom" in this place is not taken for that absolute and sovereign power of God whereby He rules all things, for that cannot be hindered, but for the kingdom of grace, which in the using of the outward means, as ministers, word, and sacraments, may be hindered by the devil, the world, and man's corruption.

3. The Wants Which Are to Be Bewailed

The wants which we in this petition are to mourn for are of two sorts: some concern our own selves; some, others. [1] That which concerns our own persons is a bondage and slavery under sin and Satan. This bondage indeed is weakened in God's servants, but none is wholly freed from it in this life. Paul complains that he is sold under sin and cries pitifully, "O miserable man that I am, who shall deliver me from this body of death?"

Question. What difference is then between the godly and the wicked? *Answer.* The evil and ungodly man in the very midst of his bondage has a merry heart. Sin is no trouble to him. Nay, it is meat and drink to him. But the godly man is otherwise minded, who, considering the power of the devil and his craft in manifold fearful temptations and seeing the proneness of his rebellious nature ever and anon to start away from God, is grieved and confounded in himself; and his heart bleeds within him that he does offend so merciful a father.

Many men live in this world, and that many years, and yet never feel this bondage under Satan and sin. Such undoubtedly cannot tell what this prayer means, but he that would have the right use of this petition must be acquainted with his own estate and be touched in his conscience that the flesh and the devil bear such sway in him. As the poor captive is always creeping to the prison door, always laboring to get off his bolts and fetters and to escape out of prison, so must we always cry to the Lord for His Spirit to free us out of this bondage and prison of sin and corruption and every day come nearer the prison door, looking when our blessed Savior will unbind us of all the fetters of sin and Satan and fully erect His kingdom in us.

(2) The wants which concern others are twofold. The former is the want of the good means which serve for the furthering of the kingdom of Christ, as preaching, sacraments, and discipline. When we shall see a people without knowledge and without good guides and teachers, or when we see one stand up in the congregation not able to teach, here is matter for mourning. This petition puts us in mind to bewail these wants. Our Savior, when He saw the Jews as sheep without a shepherd, He had compassion on them. And He wept over Jerusalem because they knew not the things which belonged to their peace (Luke 19:41–42). Therefore, when preachers want to hold up God's scepter

before the people and to hold out the word, which is as it were the arm of God to pull men from the bondage of the devil to the kingdom of Christ, then it is time to say, "Lord, let Thy kingdom come."

(3) The third want which we are to bewail is that there be so many impediments and hindrances of the kingdom of grace, as the devil and all his angels, their instruments, the pope, the Turk, and all the rest of the professed wicked of the world which by subtle enticements and tyranny keep back and repel the means whereby Christ rules as a king in His church. When the devil sees one that was sometime of his kingdom but to cast a look toward the heavenly Jerusalem, he straightway rages against him and labors quite to overthrow him. Wherefore, in regard of all these impediments we must pray, "Thy kingdom come."

4. Graces to Be Desired

(1) In this petition, we are taught, first, that we are to have a fervent desire and to hunger that God would give us His Spirit to reign and rule in our hearts and to bow them to all obedience and subjection of His will; and further, whereas our hearts have been as it were filthy [pig]sties and stables of the devil, that He would renew them and make them fit temples to entertain His Holy Spirit. "Create in me a clean heart, O God, and renew a right spirit in me, etc. Stablish me with thy free spirit" (Ps. 51:10, 12). If we shall consider the conversation of the wicked and the godly and their corrupt hearts together, we shall see little difference but in this, that the wicked are delighted and glad to sin, but the godly do wrestle as for life and death with their temptations and do resist the devil and do desire the grace of God's Spirit and cry to heaven to be freed from this bondage, howsoever their hearts are always ready to rebel against God.

(2) Forasmuch as the kingdom of grace is erected in God's church here upon earth, in this petition we are commanded to pray for the church of God and the parts thereof. "Pray for the peace of Jerusalem: they shall prosper that love thee" (Ps. 122:6). "Ye which are the Lord's remembrancers; give him no rest, until he set up Jerusalem the praise of the world" (Isa. 62:7).

And that God's church may flourish and be in good estate, we are to pray for Christian kings and princes, that God would bless them, and increase the numbers of them. For they are as nursing fathers and nursing mothers to the church [49:23]. And we especially are bound to pray for the King's most excellent Majesty, as also for other Christian kings, that they may be blessed and God's kingdom by them advanced.

And again, because ministers are the Lord's watchmen in the church, we are here also put in mind to seek their good and to pray that their hearts may be set for the building of God's kingdom, for the beating down of the kingdom of sin and Satan, and for the saving of the souls of His people. And the rather because the devil labors night and day to overthrow them in this glorious work and to resist them in their ministry, as appears in Zechariah 3:1. When Jehoshua, the high priest, stood before the Angel of the Lord, Satan stood at his right hand—namely, to resist him. Therefore, also we are to pray for them that the Lord would keep them and furnish them with gifts and withal make them faithful. "For where vision faileth, the people are left naked," says Solomon. "Brethren pray for us, that the word of the Lord may have a free passage, and be glorified" (2 Thess. 3:1).

[3] Thirdly, we must pray for all Christian schools of learning. Howsoever some think but basely of them, yet they are the ordinary means to maintain the ministry and so the church of God. A man that has divers orchards will also have a seminary full of young plants to maintain it. Schools, they are as seminaries to God's church, without which the church falls to decay, because they serve to make a supply of ministers.

(3) Thirdly, we are to desire that the Lord would hasten the second coming of Christ, as the saints in heaven pray, "Come, Lord Jesus, come quickly" [Rev. 22:20]. And therefore the godly are said to "love the coming of Christ" (2 Tim. 4:8). A penitent sinner so abhors his own corruptions and the irksome temptations of Satan that in this respect he desires that Christ would hasten His particular coming to him by death for no other cause but that he might make an end of sinning and displeasing God.

Thy Will Be Done

1. The Coherence

In the second petition, we desired that God would let His kingdom come—viz., that He would rule in our hearts. If He then must reign, we must be His subjects. And therefore here we crave that, being His subjects, we may obey Him and do His will. "If I be a father, where is my honor? If I be a master, where is my fear?" (Mal. 1:6).

2. The Meaning

Will

Here it signifies God's word, written in the Old and New Testament. For in His Word His will is revealed. Of the whole will of God, there be three special points which are in this place meant. (1) To believe in Christ. "This is the will of him that sent me, that every one which seeth the Son, and believeth in him, should have everlasting life" (John 6:40). (2) Sanctification of body and soul. "This is the will of God, even your sanctification," etc. (1 Thess. 4:3). (3) The bearing of affliction in this life. "Those which he knew before, he did predestinate to be made like to the image of his own Son" (Rom. 8:29). "That I might know him and the virtue of his resurrection, and the fellowship of his afflictions, and be made conformable to his death" (Phil. 3:10).

Thy Will
Not "mine," for man's own will is wicked and corrupt. Yea, it is flat enmity to God (Rom. 8:7).

Done
That is, obeyed and accomplished of men. Then the effect of the prayer is this: "O Lord, seeing Thou art our King, give us grace to show ourselves good subjects in obeying Thy will."

3. *The Wants to Be Prayed Against*
(1) Here, first, we are to bewail this, that our hearts are so prone to rebellion and disobedience of God's commandments. Put a match to a heap of gunpowder; on a sudden, it will be all on a flame. And as long as we add matter to the fire, it burns. So by nature we are most ready to sin, so soon as the least occasion is given. David had experience of this when he prayed, "Knit my heart to thee O Lord," etc. (Ps. 86:11), and, "Incline my heart to thy commandments" (119:36). Those which find not this want in themselves and the like affection to bewail it are in a miserable and dangerous case, even as a man that has a great disease upon him and knows not of it.

(2) Again, we must here bewail the sins of the world, as ignorance, schisms, hypocrisy, pride, ambition, contempt of God's Word, covetousness, oppression, want of love of God and His Word, etc. "Lot was vexed, and his righteous heart was vexed with the unclean conversation of the Sodomites" from day to day (2 Peter 2:7). So ought our souls to be vexed and grieved continually at the wickedness of our time, and we are to send up our prayers to God for unbelieving and unrepentant sinners that they may be brought to the obedience of God's will. In a common judgment upon Jerusalem, "They are marked in the forehead, that mourn and cry for the abominations that be done in the midst of it" (Ezek. 9:4).

(3) Here also we must humble ourselves for our unquietness of mind and impatience when God lays any cross on us. It is God's will that we should suffer affliction and withal humble ourselves under His mighty hand. Our Savior prayed that the cup might be taken away, but with submission to His Father's will (Luke 22:42). And this David had learned when he said, "But if he thus say, I have no delight in thee, behold, here I am, let him do to me as seemeth good in his eyes" (2 Sam. 15:26).

4. Graces to Be Desired

(1) The first thing which we are here to desire is that we may have grace to deny ourselves, wills, and affections, because herein we are unlike to God and like the devil. This is the first lesson that our Savior does give His disciples, that they must deny themselves and follow Him.

(2) The second thing is the knowledge of God's will. For otherwise, how shall we do it? How can that servant please his master which cannot tell what he would have done of him? Most men will have books of statutes in their houses; and if they be to deal in any great matter, they will do nothing before they have looked on the statute. In like manner, men should have the Bible—that is, the book of God's statutes—in their houses. The laws of God must be the men of our counsel. Before every action, we are to search what is the will of God and then to do it. Here then, we are taught to use the means and to pray for knowledge.

(3) Again, we are taught to have a desire in our hearts and an endeavor in our lives in all things to perform obedience to God's Word in our lives and conversations and in our particular callings.

(4) Lastly, we desire patience and strength, when it shall please God at any time to exercise us with the cross, as Paul prays for the Colossians that "God would strengthen them by the power of his might, unto all patience and long-suffering with joyfulness" (Col. 1:11).

5. Error Confuted

The Church of Rome teaches that men by nature have free will to do good, and that men, being stirred up by the Holy Ghost, can of themselves will that which is good. But if this were so, why might we not pray, "Let my will be done," so far forth as the will of man shall agree with God's will? But this cannot be, as we see in the tenor of this petition.

In Earth as It Is in Heaven

1. The Meaning

Having showed the meaning of this petition, "Thy will be done," now we are to speak of the condition, which shows in what manner we should do it. For the question might be how we would do God's will; and the answer is that His will must be done in earth as it is in heaven.

Heaven

By "heaven," here is meant the souls of faithful men departed and the elect angels. "Praise the Lord ye his angels, that excel in strength, that do his commandments in obeying the voice of his word" (Ps. 103:20).

Earth

By "earth" is understood nothing but men on earth, because all other creatures in their kind obey God. Only man, he is rebellious and disobedient. Then the meaning is, "Let Thy will be done by us on earth as the angels and saints departed do Thy will in heaven."

Question. Do we here desire to do the will of God in that perfection it is done by angels? Must we be as perfect as they? *Answer.* The words here used, "in earth as it," etc., do not signify an equality (as though our obedience could in this life be in the same degree of perfection with angels), but a similitude, standing in the like manner of obedience. Now, it may be asked, in what manner do the angels obey God? *Answer.* They do the will of God willingly, speedily, and faithfully. And this is signified in that they are said in the Scriptures to be winged and to stand continually beholding the face of our heavenly Father. And this is the manner in which we desire to perform God's will.

2. The Wants to Be Bewailed

We are here admonished to be displeased with ourselves for our slack and imperfect obedience to God and for our hypocrisy, privy pride, presumption, deadness of spirit, and many other wants which break out when we are in doing God's will. There is no servant of God but has wants in his best works. So we must understand Paul when he says, "To will is present with me, but I find no means to perform that which is good" (Rom. 7:18), where he signifies thus much in effect, that he could begin good things but not perfect them and go through stitch, as we say. When the godly do good, as here, speak God's word, pray, praise God, etc., they perform things acceptable to God. But in these actions they find matter of mourning—namely, the imperfection of the work. Therefore, David prays, "Enter not into judgment with thy servant" (Ps. 143:2). And here we may see how far wide the Church of Rome is that holds good works to be any way meritorious that be every way imperfect. If the men of that church had grace, they might see that the corruptions of the flesh were chains and fetters about their legs, that when they would fain run the ways of God's commandments, they are constrained to halt down right and to trail their loins after them.

3. Graces to Be Desired

The grace here to be desired is sincerity of heart or a ready and constant purpose and endeavor not to sin in anything, but to do God's will, so as we may keep a good conscience before God and men. "And for this counsel endeavor always to have a clear conscience toward God, and toward men" (Acts 24:16). This must we hunger after and pray for, seeing it is not sufficient to abstain from evil but also to do good and in doing good strive to come to perfection. A conformity with angels in this duty is to be sought for and to be begun in this life, that in the life to come we may be like them in glory.

Give Us This Day Our Daily Bread

1. The Coherence

Thus much of the three first petitions, which concern God. Now follow the other three, which concern ourselves. In which order we learn to pray for those things which concern God absolutely and for those things which concern ourselves not absolutely, but so far forth as they shall make for God's glory, the building of His kingdom, and the doing of His will.

But how depends this petition on the former? In the first, we are taught to pray that God's name might be hallowed, which is done when God reigns in our hearts, and His will is done. Now further, His will is obeyed in three things: first, by depending on His providence for the things of this life; secondly, by depending on His mercy for the pardon of sin; thirdly, by depending on His power and might in resisting temptations. And thus God's will is obeyed.

2. The Meaning

Bread

By "bread" in this place, many of the ancient fathers as also the Papists at this day understand the element of bread in the Sacrament and the body of Christ, which is the bread of life. But that cannot be; for St. Luke calls it "bread for the day"—that is, bread sufficient to preserve us to the present day. And by this he makes it manifest that the words of this petition must be understood not of spiritual but of bodily food, and the bread of life is more directly asked in the second or fourth petition. As for the opinion of Erasmus, who thinks that in this so heavenly a prayer made to God the Father there should be no mention made of bread—that is, of earthly things, which even the Gentiles bestow on their children—it is vain and frivolous. For it is God's will that we should not cast the care of heavenly things only, but all our care upon Him (1 Peter 5:7). And He has elsewhere commanded that earthly things should be asked at His hand (1 Kings 8:35), and the same has been asked in the prayer of Jacob (Gen. 28:20) and Solomon (Prov. 30:7). And whereas the Lord's Prayer is a perfect platform of prayer, temporal blessings must have some place there, unless we will ascribe the having and enjoying of them to our own industry, as though they were no gifts of God, which to think were great impiety.

By "bread" then we must understand properly a kind of food made of the flour of grain that is baked and eaten. And thus it must be taken in those places of Scripture where bread is opposed to water or wine. And by a figure more generally it signifies all things whereby temporal life is preserved. In this sense, goats' milk is called bread (Prov. 27:27), and the fruit of trees (Jer. 11:19), and all things that pass to and fro in traffic (Prov. 31:14). And so likewise in this place by this one means of sustaining our bodies and temporal lives all other means whatsoever must be understood, as meat, drink, clothing, health, liberty, peace, etc.

And whereas our Savior Christ under the name of bread and not under the name of any other plentiful or dainty food teaches us to ask temporal blessings, He does it for two causes. The first is that we might hereby learn frugality and moderation in our diet, apparel, houses, and be content if we have no more but bread—that is, things necessary to preserve life, which Paul comprehends under food and clothing [1 Tim. 6:8]. For we are taught in this petition to ask no more. We must not with the Israelites murmur because they had nothing but manna.

Question. Must we then use God's creatures only for necessity? *Answer.* We may use them not only for necessity, but also for honest delight and pleasure. God gives wine to make glad the heart of man and oil to make his face shine (Ps. 104:15). And our Savior Christ allowed of the fact of Mary, which took a pound of ointment of spikenard very costly and anointed His very feet so that all the house was filled with the smell, though Judas did esteem it waste (John 12:3). Yet if it so fall out that the Lord do grant us but bread—that is, so much as shall hold body and soul together—we must thankfully content ourselves therewith. "Therefore when we have food and raiment, let us therewith be content" (1 Tim. 6:8). This contentation was practiced of Jacob (Gen. 28:20).

A second cause is to teach us that there is a particular providence. All men willingly confess the general providence of God over all things; but besides that we must acknowledge another more special providence, even in the least things that can be, because every morsel of bread which we eat would no more nourish us than a piece of earth or a stone unless God give His blessing unto it.

Daily

The word in the original is thus much in effect: bread unto your essence or substances. Then the meaning is, "Give us such bread from day to day, as may nourish our substances." Thus prays Agur, "Feed me with foods convenient for me" (Prov. 30:8). Some there are which put an angelical perfection in fasting; but we are taught in Scriptures that as above all things we are to seek for life eternal, so we must in this life have care to sustain and maintain our natural life, that we may have convenient space and time to repent and prepare ourselves to the kingdom of heaven. Fasting in itself, as it is an abstinence from meat, is no part of God's worship, but in its own nature a thing indifferent. And therefore it is to be used so far forth as it shall further us in God's service, and not further. And seeing we are taught to pray for such food as shall preserve nature and maintain the vital blood, we ought not to use fasting to the hindrance and destruction of nature.

Our Bread

Question 1. How is bread ours? *Answer.* Paul shows how: "Ye are Christ's, and all things are yours" (1 Cor. 3:22). So then, by means of Christ bread is called ours. For God, having given Christ to us, does in Him and by Him give all things else to us. *Question 2.* How may I know that the things I enjoy are mine by Christ, and that I do not usurp them? *Answer.* Paul says that the creatures of God are good and that the use of them is sanctified to us by the Word and prayer (1 Tim. 4:4). Then, if we have the Word of God to tell us that we may enjoy and use them, and also if we pray to God for the right and pure use of them, we are no usurpers but indeed right owners of them not only before men, but also before God. *Question 3.* If the creatures must be made ours by Christ, how comes it to pass that the ungodly have such abundance of them? *Answer.* We lost the title and interest of the creatures in Adam; yet God of His mercy bestows temporary blessings upon the unjust as well as upon the just. But for all that, unless they be in Christ and hold the title of them by Him, they shall in the end turn to their greater condemnation.

And whereas we call it "our bread," we learn that every man must live of his own calling and his own goods. Here also is condemned all oppression, stealing, lying, cogging, and other such deceitful means which men use to get wealth and goods. Many think it no sin to provide for their families in such order, but in saying this petition they pray against themselves. "He that laboreth not, let him not eat" (2 Thess. 3:10). "He which stole, let him steal no more, but rather labor with his hands the thing that good is" (Eph. 4:28).

This Day

We say not here "this week," "this month," "this age," but "this day"—what means this? May not we provide for the time to come? *Answer.* It is lawful. Yea, a man is bound in good manner to provide for time to come. The apostles provided for the church in Judea against the time of dearth foretold by Agabus (Acts 11:28). And Joseph in Egypt in the years of plenty stored up against the years of famine. Wherefore, in these words our Savior's meaning is only to condemn all distrustful care that distracts the minds of men and to teach us to rest on His fatherly goodness from day to day in every season. This is noted unto us where the Israelites were commanded to gather no more manna than would serve for one day; and if they did, it putrefied (Ex. 16:19–20). Whereby God taught them to rest on His providence every particular day and not on the means.

Give Us

Not "me." This serves to teach us that a man must not only regard himself but also be mindful of others. For a man that has wealth is made a steward to distribute his goods to the poor and the good of God's church. True love seeks not her own things. The branches of the vine are laden with clusters of grapes not for themselves but for others. The candle spends itself to give others light.

Give

If bread be ours, wherefore are we to ask it? It may seem needless. *Answer.* Not so; for hereby we are taught to wait on God, who is the fountain and giver of all blessings. Men usually driven to any distress use evil means, as robbing, deceiving, consulting with wizards, etc. (2) Again, here we learn that though a man had all the wealth in the world, all is nothing without God's blessing. *Question.* The rich need not say, "Give us," etc. for they have abundance already. And what need they ask that which they have? *Answer.* Let a man be never so rich and want nothing that can be desired, yet if he want God's blessing, in effect he wants all. Wherefore, even kings and the greatest personages that be are as much bound to use this petition as the poorest. "God's blessing is riches," says Solomon (Prov. 10:22). "Thou mayst eat and not have enough," be clothed and not warm, earn wages and put it in a broken bag (Hag. 1:6), if God do not bless you. This blessing of God is called the staff of bread (Isa. 3:1). In bread, there be two things: the substance and the virtue thereof proceeding from God's blessing. The second—that is, the power of nourishing—is the staff of bread. For take away from an aged man his staff, and he falls. And so take away God's blessing from bread, and the strength thereof is gone. It becomes unprofitable and ceases to nourish. Lastly, here we see that all labor and toil taken in any kind of calling is nothing and avails not unless God still give His blessing (Ps. 127:1).

3. The Wants Which Are to Be Bewailed

Sins which we are taught in this petition to bewail are two especially. (1) Covetousness, a vice which is naturally engrafted in every man's heart. It is when a man is not content with this present estate. This desire is insatiable, and men that have enough would still have more. Wherefore, he which shall use this petition must be grieved for this sin and pray with David, "Incline mine heart to thy commandments, and not to covetousness" (119:36). And he must sorrow not so much for the act of this sin as for the corruption of nature in this behalf. Covetous people will plead that they are free from this vice; but mark men's lives, and we shall see it is a common disease, as David noted where he brings in the people, saying, "Who shall shew us any good?" (4:6). This then is a common sin, that we are taught to mourn for.

(2) The second want is diffidence and distrustfulness in God's providence touching the things of this life. Men also will shift this off and say they would be sorry to distrust God. But if we do but a little look into the corruption of our nature, we shall see that we are deceived. For being in prosperity, we are not troubled; but if once we be pressed with adversity, then we howl and weep. And as Paul says, "Men pierce themselves through with many sorrows" (1 Tim. 6:10). If a man shall lose a part of his goods, what then does he? Straight he goes out to a wise man. Is this to believe in God? No, it is to distrust God and believe the devil.

4. Graces to Be Desired

The grace to be desired is a readiness in all estates of life to rest on God's providence, whatsoever fall out. "Commit thy way to the Lord, and trust in him, and he shall bring it to pass" (Ps. 37:5). "Commit"—or, "roll"—"thy works upon the Lord, and thy thoughts shall be directed" (Prov. 16:3). Whereby we are admonished to take pains in our callings to get meat and drink, etc. If the Lord bless not our labor, we must be content. If He do, we must give Him thanks. Now, for this cause we are further to pray to God that He would open our eyes and by His Spirit teach us in all His good creatures to see His providence and when means fail and are contrary then also to believe in the same and to follow Paul's example (Phil. 4:12).

5. Errors Confuted

[1] Papists teach that men by works of grace may merit life eternal and increase of justification in this life. But how can this be? For here we see that every bit of bread which we eat is the free gift of God without any merit of ours. Now, if we cannot merit a piece of bread, what madness is it to think that we can merit life everlasting?

(2) They also are deceived who think that anything comes by mere chance or fortune without God's providence. Indeed, in respect of men who know not the causes of things, many chances there are, but so as that they are ordered and come to pass by God's providence. "By chance there came down a certain priest that way" (Luke 10:31).

Forgive Us Our Debts

1. The Coherence

This is the fifth petition, and the second of those which concern ourselves. In the former, we craved temporal blessings; in this and the next which follows, we crave spiritual blessings. Where we may note that, seeing there is two petitions which concern spiritual things and but one of temporal, that the care for our souls must be double to the care of our bodies. In the world, men care for their bodies. Their hearts are set for wealth and promotions. They can be content to hear the word on the Sabbath; yet neither then nor in the weekday do they lay it up in their hearts and practice it, which argues that they have little or no care for their souls.

Question. What is the cause that first we crave things for the body and in the second place those which concern the soul? *Answer.* The order of the Holy Ghost in these petitions is wonderful; for the Lord considers the dullness and backwardness of men's natures, and therefore He trains them up and draws them on by little, even as a schoolmaster does his young scholars, propounding unto them some small elements and principles and so carrying them to higher points. For the former petition is a step or degree to these two following. The ruler by the healing of the body of his child is brought to believe in Christ (John 4:53). He then that will rest on God's mercy for the pardon of his sins must first of all rest on God's providence for this life. And he that cannot put his affiance in God for the provision of meat and drink, how shall he trust God's mercy for the salvation of his soul? Here, we may see the faith of worldlings. They say that God is merciful and that they believe in Christ, which cannot be true, seeing in lesser matters, as meat and drink, they distrust God, as appears by their covetousness. Again, by this order we are taught as earnestly to seek for the pardon of our sins as we seek for temporal blessings.

2. The Meaning

Debts

By "debt," sins are meant, as it is in Luke 11:4. And they are so called because of the resemblance between them. For even as a debt does bind a man either to make satisfaction or else to go to prison, so our sins bind us either to satisfy God's justice or else to suffer eternal damnation.

Forgive

To forgive sin is to cover it or not to impute it (Ps. 32:1). And this is done when God is content of His mercy to accept the death and passion of Christ as a sufficient payment and ransom for man's sins and so to esteem them as no sins. And here under this one benefit of remission of sins all the rest of the same kind are understood, as justification, sanctification, redemption, glorification, etc.

3. The Uses of the Words

Hence we may learn many lessons. The first is that, seeing we must pray thus, "Lord, forgive," etc., we are to hold that there is no satisfaction to God's justice for sin by our works, no, not in temporary punishments, but that the doing away of our sins is of God's mere favor; for to forgive and to satisfy be contrary. Wherefore, the doctrine of human satisfactions, taught in the Church of Rome, is vile and devilish.

(2) Secondly, whereas we are taught thus to pray continually from day to day, we note the great patience and longsuffering of God, that suffers and forebears still and does not pour out His confusion upon us, though we offend His majesty day by day. This teaches us like patience toward our brethren. We ourselves cannot put up the least injury and forebear but one day, and yet we desire that God would forgive us daily to the end of our lives.

(3) Again, we may observe that there is no perfect sanctification in this life, seeing we must every day to the end crave the pardon of our sins. Therefore, wicked is the opinion of the Catharists or Puritans, which hold that men may be without sin in this life.

(4) And when we say forgive not "me" but "us," we are put in mind to pray not only for the pardon of our own sin but likewise for our brethren and enemies. "Confess one to another, and pray one for another: for the prayer of the righteous availeth much: if it be fervent" (James 5:16). And, as some think, the prayer of Steven was a means of the conversion of Saul.

(5) Also, we note that before prayers for pardon of sin must go a confession of sin; for whereas we say, "Forgive our debts," we confess before God that we are flat bankrupts and not able to discharge the least of our sins. This appears, "If we confess our sins, he is faithful to forgive us" (1 John 1:9). And it was practiced by David (Psalm 32:5; 51). The manner of making confession is this: known sins and those which trouble the conscience are to be confessed particularly, but unknown sins generally (19:12).

(6) Lastly, hence it is manifest that there is no justification by works. Our sins are debts, and so also are all works of the law. And it were a fond thing to imagine that a man might discharge one debt by another.

4. Wants to Be Bewailed

The wants to be bewailed are the burden of our sins and the corruptions of our natures and the wickedness of our lives and the sins of our youth and of our old age. "My sins have taken such hold upon me, that I am not able to look up: they are more in number than the hairs of mine head, therefore mine heart hath failed me" (40:12). Thus, with David we are to travail and groan under this burden. But this grief for sin is a rare thing in the world. Men can mourn bitterly for the things of this life, but their sins never trouble them. Again, this sorrow must be for sin because it is sin, though there were neither hell to torment nor devil or conscience to accuse nor judge to revenge.

5. *Graces to Be Desired*

The grace which we must desire is the Spirit of grace and deprecations (Zech. 12:10), which is that gift of the Holy Ghost, whereby we are enabled to call to God for the pardon of our sins. A man, having offended the laws of a prince and being in danger of death, will never be at quiet till he have gotten a pardon. Even so, they which feel and see their sins, having this Spirit, are so moved that they can never be at rest till in prayer they be eased of the burden of their sins. A man may, I grant, babble and speak many words; but he shall never pray effectually before he have this Spirit of prayer to make him cry, "Abba, Father." For worldly commodities all can pray; but learn to pray for the want of Christ.

As We Forgive Our Debtors

1. *The Coherence*

These words be a part of the fifth petition, which is propounded with a condition: forgive us, as we forgive others. And these words depend on the former as the reason thereof, which seems to be taken from the comparison of the less to the greater, thus: "If we who have but a spark of mercy do forgive others, then do Thou, who art the fountain of mercy, forgive us. But we forgive others. Therefore, do Thou forgive us." Thus Luke 11:4 has it, "Forgive us our sins, for even we forgive."[3] The Papists take it otherwise, who say, "Forgive us, as we forgive," making our forgiving a cause for which God is moved to forgive us in temporal punishments, whereas our forgiving of men is only a sign or effect that God does forgive us.

[2] *The Meaning*

Question 1. Whether is a man bound to forgive all debts? *Answer.* The word "debt" in this place is not understood of debt that is civil and comes by lawful bargaining, but of hurts and damages which are done unto us in our bodies, goods, or good name. As for the former civil debts, a man may exact them, so he do it with showing of mercy.

---

3. Rhem Test. On Luke 7:47. [NB that this was originally in text, not in the margin.]

Question 2. How may any man forgive trespasses, seeing God only forgives sins? *Answer.* In every trespass which any do to their neighbors, there be two offences: one to God; another to man. In the first respect, as it is against God and His commandment, it is called a sin; and that God only forgives. In the other respect, it is called an injury or damage, and so man may forgive it. When a man is robbed, the law is broken by stealing; and the injury that is done is against a man that has goods stolen. This injury as it is an injury a man may forgive; but as it is a sin he cannot, but God only.

Question 3. Whether may a man lawfully pray this petition and yet sue him at the law, who has done him wrong? *Answer.* A man may[4] in a holy manner sue another for an injury. And as a soldier in lawful war may kill his enemy and yet love him, so may a man forgive an injury and yet seek in a Christian manner the remedy. But in doing of this we must observe five things. (1) We are to take heed of all private revenge in inward hatred, which if we conceive, we do not forgive. (2) We must take heed of offence and have care that our doings be not scandalous to the church. (3) Our suits must be taken in hand to maintain godly peace; for if all injuries were put up, there would be no civil state or government. (4) This must be that the party offending may be chastised and be brought to repentance for his fault; for if many men were not repressed, they would grow worse. (5) Law must be the last remedy. As physicians use desperate remedies when weaker will not serve, even so must we use law as the last means when all others fail. The dealing of the world in this case is no example for us to follow. For through rage and stomach men will abide no private agreement, and therefore they use the law in the first place as the Corinthians did. But what says Paul? "It is utterly a fault among you" (1 Cor. 6:7). But if the law be used aright, a Christian man may sue his neighbor at law and love the party sued; for there is difference between dealing against a man before a magistrate and the dealing of one private man with another. For private dealing is commonly revenge and therefore unlawful.

3. The Use

The use of this clause is very profitable, for it shows us a lively sign whereby our consciences may be assured of the pardon of our sins—namely, a readiness and willing desire to forgive men. Many use these words long and often yet find no assurance of pardon. And the cause is because they have no desire of God's mercy nor willingness to forgive others, which if indeed they had, then no doubt the forgiveness of their sins should by this means be sealed unto them. Wherefore, if any would be persuaded of God's mercy in this point, let

---

4. Originally, "man."

them descend into their own souls and search narrowly if they can find their hearts as ready to forgive as they are ready to desire forgiveness at God's hand. Then they may assure themselves of God's mercy in Christ, as we are taught by our Savior Christ, "Blessed are the merciful, for they shall obtain mercy" (Matt. 5:7). Consider these comparisons. A man, walking under a wall in a cold sunny day, is heated of the wall, which first received heat from the sun. So he that shows mercy to others has first received mercy from God. Also, take a piece of wax, and put to a seal it leaves an impression or mark like itself in the wax, which when a man looks on, he does certainly know that there has been a seal, the print whereof is left behind. Even so it is in everyone that has a readiness to forgive others, by which a Christian may easily know that God has sealed to him the forgiveness of his sins in his very heart. Therefore, let men look into their hearts whether they have any affection to forgive others, for that is as it were the print in their hearts of God's mercy toward them in forgiving them.

Many there are which pray for pardon at God's hands, but they cannot brook it that they should forgive their neighbors. Hereupon come these sayings: "I may forgive him, but I will not forget him. "He may come in my Paternoster, but he shall never come in my Creed." Behold the devil's logic, which makes malice to be charity. Blind people play with the Lord's Prayer, as the fly does with the candle till she be burnt. For the more they pray these words, the more they call for vengeance against themselves (James 2:13). Neither will it help to omit this clause, as some have done in Chrysostom's days; for this is even to mock God, and if we do not forgive, we shall not be forgiven.

Lead Us Not into Temptation, but Deliver Us from Evil

1. The Coherence

It might seem to some that this petition is superfluous, for what need he care for temptations that has the pardon of his sins? But our Savior did not teach us thus to pray without special reason. (1) Because forgiveness of sins and grievous temptations be inseparable companions in this life, which thing we find to be true both in God's Word and in Christian experience; for there is no man in this world so beaten and buffeted with temptations as the penitent sinner that cries most bitterly for the pardon of his sins. This is the estate that few men in the world are acquainted with. For many are never troubled with temptation but live in all peace and quietness both in body and soul. "When the strong man armed keeps his hold, the things that he possesseth are in peace" (Luke 11:21). Whereby is signified that the wicked of the world, being possessed of Satan, are not a whit molested by him with any temptations. Neither need he trouble them, seeing he has them at commandment to do what he will. But when a man once begins to make conscience of sin and to sue unto the Lord for pardon of his offences and still continues in dislike of sin and Satan, then the enemy bestirs him and uses all means to bring that man to confusion. He offers all manner of temptations to molest him and never affords this poor sinner any rest. Hereupon, for fear of being overcome, he must pray continually unto the Lord that he may not be led into temptation.

Here, some Christian conscience may reason thus: "No man is so troubled with sin and Satan as I. Therefore, I am not in God's favor, but am a plain cast-away." *Answer.* If pardon of sin and temptations go together, all is contrary. If you had no grief for sin, no buffetings of your enemies, the flesh, the world, and the devil, you could not be in God's favor but under the power of Satan. Now, this great measure of the spiritual temptations is a sign rather of God's love. For whom God loves, the devil hates; and where God works in love, the devil works in malice.

(2) Secondly, this petition is joined with the former to teach us that as we must be careful to pray for pardon of sins past, so also we must endeavor to prevent sins to come. We must not fall again into our old sins, neither must we be overtaken with new sins.

2. The Meaning

These words be but all one petition, which has two parts, the latter being a declaration of the former. "Lead us not into temptation"—how is that done? By delivering us "from evil."

Temptation

Temptation is nothing else but the enticement of the soul or heart either by the corruption of man's nature or the allurements of the world or the devil to any sin. "God tempts no man" (James 1:13)—that is, God moves no man to sin.

Lead Us Not

Or, "carry us not" into temptation. To be led is to be overcome of the temptation when it prevails and wholly gets the victory, so as men tempted are brought to perdition. Then the meaning is this: "When we are moved or enticed to sin, Lord, keep us that we be not overcome and give Thou an issue with the temptation."

Question. God is just and cannot sin. But if He lead men into temptation, shall He not be the author of sin? *Answer.* Indeed, many, fearing to charge God with sin, read the words thus, "Suffer us not to be led." But the text is very plain, "Lead or carry us not." And the Scriptures elsewhere use the phrases of God. God is said to harden Pharaoh's heart (Ex. 9:12). The Lord moved David to number the people (2 Sam. 24:1). God sent strong delusions that men might believe lies (2 Thess. 2:11). These and such places have a special meaning thus to be gathered. There is no action of man or of the devil absolutely evil; but although in some respects it be evil, yet in some other it is good. For we are not to think that as there is a main or absolute good, so also there is a main or absolute evil. Thus then, temptation being an action, it is not in every respect evil but in some good, in some evil. And so far forth as it is good, the Lord works it. But as it is evil, He does not work it but willingly permits it to be done by man and Satan.

And there be four respects in which God may be a worker in temptations and yet be free from sin. (1) First, He tempts by offering occasions and objects to try whether a man will sin or not. A master suspecting his servant, which in work professes fidelity, lays a purse of money in his way to try if he will steal it, which, if he steals, he has found by watching him a secret thief and so has laid him open for deceiving any more. Now, this trying of him is no sin, though he sin in stealing. In the same manner, God tempts His own servants to prove and try them. "Thou shalt not hearken unto the words of the prophet or dreamer of dreams: for the Lord thy God proveth you, to know whether ye love the Lord your God with all your heart" (Deut. 13:3).

(2) Secondly, God leads into temptation by withdrawing His grace. Neither can this be a sin in God, because He is bound to no man to give him grace. And here is a difference between the tempting of God and Satan. God holds back grace when He tempts; the devil suggests evil motions.

(3) Every action so far forth as it is an action is good and of God. "In him we live, move, and have our being" (Acts 17:28). Therefore, God is a worker in temptations so far forth as they are actions. One man kills another. The very moving of the body in the doing of this villainy is of God, but the wickedness of the action is from man and the devil. A man rides upon a lame horse and stirs him. The rider is the cause of the motion, but the horse himself of the halting in the motion. So God is author of the action, but not of the evil of the action.

(4) The fourth way is in regard of the end. God tempts His servants only to correct and humble them for their sins to try how they will abide the cross and to move them the more to love Him. God afflicts the children of Israel "to try them whether they would keep his commandments" (Deut. 8:1). "He trieth Hezekiah to see what was in his heart" (2 Chron. 32:31). The devil's end in tempting is only to bring the party to destruction. Thus, we need not fear to say that God in some respects does tempt His own servants.

Deliver Us from Evil

That is, free us from the power of the flesh, of the devil, and the world. Some take evil in this place only for the devil, but we may take it more largely for all spiritual enemies. "The whole world lies in evil" (1 John 5:19)—viz., under the power of sin and Satan. These words (as I have said) are a proof and explanation of the former; for when a man is delivered from evil, he is not led into temptation. The cause being taken away, the effect ceases.

3. The Uses

(1) Hence, we learn what a righteous God Jehovah is that can work in evil actions and yet be void of sin.

(2) Whereas we say, "Lead us not," etc., we note that the devil in temptations can go no further than God permits him.

(3) We are not to pray that temptations be quite taken from us or that we be wholly freed from them, but that they do not overcome us. For it is the Lord's will that His church should be tempted. Nay, David desired some kind of temptations. "Prove me, O Lord" (Ps. 26:1). And James says, "Account it for exceeding joy, when ye shall fall into divers temptations" (James 1:2).

(4) Note also that every man by nature is the bondslave of sin and Satan. For where is deliverance, there was a bondage first. This confutes the Papists, who maintain free will; for we are dead in sin by nature as a man in a grave, and we must still pray thus till we be fully delivered.

4. Wants to Be Bewailed

The corruption which in this petition we ought to mourn for is the continual rebellion of our wicked natures and our proneness to yield up ourselves in every temptation to sin and Satan. And the remnants of the old bondage under Satan must be grievous and irksome unto us, and we must bewail them bitterly. The Jews in a bodily captivity "wept when they remembered Sion" (Psalm 137). How much more should we weep when we feel the law of our members rebelling against the law of our minds and leading us captive to sin?

5. Graces to Be Desired

The contrary blessing to be desired is that God would establish us by His free Spirit (51:12), which is so called because it sets us every day more and more at liberty out of the reach of sin and Satan.

For Thine Is the Kingdom, the Power, and Glory Forever

1. The Meaning

These words contain a reason of all the former petitions, whereby we are moved to crave things needful at God's hand.

Thine Is

Earthly kings have kingdom, power, and glory (Dan. 2:37), yet not from themselves but from God, whose vicegerents they are on earth. Therefore, to make a difference between God's kingdom, power, and glory, and those of earthly kings, it is said, "Thine is the kingdom," etc.—that is, that God has all these in Himself and from Himself, and men from Him.

The Kingdom

These words are fully expounded, "Thine, O Lord, is greatness, power, and victory, and praise: and all that is in heaven and earth is thine: thine is the kingdom, and thou excellest as head over all," etc. (1 Chron. 29:11). The kingdom is said to be God's because He is absolute possessor and owner of all things that are and also has sovereign rule over all things at His will. Now, out of the first property of God we may gather a strong motive to induce us to pray unto Him alone. For seeing all things are His, both in heaven and earth whatsoever, therefore we must come to Him for the graces and blessings which we desire.

The Power

Oftentimes earthly princes have kingdoms yet want power. But God has kingdom and power also. Yea, His power is infinite, and He can do all that He will. And more than He will as for those things which come of impotence, He cannot do them. And if He could He should not be omnipotent. And as He is omnipotent in Himself, so all the power which any creature has is from Him alone.

Question. How can this be, seeing the devil has power to sin, which is not from God?

Answer. To sin is no power but rather a want of power. Otherwise, all the strength and power Satan has is of God.

And from this second property is taken another motive to move us to pray unto God. Because all power being His, we can never do any of the things which we ask but by power received from Him.

Thine Is the Glory

The third property of God arises from the two former; for, seeing the title and interest in all things and the power whereby they are disposed and governed is of God, therefore it follows that all glory is His. Yea, in Him is fullness of glory, and the glory of the creatures is all of Him. To sinful men belongs nothing "but shame and confusion" (Dan. 9:7).

The third property ministers a third motive to induce men to pray unto God alone. For seeing all glory by right is His, therefore we must invocate His holy name that in so doing we may give Him the glory due unto Him.

Forever

The words in the original are "for ages." Now an age signifies the space of a hundred years; but here it is taken for eternity, because eternity is nothing but multiplication of ages. And as eternity is here noted by ages, so on the contrary we read that eternity is taken for a certain and distinct time. God promises Abraham to give him the land of Canaan for an everlasting possession—that is, for a long season (Gen. 17:8), for else Abraham's seed should inherit the land until this time, which it does not. Wherefore, as often the whole is put for the part—viz., eternity for a certain time—so here the part is put for the whole, ages for eternity. This also makes a difference between earthly princes and the mighty Jehovah. They have kingdom, power, and glory for a short time, but He absolutely and forever.

2. The Uses

(1)[5] Here we learn in prayer to abase ourselves before God and utterly to deny all that is in us. Kingdom, power, and glory is all His, not ours. We are no better than rebels and traitors to Him. If we have any good thing, it is from Him, even the grace whereby we pray. And he that in prayer will not confess this shall no more be heard than the insolent beggar that will not acknowledge his want.

(2) Secondly, in prayer we learn that we must be persuaded of two things and build upon them: God's power and will—His power in that He is able; His will in that He is careful to perform our request, as it was noted in the preface. The first of these is signified by kingdom and power; the second is noted in that glory is His. "For all the promises of God in him, are yea, and Amen, unto the glory of God" (2 Cor. 1:20).

(3) Again, we gather that prayer and thanksgiving must go together; for as in the five petitions we make request unto God, so in these words we praise Him and thereby give Him thanks. "But in all things, let your requests be shewed to God in prayer and supplication, with thanksgiving" (Phil. 4:6).

There is none but in want will be ready to pray; but when we have received, we are slack in giving thanks. But he which will pray aright must join them both together. And the sum of all God's praise stands in these three points: (1) that He is an absolute king; (2) that He has absolute power to rule all things; (3) that, having power and a kingdom, He has glory also, which appears in the holding of His kingdom and the showing of His power in governing of it.

(4) Whatsoever we ask, we must refer it to God's glory. This is the first thing which we are taught to crave and the last we are to perform, because it is noted both in the beginning and in the end of the prayer.

Thus much of the use of these words altogether. Now let us make use of them particularly. (1) Whereas we say, "Thine is the kingdom," magistrates and rulers must know that all the authority and rule which they have is from the

---

5. Originally, "2."

Lord. And therefore they must remember to order themselves as God's vicegerents, using their power to bring men in subjection to God's laws and referring all their callings to His glory.

(2) Where we say, "Thine is the power," we are admonished, when we are to perform any work, as to do service to God, to keep ourselves in the compass of our callings, that we have no power of ourselves. And for this cause we must ask power at God's hands, that we may be enabled to walk uprightly before Him and do our duties.

(3) In saying, "Thine is the glory," we learn that if we would have a good report and praise among men, we must above all things seek God's glory, not regarding so much our own.[6] If He give the praise among men, give Him thanks. If not, be content, because all glory is His.

Amen

1. The Meaning

We have heard the preface and the petitions, what they are. Now follows the third part, which is the assent or testification of faith required in prayer in this word "amen." And it contains more than men at the first would imagine. It signifies, "certainly, so be it, as it shall be so" (2 Cor. 1:20). It is often taken for a bare assent of the people, saying amen to the minister. But in this place it contains more, for every point in this prayer is not only a direction for public prayer but for private also and must be said as well of the minister as of the people. Now then, there being two principal things in prayer: the first, a desire of grace; the second, faith, whereby we believe that God will grant things desired. The first is expressed in the six petitions; the latter is set forth in this word "amen," carrying this sense in effect: "As we have craved these things at Thy hands, O Lord, so we do believe that for Christ's sake in Thy good time Thou will grant them to us." Therefore, this part is more excellent than the former by how much our faith is more excellent than our desire. For in this word is contained the testification of our faith, whereas the petitions are only testifications of our desires. And as it is the end, so also it is the seal of our prayers to make them authentical; and it is not only to be used (as men commonly take it) for this end to answer the minister, praying in the congregation, but also to testify our faith for the thing desired.

2. Graces to Be Desired

Hereby we are taught what grace we are to show in prayer. We must labor to give assent to God's promises when we pray and strive against doubting and unbelief.

---

6. This paragraph break is not in the original.

"Lord I believe, Lord help mine unbelief" (Mark 9:24). "Why art thou cast down my soul, and why art thou disquieted within me. Wait on God" (Ps. 42:11).

Many there are that will stand upon the strength of their faith and plead for themselves that they never doubted, but they are far wide; for true faith, being imperfect, is always accompanied with doubting more or less. Wherefore, the heart that never felt doubting is not filled with faith but with presumption. As for them which are molested with doubtings and complain of them, they have less cause to fear; for as fire and water do never strive till they meet, no more does doubting and faith till faith be wrought in the heart.

To conclude, we see what an excellent work prayer is, in which two most excellent graces of a Christian man be showed forth: hungering after mercy and faith, whereby we believe the obtaining of it. This might move men to learn to pray, prayer being the exercise of grace.

Of the Use of the Lord's Prayer

The principal use of the Lord's Prayer is to direct God's church in making their prayers in all places, at all times, and upon all occasions, though their prayers should be innumerable; and unless they be framed after this prayer, they cannot be acceptable unto God. In the using of it, there be three things required.

(1) The first is the knowledge of the Lord's Prayer and all the parts thereof.[7] He that would pray by it must understand the meaning thereof, the wants therein to be bewailed, and the graces to be desired, for which end it has been expounded.

[2] Knowing this, there is in the second place required thus much skill, that he be able to refer every want and grace to one of the six petitions. For example, feeling in himself pride of heart, he must be able to say this is a want in the first petition. And feeling a rebellion and slowness in doing God's commandments, he must be able to say this is a sin to be prayed against in the third petition. Thus, every want he must refer to his proper need. Again, he must refer every grace to be desired to one of the six petitions—as strength in temptation to the sixth; affiance in God's providence to the fourth; knowledge of God to the first, etc., and so in the rest.

(3) In the third place, he must before he pray consider what be his wants and imperfections which most trouble him, as also the graces which he would obtain. Then, for the helping of his memory, he must go to the petitions, and he must set those things first in his mind which concern the first petition. And those which concern the second petition must have the second place in his mind, and so he must proceed in order as he shall have occasion. Thus, a man,

---

7. This paragraph break is not in the original, as the additional two following.

keeping in mind the order of the petitions as they stand, shall be able by referring every grace and want to his proper head to make distinct prayer and to vary as time, place, and other occasions shall move him.

Question. Must we of necessity follow all the petitions in conceiving a prayer? *Answer.* No, but only those which do principally belong to the time, place, and occasion, as Paul makes a prayer, and all the points of it may be referred to the third and last petitions (Col. 1:9–10).

Again, a Christian man may make an excellent confession of his sins by this prayer if he shall, keeping the order of the petitions, confess and bewail the sins which every petition requires us to pray against. And it serves to make a thanksgiving to God, thus: let a man remember all the graces which he has received from God; let him then refer them to the petitions and give thanks to God after the order of them, turning every petition into a thanksgiving.

Of the Circumstances of Prayer

Question 1. Whether a man is to use a voice in prayer? *Answer.* In public prayer it is requisite that there be a voice; for the minister is the mouth of the people, and to the prayer which he conceives they give assent. For private prayer, using of voice is convenient, yet so as it may be done in silence. (1) The Lord gave us the voice as well as the heart to bless Him withal (James 3:9). (2) God created the tongue as well as the heart and so will be praised by both. (3) The voice often stirs up the heart, and again, the vehemency of affection does often draw out a voice. The voice then in private prayer is requisite, yet in some cases may be omitted, for it is not absolutely necessary. Moses and Hannah[8] prayed in silence.

Question 2. What gesture is to be used in prayer? *Answer.* The Word does not afford any particular direction. Our Savior and His disciples prayed in diverse gestures—kneeling, standing, groveling, looking up to heaven, looking down to the earth, sitting, lying, etc. (Acts 7). God respects not the gesture but the affection of the heart; yet two things must always be in gesture: first, that it be comely; secondly, that it does fitly express the affection of the heart—as when we ask mercy, to look to heaven; when we bewail our sins, to look downward and to humble our bodies, etc.

Question 3. What place must we pray in? *Answer.* The place is set down (1 Tim. 2:8). We may pray in all places, of which there is no difference. Some will say that in the time of the law the tabernacle and temple were places of divine prayer. *Answer.* The temple and tabernacle were types of Christ and His church and the unity of it; but now we, having the thing itself signified thereby, may pray in all places. Our Savior prayed in the wilderness on the Mount; Peter,

---

8. Originally, "Anna."

on the house top; Paul, by the seashore. Yet so that public prayer must be used in public places, as churches, chapels, etc., not because in them is more holiness, but for order sake.

Question 4. What is the time appointed for prayer? *Answer.* "Pray continually" (1 Thess. 5:17)—that is, upon all occasions; or when a man begins any business, whether it be in word or deed (Col. 3:17); or as Daniel, who prayed thrice every day (Dan. 9:11); or as David, who prayed at evening and morning and noontide (Ps. 55:18) and seven times a day, that is, many (119:36). Thus, we shall pray continually. Every day affords three special occasions: (1) the entrance to our callings in the morning; (2) the receiving of God's creatures at noontide; (3) the going to rest at night. Again, besides set and solemn prayers, there be certain kinds of short prayers, which the fathers call ejaculations—that is, the lifting up of the heart into heaven secretly and suddenly. And this kind of praying may be used as occasion is offered every hour in the day.

Question 5. Whether may we pray for all men or no? *Answer.* We may, and we may not. We may if all men or all mankind be taken distributively or severally. For there is no particular country, kingdom, town, person, but we may make prayers for it. And though men be atheists, infidels, heretics, yea, devils incarnate, yet for anything we know they may belong to the election of God, except they sin against the Holy Ghost, which sin is very seldom and hardly discerned of men. And in this sense must the commandment of Paul be understood: "I exhort therefore that first of all supplications, prayers, etc. be made for all men" (1 Tim. 2:1). We may not pray for all men if all men or mankind be taken collectively—that is, if all men be considered wholly together as they make one body or company and be taken as we say in gross. For in this body or mass of mankind there be some, though they be unknown to us, yet I say, there be some whom God in His just judgment has refused, whose salvation by prayer shall never be obtained.

Question 6. Whether is it possible for a man to pray in reading of a prayer? *Answer.* It pleases some to move this question, but there is no doubt of it. For prayer is a part of God's worship, and therefore a spiritual action of the heart of man standing especially in a desire of that which we want and faith whereby we believe that our desire shall be granted. Now, the voice or utterance, whether it be reading or otherwise, is no part of the prayer, but an outward means whereby prayer is uttered and expressed. Therefore, there is no reason why a form of prayer, being read, should cease to be a prayer because it is read, so be it the Spirit of grace and prayer be not wanting in the party reading and the hearers. *Objection.* To read a sermon is not to preach, and therefore to read a prayer is not to pray. *Answer.* The reason is not like in both. For the gift of preaching or prophecy cannot be showed or practiced in the reading of a sermon, and for this cause the reading of a sermon is not preaching or prophecy. But the grace and gift of prayer may be showed in reading of a prayer. Otherwise, it would go very hard with them that want convenient utterance by reason of some defect in the tongue or bashfulness in the presence of others.

Of God's Hearing Our Prayers

Hitherto we have spoken of the making of prayer to God. A word or twain of God's hearing our prayers.

Question. How many ways does God hear men's prayers? *Answer.* Two ways. The first, in His mercy, when He grants the request of such as call upon Him in the fear of His name. Secondly, He hears men's prayers in His wrath. Thus, He gave the Israelites quails according to their desire (Ps. 78:29–31). Thus, often men curse themselves, and wish that they were hanged or dead, and accordingly they have their wish.

Question 2. Why does God defer to hear the prayers of His servants? *Answer.* First, to prove them by delay. Secondly, to exercise their faith. Thirdly, to make them acknowledge that the things which they receive are God's gifts and not from themselves. Fourthly, that graces quickly given might not be lightly esteemed. Fifthly, that a hungering after grace might be sharpened and increased.

Question 3. After what manner does God hear His servants' prayers? *Answer.* Two ways. First, by granting the thing which was asked according to His will. Secondly, by denying the thing desired and by giving something proportional to it. Thus, God denies temporary blessings and in the room thereof gives eternal in heaven. Thus, He refuses to remove the cross from His servants and gives instead thereof strength and patience. Christ prays that the cup might be removed. It was not removed. He yet in His manhood was enabled to bear the wrath of God. When Paul prayed three times that the prick in the flesh might be removed, it was answered, "My strength is sufficient for thee" (2 Cor. 12:7, 9).

Question 4. Why does not God always hear men's prayers? *Answer.* There be many causes of this. The first, because oftentimes we know not to ask as we ought (Matt. 20:22). The second, because we ask amiss (James 4:3). The third, because otherwhiles the things which we ask, though they be good in themselves, yet they are not good unto us and for that cause are withheld (2 Cor. 12:7). The last, because God will for some long time defer the granting of that which we ask that He may stir up our faith and hope and our diligence in prayer, and that we might the better esteem of the gifts of God when we have them and show ourselves more thankful.

[A Collection and Exposition of Prayers from the Bible]¹

To the reader,

Paul in his epistles has set down the sum of many of his prayers. They are very gracious and heavenly, and I have here set them down that you might know them and in your prayers follow them.

Ephesians 1:16–20

"I cease not to give thanks for you, making mention of you in my prayers, that the God of our Lord Jesus Christ, the Father of glory, might give unto you the spirit of wisdom, and of revelation, in the acknowledgement of him, the eyes of your mind being enlightened, that we may know what the hope is of his calling, and what the riches are of his glorious inheritance in the saints, and what is the exceeding greatness of his power in us that believe; according to the working of his mighty power, which he wrought in Christ, when he raised him from the dead, and set him at his right hand in heavenly places."

The Exposition

In this excellent prayer, we are to mark two things: the first, to whom it is made; the second is the matter.

For the first, it is made to God the Father, who is described by two titles. The first, "the God of our Lord Jesus Christ"—namely, as Christ is man, for as Christ is God, He is equal with the Father. The second, "the Father of glory"— that is, a glorious father, and He is so called to distinguish Him from earthly fathers.

The matter of the prayer stands in two principal points. First, he asks of God [for] the Spirit of wisdom, whereby the servants of God are enabled to discern out of the Word in every business which they take in hand, whether it be in word or deed, what ought to be done, and what ought to be left undone, as also the circumstances, the time, place, manner of doing anything.

---

1. In the long Scripture passages to follow, some slight adjustment has been made to conform to modern sensibilities, without change of substance.

Secondly, he prays for the Spirit of revelation, whereby the faithful have their whole estate before God revealed unto them according to the Word, the thing itself being otherwise secret and hidden (1 Cor. 2:9–10, 12). Further, the work of this Spirit in the godly is twofold: the one concerns God Himself; the other, the things of God.

The work of the Spirit of revelation, which respects God Himself, is an acknowledgment of the Father or of Christ. Now, to acknowledge God the Father is not only to know and confess that He is a father of the faithful, but also to be resolved in conscience that He is a father to me in particular. Secondly, that Christ is not only in general a savior of the elect, but that He is in special my Savior and Redeemer.

The second work of this Spirit is an illumination of the eyes of the mind to see and know the things of God which He has prepared for them that do believe, and they are two. The first is life eternal, which is described by five arguments. (1) It is the Ephesians' hope—that is, the thing hoped for in this life. (2) It is the hope of the calling of God, because by the preaching of the gospel it is offered, and men are called to wait for the same. (3) An inheritance, properly to Christ, because He is the natural Son of God, and by Him to all that shall believe. (4) The excellency, because it is a rich and glorious inheritance. (5) Lastly, it is made proper to the saints.

The second thing is the greatness of the power of God, whereby sin is mortified, the corrupt nature renewed and mightily strengthened in temptations. This power is set forth by two arguments. The first is the subject or persons in whom this power is made manifest—"in them that believe," because none can feel this but they which apprehend Christ by faith. The second is the manner of manifesting this power in them, which is according to the working of His mighty power, which He showed in Christ. And that was in three things. First, in putting all His enemies under His feet ([Eph. 1:]20). Secondly, in raising Him from death. Thirdly, in placing Him at His right hand. Now therefore, Paul prays that this wonderful power of God, which did show forth itself in the Head, Christ, might likewise show itself in the members of Christ, first, in treading Satan and sin under their feet (Rom. 16:10); secondly, in raising them from sin, as out of a grave to holiness of life; thirdly, in advancing them in the time appointed to the kingdom of glory in heaven.

Ephesians 3:14–21

"For this cause I bow my knees unto the Father of our Lord Jesus Christ, of whom is named the whole family in heaven and earth, that he would grant you according to the riches of his glory, that ye may be strengthened by his spirit in the inner man, that Christ may dwell in your hearts by faith, that ye being rooted and grounded in love, may be able to comprehend with all saints, what is the breadth, and length, and depth, and height, and know the love of Christ, which passeth knowledge, that ye may be filled with all fullness of God. Unto him therefore that is able to do exceeding abundantly, above all that we ask or think, according to the power that works in us, be praise in the Church by Christ Jesus, throughout all generations forever, Amen."

The Exposition

These words contain two parts: a prayer and a thanksgiving. In the prayer, these points are to be marked. First, the gesture, "I bow my knees," whereby Paul signifies his humble submission to God in prayer. Secondly, to whom he prays: to the Father, who is described by two titles. The first, "the Father of our Lord Jesus Christ," and that by nature as He is God and as He is man by personal union. The other title, "of whom the whole family which is in heaven and earth is named," in which words is set down a description of the church. First, it is a family, because it is the company of God's elect children under the government of one Father (1 Tim. 3:15). It is called the house of God (Eph. 2:19). They that believe are said to be of the household of God. Secondly, the parts of the catholic church are noted—namely, the saints in heaven departed and saints living on earth. Thirdly, it is said to be named of the Father of Christ, because as the Father of Christ is the Father of this family, so also this family is called by Him (Gen. 6:2; Dan. 9:19). Thirdly, the matter of this prayer stands of four most worthy points.

The first is strength to bear the cross and to resist spiritual temptations ([Eph. 3:]16), where the strength is set out by divers arguments. First, that it is the mere gift of God, "that he would grant you." Secondly, the cause of strength, "by his Spirit." Thirdly, the subject or place where this strength must be, "in the inner man"—that is, in the whole man, so far forth as he is renewed by grace (6:14). The second is the dwelling of Christ in their hearts by faith. Faith is when a man, being seriously humbled for his sins, is further in conscience persuaded and resolved of the pardon of them and of reconciliation to God. Now, where this persuasion is indeed, there follows necessarily Christ's dwelling in the heart, which stands in two things. The first is the ruling and ordering of the thoughts, affections, and desires of the heart according to His will, as a master rules in his house. The second is the continuance of His rule. For he cannot be said to dwell in a place who rules in it but for a day.

The third is the knowledge and the acknowledgement of the infinite greatness of God's love in Christ, an effect of the former ([3:]18–19). The words are thus explained: "rooted and grounded." Here, the love of God wherewith He loves the elect is as a root and foundation of all God's benefits: election, vocation, justification, and glorification. Men are rooted and grounded in love when God's Spirit assures their hearts of God's love and does give them some inward sense and feeling of it, for then they are as it were sensibly put into the root and laid on the foundation. "With all saints"—Paul desires this benefit not only to the Ephesians but also to all the faithful with them. "What is the length, the breadth"—here is a speech borrowed from the geometricians, and it signifies the absolute greatness or infiniteness of God's love, and that it is like a world, which for length, breadth, height, and depth is endless. Here, note the order of receiving grace. First, Christ dwells in the heart by faith. Secondly, then comes a sense and feeling of God's love, as it were by certain drops thereof. Thirdly, after this arises a plentiful knowledge and apprehension of God's love and as it were the pouring out of a sea into a man's heart, that for greatness has neither bottom nor bank. "And know the love of Christ"—these words (as I take it) are an exposition of the former; for to comprehend the love of God is nothing else but to know the love of Christ, considering that all whom the Father loves, He loves them in Christ. "Which passeth knowledge"—that is, which for the greatness of it no man can fully know.

The fourth thing is the fullness of God's graces (v. 19). Here the fullness of God does not signify the fullness of the Godhead or divine nature, but the perfection of the inner man, which shall not be till after this life.

Now follows the thanksgiving or the praise of God (vv. 20–21), containing these points. The matter of praise: His power and bountifulness whereby He can work "exceeding abundantly above all we ask or think." And both these are not only to be conceived in mind, but also may be felt in the heart according to the "power that worketh in us." (2) The form of praise—"glory unto God by Christ," as all benefits are received from the Father by Christ. (3) The proper place of true praise of God, "the church." (4) The continuance of His praise "through all generations forever."

Philippians 1:9–11
"And this I pray, that your love may abound yet more and more, in knowledge and all sense, that ye may discern things that differ: to the end, ye may be pure and without offence to the day of Christ, filled with fruits of righteousness, which are by Jesus Christ, unto the praise and glory of God."

The Exposition
This prayer contains three parts. In the first, Paul prays for increase of love in the Philippians, whether it be to God or men (v. 9). And he shows the means of increase, which are two: knowledge and sense or feeling. For (to go backward) the more a godly man feels God's love and has experience of God's Word in

himself, the more he knows of God's Word and perceives His love unto him, [and] the more he loves God again and his neighbor for His sake.

The second thing prayed for is the gift of discerning, whereby men know what is true, what false; what is to be done, what to be left undone. The ends of this gift are two. The first, that by means of it they may be pure and sincere—that is, keep a good conscience before God and men in the lives and callings. The second is to be without offence—that is, innocent, giving no occasion of evil to any and not taking them offered by others. And the continuance of these is noted to the day of Christ, which is the time in which He comes to us either by our death or by the last judgment.

Thirdly, he prays that they may abound in good works, which are described by a similitude, "fruits of righteousness," Christians being fruitful trees (Isa. 61:2–3; Ezek. 47:12). By the cause efficient: "which are by Christ." (3) By the end—"unto the glory and praise of God."

Colossians 1:9–13
"I cease not to pray for you, and to desire that ye might be filled with knowledge of his will, in all wisdom and spiritual understanding, that ye might walk worthy of the Lord, and please him in all things, fructifying in all good works, and increasing in the acknowledgment of God, strengthened with all might through his glorious power, unto all patience and long-suffering with joyfulness, giving thanks to the Father which hath made us fit to be partakers of the inheritance of the saints in light, who hath delivered us from the power of darkness, and hath translated us into the kingdom of his own Son."

The Exposition
These words contain a prayer and a thanksgiving. In the prayer, three things are asked. The first is the increase of the knowledge of God's revealed will in His Word, and he divides it into two parts: wisdom, which is not only to know God's Word but also to apply it to every action for the right and holy performing thereof; and spiritual understanding, which is when by the assistance of God's Spirit do conceive the will of God in general without applying.

Secondly, Paul prays for the fruits of this knowledge, which are four. (1) To walk worthy of God, as good servants do, who in their apparel, gesture, and all their doings so behave themselves that they may credit their masters. (2) To please God in all things by approving their hearts unto Him. (3) To be plentiful in all good works. (4) To increase in the acknowledgment of God. For the more any increase in knowledge and experience in God's Word, the more shall they acknowledge God the Father to be their Father, Christ to be their Redeemer, and the Holy Ghost, their Sanctifier.

Thirdly, he prays that the Colossians may be strengthened (v. 11), where he notes the cause, "God's glorious power," and the effects, which are three: (1) patience, because it is necessary that the godly suffer many afflictions; (2) longsuffering, because oftentimes the same afflictions continue long; (3) joyfulness, because the cross is bitter.

The thanksgiving is for a benefit that God had made the Colossians fit for the kingdom of glory, and the reason is because He had made them members of the kingdom of grace.

1 Thessalonians 3:12–13

"The Lord increase you, and make you abound in love one toward another, and toward all men: even as we do toward you, to make your hearts stable and unblamable in holiness before God, even our Father, at the coming of our Lord Jesus Christ with all his saints."

2 Thessalonians 2:16–17

"Jesus Christ our Lord, and our God, even the Father which hath loved us, and hath given us everlasting consolation and good hope through grace: comfort your hearts, and stablish you in every word and good work."

1 Thessalonians 5:23

Now the very God of peace, sanctify you throughout: and I pray God, that your whole spirit[2] and soul,[3] and body may be kept blameless unto the coming of our Lord Jesus Christ.

---

2. The mind or understanding.
3. The will and affection.

A Song Gathered Out of the Psalms, Containing the Sobs and Sighs of All Repentant Sinners

Lord, hear my prayer, heark the 'plaint that I do make to Thee.
Lord, in Thy native truth and in Thy justice answer me.

Regard, O Lord, for I complain and make my suit to Thee.
Let not my words return in vain, but give an ear to me.

Behold, in wickedness my kind and shape I did receive.
And lo, my sinful mother eke, in sin did me conceive.

And I with evils many one am sore beset about.
My sins increase and so come on, I cannot spy them out.

For why, in number they exceed the hairs upon my head.
My heart doth faint for very fear, that I am almost dead.

Thus in me in perplexity is mine accumbred spright,
And in me is my troubled heart, amazed and affright.

The wicked works that I have wrought, Thou setst before Thine eye.
My secret faults, yea, eke my thoughts, Thy countenance doth spy.

O Lord, my God, if Thou shalt weigh my sins and them peruse,
What one shall Thee escape and say, I can myself excuse?

In judgment with Thy servant, Lord, oh enter not at all,
For justified in Thy sight, not one that liveth shall.

And for Thy pity plentiful, O Lord, I Thee entreat
To grant me pardon for my sin, for it is wondrous great.

O Lord, what earthly man doth know the errors of this life?
Then cleanse me from my secret sins, which are in me most rife.

And keep me that presumptuous sins prevail not over me,
And then I shall be innocent and great offences flee.

To Thee, O Lord, my God, lo I do stretch my craning hands.
My soul desireth after Thee, as doth the thirsty lands.

As handmaids watch their mistress hands, some grace for to achieve,
So I behold Thee, Lord, my God, till Thou do me forgive.

Lord, turn Thee to Thy wonted grace, my silly soul up take.
O save me, not for my deserts, but for Thy mercy sake.

My soul, why dost thou faint and quail? So sore with pain oppressed.
With thoughts why dost thyself assail? So sore within my breast.

Trust in thy Lord thy God always, and thou the time shalt see
To give Him thanks with laud and praise, for health restored to thee.

For why? His anger but a space doth last and slack again.
But in His favor and His grace, alway doth life remain.

Though gripes of grief and pangs full fore do lodge with thee all night?
The Lord to joy shall thee restore, before the day be light.

The Lord is kind and merciful, when sinners do Him grieve,
The slowest to conceive a wrath, and readiest to forgive.

And look what pity parents dear unto their children bear,
Like pity bears the Lord to such as worship Him in fear.

The Lord that made me knows my shape, my mold and fashion just,
How weak and frail my nature is, and how I am but dust.

O God, create in me a heart, unspotted in Thy sight,
And eke within my bowels, Lord, renew a stable spright.

With Thy free Spirit confirm Thou me, and I will teach therefore
Sinners Thy ways, and wicked shall be turned to Thy lore.

My soul is ravished with desire and never is at rest,
But seeks to know Thy judgments high, and what may please Thee best.

O would to God it might Thee please, my ways so to address,
That I might both in heart and voice Thy laws keep and confess.

In righteousness I do intend my time and days to serve.
Have mercy, Lord, and me defend, so that I do not swerve.

And with Thy saving health, O Lord, vouchsafe to visit me,
That I the great felicity of Thine elect may see.

And with Thy peoples' joy I may a joyful mind possess,
And may with Thine inheritance a glorying heart express.

The Lord, the God of Israel, be blest forevermore,
Let all the people say, Amen, praise ye the Lord therefore.

FINIS

The FOUNDATION Of Christian Religion Gathered into six Principles.

And it is to be learned of ignorant people,
that they may be fit to hear sermons with
Profit, and to receive the Lord's
Supper with comfort.

PSALM 119. V. 30.
The entrance into Thy words showeth light,
And giveth understanding to the simple.

Printed for *John Porter,*
1601

To all ignorant people that desire to be instructed:

Poor people, your manner is to soothe up yourselves as though you were in a most happy estate; but if the matter come to a just trial, it will fall out far otherwise. For you lead your lives in great ignorance, as may appear by these your common opinions which follow:

1. That faith is a man's good meaning and his good serving of God.
2. That God is served by the rehearsing of the Ten Commandments, the Lord's Prayer, and the Creed.
3. That you have believed in Christ ever since you could remember.
4. That it is pity that he should live which does any whit doubt of his salvation.
5. That none can tell whether he shall be saved or no certainly, but that all men must be of a good belief.
6. That howsoever a man live, yet if he call upon God on his death bed and say, "Lord, have mercy upon me," and so go away like a lamb, he is certainly saved.
7. That if any be strangely visited, he is either taken with a planet or bewitched.
8. That a man may lawfully swear when he speaks nothing but the truth, and swears by nothing but that which is good as by his faith or troth.
9. That a preacher is a good man no longer than he is in the pulpit. They think all like themselves.
10. That a man may repent when he will, because the Scripture says, "At what time soever a sinner doth repent him of his sin," etc.
11. That it is an easier thing to please God than to please our neighbor.
12. That you can keep the commandments as well as God will give you leave.
13. That it is safest to do in religion as most do.
14. That merry ballads and books, as *Scogin, Bevis of Southampton*, etc., are good to drive away time and to remove heart-qualms.
15. That you serve God with all your hearts, and that you would be sorry else.

16. That a man need not hear so many sermons except he could follow them better.

17. That a man which comes at no sermons may as well believe as he which hears all the sermons in the world.

18. That you know all the preacher can tell you. For he can say nothing but that every man is a sinner, that we must love our neighbors as ourselves, that every man must be saved by Christ; and all this you can tell as well as he.

19. That it was a good world when the old religion was, because all things were cheap.

20. That drinking and bezelling in the alehouse or tavern is good fellowship and shows a good, kind nature and maintains neighborhood.

21. That a man may swear by the Mass because it is nothing now, and by our Lady because she is gone out of the country.

22. That every man must be for himself, and God for us all.

23. That a man may make of his own whatsoever he can.

24. That if a man remember to say his prayers in the morning (though he never understand them), he has blessed himself for all the day following.

25. That a man prays when he says the Ten Commandments.

26. That a man eats his Maker in the Sacrament.

27. That if a man be no adulterer, no thief, nor murderer, and do no man harm, he is a right honest man.

28. That a man need not have any knowledge of religion because he is not book-learned.

29. That one may have a good meaning, when he says and does that which is evil.

30. That a man may go to wizards, called wise men, for counsel, because God has provided a salve for every sore.

31. That you are to be excused in all your doings, because the best men are sinners.

32. That you have so strong a faith in Christ, that no evil company can hurt you.

These and such like sayings—what argue they but your gross ignorance? Now, where ignorance reigns, there reigns sin. And where sin reigns, there the devil rules. And where he rules, men are in a damnable case.

You will reply unto me thus, that you are not so bad as I would make you. If need be, you can say the Creed, the Lord's Prayer, and the Ten Commandments;

and therefore you will be of God's belief, say all men what they will, and you defy the devil from your hearts.

I answer again that it is not sufficient to say all these without book, unless you can understand the meaning of the words and be able to make a right use of the Commandments, of the Creed, of the Lord's Prayer by applying them inwardly to your hearts and consciences and outwardly to your lives and conversations. This is the very point in which you fail.

And for a help in this your ignorance to bring you to true knowledge, unfeigned faith, and sound repentance, here I have set down the principal point of Christian religion in six plain and easy rules, even such as the simplest may easily learn; and hereunto is adjoined an exposition of them word by word. If you do want other good directions, then use this my labor for your instruction. In reading of it, first learn the six principles; and when you have them without book and the meaning of them withal, then learn the exposition also, which, being well conceived and in some measure felt in the heart, you shall be able to profit by sermons, whereas now you cannot, and the ordinary parts of the catechism—namely, the Ten Commandments, the Creed, the Lord's Prayer, and the institution of the two sacraments—shall more easily be understood.

Yours in Christ Jesus,
William Perkins

The Foundation of Christian Religion, Gathered into Six Principles

The First Principle[1]

Q. *What do you believe concerning God?*
A. There is one God, Creator and Governor of all things, distinguished into the Father, the Son, and the Holy Ghost.

Proofs Out of the Word of God

1. There is a God.

> "For the invisible things of Him, that is, His eternal power and Godhead, are seen by the creation of the world, being considered in His works, to the intent, that they should be without excuse" [Rom. 1:20].

> "Nevertheless, He left not Himself without witness, in that He did good and gave us rain from heaven, and fruitful seasons filling our hearts with food and gladness" [Acts 14:17].

2. This God [is] one.

> "Concerning therefore meat sacrificed to idols, we know that an idol is nothing in the world: and there is none other God but one" [1 Cor. 8:4].

3. He is Creator of all things.

> "In the beginning God created the heaven and the earth" [Gen. 1:1].

> "Through faith we understand, that the world was ordained by the Word of God: so that the things which we see, are not made of things which did appear" [Heb. 11:3].

4. He is Governor of all things.

> "The eyes of the Lord in every place behold the evil and the good" [Prov. 15:3].

> "Yea, and all the hairs of our head are numbered" [Matt. 10:30].

---

1. NB that because of the format of both the "Foundation" and "Exposition" of the six principles here and below, herein I have taken liberty to adjust spacing and layout to accommodate modern sensibilities, though without changes of content.

5. Distinguished into the Father, the Son, and the Holy Ghost.

"And Jesus when He was baptized, came straight out of the water, and lo, the heavens were opened unto Him, and John saw the Spirit of God descending like a dove and lighting upon Him" [Matt. 3:16].

"And lo, a voice came from heaven, saying: this is my beloved Son, in whom I am well pleased" [3:17].

"For there are three, which bear record in heaven, the Father, the Word, and the Holy Ghost: and these three are one" [1 John 5:7].

The Second Principle

Q. *What do you believe concerning man and concerning your own self?*
A. All men are wholly corrupted with sin through Adam's fall and so are become slaves of Satan and guilty of eternal damnation.

1. All men are corrupted with sin.

"And it is written, there is none righteous, no not one" [Rom. 3:10].

2. They are wholly corrupted.

"Now the very God of peace sanctify you throughout, and I pray God that your whole spirit, and soul, and body, may be kept blameless unto the coming of our Lord Jesus Christ" [1 Thess. 5:23].

"This I say therefore and testify in the Lord, that ye henceforth walk not as other Gentiles walk in vanity of their mind" [Eph. 4:17].

"Having their cogitation darkened, and being strangers from the life of God, through the ignorance that is in them, because of the hardness of their heart" [v. 18].

"When the Lord saw that the wickedness of man was great in the earth, and all the imaginations of the thoughts of his heart were only evil continually" [Gen. 6:5].

3. Through Adam's fall.

"Wherefore as by one man, sin entered into the world, and death by sin, and so death went over all men, for so much as all men have sinned" [Rom. 5:12].

4. And so are become slaves of Satan.

"Wherein in time past ye walked according to the course of the world, and after the prince that ruleth in the air, even the spirit that now worketh in the children of disobedience" [Eph. 2:2].

"For as much then as the children were partakers of flesh and blood, He also Himself likewise took part with them, that He might destroy through death, him that had the power of death, that is, the devil" [Heb. 2:14].

"In whom the God of this world hath blinded the minds, that is of infidels, that the light of the glorious gospel of Christ, which is the image of God, should not shine unto them" [2 Cor. 4:4].

5. And guilty of eternal damnation.

"For as many as are of the works of the law, are under the curse, for it is written: cursed is every man that continueth not in all things, which are written in the book of the law to do them" [Gal. 3:10].

"Likewise then as by the offence of one, the fault came on all men to condemnation; so by the justifying of one, the benefit abounded toward all men to the justification of life" [Rom. 5:18].

The Third Principle

Q. What means is there for you to escape this damnable estate?
A. Jesus Christ, the eternal Son of God, being made man, by His death upon the cross and by His righteousness has perfectly alone by Himself accomplished all things that are needful for the salvation of mankind.

1. Jesus Christ [is] the eternal Son of God.

"And the Word was made flesh and dwelt among us, and we saw the glory thereof, as the glory of the only begotten (Son) of the Father full of grace and truth" [John 1:14].

2. Being made man.
"For He in no sort took the angels, but He took the seed of Abraham" [Heb. 2:16].

3. By His death upon the cross.

"But He was wounded for our transgressions, He was broken for our iniquities, the chastisement of our peace was upon Him, and with His stripes we are healed" [Isa. 53:5].

4. And by His righteousness.

"For as by one man's disobedience many were made sinners, so by the obedience of one, shall many also be made righteous" [Rom. 5:19].

"For He hath made Him to be sin for us which knew no sin, that we should be made the righteousness of God in Him" [2 Cor. 5:21].

5. Has perfectly.

"Wherefore He is able also perfectly to save them that come unto God by Him, seeing He ever liveth to make intercession for them" [Heb. 7:25].

6. Alone by Himself.

"Neither is there salvation in any other, for among men there is given none other name under heaven, whereby we must be saved" [Acts 4:12].

7. Accomplished all things needful for the salvation of mankind.

"And He is the reconciliation for our sins, and not for ours only, but also for the sins of the whole world" [1 John 2:2].

The Fourth Principle

Q. *But how may you be made partaker of Christ and His benefits?*

A. A man of a contrite and humble spirit, by faith alone apprehending and applying Christ with all His merits unto himself, is justified before God and sanctified.

1. A man of a contrite and humble spirit.

"For thus saith He, that is high and excellent, he that inhabiteth the eternity, whose name is the Holy One, I dwell in the high and holy place, with him also that is of a contrite and humble spirit, to revive the spirit of the humble, and to give life to them that are of a contrite heart" [Isa. 57:15].

"The sacrifices of God are a contrite spirit, a contrite and a broken heart, O God, Thou wilt not despise" [Ps. 51:17].

2. By faith alone.

"As soon as Jesus heard that word spoken, He said unto the ruler of the synagogue, be not afraid, only believe" [Mark 5:36].

"So Moses made a serpent of brass, and set it up for a sign, and when a serpent had bitten a man, then he looked to the serpent of brass and lived" [Num. 21:9].

"And as Moses lifted up the serpent in the wilderness, so must the Son of Man be lifted up" [John 3:14].

"That whosoever believeth in Him, should not perish, but have eternal life" [3:15].

3. Apprehending and applying Christ with all His merits unto himself.

"But as many as received Him, to them He gave power to be the sons of God, to them that believe in His name" [John 1:12].

"And Jesus said unto them, I am the bread of life, he that cometh to Me shall not hunger, and he that believeth in Me shall never thirst" [6:35].

4. Is justified before God.

"For what saith the Scripture, Abraham believed God, and it was counted to him for righteousness" [Rom. 4:3].

"Even as David declareth the blessedness of the man, unto whom God imputeth righteousness, without works, saying: Blessed are they whose iniquities are forgiven, and whose sins are covered" [vv. 6–7].

5. And sanctified.

"And He put no difference between us and them, after that by faith He had purified their hearts" [Acts 15:9].

"But ye are of Him in Christ Jesus, who of God is made unto us wisdom, and righteousness, and sanctification, and redemption" [1 Cor. 1:30].

The Fifth Principle

Q. What are the ordinary or usual means for the obtaining of faith?
A. Faith comes only by the preaching of the word and increases daily by it, as also by the administration of the sacraments and prayer.

1. Faith comes only by the preaching of the word and increases daily by it.

"But how shall they call on Him, in whom they have not believed: how shall they believe in Him, of whom they have not heard: and how shall they hear without a preacher?" [Rom. 10:14].

"Where there is no vision the people decay, but he that keepeth the law is blessed" [Prov. 29:18].

"My people are destroyed for lack of knowledge: because thou hast refused knowledge, I will also refuse thee, that thou shalt be no priest to me, and seeing thou hast forgotten the law of thy God, I will also forget thy children" [Hos. 4:6].

2. As also by the administration of the sacraments.

"After He received the sign of circumcision, as the seal of the righteousness of the faith, which he had when he was uncircumcised, that he should be the father of all them that believe not being circumcised, that righteousness might be imputed to them also" [Rom. 4:11–12].

"Moreover brethren, I would not that ye should be ignorant, that all our fathers were under the cloud, and all passed through the sea," etc. [1 Cor. 10:1].

3. And prayer.
"For whosoever shall call upon the name of the Lord shall be saved" [Rom. 10:13].

The Sixth Principle

Q. *What is the estate of all men after death?*
A. All men shall rise again with their own bodies to the last judgment, which being ended, the godly shall possess the kingdom of heaven; but unbelievers and reprobates shall be in hell, tormented with the devil and his angels forever.

1. All men shall rise again with their own bodies.
"Marvel not at this, for the hour shall come, in the which all that are in the graves shall hear His voice" [John 5:28].

"And they shall come forth that have done good, unto the resurrection of life: but they that have done evil, unto the resurrection of condemnation" [v. 29].

2. To the last judgment.
"For God will bring every work unto judgment, with every secret thing, whether it be good or evil" [Eccl. 12:14].

"But I say unto you, that of every idle word that men shall speak, they shall give account thereof, at the Day of Judgment" [Matt. 12:36].

3. Which being ended, the godly.
"And delivered just Lot, vexed with the unclean conversation of the wicked" [2 Peter 2:7].

"And the Lord said unto him: go through the midst of the city, even through the midst of Jerusalem, and set a mark upon the foreheads of them that mourn and cry for all the abominations that be done in the midst thereof" [Ezek. 9:4].

4. Shall possess the kingdom of God.

"Then shall the King say to them on his right hand, Come ye blessed of My Father, inherit ye the kingdom prepared for you, from the beginning of the world" [Matt. 25:34].

5. But unbelievers and reprobates shall be in hell, tormented with the devil and his angels.

"Then shall He say unto them on the left hand, depart from Me ye cursed into everlasting fire, which is prepared for the devil and his angels" [Matt. 25:41].

The Scriptures for proof were only quoted by the author to move you to search them. The words themselves I have expressed at the earnest request of many, that you may more easily learn them. If yet you will be ignorant, your malice is evident. If you gain knowledge, give God the glory in doing of His will.

Thine, T.S.

The Exposition of the Principles

The First Principle Expounded

Q. What is God?
A. God is a spirit [John 4:24], or a spiritual substance, most wise, most holy, eternal, infinite.

Q. How do you persuade yourself that there is such a God?
A. Besides the testimony of the Scriptures, plain reason will show it.

Q. What is one reason?
A. When I consider the wonderful frame of the world [Acts 14:17; Rom. 1:20], I think[2] the silly creatures that be in it could never make it, neither could it make itself. And therefore besides all these, the Maker of it must needs be God. Even as when a man comes into a strange country and sees fair and sumptuous buildings and yet finds no living creatures there besides birds and beasts, he will not imagine that either birds or beasts reared those buildings; but he presently conceives that some men either are or have been there.

Q. What other reason have you?
A. A man that commits any sin, as murder, fornication, adultery, blasphemy, etc., albeit he does so conceal the matter that no man living know of it, yet oftentimes he has a gripping in his conscience and feels the very flashing of hellfire, which is a strong reason to show that there is a God, before whose judgment seat he must answer for his acts [Gen. 3:8, 10; 42:21; Rom. 2:15].

Q. How many Gods are there?
A. No more but one [1 Cor. 8:9].

Q. How do you conceive this one God in your mind?
A. Not by framing any image of Him [Deut. 4:16; Amos 4:13], as ignorant folks do that think Him to be an old man sitting in heaven; but I conceive Him by His properties and works.

Q. What be His chief properties?
A. First, He is most wise [Job 12:13], understanding all things aright and knowing the reason of them. Secondly, He is most holy [Ex. 20:5–6; Isa. 6:3], which

---

2. Originally, "methinks."

appears in that He is most just and merciful unto His creatures. Thirdly, He is eternal [Isa. 41:4], without either beginning or end of days. Lastly, He is infinite [Ps. 139:12], both because He is present in all places and because He is of power sufficient to do whatsoever He will [Deut. 10:17; Job 9:4].

Q. How know you that God governs every particular thing in the world by His special providence?
A. To omit the Scriptures [Matt. 10:30; Prov. 16:33], I see it by experience [Lev. 26:26; Matt. 4:4]: meat, drink, and clothing, being void of heat and life, could not preserve the life of man unless there were a special providence of God to give virtue unto them.

Q. How is this one God distinguished?
A. Into the Father, which begets the Son; into the Son, who is begotten of the Father [Matt. 3:17; 1 John 5:7]; into the Holy Ghost, who proceeds from the Father and the Son [John 15:26].

The Second Principle Expounded

Q. Let us now come to ourselves; and first, tell me what is the natural estate of man?
A. Every man is by nature dead [Eph. 2:1; 1 Tim. 5:6] in sin as a loathsome carrion or as a dead corpse lying rotting and stinking in the grave, having in him the seed of all sins.

Q. What is sin?
A. Any breach of the law of God [Rom. 7:7; Gal. 3:10; 1 John 3:4], if it be no more but the least want of that which the law requires.

Q. How many sorts of sin are there?
A. Sin is either the corruption of nature or any evil actions that proceed of it as fruits thereof [Ps. 51:5; Col. 3:9].

Q. In whom is the corruption of nature?
A. In all men, none excepted [Rom. 3:10].

Q. In what part of man is it?
A. In every part both of body and soul [Gen. 6:5; 1 Thess. 5:23], like as a leprosy that runs from the crown of the head to the sole of the foot.

Q. *Show me how every part of man is corrupted with sin.*

A. First, in the mind there is nothing but ignorance and blindness concerning heavenly matters [Rom. 8:5; 1 Cor. 2:14]. Secondly, the conscience is defiled [Isa. 57:20; Eph. 4:18; Titus 1:15], being always either benumbed with sin or else turmoiled with inward accusations and terrors. Thirdly, the will of man only wills and lusts after evil [Job 15:16; Phil. 2:13]. Fourthly, the affections of the heart, as love, joy, hope, desire, etc. [Gal. 5:24], are moved and stirred to that which is evil to embrace it. And they are never stirred unto that which is good, unless it be to eschew it. Lastly, the members of the body are the instruments and tools of the mind for the execution of sin [Rom. 6:19].

Q. *What be those evil actions that are the fruits of this corruption?*

A. Evil thoughts in the mind [Gen. 6:5], which come either by a man's own conceiving or by the suggestion of the devil [1 Chron. 21:1; John 13:2; Acts 5:3], evil motions and lusts stirring in the heart, and from these arise evil words and deeds, when any occasion is given.

Q. *How comes it to pass that all men are thus defiled with sin?*

A. By Adam's infidelity and disobedience in eating the forbidden fruit [Genesis 3; Rom. 5:12, 18–19], even as we see great personages by treason do not only hurt themselves but also stain their blood and disgrace their posterity.

Q. *What hurt comes to man by his sin?*

A. He is continually subject to the curse of God [Gal. 3:10] in his lifetime, in the end of his life, and after this life.

Q. *What is the curse of God in this life?*

A. In the body, diseases, aches, pains [Deut. 28:21–22, 27, 65–67]; in the soul, blindness, hardness of heart, horror of conscience; in goods, hindrances and losses; in name, ignominy and reproach; lastly, in the whole man, bondage under Satan, the prince of darkness.

Q. *What manner [of] bondage is this?*

A. This bondage is when a man is the slave of the devil and has him to reign in his heart as his god [Luke 11:1; 2 Cor. 4:4; Eph. 2:2; Heb. 2:14].

Q. *How may a man know whether Satan be his god or not?*

A. He may know it by this: if he give obedience to him in his heart and express it in his conversation.

Q. And how shall a man perceive this obedience?
A. If he take delight in the evil motions that Satan puts in his heart and do fulfill the lusts of the devil [John 8:44; 1 John 3:8].

Q. What is the curse due to man in the end of this life?
A. Death [Rom. 5:12], which is the separation of body and soul.

Q. What is the curse after this life?
A. Eternal damnation in hellfire [Rom. 3:19; Gal. 3:10], whereof every man is guilty and is in as great danger of it as the traitor apprehended is in danger of hanging, drawing, and quartering.

The Third Principle Expounded

Q. If damnation be the reward of sin, then is a man of all creatures most miserable. A dog or a toad, when they die, all their misery is ended. But when a man dies, there is the beginning of his woe.
A. It were so indeed, if there were no means of deliverance. But God has showed His mercy in giving a savior to mankind.

Q. How is this Savior called?
A. Jesus Christ [Matt. 1:21].

Q. What is Jesus Christ?
A. The eternal Son of God [John 1:14; Heb. 2:16], made man in all things, even in His infirmities like other men, save only in sin [Mark 13:32; Heb. 5:7].

Q. How is He made man void of sin?
A. He was conceived in the womb of a virgin and sanctified by the Holy Ghost at His conception [Matt. 1:18].

Q. Why must our Savior be both God and man?
A. He must be a man, because man has sinned, and therefore a man must die for sin to appease God's wrath [1 Tim. 2:5–6]. He must be God to sustain and uphold the manhood to overcome and vanquish death.

Q. What be the offices of Christ to make Him an all-sufficient savior?
A. He is a priest, a prophet, a king [Deut. 18:17–19; Ps. 47:7; Psalm 110; Luke 1:33; 4:8].

Q. Why is He a priest?
A. To work the means of salvation in the behalf of mankind.

Q. How does He work the means of salvation?
A. First, by making satisfaction to His Father for the sin of man; secondly, by making intercession [Matt. 20:28; Heb. 7:15–16].

Q. How does He make satisfaction?
A. By two means, and the first is by offering a sacrifice.

Q. What is the sacrifice?
A. Christ Himself [Isa. 53:10] as He is a man, consisting of body and soul.

Q. What is the altar [Heb. 13:10; Rev. 8:3]?
A. Christ as He is God is the altar on which He sacrificed Himself.

Q. Who was the Priest?
A. None but Christ [Heb. 5:5–6], and that as He is both God and man.

Q. How oft did He sacrifice Himself?
A. Never but once [9:28].

Q. What death did He suffer when He sacrificed Himself?
A. A death upon the cross, peculiar to Him alone; for besides the separation of body and soul, He felt also the pangs of hell in that the whole wrath of God due to the sin of man was poured forth upon Him [Isa. 53:5; Luke 22:44; John 12:27; Rev. 19:15].

Q. What profit comes by His sacrifice?
A. God's wrath is appeased by it [Heb. 9:26].

Q. Could the sufferings of Christ, which were but for a short time, countervail everlasting damnation and so appease God's wrath?
A. Yea; for, seeing Christ suffered [Acts 20:28; 2 Cor. 5:15], God suffered, though not in His Godhead. And that is more than if all men in the world had suffered forever and ever.

Q. Now tell me the other means of satisfaction.
A. It is the perfect fulfilling of the law.

Q. How did He fulfill the law?

A. By His perfect righteousness [Rom. 3:25; 1 Cor. 1:30; 2 Cor. 5:21], which consists of two parts: the first, the integrity and pureness of His human nature; the other, His obedience in performing all that the law required [Rom. 4:8; 5:19].

Q. You have showed how Christ does make satisfaction. Tell me likewise how He does make intercession.

A. He alone does continually appear before His Father in heaven, making the faithful and all their prayers acceptable unto Him by applying of the merits of His own perfect satisfaction to them [Rom. 8:38; 1 Peter 2:5].

Q. Why is Christ a prophet?

A. To reveal unto His church the way and means of salvation [Matt. 3:17; John 6:45], and this He does outwardly by the ministry of His word and inwardly by the teaching of His Spirit.

Q. Why is He also a king?

A. That He might bountifully bestow upon us and convey unto us all the aforesaid means of salvation [Isa. 9:7].

Q. How does He show Himself to be a king?

A. In that, being dead and buried, He rose from the grave, quickened His dead body, ascended into heaven, and now sits at the right hand of His Father with full power and glory in heaven [Eph. 4:8; Acts 1:9; 10:40].

Q. How else?

A. In that He does continually inspire and direct His servants by the divine power of His Holy Spirit according to His holy Word [Isa. 9:7; 30:41].

Q. But to whom will this blessed King communicate all these means of salvation?

A. He offers them to many [Matt. 20:16; John 1:11], and they are sufficient to save all mankind. But all shall not be saved thereby, because by faith they will not receive them.

The Fourth Principle Expounded

Q. What is faith?

A. Faith is a wonderful grace of God [John 1:12; 6:35; Gal. 3:27; Col. 2:12] by which a man does apprehend and apply Christ and all His benefits unto himself.

Q. How does a man apply Christ unto himself, seeing we are on earth, and Christ in heaven?
A. This applying is done by assurance when a man is verily persuaded by the Holy Spirit of God's favor toward himself particularly and of the forgiveness of his own sins [Rom. 8:16; 2 Cor. 1:21–22].

Q. How does God bring men truly to believe in Christ?
A. First, He prepares their hearts that they might be capable of faith, and then He works faith in them.

Q How does God prepare men's hearts?
A. By bruising them [Ezek. 11:19; Hos. 6:1–2], as if one would break a hard stone to powder. And this is done by humbling them.

Q. How does God humble a man?
A. By working in him a sight of his sins and a sorrow for them.

Q. How is the sight of sin wrought?
A. By the moral law [Rom. 3:20; 7:7–8], the sum whereof is the Ten Commandments.

Q. What sins may I find in myself by them?
A. Ten.

Q. What is the first?
A. [Com. 1] To make something your God which is not God by fearing it, loving it, so trusting in it more than in the true God.

Q. What is the second?
A. [2] To worship false gods or the true God in a false manner.

Q. What is the third?
A. [3] To dishonor God in abusing His titles, words, and works.

Q. What is the fourth?
A. [4] To break the Sabbath in doing the works of their calling and of the flesh and in leaving undone the works of the Spirit.

Q. *What be the six latter?*

A. To do anything that may hinder your neighbor's [5] dignity, [6] life, [7] chastity, [8] wealth, [9] good name—though it be [10] but in the secret thoughts and motions of the heart, unto which you give no liking nor consent.

Q. *What is sorrow for sin?*

A. It is when a man's conscience is touched with a lively feeling of God's displeasure for any of these sins [Acts 2:37–38], in such wise that he utterly despairs of salvation in regard of anything in himself, acknowledging that he has deserved shame and confusion eternally [Ezra 9:6–7; Luke 15:21; 1 Tim. 1:15].

Q. *How does God work this sorrow?*

A By the terrible curse of the law.

Q. *What is that?*

A. He which breaks but one of the commandments of God [Gal. 3:10], though it be but once in all his lifetime, and that only in one thought, is subject to and in danger of eternal damnation thereby.

Q. *When men's hearts are thus prepared, how does God engraft faith in them?*

A. By working certain inward motions in the heart, which are the seeds of faith and of which it breeds.

Q. *What is the first of them?*

A When a man, humbled under the burden of his sin, does acknowledge and feel that he stands in great need of Christ [Isa. 55:1; John 7:27; Luke 1:53].

Q. *What is the second?*

A. A hungering desire and a longing to be made partaker of Christ and all His merits [Matt. 5:4; Rev. 21:6].

Q. *What is the third?*

A. A flying to the throne of grace from the sentence of the law pricking the conscience [Heb. 4:6].

Q. *How is it done?*

A. By praying with sending up loud cries for God's favor in Christ in the pardoning of sin and with fervent perseverance herein, till the desire of the heart be granted [Matt. 15:22–23, etc.; Luke 15:18–19; Acts 8:22; 2 Cor. 12:8].

Q. *What follows after this?*
A. God then according to His merciful promise lets the poor sinner feel the assurance of His love wherewith He loves him in Christ, which assurance is a lively faith [Isa. 65:24; Job 33:26; Matt. 7:7].

Q. *Are there divers degrees and measures of true faith?*
A. Yea [Luke 17:5; Rom. 1:17].

Q. *What is the least measure of true faith that any man can have?*
A. When a man of a humble spirit by reason of the littleness of his faith does not yet feel the assurance of the forgiveness of his sins, and yet he is persuaded that they are pardonable and therefore desires that they should be pardoned and with his heart prays to God to pardon them [Isa. 42:3; Matt. 17:20; Luke 17:5].

Q. *How do you know that such a man has faith?*
A. These desires and prayers are testimonies of the Spirit [Matt. 5:6; Rom. 8:23, 26; Gal. 4:6], whose property it is to stir up a longing and a lusting after heavenly things with sighs and groans for God's favor and mercy in Christ [Rom. 8:9; Eph. 3:17]. Now, where the Spirit of Christ is, there is Christ dwelling; and where Christ dwells, there is true faith, how weak soever it be.

Q. *What is the greatest measure of faith?*
A. When a man, daily increasing in faith, comes to be fully persuaded of God's love in Christ toward himself particularly and of the forgiveness of his own sins [Song 8:6; Rom. 8:38–39].

Q. *When shall a Christian heart come to this full assurance?*
A. Not at the first, but in some continuance of time [Ps. 1:2–4, etc.; 23:6; 2 Tim. 4:7–8], when he has been well practiced in repentance and has had diverse experiences of God's love unto him in Christ. Then, after them will appear in his heart the fullness of persuasion, which is the ripeness and strength of faith [Rom. 4:19–21].

Q. *What benefits does a man receive by faith in Christ?*
A. Hereby he is justified before God and sanctified [Acts 15:9; Rom. 4:3; 1 Cor. 1:30].

Q. *What is this to be justified before God?*
A. It comprehends two things: the first, to be cleared from the guiltiness and punishment of sin [Rom. 8:33]; the second, to be accepted as perfectly righteous before God.

Q. How is a man cleared from the guiltiness and punishment of his sins?
A. By Christ's sufferings and death upon the cross [Col. 1:22; 1 Peter 2:24; 1 John 1:7].

Q. How is he accepted righteous before God?
A. By the righteousness of Christ imputed to him [2 Cor. 5:21].

Q. What profit comes by being thus justified?
A. Hereby and by no other means in the world, the believer shall be accepted before God's judgment seat as worthy of eternal life by the merits of the same righteousness of Christ [Rom. 4:17; Rev. 21:17].

Q. Do not good works then make us worthy of eternal life?
A. No; for God, who is perfect righteousness itself, will find in the best works we do more matter of damnation than of salvation. And therefore we must rather condemn ourselves for our good works than look to be justified before God thereby [Job 9:3; Ps. 143:2; Isa. 64:6].

Q. How may a man know that he is justified before God?
A. He need not ascend into heaven to search the secret counsel of God [Rom. 8:1; 1 John 3:9], but rather descend into his own heart to search whether he be sanctified or not.

Q. What is it to be sanctified?
A. It comprehends two things: the first, to be purged from the corruption of his own nature; the second, to be endued with inward righteousness.

Q. How is the corruption of sin purged?
A. By the merits and power of Christ's death, which, being by faith applied, is as a corrosive to abate, consume, and weaken the power of all sin [Rom. 6:4; 1 Peter 4:1–2].

Q. How is a man endued with inherent righteousness?
A. Through the virtue of Christ's resurrection, which, being applied by faith, is as a restorative to revive a man that is dead in sin to newness of life [Rom. 6:5–6; Phil. 3:10].

Q. In what part of man is sanctification wrought?
A. In every part of body and soul [1 Thess. 5:23].

Q. *In what time is it wrought?*
A. It is begun in this life, in which the faithful receive only the firstfruits of the Spirit, and it is not finished before the end of this life [Rom. 8:23; 2 Cor. 5:2–3].

Q. *What graces of the Spirit do usually show themselves in the heart of a man sanctified?*
A. The hatred of sin and the love of righteousness [Ps. 40:8; 101:3; 119:113; Rom. 7:22].

Q. *What proceeds of them?*
A. Repentance, which is a settled purpose in the heart with a careful endeavor to leave all his sins and to live a Christian life according to all God's command-ments [Ps. 119:57, 112].

Q. *What goes with repentance?*
A. A continual fighting and struggling against the assaults of a man's own flesh, against the motions of the devil, and the enticements of the world [Gal. 5:17; Eph. 6:11–12; 2 Tim. 4:7–8].

Q. *What follows after a man has gotten the victory in any temptation or affliction?*
A. Experience of God's love in Christ and so increase of peace of conscience and love in the Holy Ghost [Rom. 5:3–4; 2 Cor. 1:5].

Q. *What follows if in any temptation he be overcome and through infirmity fall?*
A. After a while there will arise a godly sorrow [Matt. 26:75; 2 Cor. 7:8–9], which is when a man is grieved for no other cause in the world but for this only, that by his sin he has displeased God, who has been unto him a most merciful and loving father.

Q. *What sign is there of this sorrow?*
A. The true sign of it is this: when a man can be grieved for the very disobedi-ence to God in his evil words or deeds, though he should never be punished and though there were neither heaven nor hell [1 Peter 2:19].

Q. *What follows after this sorrow?*
A. Repentance renewed afresh [2 Cor. 7:11].

Q. *By what signs will this repentance appear?*
A. By seven: [1] a care to leave the sin into which he is fallen; [2] an utter con-demning of himself for it, with a craving of pardon; [3] a great anger against

himself for his carelessness; [4 a fear lest he should fall into the same sin again; [5] a desire ever after to please God; [6] a zeal of the same; [7] revenge upon himself for his former offence [2 Cor. 7:11].

The Fifth Principle Expounded

Q. *What outward means must we use to obtain faith and all the blessings of God which come by faith?*
A. The preaching of God's word [Prov. 29:18; Matt. 28:19–20; Rom. 10:14; 2 Tim. 3:16] and the administration of the sacraments and prayer.

Q. *Where is the word of God to be found?*
A. The whole word of God needful to salvation is set down in the Holy Scriptures.

Q. *How know you that the Scriptures are the word of God and not men's policies?*
A. I am assured of it, first, because the Holy Ghost persuades my conscience that it is so [Eph. 1:13]. Secondly, I see it by experience; for the preaching of the scriptures have the power of God in them to humble a man when they are preached and to cast him down to hell and afterward to restore and raise him up again [1 Cor. 14:35; Heb. 4:12].

Q. *What is the use of the word of God preached?*
A. First, it breeds and then it increases faith in them which are chosen to salvation [Rom. 1:17; 2 Cor. 2:16; Heb. 4:2]. But unto them that perish it is by reason of their corruption an occasion of their further damnation.

Q. *How must we hear God's word that it may be effectual to our salvation?*
A. We must come unto it with hunger-bitten hearts, having an appetite to the word. We must mark it with attention, receive it by faith, submit ourselves unto it with fear and trembling, even then when our faults are reproved. Lastly, we must hide it in the corners of our hearts, that we may frame our lives and conversations by it [Ps. 119:11; Isa. 66:2; Luke 2:51; Acts 16:14; Heb. 4:2; James 1:19].

Q. *What is a sacrament?*
A. A sign to represent, a seal to confirm, an instrument to convey Christ and all His benefits to them that do believe in Him [Gen. 17:11; Rom. 4:11; Gal. 3:1].

Q. *Why must a sacrament represent the mercies of God before our eyes?*
A. Because we are dull to conceive and to remember them.

Q. Why do the sacraments seal unto us the mercies of God?
A. Because we are full of unbelief and doubting of them.

Q. Why is the sacrament the instrument of the Spirit to convey the mercies of God into our hearts?
A. Because we are like Thomas. We will not believe till we feel them in some measure in our hearts.

Q. How many sacraments are there?
A. Two and no more [1 Cor. 10:1–3, 5]: baptism, by which we have our admission into the true church of God; and the Lord's Supper, by which we are nourished and preserved in the church after our admission.

Q. What is done in baptism?
A. In the assembly of the church, the covenant of grace between God and the party baptized is solemnly confirmed and sealed [Matt. 28:19; Acts 2:38; 21:16; Titus 3:5].

Q. In this covenant, what does God promise to the party baptized?
A. Christ with all blessings that come by Him [Gal. 3:27; 1 Peter 3:21].

Q. To what condition is the party baptized bound?
A. To receive Christ and to repent of his sin [Mark 16:16].

Q. What means the sprinkling or dipping in water?
A. It seals unto us remission of sins and sanctification by the obedience and sprinkling of the blood of Christ [1 Peter 1:2].

Q. How comes it to pass that many after their baptism for a long time feel not the effect and fruit of it, and some never?
A. The fault is not in God, who keeps His covenants; but the fault is in themselves in that they do not keep the condition of the covenant to receive Christ by faith and to repent of all their sins.

Q. When shall a man then see the effect of his baptism?
A. At what time soever he does receive Christ by faith, though it be many years after, he shall then feel the power of God to regenerate him and to work all things in him, which He offered in baptism [Heb. 10:20; 1 Peter 3:21].

Q. How if a man never keep the condition, to which he bound himself in baptism?
A. His damnation shall be the greater, because he breaks his vow made to God [Deut. 23:21–22; Eccl. 5:4].

Q. What is done in the Lord's Supper?
A. The former covenant, solemnly ratified in baptism, is renewed in the Lord's Supper between the Lord Himself and the receiver [1 Cor. 11:23–24; 12:13].

Q. What is the receiver?
A. Everyone that has been baptized and after his baptism has truly believed in Christ and repented of his sins from his heart [1 Cor. 11:28, 31; Matt. 5:23–24; Isa. 66:2–3].

Q. What means the bread and wine, the eating of the bread, and drinking of the wine?
A. These outward actions are a second seal set by the Lord's own hand unto His covenant [1 Cor. 10:16–17]. And they do give every receiver to understand that as God does bless the bread and wine to preserve and strengthen the body of the receiver, so Christ apprehended and received by faith shall nourish him and preserve both body and soul unto eternal life.

Q. What shall a true receiver feel in himself after the receiving of the Sacrament?
A. The increase of his faith in Christ, the increase of sanctification, a greater measure of dying to sin, a greater care to live in newness of life [1 Cor. 10:16–17; 11:24].

Q. What if a man, after the receiving of the Sacrament, never find any such thing in himself?
A. He may well suspect himself whether he did ever repent or not and thereupon is to use means to come to sound faith and repentance.

Q. What is another means of increasing faith?
A. Prayer.

Q. What is prayer?
A. A familiar speech with God in the name of Christ [1 John 5:14] in which either we crave things needful or give thanks for things received [Phil. 4:6; 1 Tim. 2:1].

Q. In asking things needful, what is required?
A. Two things: an earnest desire and faith.

Q. What things must a Christian man's heart desire [Mark 11:24]?
A. Six things especially.

Q. What are they?
A. [1] That he may glorify God. [2] That God may reign in his heart and not sin. [3] That he may do God's will, and not his lusts of the flesh. [4] That he may rely himself on God's providence for all the means of this temporal life. [5] That he may be justified, and be at peace with God. [6] That by the power of God he may be strengthened against all temptations.

Q. What is faith?
A. A persuasion [amen] that these things which we truly desire, God will grant them for Christ's sake.

The Sixth Principle Expounded

Q. After that a man has led a short life in this world, what follows then?
A. Death, which is the parting asunder of body and soul.

Q. Why do wicked men and unbelievers die?
A. That their bodies may go to the earth, and their souls may be cast into hell-fire [Luke 16:22–23].

Q. Why do the godly die, seeing Christ by death has overcome death?
A. They die for this end, that their bodies may rest for a while in the earth, and their souls may enter into heaven immediately [Luke 23:43; Acts 7:60; 1 Cor. 15:51–52; 1 Thess. 4:13; Heb. 2:14].

Q. What follows after death?
A. The day of judgment.

Q. What sign is there to know this day from other days?
A. Heaven and earth shall be consumed with fire immediately before the coming of the Judge [2 Peter 3:11–12].

Q. Who shall be the Judge?
A. Jesus Christ, the Son of God.

Q. What shall be the coming to judgment?
A. He shall come in the clouds in great majesty and glory with infinite company of angels [1 Thess. 4:16–17].

Q. How shall all men be cited to judgment?
A. At the sound of a trumpet [Matt. 24:31], the living shall be changed in the twinkling of an eye, and the dead shall rise again, everyone with his own body [Job 19:24], and all shall be gathered together before Christ. And after this, the good shall be severed from the bad [Matt. 25:32–33], these standing on the left hand of Christ, the other on the right.

Q. How will Christ try and examine every man's cause?
A. The books of all men's doings shall be laid open [Dan. 7:10; Rev. 20:12]. Men's consciences shall be made either to accuse them or excuse them, and every man shall be tried by the works which he did in his lifetime, because they are open and manifest signs of faith or unbelief [John 3:18; 5:24].

Q. What sentence will He give?
A. He will give sentence of salvation to the elect and godly [Matt. 25:31, 41], but He will pronounce sentence of damnation against unbelievers and reprobates.

Q. What state shall the godly be in after the day of judgment?
A. They shall continue forever in the highest heaven in the presence of God, having full fellowship with Christ Jesus and reigning with Him forever [Matt. 25:31; Rev. 21:3–4].

Q. What state shall the wicked be in after the day of judgment?
A. In eternal perdition and destruction in hellfire.

Q. What is that?
A. It stands in three things especially: first, a perpetual separation from God's comfortable presence; secondly, fellowship with the devil and his angels; thirdly, a horrible pang and torment both of body and soul, arising of the feeling of the whole wrath of God, poured forth on the wicked forever world without end [Isa. 66:24; 2 Thess. 1:9; Rev. 21:8]. And if the pain of one tooth for one day be so great, endless shall be the pain of the whole man, body and soul forever and ever.

FINIS

Scripture Index

Joshua

5:13	62
7:24	179
10:12	77
10:24	283

Judges

4:19	191
14:6	125
15:18	191

1 Samuel

1:15	189, 425
2:6	233
2:22	4
2:25	316
2:26	4
10:26–27	285
15:29	332
15:31	435
17:37	81
24:6	285
27:12	323
30:6	82, 194

2 Samuel

6:11	322
10:12	82
12:11	78, 357
15:26	37, 447
16:10	80
16:11	78
17:23	149
18:5	34
18:33	34
21:6	181
23:15–16	285
24:1	78, 460

1 Kings

1:39–40	285
1:40	410
2:19	270
5:5	439
8:10–11	261
8:27	55, 436
8:35	450
17:1	79
18:45	77
19:5	61
19:7	61
19:14	376
19:18	350, 376
20:31	397
21:29	425
22:22	77

2 Kings

1:3	61
1:13–14	220
2:8	77
2:12	419
2:23–24	188
4:10	270
4:23	378
5:3	244
5:13	244
5:14	77
6:6	77
6:16	391
6:17	64
13:21	229
18:36	188
19:35	62, 239
20:6–7	46

1 Chronicles

13:2	81
21:1	496
29:11	463

2 Chronicles

7:14	432
11:4	78
11:14	384
15:2	432
15:3	376
16:12	21
16:9	75
19:6	143

Subject Index

Joseph of Arimathea, 223–25, 227–28
Joshua, 98
joy
    as fruit of the Spirit, 317
    fullness in heaven, 410–11
jubilee, 207–8
Judas, treason of, 152–53
judgment, 52
judgment of certainty, 333
judgment of charity, 333
Julian the apostate, 188, 349, 435
justice of God, 195, 399
    and decree of reprobation, 346
    in execution of reprobation, 352
    in predestination, 325
    and punishment, 76
justification, 350–51, 491, 502–3
    by works, 380, 456

keys of heaven, 264–65
kingdom of darkness, 442
kingdom of glory, 443, 476
kingdom of God, 166–67, 493
    coming of, 442–46
    desire for, 462–63
    waiting for, 225
kingdom of grace, 443–44, 476
kingdom of heaven, 388, 442
kings, Christians as, 107
knowing Christ, 256–57
knowledge (part of faith), 9, 11
knowledge (providence), 75
knowledge of God, 20, 22, 352, 441
    perfect in life to come, 409
knowledge of will of God, 448, 475

last judgment, 261, 286–305, 492
Lazarus, raising of, 248, 254, 400, 404
learning by hearing not seeing, 261
legal descent, 136
leprosy, 291–92
Libertines, 59, 382
life everlasting. *See* eternal life
living under the cross, 373–74
local descent, xv

longsuffering, as fruit of the Spirit,
    318–19
Lord's Day, 242
Lord's Prayer, 466, 484–85
    as catechetical tool, xvi
    as model for prayer, 428
    outline of, 421–22
    preface to, 429–38
    first petition, 438–42
    second petition, 442–46
    third petition of, 446–50
    fourth petition, 450–54
    fifth petition, 455–57
    sixth petition, 459–61
Lord's Supper, 55, 388, 506–7
Lord (title), 115–18
love
    for brethren, 435–36
    of a Christian, 340
    duties of, 393–94
    as fruit of the Spirit, 317
    for God, 438
    in heaven, 409–10
    increase of, 474
Low Countries, churches of, 383
Lucidus, John, 49
lusts of the flesh, 508
Luther, Martin, 49, 427
Lutherans
    errors of, 367, 379
    as part of true church, 382
    on sacraments, 367, 382–83
lying, 70, 452

magistrates
    and flourishing of the church, 445
    as gods, 20
    maintains religion with the sword,
        154
    obedience to, 226
making election sure, 354
malignant church, 385
man
    creation of, 64–72
    dignity of, 66–67

on supremacy of Peter, 247
on transubstantiation, 187
on works of merit, 454
on worship of images and saints,
380–81
rule of faith, 4, 8

Sabbath
change of day, 241–42, 258
perpetual in heaven, 410
sanctification of, 51–52
in state of innocence, 67–68
sacraments, 207, 388, 505–6
Lutherans on, 382–83
as means of furthering the kingdom, 444
as pipes and conduits to grace, 254
strengthen faith, 492
Sadducees, 59
saints, not mediators in prayer, 275,
426, 431
salt of the earth, 208–9
Samosatenians, 382
sanctification, 126–27, 370, 446, 456,
491, 502, 503–4
not perfect in this life, 91
and predestination, 335
and resurrection of Christ, 253
Satan
bondage to, 198–99, 262, 444, 496
as father of corruption, 29–30
obedience to, 496–97
temptation of, 460
saving faith, 12
Savoy, churches of, 383
schisms, 447
Scotland, churches of, 383
scribes and Pharisees, 150
second Adam, 127
second causes, 45–46
second commandment, 500
second death, 197, 198, 256, 403
seed of Abraham, 324, 326
seed of the serpent, 96
seed of the woman, 96

seeking heavenly things, 257, 414, 437
self-abasement, 93, 464
self-denial, 22, 106, 448
Sennacherib, 200
separation, from a church, 384–85
serpent in the wilderness, 183
service of God, 106
serving for the glory of God, 106,
199–200, 309
seventh commandment, 501
sheep and goats, separation of,
295–96
Shilo, 123
sickness, 268
signs, of last judgment, 288–91
Simon Magus, 9, 11
Simon of Cyrene, 180
sin, 82–92, 495–96
burial of, 229
disliking of, 313–14
forgiveness of, 458
God's will and decree of, 45
governed by God, 75–76
greatness and wretchedness of,
141, 291
guilt of, 83
imputed to Christ, 388
not all equal, 83
permitted by God, 75
restrained by God, 76
of the world, 447
sins to come, prevention of, 460
sixth commandment, 501
sobriety, 291
Son
eternal generation of, 24–26,
108–9, 113
as our Redeemer, 27
personal properties of, 24
as Word of the Father, 47
work of creation, 42–43, 110
Son of God (title), 108–15
sons of God, 33, 95, 113, 114
sons of men, 95
sorrow for sin, 501